# A2 Sociology for AQA

## Chris Livesey & Tony Lawson

# Hodder Arnold

A MEMBER OF THE HODDER HEADLINE GROUP

Orders: please contact Bookpoint Ltd, 130 Milton Park, Abingdon, Oxon OX14 4SB. Telephone: (44) 01235 827720. Fax: (44) 01235 400454. Lines are open from 9.00 – 5.00, Monday to Saturday, with a 24 hour message answering service. You can also order through our website www.hoddereducation.co.uk

If you have any comments to make about this, or any of our other titles, please send them to educationenquiries@hodder.co.uk

*British Library Cataloguing in Publication Data*
A catalogue record for this title is available from the British Library

ISBN-10: 0 340 912 553
ISBN-13: 978 0 340 912 553

Published 2006
Impression number   10 9 8 7 6 5 4 3 2 1
Year                2010 2009 2008 2007 2006

Hodder Headline's policy is to use papers that are natural, renewable and recyclable products and made from wood grown in sustainable forests. The logging and manufacturing processes are expected to conform to the environmental regulations of the country of origin.

Typeset by Fakenham Photosetting Ltd, Fakenham, Norfolk
Printed in Spain for Hodder Arnold, an imprint of Hodder Education, a member of the Hodder Headline Group, 338 Euston Road, London NW1 3BH

# Contents

# Acknowledgements

While writing can, at the best of times, be a solitary experience, a number of people have helped me through the long, dark, winter months.

On a personal level, I want to recognise the help and support of:

Julia, my wife.
Anne and John, my parents.
Keith and Kevin, my brothers.

On a professional level I'd like to thank everyone at Hodder who's been involved in some way in the production of the text. In particular, I'd like to acknowledge the help (and patience) of Colin Goodlad, Matthew Sullivan and Matthew Smith (the person responsible for originally getting this show on the road).

On both a personal and professional level I'd also like to acknowledge (and thank) Tony Lawson for his contribution to the text. I'd like to think it's a much better effort for his able assistance.

Finally, to paraphrase the mighty Arcade Fire:

Consider this text a tunnel.
Yeah, a tunnel – From my window to yours.
Meet me in the middle, the empty middle ground.
And since there's no one else around,
We'll let our time grow long,
And remember everything we've come to know.

Chris Livesey

The publishers wish to thank the following for permission to use copyright material:

TopFoto.co.uk for photographs on p. 7, p. 95, p. 228, p.324, p. 386 and p. 503.
Anthony Harvey/PA/Empics for photograph on p. 15.
Everett Collection/Rex Features for photograph on p. 27.
Pier Paolo Cito/AP/Empics for photograph on p. 43.
Sipa Press/Rex Features for image on p. 48.
Francoise Sauze/Science Photo Library for photograph on p.52.
EDPpics/D. Bradley/Rex Features for photograph on p. 62.
Sinopix/Rex Features for photograph on p. 72.
TopFoto/Empics for photographs on p. 106 and p. 166.
Peter Jordan/PA/Empics for the 'anti-fox hunting' photograph on p. 113.
National Pictures/TopFoto.co.uk for the 'pro-fox hunting' photograph on p. 113.
TopFoto/UPP for photograph on p. 136.
BBC Photo Library for photograph on p. 142.
TopFoto/KPA for photograph on p. 145.
PA/Empics for photographs on p. 173 and p. 377.
Ingram for photographs on p. 185 and p. 224.
Apichart Weerawong/AP/Empics for photograph on p. 191.
Photodisk for photograph on p. 210.
Removing Unfreedoms (www.removingunfreedoms.org) for 'measuring unfreedoms' table on p. 215

The Image Works/TopFoto.co.uk for the photograph on p. 235.

Dr David Gatley/Staffordshire Record Society for 'Age-Sex Pyramid for Stoke-upon-Trent (UK), 1701', p. 256.

Global Forum for Health Research for 'Yearly health spending per capita' table on p. 258

20th Century Fox/Everett/Rex Features for photograph on p. 278.

Richard Gardner/Rex Features for photograph on p. 294.

BSIP, Chassenet/Science Photo Library for photograph on p. 306.

Science & Society Picture Library for photograph on p. 366.

Professor Jock Young for 'The square of crime', p. 396.

Jacquemart Closon/Rex Features for photograph on p. 408.

Caroline Hodges Persell for 'Wright and Perrone's class schema', p. 457.

Richard Young/Rex Features for photograph on p. 460.

24/7 Media/Rex Features for photograph on p. 463.

TopFoto/Keystone for photograph on p. 467.

Oxford University Press for 'Hakim's (2000) classification of women's work-lifestyle preferences in the 21st century', p. 490.

All other cartoons are by © Barking Dog Art.

National Office of Statistics Material is reproduced under the terms of the Click-Use License.

Every effort has been made to trace and acknowledge ownership of copyright. The publishers will be glad to make suitable arrangements with any copyright holders whom it has not been possible to contact.

# CHAPTER 1

# Religion

In this chapter we're going to examine the concept of religion from a variety of angles, from thinking about different types of religious organisation (such as churches and sects), through the role of religion in society (as a force for conservation or change, for example), to the relationship between religious beliefs and behaviours. In the concluding section we will examine the question of whether or not religion is a declining force in contemporary societies.

In this opening section, however, we're going to look at two broad areas. First, how we can define religion, and second, different explanations for the existence and persistence of religious beliefs and practices in human societies.

## 1. Different theories of religion

### WARM-UP: THE MEANING OF RELIGION

Individually, take a few minutes to think about:

- what religion means to people (including yourself)
- how people practise their religious beliefs
- how people join together to celebrate and affirm their religious beliefs (through ceremonies and festivals, for example).

Make brief notes about your thoughts and, as a class, discuss the different beliefs and practices involved in the concept of religion (identifying, if possible, any 'core themes' to religious behaviour – possible beliefs or behaviours that might be a fundamental aspect of religion).

### Preparing the ground: Defining religion

As you will probably have discovered, identifying different features of religion is relatively easy; defining the 'essential features' of religion – the things that make it different to other kinds of social behaviour – is, however, more difficult. **Hutchinson** (1981) suggests: 'Definitions of religion are as numerous ... as there are students of religion. Often such definitions illustrate the oriental parable of the blind men describing the elephant, each taking hold of part of the beast and defining the whole in terms of this part. Like the elephant, religion is a large and complex phenomenon'.

### Weeding the path

The difficulties involved in defining religion can be summarised in a couple of ways:

- **Diversity**: Although it's tempting to see religion as a single (*homogeneous*) entity,

in reality there are wide variations in both *beliefs* and *practices*:

- **historically** – in the same society over time
- **contemporaneously** – in the same society at the same time
- **cross-culturally** – between different societies.

For example, in terms of:

**Beliefs**, some forms (such as Christianity, Judaism and Islam) involve the worship of a single god (*monotheism*), whereas other forms (such as paganism) involve the worship of many different gods (*polytheism*) – and some forms don't involve worshiping 'god' at all (the North American Sioux, for example, understood the world in terms of *Waken Beings or Powers* – the expression of anything 'incomprehensible'). In terms of:

**Practices**, some forms allow direct communication with God through prayer, but others do not.

- **Constituency**: McGuire (2002) suggests

religion is difficult to define because of its 'dual character' – it is, for example, both:

- **Individual** in that it involves a diversity of beliefs and practices and a variety of ways to 'be religious', some of which involve the communal practice of religious beliefs, such as attending religious ceremonies; others of which do not (it is possible, for example, to consider yourself a 'Christian' without ever setting foot inside a church).
- **Social** in the sense that religions perform certain *functions* for the society in which they exist – things like *socialisation* (*moral values*, for example), *social solidarity* (giving people a sense they have things in common) and *social control*.

## The potting shed

Identify and briefly explain one function of religion for individuals and one function for society.

## ✳ SYNOPTIC LINK

**Theory and methods: McGuire's** distinction reflects what **Leming** (1998) characterises as the idea that people both create and are created by society. This reflects a common theme throughout the A level course – the distinction between structure and action.

Ideas of concept diversity and constituency are reflected in the fact that we can outline three standard types of definition of religion.

## Substantive

**Substantive** definitions focus on the content (or *substance*) of religion – the things (beliefs, ceremonies and the like) that are distinctive in religious behaviour and which, in turn, mark religious behaviour as different to other behaviours (such as shopping or going to school). **Beckford** (1980) characterises this type as '… restricting the term "religion" to phenomena displaying definite properties which do not occur together in other phenomena. The strongest form of substantive definitions holds that religion has an essential nature'.

Normally, this 'essential nature' involves a concept of 'the *sacred*', something **Maguire** (2001) defines as 'the word we use for that which is utterly and mysteriously precious in our experience'. In other words, the single (or essential) characteristic that separates religion from other forms of belief is that something should be *venerated* (respected or revered in some way). We can develop this type of definition by noting some of the 'essential characteristics' of religion suggested by different writers.

**Eliade** (1987) suggested that religion involved:

- distinguishing between 'the sacred' (or special) and 'the profane' (or everyday) – a distinction originally made by Emile **Durkheim** (1912)
- a code of values with a sacred origin
- communication with the supernatural (through mechanisms such as prayer).

**Bilton et al.** (1996) added the idea of:

- a system of beliefs about the individual's place in the world, providing order to that world and a reason for existence within it.

**Giddens** (2001) additionally noted that religion involved:

- symbols invoking feelings of reverence or awe linked to rituals or ceremonies (such as church services) practised by a community of believers
- ceremonials practised collectively by believers that normally occur in special places – churches, temples or ceremonial grounds.

## Functional

**Functional** definitions focus on what religion *does* as a way of identifying its general characteristics. **Cline** (2005) notes: 'For those who focus on functional definitions … if your belief system plays some particular role either in your social life, in your society, or in your psychological life, then it is a religion; otherwise, it's something else.'

**Haviland et al.** (2005) identify examples of two types of religious function when they note the significance of:

**Religious rituals** (such as christenings, marriages and funerals). These 'ritualistic aspects' of social life play a significant role in 'marking important life transitions'. In some forms of Judaism, for example, the *Bar Mitzvah* (for boys aged 13) and *Bat Mitzvah* (for girls aged 12) symbolise a *rite of passage* (a ceremony marking the passing between life stages) between childhood and adulthood.

**Intensification rites**, meanwhile, function to 'mark *group* occasions' and involve the 'expression and affirmation of common values' – in other words, religious ceremonies (such as church services) or festivals (such as Christmas) have an *integration* function, binding people together through the beliefs and practices they share.

In this respect, functional definitions are broader in scope and include a wider range of ideas and beliefs under the general heading of religion than their substantive counterparts.

## Interpretive

**Interpretive** definitions focus on how people (in different societies and at different times) 'define a situation' as being religious or not religious. In other words, rather than a sociologist, for example, creating a 'definition of religion' against which to measure the extent to which some forms of behaviour are considered 'religious', definitions develop, according to **Blasi** (1998), out of how people define their behaviour. In this respect, 'religion' and 'religious behaviour' are effectively whatever people claim them to be.

## ⚠ Digging deeper: Defining religion

Sociological approaches to understanding the role of religion can be broadly classified in terms of two general categories (*inclusive* and *exclusive*):

**Inclusive approaches** consider religion in the broadest possible terms, in order to explore the forms and functions of 'religious-type' belief systems (*ideologies*). This approach, therefore, focuses on identifying and explaining the social and individual purposes religious beliefs and organisations exist to satisfy, which would include ideas like:

- **social integration** – exploring, for example, how religious-type beliefs promote common norms and values
- **social solidarity** – examining, for example, how a common religious-type belief system serves as a source of personal and social identity.

This approach, therefore, considers religion both in terms of how we see it conventionally (a belief in the existence of god, for example) and in forms we generally *don't* consider to be 'religious'; political ideologies (such as communism) could, for example, be included as 'religious-type' belief systems here, mainly because they involve elements of:

**Faith**: Like conventional forms of religion, political ideologies require their followers to obey certain articles and principles of faith, often in return for some promised goal. For some religions the promised goal might be a place in heaven (Christianity) or rebirth into a higher social position (Hinduism) whereas in a 'political faith' such as communism the promised goal is a fairer, more equal (*egalitarian*) society.

**Function**: The way beliefs differ in terms of their specific content is less important than the fact that they function in similar ways – sharing beliefs, for example, promotes the idea of belonging to a community of 'like-minded individuals' bound together by what they have in common (their beliefs, norms and values).

## ✳ SYNOPTIC LINK

**Theory and methods:** Some inclusive approaches classify science as a form of religion because it involves the idea of faith – a belief, for example, that the natural world is governed by particular physical laws of development.

Although inclusive approaches are generally associated with functionalist theories of religion, they extend into many other theoretical areas. The interactionist sociologist Thomas **Luckmann** (1967) argues that *any* system of belief that explains the nature of the social or natural world is a form of religion.

**Exclusive approaches** consider religion in a narrower way, insisting on a more selective (*substantive*) range of beliefs – such as a belief in god or the supernatural – as being representative of religions. In this respect, religious beliefs are considered *qualitatively* different to other forms of belief and this approach is generally characteristic of Marxist and Weberian explanations of religion.

Different approaches to defining religion impact, to some extent, on explanations of religious behaviour, and to reflect the distinction we can examine a range of theories broadly divided into *inclusive* approaches (such as functionalism, interactionism and postmodernism) and *exclusive* approaches (such as Marxism).

## Preparing the ground: Functionalist theories of religion

Classical functionalist theories, associated with the work of writers like **Durkheim** (1912), **Malinowski** (1926) and **Parsons** (1937), generally see religion as a:

**Cultural institution** – religion is mainly concerned with the creation, promotion and maintenance of cultural values – something that it relates to ideas about:

**Social order**: Cultural institutions (that in contemporary societies include education and the mass media) help to create and maintain a sense of order and continuity in society – their main function (or purpose) being to provide people with a set of meanings (beliefs and values, for example) that help them make sense of both the social world and their place in that world. Religions serve to both originate new ideas and categories of thought and reaffirm existing social values.

Cultural institutions, therefore, primarily function to encourage people to believe they belong to that collective group we term 'society'; they promote, in other words:

**Social solidarity** – the belief that we are connected into a larger network of people who share certain beliefs, identities and commitments to each other. For such feelings of *solidarity* to develop, however, societies have to create mechanisms of:

**Social integration**: A sense of solidarity and commitment has to be nurtured and encouraged (through socialisation processes, for example) to create a sense of social purpose and cohesion.

# Functions

For **Alpert** (1939), religion served four major functions:

**Discipline**: Religions require various forms of self-discipline and adherence to moral rules and codes (*common values*), which translate into wider social relationships by creating both a sense of *commitment* (the individual connected to a greater whole – 'society') and an understanding of the individual's place in society. For **Parsons** (1937), religion is a social mechanism for originating and propagating common values for two reasons:

- **Authority**: When people follow 'a god' they submit to a 'higher authority' and power – something that translates into the idea of observing society's norms/laws.

- **Collective ceremonies**: Common values are reinforced and given meaning through collective behaviour (such as the singing of hymns in the Protestant church).

**Cohesion**: Religious ceremonies bring people together in situations where they 'put into practice' their shared norms, values and experiences, thereby cementing and reinforcing *social solidarity*. In addition, ceremonies – such as a marriage or funeral – involve:

**Symbols** with shared meanings (a wedding ring, for example). Thus for **Ricoeur** (1974) a symbol '... by expressing one meaning *directly*, expresses another *indirectly*'.

## ✳ SYNOPTIC LINK

**Theory and methods:** This idea of symbolic meaning is related to semiological research methods.

For **Durkheim** (1912), religious symbols reflected a significant distinction between:

- **the sacred** – that which is 'special' or important, and

- **the profane** – the 'everyday', the commonplace and the unimportant.

For **Durkheim** the form taken by 'the sacred' was not significant; anything – from *things* (such as a book or an animal) to *ceremonies* (like a wedding) or *places* (a building, for example) could be considered sacred. The function of 'the sacred' was simply to help people develop shared values – the things on which they could agree and, by so doing, be drawn closer together as a group or society.

**Vitalisation**: Common values and beliefs represent *vital* dimensions of culture, socialisation and, of course, social control. This follows because groups – and societies – can use the 'ideas that bind them together' as sources of:

- **Identity** ('vitalisation'): People 'understand who they are' through their membership of social groups.

- **Revitalisation** – a common culture can be transmitted from one generation to the next, thereby providing social continuities through things like traditions and customs.

**Euphony** (*soothing* or *harmonious*) reflects the idea that people may undergo periods of pain and crisis, requiring an individual or collective need to re-establish a sense of normality. The *euphonic function* of religion is expressed in terms of things like:

**Tension management**: Both **Parsons** (1937) and **Malinowski** (1926) noted how the religious rituals surrounding death serve to manage this potentially tense and traumatic situation by, for example, providing a social structure (the funeral) that permits and encourages certain forms of *social action* (such as grieving for a certain length of time).

**Meaning**: In his study of the Trobriand Islanders, **Malinowski** (1926) noted how religion provided 'explanations for the inexplicable', an idea **Thompson** (1986) expresses in the following terms: 'In a society full of dangers and uncertainty ... where there was a continual threat of injury, disease and death, there was always an element of the inexplicable, the "unknowable". Religion and magic served to offer an explanation of the events for which other frameworks could not account.'

More recently, **Luhmann** (1977) argues that a major function of religion in modern societies is to 'explain that which is not currently known or understood' or, to use **Bežovan's** (2004) wonderfully unintelligible phrase: 'the transformation from indeterminable to determinable complexity'.

## Neo-functionalism

More recently, neo-functionalists have explored how the functions of religion have evolved in *postmodern* society – for example, in terms of the way our society has changed, economically, politically and culturally, over the past 50 years or so. Two initial points can be usefully noted here:

- **Diversity**: As our society has become more culturally diverse, the focus of interest for neo-functionalists has generally been on the role of religion considered in terms of its functions for individuals and groups rather than 'society as a whole'.

- **Decline**: As our society has evolved in terms of diversity, the social significance

## ⚠ Growing it yourself: Death of a princess

Although widespread expressions of grief and mourning are relatively rare in our society, the death of **Diana, Princess of Wales** in 1997 provoked a vast outpouring of public grief for a number of days.

Use Alpert's four functions of religion (discipline, cohesion, vitalisation and euphony) to write a brief analysis (around 100 words for each function) of how this public display of national mourning could be explained by functionalist approaches to religion.

Thousands of wreaths and flowers were left outside Buckingham Palace as a final tribute to Princess Diana

of organised religion (such as the Church of England) has declined and, according to **Kung** (1990), the functions of religion have similarly evolved in terms of:

**Identity**: **Gans** (1971) suggests the theoretical focus has changed from thinking about how religion may be functional for some groups but not necessarily others, so that: 'In a modern heterogeneous society few phenomena are functional or *dysfunctional* for society as a whole, and most result in benefits to some groups and costs to others.' Membership of a religious group or organisation may, therefore, confer certain benefits to individuals (by defining who they are, promoting clear moral guidelines and satisfying psychological, social and spiritual needs, for example) – things, as **Perry** and **Perry** (1973) note, '… particularly important in times of rapid social change, in which problems of identity are critical'.

**Dysfunctions**: **Merton's** (1957) argument that something in a society may be harmful (*dysfunctional*) further suggests religion is not inevitably functional. In a culturally diverse society it can be dysfunctional when it creates conflict – some Christian groups in the USA, for example, are violently opposed to abortion. As **Bruce** (1995) observes: 'Social scientists have long been aware of the role of religion as social cement; shared rituals and shared beliefs that bind people together … What is not so often noted is the logical accompaniment to the idea that a commonly worshipped God holds a people together: religion often divides one group from another.'

## The potting shed

**Identify and briefly explain one additional way religion may be dysfunctional to the individual or society.**

**Social change**: Religion can be a mechanism for change, in that membership of a religious organisation may provide oppressed people with the social solidarity and sense of purpose they need to challenge unjust laws. The Black Civil Rights movement in the USA in the 1960s was partially organised and articulated through Christian church membership.

**Psychological support**: **Farley** (1990) notes how 'religion serves as a source of psychological support during the trying times of a person's life. Not only do religious rites mark the most stressful and major transitions throughout a person's lifetime, but they offer tremendous support during unexpected crises'.

## Digging deeper: Functionalist theories

Although various forms of functionalist theory have been influential for our understanding of religion, this is *not* to say the perspective is without problems. For example:

**Methodologically** an initial question is how it is possible to test or measure (*operationalise*) the concept of function: how, for example, do we know whether something like religion is functional? We can illustrate this problem using **Merton's** (1957) distinction between different types of function:

- **Manifest functions** represent the *intended consequences* (the consequences people see or expect) of behaviour. Thus, the manifest function of prayer is to communicate with or influence the behaviour of a deity.

- **Latent functions**, however, represent *unrecognised and unintended consequences* (in the sense that the effect of behaviour may be unplanned). A classic example is **Durkheim's** (1912) argument that the worship of 'God' is actually the unintended worship of 'society'; as **Adams** and **Sydie** (2001) note: 'For Durkheim, the sacred comes from society, from the members of the society who collectively believe the object or ritual to be sacred and endow it with meaning. Thus religion becomes … the "worship of society".'

A *latent function* of religion therefore is that religious behaviour is, ultimately, directed towards the creation, maintenance and policing of 'society' – but the problem here is, how can this be proven or disproven? Similar methodological problems arise with the concept of:

**Dysfunction**: For classical Functionalism, something like religion was functional 'because it existed' – an assumption, not unreasonably perhaps, based on the idea that if religion had no purpose it would have little or no point in existing. The task, therefore, was to explain the purpose of something (like attendance at religious services) by identifying and understanding its benefit for the individual and/or society. However, the introduction of the concept of *dysfunction* – some forms of behaviour, rather than contributing to social *order* could

contribute to social *disorder* – raises a further problem, namely how to disentangle functional behaviour from dysfunctional behaviour: is religion, for example, functional or dysfunctional to atheists? And are Islamic beliefs functional or dysfunctional for Christianity?

## ❊ SYNOPTIC LINK

**Crime and deviance:** The problem of how to disentangle *function* from *dysfunction* is illustrated by **Durkheim's** (1897) argument that 'too much criminality' in society was potentially *dysfunctional*, even though crime itself was broadly *functional*.

## Weeding the path

Any process of social interaction may, by definition, be potentially both functional and dysfunctional. Crime, for example, may be *functional* to me if, by stealing some money from you, I profit – you, on the other hand, may feel my act to be *dysfunctional*. The question here, therefore, is not who is right or wrong (we're both right in our different ways), but how can you differentiate between the 'functions' and 'dysfunctions' of behaviour in any objective way?

## ❊ SYNOPTIC LINK

**Crime and deviance:** The evaluative problems we've identified can be equally applied to functionalist explanations of crime and deviance.

A further problem we can note involves the idea of:

**Inclusive theory**: Functionalist theories

generally focus more on what religion *does* (its functions) than on what it *is* (what features, for example, makes religion a unique cultural institution?). This means that any social institution can be considered 'a religion' if it performs the functions associated with religious institutions. This idea is both *confusing* – it's not clear why religion (considered in the conventional sense of spiritual beliefs, and so forth) should be considered a distinct object of study – and *convenient*, because it allows functionalists to explain seemingly *contradictory* or *mutually exclusive* observations by using the concept of:

**Functional alternatives**: For example, if religious observance and practice is widespread in a society, this is evidence for the function of religion. However, if such things go into decline (in the UK, for example, Christian church attendance has declined steeply over the past century), the general theory is *not* considered false because it can be saved by reference to 'other social institutions' (or *functional alternatives* to religion) that take over the role it previously performed – an example being something like football performing a *social solidarity* function (large numbers of people sharing and showing their support for the national team).

## The potting shed

Identify and briefly explain one way the mass media or education might represent a 'functional alternative' to religion.

## Preparing the ground: Interactionist theories

For interactionist sociology the general focus is on understanding what religion *means* (interpretively), considered on two levels:

- **The individual**: This examines the 'meaning of religion' for individual social actors – to study, for example, the motivations, behaviours and beliefs of those who classify themselves as religious.

- **The social**: This might involve looking at the 'collective religious beliefs' existing in a particular society and how these beliefs influence the development of cultural identities, legal systems and the like.

Although the individual level of analysis is important, the focus here is on the social level, mainly because we're generally interested in the role of religion in *society* and, in particular, the idea that the main thing 'religions' have in common is their organisational power, based around the concept of:

**Belief systems** (or **ideological frameworks**) – ways of organising knowledge and understanding. **Berger** (1973) views religion as a framework for the interpretation and understanding of the world: in pre-modern (pre-scientific) societies, religion provided a comprehensive framework for the interpretation and imposition of meaning in a (potentially) chaotic and threatening world – a means by which people imposed a sense of order on their world when threatened by 'inexplicable' phenomena (such as death, disaster and disease).

By its ability to 'explain the inexplicable' (something that's similar to **Luhmann's** (1977) ideas about religion), an important role of religion is to encourage *certainty* – there is nothing that cannot be explained by religion which, in **Berger's** terms, makes it a:

**Cosmology** – a complete body of knowledge about the world supported by various forms of practice and expression (ceremonials and the like – which links, to some extent, with **Durkheim's** (1912) ideas about the functions of religion). On a more specific level, we can understand how this organisational framework works in terms of:

**Culture mapping**: This represents 'mental maps' of the world and our place in that world articulated through, for example, religious beliefs and practices. Such organisational maps enable us to:

- **explain** our experiences
- **interpret** their meaning and significance
- **create** shared, stored (cultural) meanings.

**Jarvis** (1995) notes how mental mapping helps people build '. . . an objective and moral universe of meaning'. In other words, for interactionists the world is:

**Socially constructed** – without clear and strong instincts to guide behaviour we create a sense of order and predictability through other means (such as the socialisation process) and, as such, we're all socialised into some form of universe of meaning (religious, political, magical, scientific or, in modern societies, a possible mixture of these) that explains the world. We can understand this idea a little more easily by the use of an analogy.

Interactionists like to compare people to actors, so imagine 'life as a television soap opera' (such as *Coronation Street*). In this world, scriptwriters are powerful social actors – they write the lines spoken by the actors. The actors too are powerful, in their own way, since their job is to bring a script to life and make it believable.

The 'soap opera world' is a clearly defined one, tightly controlled by the participants (by the writer in particular), and is subject to various conventions (which are like traditions and customs). The actors and writers are also socialised into obeying these

## ⚠ 🌱 Growing it yourself: Cultural maps

In small groups, use the following table as a template to identify some of the ways religious beliefs and practices help people create 'cultural maps' of their world (we've given you some examples to get you started).

| Explain our experiences | Interpret meaning | Create shared meanings |
|---|---|---|
| What happens when we die? | Why is there suffering and unhappiness? | Murder is wrong |
| **Further examples?** | | |

conventions (a western soap opera has different conventions to a hospital-based soap opera). In this small world there is only one universe of meaning and the actors 'take this world for granted'. Actors in a police drama, for example, do not suddenly start acting as if they were in a western. To do so would be inconceivable within the conventions set by the particular *genre* (type). We can apply these ideas to the distinction developed by **Weber** (1905), when he talked about different types of society:

**Traditional** or **pre-modern** societies may involve only one universe of meaning because they are *closed systems* – societies where one belief system is continually emphasised and socialised into individuals, to the exclusion of all other belief systems. The role and behaviour of the Roman Catholic Church in Britain in the Middle Ages is an example here since it was able to monopolise knowledge about the world (in the absence of alternative belief systems such as science) and, most importantly, *use* this knowledge to suppress alternative belief systems. **Boronski** (1987) notes how the Catholic Church tried to prevent the spread of **Galileo's** scientific ideas about the nature of the universe because they posed a threat to the prevailing religious *cosmology*.

**Modern societies**, such as contemporary Britain, involve many possible 'universes of meaning' – religion, science, politics, and so forth. These 'universes' are not necessarily:

- **separate** – political ideas may be rooted in religious beliefs – or
- **homogeneous**: There are a variety of religious universes, both *within* religions like Christianity (Roman Catholicism and Protestantism, for example) or Islam

(Sunni and Shia) and *between* religions (such as Hinduism and Sikhism).

## Inclusiveness

For interactionists, religion in modern societies is but one cosmology in an increasingly diverse system of competing cosmologies, and in this respect they tend to adopt a generally:

**Inclusive approach** to religion by focusing on the role of religion as a belief system; for example, their interest lies in exploring how religious ideologies provide an organising structure to our lives. The specific content of religious beliefs is, consequently, not of primary significance. One reason for this, perhaps, is expressed in the concept of:

**Plausibility**: For interactionists (as, to some extent, with postmodernists) religious beliefs persist only for as long as they are believed (*plausible*). In this respect, **Luckmann** (1967) suggests we should distinguish between two 'plausibility spheres':

- **The public** – where religions are forced to 'compete' with other belief systems in terms of how they explain the social and natural worlds.
- **The private** – the realm of individual beliefs. In this sphere, questions of personal identity, what happens when you die, and so forth, are reduced to private, personal concerns to which religion may provide plausible answers (sometimes in the absence of any other sort of answer).

### Digging deeper: Interactionist theories

The inclusive nature of interactionist approaches leads **Berger** (1967) to argue that religion takes on the form of a:

**Sacred canopy**, an idea that involves '… an all-embracing sacred order … capable of maintaining itself in the ever-present face of chaos'. Religious beliefs and practices, in other words, resemble a *shield* people use to protect themselves from psychological harm. As **Wuthnow** (1992) puts it: 'Religion is a symbol system that imposes order on the entire universe ("cosmos"), on life itself, and thereby holds chaos (disorder) at bay.' Alternatively, **Leming** (1998) characterises this view of religion as '… the audacious attempt to conceive of the entire universe as being humanly significant'.

**Social change**: From this position, the persistence of religion in human society is *not* tied to specific notions of *functionality* (the purpose religion is supposed to serve). There is, for example, no sense of religion performing functions that no other cultural institution can perform. By tying religion into *beliefs*, interactionists can explain both the:

**Persistence** of religion in human societies (its ability to provide a 'universe of meaning') and

**Change** (how and why religious forms of belief and expression change). Unlike functionalist inclusive approaches, interactionists do not necessarily see 'competition' between different belief systems as being *oppositional* (based on conflict); scientific beliefs, for example, do not automatically cancel out religious beliefs, and different belief systems may coexist by:

- **explaining** different things in different ways (religion, for example, is arguably better placed than science to explain 'life after death')

- **changing** their form to accommodate

different belief systems. As **Luckmann** (1967) argues, the form taken by religion in modern societies is more privatised and individualistic (*fragmented*) than in the past – something that reflects the way it evolves to meet new challenges from alternative belief systems.

## ⚠ Weeding the path

Despite these ideas, there are weaknesses and inconsistencies in this general perspective we can usefully note.

**Plausibility structures**: Although 'plausibility' represents a way of comparing one form of knowledge against another (for example, does theory X explain something better than theory Y?), it's not so useful when considering the *internal plausibility* of something like religious belief.
The main problem here is that we have no way of knowing which comes first – the ideas that sustain a 'plausibility structure' or the structure itself. In other words, do people continue to hold religious beliefs *because* these beliefs are plausible (they explain something no other belief system can explain) or are such beliefs plausible simply because they are believed? This leads us to consider the concept of:

**Social structures** and the idea that interactionists underplay the role of social structures (and overplay the role *of social actions*) in the persistence of religion. As **Wuthnow** (1992) notes: 'Social interaction is surely important in maintaining religious realities, but putting the matter in these terms leaves the influence of social conditions largely indeterminate. For example, when research finds Christian friendships reinforce Christian convictions, the question still remains why some people choose Christian friends and others do not.' In other words, the suggestion is that specifically religious beliefs persist because they serve important and significant functions for both the individual and society.

**Conflict**: Although we've talked about conflicts between different belief systems (such as those of religion and science) it is clear there are also conflicts within religion as a belief system. New Age religions (involving things like crystal healing) have little or nothing in common with traditional religions (such as Christianity or Islam), aside from their general classification as 'religions', and this makes it difficult to support the idea of religion as a single belief system or universe of meaning.

## Preparing the ground: Postmodernist approaches

As **Grassie** (1997) notes, 'postmodernism represents a great range of philosophical points of view' and reflects what he terms 'a broad and elusive movement of thought'. It is, in other words, an *approach* to thinking about the social world that encompasses a wide range of different viewpoints gathered under the theoretically convenient (but potentially misleading) banner of postmodernism. This does present us with a couple of problems, of course, the main one being that, when thinking specifically about religion, postmodernism doesn't present a particularly unified face to the world. This 'lack of theoretical unity' is reflected in **Taylor's** (1987) observation that 'for some, postmodernism suggests the death of God and the disappearance of religion, for others, the return of traditional faith, and for others still, the possibility of recasting religious ideas'.

Although this makes it particularly difficult to talk convincingly about postmodernist approaches to religion, there are arguably a range of general concepts employed by postmodernists that can be applied to an understanding of such behaviour. In this respect, a couple of concepts are initially significant.

**Narratives**: This idea holds, rightly or wrongly, that knowledge consists of *stories* that compete with one another to explain something. From this position religion represents just another form of *narrative* – one that, more importantly, can sometimes be considered a:

**Metanarrative** (or 'big story'): Narratives sometimes break out of small-scale storytelling and become all-encompassing stories that seek to explain 'everything about something' (or, in some cases, 'everything about everything', to paraphrase **Vaillancourt-Rosenau's** (1992) characterisation of the 'religion metanarrative'). Religious metanarratives, in this sense, represent a general structure or framework around which individual beliefs, practices and experiences can be orientated and, of course, ordered. It also follows from this that metanarratives invariably involve a claim to *exclusive truth* about whatever it is they're explaining.

The idea of religion as a metanarrative has two significant implications. First, for **Lyotard** (1979), the postmodern condition involves an 'incredulity toward metanarratives' – a general disbelief that any single set of beliefs has a monopoly of truth. Second, **Ritzer** (1992) argues that postmodern approaches represent an 'assault on structure ... and structural approaches' to understanding and explanation.

In general terms, therefore,

postmodernists argue that the structural frameworks that in the past supported *organised religions* (their ability to explain the nature of the world, for example) increasingly come under attack from competing world views – from the sixteenth century onwards in Western Europe, for example, this has involved the rise of scientific explanations. Many things that were once plausibly explained by religion are now *more plausibly* explained by scientific narratives – and, in consequence, the metanarrative foundations of organised religions are undermined by competing explanations and systematically:

**Deconstructed**: That is, broken down, in two ways: a decline in the ability of religion to exert power and control over people's lives and a gradual retreat into what are termed 'local narratives', or small stories about people's situations and circumstances. In other words, religion, where it continues to exert influence, does so in terms of individual:

**Identities**: In postmodern society people are exposed to a variety of sources of information and ideas that compete for attention – the world is no longer one where meaning and truth can be imposed and policed by elites, for example. On the contrary, people are increasingly presented with a range of choices and critiques that encourages:

- **scepticism** towards metanarratives – for every 'big story' there is a multitude of 'alternative stories'
- **hybridity**: Postmodern society encourages the development of *cultural hybrids* – *new* ways of thinking and acting that develop out of the combination of *old* ways of behaving.

In this respect, **Jencks** (1996) notes how 'the Post-Modern Age is a time of incessant choosing. It's an era when no orthodoxy can be adopted without self-consciousness and irony, because all traditions seem to have some validity . . . Pluralism, the "ism" of our time, is both the great problem and the great opportunity'.

The outcome of choice – and a plurality of opportunities, meanings and behaviours – is that religious symbols, for example, lose much of their original meaning and power as they are adopted into the everyday (*profane*) world of fashion and display. An example here is the co-option of Rastafarian religious signs and symbols (such as dreadlocks) into some parts of mainstream fashion.

Religious practice, therefore, no longer holds a central place in people's everyday life or identity; instead, it lives on as a set of accoutrements and adornments to the construction of identity – something that occurs not only in the world of *objects* (rings

Dreadlocks were originally popularised by the Rastafarian movement in the 1960s – although their origins seem to go back to places such as Ancient Egypt . . .

and pendants, for example), but also in the world of *beliefs*.

New forms of religious belief develop *not* as metanarrative but as part of *individual narratives*. These, as with the objects that accompany them, are 'picked up, worn for a time and then discarded', much as one might wear a fashionable coat until it becomes unfashionable.

## Digging deeper: Postmodernist approaches

Postmodernism reflects (or possibly encourages) a contradictory set of ideas about the significance of religious ideas, practices and organisations in both the past and the present. At one and the same time, for example, we see the ideas of religious:

**Decline** – as organised religions lose their ability to control and influence events in the *secular* (non-religious) world, and

**Development** – in that religious beliefs and practices shift and change, reflecting

# Discussion point: Lifestyle shopping?

## Wearing Kabbalah

Source: http://www.metronews.ca

### Fashion designers going with religious flow

Shopping for Kabbalah is the newest new age mantra of anyone who wants to attach themselves to the craze, but doesn't necessarily want to invest years in earnest study. While most of us will never fully appreciate the intimacies of the ancient mystical Jewish religion, enthusiastic consumers often argue that the ritual and the ecstasy of shopping is nothing short of a religious experience.

Sharon Chalkin-Feldstein describes the lounge-wear collection as versatile 'lifestyle dressing' perfect for yoga, mediating and shopping ... Take your cue from the flock of A-list celebrities, from Madonna and David Beckham to Demi Moore, who wear their devotion to Kabbalah on their wrists (always in the form of a red string, believed to ward off evil).

The above suggests some forms of religious belief and practice are bound up with the idea of consumption – that religion, for example, has meaning in terms of fashion and lifestyle. Think about and discuss the following:

- What examples of 'religious lifestyle shopping' can you identify?
- To what extent do you think 'religious symbols' have become fashion items to adorn a particular lifestyle?
- How does the combination of religious beliefs and individual lifestyle choices reflect postmodern ideas about the role of religion in contemporary societies?

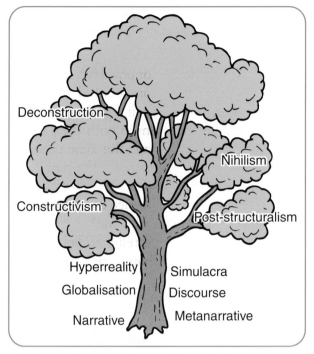

**The postmodern tree of knowledge**

perhaps basic beliefs in 'supernatural phenomena', but expressed in ways that are far removed from organised religious services. In this respect, religion (or, perhaps more correctly, *religions*) is viewed as being constantly *reinvented* to reflect the ways people choose and discard different forms of *personal identity* (the currently fashionable Kabbalah religion being a case in point).

In addition, further contradictions are evidenced in relation to the:

**Privatisation and deprivatisation** of religion: Although there are clear signs of a move towards *privatised* forms of religious belief (religion as something practised in the private rather than the public sphere), organised religion stubbornly refuses to disappear. On the contrary, there is evidence (with some forms of Islam and Christianity in particular) of a contrary process of organised forms of religion re-emerging as significant aspects of public life.

## ⚠ Weeding the path

This diversity of thought makes it difficult, in some ways, to evaluate postmodern approaches to religion because, as we've suggested, a common set of unifying principles is absent. This is not to say, however, that we can't offer up some observations about postmodern approaches.

**Metanarratives**: **Callinicos** (1991) argues that postmodernism is itself a form of the 'metanarrative thinking' postmodernists claim to dismiss as being unsustainable. More significantly, postmodernism's *inclusive approach* to metanarratives – placing scientific ideologies (such as *positivism*) on a par with religious ideologies – has the (unintended) effect of actually *strengthening* the position of religion; if both science and religion have the same metanarrative status (and postmodernists such as **Lyotard** (1997) suggest we should be equally sceptical about the respective claims of both), it follows that religious beliefs and explanations are *no less valid* than scientific beliefs and explanations. Something like *creationism* (or 'intelligent design', a belief about how the earth was created based on a literal interpretation of the Christian Bible), for example, can claim the same explanatory status as something like *evolutionary theory*.

This idea leads us to consider a further question, namely:

**Resacralisation**: One of the enduring contradictions described by postmodern approaches is noted by **McLeod** (1997) when he observes that postmodernity is an 'era of religious fragmentation, characterised by religious pluralism and conflicting evidence of both secularisation and sacralisation'. In this respect, a general decline in overt forms of religious practice (such as attendance at religious ceremonies) sits alongside a *reinvigoration* of both public and private religious practice (in the USA, for example, church attendances are generally rising). The basic idea here, therefore, is that religion actually becomes *less important* to people in terms of *practice*, but *more important* as a source of personal and social identity. In a world that appears increasingly confusing and unstable, religions become beacons of order and stability by their ability to produce moral certainties.

Thus, in a world of *moral relativism* – where one set of beliefs and values is as good (or bad) as any other – religions are reinvigorated precisely because what they have to offer is no worse than any other form of explanation (and, possibly, a good deal more attractive than some). In this respect, **Bauman** (1992) argues, 'postmodernity can be seen as restoring ... a re-enchantment of the world that modernity tried hard to disenchant'. **Bauman** (1997) also addresses the issue of religious:

**Fundamentalism**: This represents a form of religious belief and organisation that advocates a strict observance of the 'fundamental beliefs' of a religion, whether it be of the Christian variety in the USA or the Islamic variety in Iran. For **Bauman**, fundamentalist religions draw their strength from the ability to provide *certainties* in an uncertain world – from a belief in the principles laid down in the Old Testament of Christianity (an 'eye for an eye', for example) to the clear specification of how men and women should dress and behave in Islam. **Bauman's** ideas, in this respect, link to **Beck's** (1992) concept of:

**Risk** in the sense that fundamentalist religions, by removing *choice*, also remove *risk*. The individual, by being given clear moral guidelines, has the 'dread of risk taking' (and the consequences of those risks) removed.

## Weeding the path

Ideas about the relationship between postmodernity and religious fundamentalism need to be considered in relation to two ideas; first, that such fundamentalism is not necessarily new (it has existed at various times throughout history) and second, whether contemporary forms of fundamentalism are actually linked with postmodernity, per se, or some other socio-economic processes.

The final idea we can note is:

**Meaning**: For many postmodernist writers, religious signs and symbols have lost their 'original' meaning – they become, in **Baudrillard's** (1998) terms:

**Simulacra**, or things that simulate something that may once have been real. These simulations are *not* imitations; they are just *as real* as the things they simulate – televised religious services, for example, give the *appearance* of participation in a real religious service, although, of course, the two experiences are quantitatively and qualitatively different. For **Baudrillard**, *religious simulacra* give the appearance of religiosity (wearing a cross, for example), but are, he argues, actually empty and devoid of any original meaning they once had – they 'simulate divinity', as he puts it, and in so doing devalue both the meaning and substance of religion. **Sedgwick** (2004), meanwhile, suggests this argument is overstated when he notes the distinction between:

- **organised religions**, such as the Catholic Church, and

- **'disorganised' religions** which involve a certain level of *spirituality* – a belief in the supernatural, for example – but which are not always explicitly practised in the same way as organised religions.

As he notes: 'We are often told that people are wide open to the idea of the spiritual – the religious, the numinous, call it what you like – but have no time for organised religion. And so the churches are emptying while they pursue their quest elsewhere.' He suggests people are '. . . looking for private religion – that is, religion they can practise with minimal interruption to their normal routine and without having to bother about burdensome responsibilities. "I want the feel-good factor, but not the cost of commitment" – that, in reality, is what such people are saying. Putting it bluntly, private religion is essentially selfish religion'.

**Bauman** (1997) is equally scathing of 'the new spiritualism': 'Postmodernity is the era of experts in "identity problems" of personality healers, of marriage guides, of writers of "how to reassert yourself" books; it is the era of the "counselling boom". Business executives need spiritual counselling and their organizations need spiritual healing. Uncertainty postmodern-style begets not the demand for religion . . . [but] the ever rising demand for identity-experts.'

Having covered a range of inclusive approaches, we can turn now to consider some *exclusive* approaches to understanding religion.

## Preparing the ground: Marxist theories

Marxists generally (and **Marx** in particular) take an *exclusive* view of religion, preferring to study its impact on society by focusing on the particular qualities of religions – most notably the experience of 'the sacred' (what **Eliade** (1969) called the 'irreducibly religious' element of religion) that can only be found in 'religious experience'. In this sense, therefore, Marxists have examined how religious beliefs and practices are *qualitatively* different to other forms of belief and practice. Thus, for Marxists religion is an important object of study in its own right, albeit one located in the general structure of (capitalist) society. To understand the significance of religion, therefore, we need to think about its:

**Institutional role** as part of the general structure of society, which involves thinking about how Marxists theorise the relationship between economic, political and ideological institutions (such as religion). In this respect, capitalist societies are theorised in terms of the relationship between 'base and superstructure':

- **Economic base**: This is the foundation on which any society is built. It is the world of work and involves particular types of *relationships* (owner/manager/wage labourer, for example) and *organisation* (based on things like wages in capitalist societies).

- **Political** and **ideological superstructure**: This 'rests' on the economic base and represents things like *government* and formal agencies of social control (political institutions) and *cultural institutions* like religion, education and the mass media

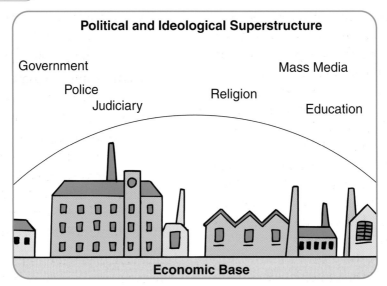

**Political and Ideological Superstructure**

Government

Mass Media

Police

Judiciary

Religion

Education

**Economic Base**

It can help to think about society as a dome resting on economic foundations – the dome itself involves ideological institutions such as religion.

(which Marxists call ideological institutions).

Our focus here is on the ideological role of religion in society.

## ✳ SYNOPTIC LINK

**Stratification and differentiation:** These ideas are explained in greater detail in the section on Marxist theories of stratification.

## ⚘ Growing it yourself: Not rocking the world?

In small groups, identify some of the ways religions have supported the status quo (especially, but not exclusively, in the past). For each idea you identify, briefly note how it tries to prevent social change. We've given you a couple of examples to get you started (because we're nice).

| | |
|---|---|
| Ten Commandments | Not stealing or being jealous of the things owned by others |
| God | All powerful – He made the world for a reason |
| Reincarnation | In the Hindu religion, if you obey religious law in this life you will be reborn in a higher social position in your next life |
| **Further examples?** | |

From this position religion is seen as an:

**Ideological framework** (or belief system) that helps to shape the way people see the world; its role, in capitalist society, is to 'represent the world' in a way that reflects and supports the existing economic order. In other words, religious ideologies represent:

**Legitimating myths** about the world – 'propaganda stories', in other words, whose ultimate aim is to explain and justify the way society is ordered. Its role, in common with other cultural/ideological institutions in capitalist society, is to uphold the *status quo* (to keep things as they are).

In this respect, therefore, the role of religion in society is seen as both *oppressive* and *repressive*.

- **Oppressive**: As **Marx** (1844) argued, religion represented an 'illusory happiness' that prevented people finding 'real happiness'. The 'need for illusions' about the world, he argued, stemmed from the conditions under which people lived. For most people living in Victorian Britain, conditions were grim, and for **Marx** the solution to their unhappy situation was to remove the conditions that caused this (economic exploitation).

- **Repressive**: Although, like **Durkheim** (1912), **Marx** saw religion as having an *integrating* function, he also saw it as an (ideological) agency of social control – one that teaches people to accept both the world 'as it is' and, of course, their position in that world. Religion, therefore, served the interests of a ruling class by enforcing their ideological domination of other classes – in Victorian Britain, for example, religion promoted these interests by:

  - **upholding the status quo**: The social world could legitimately be portrayed as 'god-given' and consequently beyond the power of people to change

  - **legitimising economic exploitation**: If God made the world, it was not the place of people to question this scheme

  - **justifying poverty and inequality**: Poverty could be portrayed as a *virtue* – something to be endured in an uncomplaining fashion, since it was a means of achieving true spiritual riches in the afterlife (heaven).

The power of religious ideology, for **Marx**, wasn't simply that it was 'believed uncritically' – its real power to convince was based on the fact that it could 'do something' for believers, such as 'dull the pain of oppression' with its promise of eternal life (Christianity) or reincarnation into a higher social *caste* (Hinduism) – as **Marx** (1844) expressed it: 'Religious suffering is, at one and the same time, the *expression* of real suffering and a *protest* against real suffering. Religion is the sigh of the oppressed creature, the heart of a heartless world, and the soul of soulless conditions. It is the *opium* of the people.'

## Discussion point: Drugged up?

In small groups, think about the following:

- What do you think Marx meant by the phrase 'religion is the opium of the people'?

- Identify some ways religion is like a powerful drug.

- If the religious are like (metaphorical) drug addicts, who supplies the drug and how do these 'drug dealers' profit from religion?

## ❊ SYNOPTIC LINK

**Stratification and differentiation:** The caste system is discussed in more detail as a form of social stratification in the 'Theories of stratification' section.

For traditional forms of Marxism, therefore, religion represents a form of:

**False consciousness** – people are *unaware* they are being tricked into accepting a situation that exploits them. By believing religious ideas people fail to see or understand the real causes of their misery and oppression – an exploitative economic system. **Foucault** (1983) captures this idea quite neatly when he notes: 'People know what they do; they frequently know why they do what they do; but what they don't know is what they do does.' (Think about it – but not for too long.)

Marx didn't simply believe that by exposing the oppressive role of religion people would come to see their true interests. Religious beliefs, like any form of ideology, don't just exist as ideas imposed on the gullible. On the contrary, such beliefs are rooted deeply in the condition under which people live in capitalist society:

**Alienation:** In a competitive, exploitative society people gain little or no satisfaction or fulfilment from either the work they do or the relationships they form – they are, in this respect, alienated from both themselves and each other. In this situation, **Marx** (1844) argued, religion provided – at least at the time he was writing – a sense of meaning and purpose to life (albeit a false and illusory meaning).

## 🍴 Weeding the path

At this point, you may be thinking that even if alienation is 'part of the problem' it no longer seems very plausible (when thinking about Britain in the twenty-first century) to see religion playing the kind of role described by **Marx** – and you'd probably be right (which is as good a reason as any to look at both an evaluation of classical Marxism and some more-modern (neo) Marxist thinking about religion).

## ⛏ Digging deeper: Marxist theories

When we dig deeper into classical Marxist theories of religion we can identify two major problems, the first of which is:

**False consciousness:** There are a couple of critical dimensions here:

- **Historical:** For false consciousness to be a factor in people's oppression it is necessary for 'the oppressed' to be 'religious' in terms of their beliefs and practices. **Turner** (1983), however, has argued that, historically, the working classes have never been particularly religious (if you measure religious conviction in terms of church attendance, involvement in and membership of religious groups and the like).

- **Contemporary:** Although there is a diversity of religious beliefs and practices in modern Britain, it's arguable that, in terms of Christianity at least, religion plays a relatively *peripheral* and *superficial* role in the lives of most people (one restricted, in many instances, to attending things like weddings and funerals). In this respect, it's difficult to see religion as having much ideological significance for the majority of people.

The second problem is that, for classical Marxism, religion was a largely *conservative force* (in the sense of broadly supporting the status quo). However, this is not necessarily the case, as the following examples show:

- **The Iranian Revolution** in 1979 involved the overthrow of the (secular) regime of the Shah of Persia.

- **Liberation theology**: **Boff** and **Boff** (1987) note the involvement of Roman Catholic clerics in revolutionary political movements in parts of South America from the 1960s onwards.

- The **Civil Rights Movement**: In the USA, from the 1960s onwards, social change was promoted and supported by Black religious activists and leaders (such as Martin Luther King).

## Weeding the path

**Seiler** (2004) argues that the overall picture of the relationship between religion and its ability to promote social change is complicated – he notes, for example: 'Freedom is relative because it has its limits. In the case of Liberation Theology, for example, the Catholic Church hierarchy has not welcomed this ideological form and has tried, with varying degrees of success, to limit its impact.'

**Neo-Marxist theories** of religion attempt to resolve these problems through, initially, the concept of:

**Hegemony** – an idea put forward by **Gramsci** (1934) and elaborated by, among others, **Poulantzas** (1974). *Hegemony* involves the idea that beliefs about the world are not simply imposed 'from above' (by a ruling class onto all other classes). Rather, as **Strinati** (1995) suggests, dominant groups are able to maintain their dominant position through the 'consent' of subordinate groups. This 'consent' (for the leadership in society by those who are led) is created through *socialisation* and *force*.

**Socialisation**: Consent is 'manufactured' through ideological institutions (of which religion is but one). **Althusser** (1972) argued that we should see this aspect of 'consent manufacture' in terms of the concept of:

- **ideological state apparatuses** (ISAs) – socialisation processes carried out by cultural institutions such as religion, education and the media.

**Force**: This aspect may come into play *directly* (through agencies such as the police playing a repressive role in society), but one of the subtleties of hegemonic arguments is that 'consent to leadership' doesn't actually have to involve support for 'dominant ideas'. On the contrary, it's possible to *oppose* dominant ideas – but if you're unable to do anything to change them you are effectively lending them your consent. **Althusser** argued we should see this aspect of 'consent manufacture' in terms of:

- **repressive state apparatuses** (RSAs), involving groups such as the police, social workers and the armed forces.

The concept of hegemony makes it possible for 'religious ideas' to be seen as influential in contemporary societies without necessarily having to show that 'the majority' of people either believe or support them, an idea **Strinati** (1995) expresses thus: '... **Gramsci's** theory suggests subordinated groups accept the ideas, values and leadership of the dominant group not because they are physically or mentally induced to do so, nor because they are ideologically indoctrinated, but because they have reason of their own.'

We can build on the concept of *hegemony* by noting that, for traditional Marxist theory, religion formed part of a:

**Dominant ideology** – a set of ideas, sanctified by God, that explained and justified the nature of the social world. Consequently, it represented an:

**Integrating social force**: By providing a set of beliefs and practices to which everyone was either subject or to which they could aspire, religion helped provide the 'social glue' binding people together in terms of shared norms, values, traditions, customs and the like.

For neo-Marxists, as **Turner** (1983) notes, the ideological impact of religion is more subtle in that, rather than seeing religious ideas and rationalisations as an instrument of ideological oppression, they suggest it represents a:

**Cohesive force** for a *ruling class* in capitalist society. In other words, religion represents one way (significantly more important in the past, perhaps) that the various elements and members of a ruling class are integrated *as a class*. Religion, in this respect, provided a set of universal, moral guidelines for ruling-class behaviour – in relation to areas such as marriage and the inheritance of property (Christianity, for example, laid down the rules for legitimate relationships and hence for the inheritance of property).

## Weeding the path

Although neo-Marxism provides a different view of the role of religion in capitalist society to its traditional counterpart, a significant criticism of this position involves the idea of:

**Reductionism**: That is, the explanation for the existence and role of cultural institutions like religion ultimately comes down – or is *reduced* – to what **Pals** (1996) calls 'the material facts of the class struggle and alienation. Since these burdens form the reality behind the illusions of belief, [Marxists] explain religion best only when [they] reduce it to the forces of economic life that have created it'. In other words, whether from a traditional or a neo-Marxist position, the significance of religion is ultimately judged in terms of how it performs an ideological role in support of a capitalist economic system.

## Moving on

We have, at various points, touched on the question of whether religion acts as a *conservative social force* – limiting and inhibiting social change in support of the political and economic status quo – or as a potential *force for change*. In the next section, therefore, we can look at both sides of this argument in more detail.

## 2. The role of religion as a conservative force and as an initiator of change

The relationship between religion and social change is interesting because it provides an insight into the dynamics of religious beliefs, practices and organisation and enables us to look at religion in terms of its influence on a range of societies, as a possible initiator of change or as a conservative social force. Before we explore these ideas in more detail, however, we need to clarify a few ideas.

**Social change**: This idea can be interpreted in a couple of ways (*historically* and *localised*).

**Historical movements** refer to large-scale, far-reaching changes to the way of life in a society. Examples here might include the French and American revolutions in the eighteenth century, the Russian Revolution(s) in the twentieth century or the transition from feudal to capitalist societies that began, in Western Europe, in the seventeenth century.

**Localised movements** refer to the relatively small ways a society changes over time. Britain in the twenty-first century, for example, is a substantially different society to Britain in the middle of the twentieth century. Although there have been no great historical changes of the type just noted over this period, changes in terms of technological developments, social class, gender relationships and the like have certainly taken place.

The meaning of 'social change' is, in this respect, not always clear and precise and different writers make different assumptions about what it involves. In this section, however, we're going to focus on the former meaning of social change in order to

## WARM-UP: PERSPECTIVES ON CHANGE

When we looked at theories of religion we considered some of the implications of each in terms of whether or not religion was likely to support the status quo in society. In small groups, use the following table as the basis for identifying how each theoretical perspective mainly sees the role of religion.

| Perspective | Does this perspective suggest religion is mainly: | | |
|---|---|---|---|
| | Conservative? | Initiator of change? | Possibly both? |
| Classical Marxism | ✓ | ✗ | ✗ |
| Neo-Marxism | | | |
| Functionalism | | | |
| Interactionism | | | |
| Postmodernism | | | |

Once you've done this, briefly discuss among the group the reasons for your choices.

As a class, discuss your choices and reasons to arrive at a general picture of the role of religion in society from a variety of sociological perspectives.

examine a range of 'classical sociological perspectives' on the relationship between religion and social change.

**Conservative force**: There are two basic meanings we need to note for this idea. The first, relatively straightforward, one is the role of religion in:

- **Preventing social change**: In other words, its role in maintaining the status quo in society.

The second, less straightforward, meaning involves the idea of 'conservative' in the sense of promoting a set of:

- **Traditional values and beliefs**: This involves religion asserting or reasserting a set of values and practices that belong 'to the past' and an example here might be attempts to recreate a way of life based on traditional values and morality (real or imagined). A classic illustration of this idea is the 1979 Iranian Revolution, involving the replacement of a secular regime with an Islamic political, legal and moral order. Although religion was involved in promoting social change, it was a *conservative* form of change, designed to assert a particular (non-Western), socially conservative political order.

## ⚠ Preparing the ground: Marxist perspectives

As we've suggested in the previous section, the general Marxist view of the relationship between *economic* institutions (such as work and the production process) and *cultural* institutions (such as religion) is that the latter are supportive of – and in some respects dependent upon – the former. For neo-Marxists like **Balibar** and **Althusser**

(1970) or **Poulantzas** (1973), the economic sphere should always be considered *determinant 'in the last instance'* (in other words, in any final reckoning over a clash of interests, those holding economic power would always triumph over those wielding ideological power alone). What this means is that Marxists generally view religion as a *conservative social force*, expressed in two main ways:

- **False consciousness**, which we've already discussed in relation to classical Marxism (religion is partly responsible for mystifying the nature of the social world), and

- **System maintenance**: There are times when capitalist societies undergo economic crises that threaten their stability. In such moments, the conservative role of religion may actually act as a channel for social dissent that, somewhat ironically perhaps, helps to *preserve* the overall status quo in society by promoting a (limited) but crucial amount of social change. If this is a little unclear, an example should help.

**The black Civil Rights Movement**: In the USA in the 1950s the systematic oppression of black minorities by the white majority threatened the stability of American society (and, perhaps more significantly, American capitalism) as black discontent and unrest was manifested in civil unrest. A number of factors, as **Farley** (1990) notes, 'heightened the black sense of relative deprivation'. These included:

- **Urban ghetto life**, which 'facilitated communication and organisation', and
- **Military service** in the Second World War where '... African-American soldiers

**Rosa Parks' protest in 1955 was a potent symbol of the American Civil Rights Movement**

fought for their country, only to return to a society that did not regard them as full citizens'.

In this situation we have a conventional Marxist scenario – economic and political deprivation leading to a sense of injustice and unrest – that required a *catalyst* to produce change. This, arguably, came from the experience of **Rosa Parks** '... arrested for refusing to give up her seat to a white person on a bus'.

**Farley** suggests '... black churches were largely responsible for organising the massive bus boycott that followed ... **Parks** had discussed her plans and their possible consequences with church leaders and civil rights organisations', including Dr **Martin Luther King** (who, you might be interested to learn, was a sociology graduate) and the Southern Christian Leadership Conference. In the wider context, **Pyle** and **Davidson** (1998) suggest: 'Perhaps more than any other institution, religion illustrates the diversity of strategies that African Americans have adopted in attempting to address racism and class inequality.'

From a Marxist position, therefore, religion played a role in social change by functioning as a:

**Channel** through which protest was organised and focused; this resulted, eventually, in major changes to the relative social positions of black and white Americans. However, it could also be argued that such change was, essentially, *conservative* in that it left the economic structures of US society largely untouched.

### ⚠ Digging deeper: Marxist perspectives

Although Marxists traditionally see religion as a broadly conservative social force, there are, as we've suggested, differences of interpretation within this perspective. These stem partly from the way our society has developed historically and partly from a change of theoretical emphasis within

Marxism itself. We can illustrate both this idea and the different preoccupations of classical and neo-Marxism in the following way.

**Classical Marxism** has traditionally focused on the analysis of:

**Social transformations** – large-scale, widespread change that transforms, in some way, the nature of a society. This may occur slowly, as in Britain from the seventeenth century onwards (the change from a feudal to a capitalist system), or rapidly, as in the French Revolution (the change from a monarchy to a republic) or the Iranian Revolution (the change from a Westernised dictatorship to an Islamic republic).

## Neo-marxism

**Neo-Marxism**, while not neglecting this area of study, has tended to focus more on:

**Social transitions** – situations where, although the basic (economic and political) structure of society doesn't change, the relative positions of people and groups within a society does. The civil rights illustration we've just used is an example of this type of change. Similarly, in our society we could think of *social transitions* in terms of areas like gender or age and changes in the position of different groups over the last 50 years or so.

In terms of *social transformations*, therefore, we can look briefly at the classical Marxist analysis of the change from feudalism to capitalism in Britain from the seventeenth century onwards (a good example of how classical Marxists saw religion as a conservative social force and useful as a point of comparison when we examine Weberian perspectives on religion and change). In the transformation of British society – over a period of 200 years or more, beginning around the middle of

the seventeenth century – we see a major social change:

**Feudal society** was characterised by:

- **stratification** – a rigid (closed) system of social stratification that involved little or no movement up or down the class structure

- **land ownership** (the main source of income and power) concentrated in a relatively small number of aristocratic hands

- **an obligatory system** involving rights and responsibilities, mainly concerning the exchange of land rights for service

- **monarchy** – a dictatorship based around a king or queen who was an absolute ruler (their authority derived from God).

---

## ✳ SYNOPTIC LINK

**Stratification and differentiation:** The structure of feudal society is outlined in more detail in relation to theories of stratification.

---

**Capitalist society**, meanwhile, was characterised by:

- **stratification** – a fluid, open system of stratification

- **technology** – factory ownership and machine production became the main source of income and power

- **contract** – economic and social relationships based on exchange (money) involving owners and non-owners, employers and employees

- **democracy** – political power and representation was increasingly spread throughout society, based eventually, over a few hundred years, on a system of universal suffrage ('one person one vote').

**Marx** characterised feudalism as a system in which one section of a ruling class (an old feudal aristocracy) was supported by the Catholic Church – a powerful force in this society – in three main ways:

- **economically** – as a major landowner
- **politically** – because of its relationship with – and power over – the monarchy and aristocracy
- **ideologically** – its teachings stressed an acceptance of the 'natural order' in society (involving respect for and deference to 'social superiors') that was God-created and immutable (impossible for people to change).

Technological development (the invention and application of machinery and new forms of power such as gas and electricity – the Industrial Revolution) led, according to **Marx**, to the development of a *new section* of the bourgeoisie – a 'merchant class' that took advantage of the opportunities created by emerging technologies to advance their economic power (at the expense of both the old feudal aristocracy and the peasantry). For **Marx**, as this 'class within the ruling class' became economically powerful, it needed an:

**Ideology** that allowed it to challenge the 'old existing social order' – one that would allow the emergent bourgeoisie to legitimately translate their *economic power* into *political power* – and two different forms of the Protestant religion (*deism* and *Calvinism*) fitted the bill quite neatly in this respect:

- **Deism:** A form of religious belief that argued that although God had made the world, He gave people the freedom to find their own way to ultimate salvation. In this respect, people were to be finally judged on the basis of their good works – and their sins – during their lifetime.
- **Calvinism** (named after its founder, John **Calvin**) was based on the concept of:
  - **Predestination** – the idea that an individual's life was predetermined by God. Nothing the individual did in life could change or influence a decision that had already been made. However, Calvinism also argued that leading a successful and productive life was a sign, from God, that the individual would go to Heaven when they died (on the not unreasonable assumption, perhaps, that those who were unsuccessful and unproductive were not likely to be predestined for Heaven).

Both deism and Calvinism, in their different ways, provided a set of ideological tools that supported the efforts of the bourgeoisie to develop the political power and influence to reflect their emerging economic power.

## Weeding the path

Although a major social transformation (between feudalism and capitalism) clearly occurred in Britain, **Marx** argued the Protestant religion did *not* initiate social change; rather, one set of religious ideas was used by one section of the ruling class (the bourgeoisie) as a *rationalisation* for their economic and political dominance over another section – the aristocracy. The *cause* of social change was *economic* – changes in the way things were produced, distributed and exchanged led to changes in the way society was organised.

Thus, for classical Marxists, ideas about the nature of the world arose out of people's *experience* in the world (not the other way round) and social change arose out of economic conflicts between and within social classes. Religious ideas played a significant role *only* in relation to the differing abilities of powerful economic classes to use such ideas as a rationale for change.

In a contemporary context, **Azad** (1995) has applied a similar analysis to social transformations such as the Iranian Revolution (1979). The overthrow of the 'old order' (a tyrannical, secular dictatorship, supported by countries such as Britain and the USA) was seen to occur through an alliance of 'progressive elements' among the working classes and (Islamic) religious organisations. Only *after* the Shah of Persia was deposed, **Azad** argues, did a power struggle for control emerge in which religious leaders proved the stronger. However, even in this particular context, **Azad** suggests that, fundamentally, no major transformation took place in Iran: 'In 1979 the Iranian economy was a capitalist economy. Sixteen years later, despite many religious edicts, that is still its essence.'

For neo-Marxists, greater emphasis in recent times has been placed, as we've suggested, on the analysis of *social transitions* where, although religion is still seen as an essentially conservative force, it may, at certain times, become a popular channel for dissent and social change. In addition to the civil rights movement illustration we mentioned earlier, a further example to support this particular interpretation of the role of religion is:

**Northern Ireland**: The conflict between, on the one hand, Roman Catholics who wanted a united Ireland and, on the other, Protestants who wanted to remain part of the United Kingdom, appears, on the face of things, to be a clear-cut example of religious identification and affiliation playing a major role in social change. However, the general Marxist interpretation of this conflict suggests *social class* was the prime mover – the majority of Catholics, for example, were drawn from the working classes while the majority of Protestants were middle or upper class.

Finally, it's useful to note **Robinson's** (1987) argument that there are 'six conditions that shape the likelihood of religion becoming a force for social change':

- A **religious world view** shared by the revolutionary classes.
- **Theology** (religious teachings and beliefs) that conflicts with the beliefs and practices of the existing social order.
- **Clergy** who are closely associated with revolutionary classes.
- A **single religion** shared by the revolutionary classes.
- **Differences** between the religion of the revolutionary classes and the religion of the ruling classes (such as one being Catholic and the other Protestant).
- **Channels** of legitimate political dissent blocked or not available.

## Weeding the path

We can identify a couple of problems with the general Marxist position on religion and social change:

- **Reductionism**: As we've previously noted, everything is ultimately reduced to (economic) class struggle. Thus, even in a situation such as Northern Ireland in the 1980s (where religious affiliation played a role in establishing group cohesion and sense of identity), social change is seen in terms of *class* rather than *religious identity*.

- **Religion and revolt: MacCulloch** and **Pezzini** (2002) question the relationship, suggested by Marxists, between religious beliefs and acceptance of the prevailing social order – their research, for example, found that in democratic societies there was little or no difference between religious believers and non-believers on the need for major social change. This suggests that, at best, there is no simple link between levels of religious belief and acceptance or rejection of the status quo.

## Preparing the ground: Functionalist perspectives

As with Marxism, we can consider functionalist accounts of religion and social change in terms of its classical and newer variations.

**Classical functionalism:** For **Durkheim** (1912), one of the fundamental features of human behaviour was the idea of:

*Homo duplex:* In basic terms, this involves human beings (*homo*) having 'two sides' (*duplex*): an 'individualistic' or 'selfish' side (similar to what the interactionist sociologist **G.H. Mead** (1934) called the 'unsocialised self') and a 'social' or 'communal' side (the 'socialised self'). In other words, we all have two aspects to our lives; while we are all biological animals, we become 'recognisably human' only through our relationships with other people. Without 'society', therefore, we can't express our unique, human, individuality. Thus, in order to 'become human individuals' we must immerse ourselves in *social groups,* and to achieve this we must give up some aspects of our 'selfish side' (the desire to behave as we want, when we want)

to 'society' – to create what **Bental** (2004) terms '. . . a strong attachment to society . . . to guide [our] behaviour', and which, for **Durkheim**, was represented by the:

**Collective conscience** – the 'will of society' people experience as an 'external force' that controls and coerces our behaviour. Just as each individual has a conscience, so too society has a 'conscience' – the 'collective presentations', as **Bental** puts it, 'that hold society together' – expressed through a range of norms and values (such as prescriptions against murder). For classical functionalism, religion plays an important role in maintaining the collective conscience through:

- **Moral codes:** Religion provides a source of morality that cannot be realistically challenged, since it derives from a power higher than the individual (such as 'God').

- **Collective ceremonies:** Through participation in ceremonies (such as religious services) society is given substance or 'made real'; through collective behaviour we gain a necessary sense of our relationship to – and dependence on – others. **Bental** also notes that 'participation in rituals brings about the psychological phenomenon of *collective effervescence*' – an emotional high and feeling we are part of something bigger than ourselves'.

## Weeding the path

Some functionalists argue that in modern, diverse societies, traditional forms of religion no longer have a 'monopoly of faith' and therefore cannot integrate people into society as a whole. **Bellah** (1967) developed the concept of:

## Growing it yourself: Civil religion in Britain

In small groups, use the following table as a template to identify some possible components – both religious and non-religious (secular) – of a 'civil religion' in Britain.

| Religious components? | Secular components? |
| --- | --- |
| The existence of a 'higher power'<br>Prayer | Democracy<br>National anthem |
| **Further examples?** ||

Civil religion to refer to a set of common ideas, shared by the vast majority of people in a society, that have both religious and secular aspects. In Britain, for example, there are a variety of religions, but the one thing they all arguably have in common is a belief in some form of 'god'; this general belief – rather than specific beliefs about the actual form and nature of god – represents an aspect of *civil religion*. In a different way, ideas like 'innocent until proven guilty' or a belief in the 'democratic process' can all be considered part of a British civil religion.

As **Wimberley** and **Swatos** (1998) note, **Bellah's** definition of civil religion represents 'an institutionalised collection of sacred beliefs', whether these beliefs be overtly religious or overtly secular.

### Digging deeper: Functionalist perspectives

Classical functionalism generally views religion as a *conservative social force* (on the basis that it functions as both a source of:

- **social solidarity** (by providing moral codes, a common value system, and so forth), and
- **social integration** through such things as collective ceremonies.

**Neo-functionalist** writers, such as **Alexander** (1985), however, suggest that religion may, under some conditions, initiate social change in contemporary societies. Drawing on (and revising) the work of **Parsons** (1951), **Alexander** sees societies in terms of:

**Functional subsystems** – groups of institutions carrying out different, but interrelated, functions. The *cultural subsystem*, for example, includes institutions such as education, the media and religion, and is related to subsystems such as work, the family and the political process. This subsystem is seen – borrowing from (neo-Marxist) writers such as **Althusser** (1972) and **Poulantzas** (1973) – to have a degree of:

**Relative autonomy** (or freedom) from other parts of the social system, mainly because it involves institutions whose primary function is *socialisation* and the creation/propagation of cultural values. Under certain conditions, therefore, cultural institutions have the potential to instigate social change. This follows, for **Alexander,** because religion contains theories not just of the *past* (where we've been) and the *present* (how we've got here), but also of the *future* (where we are ultimately going), which means religions are not just concerned with questions of social order and stability, but also social change. We can illustrate this idea using the:

**Jehovah's Witnesses**: This particular religious group has a theory of the:

- **Past**: The world was created by Jehovah ('God'): 'The very existence of the intricately designed wonders in the universe surrounding us reasonably argues that a supremely intelligent and powerful Creator produced it all.'

- **Present**: We now live in the 'time of the end' in which 'Satan is the invisible ruler of world'. Witnesses believe the Earth will never be destroyed, but the people who populate it can die (and, mainly, go to Hell).

- **Future**: Witnesses believe in the 'Second Coming' of Christ, a time when human beings will be destroyed and True Believers (i.e. Jehovah's Witnesses) will be resurrected to enjoy the Kingdom of Heaven ('paradise') on earth.

In this respect, many (not necessarily all) religions contain the possibility, not always realised, of initiating social change, either:

- **transformative**: For Jehovah's Witnesses, the aim is to transform society. For some followers of Islam, the aim is to create societies based on Islamic Law (the Sharia), or

- **transitional** – for example, changing Christian attitudes to homosexuality or the ordination of female priests.

In this respect, neo-functionalists generally characterise modern societies as being in a state of:

**Moving equilibrium**: That is, they are constantly changing in a variety of ways, normally – but not exclusively – in the form of structural adjustments and realignments; a classic example here is the development of education systems in modern societies. In Britain, for example, formal schooling developed during the nineteenth century as a structural response to changes in the workplace (such as the need for a literate and numerate workforce).

## ✳ SYNOPTIC LINK

**Education:** This idea (and the one that follows) represents a functionalist explanation for the development of formal systems of education.

Social change, for neo-functionalists, is explained in terms of:

**Structural differentiation** – an idea borrowed from **Parsons** (1937) that argues that social institutions have progressively lost many of the functions they performed in the past; they become differentiated ('separated'), but in the process also become more *specialised*; that is, more tightly focused on the ('core') functions they perform most effectively. For example, in the past in our society religion (in the shape of Christianity) performed a range of functions (such as education) that have increasingly been taken over by specialist institutions (such as schools). The Christian Church, although still involved in education ('faith schools'), mainly focuses on serving the spiritual needs of its parishioners.

Writers such as **Luhmann** (1977) and **Bettinger** (1996) have developed the idea of *core functions* to suggest social change may come about through:

**Negative feedback** – an evolutionary process that sees social change resulting from the clash of (cultural) ideas and experiences. A classic example here might be the 'ideological clash' between the ideas of Western secular societies and Islamic religious groups.

 Weeding the path

We can note some general criticisms of the functionalist approach in terms of:

- **Social change**: This is generally theorised as being slow, gradual and evolutionary and this perspective has difficulty explaining rapid, revolutionary social transformations and the development of new value systems.

- **Tension management**: Although societies are considered to evolve and adjust through *structural differentiation*, it's not always clear how and why tensions arise in society. If a society is 'balanced', then how and why do tensions appear?

- **Evolution**: Social change, when it occurs, is generally viewed positively – mainly because there is no real way, within this perspective, to evaluate such change.

## Preparing the ground: Religion as an initiator of social change

We can begin by outlining the arguments put forward by **Weber** (1905) in his analysis of *social transformations* (in this instance from feudal to capitalist society) to support his argument that religion could be an initiator of social change. In this respect, **Giddens** (1993) notes: '**Weber's** writings on religion differ from those of **Durkheim** in concentrating on the connection between religion and social change, something to which **Durkheim** gave little attention. They contrast with **Marx** because **Weber** argues that religion is not necessarily a conservative force; on the contrary, religiously inspired movements have often produced dramatic social transformations.'

Unlike the Marxist analyses at which we've just looked, **Weber** was interested in developing a:

**Multi-causal** analysis of change. In other words, he explored how a multitude of possible factors – economic, political and ideological – could, at certain times and under certain conditions, *combine* to promote change. He chose to explain, as an example of this approach, the social changes that first occurred in Britain from the seventeenth century (the development of capitalist society).

**Weber** wanted to understand how and why capitalism developed in some societies but not others, even though they had reached similar levels of economic and technological development. Both China and the Roman Empire once developed sophisticated technologies hundreds of years in advance of anything seen in Britain, yet neither developed beyond a feudal economic and political system.

# ⚠ Growing it yourself: The problem of predestination

In small groups, your task is to relate general observations about Calvinism to technological developments in seventeenth/eighteenth-century Britain to understand how religion could potentially be a source of social change. Read the following statements:

| Calvinism | Economic opportunities |
|---|---|
| 1. God was omniscient ('all-knowing'). He knew both an individual's past and their future – who would go to Heaven and who would not. | 1. In feudal society, land ownership (mainly by the aristocracy) was the main source of economic and political power. |
| 2. Predestination: God predetermined every individual life. It was not possible for people to influence how their life developed or know whether they would achieve salvation (in Calvinist terms, whether they were one of God's 'Elect'). | 2. Calvinists had few opportunities to acquire land. |
| 3. Church ministers had no 'special relationship' with God; they could not 'absolve sins' and could not act as an intermediary between God and the individual (through prayer, for example). | 3. Technological developments – the invention of machines, for example – created opportunities for enterprising individuals to generate wealth through the application of 'new technologies'. |
| 4. God would allow only those who had led a spiritually pure life to go to Heaven. Those who were 'God's Elect' would, therefore, show signs of their 'chosen status' during their lifetime. | 4. Wealth creation involved the investment and reinvestment of money and effort in the productive process. Exploiting new developments was a means towards creating, keeping and expanding wealth. |
| | 5. Making profits – and becoming wealthy – was a sign of success. The continued reinvestment of profits in a business ensured its continued success. |

Think about/discuss the following:

1. What picture of 'the Calvinist' is portrayed here?
2. How did technological developments produce new opportunities for moneymaking?
3. Why were Calvinists in a good position to exploit the opportunities presented by technological innovations?
4. How do these ideas show religion to be a potential initiator of social change?

What **Weber** suggested was that religion (or a particular form of Protestant religion – *Calvinism*) provided the 'final push', allowing a society with a particular level of technological development to 'break through' the invisible barrier dividing relatively poor, agriculture-based, feudal dictatorships from the relatively affluent, industry-based, capitalist democracies.

Calvinism, **Weber** argued, provided the necessary 'spirit of capitalism' – a set of ideas and practices that promoted a strong and lasting social transformation.

## ✳ SYNOPTIC LINK

**Weber** concluded religion was a potential source of social change because, in this instance, two things came together at the right moment: *technological changes* that provided opportunities to create wealth in a new and dynamic way, and a group of people with *the ideological orientation* and impetus to exploit these opportunities. As **Bental** (2004) puts it: 'Here we have a category of people – the early Protestants [Calvinists] – who associated morality and Godliness with hard work, thriftiness, and reinvestment of money. Given that Western Europe and America served as home for these people, should we be surprised capitalism took off in the West?'

### ⚠ Digging deeper: Religion as an initiator of social change

We can look a little more closely (and critically) at **Weber's** general analysis in a range of ways.

**Methodology:** Criticism here focuses on the question of whether or not the development of Calvinism was a 'cause of capitalism'. **Tawney** (1926) argued that capitalism developed in places like Venice

and Germany *prior* to the development of Protestantism. This led him to argue that capitalism developed in Protestant countries like Holland and England in the sixteenth and seventeenth centuries due 'not to the fact they were Protestant powers but to large economic movements, in particular the discoveries and the results which flowed from them'. **Fanfani** (2003) supports this general argument when he notes: 'Europe was acquainted with capitalism before the Protestant revolt. For at least a century capitalism had been an ever growing collective force. Not only isolated individuals, but whole social groups, inspired with the new spirit, struggled with a society that was not yet permeated with it.' If these arguments are valid they call into question – in this context at least – the role of religion as an initiator of change.

**Calvinism: Viner** (1978) argues that where Calvinism was the dominant religion in a society it acted as a largely *conservative social force* that put a *brake* on economic development and change. **Marshall** (1982), however, disputes this interpretation (especially in relation to Scotland, where he argued Calvinism provided an impetus for social change that was held back by a variety of localised factors, such as the lack of capital available for investment).

### ⚠ Weeding the path

Although these ideas call into question both the causal relationship between Calvinism and the development of capitalism and the role of religion in social change, **Pierotti** (2003) argues we should not ignore or necessarily reject Weber's analysis: 'None of the critics I have read managed to destroy the basic premise by which **Weber** sought to explain the growth of capitalism. Something happened in the long sixteenth century that saw an explosion of capitalist economic activity, free thought, and religious rebellion. Whether the relationship among these is causal or coincidental will be grounds for conjecture for years to come.'

If this particular example of the role of religion as an initiator of social change is, at best, inconclusive, there are other, contemporary examples that suggest the main role of religion in social change is as a:

**Focus for dissent**: Although religion itself is not necessarily the prime mover for change, it is a *channel* through which dissent can be expressed and thus find an outlet that results in some form of social change. We can explore this idea a little further through:

**Liberation theology**: We've previously referred to the development of liberation theology in South American countries such as Brazil – a situation (to oversimplify somewhat) that involved *some* Catholic priests forming political alliances with revolutionary groups to oppose government policies (normally against the wishes of the Catholic Church hierarchy). **Bruneau** and **Hewitt** (1992) argue in the case of Brazil: 'For its proponents, the theology of liberation becomes the only way to understand the church and its mission … the church must be involved, it must opt for the poor, and it must use its resources to assist the poor in their liberation. Churches, for their part, become the privileged vehicle to work with the poor and promote their awareness, mobilization, and organization.' Although it's difficult to evaluate the success or otherwise of liberation theology in bringing about social change, its existence does demonstrate that, in theory at least,

religions may play a role in the (multi-causal) explanation of change.

## Contradictions

**Canin** (2001) argues it's a mistake to see religion and its relationship to change as *either* conservative *or* radical. Instead, he suggests it may play a:

**Contradictory role**: His research into the Santo Domingo fiesta in Nicaragua suggested religious organisations have in recent years faced the dilemma of pursuing their:

- **Conservative role** – the 'traditional paternalistic control of the faithful … focusing their attention away from poverty and suffering in this world and toward miracles and salvation in the next world', and a

- **Liberation role** that grew, at times, out of peasant discontent. As **Canin** argues: 'Beyond merely functioning as an "escape valve" for dissent against the status quo, this ritual rebellion [the Santo Domingo fiesta] has exploded into actual rebellion … at specific historical moments that have preserved a historically forged culture of rebellion. More than providing the sensation of liberation, rituals such as the … fiesta provided the framework, if not the material conditions, for the transformation of the social order.'

The material in this section suggests that, in many different ways, religious organisations are intimately involved, at various times and in various contexts, in both the promotion of change and the maintenance of social order – and, as we've seen with the example of liberation theology and the Catholic Church, the two processes may occur within the same religious organisation. We can develop

# ⚠ Growing it yourself: Channel for dissent

We can develop a synoptic link between religion/crime and deviance by applying a theory (originally formulated to explain deviance) to explain the role of religion as a possible channel of dissent and social change. In small groups:

1 Familiarise yourself with Lea and Young's (1984) New Left realist theory of deviance that used three related concepts (for more information see 'Different explanations of crime'):

- Subculture: A group of people in a similar social situation – a political dimension to people's social situation.

- Relative deprivation: A feeling that, in relation to the rest of society, a group is economically disadvantaged – an economic dimension to people's social situation.

- Marginalisation: A situation where a group of people find themselves pushed to the edges of society, where they lack any real form of political representation or expression for their needs – an ideological (or cultural) dimension to people's social situation.

2 Each group should choose one of the following situations:

- Northern Ireland: The relationship between Catholics and Protestants
- Brazil: Liberation theology
- Nicaragua: Before and after the Sandinista revolution
- America: Civil Rights Movement
- Iran: The Islamic revolution
- Poland: Solidarity movement
- South Africa: Apartheid

Discover as much as possible about the society, role of religious organisations and types of social change that occurred in each.

Explain how social change was related (or not) to the three concepts identified by Lea and Young.

this idea a little further through the concept of:

**Religious fundamentalism: Sahgal** and **Yuval-Davis** (1992) suggest some basic features '... common to all fundamentalist religious movements' which, in combination, define this type of religious ideology:

- **Truth**: Fundamentalist religious movements 'claim their version of religion to be the only true one'.

- **Fear**: The movement feels threatened by alternative (secular) views of the world and, by extension, alternative religious interpretations.

- **Social control**: Such movements use a

variety of political means – some democratic and some not – 'to impose their version of the truth on all members of their religion'. For some fundamentalist groups this desire for control extends outwards to a desire to control the behaviour of all aspects of secular society.

In this respect, **Sahgal** and **Yuval-Davis** see fundamentalist movements as '... basically political movements which have a religious imperative and seek in various ways ... to harness modern state and media powers to the service of their gospel' and in this respect they make an interesting distinction between religion as a form of belief and practice and *fundamentalist religion*, which seeks – forcibly or otherwise – to change society in ways that accord with the particular ideological interpretations of the movement. Thus: 'By fundamentalism we are not referring to religious observance, which we see as a matter of individual choice, but rather to modern political movements which use religion as a basis for their attempt to win or consolidate power and extend social control.'

**Berer** and **Ravindran** (1996) develop this when they point out that 'fundamentalism' was originally used to describe nineteenth-century 'Protestant religious and political movements, which attempted a literal or "fundamental" interpretation of Biblical scripts'. In modern-day usage the term has been both widened – to include a large range of religious groups which possess 'fundamental beliefs' – and loosened (especially in the media) following the attack on the World Trade Center (9/11), where the association is with 'terrorism' rather than any other form of political protest or change.

**Giroux** (2004) talks about the rise of the religious right in contemporary America 'imbued with theocratic certainty and absolute moralism' in a situation where 'right-wing religion conjoins with political ideology and political power' to 'legitimate intolerance and anti-democratic forms of religious correctness and lay the groundwork for a growing authoritarianism ... How else to explain the growing number of Christian conservative educators who want to impose the teaching of creationism in the schools, ban sex education from the curricula, and subordinate scientific facts to religious dogma'. He explains the contemporary development of fundamentalist religious movements in both the USA and elsewhere in terms of globalisation.

## Globalisation

In this context, globalisation has two main consequences. First, it creates a situation (postmodern society) where people are exposed to different views and belief systems. In such a situation, to use **W.B. Yeats'** (1921) famous poetic phrase, 'things fall apart; the centre cannot hold' – the things that seemed to bind people in modern society, such as faith in science and progress, no longer seem either attractive or believable.

One consequence of this 'loss of faith' is a moral vacuum (filled, as critics of postmodernism claim, with a *moral relativism* – the idea that 'anything goes' and no one form of explanation can be shown to be superior to any other), expressed neatly by **Yeats** with the phrase: 'Mere anarchy is loosed upon the world.' The world, in other words, appears a more frightening and dangerous place once the great centres – religion, science, politics, and so forth – can no longer hold centre stage.

**Giroux** expresses this 'sense of loss' in terms of two main ideas:

- **Isolation**: The 'collapse of the centre' in postmodern society leaves people feeling alone, vulnerable and largely unconnected with those around them. In this situation, 'fundamentalism taps . . . into very real individual and collective needs'. In other words, it provides a sense of belonging based on the ideas of:

  - **Tradition**: As **Berer** and **Ravindran** (1996) put it, fundamentalist religions seek to raise their adherents 'above the political on the basis of divine sanction or by appealing to supreme authorities, moral codes or philosophies that cannot be questioned', and

- **Social solidarity** (or 'community'): **Giroux** argues that fundamentalist movements give people a sense of *identity* by providing – through their literal interpretation of religious texts as expressions of 'God's will' – a clear and incontestable sense of meaning based on the rigorous enforcement of a particular moral code. As **Castells** (1997) puts it, religious fundamentalism involves 'the construction of [a] collective identity [by] the identification of individual behaviour and society's institutions [with] norms derived from God's law, interpreted by a definite authority that intermediates between God and humanity'.

## Moving on

How we interpret the meaning of religious behaviour – as a conservative force, a radical force or, as in the case of fundamentalist groups, a 'radical conservative' force – affects our perception of the role of religion in modern societies. For this reason, the next two sections focus on exploring different types of religious organisation and the ways religious beliefs relate to questions of identity (such as class, gender and ethnicity) in contemporary societies.

# 3. Cults, sects, denominations and churches and their relationship to religious activity

In previous sections we've looked at the concept of 'religion' in a *relatively undifferentiated* way. That is, we've talked about religion in terms of its general features, how it differs from non-religious world views, and so forth. In this section, however, the focus is on some major differences *within* religions; we are, in other words, going to examine some of the ways religions can be *differentiated*, mainly – but not exclusively – by outlining different types of *religious organisation*. There are two main reasons for this:

Firstly, religious organisations involve a range of ideas, from things like how they are physically organised to the general view of the world they seek to propagate.

Secondly, it allows us to identify 'essential differences' between various religious types – to think, for example, how a church might be different to a cult (even though they are both, nominally, religious organisations).

## WARM-UP: RELIGIOUS ORGANISATIONS

We've just identified four basic types of religious organisation and it would be useful to discover what you already know about each.

In small groups, use the following table as a template to identify what you know/think are the main features of each type – we've given you an example of each to get you focused/stimulate some thoughts.

| Church | Denomination | Sect | Cult |
|---|---|---|---|
| (Catholicism) | (Methodism) | (Jehovah's Witnesses) | (Astrology) |
|  |  |  |  |

## Preparing the ground: Religious organisations – church, denomination, sect and cult

**Church-type**: This refers to a particular *organisational type* whose defining features involve:

**Size**: This type is, almost by definition, *large* when considered in terms of membership and attendance. According to **Barrett et al.** (2001), Christian churches worldwide have around 2 *billion* adherents (around 30% of the world's population).

## Weeding the path

We can note a couple of qualifications to these statistics:

**Reliability**: Precise measurement of 'church size' is notoriously difficult and involves a range of factors and qualifications discussed throughout this section. For the moment, the figures just quoted should be considered, at best, *rough estimates*.

**Validity**: Church-type membership figures, for example, don't differentiate between *active members*/attendees and those simply counted as members on the basis of being born in a country where a particular church is the official (*state* or *established*) religion. If you're born in England, for example, you're classed as a member of the Church of England unless you – or your parents/guardian – decide otherwise.

**Scope** refers to the reach or influence of the organisation on both secular authorities and other religious organisations. According to **Bruce** (1995), church-type organisations have traditionally tried to *dominate* the religious – and frequently the secular – sphere in society. They have, in other words, traditionally assumed a:

**Monolithic form**, where the aim was to be the *only* form of religious organisation recognised and allowed in a society (think, for example, about British history and the battles between the Protestant and Catholic Christian churches). Alternatively, in countries such as Iran, Islam represents this type of organisation – the church is involved in both religious matters and the affairs of state.

In modern societies, however, religious influence in secular matters has generally declined in a way that reflects a changing role for religion. As **Bruce** notes: 'The gradual distancing of the state churches from the state ... allowed the British churches to rediscover the prophetic role of religion ... but that freedom has been bought at the price of the government listening to them.'

**Authority structure**: As befits a large (national and *transnational*) organisation, the church-type is characterised by a relatively formal internal structure that may include:

- **Bureaucratic structures:** In **Weber's** (1922) terms, this involves a rational organisation of a church in terms of specifying such things as the dates of religious services, the organisation of ceremonies and the collection of 'taxes' (or donations) from congregations. The Roman Catholic Church, for example, has a centralised structure based around the figure of the Pope, the authority of Cardinals, and so forth.

- **Hierarchies of power** that derive from this bureaucratic organisation. This can involve paid officials (who may or may not have a religious function), organised in terms of their different statuses.

Traditional church-type organisations are generally:

**Exclusive** in terms of both their ministry (who is authorised to tend to the religious

needs of a particular population) and their relationship to other forms of religious organisation (such as cults). In recent times, this exclusivity has generally weakened, leading to a toleration of (and, at times, active cooperation with) other, similar church-types. In general, however, church-types tend to oppose some forms of *sect* and *cult* organisation (although the situation is complicated by some church types being tolerant of sects – although rarely cults – within their overall organisation). **Staples** (1998) notes how the Protestant Church is characterised by what he terms 'substantial levels of internal pluriformity' – different groups, with varying degrees of autonomy, existing within the same general organisation.

**Inclusiveness**: Church-types are inclusive in the sense that they generally allow anyone to join and membership is often *assumed* rather than the result of a conscious individual choice (as we've noted with the Church of England).

Inclusion is further encouraged by ceremonies such as baptism and confirmation (in Christian churches), and conversions from one religion to another are normally welcomed, if not always actively pursued. Consequently, there tend to be few, if any, membership tests or entry qualifications (something shared with *denominations* but not with sects).

**Social capital** refers to the ways people are connected (or disconnected) from *social networks* and the implications these connections have for what **Putnam** (2000) calls 'norms of reciprocity' (what people are willing to do for each other). Many forms of religious organisation and behaviour involve social capital (as writers such as **Durkheim** (1912), for example, have recognised).

**Benedict XVI calls for the unification of Christians**

At his first Mass, Pope Benedict extended the notion of inclusiveness to all forms of religion: 'I would like to greet all those, including those who follow other religions . . . to reassure them that the Church wants to continue with its open . . . sincere dialogue looking for the true good of man and of society.'
(Source: www.cnn.com, 21/4/05)

However, **Putnam** makes a distinction between *two types* of social capital relevant to our present analysis:

- **Bridging capital** relates to ideas about *inclusiveness* involving notions of cooperation, trust and institutional effectiveness. Church-type organisations are more likely than sects and cults to utilise this type of social capital. This, as **Zmerli** (2003) argues, has the effect of making them 'outward-oriented and their composition can be more heterogeneous. They enhance broader identities and reciprocity. Examples of these networks are civil rights movements and ecumenical [cross-church] religious organisations'.

- **Bonding capital** is a more *exclusive form*, one that, while serving to bond particular group members, sets an organisation apart from other organisations – cult members, for example, form strong bonds with each other that set them apart from wider society.

**Ideology**: Church-type organisations are more likely to be in tune with the secular values of the society in which they exist than organisations such as sects or cults. In other words, because of the way they operate in modern societies, church-type organisations are more *accommodating* than either sects or cults to secular cultures. Historically, this has meant churches have frequently aligned themselves with the ruling powers in society by offering their support to the political and economic objectives of ruling groups.

**Orientation**: The ideological attachments of churches, in this respect, tends to see them integrated into the secular world; sects and cults, however, tend to maintain a certain level of detachment from the world.

**Examples**: Most of us are probably quite familiar with examples of the church-type organisation (just as many of us, either through choice or inertia, will be members of this type of organisation). The Protestant and Roman Catholic versions of Christianity qualify, as does Islam, and, in some respects, Judaism.

## Denomination-type

The denomination-type is normally well established in a society and shares many of the features of the church-type, which is not too surprising given that, in many cases, church-types are also denominations: Roman Catholicism and Protestantism, for example, are denominations of Christianity, while Sunni and Shia are denominations of Islam. Hinduism, on the other hand, doesn't recognise a single set of beliefs or practices and involves a multitude of groups built around the central idea of a 'universal soul'. In this sense, therefore, a denomination is a subgroup that forms within a religion, characterised by a number of features.

**Ideology**: Denominations frequently begin as a breakaway group within a church for reasons that may include ideological/political differences or geographic isolation and separation leading to differences in beliefs and practices – differences that result in a split (schism) from the main church. Examples here are Christianity (with the development of Protestantism in the sixteenth century) and Islam (with the Sunni/Shia split in the seventh century).

**Scope**: Denominations generally tend to be looser-knit groups than churches; they may, for example, unite a geographically (and in some cases ideologically) dispersed group of congregations (people who generally share similar beliefs and practices). In some ways, a denomination represents an administrative system – one that links and serves a relatively disparate set of religious organisations – that enables cooperation between the various elements of the denomination for activities such as missions, welfare efforts, and so on. Denominations – partly perhaps because of their 'looser structure' – rarely claim a monopoly of religious truth. Consequently, they tend to be more tolerant of alternative religious organisations, beliefs and practices.

**Inclusiveness** follows the general church-type line in that people may choose to join or they may be born into an organisation (through their parents' membership, for

example). Denominations do not have membership tests and make similar demands on their members to churches – all they generally require is some form of implicit commitment to the organisation (which may be as little as a 'belief in God') rather than the overt demonstrations of commitment demanded by sects and cults.

**Authority structure**: Although there are variations in the organisation and distribution of power and authority within and between denominations (Baptist congregations, for example, have generally been allowed to develop different beliefs and practices within the overall structure of the organisation), denominations normally develop a professional clergy with responsibility for tending to their members. Some denominations are more democratically organised than others (some allow all members to contribute to discussion about church affairs, others do not), but generally denominations are a more democratic type of organisation than churches, sects or cults.

**Examples**: Denominations are a common form of religious organisation across the globe and examples aren't hard to find (think in terms of Presbyterians, Baptists and Methodists within the Protestant Christian religion or Wahhabi and Alawite for Islam). This diversity, it could be argued, is indicative of:

**Religious pluralism** – a situation where, although different denominations compete for members, there is a general *tolerance* of other forms of religious behaviour (both within and between religions), just as there is a general tolerance for those who hold no religious beliefs (*atheists*). **Bruce** (1995) argues this 'pluralist feature' of denominations represents a major difference between this type of organisation and sects (which, ironically perhaps, tend to be the initial origins of a denomination – *sectarian* disputes leading to schisms within churches, for example). He also sees *tolerance* and *respectability* (especially in the eyes of the media) as significant ways of distinguishing denominations from sects and cults.

## Sects

Although sects and denominations share some general organisational features (*Methodism*, as **Cody** (1988) points out, originated as a sect before evolving into a denomination), we shouldn't overstate the similarities between the two forms; sects are sufficiently different in organisation and outlook to be considered a separate form of religious organisation. We can, therefore, examine some of their essential characteristics in the following terms.

**Development**: **Glock** and **Stark** (1965) argue the emergence of a sect is normally based around two types of *dissent*:

- **Religious**, which involves either dissatisfaction (or *disenchantment*) with the prevailing religious orthodoxy or the 'compromising' of religious ideals by a religious organisation's contacts with secular authorities. This type relates to the schismatic development to which we referred earlier.

- **Social**, which involves, at either an individual or a collective level, feelings of discontent, deprivation and protest.

This 'dissention explanation' is tied to what **Niebuhr** (1929) identified as the *Church–Sect dynamic*; as a religious organisation becomes established, it's forced to compromise with the secular order. A classic example is the Mormon religion and its initial advocacy of:

**Polygamy** (a man being married to more than one woman). According to **Lyman** (1986), Mormon polygamy was a major political stumbling block in Utah's quest for statehood (and a measure of independent government) in mid-nineteenth-century America. Luckily – and probably coincidentally – a 'new revelation from God' banned polygamy within the religion and statehood was granted. This resulted, however, in the breakaway from the main body of Mormonism of a number of *polygamous sects*.

In terms of sects that develop out of social dissent, **Glock** and **Stark** identified five kinds of:

**Deprivation** that, if experienced, may contribute to the decision to join or establish a sect:

- **economic** – both real (as in 'being poor') and *relative* (as in 'compared with others')

- **social** – when desired cultural assets, such as status, prestige and power, are unequally distributed

- **organismic** – refers to *status differences* in physical and mental ability (those classified as 'mentally ill', for example, may have a different social status to those not so classified)

- **ethical** – refers to the idea of value conflict. More specifically, such deprivation occurs when the values of the individual are not compatible with those of the group or society in which they live

- **psychic** – refers to a 'search for meaning' – the idea, for example, that 'there must be more to life than working in an office, nine to five'.

For **Glock** and **Stark** 'deprivation', although a *necessary* precondition, was not in itself *sufficient* to lead to the development of a religious sect. They argued the latter would develop only if certain other conditions were present, which included:

- **shared** feelings of deprivation
- **alternative** channels for problem resolution being unavailable
- **leaders** with an 'innovative solution' to the problem emerging.

## ✳ SYNOPTIC LINK

**Crime and deviance:** Note the similarities between **Glock** and **Stark's** conditions that lead people into religious sects and **Lea** and **Young's** (1984) argument about the conditions that lead to deviant behaviour (a link further enhanced by **Stark** and **Bainbridge's** (1987) argument that a sect is a 'deviant religious organization with traditional beliefs and practices').

**Wilson** (1982) suggests sects are more likely to develop in situations of *social change* and *disruption* – conditions, in other words, related to:

Anomie, where rapid social and/or technological changes disrupt traditional social norms and create, in some people, feelings of confusion and despair. Sects offer a 'solution' by providing a stable belief system to the one disrupted by change. In this situation, sects are more likely than established denominations to attract adherents because they are less likely to be associated with the secular order seen as responsible for disruptive change.

## ✳ SYNOPTIC LINK

**Crime and deviance:** Anomie has also been put forward (by **Merton** (1938), for example) as an explanation for crime and deviance.

**Wilson** points us towards some basic characteristics of sect-type organisations:

- **Exclusiveness** in terms of the demands they make on their members (such as levels of group commitment and their claim to 'exclusive knowledge' – a monopoly on religious truth). Part of this exclusivity also relates to the demand for complete allegiance of members and sanctions (including expulsion) against those who break the rules.

- **Organisation** tends to be less formal than with church- or denomination-types and is characterised by the absence of a division of labour in religious practice (no clergy, for example).

- **Authority**: Sects generally place more emphasis on the role of *leaders* (many of whom claim *divine authority*) than on a professional clergy. Individual behaviour tends to be highly regulated (and while this sometimes involves the development of an administrative class, more usually control is exerted through strict rules enforced by sect members on each other).

- **Protest**: **Wilson** argues sect development occurs as the result of different kinds of protest, be it at the group level (a protest against the way a church-type religion is developing, for example) or on an individual level (such as a protest against status denial).

- **Size**: Sects are traditionally comparatively small religious organisations when compared with churches or denominations, although, as ever, we need to keep in mind the difficulty of measuring levels of affiliation. Both sects and cults present their own slightly different 'problems of measurement' for a couple of reasons:

- **Attendance**: Many sects don't hold the type of services common to churches and denominations, something that makes counting members or attendees difficult.

- **Membership**: For a variety of reasons sects may decline to disclose their membership numbers. Where they do provide such information we have to take its accuracy on trust.

- **Inclusiveness**: Sects are fairly exclusive organisations in terms of membership, which is generally characterised by:

  - **choice**, rather than birth

  - **commitment** shown to the values and goals of the sect.

Entry often involves a 'probationary period', followed by some form of testing before full sect membership is granted. *Scientology* is a good example here – people ('*preclears*') are *invited* to join, but their continued membership is dependent on moving through the various 'levels of knowledge' available. Scientology students (such as the US film stars John Travolta and Tom Cruise) buy courses of instruction and submit to tests (called 'audits') of their abilities and understanding before being allowed to pass to the next knowledge level.

**Ideology**: Sects generally lay claim to either knowing the 'one true way to the afterlife' or to some special religious knowledge denied to non-members. For Scientology, this 'special knowledge' is actually knowledge of oneself – how the problems of an individual's 'past lives' have created problems in their current life that need to be identified ('audited') and removed ('cleared'). Although sects are diverse organisations, familiar ideological themes include:

- **Heaven on Earth** for the 'chosen' (Jehovah's Witnesses)

- **catastrophe** – usually involving an 'end-of-the-world' scenario (The People's Temple)

- **millenarianism**, involving ideas such as a belief in a return to a spiritual homeland (Rastafarians).

## Types

Much of the writing on sect membership and activity, in this respect, has focused on the way the different needs of sect members produce different religious responses to the satisfaction of such needs. **Yinger's** (1957) classic (and idealised) categorisation of sects involves the idea that sect members seek answers to the problem of an undesirable situation that can be resolved in one of three basic ways:

- **Acceptance** sects are largely middle class and life has been personally good to them. The 'key problems' sect members face are more philosophical ('the meaning of life') than economic (poverty) and, consequently, members tend to see the resolution of social problems in terms of individual and collective faith, self-help, and so forth.

- **Opposition** (sometimes called **aggression** sects) are a radical reaction to problems of poverty and powerlessness; their membership is usually drawn from the lower social classes.

- **Avoidance** sects downgrade the significance of this present life by projecting their hopes into the supernatural world; they address problems by appealing to a higher social order and, in consequence, cannot be so easily confronted by failure. They also avoid direct contact with secular society – *Exclusive Brethren*, for example, physically separate themselves from both secular and other religious society.

**Authority structure**: Sects can be differentiated from cults in terms of what **Price** (1979) calls:

**Epistemological authoritarianism**, where 'the beliefs of members derive from the dictates of their leader'.

## Classification

**Orientation**: **Wallis** (1984) argues we can classify sects into three broad (ideal) types, based around their orientation to and relationship with the 'outside world':

- **World-rejecting** sects are critical of the secular world and withdraw, as far as possible, from contact with that world. This usually involves sect members in some form of communal living. An example here is the Heaven's Gate sect, whose members believed they were extra-terrestrial beings 'using' human form as a 'vehicle' through which to carry out their studies on Earth. In 1997, they believed a spaceship, shadowing the appearance of the Hale-Bopp comet, had arrived to transport them away from Earth and their earthly forms were duly 'discarded' in the mass suicide of 39 sect members.

  In a similar way to **Yinger's** 'opposition type', **Smith** (2005) notes how this type '. . . always find themselves in a

The home page of the Heaven's Gate sect. Last update: 27 March 1997

confrontation with the "evil world" they despise and this normally ends with tears before bedtime in terms of the confrontation between their world and that of an increasingly secular society'.

- **World-accommodating** sects, according to **Björkqvist** (1990), 'draw a clear distinction between the spiritual and the worldly spheres' and neither reject nor promote the secular world.

- **World-affirming** sects: **Björkqvist** suggests this type may not possess the kinds of things we normally associate with religions – 'may have no ritual, no official ideology, perhaps no collective meetings whatsoever'. However, its key characteristic is its claim to 'unlock people's hidden potential, whether spiritual or mental, without the need to withdraw from or reject the world' – a classic example being Scientology.

**Marczewska-Rytko** (2003) offers a more contemporary take on what she calls 'religious communities' and 'their attitude to the outside world'. She treats them as:

**Interest groups** – goal-orientated groups, pursuing some form of incentive or benefit for group members. People derive benefits from their membership and they attempt to 'share' such benefits with the rest of society (Jehovah's Witnesses, for example, whose task in life is to give people the opportunity to be saved from damnation). This relates to **Stark** and **Bainbridge's** (1987):

**Rational choice** theory of religious group membership, when they argue that sect members, for example, consciously weigh up the likely costs and potential benefits of group membership. *Incentives* to join might involve feelings of superiority through access to 'hidden knowledge', while *benefits* might involve the feeling of belonging to a strong, supportive, moral community.

## Orientation

**Marczewska-Rytko** identifies four main sect orientations:

- **Reformative**: The objective here is to change people (in terms of their spiritual awareness) and, by so doing, 'reform the secular world'. The main focus is to convert as many people as possible to the sect's world view.

- **Revolutionary**: The objective here is to change a condemned social order, usually by awaiting some form of 'divine intervention' in the form of an apocalyptic, 'end-of-the-world' scenario. Some sects are happy to await Doomsday (Jehovah's Witnesses, for example) whereas others are equally happy to try to help things along a little – in 1995 members of the *Aum Shinrikyo* sect (whose leader, Shoko Asahara, had issued a number of 'doomsday prophesies') released Sarin nerve gas in the Tokyo underground system, killing 12 people and injuring around 5000 more.

- **Introvert**: This type generally looks inwards to the spiritual well-being and welfare of members, who derive strength from feelings of 'moral superiority' over the outside world. These sects focus on personal development as members strive for spiritual enlightenment.

- **Manipulative**: This type of community – sometimes seen as a cult – focuses on the manipulation of things like the occult (magic, for example) for the benefit of its practitioners. In some ways these communities are *acceptance sects* because practitioners desire 'success' (economic, personal, and so forth), which they feel can be achieved through the mastery and practice of rituals and ceremonies. Included in this group might be various forms of paganism, neo-paganism, and so on.

## Cults

A cult is a loose-knit social group that collects around a set of common themes, beliefs or interests, where religious experience is highly individualistic and varies with an individual's personal experiences and interpretations. Cults differ from sects (which they loosely resemble) on the basis that they lack a clearly defined, exclusive belief system for all their followers.

**Size**: The general lack of formal organisational structures (clerical hierarchies, meeting places, official records and the like) makes it difficult to specify a minimum or maximum size for a cult – a difficulty compounded by the fact that cult followers resemble *consumers* rather than members. There is rarely any formal joining mechanism and those interested in a particular cult activity (Transcendental Meditation, for example) are encouraged to buy into the cult to varying degrees (Transcendental Meditation sells stages to spiritual enlightenment the consumer can buy as and when they want).

## Weeding the path

The diversity of cult-type relationships (**Lewis** (1998) identifies more than 1000 such groups worldwide) means there is also room within this general definition for 'communities of believers' to exist in an organised relationship that, in some respects, resembles a sect. The very looseness of the definition is both a strength – it encompasses a wide range of different beliefs, behaviours and practices – and a weakness, since it makes it difficult to pin down the 'essential characteristics' of a cult and, in some respects, difficult to disentangle cults from sects (a problem we'll address in a moment when we explore New Religious Movements).

**Scope: Hume** (1996) notes 'various scholars have attempted to give definitions of the term "cult" but there has been little agreement to date' and **Robbins** and **Anthony** (1982) warn against seeing cults in terms of an 'illusionary homogeneity' that characterises them as 'authoritarian, centralized, communal and "totalistic"' (a 'total institution' is one, like a prison, that attempts to control all aspects of an individual's life). Classifying cults is, therefore, difficult; the table on the following page, however, identifies the main features of two different examples of cult classifications.

## Weeding the path

It's possible to identify some general features of cults that distinguish them from other religious organisations, although we need to keep in mind a couple of potential problems, both:

- **practical** – cult diversity and the fact that many cults have little or no obvious organisational structure make it difficult to actually research their behaviour – and

- **methodological**: Some forms of religious organisation (such as Scientology) cut across both the 'cult/sect' dynamic (Scientology, it could be argued, shows features of both) and the various categories defined by writers like **Stark** and **Bainbridge**.

Scientology has elements of all three types, reflecting perhaps the internally diverse nature of its teachings and practices. Some members are highly committed (*movement*); others show less commitment but take some of the courses on offer (*client*); while others simply share a general interest in the kinds of ideas Scientology seeks to popularise (*audience*).

**Giddens** (2001) argues that cults 'resemble sects', although there are differences in areas like:

- **Values** that reject those of mainstream society. In some cases rejection is outright (as with survivalist cults in North America, some of which have their own websites where practitioners can buy maps, guns, a handbook on *How to Survive a Nuclear Blast* . . . ), whereas in others the cult simply uses alternatives to conventional values – using magic, for example, to get that new car rather than the more usual methods.

- **Individual experience** is a major area of difference; cults are focused on the individual (their rights and responsibilities, for example) within a

| Cult classification | | |
|---|---|---|
| **Stark and Bainbridge (1987)** | **Examples** | **Van Leen (2004)** |
| **1. Movement**<br>Well organised and often highly centralised, with a particular philosophy to 'sell' (sometimes literally) | Many cults (sometimes called **syncretic**) gather 'the best bits' of different philosophies to create something 'new'. Characteristic of groups such as Hare Krishna or the Divine Light Mission | **1. Explicitly religious**<br>Includes cults offering interpretations of Christianity to those offering a mix ('*syncretism*') of different philosophies |
| **2. Client**<br>Focus on providing a 'service' to members/practitioners, usually with a 'provider–client' relationship between different followers | No concept of a deity external to people. Instead, focus on 'inner spirituality' revealed through the right teachings and practices (as with Transcendental Meditation) | **2. Human potential**<br>Exists to help individuals 'fulfil their potential', either in terms of an *immanent* view of religion ('God' is inside us) or as a way of leading a 'better, happier, more fulfilled' life |
| **3. Audience**<br>Rarely have any organisational structure and involve a 'producer–audience' relationship where 'cult members' share a general interest about something (such as astrology) | Audience cults involve people with a common interest in some aspect of religious experience, such as 'alternative medicine' or tarot reading.<br>New Age cults embody beliefs that can be picked up – and discarded – almost at will (syncretic philosophies such as Eastern Mysticism are popular and people may follow these ideas without ever formally joining a cult) | **3. New Age/Mystical**<br>A very diverse category with a wide range of teachings and practices united only by their general foundation in various forms of 'ancient' religions and beliefs |
| | The use of magic can involve loose communal organisation (group ceremonies, for example) and some groups have hierarchical organisational structures (different levels of priesthood or ability, for example). In the main, however, occultism is mainly practised individually. Examples here include paganism, neo-paganism and satanism | **4. Occult groups**<br>A category that doesn't fit particularly neatly with **Stark** and **Bainbridge's** classification, but which involves the attempt to influence the world – for good or bad – by a range of magical means |

loose, supporting framework of ideas over which there may be discussion and dispute. Cults also tend to attract people looking for relatively short-term solutions to specific problems.

**Inclusiveness**: In one sense cults are highly inclusive – they rarely have any formal joining conditions. 'Members' could more accurately be described as practitioners who subscribe to particular beliefs and perform certain practices – from tantric sex (don't ask) to witchcraft or the ever-popular ear-candling.

Their appeal, for **Zimbardo** (1997), is simple: 'Imagine being part of a group in which you will find instant friendship, a caring family, respect for your contributions, an identity, safety, security, simplicity, and an organized daily agenda. You will learn new skills, have a respected position, gain personal insight, improve your personality and intelligence. There is no crime or violence and your healthy lifestyle means there is no illness . . . Who would fall for such appeals? Most of us, if they were made by someone we trusted, in a setting that was familiar, and especially if we had unfulfilled needs.'

**Ideology**: Cult diversity makes it difficult to pin down definitive ideological content, but one unifying theme is reflected in **Price's** (1979) concept of:

**Epistemological individualism** – 'individualism' is a *necessary* characteristic of the cult-type.

**Authority structure**: In terms of **Stark** and **Bainbridge's** (1987) classification we can note differences in authority structures between different types of cult.

**Movement cults** generally conform to **Robbins** and **Anthony's** (1982) characterisation of their internal authority structure as:

- **Authoritarian**: **Enroth's** (1993) study of US cults revealed situations where 'the leaders have justified the use of abusive authority in order to follow Jesus. They demand submission even if the leaders are sinful and un-Christlike'.

- **Centralised**: Authority is concentrated in a relatively small group at the top of the organisation. **Van Leen** (2004) characterises this as being 'leader, or leadership, centred, usually by persons claiming some divine appointment or authority – while members are accountable to the leadership the leadership is not accountable to anyone else and often make significant decisions for members'.

- **Total**: Communal living – often isolated, both geographically and philosophically, from the secular world – is a control mechanism where all aspects of the member's life can be regulated. **Van Leen**

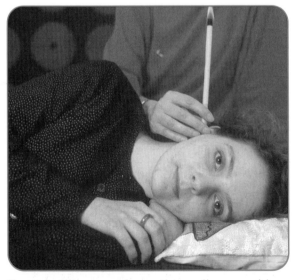

Ear-candling – performed to relieve a wide range of ear-related problems. Obviously.

# ⚘ Growing it yourself: Compensation culture

Stark and Bainbridge's *Exchange Theory* is based around the idea of compensators – something that compensates the individual for their failure to receive desired rewards. Evans and Campany (1985) argue 'entry to heaven' is a *compensator* for death. Hak (1998) suggests 'religious people want rewards against low costs, and if rewards are scarce or not there at all, they will take compensators or IOUs for rewards'.

In small groups, use the following as a template to identify possible compensators for participating in cult activity (we've provided an example of each to get you started).

| Movement cults | Client cults | Audience cults |
|---|---|---|
| Belonging to a group | Taking control of your life | Influencing the future |

Once you've completed the above, do the same for the following:

| Denomination | Sect | Football club |
|---|---|---|
| | | Feeling part of a group |

argues control often extends to 'criticism of natural parents and family members' and the depiction of the cult as a 'family'.

## Brainwashing

Some critics have argued that cults use:

**Brainwashing** techniques to recruit and keep members. **Galper** (1982) notes how 'allegations of coercive brainwashing have been made by concerned parents whose children have been exposed to cult recruitment'. In addition, **Singer et al.** (1996) claim: 'Cults have used tactics of coercive mind control to negatively impact an estimated 20 million victims [in America]. Worldwide figures are even greater.' **Richardson** and **Ginsburg** (1998), however, suggest 'brainwashing' is not a particularly useful or convincing explanation of the attraction of cults. They argue that although there's *anecdotal* and *emotive* 'evidence' for brainwashing, *empirical* evidence is generally lacking.

**Zimbardo** (1997) also argues 'cult methods of recruiting, indoctrinating and influencing their members' are little different to the socialising methods employed in *any* group or organisation. The attraction of cults, he suggests, can be explained by the fact that 'cult leaders offer simple solutions to the increasingly complex problems we all face daily … the simple path to happiness, to success, to salvation by following their simple rules, simple group regimentation and simple total lifestyle'.

**Audience** and **client cults** often have little or no organised authority structure, mainly because, as we've noted, they involve 'producer–consumer' type relationships. Authority, in this respect, relates to the way cult promoters provide a 'design for living' or advice relating to a way of life. **Fraser** (2005) argues that 'spirituality shopping' 'offers a language for the divine that dispenses with all the off-putting paraphernalia of priests and church … it's not about believing in anything too specific, other than some nebulous sense of otherness or presence. It offers God without dogma'.

**Orientation**: Where a cult sells some special aspect of spiritual enlightenment, 'customers' are rarely retained in the long term (although a general interest in the ideas being sold may continue) for two main reasons:

- **Socialisation**: Cults lack the socialising mechanisms available to other religious organisations and, consequently, their ability to exercise social control or recruit new members is curtailed.

- **Knowledge**: Once someone has learnt the basics required to do something (how to relax using Transcendental Meditation or yoga, for example) they may have little reason for continued formal involvement.

With more aggressive cults, their general orientation to both members and the outside

world is more *defensive*. Hostility to criticism is a frequent feature (**Enroth** (1994), for example, details the harassment he suffered at the hands of the Jesus People in America). **Price** (1979) also notes the (ambivalent) orientations of cults such as the Divine Light Mission: 'Without doubt the beliefs of members of DLM derive from the dictates of their leader, indeed the knowledge they possess is his knowledge.' Even in such a situation, however, 'many adherents hold a more idiosyncratic position, accepting only parts of the belief system and choosing the degree to which they conform to accepted practice'.

### ⚠ Digging deeper: Religious organisations (New Religious Movements)

Although we've just noted differences between different types of religious organisation and activity (as well as similarities), the usefulness of thinking in terms of church, denomination, sect and cult is open to question in a couple of ways:

**Typologies**: How useful, for example, are these categories 'in the real world' (where religious organisations develop, evolve and disappear)? In particular, there are two main areas of concern.

- **The church–denomination** distinction: We need to think about how useful – in an increasingly global and diversified world – the concept of 'church' (as opposed to denomination) is likely to be. Although we can talk generally about 'Christianity' or 'Islam', the *differences within* these broad organisations are probably of more significance. For example, within some categories of church the 'unity of beliefs and practices' is more apparent than real. **Levinson** (1998) notes how 'Hinduism' consists of 'thousands of different religious groups that have evolved in India since 1500 BCE' – it has no single founder, theology, morality or central organisation.

- **The sect–cult distinction**: The diversity of sects and cults makes it difficult to maintain a clear separation between the two forms – some sects act in some ways, but not others, like cults, and vice versa.

**Diversity and homogeneity**: It's difficult to sustain the sect–cult distinction in the face of empirical evidence from the behaviour of different religious groups and movements – they are increasingly sophisticated in the way they recruit and retain members, and internally diverse in terms of how they operate. The internet (as well as the more traditional recruitment methods) allows movements to diversify in terms of what they offer to converts and how they offer it. Scientology has been particularly sophisticated in this respect, marketing itself by forging many different types of relationship with members.

In addition, there are huge organisational and behavioural differences within categories like 'sect' and 'cult' – they are not homogeneous classifications and it may be more useful to reflect this diversity by being more selective in our (sociological) categorisation. We also need to consider the way labels such as 'sect' and 'cult' have acquired, over the years, a negative (*pejorative*) meaning, especially in the media. **Barker** (1999) suggests we strip away the cultural and emotional baggage surrounding

these labels and develop a different way of classifying these religious organisations in terms of:

**New Religious Movements** (NRMs), a classification system developed for two main reasons:

- **Stigma**: As **Barker** argues: '. . . The media and the general public tend to employ the word "cult", which has negative overtones, often implying bizarre beliefs, sinister and deceptive practices, mind control or psychological coercion and, perhaps, sexual abuse and violent tendencies.'

- **Theoretical clarity**: Such is the overlap between sects and cults that the distinction 'on the ground' (when studying their activities) is less than useful. In this respect, 'NRM' becomes a kind of generic (umbrella) term for a range of religious organisations that don't fit easily into the church or denomination category.

## Weeding the path

The term 'NRM' has itself been questioned. Religious historians such as **Melton** (1993) and **Miller** (1995) suggest 'alternative religions' or 'non-conventional religions' would be more accurate because some 'new' religious movements simply involve a reworking of traditional religious ideas and practices. **Barker** (1999) justifies the use of NRM when she argues they can be '. . . defined as groups which have become visible in their present form since the Second World War, and which are religious in so far as they offer an answer to some of the ultimate questions traditionally addressed by mainstream religions: Is there a God? What is the purpose of life? What happens to us after death?' **Chryssides** (2000), however, points to a number of problems with this categorisation:

**New**: The starting point for classification is important because it may arbitrarily exclude movements (such as Jehovah's Witnesses) that are worthy of classification and study. **Chryssides** suggests 'a more liberal 150 year time scale'.

**Religious**: The objection here is 'there must be something plausibly religious about a movement . . . for it to count as a religion and hence an NRM'. He suggests we should include as NRMs only movements that satisfy four basic criteria:

- **answering** fundamental questions (like those posed by **Barker**)
- **rites of passage** that mark 'key life events'
- **life-coping strategies** that address 'problems of existence' rather than simply personal life issues (such as how to be more successful in business)
- **ethical codes** that set out how one's life should be lived.

To be defined as an NRM, therefore, a movement should be 'substantively' (rather than functionally) religious.

**Movements**: **Chryssides** suggests there are groups which reject the label of 'religion' and which, as a consequence, should not be classified as an NRM: 'The New Age Movement is one such example. It is nebulous, with little formal organization or membership, and its followers often explicitly reject organized religion, particularly traditional Christianity.'

The above notwithstanding, we can examine NRMs in terms of two ideas: *characteristics* (defining features) and *explanations* for their existence.

## Characteristics

Following **Barker's** (1999) lead ('There are . . . some characteristics which tend to be found in any movement that is both *new* and *religious*'), we can identify a number of NRM features in terms of:

**Converts**: With 'new movements' many recruits will be first-generation converts; they were neither born into the religion nor have a family history of involvement. 'Early adopters' tend to be committed, highly enthusiastic and, in many cases, *proselytizing* – keen to sell their movement and convert others to their faith (groups like Scientology and Hare Krishna use a variety of techniques to spread the word, from street selling to mail drops).

**Membership**: Recent (post-1970) NRMs attract young, middle-class recruits in disproportionate numbers to other religious organisations. This is partly because the young, in particular, are more open to – and desirous of – new experiences, while this age group is also more likely to be targeted for recruitment by NRMs.

**Authority**: Many NRMs are led by a founder with the *charisma* to attract followers in the first instance, something that often gives such movements an autocratic, rather than democratic, structure. A leader may control all, some or very little of the day-to-day life of converts, but many NRMs have the characteristics of a:

**Total institution**, which **Goffman** (1961) defines as 'a place of residence and work where a large number of like-situated individuals, cut off from the wider society for an appreciable period of time, together lead an enclosed, formally administered round of life'. However, unlike some other total institutions (prisons, for example) an important characteristic of NRMs is their:

**Voluntarism** – how people make choices about their behaviour and, although, as **Francis** and **Hester** (2004) note, choices are always made against a social background that gives them meaning and context, converts may *consciously choose* to become part of a total institution for many different reasons. In *Shopping for Faith* (2002), one of **Cimino** and **Lattin's** respondents stated: 'If all the gospel of Jesus Christ is going to do is change my Sunday schedule, then I'm not interested. I want something that is going to change my finances, my sex life, the way I work, the way I keep my house and the way I fix my yard.'

**Certainty**: NRMs normally promote a particular version of 'truth' that is more dogmatic and less open to questioning than the 'truths' promoted by their older counterparts.

**Identity**: A sharp distinction is invariably made between 'Us' (the movement's members) and 'Them' (non-members or unbelievers), partly on the basis of the certainty and truth underpinning the faith of members. This concept of group and, by extension, individual identity is based on a distinction between the members' sense of:

- **self** (who they are, what they believe and so forth), and their perception of
- **the other** (people, in effect, who are 'not like us').

In this respect, a sense of 'ourselves' as 'homogeneously good and godly' is arguably sustained by a sense of 'others' as 'homogeneously bad'. If this is the case, it is not particularly difficult to see why the final characteristic of NRMs is:

**Antagonism** (and suspicion) between a particular NRM, wider society and other religious organisations. This follows, perhaps, because an important way for an NRM to both carve out a clear identity in an increasingly crowded 'religious marketplace' and maintain a strong sense of self once a niche has been created is to, in Old Religious Movement terms perhaps, 'demonise your competitors'.

## Typology

**Daschke** and **Ashcraft** (2005) suggest a typology of NRMs based around 'five interrelated *pathways*', each of which identifies the unique features of a range of NRMs:

- **Perception**: This identifies movements that involve a *new way* of looking at the 'problem of existence and understanding'. Their focus – and attraction – is on philosophical questions (like the meaning of life).

- **Identity** overlaps with *perception* in the sense it focuses primarily on the Self. However, 'identity movements' are less likely to address questions relating to 'the cosmos' (the scheme of things) and more likely to focus on human potential – in particular, the development of new personal identities. These movements attract those who seek personal enlightenment through the mastery of certain techniques and practices designed to release their 'inner spirituality'.

- **Family** types focus on the *social solidarity* aspect of religious practice; their primary attraction is the offer of a sense of community and well-being through the development of close, personal relationships with like-minded

## 🌸 Growing it yourself: Building a brand

'We are building a religion,
We are building it bigger
We are widening the corridors
and adding more lanes
We are building a religion.
A limited edition'

**Cake 'Comfort Eagle': Columbia Records, 2001**

In this exercise, the task is to create and market a New Religious Movement. In small groups, design a campaign aimed at publicising the new product and attracting converts. You can do this in any way you decide, but you should include the following information:

- **Product name:** Time to think of a catchy title ...

- **Content:** What is it you're trying to sell? Identify some features of the NRM you think will make it attractive to potential converts – the only proviso is that content must have some religious basis.

- **Unique selling point:** What features of your brand make it different to what's already available?

- **Target audience:** To whom are you marketing your brand (and why)?

- **Marketing:** How will you sell your new product (word of mouth? Advertising? The internet?).

Once this stage is completed, each group should 'pitch' their ideas in turn to the class as a whole.

individuals. In this category people want to explore different ('alternative') ways of living and working, usually by distancing themselves, as a group, from wider society.

- **Society movements** focus group solidarity outwards rather than inwards – a major attraction here is the possibility of changing society to align it more closely with the (spiritual) beliefs of the group. This involves transforming social institutions (such as work, school and the family) through the application of a particular moral or ethical code (a 'design for living', if you like).

- **Earth movements**: The goal here is to transform the whole *world*. Some of these movements focus on:

  - **Planet transformation**, usually through beliefs in an *apocalyptic* end to the earth and, from the ruins, the creation of a new 'golden age' (whether this is through supernatural or human intervention). Other variations focus on:

  - **Group transformation** – the idea, for example, that the group will be transported to a new planet (what are sometimes called 'exit-orientated' movements).

# Explanations

The final question we need to consider is how to explain the existence and development of NRMs – something that links with the work we've done on religion and social change by reversing the focus of that work. Rather than looking at the role of religion in promoting social change, however, we can consider the *role of social change* in the development of religious movements.

**Technological change**: **Wuthnow** (1986) explains the rise of NRMs in the post-Second World War period (in Western Europe and the USA in particular) in terms of the effect of rapid developments in science and technology. The strong development of a secular ideological framework ('science'), he argues, challenged the *hegemonic* role of religion and forced changes in the way mainstream churches and denominations interpreted their relationship to the secular world, resulting in established religions becoming increasingly *liberal* in their interpretation of religious scriptures. These changes within religious organisations produced *schisms* ('counter-movements') whereby those who opposed liberalisation split from established religions, leading to an increase in NRMs. As the rate of technological and educational growth declined, NRM growth and activity also declined (or 'solidified').

**Globalisation**: Rapid forms of political, economic and cultural change at the end of the twentieth century have created, according to **Baudrillard** (2001), a situation of 'postmodern uncertainty' that has led some to seek certainties in the teachings and moralities of both traditional and non-traditional religions – a situation that has arguably led to a *revitalisation* of NRMs in the 'postmodern age'.

**Economic change**: **Arjomand** (1986) considered the impact of social change on non-Christian religions (such as Islam) and identified processes 'which are likely to strengthen disciplined religiosity [levels of religious commitment] and, under favourable conditions, give rise to movements of orthodox reform and renewal of Islam':

- **Social integration**: As Islamic societies become integrated into the international economic system they face increasing competition from Western secular and religious ideas and philosophies.

- **Communication**: The development of transport, communication and the mass media (including the internet) exposes populations to a range of new – and in many cases radically different – ideas.

- **Urbanisation** creates pressure for change where people react to worsening economic situations by developing new responses – which include both NRMs and a reinvigoration/reinterpretation of traditional religious movements.

- **Education**: As populations become more literate and formally educated they are exposed to a range of ideas that promote the development of new ways of interpreting the world.

**Social unrest**: **Eyre** (1996) suggests, in relation to the USA particularly, that NRM growth during the 1960s resulted from *disillusionment*, especially among the young, with both involvement in the Vietnam War and a general questioning of the materialistic values of US society. One aspect of this 'rebellion' was to explore a range of alternative lifestyles and beliefs.

**Immigration**: The movement of people across different cultures and the introduction of new – and different – ideas into the host culture challenges *religious orthodoxy* ('the things people have always believed') and leads to the development of 'new religions' through a process of:

**Cultural hybridisation** – the idea that different cultures meet, mix and produce something different. In the 1960s, for example, **Eyre** notes how a range of Eastern 'faiths and philosophies' met Western faiths and resulted in hybrid philosophies that subsequently developed into NRMs.

## Weeding the path

'Social change/social unrest' explanations have been criticised on the basis that the major period of NRM growth occurred in the 1950s, a period of relative political and economic stability. More importantly, perhaps, we can question the extent to which NRM 'growth' is actually an *illusion*. **Beckford** and **Levasseur** (1986) suggest this when they focus on the development of:

**Communication technology**: Improvements in the means of communicating ideas in the post-war period allowed NRMs to reach a mass audience. Effectively, this meant the overall *visibility* of various NRMs was increased, without there necessarily being an increase in their number. The development of internet technologies – *websites* and *email* in particular – may have accelerated or amplified this process.

## ✳ SYNOPTIC LINK

**Crime and deviance: Beckford** (1994) suggests the behaviour and activities of

NRMs are subject to a process of 'media amplification', similar to that relating to the amplification of deviance.

---

**Beckford** and **Levasseur** argue there hasn't been a 'sudden, significant, explosion of NRMs' that needs to be explained. Rather, NRMs were simply following a 'traditional path' of emergence and growth; their *apparent* development can be explained by the fact they were able to 'get their message' across to a larger audience – the 'growth' of NRMs was the result of improvements in publicity and advertising.

The traditional audience for NRMs – mainly the urban young – are precisely the people most affected by technological/social change and, in consequence, most receptive to 'new' ideas about the nature of the world. For **Beckford** and **Levasseur** (as for writers such as **Bruce**, 2002), NRM membership was – and remains – relatively small and *transient* (people move into – and out of – these groups with great frequency). This suggests, perhaps, that a more useful question here is not *why* people are attracted to NRMs, but rather why so many people are *not* attracted to the kinds of 'solutions' they appear to offer.

## New Age Movements (NAMs)

NAMs are often confused with NRMs, partly because they are both relatively recent phenomena and partly because NAMs sometimes have a 'religious' frame of reference. **Melton** (2001) argues that 'the term New Age refers to a wave of religious enthusiasm that emerged in the 1970s ... only to subside at the end of the 1980s'. We should, however, note that the 'religious' aspects of NAMs are subtly different to those of NRMs, which is why we need to

# The potting shed

| NRM | Page hits |
|---|---|
| 'Divine Light Mission' | 4600 |
| 'Unification Church' | 121,000 |
| 'Children of God' | 676,000 |
| 'Scientology' | 1.5 million |

Identify and explain one reason why these results support **Beckford** and **Levasseur's** argument and one reason why they might be evidence against their argument.

explore them as a separate – but interrelated – aspect of the 'new religiosity'. In this respect, NAMs, according to **Cowan** (2003), have a couple of defining characteristics:

**Salvation** is interpreted in terms of 'this world' with the focus of involvement being on finding solutions to problems through *personal agency* – in **Brown's** (2004) terms, a commitment to the 'transformation of both self and society'. **Brown** identifies a range of disparate movements within the general 'New Age' category ('astrology, channelling (direct communication with spirits), work with one's "inner child" ... and a laundry list of unconventional healing techniques') and suggests: 'Some scholars have labelled the New Age an '*audience cult*,' rather than a kind of religion in the conventional sense, because of its diffuse, networklike quality.'

**Focus** on 'personal salvation' is a key element of NAMs, expressed, as **Cowan** argues, through different preoccupations and concerns, including:

- peace of mind
- positive self-image
- physical health
- personal empowerment
- enlightenment/insight.

**Brown** further notes that NAMs have a couple of qualities *not* shared by other types of religious movement/organisation:

**Orientation**: The focus is on the ability (or otherwise) to influence future events (both personal and social).

**Individualism**: **Brown**, like **Fraser** (2005), argues that NAM adherents are 'less inclined to accept the personal compromises needed to maintain a stable group', something that gives NAMs the appearance of 'consumerist movements' – loose collections of individuals whose most cohesive feature is the desire to buy into a particular belief system.

**Langone** (1993) identifies four main 'streams' within New Age Movements:

- **Transformational training** that involves the ability to transform personal life through a range of techniques and practices.

- **Intellectualism**, where the main interest lies in the exploration of 'alternative beliefs' rather than the practice of such beliefs.

- **Lifestyle**, with a focus on the transformation of society through behavioural changes (such as anti-globalisation movements or environmentalism).

- **Occult** that involves both 'conventional' beliefs and practices such as witchcraft ('Wicca') and areas such as astrology, palmistry, crystal healing and so forth.

These categories may in some instances overlap (occult practices, for example, might involve beliefs about lifestyle changes), but **Langone** argues that one feature common to all NAMs is the belief that '. . . spiritual knowledge and power can be achieved through the discovery of the proper techniques'.

NAMs appear to represent a variety of disparate beliefs and practices that are rarely, if ever, organised into a stable 'community of believers'. We could, therefore, argue that NAMs (and possibly NRMs) epitomise a postmodern perspective on the world. NAMs in particular seem to fulfil a range of requirements for a postmodern religion:

- **Diversity**: There are numerous variations on a New Age theme available.

- **Fragmentation**, in the sense of diversity *between* and *within* different NAMs (think, for example, of the possible differences between pagans and neo-pagans, white Wicca and black Wicca, etc.).

- **Metanarrative breakdown**: Organisational diversity makes it difficult to identify – or sustain – a consistent world view among NAMs. In addition, the overwhelming sense of individualism – different people seeking personal solutions to their particular problems – makes the idea of a 'New Age metanarrative' difficult to pin down.

- **Choice**, not only in terms of 'ready-made' movements, but also in a kind of 'pick-and-mix' approach where, if you don't like what's on offer, you can start your

Pagans? Neo-pagans? Or just people who like to get dressed up on a Saturday night?

own movement by choosing whatever philosophical bits and pieces take your fancy – something that leads to the idea of NAM consumers as:

**Spiritual shoppers** – people looking to buy solutions and willing to consider whatever particular movement happens to take their fancy. There is, unlike with traditional churches or denominations, little sense of 'brand commitment' or consumer loyalty. This suggests one feature of the 'new age of religion' is the consumer experience – religion is:

**Experiential** – you 'go with the flow' and if it 'works for you' then you don't question the rationality of the experience; consumers buy into a brand, use it as and when they want and discard it when it no longer serves its purpose. Whether or not this is a particularly accurate representation of 'postmodern religion', the idea of:

**Shopping for faith** is an interesting one. **Cimino** and **Lattin** (2002) express the essence of this idea when they note: 'Whether soul-shaking experiences and religious conversions are the true action of the Holy Spirit, hypnotic trance states, or some other psychological trick makes little difference. They feel real. They inspire people to change their lives and commit themselves to another power, whether it's a higher power outside themselves or an inner voice crying out from the depths of their soul.'

## Weeding the path

Some features of NAMs give substance to this idea. **Langone**, for example, argues that 'New Age mysticism' appeals to a wide range of consumer groups, from secularists who want to explore aspects of 'spirituality' without necessarily committing to traditional religions, to those searching for 'meanings' religions have failed to supply.

New Age ideas about magic, personal fulfilment and the like have also found their way into modern business practices – from salespeople who buy into 'transformational training' to improve their self-esteem and ability to sell, to 'management gurus' (note the religious terminology) who sell whatever version of 'business wisdom' happens to be in fashion at the time, using a variety of New Age techniques.

**Ammerman** (1997) captures the overall flavour of this particular NAM discourse when she argues: 'Rather than either/or categories like sect/church … we may begin to imagine ways of describing the much more complicated reality we encounter in a world where actors are constantly choosing their ways of being religious.' She also argues:

**Mediated** religious influences such as books, magazines, television and the internet '… provide models of behaviour, pieces of rhetoric, bits of belief, from which individuals construct the routines they enact' – what **Roof** (1996) labels 'pastiche religion', to reflect its fundamental character as an individual 'construction'. Alternatively, we might apply the concept of:

**Bricolage religions** (the idea of making something new by combining different sources) to the concept of NAMs to reflect both their postmodernity and, more importantly, the idea of their construction and reconstruction at the hands of different individuals and groups.

### Moving on

In this section we've touched on the relationship between religious organisations and beliefs. In the next section, we can develop this relationship in terms of social groups based around concepts such as class and age.

# 4. Explanations for the relationship between religious beliefs, religious organisations and social groups

This section is based around the key variables of **class**, **age**, **gender** and **ethnicity.** We can begin by looking at how and why religious beliefs and organisations are related to these social categories.

## WARM-UP: INDICATORS OF RELIGIOUS COMMITMENT

In this exercise we're going to look, individually at first and then as a class, at four basic types of religious indicator, partly to explore your religious beliefs, attachments and practices and partly to introduce some problems involved in the identification and measurement of such things.

Listed below are some selected indicators of religious commitment. Tick (✓) any you feel apply directly to you and put a cross (✗) against any you feel do not apply to you.

| Disposition | Orthodox belief | |
|---|---|---|
| Do you:<br>Often think about the meaning of life<br>Think life is meaningless<br>Often think about death<br>Often regret doing wrong<br>Need moments of prayer, etc.<br>See yourself as a religious person<br>Draw comfort/strength from religion<br>Think God is important in your life<br>Have spiritual experiences<br>Have superstitions<br>Believe in predestination | *I believe in:*<br>God<br>Sin<br>Soul<br>Heaven<br>Life after death<br>A spirit or life force<br>The devil<br>*I accept commandments demanding:*<br>No other gods<br>Reverence of God's name<br>Holy Sabbath | |
| Moral values | Institutional attachment | |
| Absolute guidelines exist on good and evil<br>*I accept commandments against:*<br>Killing<br>Adultery<br>Stealing<br>Lying<br>Terrorism may be justified<br>*The following acts are never justified:*<br>Claiming benefits illegally<br>Accepting a bribe<br>Taking illegal drugs<br>Homosexuality<br>Euthanasia<br>I always respect those in authority<br>Capital punishment is wrong | I have great confidence in the church/synagogue/temple/mosque<br>*Church/synagogue/temple/mosque answers my:*<br>Moral problems<br>Family problems<br>Spiritual needs<br>I attend a religious service monthly at least<br>I identify with a particular religion<br>*I believe religion:*<br>Is important for my society<br>Will be more important in future<br>Will be less important in future<br>I believe in one true religion<br>Religious faith is an important value to develop in children<br>People should marry only in a religious setting<br>Religion has a political role in society | |

Once you've completed the table, as a class discuss the following:

- Judging by the results, how religious are the people in your class?
- What problems did you discover in terms of completing the table and interpreting the results?

Source: Adapted from **Abrams et al.** (1985)

## Preparing the ground: Religiosity

This exercise has introduced:

**Religiosity** – a concept that suggests the possibility of identifying and measuring the various qualities involved in 'being religious' ('religiousness') and the exercise will have sensitised you to two aspects of *religiosity*:

- **Social indicators** are areas (such as whether people attend religious services) that can be observed and measured as indicators of people's thoughts and behaviour.

- **Belief and belonging**: Davie (1994) makes this distinction to suggest we need to recognise that people can hold religious *beliefs* while simultaneously showing little or no commitment to religious *organisations* or *practices*. We can, for example, quite happily believe in God without ever attending a religious service. People may also attend religious services without necessarily having any strongly developed sense of religious belief; religious practice may have secular functions, with people attending services for reasons of friendship, social status, tradition and so forth.

This difference between *belief* and *belonging* is an important distinction since it suggests that to understand patterns of religious commitment we can't *simply* look at

indicators like membership of religious groups or attendance at religious services as prima facie ('at first sight') evidence of *religiosity* – although these may, of course, be important dimensions of any explanation of religiousness.

## Digging deeper: Religiosity

**Glock** and **Stark** (1965) argue that religious behaviour has *five dimensions* which reflect **Davie's** (1994) contention that it's possible to 'believe without belonging' (someone may, for example, have a deep (*intellectual*) interest in religious texts without necessarily having any *emotional* or *ritualistic* interest in religion).

- **Ritual** activities include things like attending religious services and ceremonies.

- **Ideological** refers to the commitment someone has to the essential beliefs of a religion.

- **Experiential** represents a measure of 'emotional' identification and attachment on the basis that religion is not simply about 'thinking' and 'doing'; it's also about 'feeling' – and this dimension considers things like the extent to which people identify with a particular religious group (the *solidarity* function of religion).

- **Intellectual** dimensions measure people's knowledge and understanding of their religion's beliefs and practices.

- **Consequential** dimensions look at how all of the above affect the individual's life. In other words, it's a (complicated) measure of the impact religious beliefs, practices and attachments have on everyday life.

**Smith** (1996) fine-tunes **Davie's** (1994) distinction 'to allow for other forms of relationship between the two terms'.

This type of multidimensional grid increases the range of commitments and attachments it's possible to identify in a particular community. Something like New Age (religious) movements involve very

high – often evangelical and proselytising (actively trying to convert others) – levels of belief without adherents necessarily having a strong sense of belonging to a religious organisation: As **Smith** argues: 'Belonging if it exists at all is to loose, ever-changing networks, or to the electronic church.'

**Engs** (2002) suggests that a more general measure of religiosity in the twenty-first century needs to take account of a number of ideas:

- **Belief** refers to the extent to which someone accepts the 'traditional beliefs' of a religion.

- **Difficulty** refers to how individuals relate to a religion – do they, for example, have difficulties and anxieties about certain

| Greg Smith (1996): The Unsecular City | | | | |
|---|---|---|---|---|
| | **Believing** | | | |
| | Low ——————————————————→ High | | | |
| **Belonging** ↓ | 1 | 2 | 3 | 4 |
| | No belief in God | Common or folk religion | Formulaic orthodoxy | Committed/life changing |
| A. Minimal (by birth or ascription) | Never go to church | 'C of E' | Lapsed Roman Catholic | New Age activist |
| B. Nominal allegiance/ occasional participation | 'Not religious' ('weddings only') | Christmas/ Easter | Weekly mass | TV congregation |
| C. Active involvement/ paid-up membership | Humanist society | Parish work | Cynic | Evangelist preacher |

aspects of doctrine (such as abortion, female clergy and homosexuality)?

- **Apathy** and **boredom** consider an individual's willingness to withdraw from a religion when it loses its relevance – a measure, in effect, of *religious attachment*.

- **Satisfaction** represents an assessment of whether people feel they gain something from involvement in religious activities, ceremonies and relationships.

- **Conscience** looks at the feelings people have about the general role of their religious organisation in society – should it, for example, involve itself in secular affairs or concentrate on spiritual matters?

## ✳ SYNOPTIC LINK

**Theory and methods: Engs** suggests an 'inventory' of religious commitment can be constructed using a **Likert scale** – a questionnaire technique designed to measure *attitudes* that involves asking respondents to express their level of agreement/disagreement about a statement on a five-point scale (from 'Strongly Agree' at one end to 'Strongly Disagree' at the other).

The variety of typologies available suggests there's no real agreement about how to *reliably* and *validly* measure a concept like religiosity – something we need to keep in mind as we look at how this idea relates to different social groups.

## ⚠ Preparing the ground: Social class

Much of the information we have about the relationship between class and religiosity is based on survey material from sources such as:

- **Government departments** like the **Home Office's** citizenship survey and the ten-yearly census.

- **Private polling organisations** – YouGov, the internet-based polling organisation, for example.

- **Religious organisations**: Organisations like the Church of England produce yearly attendance and membership figures.

When thinking about these and other forms of data we need to keep in mind, as always, the basic methodological questions of:

- **Reliability**: How data are collected – and for what purpose – are always important questions. Data from religious organisations, for example, often involve different definitions of what constitutes 'membership' and 'attendance'. Church of England attendance figures are 'based on average Sunday attendance, collected over a four-week period each October' (**Barley**, 2005). For comparative purposes, however, we need to be aware, as **Bates** (2005) notes, that in the past attendance figures have been compiled by 'accepting a vicar's assessments or headcounts on a particular day'.

- **Validity**: Opinion poll or interview data are a snapshot of people's opinions at a particular time and the data produced may be subject to a variety of interview/interviewer effects. **Hadaway** and **Marler** (1998) note how poll data in the USA about 'religious attendance' showed significant discrepancies between the numbers 'claiming to attend services' and those who actually attended.

We can note some features of the relationship between class and Christian religiosity (mainly because 70–80% of the UK population identify their religious affiliation – 'a present or past personal or familial connection to a religion' (O'Beirne, 2004) – in such terms), as reported by YouGov (2004).

Belief: There is little significant class difference in beliefs surrounding ideas such as:

- God/gods/supreme being.

- Religious affiliation: The working class are slightly more likely to describe themselves as Protestant or Roman Catholic, whereas the middle classes are slightly more likely to describe themselves as 'other Christian' (Jews, however, are three times more likely to be middle class than working class).

- Prayer: Slightly more middle-class people believe in praying.

- General beliefs: There seems to be no significant class difference in terms of belief in things like heaven, life after death, the devil and hell.

Practice: In terms of attendance at religious services:

- Regular attendees (weekly or monthly): Approximately three times more of the middle classes classify themselves in this way.

- Occasional attendees: Little significant class difference.

- Never attend (outside of ceremonies such as weddings and funerals): The working class are slightly more likely to 'never attend'.

To keep this in context, in a 2003 Mori opinion poll ('Faith in the UK', 2003) only 18% of respondents classified themselves as a 'practising member of an organised religion'.

## Characteristics

When we look at the general social characteristics of different faith groups (O'Beirne, 2004), we can note:

- Occupation: *Christians* were more likely than any other faith to be employed in middle-class (managerial and professional) occupations. *Muslims* were most likely to report never having worked (something, as we will see, that relates to class, gender and age – 35% of Muslim women, for example, reported never having worked, a figure that increased to 63% of those aged 50+).

- Education: General levels of education were higher among those with no religious affiliation than among their religious counterparts. Among faith groups, *Jews* and *Hindus* were more likely to have higher-level qualifications (such as a university degree). *Christian* and *Muslim* faiths had the 'smallest proportions of respondents with the highest educational qualifications' and were most likely, of all faith groups, to have no formal educational qualifications.

- Civic participation (such as membership of voluntary groups): With the exception of 'Christian respondents of black or mixed race ethnicity', religious affiliation made no appreciable difference to participation levels.

One important point to keep in mind here is that the differences and similarities we've identified largely relate to those who profess some form of religious belief and a significant number of people in our society *do not* define themselves as 'religious'.

## ✱ SYNOPTIC LINK

**Stratification and differentiation:** Both polling organisations and government departments use 'class scales' to define and categorise social class. However, different scales may be used by different organisations. **YouGov**, for example, uses a variation of the Registrar General's scale whereas the **Home Office** use the much-newer NS-SEC categories.

## Digging deeper: Social class

O'Beirne (2004) notes that 'respondents affiliated to particular faiths share certain socio-economic experiences and characteristics', and we can dig a little deeper into this idea by examining some possible explanations for the relationship between religious affiliation and social class.

**Status**: In the past, in our society, religion was a source of status for both the upper and middle classes – the former in terms of their positions within powerful religious institutions (such as the Church) and the latter in terms of using things like church attendance as a synonym for 'respectability'. It's arguable whether either of these class functions of religion applies any more.

**Identity**: The decline, noted by **Bruce** (2001), in the significance of religion as a source of *group* (as opposed to *individual*) identity is important in terms of the 'uses of religion' for things like status, social control and the like. When **Colls** (2005) talks about 'a post-industrial, post-colonial, post-masculine, post-Christian world of fluid identities ... ', he argues that the 'religion and respectability' *class markers* of the past no longer have the power and resonance

they once had. **O'Beirne** found little evidence of religious belief/practice forming a significant part of self-identity – only 20% of respondents considered religion 'an important part of their personal description' (and even then religion came somewhere down the scale of significance after family, age, work and interests).

If religion as a source of class identity has little or no resonance for Christians, it was, according to **O'Beirne,** significant for some minority faith communities (Muslims and Hindus, for example). However, this broadly cut across class boundaries – it was mainly a source of *ethnic* identity for all social classes.

**Deprivation**: With one major exception, **O'Beirne's** respondents with religious affiliations '... lived in places with low-to-moderate levels of area deprivation' – something that suggests both the changing nature of class relationships (these are not presently played out – unlike in the past perhaps – in relation to strong concepts of social inequality and deprivation) and the changing nature of established religions; they no longer represent a source of 'hope' for the most deprived in our society. The exception, however, is the Muslim faith – associated with 'the highest levels of area deprivation'.

This suggests UK Muslims largely inhabit the lowest social strata and that religious belief, practice and commitment are an integral part of 'Muslim life' in terms of providing moral codes for a community and as a mode of group/individual identity represented by a strong and vital religious organisation.

## Weeding the path

Although people are generally less inclined to 'join organisations', the fact that some

# Discussion point: Deprivation and deviance?

The relationship between 'deprivation' and 'religiosity' is interesting for two reasons:

1 Deprivation alone doesn't explain why people are religious (working-class Muslims have higher levels of religiosity than working-class non-Muslims).

2 Deprivation – although significant – combines with other social factors (such as political marginalisation and a sense of (sub)cultural identity) to produce certain kinds of cultural response (whether this be deviance, religious behaviour or, in some cases, both).

It would be useful, therefore, to discuss the following questions:

● What parallels are there between deviance and religious belief/behaviour as 'responses' to an individual or group's social situation (how is deviant behaviour sociologically similar – or different – to religious behaviour)?

● What factors can you identify to explain why some people/groups embrace religion?

religious organisations can demonstrate increased levels of membership and attendance might suggest the 'problem' lies less with society and more with what (Christian) religions are currently offering people.

**Fragmentation**: Postmodern societies are different in terms of two kinds of relationship:

● **Individual**: People are less likely to define themselves in terms of class and, consequently, less likely to behave in ways that (perhaps) reflect their perception of class relationships. **Petre** (1999) encapsulates this idea when he quotes Douglas Bartles-Smith, the Archdeacon of Southwark, explaining the repeated fall in Christian church attendance and membership in the UK: 'There has been a general flight from institutions. Trade union membership is down, as is that for political parties and voluntary organizations. It is difficult to find any institution that has not suffered.'

● **Institutional**: This dimension is taken up, in their different ways, by both postmodernists and *exchange theorists* (such as **Finke** and **Stark**, 2004). The basic idea here is that *religious pluralism* is a feature of contemporary societies in terms of the choices available to the 'religious consumer' – both *between* religions (Christianity or Islam, for example) and *within* religions (such as liberal or fundamentalist Christianity). If we include NRMs, the range of consumer choices is even greater.

The argument here is that religious affiliation now relates to 'individual, personal identities' rather than the 'collective, social identities' of the past. The weakening of 'traditional class associations', coupled with increased consumer choice, explains why social class no longer correlates very closely with affiliation. As **Bruce** (2001) argues, the logic of this argument is that 'competitive free markets [in religion] are supposed to be better at meeting not only material but also spiritual needs'.

*Fragmentation* and *pluralism* also have consequences for:

**Partisan dealignment**, which can be related to the association between religious organisations, social groups and voting behaviour. In the past, for example, we find quite strong correlations between class, religious affiliation and political affiliation. Catholicism in the UK drew large numbers of adherents from the working classes who tended to support left-of-centre political parties, and **Dogan** (2004) argues that 'social changes in the last few decades' have altered this situation to one where both class and religion have declined in significance as explanations for political alignments.

**Lifestyle**: **Stark** and **Bainbridge** (1987) argue that cults draw their members from the higher social classes, whereas **Kelly** (1992) has suggested that NRMs are founded and populated by the educated middle classes. **Adler's** research (1979) has drawn attention to the fact that, in the USA at least, members of witch covens are drawn predominantly from the professional middle classes. On a different note, **Bader** (2003) notes how two-thirds of those who claim to have been abducted by aliens previously held middle-class occupations.

The last word here should perhaps go to **Bruce** (1995) for his amusing – if dismissive – explanation for middle-class affiliation with NAMS and, to some extent, NRMs: 'Spiritual growth appeals mainly to those whose more pressing material needs have been satisfied. Unmarried mothers raising children on welfare tend to be too concerned with finding food, heat and light to be overly troubled by their inner lights, and when they do look for release from their troubles they prefer the bright outer lights of bars and discotheques.'

## Preparing the ground: Age

The relationship between religiosity and age is, as you might expect, rather more methodologically straightforward and there's a range of interesting data available relating to religion and age. On a *nominal* level (in terms of what people *say* they believe), identification with religious beliefs, practices and organisations varies considerably in terms of:

**Intergenerational** differences (between age groups): If we look at Christian affiliation (the primary UK faith community):

While data like this don't tell us much about either the relative strength of people's beliefs or the extent to which 'Christians' are committed to their faith, they broadly accord with both **Hunt's** (2002) observation that Christian affiliation tends to rise with age and **O'Beirne's** (2004) research which found those affiliated to a religion were generally older (50+), on average, than those who had no affiliation.

All major UK faith communities (Muslim, Hindu, Jewish, Sikh and Buddhist) showed increasing affiliation with age. However, this should be qualified by noting that, with the exception of Jews, these communities currently have fewer elderly (50+) than younger (25–50) adherents, a discrepancy that can be explained *demographically* (see table on the following page):

**Immigration**: With the exception of Jewish communities (who share a similar demographic profile to Christians), other

| Christian and no religious identification by age (Great Britain) | | | | |
|---|---|---|---|---|
| Age group | Christian | | No religion | |
| | % | Millions | % | Millions |
| 0–15 | 18 | 7.3 | 19 | 2.1 |
| 16–34 | 22 | 8.9 | 23 | 3.3 |
| 35–64 | 41 | 17.0 | 12 | 2.7 |
| 65 and over | 19 | 7.8 | 4 | 0.4 |

Source: Census 2001: Office for National Statistics, 2003; General Register Office for Scotland, 2003

faith groups tend to have a lower age profile because, as the **Office for National Statistics** (2001) notes, 'migrants are mainly young adults'. Between 1997 and 1999 the average age for the majority population was 37, whereas for ethnic minority groups it was 26.

**Fertility**: The birth rates for many minority ethnic groups are higher than the norm for the UK population. **Office for National Statistics** (2001) data show that between 1997 and 1999 '. . . the number of people from minority ethnic groups grew by 15% compared to 1% for white people'.

**Beliefs** show marked generational differences. **YouGov** (2004) found belief in God was highest in the 55+ age group and lowest among the young (18–34). The reverse was true for non-belief. Nearly twice as many elderly as young respondents expressed a belief in prayer and personal experience of praying. In terms of 'basic Christian beliefs' there was little appreciable age difference.

However, one of the most striking features of 'belief' is arguably that a

significant and consistent *majority* of young people (60+% in this survey, 60+% according to the **British Social Attitudes Survey** (2000) and 65% according to **Park et al.**, 2004) expressed no positive religious belief or affiliation. **Park et al.** also note the growth (from 39% to 43% in the past 10 years) in the number of adults with no religious affiliation. This suggests there is no simple relationship between *age* and *affiliation* per se (although religiosity increases with age for believers, young 'non-believers' don't become elderly 'believers').

**Practice**: **Brierley** (1999) concludes that not only are churchgoers 'considerably older than non-churchgoers', but the age gap, as **Bruce** (2001) confirms, has widened over the past 25 years. This trend, he argues, is consistent across all major Christian faiths.

One explanation for this decline, **Bruce** argues, is the inability of the established church to socialise young people into religious belief and behaviour. The decline in Sunday School membership, for example – from 55% of the population in 1900 to 4% in 2000 – is indicative of the inability of established churches to capture and keep young adherents. **Petre** (1999) also suggests the numbers of those under 15 who attend church services is similarly declining (under 20% at present), with fewer than 5% of people in their twenties classifying themselves as 'churchgoing'. The **British Social Attitudes survey** (2001) found the average age of churchgoers is older than that of the general population and, perhaps more significantly, is rising (from 38 in 1989 to 43 in 2000).

## Digging deeper: Age

The '*generation gap*' refers to age-related differences in attitudes and behaviour, and when it comes to religiosity there's a clear, persistent and (arguably) widening gap between the religious behaviour of different generations in our society. As **Jowell** and **Park** (1998) put it: 'All the differences between age groups . . . are minor in comparison with those on religion. The fact is the young are overwhelmingly less religious than their elders.' There is a range of possible explanations for generational differences.

**Disengagement**: The argument here is that as people get older they progressively 'retreat' from a society that, in turn, disengages from them. The ageing process, for **Cumming** and **Henry** (1961), involves a (functional) 'coming to terms' with death – the ultimate disengagement – and religious belief (if not necessarily practice) increases as a means of psychological *coping* with the trauma of death. A decline in religious *practice* in our society among the 65+ age group can be explained in terms of reduced physical mobility.

## Weeding the path

When we look at the relationship between age and religious belief we consistently find that the elderly are more religious than the young. The question here, however, is whether religious belief *increases* with age (that is, whether people who were non-believers in their youth 'start to believe' as they age) and the evidence, according to **Hunsberger** (1985), is that this is not the case.

## The potting shed

Identify and explain one way we could test the argument that religious belief increases with age.

**De Geest** (2002), however, relates elderly disengagement to:

**Identity**: Religion '. . . may especially impact on older adults, as many may be disengaging from formal group connections . . . the older adult still may require some form of group connection and may find it through religion'. **Stuckey's** (1997) research into older female involvement in Sunday School classes suggests this may be the case.

**Lifestyle**: Traditional forms of belief and practice appeal less to the young than to the elderly, which may reflect lifestyle situations and choices. **O'Beirne** (2004) argues the young have less time to commit to religious practice – 'declining activity or interest in work, sports or school-related matters has been identified as a possible explanation for more engagement with a faith community'.

Alternatively, the perception of traditional religion among the young (in the

# The potting shed

**Identify and explain two reasons why evangelical religious services are attractive to young people.**

words of one respondent (**Robins et al.**, 2002), 'It's not cool to be a Christian') may also be a factor here – an explanation supported, in some respects, by the attraction of evangelical missions within the Church of England. The most notable of these in recent times is St Thomas' Church in Sheffield where, as **Cooke** (2003) describes it: 'Every Sunday night, between 800 and 1,000 people – the vast majority under the age of 35 – pile into this ... warehouse in the heart of the inner city. Once inside, they celebrate the love of Jesus with the help of synthesisers and guitars, light shows and overhead projectors, a nightclub-style production masterminded by the church's "worship director"'.

**Alternative ideologies**: Organised religions no longer have a 'monopoly of knowledge' and have consequently lost some of their ability to control how people think about and see the world.

Scientific/rationalist narratives, for example, effectively compete against – and in many ways undermine – religious explanations, making them both less mysterious and, potentially, less attractive as explanations.

**Fanaticism**: Although the absolutes and certainties of religion can be attractive for some (as a source of social and psychological stability), the reverse may also be true; prescriptive moral codes (such as the anti-abortion, anti-contraception and anti-gay teachings of some religions) may, in the words of another of **Robins et al.'s** (2002) young respondents, become 'a big turn-off'.

## Weeding the path

Not all sociologists agree with **Bruce's** (2001) claim that there is 'compelling evidence of a general and persistent decline in religiosity' across all age groups. For some writers, seeking evidence of a lack of religiosity is like looking for the wrong things, in the wrong places in the wrong ways. Instead, they emphasise the idea of:

**Resacralisation**: **Stark** (1999) argues that religiosity in contemporary societies is less likely to be expressed through 'traditional forms of association and membership' and, therefore, is less likely to be reliably picked up by surveys (both *qualitative* – opinion surveys – and *quantitative* – attendance surveys) that focus on traditional faiths such as Christianity and Islam. NRMs, in particular, are notoriously difficult to research, although as **Bader** (2003) notes, what research there is generally shows affiliation to NRMs and NAMs is more popular among the young. **Stark** and **Bainbridge** (1987), however, found evidence that NAMs were popular among older age groups, and **Francis** and **Robbins** (2004) have produced extensive survey data (among males aged 13–15 years) to show evidence of what they term:

**Implicit religion** – the idea that 'believing without belonging' is an increasingly significant trend in contemporary societies among the young, for reasons like:

- **lifestyle**: Being too busy to attend religious services and having other things to occupy their time

- **peer group** pressures that see overt forms of mainstream religious practice as 'uncool'.

## Preparing the ground: Gender

**Walter** and **Davie's** (1998) observation that 'in western societies influenced by Christianity, women are more religious than men on virtually every measure' is a useful starting point for any examination of the relationship between gender and religiosity. As with the two previous categories, we can look at patterns in a similar way, focusing first on:

**Affiliation**: According to **O'Beirne** (2004), across the major UK religions, more women (83%) than men (74%) claimed some form of affiliation. Within the major UK faith communities, the split is 54–46% in favour of women; however, apart from Christians (54% female) and Sikhs (53% female), men are in the majority across the remaining major faith communities. Of those classed as non-religious, 60% were men.

These figures confirm a trend, noted by successive **British Attitudes Surveys**

(1983–1999), that men are less religious in terms of their affiliation levels. Affiliation is also declining among men – from 61% in 1983 to 43% in 1999.

According to **Census 2001**, women also have greater levels of involvement in non-traditional religions such as spiritualism and Wicca (both nearly 70% female), although variations were evident (Rastafarianism, for example, was 70% male).

**Belief**: Although the validity of data about religious beliefs is often questionable – **Furlong** (2002) noted, '. . . people questioned about how much they go to church, give figures which, if true, would add up to twice those given by the churches' – the general evidence from opinion polls (such as **YouGov**, 2004) is that women have higher levels of belief in:

- God: **Crockett** and **Voas** (2004) found 36% *more* women than men believed in the certainty of God's existence

- prayer – 44% of women (and 29% of men) personally believe in prayer

- life after death, heaven, the devil and so forth.

**O'Beirne** also notes more women (57%) than men (42%) affiliated to a faith community defined themselves in terms of their religion. However, we shouldn't ignore the fact that the majority of men and women in our society professed little or no religious belief (in other words, religion was of little or no importance in terms of identity).

**Participation**: Women generally participate more in religious activities (such as attendance at services and clubs) than men:

- **Attendance**: **Crockett** and **Voas** (2004) estimate that women in the 21–40 age group were far more likely (40%) than their male counterparts to attend services.

- **Participation: O'Beirne's** research found Christian women slightly more likely (24–17%) than men to participate 'in groups or clubs with a religious link'. Although the reverse was true for Muslims (30–40% respectively), this may reflect *gender norms* – Muslim women not being allowed to participate independently of men in religious activities, for example – rather than any significant difference in religiosity.

This pattern of attendance and participation is not restricted to the UK and Western Europe. Among Americans, **Barna** (1996) noted that the difference was even more marked, with 'women twice as likely to attend a church service during any given week [and] 50% more likely than men to say they are "religious" and to state they are "absolutely committed" to the Christian faith'. Similarly, if we include NRMs, **Bader** (2003) suggests NRMs (and NAMs) generally have a higher ratio of female-to-male participants.

Finally we can note that men, by and large, hold positions of power and authority within the major world religions. As **Malmgreen** (1987) points out: 'In modern Western cultures, religion has been a predominantly female sphere. In nearly every sect and denomination of Christianity, though men monopolized the positions of authority, women had the superior numbers.'

## Digging deeper: Gender

Traditional sociological explanations for the greater levels of female religiosity focus on the concept of *gender socialisation*, which examines how the behaviour of cultural groups is conditioned by the values and norms developed by – and taught to – different group members. In this respect, the idea that men and women in our society develop different cultural identities has been used by feminists in particular to explain gender differences in participation in ways related to the concept of *patriarchy*.

**Roles**: Christianity, **Steggerda** (1993) notes, promotes concepts of love and care that are more attractive to women who 'interiorise the role of the mother' and translate their general family role into religious behaviour, whereas levels of religiosity between *working* males and females are very similar.

**Participation**: **Daly** (1968) argues that patriarchal forms of religion have a certain attraction (for both men and women) in terms of offering the prospect of things like:

- **order**: Religious beliefs and institutions provide *certainties* in an increasingly 'senseless and confusing world'
- **rules** that clearly specify the limits of acceptable behaviour.

In this respect, as long as both men and women 'understand, know and accept' their place in this moral order, religions also provide:

- **shelter** – a 'home and haven' in a male-dominated world
- **safety** in a threatening world
- **belonging**, which incorporates all of the above into a sense of finding personal identity through group membership.

These 'benefits' come, according to **Daly** (1973), at a price for women; the price they pay is submission to *patriarchal control* since, she argues, religions are male-dominated, hierarchical institutions that '. . . serve the interests of sexist society'. This applies to:

- **Traditional religions**, such as Islam and Christianity, where women are rarely found in positions of power and influence (although the Church of England has allowed women priests since 1992) and

- **NRMs**, which are similar to traditional religions in their general male domination. **Palmer** (1994) says the type of women they attract are not particularly seeking power and, like **Daly**, suggests that 'women join NRMs to bring order to their lives'. In some ways, therefore, the price women are willing to pay for a sense of cultural identity and stability is patriarchy. **Palmer** suggests this 'patriarchal order' is played out in terms of three basic types of NRM, based on their views relating to sexuality, bodies and gender roles:

  - **Sex complement**: Each gender has different spiritual qualities which, when combined (in marriage, for example), serve to complement each other.

  - **Sex unity** groups emphasise 'inner spirituality' as being 'sexless' – a belief that rests on recognising traditional forms of gender/sex division in the 'non-spiritual' world.

  - **Sex polarity** groups emphasise essential, different and non-complementary qualities in men and women with, **Palmer** argues, men being seen as the superior sex.

- **Fundamentalist** sects and denominations, the majority of which – Christian and non-Christian – emphasise an

exaggerated form of 'traditional' gender roles and relationships. A classic example here might be something like:

**Promise Keepers**: **Bartkowski** (2000) notes the driving theme behind this US-based sect is the 'rejuvenation of godly manhood' united around two forms of masculinity:

- **Instrumentalist**, involving the development of a religious organisation as a 'tool' benefiting men at the expense of women. This type of masculinity emphasises 'traditional masculine roles' as breadwinner and provider.

- **Expressive** in the sense that both genders see male control as being the medium through which to understand 'natural roles and responsibilities'. 'Masculinity', in this sense, is expressed through the ability to perform 'traditional male roles'.

## Weeding the path

We need to keep in mind that very few men or women in our society actually *practise* their religious beliefs. Of the 37 million who identified themselves as 'Christian' in **Census 2001**, around 3% (1.1 million) on average attend a weekly service.

**Partial participation**: An alternative way of looking at participation is, following **Nason-Clark** (1998), to see some forms of female involvement in religious organisations as 'challenging the institution from within'. In other words, we shouldn't simply see 'participation' in terms of what postmodernists call:

**Binary oppositions** (in this instance, participation/non-participation or patriarchal/non-patriarchal). Rather, as **Winter et al.** (1994) argue, we should look at how both women – and men – are involved in changing the nature of religious faith and practice through what they term:

**Defecting in place** – the idea that various forms of feminist theology (such as critiques of patriarchal practices and images) are promoting changes *within* traditional religions, such as female-centred:

- **Spaces** within religions – the idea that women are able to carve out areas of religious belief and activity that relate specifically to female interests and concerns.

- **Religions** and the development of ideologies supporting female authority within religious movements. Some forms of 'ecofeminism', for example, link a range of themes (such as environmentalist politics, spirituality and animal rights) to what **Spretnak** (1982) terms concepts of 'prepatriarchal myths and religions that had honoured women'. **Neitz** (1998) notes how such NRMs are '... oriented primarily to ... female deities ... exploring how these woman-affirming beliefs, symbols, and rituals may be empowering to women'.

## Weeding the path

Matriarchal/matrifocal religious movements are small in number even in the context of those who actually practise their religious beliefs. Of more immediate significance, perhaps, is a process that **Swatos** (1998) calls the:

**Feminisation** of religions – the idea that religions in Western Europe and the USA are currently undergoing a 'fundamental orientational change' in which 'feminine (rather than masculine) images of the nature of deity and the role of the clergy come to predominate. God is seen as loving and consoling rather than as authoritarian and judgemental; similarly, members of the clergy are seen as 'helping professionals' rather than as 'representatives of God's justice'.

A different perspective on gender differences in religious belief and behaviour is provided in terms of:

**Physiology and faith**: The general argument is that sex-role socialisation fails to explain adequately gender differences in religious/irreligious belief and behaviour. As **Stark** and **Finke** (2000) note: 'Traditional explanations are that women are more religious because they are more involved in socialising children, less involved in their careers, and more likely to join social groups', whereas **Miller** and **Stark** (2002) argue there is little empirical evidence to support the idea that 'gender differences in religiousness are a product of differential socialization'. In its place, Stark and others draw on a variety of New Right Realist perspectives and apply a range of:

**Evolutionary psychological** ideas, put forward by writers such as **Kanazawa** and **Still** (2000). One essential difference between males and females, from this position, is that 'like crime, *irreligiousness* is an aspect of a general syndrome of short-sighted, risky behaviours'. In other words, men are more likely to indulge in *risky behaviour* (such as not believing in God) because of their biological evolution – a conclusion drawn by **Stark** (2002) on the basis that 'in every country and culture men were less religious than women'.

## ⚠ Weeding the path

**Lizardo** and **Collett** (2005) reject the general conclusion that a 'gender difference in risk preference of physiological origin might explain' male and female religiosity and, as evidence, they point to the work of **Hagan et al.** (1988) in relation to:

**Power control theory**: Although there are differences in 'risk-taking behaviour' between men and women, there are also differences in such behaviour between different groups of men and between different groups of women. What this theory argues is that '... gender differences in risk-preference' are closely related to '... class-based differences in the socialization of children, with women raised in patriarchal families more likely to be risk-averse than men raised in the same type of households and women raised in more egalitarian households'. **Lizardo** and **Collett's** research demonstrated that:

- women raised by highly educated mothers show lower religiosity than those raised by less-educated mothers

- mother's education has little effect on men's chances of being irreligious

- father's education has little effect on gender differences in religiosity.

In other words, levels of gender religiosity could be explained in terms of (class-based) differences in socialisation and, contrary to **Stark's** argument about the lack of evidence for secular attitudes in modern societies, young people as a group (or *cohort* if you prefer) appear to have *converging* gender attitudes to religion (something that shouldn't happen if religious belief is based on fundamental evolutionary differences between the sexes).

## ⚠ Preparing the ground: Ethnicity

We can begin by outlining the general relationship between different ethnic groups and religiosity in terms of their religious affiliations.

The data in the table on the following page comes from the *decacentennial* (ten-yearly) national **census** (2001) and are based on the question 'What is your religion?' We can use this data to explore some important methodological issues relating to data reliability and validity.

Although this type of data doesn't tell us a great deal about people's beliefs or the strength of their affiliation (the 76% of 'White British' who classify themselves as 'Christian' are unlikely to share similar levels of affiliation), there are some useful points that can be drawn from it.

**Diversity**: Our society has a range of ethnicities and religious affiliations, considered not just in terms of different ethnic groups associating themselves with different religions, but also in terms of the diversity of affiliation *within* some ethnic groups (Indian, for example). This leads us to note the:

**Heterogeneity** of religious affiliation within and between different ethnic groups. This raises questions about:

**Ethnicity**: In particular, when comparing two apparently 'similar' ethnic groups (such as Indian and Pakistani, often grouped as 'South Asians'), wide disparities of affiliation exist. The different forms of affiliation (Hindu, Muslim and Sikh, for example) found among Indian respondents suggests a

| Selected UK ethnic groups and religious affiliation | | | | | | | |
|---|---|---|---|---|---|---|---|
| | Christian | Hindu | Muslim | Sikh | Jewish | Buddhist | None/ Unstated |
| Ethnic group | Percentage Thousands | | | | | | |
| White British | 76 38,100 | | 0.1 25 | | 0.4 225 | | 23 11,500 |
| White Irish | 86 592 | | | | | | 14 100 |
| Other White | 63 896 | | 08 117 | | 02 33 | | 25 350 |
| Black Caribbean | 74 417 | | | | | | 24 130 |
| Black African | 69 333 | | 20 97 | | | | 10 49 |
| Indian | | 45 472 | 13 133 | 29 307 | | | 06 67 |
| Pakistani | | | 92 686 | | | | 07 50 |
| Bangladeshi | | | 92 261 | | | | |
| Chinese | 21 51 | | | | | 15 37 | 62 150 |

**Note:** A blank box means less than 5% of respondents affiliated themselves with a particular religion. This does, of course, highlight data discrepancies. For example, 25,000 White British respondents (0.1%) identified themselves as Muslim, whereas 4.9% of Indians identified themselves as Christian (8,000 respondents).

Source: Census 2001 (Office of National Statistics, 2004)

higher level of ethnic *fragmentation* among this group than among Pakistanis, for example. How significant this might be, in terms of study and behaviour, needs to be related to questions of:

**Identity:** Questions of *ethnic identity* are

# ⚠️ Growing it yourself: Methodological issues

In small groups, think about the following questions in relation to the data provided in the 'religious affiliation' table and explain how they relate to issues of reliability and validity:

1 **Completion:** The questionnaire is completed by the 'head of household', not individual family members.

2 **Optional:** The question was not compulsory (why, for example, might people decide not to state their religion?).

3 **Ethnic (self-) classification:** What potential problems might there be with people of different generations classifying themselves in terms of their ethnic background?

4 **Phrasing:** Answers to questions on religion are sensitive to how such questions are worded and, as the Office for National Statistics notes: 'Slight differences in question wording can produce large differences in the proportion of people who say they are Christians or have no religion, although the proportion of people from other religions tends to be more stable.' How might this and other possible factors have affected data validity?

frequently conflated with *religious identity*. This can have serious consequences (the tendency for many national newspapers, for example, to equate 'Muslims' with both 'religious fundamentalism' and 'terrorism'). In addition, just as we'd avoid claiming that the white majority, as Christians, share similar norms, values and beliefs, we should also be wary of attributing this to ethnic

minority groups. **O'Beirne** (2004), however, has noted that religion is a relevant factor 'in a person's self-description, particularly for people from the Indian subcontinent'.

**O'Beirne** (2004) suggests 'religion is important to migrant minority ethnic groups because it is integral to their cultural and ethnic identity'. However, when we break down identity in terms of *religion*, differences

| Top things important about respondents' identity by ethnicity | | | |
|---|---|---|---|
| Rank | White | Black | Asian |
| 2 | Work | Ethnicity/culture | **Religion** |
| 3 | Age | **Religion** | Ethnicity/culture |
| 10 | **Religion** | Nationality | Skin colour |

Source: Census 2001 (Office of National Statistics, 2004)

| | | | Things saying something important about respondents by religious affiliation | | | |
|------|-----------|--------------------|--------------------|--------------------|-----------|-----------|
| Rank | Christian | Muslim | Hindu | Sikh | Jewish | Buddhist |
| 1 | Family | Family | Family | Family | **Religion** | Work |
| 2 | Work | **Religion** | **Religion** | **Religion** | Family | Family |
| 3 | Age | Ethnicity/ culture | Ethnicity/ culture | Ethnicity/ culture | Education | **Religion** |
| 7 | **Religion** | Nationality | Age | Age | Age | Education |

Source: Census 2001 (Office of National Statistics, 2004)

between faith communities are fairly negligible – except in relation to Christians.

We need to note there are significant variations in affiliation (and strength of belief) based on categories such as gender and age – the latter, in particular, is significant when comparing the experiences of different generations within (recent immigrant) ethnicities; although **Cook** (2003) notes: 'Collecting data on ethnicity is difficult because … there is no consensus on what constitutes an "ethnic group".'

**Generational differences** among minority groups are present in the different ways young and old (or first- and second-/third-generation groups) classify themselves. First-generation immigrants are more likely to identify with their country of origin, whereas third-generation individuals are more likely to classify themselves in:

**Hybrid** terms – the use, by some young Asians, of the term 'Brasian' (British Asian) is a case in point here.

**Non-religious affiliations**: The optional nature of the census question means it's impossible to know exactly how many of those who chose not to state their religion did so because they considered it a private matter, didn't know how to classify themselves or whatever. However, it's interesting to note both the relatively high number in some ethnic groups who claim no affiliation (British and Chinese, for example) and the relatively low number in other groups (Pakistani, for example) who claim to be non-religious.

## Weeding the path

The census classifies NRMs as 'other religions' involving relatively small numbers (approximately 160,000 respondents across all ethnic groups – 115,000 White British being the largest group). However, we need to be aware that NRM respondents may not see their beliefs in 'conventional religious' terms or they may have used the 'not stated' category as a way of recording their beliefs.

## Digging deeper: Ethnicity

There are a range of explanations for the relationship between ethnicity and religiosity we can explore, starting with:

**Deprivation**: As we've seen, the highest levels of religious affiliation are found among Pakistani (92%) and Bangladeshi (92%) minorities. Both **Dorsett** (1998) and **Berthoud** (1998) have shown these ethnic groups to be among the very poorest in our society.

While this correlation is interesting, deprivation of itself is not a sufficient explanation for higher levels of religiosity (measured in terms of both affiliation and practice). Although Christians generally profess high levels of affiliation, this does not translate significantly into religious practice. As **Crockett** and **Voas** (2004) put it: 'All major ethnic minority populations are more religious than British-born whites.' Since high levels of deprivation exist in places among the white working class, the question here is why do some ethnic groups – but not others – display high levels of religiosity under similar economic circumstances?

The answer is bound up in ideas and issues related not simply to ethnicity, but also to the *experience* of being an 'ethnic minority' within a society; in other words, the key to understanding levels of ethnic group religiosity (both majority and minority) is found in two areas:

- **Inter-group relationships**: How, for example, different minority groups relate to both other minorities and to the ethnic majority.

- **Intra-group relationships**: Differences, for example, within ethnic minority groups (such as those of class, gender and, in particular, age) that relate to how these groups interact with, for example, the ethnic majority.

These different experiences, therefore, relate to questions of:

**Identity** – considered in terms of both the self-perception of different ethnic groups and, of course, the various social factors that go into the 'constructive mix' of such identities. We can illustrate this idea by contrasting the experiences of the 'White British' majority ethnic group in the UK, following a predominantly Christian faith, and the Pakistani minority, following a predominantly Muslim faith. The measured differences in religiosity between these two groups are explained conventionally in terms of a distinction between two types of believer:

- **Nominal**: A situation where people are 'born into a religion' (such as the Church of England) and generally, when asked, associate themselves with this religion without having much of a firm faith or commitment to it. The majority of UK Christians, by and large, fall into this category.

- **Authentic**: People who demonstrate their firmly held beliefs through various forms of practice and commitment. Pakistani Muslims generally fall into this category.

## Weeding the path

This distinction begs the question of why *nominal belief* should be considered 'less authentic' than *overtly practised* beliefs – to argue that the latter group are *necessarily* 'more religious' ignores two things:

- **Private beliefs** may be sincerely held without the need to have them continually and publicly affirmed and reaffirmed.

- **Public practice** may be indicative of social processes (such as status considerations or peer pressure) other than strict religious belief.

**Bruce** (1995) develops these ideas by arguing that in modern, secular societies a distinction arises between two spheres of behaviour and practice that involve different basic values and norms:

- **The public sphere** is governed by ideas of rationality, instrumentalism and, most importantly, universal values and norms (as he argues: 'Supermarkets do not vary prices according to the religion, gender or age of the customer'). This sphere can be described loosely as that of the *community* – a space where people meet, greet and interact according to a set of shared ideas and beliefs.
- **The private sphere** is characterised by ideas of expression and affection. It is also private in the sense of not being wholly part of the communal sphere – it represents space where the individual is, to some extent, set apart from the communal, public sphere.

Using this distinction, Christianity has evolved to accommodate itself to *secular* changes, especially in the *public sphere* (the development of secular politics, the demands of economic globalisation and cultural diversity, for example). In so doing, it has slowly retreated from the public sphere of religious *practice* into the private sphere of religious *belief*. This is not to say that services and ceremonies are no longer attended (around 1 million Christians attend church services each week); rather, it's to argue that the Church has had to come to terms with the idea that, for the ethnic majority, the role and function of organised religion has slowly changed. This group no longer (if indeed it actually ever did, as a society) needs religion to perform functions like:

- **Communality**: Bringing people physically together to promote:
- **Social solidarity** – the idea that people have things in common which bind them together as a group or society, and
- **Identity** – the idea that we become 'centred' (reasonably secure in the knowledge of 'who we are') through something like communal religious practices.

## Private religion

Although we still require these things, they are increasingly satisfied by other institutions and activities (from the media, through shopping, to sport). Thus, as the Christian Church loses its *public functions*, attendance and practice also decline – but religion doesn't necessarily disappear from people's lives; rather, Christianity has, **Bruce** (1995) argues, been '. . . reworked so as to confine it to the private sphere'.

**Davie** (2001), however, argues that religious practice often remains important even in situations where religiosity has become largely confined to the private sphere – people still feel the need to make public affirmations, the most obvious and widespread being the classic 'christenings, weddings and funerals' trinity in our society. These are important:

**Life events** that require *both* private and public acknowledgement.

For minority groups, **Bruce** (1995) suggests the situation is somewhat different; such groups in the UK have moved from a

## Discussion point: A church without walls?

A Church of Scotland Report, 'Church without Walls' (2001), identifies a number of ways the Christian Church should adapt to meet the changed needs of its potential parishioners. These include:

- focusing on getting the Christian message across in ways other than attending church

- going where people are rather than waiting for people to come to church

- encouraging churches to work together

- putting the local church at the centre of the community.

Thinking about these ideas:

- Does this type of report reflect a change in the way churches see their own organisation and the changing needs/requirements of potential and actual adherents? If so, in what ways?

- Do you think these types of changes will be successful in 'bringing Christianity to more people'? Why/why not?

- What changes in religious organisations can you suggest to 'make them more attractive' to potential religious consumers?

Source: www.churchwithoutwalls.co.uk

situation in which 'their religion was dominant and all-pervasive to an environment in which they form a small, deviant minority, radically at odds with the world around them'. Recent immigrant groups especially find themselves in, at best, an indifferent world, and, at worst, one that's hostile and uninviting.

In such a situation, it's hardly surprising that Pakistani minorities, for example, look to the things that are familiar and certain in their lives. These involve various traditions, customs, particularistic values and norms, which in turn require affirmation and reaffirmation through communal gatherings that promote both social solidarity and a sense of ethnic identity. Religion, through communal practices and beliefs, provides an outlet for such things, and it can also be

argued that religious practices are a source of protection – both physical and psychological – in a hostile and challenging world.

Religions such as Islam, therefore, are articulated in the public sphere (as **Davie** (2001) notes: 'Islam is not a religion that lends itself to private expression') and relate to a sense of:

**Belonging** – not just in the literal sense of 'belonging to a religion or organisation', but also of belonging to a specific, definable group, membership of which is affirmed through public practices.

In this respect we can note how, for ethnic minority groups in particular, religiosity performs significant services and functions in terms of:

**Social identities**: As we've suggested, one function of religious organisations for many ethnic minority groups is that of providing a sense of homogeneity, shared purpose and, indeed, a sense of permanence for a particular group. The concept of identity implies both a sense of *self* ('who we are') and, by definition, a sense of *other* ('who we are not') that is sustained both:

- **internally**, in terms of the particular beliefs and practices of the group, and
- **externally**, by contrasting these beliefs and practices with groups who are 'not like us'.

**Emotion** refers to the psychosocial sense of belonging and well-being created by membership of – and acceptance within – a particular group (such as a religion). For some minority groups the emotional aspect of religious belief and practice is valued in a world that may, at various times, seem hostile and dangerous.

**Power**: In the type of situation just described – especially among politically and economically marginalised groups – belonging to a coherent group in which you are valued confers a sense of power and sustenance through which to face the world.

## Moving on

In this section the discussion of the relationship between religious beliefs, organisations and social groups has laid the ground for the final section that explores the concept of secularisation – the question of whether or not religious beliefs, practices and affiliations are in general decline in modern societies.

# 5. Different definitions and explanations of the nature and extent of secularisation

At various points throughout this chapter we've touched on the question of whether or not 'religion' is in decline in modern societies. In this final section, therefore, we address the question head-on by examining the concept of 'religious decline' in terms of the different ways secularisation has been defined, measured and explained.

## Preparing the ground: Defining secularisation

Secularisation is a concept that's easier to describe than it is to operationalise and explain – as **Sachs** (2004) notes: 'The origin of the word is one of the few things about it that is relatively unmuddled.' It refers to the idea that the 'influence of religion' has declined – and continues to decline – in contemporary societies. As **Swyngedouw** (1973) puts it, the concept represents a '... generic term to designate the whole process of change occurring in contemporary society, with special regard to what has traditionally been called "religion"'.

## Weeding the path

The general problems surrounding the concept of secularisation can be summarised in terms of:

**Measurement**: Ideas like 'decline' have a certain *quantitative* substance to them, given that they involve *comparing* some feature of 'past behaviour' with the same feature of 'present behaviour'. However, for this we

## WARM-UP: SECULAR EVIDENCE

Divide the class into two groups (four if the class is large). Each group should brainstorm ideas about *one* of the following for our society (we've given you a couple of ideas to get you started).

Once you've done as much as you can, each group should take it in turns to state – and discuss – the evidence they've identified. Once the discussion is complete, group the different ideas you've identified into categories (for example, those dealing with the Church as an institution, attendance patterns/levels etc.).

| Evidence for/indicators of a decline in significance of religion | Evidence for/indicators of the significance of religion |
|---|---|
| Fewer people attending Christian church services | Some forms of religion (such as Evangelical Christians) seem to be flourishing |
| **Further examples?** ||

need access to accurate, reliable and valid information about people's behaviour – something can't be taken for granted in either the past or the present. In addition, two furthers dimensions of measurement include:

- **what** features of religion we measure to test 'decline'
- **how** we go about measuring such features (what, for example, counts as religious practice).

**Definitions** of secularisation are many and varied, which makes it difficult to identify a 'definitive definition'. We can, however, identify some *common themes* running through the debate and a classic starting point for this is **Shiner's** (1967) argument that secularisation – if it exists – would be manifested in areas such as:

## Religious decline

The most obvious meaning of secularisation

is that religion has become less important in contemporary (usually Western) societies. There are, as you might expect, different versions of this general view, with the emphasis on either:

- **Decline**, in the sense of religion continuing to exist within broadly secular societies but relegated to the role of 'minority interest', much as certain sports and pastimes attract a small but highly specialised audience. The majority of pro-secularisation sociologists probably fall into this camp.

- **Disappearance**, in the sense that society becomes truly secular. Very few, if any, sociologists subscribe to this particular view however.

- **Conformity**: In this scenario, religions gradually come to lose their 'supernatural' preoccupations; rather than disappearing, religions 'accommodate themselves' with secular society, turning their attention and ministry to looking after secular needs. The Church of England, for example, has in recent times examined areas like poverty – the 'Faith in the City' report (1985) was highly critical of the **Thatcher** government's policies towards the poor.

- **Disengagement**: In this scenario, secularisation involves a progressive distancing of the institutions of secular society (government, education and so forth) from religious organisations. Religions lose their role in the public sphere (the power to either govern in their own right or to influence or dictate the direction of secular policies). Religion doesn't disappear, as such, but is instead largely restricted to the private sphere of personal beliefs – it becomes purely a matter for individual conscience.

- **Transposition** involves the idea of ideological challenge and change, the classic example of which, in modern times, has been the rise of *scientific* forms of explanation. What was once explained in religious terms is explained, increasingly, in ways considered more plausible by secular society.

## ⚠🏠 The potting shed

Identify and explain two examples of things which in the past were explained by religion but which are now more plausibly explained by science.

**Desacralisation** points to the idea that the social and natural worlds become progressively 'demystified'; in the natural world, for example, sciences like chemistry explain the world in a rational way that leaves no room for *metaphysical* (religious) explanations. Social sciences, such as sociology, meanwhile, provide explanations for individual and group development that similarly leave little or no space for religious explanations. On a political level, *desacralisation* involves the removal of religious authorities and religious laws from secular affairs.

**Movement** relates to the way societies develop – from the simple to the complex and the sacred to the secular. In other words, where small-scale, relatively simple and undifferentiated societies were once dominated by notions of 'the sacred', large-scale, complex and relatively differentiated societies place the secular at their centre.

## Dimensions

Although **Shiner's** observations are nearly 40 years old, they point the way to the subsequent development of the 'secularisation debate' in the sense that they help to identify three major *dimensions* of religion around which the debate has been framed:

- **Institutional**: This dimension looks at the role played by religious organisations in the general governance of (secular) society and its focus is on the power wielded by religious organisations. We can think of this dimension, in terms of **Shiner's** categories, as relating to ideas such as *institutional disengagement*, religious *movement* and *conformity*.

- **Practical**: This dimension looks at the extent to which people practise their religious beliefs through things like attendance at religious services or membership of religious organisations. This, in **Shiner's** terms, involves ideas about religious *decline* and the *desacralisation* of society.

- **Ideological**: The final dimension is the extent to which people hold religious beliefs – either in tandem with or separated from – religious practice. As we've seen, it's possible for people to hold strong religious beliefs without ever wanting or needing to practise such beliefs. In terms of **Shiner's** argument, this involves ideas about *disengagement* and *transposition*.

## Themes and issues

**Wilson** (1982) echoed the above categories with his characterisation of secularisation potentially involving a number of interwoven themes and issues.

**Institutional** themes involved the extent to which there is a secular takeover of powers formerly exercised by religious institutions (such as definitions of crime and punishment). Alternatively, the development of the welfare state in Britain is an example of the way secular institutions might effect a shift of power and control away from religious institutions, in the sense that the state, rather than the Church, assumed responsibility for the poor.

**Organisational** issues involved questions of whether there was a general decline in the time and energy people devoted to religious practices and concerns and the extent to which behaviour was governed and controlled by secular, as opposed to religious, norms and values.

**Ideological**: **Wilson** argued an important

(individual) dimension of secularisation was whether the level of people's understanding about the natural and social world changed, moving away from a *magical* (spells and charms) or *religious* (prayer) consciousness towards a secular, rational consciousness.

## Processes

Similarly, **Casanova** (1994) argues secularisation involves the study of three different processes:

- **Differentiation** involves thinking about the extent to which religious institutions become separated from secular institutions and spheres of influence.

- **Decline** examines whether or not religious beliefs have any great influence over the individual or society. In addition, we need to consider whether religious practices decline in terms of both the numbers involved and their social significance. Weddings, for example, may be seen more as secular, as opposed to religious, occasions.

- **Distance** relates to whether religion has retreated into the private sphere and, if so, whether it signals disengagement between religious ideas/practices and the secular world.

**Bruce** (2002) echoes the above and takes them slightly further when he argues that '... secularisation is a social condition manifest in' two different types of decline:

- **Institutional** – reflected in religious organisations having little or no involvement in areas such as government and the economy. In addition, 'the social standing of religious roles and institutions' declines as secularisation takes hold.

- **Organisational** – measured in terms of a fall in the significance of religious conduct, as covered by ideas relating to behaviour, practice and beliefs. In this respect, the general plausibility of religious ideas and practices would, if secularisation is taking place, be generally called into question.

## Weeding the path

These definitions generally focus on the idea of secularisation operating at the level of institutions, practices and behaviours (as **Wilson** (1966) puts it: 'Secularisation is a process whereby religious thinking, practices and institutions lose their significance in society'). **Marshall** (1994), however, argues that the focus should be on the concept of beliefs, considered in terms of their:

**Nature**: Traditionally, sociologists have looked at 'religious beliefs' in terms of how they have been reflected in religious practice – to put it crudely, the number of people attending religious services. **Marshall** argues, however, that to understand the secularisation question we must take account of possible changes to the nature of religious belief. We need to consider, therefore, the 'privatisation of belief' as a measure of secularisation.

**Extent** relates to how widely – or narrowly – we define both religion and religious practice. For example, whether we hold *inclusive* or *exclusive* definitions of religion or see evidence of religious practice in either overt terms (such as attending ceremonies) or implicit terms (such as moral beliefs) will affect our perception of secularisation.

**Intensity**: Finally, we need to consider how strongly individual religious beliefs are

## The potting shed

Identify and briefly explain one example of an overt religious practice and one example of an implicit religious practice.

held (both in the past and in the present). For **Marshall**, therefore, the focus of secularisation theory is that of people's 'core beliefs', expressed in terms of 'three causally related things':

- the **importance** of religion in any society
- the **number** of people who take it seriously and, most significantly
- **how seriously** people take it.

These ideas open up a range of possibilities and problems when we consider how to operationalise the concept of secularisation.

## Digging deeper: Operationalising secularisation

Although it's not possible to directly measure 'religious decline', we can identify *indicators* of decline by comparing changes to institutional, organisational and individual religious behaviours and beliefs. In this respect we need to consider how we can *quantify* ideas like religious decline:

**Indicators**: A major question here is which indicator – among many – is most important. **Dobbelaere** and **Jagodzinski** (1995) suggest 'a *quantitative* decline in the number of people attending religious services' – but although it's possible to show that fewer people attended religious services in Britain in 2005 than they did in 1805, does this mean secularisation has occurred?

Alternatively, we have to consider the question of whether or not it's necessary to show that all possible indicators (institutional, organisational and individual) have declined in order to conclude secularisation has taken place.

**Timescale**: Comparisons can turn on the timescale used. Do we, for example, pick a date from the distant past (if so, which one?) as the starting point for our comparison? Alternatively, do we sample a range of dates to see whether it's possible to arrive at an 'average view' of secularisation?

**Levels of secularisation**: Dobbelaere (1981) notes three basic levels that could be investigated, reflecting the institutional/organisational/individual distinction we've made previously:

- **Macro**: This examines society as a whole, with the focus on institutional processes and changes (such as changes to religious involvement in government).
- **Meso**: The organisational ('middle') level that focuses on changes in religious organisations and practices.
- **Micro**: The level where the focus is on individual religious beliefs.

**Dobbelaere**, while seeing these levels as 'inextricably linked', suggests the *macro* level is most significant as an indicator of secularisation, mainly because it involves behaviour that impacts on *all levels* of society.

## ⚠ Weeding the path

**Bruce** (2002) suggests that fundamental arguments over which indicators to use to operationalise secularisation means there is no longer a single 'secularisation theory', but rather a series of theories – a problem compounded by the fact that any attempt to measure secularisation involves comparing the past with the present. This, in turn, raises practical problems of:

**Reliability**: On a basic level there is a lack of accurate data about people's behaviour and beliefs 'in the past', and even contemporary records, such as levels of church attendance, suffer from problems relating to who to count and when to count them. There are, for example, three areas in which data reliability about religious practice is questionable:

- **availability**: Some religions collect attendance and membership data, some do not
- **distribution**: Some organisations make this data freely available, others do not
- **counting**: Statistics are collected and counted in a variety of ways (and the way something like attendance is counted may also change over time).

Although it's not difficult – as we've seen – to quantify people's current beliefs (using methods like questionnaires and interviews), this is not true of even the recent past. As **Hadden** (1987) notes: 'Public opinion polling has only existed for about sixty years. Much of the archived literature is difficult to assess because different methodologies and different sampling techniques do not make the data directly comparable.'

**Validity**: One problem that may be overlooked when considering quantitative data is that it still needs to be *interpreted*. Even if we could be certain church attendance figures over the past 200-odd years were totally reliable (and, for the sake of argument, we could assume the figures showed a significant decline in attendance),

# Growing it yourself: Counting converts?

1 In the following extracts, find examples of the following issues:

**Reliability differences**
- definitions
- counting techniques
- time periods.

**Validity differences**
- interpretations of attendance
- measurement of attendance
- accuracy of measurements.

2 Write a paragraph on each of the differences you've identified, detailing and describing how such issues relate to the measurement of secularisation. Each paragraph should have the following format:
- opening statement of the issue
- explanation of why it is a potential problem
- outline of the evidence to support your argument
- brief conclusion about how your argument relates to secularisation.

## Parishes attack Church's 'greed and arrogance': Jonathan Petre

Source: www.telegraph.co.uk, 2 July 2000

There was also a feeling among parishes ... that 'the Church of England has not been entirely honest about declining congregations'. Officials suspended the Sunday church attendance statistics for two years, saying they did not fairly reflect the changing patterns of worship. When they were finally released they showed the figure had fallen below a million for the first time, which officials said was an underestimate.

## Counting sheep: Paddy Benson

Source: www.tfh.org.uk

Newspaper headlines would have us believe that Christianity is a spent force in this country and our days of influence, or even existence, are numbered. However, this survey of church attendance statistics shows that the announcement of our demise may be premature. Regular weekly numbers are declining but there are also a growing number of ... 'casual attendees'. Over a two-month period, typically half of the total congregation may only come on a single Sunday. We need to recognise that these people make up a substantial part of our flock.

## Vital statistics 2002: Stephen Cottrell and Tim Sledge

Source: www.evangelism.uk.net

Cottrell and Sledge helped organise detailed registers of all people attending church over an eight-week period in a Deanery in Wakefield Diocese ... the actual attendance was 37% higher than the average attendance – people's pattern of attendance varied. Across a whole Deanery, only 144 people attended church on each of the eight Sundays. Across the Deanery over eight Sundays there were 1776 one-off attendees.

If the figures for total regular attendance are taken (rather than Average Sunday Attendance) is church growing? Or, what about those who cannot or will not attend on Sunday (work, leisure, sports, family, shopping) – are there ways in which they can embrace Christian community and worship at other times or in other ways?

a validity problem remains – namely the assumption that people in the past and the present attended religious services for the same reason. Thus, it's possible for the same data to demonstrate two mutually exclusive things:

- **Decline**: An absolute decline in the number of people attending services could be taken as evidence of secularisation (at least in relation to organisational practice). **Bruce** (2001), in his analysis of pre-industrial Britain, and **McLeod**'s (1993) research into Victorian Britain both suggest religious attendance was significantly higher in the past than it is in the present.

- **Increase**: **Coleman** (1980) argues 'Victorian England, and in particular its cities, experienced a breakdown of religious practice and what amounted to a secularisation of social consciousness and behaviour'. In other words, although religious attendance may have been significantly higher in the past, the *quality* of present-day attendance is significantly greater – people nowadays, it could be argued, show greater levels of religiosity because attendance has been stripped of many of its earlier, non-religious attributes (compulsion, entertainment, leisure and so forth).

## Weeding the path

Thus far we've looked at some 'practical problems' of methodology, but this isn't the only dimension we need to consider. The secularisation debate involves two other types of question.

**Ontological** questions refer to different basic groups of beliefs – those broadly 'pro'

and 'anti' the secularisation thesis in this context. Where a writer stands in relation to this debate conditions how they interpret data; **Bruce** (2002), for example, is broadly pro-secularisation, whereas **Finke** and **Stark** (2004) (anti-secularisation) dispute **Bruce's** interpretation of the *same* evidence.

**Epistemological**: This type of problem revolves around two ideas: what we claim to know and the general proof we will accept in support of this claim. Consideration of this problem leads us, therefore, into some slightly murkier waters when we consider a range of 'operational problems'.

## Problems

**Definitions**: The most obvious *epistemological* problem here is how to decide which of the many competing definitions to accept as definitive for measurement purposes. Although there is a general agreement that issues like institutional, practical and ideological decline are significant, there is little agreement about which of these areas (if any) are *most* significant. In epistemological terms, therefore, the 'problem of operationalisation' turns not so much on the existence of different definitions, but on different forms of:

**Interpretation**: In other words, even where a general agreement exists over what needs to be studied, tested or measured, there is little or no agreement over the meaning and significance of changes in areas such as religious practice. As **Taylor** (2000) argues, many interpretations of secularisation 'depend largely on church attendance statistics', and their steady decline '. . . is still read as conclusive evidence' of the decline of religious practice and the privatisation of religious belief 'in a vicious spiral of inevitable demise'.

Alternatively, **Glasner** (1977) has observed: 'The assumption is that, since a common usage definition of Christianity, for example, is concerned with Church attendance, membership and the presence of rites of passage, these constitute significant elements of a definition of religion and that any move away from this institutional participation involves religious decline.'

## Controversies

Secularisation theory, in this respect, has been dogged by controversies of interpretation leading some, such as **Spickard** (2003), to question whether it's possible to measure secularisation empirically. **Spickard**, from a broadly postmodernist position, rejects the idea we can see secularisation as a 'paradigm, theory or any other scientific-sounding word'; instead, he argues, we should view it as:

**Narrative** because, he suggests, 'scholars … are led by their imaginations. Not that they ignore data … But isolated data do not make sense all by themselves. No, data make sense only when they are imbedded in a story that gives them meaning'.

To support this argument he notes how the same 'secularisation data' can have different meanings, depending on the interpretation of a particular observer. Thus: 'The membership declines of American mainline Protestant denominations, for example, can be interpreted as the result of growing secularisation or as the result of increased fundamentalism … or as a sign of growing religious individualism, or as the result of these denominations' failure to deliver a religious product that appeals to American consumers. Or, it can be all of these … '

At the centre of this overall debate, therefore, is not the extent or quality of specific forms of secularisation data, but rather the idea that 'data alone do not tell us which of these is the "correct" story. Getting from data to narrative requires an imaginative leap: the discernment of a pattern that makes various data hang together. Most scholarly conflicts arise from different leaps, not from different facts'.

## Preparing the ground: Explaining secularisation

In general terms, the 'secularisation debate' is broadly organised around three basic positions

- **Pro-secularisation**: Religion has declined in significance – from the past, when it dominated all aspects of political, economic and cultural life, to the present where its influence is marginal to the first two ideas and increasingly marginal to the third.

- **Anti-secularisation** theorists dispute this interpretation, from a variety of positions:

  - **Overstatement**: The influence of religious organisations and beliefs in the past has been *overstated* and the contribution made by religion to contemporary societies *understated*.

  - **Religious influence** in modern societies is still strong. It provides, for example, the basic rationale for moral codes underpinning political life and takes the lead in arguing for *ethical* practices to inform economic life. There is also a strong undercurrent of individual religious beliefs even in secular societies.

- **Evolution**: Religion has changed, rather than 'declined' in influence. People are, for example, less likely to follow the overt practices common in the past because these served functions that are either no longer needed or are performed by other institutions.

- **Post-secularisation** theories cover a range of positions, a number of which acknowledge both the previous positions – 'pro-secularisation' in the sense of seeing a decline in the influence of religion in *some areas* of social life (such as government and economic activity), but 'anti-secularisation' in the sense that religion still makes significant contributions to other areas of social life (culture, personal morality, beliefs and so forth). **Yip** (2002) characterises this general position as being one where religion is seen to be '… in a constant state of transformation (and persistence)'.

Having broadly sketched these three basic positions, we can look at each in a little more depth.

## Pro-secularisation

**Crockett** and **Voas** (2004) argue that *social change* and, in particular, the gradual transformation of *pre-modern* society into *modern* society creates a situation where 'the social significance of religion, and religious participation as a result, declines as modernity advances', due mainly to three things:

- **Social transitions** – from small-scale communities, where informal social controls held sway over people's lives, to large-scale, complex societies in which people could both develop a range of ideas

and behaviours and exercise choice over what they believed and how they behaved.

- **Knowledge** – in particular the 'increasing sense of mastery over fate' that came with the development of science-based knowledge.

- **Religious pluralism**: As people developed a more individualistic outlook, their choices of behaviour and belief were (and indeed remain) reflected in different forms of religious and non-religious belief.

**Modernisation, Crockett** and **Voas** argue, undermines the 'plausibility of any single religion', leading to a general decline in religious influence. This follows because *religious diversity* means religious organisations can no longer present a 'united ideological front' to the world – their ability to impose religious discipline and sanctions, influence social and economic policies or challenge scientific rationalism is, therefore, seriously weakened.

**Hadden** (2001) argues that although early sociological theorists (such as **Marx** and **Weber**) tended to view *modernisation* as 'impacting the totality of human culture' (that is, affecting all areas of society

Are football grounds like Hampden Park, Glasgow, the 'new cathedrals' of the twenty-first century?

equally), we can best understand secularisation by thinking in terms of its impact on three main dimensions of behaviour in which the influence of religion is either seriously weakened or in general decline:

- **Cognitive** dimensions focus on how information and beliefs are organised. People in *modern society* think very differently about the nature of god, the social and natural worlds and the like, to people in *pre-modern society*. From this perspective, the plausibility of religious explanations declines inexorably.

- **Institutional** dimensions: Increasing institutional development and differentiation in the modern world results in many of the functions performed by religion in pre-modern society being taken over by secular institutions. As **Hadden** argues: 'Corporate structures and the secular political state appear as the locus ['centre'] of power and authority in the modern world.'

- **Behavioural** dimensions: Religious behaviour retreats from the public to the private sphere.

## Evidence

For *pro-secularisation* theorists, therefore, religious decline is evidenced in terms of:

- **Participation**: In the UK there has been a long-term decline in attendance since the nineteenth century (with a particularly sharp decline since the 1950s).

- **Membership**: A minority (around 10%) of the general population are, for example, members of the Church of England.

- **Privatised beliefs**: 'Religion' is relegated to ad hoc beliefs about 'God' and 'Heaven' that have little or no meaning outside of 'personal crises' (such as illness and ill health).

- **Loss of functions**, such as the ability to provide social cohesion or the monopoly of knowledge in society.

**Bruce** (2001) suggests further reasons for believing that secularisation has been – and continues to be – a defining movement in *Western Europe*:

- **Clergy**: Over the past 100 years in the UK – a period when the general population has doubled – the number of full-time, professional clergy has declined by 25%.

- **Rites of passage**: The trend here, in relation to areas such as baptisms, confirmations and weddings, is one of decline. **Brierley** (1999) notes: 'In 1900, 67% of weddings in England were celebrated in an Anglican church; in 2000, it was 20%.'

**New Religious Movements** are frequently cited as evidence of both religious:

- **transformation** – people expressing their religiosity in non-traditional ways – and

- **revitalisation** – a growth area in terms of numbers.

However, **Bruce** argues that if NRMs were 'religious *compensators*' we should have seen 'some signs of vigorous religious growth'. This hasn't happened since 'the new religious movements of the 1970s are numerically all but irrelevant'.

**Belief**: Although 'believing without belonging' is sometimes seen as evidence against secularisation, **Bruce** argues the evidence for a general decline in religious beliefs is strong – it simply 'lags behind' the decline in religious practice.

**Gill et al.** (1998), in their analysis of British survey data over the past 70 years, conclude: 'The results show an increase in general scepticism about the existence of God, the related erosion of dominant, traditional Christian beliefs, and the persistence of non-traditional beliefs.'

## Weeding the path

The relationship just suggested between modernity and secularisation has, in recent times, been challenged. **Brown** (2001) argues that 'modernity' is too broad an explanation for secularisation within Christianity and that, in its place, we should understand changes in Christianity based around:

**Gender** and, in particular, *female religiosity*. **Brown's** research, for example, shows that from the late eighteenth century, the Christian Church in Britain was predominantly supported and maintained by *women*. The post-1945 decline in church attendance is explained by changes in female lives and self-perceptions, which resulted in a questioning of both religious practice and beliefs as the lives and experiences of this social group changed. In other words, any 'decline in religiosity' could be explained in terms of 'a remarkably sudden and culturally violent event' in the shape of feminism.

## Anti-secularisation

Although **Hadden** (2001) notes, 'secularization theory was the dominant theoretical view of religion in the modern world for most of the 20th century', over the past 30 years, a number of writers, especially – but not exclusively – in the USA, have challenged the notion of secularisation itself, in terms of both empirical and interpretive evidence.

**Empirical evidence**: **Warner** (1993) proposed a reassessment of traditional secularisation theory based on the fact that '... the proportion of the population enrolled in churches grew hugely throughout the 19th century and the first half of the 20th century, which, by any measure, were times of rapid modernization'; and Peter **Berger** (1999) – significantly, given his earlier support for secularisation theory – has noted that declining congregations in Western Europe was not a trend replicated in the USA. **Kelley** (1972) added a controversial idea into the general mix when he argued that secularisation, where it had occurred, was the result *not* of modernity and rationality but rather the outcome of:

**Accommodations** made by religious organisations to the secular world. In other words, religious practice *declined* only in organisations that were:

- **image conscious** – appealing to the widest range of people
- **democratic** in their internal affairs
- **responsive** to people's needs
- **relativistic** in terms of their teaching and morality.

Religious growth, according to **Kelley**, was found in religious organisations that offered their adherents a set of basic ideas and principles that were:

- traditional
- autocratic

- patriarchal
- morally absolute.

Although not empirically convincing – **Roozen** (1996), for example, has linked increases in religious attendance to *demographic factors* such as the post-war 'Baby Boom' (more people in a population, allied to the elderly being more religious, means a (temporary) increase in religiosity) – **Kelley** introduced a significant element into the discussion of secularisation, namely the idea that religious practice has a:

**Consumer orientation** – the idea that people will 'buy into' things they find attractive and useful. This relatively simple idea, however, opened the door to a different way of approaching the secularisation debate by thinking about religion as both a:

- **cultural institution**, in terms of propagating values, and an
- **economic organisation** – one that was actively engaged in 'selling religion' and, in consequence, could be studied in a similar fashion to non-religious business organisations.

## Theory

The idea of analysing religion in this way developed, in the 1990s, into a specific form of theory related to:

**Interpretive evidence**: The most influential and wide-reaching current forms of anti-secularisation analysis are based around:

**Religious economy theory** (and its variations *rational choice/supply-side* theory): Rather than deny 'secularisation theory', as such, this theory suggests secularisation is *inadequate* as a theory for explaining

developments in contemporary (*postmodern*) society. The basic ideas underpinning a theory made popular by writers like **Iannaccone** (1994) and **Stark** and **Finke** (2000, 2004) are:

- **Religious pluralism** – encourages organisations to compete for 'customers' in the religious marketplace.
- **Competition** – encourages both *innovation* (religious organisations have to find new ways to appeal to customers) and *reinvigoration* (organisations are continually reinventing both themselves and their services as a way of 'keeping ahead of the competition').
- **Monopolies**: In societies where one religious organisation has a 'monopoly of belief' (such as, for example, in Britain where the Church of England is the 'official state religion'), competition is discouraged (new religious organisations find it difficult to break into the religious market) and state religions become 'lazy' (they take their customers for granted). In other words, they stop being *innovative* in the face of declining congregations and focus their efforts on retaining their monopoly position rather than finding new ways to attract adherents.
- **Schisms** or **sectarian** movements represent a 'natural' form of market adjustment – breaking up moribund, stagnating organisations and breathing new competitive life into the marketplace.
- **NRMs**: Their role takes two basic forms. First, they offer 'non-mainstream' alternatives to potential customers; second, they provide a radical alternative

to traditional religious organisations. Their 'innovative methods' also serve as testing grounds for ideas that can subsequently be exploited by mainstream religions (as with evangelical movements within the Church of England).

**Crockett** and **Voas** (2004) note the use of economic concepts like:

- **Supply and demand** – religious organisations, if they are to survive and prosper, have to meet the (changing) demands of their actual and potential customers – and

- **Rational choice**: People are attracted to (or turned off by) religious organisations on a cost/benefit basis. If the perceived benefits of joining outweigh the costs, then an individual will join; if they do not, they won't. The task of religious organisations, therefore, is to orientate themselves towards making the benefits of membership more attractive than the costs.

## Weeding the path

This 'theory of *resacralisation*' has caused a great deal of controversy and argument.

**Proponents** argue it explains things like the growth of fundamentalist religious movements (Christian and Islamic, for example), as well as the fact that, as **Greeley** and **Jagodzinski** (1997) note, in many countries around the world religious beliefs and practices are, at worst, not declining, and, at best, flourishing.

**Antagonists**, however, point to a number of problems. **Crockett** and **Voas** (2004) note that in the UK 'British religious markets have become more competitive' through the influence of ethnic groups, but there has been little or no corresponding rise in overall religious practice or belief. **Norris** and **Inglehart's** (2004) research goes further to argue that in Europe, countries with the *closest* links between Church and State have the highest levels of practice (contrary to supply-side theories).

Given the differences between both sides of this particular argument, you may be forgiven for thinking that the 'secularisation thesis' is one bound up in the value systems of different sociologists – either you believe secularisation is occurring or you don't. There are, however, possible ways out of this theoretical impasse we can explore briefly in the final part of this section.

## Digging deeper: Explaining (post-) secularisation

The work we've just done suggests two things:

**Non-linearity**: Secularisation is not a simple, linear process (a movement from 'the religious' to 'the secular').

**Dimensions**: The institutional, organisational and individual dimensions of religion are interconnected. For example:

- **Pro-secularisation** theory takes a 'top-down' approach, whereby institutions become secularised, followed by organisational practices and, eventually, individual beliefs.

- **Anti-secularisation** theory effectively reverses this process, with individuals seen as being 'prone to religion'; in other words, religion is a cultural universal serving some form of human need (think in terms of something like **Maslow's** (1943) 'hierarchy of need', for example, where the 'safety' people derive from religion is a significant *psychological* need). In situations where people are able to express their religiosity, religious organisations exist and develop and, in turn, this behaviour spreads throughout political and economic life. A classic example, here, might be contemporary US society.

## Post-secularisation

This theory attempts to resolve this argument by redefining secularisation and simultaneously severing the (causal) links between different dimensions. **Phillips** (2004) argues that this position is based initially around the idea of:

**Differentiation**: Social structures and institutions that were, at one time, heavily under the influence of – or, in some instances, controlled by – religious organisations and ideas become secularised. In other words, a *separation* between religious and non-religious institutions occurs in modern societies. However, the general thrust and extent of secularising tendencies is limited to institutions and practices. In other words, *post-secularisation* theory argues that differentiation also involves a:

**Separation** between social structures and individual sociologies. This makes it possible to chart the secularisation of two dimensions of religiosity (social institutions and religious organisations/practice) by arguing that a third dimension (individual beliefs) should be left out of the equation, for reasons relating to:

**Social actions**: The question of whether, in an institutionally secularised society, people hold religious-type beliefs is considered relatively unimportant. These beliefs are significant only if they inform people's general social actions; in other

words, it's not the fact of people saying they believe in such ideas as 'God' that's significant; rather, it's what they do – or fail to do – on the basis of such beliefs that is sociologically significant. If, for example, religious beliefs are so strongly held that they form the basis for *social action* – such as the creation of, and active involvement in, political parties that advocate strict religious laws and observances – then this becomes a matter that must be addressed by secularisation theory. However, in such a situation the question of 'individual beliefs' is transformed into a *structural question* (relating to areas such as group identities, how and why they are created and the functions they perform), not an 'individual question', and hence becomes a matter for study and explanation.

If, however, religious beliefs are 'simply' matters of *personal preference* that have little or no impact on social structures, then for post-secularisation theory they are effectively considered irrelevant. **Casanova** (1994) notes that secularisation, under these terms, involves the liberation of secular spheres (politics, economics, etc.) from the influence of religious organisations, values and norms – it does not necessarily involve the disappearance of personal religious beliefs. Similarly, **Tschannen** (1994) suggests that, for post-secularisation theory, the main object of study is the changing position of religion, as an institution, in society; whether or not people 'believe' or 'disbelieve' religious ideas on a personal basis is conceptually unimportant – or, as **Sommerville** (1998) argues, institutional differentiation is not something that 'leads to secularisation. It *is* secularisation'.

**Phillips** (2004) characterises this general position as one where 'post-secularization is an attempt to lift the baby of differentiation from the bathwater of predicted declines in personal religiousness' – an idea that leads us to consider briefly what **Crockett** and **Voas** (2004) note as an interesting development in post-secularisation theory.

## Social capital

The **Putnam Thesis**: In his influential article (and book) *Bowling Alone* (2000), **Putnam** reworks the concept of 'believing without belonging' (and, if we're being picky, **Bourdieu's** concept of *cultural capital*) to interesting effect. His basic argument is that:

**Social capital** refers to the extent to which individuals are connected. In other words, it represents the idea of:

- **social networks** and, most significantly, the extent to which people:
- **participate** in social/communal activities and trust each other.

Social capital, therefore, refers to what **Durkheim** (in another context) referred to as the '*social glue*' that binds people together as a *society* (rather than as a collection of isolated individuals) – the roles, values, norms and so forth developed to facilitate communal living. More technically, **Cohen** and **Prusak** (2001) suggest that social capital '. . . consists of the stock of active connections among people: the trust, mutual understanding, and shared values and behaviours that bind the members of human networks and communities and make cooperative action possible'.

## Modernity

The basic idea here is that the 'decline of religion' is related to *modernity*, as traditional

secularisation theorists argue. However, more specifically, any *decline* in religious *participation* is linked to wider questions of social participation across all social groups (such as trade unions, political parties and the like). The *secularisation of participation*, therefore, is not simply a question of religious transformation, but one of a general social transformation.

In other words, we can explain the relative decline in religious participation in terms of a general 'process of withdrawal from the public sphere' in modern societies – hence **Putnam's** use of the *Bowling Alone* metaphor to describe how the traditionally social activity of ten-pin bowling in US society has, in his view, been transformed into an individual activity. This metaphor has, it should be noted, been challenged in a variety of ways, especially by **Crockett** and **Voas'** (2004) observation that 'unlike bowling, people are not "praying alone"'.

The implication of this idea (one shared, with some crucial differences, by **Davie**, 2002) is that post-secularisation theorists do not need to account for any decline – or increase – in religious practice/participation in *religious* terms (the activities of religious organisations, the influence of secular ideas and so forth). Rather – and somewhat counter-intuitively perhaps – it can be explained in terms of *social capital* and a decline in general social cohesion (measured in various ways, such as through participation rates in voluntary work and the like).

## Problems

**Putnam's** (2000) thesis is not, of course, without its critics. Both **Turner** (2001) and **Wuthnow** (2002) have questioned the extent to which social capital in the USA, for example, has declined. **Wuthnow** argues: 'There has been some decline in social capital in the United States over the past two or three decades; however, evidence does not indicate that social capital has declined drastically or to radically low levels, nor does it show that social capital of all kinds has declined.' In addition, questions remain over the extent to which the apparent revival in religious participation in some parts of the USA and in some religious organisations can be related to different levels of social capital – but this is probably an area that requires further investigation rather than being something that necessarily falsifies the general argument.

## Beyond secularisation

To conclude we can note a couple of further ideas about the secularisation debate. First, referring to both the secularisation thesis and the nature and extent of religiosity, **Harper** and **LeBeau** (1999) note: 'The evidence is pervasive and clear; religion has disappeared nowhere but changed everywhere' – and this, as far as we're concerned, perhaps, is part of the problem. Both religion and secularisation frequently have different:

- definitions
- measurements
- interpretations.

For this reason, therefore, rather than try to come to firm conclusions about the secularisation thesis, it might be useful to note **Spickard's** (2003) observation that the sociology of religion generally consists of six main *narratives*:

- **Secularisation**: The 'decline and loss of influence' story, backed up to some extent by evidence relating to 'European religion (and its decline), the relative decline of American mainline churches, and a biographic loss of religiosity on the part of many intellectuals...'

- **Fundamentalisms**: The idea, mainly perpetuated through the media, that religion is becoming 'increasingly Fundamentalist – A resurgent Islam certainly makes this story plausible. So does the intrusion of American right-wing religion into national politics. But these are only two views'.

- **Reorganisation** suggests the shape of religious organisations is changing, rather than declining or becoming more fundamentalist. The phenomenon of 'cell churches' (where people meet in small groups in each other's houses rather than in a church) is an example here.

- **Individualisation** sees religion as increasingly 'a matter of personal choice' – not only in terms of things like worship and practice, but also in terms of a 'pick-and-mix' approach to religions (combining various ideas and philosophies to create personalised forms of belief). Such individualisation evolves to satisfy religious yearnings in situations where individuals 'can no longer rely on social institutions'.

- **Religious markets**: This story, as we've seen, relates to a resurgent anti-secularisation message that involves a plurality of organisations servicing a range of religious needs.

- **Globalisation**: In a sense, a catch-all type of story that sees the ease of communication coupled with economic and cultural globalisation contributing to the rise – and decline – of religious organisations, fundamentalism and the like around the globe.

# Discussion point: Operationalisation

Read the following parable (in which you may, incidentally, be able to spot examples of different religious/secularisation narratives). What difficulties does the parable illustrate relating to how we can define and operationalise the concepts of:

- religion?

- secularisation?

Once upon a time two explorers came upon a clearing in the jungle. In the jungle were growing many flowers and many weeds. One explorer says, 'Some gardener must tend this plot.' The other disagrees: 'There is no gardener.' So they pitch their tents and set a watch. No gardener is ever seen. 'But perhaps he is an invisible gardener.' So they set up a barbed-wire fence. They electrify it. They patrol with bloodhounds (they remember how H. G. Wells's 'Invisible Man' could be both smelt and touched though he could not be seen). But no shrieks ever suggest that some intruder has received a shock. No movements of the wire ever betray an invisible climber. The bloodhounds never give a cry. Yet still the Believer is not convinced. 'But there is a gardener, invisible, intangible, insensible to electric shocks, a gardener who has no scent and makes no sound, a gardener who comes secretly to look after the garden which he loves.' At last the Sceptic despairs. 'But what remains of your original assertion? Just how does what you call an invisible, intangible, eternally elusive gardener differ from an imaginary gardener or even from no gardener at all?'

Source: Antony Flew (1971)

# CHAPTER 2

# Power and politics

In this chapter we consider the relationship between *power* and *politics* in a range of ways.

This section introduces the idea of political process by looking at how political behaviour in our society is structured through parties, groups and movements. Subsequent sections develop this idea to include political actions, such as voting, and political ideologies. They also examine the concept of power in terms of its definition and social distribution (which groups have power and why, for example), something that includes an exploration of how ideas about power and politics relate to theories of the role of the modern state.

This opening section, as we've just noted, explores some of the ways in which power is socially organised and exercised through political processes and actions.

## 1. The role of political parties and movements, pressure/interest groups and the mass media in the political process

### WARM-UP: PLAYING POLITICS

The objective of this exercise is to get yourself elected as 'Class President' and to do this you've got to build an alliance by convincing people you are the right person for the job. Your teacher takes the role of 'Head of the Class' – their job is to keep order, time each round and ensure fair play.

**Round 1**: Everyone has ten minutes to recruit fellow students to their cause. This is achieved through negotiation – how you do this is up to you: make promises, convince them through argument, offer them bribes . . . Once someone has agreed to support you,

they are part of your alliance and cannot be recruited by other alliances. They should form an orderly group behind their leader and can contribute to the recruitment of others to the alliance.

**Round 2**: If one alliance has 50%+ of class members, they are the winners. If not, the alliance with the least members is eliminated and they return to being unaligned. The remaining alliances have a further five minutes to recruit members.

**Round 3**: This process continues until an alliance reaches the required 50%+ of class members. If this proves impossible, the teacher declares the largest alliance the winner.

**Round 4**: The members of the winning alliance then have five minutes to canvas votes from each other, after which a vote is taken from among the members of the winning alliance. The person with the most votes is declared 'Class President'. In the event of a tie, there are five minutes of further negotiation. If no winner emerges, your teacher (as Head of Class) will choose the winner.

**As a class**: What issues about 'the democratic process' did this activity raise?

## ⚠ Preparing the ground: Defining political groups

We can begin by outlining some of the general characteristics of the different types of political groups in our society.

### Political parties

Although the concept of a political party (such as Labour or the Liberal Democrats in the UK) is a familiar one, defining this concept is not particularly straightforward, mainly because parties are complex organisations that potentially take a number of forms. Rather than constructing a specific, *inclusive* definition, therefore, it would be more useful to define this type of organisation in terms of what it sets out to do (its general *functions* in democratic societies). In this respect, we can identify a number of characteristics that *differentiate* parties from other types of political organisation:

- **Power**. Parties are organisations that seek to achieve political power and this, in a democracy, involves fighting elections for control of:
- **Government**. The main objective, in this respect, is to take control of the administration and machinery of government in order to put into practice a particular:
- **Ideology**. Parties function to bring together people who share a particular political philosophy. In addition, since a

major objective of parties is to win power (through, for example, democratic means), they also represent ways that ideas are *articulated* (presented to the electorate through the media, for example) in terms of specific policies.

- **Representation**. This takes two broad forms.

  - **Membership**: Party organisations reflect the broad ideological principles of their members (who normally pay a subscription to the party). Members may play a variety of roles within different parties (such as fundraising, policy development, selection of political representatives and so forth). In terms of the latter, therefore, one function of parties is to select candidates – people who represent the party and for whom an electorate votes (or doesn't, as the case may be).

  - **The electorate**: Representation extends, of course, to appealing to like-minded members of the electorate and, in this respect, a party reflects the

Each of the main UK political parties currently holds a week-long conference attended by delegates, selected by its membership, who may be able to influence the development of party policy – something some find more tiring than others ...

broad ideological principles of those who vote for its representatives. It may not necessarily be the case that electors (or indeed party members) share every single aspect of a party's ideological principles – each of the three main UK political parties (*Labour*, *Conservative* and *Liberal Democrat*), for example, contain members with opposing views on the UK's relationship to the European Union.

In terms of representation, parties function as conduits through which both members and voters can potentially influence decision-making in relation to government policy. In addition, parties serve as channels for the interests of a range of other organisations, such as interest groups and new social movements.

## Pressure or interest groups

A different type of political organisation is the:

**Pressure** or **interest group** that **Wilson** (1990) defines as 'organizations, separate from government, that attempt to influence public policy'. The difference (if any) between a *pressure* and an *interest* group is not one we're going to pursue here – although it's sometimes argued that an *interest group* doesn't necessarily try to apply 'pressure' to political parties/governments. **Smith** (1995) suggests the two terms are often used *interchangeably*, mainly because such groups 'seek to represent the *interests* of particular sections of society in order to *influence* public policy making'. Whatever the niceties of the possible difference, if we accept **Smith's** characterisation, a

pressure/interest group's main objective is to *influence* the decisions made by political parties (rather than to seek representation and power through elections) and they do this in a couple of ways:

- **Direct action** involves trying to influence government behaviour *directly*, through demonstrations, political events and the like.
- **Indirect action** involves trying to influence the general political philosophy of a party (to persuade a party to adopt a policy that reflects the interests of the pressure group, for example).

A recent example of how some interest groups use a combination of these two forms of action is the *Countryside Alliance*, a pressure group initially formed to try to stop the government banning fox hunting with dogs (unsuccessfully as it turned out – this activity was banned in 2005). Its *direct actions* involved mass public demonstrations and 'political events' (such as interrupting a parliamentary debate), while it also campaigned *indirectly* through the media and the efforts of pro-fox hunting MPs to prevent a ban.

Like the political parties they seek to influence, interest groups reflect a range of political ideas, but we can broadly classify them in terms of two basic types (with a range of associated subdivisions):

- **Sectional or protective** interest groups exist to represent the common interests of a particular social group. An example here might be a trade union or professional association (such as the British Medical Association). Organisationally, sectional groups tend to have members who have direct involvement in the particular interests being promoted (a relatively *closed membership*).

- **Causal** or **promotional** groups exist to promote a particular *cause* – in other words, they are interest groups representing the interests of the 'neglected or politically unrepresented', something they may do in a variety of ways:

  - **Demonstrations** and **public meetings** can include **direct action** – in 2000, 28 Greenpeace supporters destroyed a field of genetically modified maize as a protest against GM crops – and

  - **Publicity stunts** – *Fathers 4 Justice*, for example, specialised in public events designed to bring its argument (what its members saw as a discriminatory lack of access to their children following divorce) to media and hence public attention.

Organisationally, the general membership/ support for this type of group is *more likely* to have an indirect (non-personal) interest in the particular cause being promoted (what's sometimes called an *open membership*), although an exception here might be an off-shoot of this general type, the:

**Episodic group**, an interest group formed to support or oppose a specific cause or issue (such as the proposal to build a new motorway). Once the issue has been resolved, the group disbands.

## The potting shed

Identify any interest/pressure groups to which you give either direct or indirect support. What sort of involvement do you have with these groups?

## Social movements

The third type of political 'organisation' we need to think about is the social movement. A 'movement', by its very nature, is not something that can be easily pinned down since, as **Glaser** (2003) suggests, it represents a 'loose community of like-minded people who share a broad range of ideas and opinions'. This type of definition, therefore, covers a range of behaviours, a good example of which might be something like the 'environmentalist movement' – a very broad category of people who, in a variety of ways, are concerned with protecting the physical environment.

**Della Porta** and **Diani** (1999) refine this general idea by thinking about social movements in terms of:

**Informal networks** – the movement as a whole is loosely structured. People come together, at various times, on the basis of:

**Shared beliefs** and **support** for a general set of ideas, usually based around:

**Conflictual issues**, especially, although not necessarily, issues of *national* and *global* significance.

Part of the reason for social movements is that issues of concern to movement adherents/members are either not being addressed by political parties or, if they are, the movement's adherents are strongly opposed to the policies being proposed/enacted. This is one reason why such movements often involve:

**Protest** in a range of forms (such as civil disobedience, demonstrations or publicity stunts). In other words, as **Schweingruber** (2005) puts it, social movements involve: 'Continuous, large-scale, organized collective action, motivated by the desire to enact, stop, or reverse change in some area of society.'

In general, sociologists tend to talk about two basic types of social movement:

- **Old social movements**: OSMs were (and still are, to some extent) involved in what **Barnartt** and **Scotch** (2002) term 'issues of rights and the distribution of resources', classic examples being the *American Civil Rights movement* in the 1960s and the *trade union movement* in the UK. In this respect the prefix 'old' refers to the general focus, behaviour, concern and organisation of these types of movement rather than to the idea that they no longer exist.

- **New social movements**: Unlike their OSM counterparts, **Barnartt** and **Scotch** suggest NSMs are more concerned with 'values (postmodern and post-materialistic), lifestyles, and self-actualization, especially among marginalized groups'. In other words, this type of movement focuses, to use **Anspach's** (1979) phrase, on 'identity politics'.

## ⚠ The potting shed

Aside from those just mentioned, identify and briefly explain one example of an old social movement and one example of a new social movement.

This distinction is theoretically useful because it suggests different broad types of social movement have developed to address different concerns, even though we should be wary, perhaps, of overemphasising possible differences – the 'rights' (OSM) and 'lifestyles' (NSM) distinction is too restrictive, given that many NSMs address 'old problems' like unemployment and poverty. In addition, as **Bottomore** (1991) notes, some forms of new social movement have developed out of – and in some respects alongside – old social movements.

**Ecofeminism**, for example, represents what **Spretnak** (1990) terms 'a joining of environmental, feminist, and women's spirituality concerns' that extend across national/state boundaries. However, this NSM has its origins in (feminist) OSMs of the past, where the emphasis was on women's *rights* (such as the right to vote that created a focus for first-wave feminism in the late nineteenth/early twentieth centuries) and their share of resources, such as 'payment for housework' that featured among some second-wave feminist demands.

## ✳ SYNOPTIC LINK

**Theory and method:** Different waves of feminism are discussed in more detail in relation to modernity and postmodernity.

We can refine this basic categorisation by thinking about social movements generally in terms of:

**Political change**, an idea taken from **Schweingruber** (2005) that involves classifying movements in terms of both the general *level* of change they advocate and the *target* of such change (see table on page 110).

We can explain these different types of movement in the following terms:

- **Alternative**: This type provides an alternative to prevailing social norms. The focus of political *change*, therefore, is on developing different ways of doing things, such as the example we've suggested in the table, of home schooling as an alternative to state schooling.

| Classifying social movements and political change: Schweingruber (2005) | | |
|---|---|---|
| | **How much change?** | |
| **Who is changed?** | **Limited** | **Radical** |
| **Particular individuals** | **Alternative** <br> Home schooling | **Redemptive** <br> Born-again Christians |
| **Everyone** | **Reformist** <br> Civil rights/women's rights | **Revolutionary** <br> Communism/anarchism |

- **Redemptive** movements focus on 'redeeming others'; in the example we've used, a new form of Christianity focuses on changing people's lives by requiring them to embrace a different form of religious behaviour (a literal interpretation of the Bible, for example).

- **Reformist** movements seek to change society in some way – either, as in the case of the American Civil Rights movement, the relative position of ethnic groups or, as with second-wave feminism,

relative gender positions. Change may be far-reaching, but this type of movement doesn't seek the revolutionary overthrow of the existing order. Change, in other words, is *incremental* (one step at a time).

- **Revolutionary** social movements, such as communism or fascism, have as their political objective the overthrow (violent or otherwise) of an existing political order and its replacement by a new and different type of order.

# Growing it yourself:
## Social movements

Make a copy of the following table and identify some further examples of:

| Old social movements | | New social movements |
|---|---|---|
| | Alternative | |
| | Reformist | |
| | Redemptive | |
| | Revolutionary | |

## ⚠ Digging deeper: The role of political groups

Although we've outlined some basic ideas about different types of political organisation, we need to think about how each relates to the other in terms of the general political process in our society. When we talk about 'the political process' we are implicitly thinking about how, in democratic societies, there exists a:

**Plurality** of political organisations, each pursuing a range of aims and purposes. In addition, we need to think about how each type of organisation impacts on other types of related organisation. Thus **political parties**, as **McKay** (2005) notes, perform a number of roles in terms of their contribution to the political process. These include:

- **Demand aggregation**: Democratic societies contain a variety of groups with different interests to 'promote and defend'. The political party, in this respect, represents an organisation through which these group demands can be brought together (*aggregated*) and expressed, both through the process of elections and control of government and the administration of the state (such as a civil service).

- **Reconciliation**: In a situation where competing interests and political perspectives exist, parties provide a mechanism through which such competition can be *reconciled*, both *within* a particular party (where different factions develop broad agreements on the policy platform they present to the electorate) and *between* different political philosophies (in the sense that these competing interests tacitly agree to engage in the political process, whereby the electorate make the final choice).

- **Government**: One obvious function of parties is to take control of the general machinery of government and, by so doing, provide a (functional) link between government and the governed. This reflects what is sometimes called a:

  - **Social contract theory**, whereby the electorate effectively places politicians and parties in a position of trust (government) and, in return, require politicians to be accountable by submitting, periodically, to a renewal of trust through elections.

- **Political stability**: In this respect, the political process that involves parties and elections contributes to an overall sense of both *political stability* (in that different parties may represent different interests in a relatively orderly way) and *social stability*, in the sense that the orderly operation of politics (free and fair elections, the transfer of power between elected and dismissed governments, and so forth) represents a form of *political socialisation* whereby the perceived legitimacy of the political process also, in turn, is legitimised by people's acceptance of such a process.

Although parties, from this general perspective, are the *main* focus of the political process, other groups contribute in a variety of ways. **Pressure groups**, for example, have a distinctive role to play in that they both support and enhance the political process in ways that are generally outside the scope, role and purpose of parties. In this respect, parties and pressure groups have a:

**Symbiotic relationship** – each gains in some way from their relationship. Parties, for example, may develop ideas and policies from the input of pressure groups whereas pressure groups may gain political influence for either their members or the interests they exist to represent.

## Functions

From the general position we've outlined, therefore, we can note a number of functions performed by pressure/interest groups in democratic societies:

- **Mediation**: Pressure groups represent an important bridge between government/the state and the interests of relatively disadvantaged or powerless groups (such as the homeless).

- **Agency**: Some groups act as conduits and sounding boards for government policies; as organised representatives of different interests it may be useful for both the government and political parties to consult widely to develop popular policies. Trade unions and business organisations (such as the Confederation of British Industry), for example, perform this role in the political process. They may also, of course, act as originators of political policy for different parties.

- **Opposition**: Some groups function to provide expert advice and information that acts as an 'oppositional force' to political parties (although parties outside government may also play this role). Both explicit pressure groups (such as Greenpeace) and implicit pressure groups (such as the media) play roles that provide 'checks and balances' to political power.

- **Participation**: Our society is sometimes considered to have a 'democratic deficit' in the sense that most people's political participation is limited to voting in (general and local) elections.

Involvement in pressure groups, especially on a voluntary basis, serves to cut this deficit and make for a more *active* political process through the involvement of different people at different levels.

- **Education**: By publicising issues (through the media, for example), public awareness and understanding of social problems may be increased.

- **Ideas**: Pressure groups contribute to the overall vitality of the political process, both in terms of originating ideas for parties to consider and in terms of providing a further layer of political diversity. Highly sensitive issues, for example, can be promoted by interest groups in situations and ways that are not necessarily open to parties. Childline, for instance, campaigns against child abuse and bullying.

## Weeding the path

In the same way that not all parties have similar levels of electoral support and access to power, the same is true of pressure groups. We can make a relatively simple distinction, for example, between those groups which exist 'inside the game' (they have *direct access* to politicians and government departments) and those groups which, for whatever reason, exist 'outside the game' (they have little or no access to government). *Access differences*, therefore, affect how such groups operate and, of course, their particular roles in the political process.

**Insider groups**, for example, are usually seen as an integral part of the political process for ruling parties and politicians. Such groups may be able to directly *lobby* significant (politically powerful) politicians on a face-to-face basis. This 'access to power' gives such groups a potentially powerful advantage, but also blurs the distinction between parties and pressure groups. Also, as **Blumenthal** (2005) has noted, it raises questions of possible 'undue political influence' and corruption – those closest to political power have the potential to use their proximity to further both their own interests and those of powerful (and not necessarily politically representative) groups.

**Outsider groups**, since they have no direct access to government and political power, adopt different techniques of influence. These usually involve attempts to publicise their particular area of interest by and through the media – the former in terms of advertising campaigns, for example, and the latter in terms of 'creating media events', such that the group's message will be reported (obvious examples here being political demonstrations, publicity stunts and various forms of 'direct action').

## The media

**Besley et al.** (2002) identify some conventional ways the media contribute to the political process in terms of:

- **monitoring** the activities of political parties, groups and factions

- **reporting** political activities and events and, by so doing, encouraging public participation in the political process

- **interpreting** the significance and meaning of various forms of political behaviour

- **informing** the political process by performing a 'surveillance role' that makes politicians:

- **accountable** and responsive to the electorate.

Two forms of outsider protest that created interest in the UK media in 2005
Anti-fox hunting

Pro-fox hunting

In other words, the role of the media in the political process is that of overseeing behaviour in the political sphere. This general role, however, is not necessarily a politically neutral one. It involves, for example, three distinct processes:

- **Sorting** refers to the different kinds of information presented to the public. This might include *positive spins* on particular policies, politicians and groups, just as it might involve *negative* coverage and perceptions. This process itself can, therefore, be significant in terms of the type of information the media are able (or willing) to place in the public domain.

- **Discipline** refers to the extent to which the media are able to 'act independently' of political controls – both *overt* (in the sense of *censorship*) and *covert* in terms of the particular relationship different media forms have with parties and groups. The nature of this relationship may result in favourable political coverage, negative coverage or, indeed, no coverage at all.

- **Salience**: Although *news agendas* are often set by events (war, natural disasters and so forth), there are many times when they are not and *salience* refers to the way different issues are presented or ignored within different media. Some types of story/information, do, of course, have different levels of salience at different times in the political process, but the significant point here is the role of media representatives and organisations in 'setting the political agenda' (deciding, in effect, what issues are – and are not – politically significant).

## ✳ SYNOPTIC LINK

**Mass media:** Issues relating to the role and effect of the mass media in modern societies are discussed throughout Chapter 3 in the AS book.

**Social movements** tend to appear towards the bottom of any 'hierarchy of significance' when we consider the general political process, mainly because, of all political organisations, these are generally the least organised in terms of their political

structure. Unlike parties, pressure groups and the media, social movements tend, almost by definition, to be loose-knit 'groups' of like-minded individuals without an obvious organisational structure (although, as we've seen, there are exceptions to this rule). In this respect, many social movements represent 'mobilisations of ideas' which are either picked up or rejected by more structured political agencies.

Historically, therefore, social movements have been portrayed in terms of their:

**Pre-political** functions (in the sense of not being politically organised in the way parties and interest groups are organised to either directly exercise political power or influence how it is distributed). In addition, OSMs (such as trade unions) have been conceptualised in terms of how they are generally:

**Integrated** into conventional political processes and organisations. Trade unions in our society, for example, have moved from (illegal) workplace representation of the working classes in the nineteenth century, through sponsorship of a 'working class, socialist' political party (*Labour*) to their current role as, arguably, a form of interest group for their members. Conventionally, therefore, the role of social movements in the political process is seen in terms of:

**Dissent**. Such movements have, for example, historically developed to 'fill a political vacuum' by providing 'channels and voices' for a range of social groups (the working classes through trade unions, alternative sexualities through the gay liberation movement, women through feminist movements, and so forth).

In this respect, one function of OSMs (in particular) has been:

**Representation** by providing an outlet for

the 'politically marginalised' – those who, for whatever reason, have been 'pushed to the political margins' in terms of how their ideas and interests are represented (or not, as the case may be) by parties and pressure groups. Such movements have also represented:

**Mechanisms for change**, both in the sense of providing alternative sources of political dissent, ways of living and associating, and so forth, and in terms of the generation of 'new ideas' and 'ways of seeing' the world.

## ⚠ Preparing the ground: New political processes

Thus far we've presented a fairly conventional picture of the political process in democratic societies – one that involves seeing the role of political organisations in terms of their general objectives (either achieving political power through government or exerting influence on parties and government). In this respect we've characterised the political process as:

- **Pluralistic** in that it involves a number of broad organisational forms (parties, pressure groups and movements), sub-divided into competing groups (in the UK for example, there are three main parties, plus a range of smaller nationalist and other groups, represented in Parliament).

- **Hierarchical** in the sense that each organisational form is differentially placed in terms of its access to government-based forms of power and influence. Thus parties have *direct access* to political power whereas interest groups, the media and social movements have *mediated*

*access* (their power comes from the ability to influence the behaviour of parties and governments).

- **Functional** in that 'the political process' can be represented as a *system* within which different groups develop different (related and interlinked) roles that contribute to the overall maintenance and reproduction of the political system.

## Social change

However, although this gives us one picture of the political process, it's possible to argue that the relatively recent development of new forms of social movement may change the way we view this process, in the light of two major social changes:

- **Focus**: First, we can argue that NSMs represent a significant political development, one that has important ramifications for the general political process in that, as we've suggested, their focus is both:

  - **Individualistic**, in the sense of a preoccupation with the development of identity-based politics, and

  - **Global**, in the sense of representing movements capable of transcending national forms of political organisation and process. In other words, rather than simply seeing political processes in *national* terms, we should consider how the ability of NSMs to reach out to people across national (*nation state*) borders impacts on the type of political process we've described.

- **Milieu**: The general idea here is that the *economic*, *political* and *cultural setting* within which traditional forms of party, pressure group, social movement and media have developed historically is undergoing a *transformation*. In particular, two related ideas have significant implications for our understanding of both the way the political process is organised and the respective roles of different types of political organisation:

- **Post-industrial society**: The idea that economic changes in the structure of our society (and the growth of a 'new middle class') have far-reaching consequences for both the theory and practice of politics.

- **Globalisation**: In particular, the development of worldwide communication networks (such as the internet) – potentially open to all – that cut across boundaries of time and space. As **March** (1995) puts it: 'The Internet is no mere static repository of information, but a place of action ... The reachable "audience" grows daily. This opportunity and ability to influence public opinion should not be ignored.'

## ✳ SYNOPTIC LINK

**Theory and method/Stratification and differentiation:** The concept of post-industrial society is explained in more detail in terms of modernity and postmodernity and applied in relation to contemporary changes in the class structure.

In short, the argument we need to explore is whether the 'rules of the political game' are changing since, as **Patten** (2000) puts it, 'The defining feature of contemporary social movements is their commitment to cultural transformation at the level of social relations and political identities'. The question here, therefore, is, are we experiencing a form of *postmodern politics* where the ideas, activities and behaviours of new social movements have far-reaching consequences for both national and international political processes?

## ⚠ Digging deeper: New political processes

NSMs are a significant development for our conceptualisation and understanding of the political process in late/postmodern societies on a number of levels.

**Issues**: NSMs embrace a diversity of issues traditionally viewed in terms of categories such as class, gender and ethnicity (from antiglobalisation, through sexualities, to issues of black power and beyond). However, what sets them apart (as *new* social movements) is a broadly different interpretation of:

**Power**, embraced and expressed in terms of ideas like identity and lifestyles, as opposed to the conventional concerns of OSMs, parties and pressure groups with *economic* forms of power.

**Process**: The focus on *universal* issues (such as the meaning of identity) is not coincidental in that it has arisen at the moment when instantaneous global communication systems have started to develop that facilitate 'connected networks' of like-minded individuals across the globe. In this respect, **Carroll** (1992) suggests the significance of NSMs for our understanding of the political process is rooted in the idea that they represent movements ' ... through which new identities are formed, new ways of life are tested, and new forms of community are prefigured'. These ideas impact on the nature of NSM:

- **Organisation**. As we've suggested, one distinguishing feature of NSMs is their lack of formal organisational structure, something that's important in the context of conventional forms of political process – governments, for example, generally relate to *organisations*, which effectively means NSMs are excluded (through both choice and circumstance) from this process. However, although NSMs may lack conventional organisational structures, this doesn't mean they are 'disorganised'; rather, they frequently function, as we've just noted, in terms of:

- **Decentralised networks**. As **Patten** (2000) puts it, NSMs are constructed around 'non-institutionalized networks of groups and individuals' – a significant idea in terms of the role played by the *media* in the development of NSMs.

Thus far we've considered the role of the media in terms of how information is *produced* (by corporate organisations, for example) and *consumed* by a general population. However, when dealing with NSMs, two significant factors come into play.

First, the role of the media, in terms of how it can be *used* by the consumer to make communication easier, and second, how developments like the internet facilitate different organisational forms. As **March** (1995) notes: 'Community activists get together regularly online . . . to connect at some shared level. Meeting in cyberspace can be an activist's "ultimate conference call" . . . new social movements, by the nature of their organizational structure, are perfect candidates for using this forum . . . Issues and concerns can be brought to the attention of both the local, and global, community.'

## Discussion point: Making the connection

Imagine (it's easy if you try) you were starting a new social movement.

- How could you use new technologies, such as the internet, both to spread your important message across the globe and to make contact with people who share your political message?

What are the general advantages and disadvantages of a political movement developing in this way?

The organisational structures of NSMs reflect, in turn, how they operate in terms of both:

- **Physical operation**, using modern communication methods (such as mobile phones and computers) in a variety of ways to connect the various disparate 'members' of NSMs

- **Mental operation** in terms of what **Welsh** (2001) calls 'agents of innovation and transformation inescapably within but apart from systems'.

In other words, the various ways NSMs operate – both in terms of how they mobilise for political ends and the aims of political action – are indicative of a different form of 'political operation' located within a different form of political process. The objective is not merely to control or influence 'governments'; rather, it is to develop new and different forms of association, relationship and political practice, an idea that leads **Cox** (1996) to argue we should move 'beyond the language of social movements' to embrace the idea of NSMs as:

**Counter-cultures**, whose objective is not simply to influence *national* political processes, but rather to influence the development of *globally networked* political processes that address 'global problems' – environmental destruction, poverty, slavery, sweated labour, disease, and so forth.

This idea dovetails neatly with **Melucci's** (1996) argument that we should view NSMs not as discrete, 'issue-based' movements, but rather as:

**Networks within networks** – in other words, movement 'members' (or activists) are generally buying into a 'political worldview' rather than a particular issue (such as 'Saving the Whale').

While an interest in such issues frequently represents a way into political networks, once inside, the individual is linked into a wide range of related issues and areas. 'Activists', as **Wall et al.** (2002) note, 'have multiple concerns ... In our study we found ... an activist in the anti-capitalist network was also a key organizer of a protest against the imprisonment of asylum seekers.'

## Weeding the path

Notwithstanding the potential significance of this 'new development' in the behaviour and scope of social movements, not everyone shares this general interpretation. **Patten** (2000), for example, suggests:

**Differences** between NSMs and traditional forms of pressure-group behaviour should not be overstated. Although usually they may use different methods and be organised differently, their general objectives (to influence national government policies) frequently converge.

**Democracy**: NSMs are not automatically 'more democratic' than other types of political organisation. They can, for example, 'reflect specific interests just as easily as parties and pressure groups'.

**Representation**: The particular role of NSMs in the political process is open to interpretation. **Galipeau** (1989), for example, has argued that we should view 'parties, pressure groups and social movements' as the central core of different forms of representation. Whereas parties and groups operate at:

**Institutional levels** of representation ('elections, parliament and bureaucratic networks' of state policy-making), social movements operate at the level of the:

**Non-institutionalised margins** of the political process – they represent innovative political organisations that, as **Patten** (2000) notes, ' ... aim to alter how we think about politics, political identities and political interests'.

In this sense, the three types of political organisation we've outlined (parties, pressure groups and social movements) exist in a form of 'functional interdependence'; while each may perform different roles, these are, in the greater scheme of things, functionally connected as separate, but significant, aspects of the overall political process in democratic societies. **Patten**, however, disputes this interpretation when he argues that parties and movements should be seen as being in competition with each other, for two main reasons:

- **Engagement**: New social movements frequently attempt to influence national political processes and parties – they do not simply 'bypass' these significant political channels of influence.

- **Transgressive politics**: Just as new social movements may attempt to form political parties, established parties and pressure groups have responded (albeit more slowly, perhaps) to the 'changing national and global political landscape' by focusing on issues, such as environmentalism and identity politics, that have conventionally been the preserve of new social movements.

## Moving on

In this opening section we've looked at the political process in terms of the relationship between different types of political organisation and how they attempt to influence this general process. In the next section, therefore, we need to look more closely at the object of this process – power, its social distribution and the role of the state.

# 2. Explanations of the nature and distribution of power and the role of the modern state

This section focuses on the concept of power, considered in two main ways. First, we look at how it is defined, and second, at explanations for its distribution. As a way of thinking about how these ideas can be applied we then explore theories of the role of the modern state.

We can start by suggesting that power is something with which we are all familiar, mainly because we experience it in terms of how our behaviour – and that of others – is controlled.

## Preparing the ground: The nature of power

We can begin by noting two ideas:

- **Politics**: Although we tend to think about 'politics' in terms of political parties and governments, sociologists spread the net wider by thinking about politics in terms of how *power* is organised and employed in relation to *decision-making* – sometimes on a grand scale (such as the decision to declare war), but more frequently on a relatively minor, day-to-day scale (such as choosing our friends).

Political behaviour, therefore, extends far deeper into the fabric of our lives than the activities of politicians.

- **Power**: If politics involves decision-making then power is the vehicle through which it is expressed. It represents, in crude terms, the way to 'get things done' – or as **Dugan** (2003) puts it, 'the capacity to bring about change'. **Giddens** (2001), for example, suggests power involves 'the ability of individuals or groups to make their own concerns or interests count, even where others resist', while **Weber** (1922) puts this more forcibly: 'Power is the probability that one actor within a social relationship will be in a position to carry out his [sic] will despite resistance.'

## Types

Power and politics, therefore, are closely related in that politics is the means by which power is given *shape*, *expression* and *direction*, which suggests power needs to be understood in:

**Relational terms** – how people use it to control or influence the behaviour of *others*, or, as **Arendt** (1970) expresses it: 'Power corresponds to the human ability not just to act but to act in concert ["as a group"].' This leads us to think about different *types* of power since there are many different ways people 'act together' (willingly or unwillingly) to bring about change. **Boulding** (1989), for example, identifies 'three faces of power':

- **Coercive** power involves threat – someone obeys because they fear the consequences of disobeying, a situation where someone has *power over* others.

- **Exchange** involves the power of negotiation ('if you do something I want, I will do something you want'). This form represents *power with* others because it is exercised to mutual benefit.

- **Integrative** power can be expressed by thinking about the power of love – if someone loves you they may be willing to do things to help or please you – neither threat nor exchange is necessarily involved. This form has further possibilities, of course. It may involve an individual with the *power to* accomplish some desired goal on the basis of their personal abilities or characteristics (physical or mental).

## The potting shed

Identify and briefly explain one example, from any area of the Specification, of each of **Boulding's** faces of power.

## Digging deeper: The nature of power

We can think about power in a more detailed way in terms of the distinction between:

**Power** and **authority**. **Weber's** (1922) classic definition is always worth considering here, mainly because it distinguishes between two types of power: *coercion* and *consent* (*authority*):

- **Coercion** means people are forced to obey under threat of punishment. Obedience, therefore, is based on *threat* (real or imagined).

- **Authority**, however, is where people obey because they believe it right and proper to conform.

**Weber** distinguished three types of authority:

- **Charismatic**: People obey because they *trust* the person issuing the command, something that stems from the personal qualities of leadership they see in that person. A charismatic individual may be someone *exemplary* or *heroic* (a religious leader or army commander, for example), or they may simply be someone in our life we admire and want to please.

- **Traditional**: This type of authority is based on custom – 'the way things have always been done'.

- **Legal**: People give orders (and expect they will be obeyed) because their *position* in an *authority structure* (a school, workplace or army battalion, for example) gives them this power. This is sometimes called *bureaucratic power* because it's based on the existence of *rational rules* and *procedures* that apply to all members of an organisation; orders are to be obeyed only if they are relevant to the situation in which they are given. A teacher, for example, could reasonably expect the order to 'Complete your

## 🌷 Growing it yourself: Types of power

Identify further examples of each of Weber's four types of power (we've given you one to start):

| Coercive | Charismatic | Traditional | Legal/Rational |
|---|---|---|---|
| Police officer | Rock singer | Parent | Teacher |

In the above you will probably have discovered that many people/occupations could fit into different categories (a police officer, for example, exercises both *legal* and *coercive* power). This is because power can potentially take different forms, depending on the *context* in which it's exercised, an idea reflected in:

**Dimensions of power. Lukes** (1990) defines power in terms of *decision-making* and suggests we can understand it in terms of three dimensions, involving the ability to:

- **Make** decisions – teachers, for example, have power because they can decide what their students do in the classroom.

- **Prevent** others making decisions – a further dimension is the ability to stop others making decisions. In the classroom a teacher can stop their students doing things they might like to do (such as gaze out of the window).

- **Remove** decision-making from the agenda – this involves the ability to prevent others making decisions because you have the power to convince them no decisions are necessary; change, in other words, is not up for discussion. This suggests the powerful are able to *manipulate* the powerless in ways that prevent challenges to their power (the powerless, in effect, are unaware of any need for change).

homework by Thursday' to be obeyed by a student in their class. However, they couldn't reasonably expect the student's parent to obey this order. Unlike the other types, which exist in all known societies, legal authority was, for **Weber**, a characteristic of – and the dominant form in – modern societies.

## ✳ SYNOPTIC LINK

**Families and households: Lukes'** dimensions of power can be applied to an understanding of gender relationships within families (think about who has the power to make decisions in this institution, for example).

**Lukes'** third dimension of power links into the final definition we're going to consider since, for someone like **Foucault** (1980, 1983), power in *contemporary societies* has a couple of features that differentiate it from power in *past societies*.

**Opacity**: Power is 'difficult to see' in the sense that we are *unaware* of the power others (especially governments) hold over us. This is not because the nature of power itself has changed – coercive and authoritative forms still exist, for example – but rather that the way we *experience* and *think* about power in our everyday existence has changed.

In the past, for example, control was largely based on 'raw (coercive) power' – from a monarch exercising supreme power to prison systems that maintained total control over the body. In contemporary societies raw power still exists, but its form has been transformed into increasingly subtle modes of domination, from the expansion of technological (*overt*) surveillance such as CCTV to the ultimate form of *covert*

surveillance, the construction of knowledge and language itself, which **Foucault** expresses in terms of:

**Discourse**s. These are systems of belief that control behaviour by controlling how we *think* about the world, and these are constructed around:

**Knowledge** or beliefs about the 'nature of things'. For example, knowledge in contemporary Western societies is constructed around *binary oppositions* – we 'think about things' in terms of what something *is* ('truth', for example) and what it *is not* ('falsity'). These oppositions are all around, from male and female, through good and evil, to law-abiding and criminal.

## ✳ SYNOPTIC LINK

**Theory and methods:** The idea of binary oppositions is, according to postmodern writers, a fundamental feature of modernist thinking.

**Language**: This is how we express our thoughts about things. If we believe in ideas like male and female, this conditions how we behave as males and females.

## ⚠🏠 The potting shed

A simple example to illustrate this idea is to think about the word 'terrorist'. Describe the images and ideas that pop into your head when you read this word.

**Foucault** argues that power works 'through people rather than on them', in that discourses specify *moral ideas* about right and wrong which are, of course, powerful, if subtle and opaque, forms of control.

**Pervasiveness**: For **Foucault**, 'power is everywhere' – it's not just something, as **Gauntlett** (1998) notes, 'possessed by certain people and not ... by others'. Rather, power works through people in the sense that it is both:

- '**Out there**' – created through our relationships, both *personal* (family and friends, for example) and *impersonal* (how the government attempts to control our behaviour) – and

- '**In here**' – such as how we exercise control over our own behaviour.

Power, therefore, is not something embedded in social structures ('I am male, therefore I have power over you'); rather, it resembles a:

**Network**, embedded in individual belief systems (the way we see, think about and make sense of the world) that spread outwards to encompass all aspects of daily life. People become, in other words, their own police, patrolling and controlling perceptions of normal and abnormal, for example. Power, therefore, is like a net that spreads ever further until we are completely surrounded, by which point the net is closed and we see no way (and, for most of us, no reason) to break free.

## ✳ SYNOPTIC LINK

**Crime and deviance:** These ideas link to policing and surveillance in modern societies. Refer, for example, to both **Cohen's** (1979) ideas about the extension of social controls (how the 'net widens', for example) and **Shearing** and **Stenning's** (1985) work that

uses the example of Disney World to demonstrate modern forms of surveillance.

We can develop ideas about the nature and distribution of power by relating it to a concrete example – that of the *role of the state* and, to do this, we need first to define 'the state'.

## ⚠ Preparing the ground: The modern state

We can begin by thinking about a basic definition:

**The State** refers to a set of *organisations* and *institutions* related to the function of government (how order is created and maintained, for example). In this respect, the *state* 'exists' in terms of:

**Practices**; in other words, we can define it by what it *does* in terms of, for example:

- **Social order**: The modern state creates and maintains order in a number of ways, both explicitly, through the police and armed forces, and implicitly, by creating the conditions under which people can go about their daily lives in relative safety and security.

- **Policy-making**: This relates to something like the creation of laws which, in democratic societies, apply equally to all.

**Services**: Modern states are, at various times, responsible for a range of public services (and private services paid for by the state). These include:

- **Direct services**: These might involve something like those provided, until recently in the UK, by *nationalised* (state-owned) industries. In the 1970s, for example, the state owned coal mines, car manufacturers, gas provision and telecommunications. In the 1980s, the Conservative government *privatised* (sold into private ownership) these examples of nationalised industries.

- **Indirect services**: A range of things could be included here, depending on how widely you want to draw the distinction between ownership and control. The state, for example, provides (compulsory) education and a National Health Service, employs social workers and traffic wardens (through local government), and so forth.

**Revenue**: In the UK, for example, the state raises a range of taxes (from income tax and national insurance, through VAT, to corporation tax on business profits). State revenue is used for a variety of purposes (from paying politicians and civil servants to building prisons).

**Representation**: This can be expressed in two basic ways:

- **Internal**: Modern democratic states provide a system of political representation whereby people and their views are politically represented (in Parliament, for example).

- **External**: This refers to the various ways a state represents itself to other states. These relationships take a number of forms, from trade agreements, through treaties, to wars.

## Digging deeper: The modern state

Defining the state in terms of 'what it does' points us towards an initial problem: the idea of the state having an:

**Ambiguous status**: – that is, the state is an *abstract concept* in the sense that it has no distinctive *empirical reality* (we can't, for example, point to something concrete called 'the state'). This reflects, according to **Jessop** (1990), a central paradox, namely that 'the

## Growing it yourself: What has the state ever done for you?

Construct the following table and identify examples of state functions:

| Social Order | Policy-making | Services | Representation | |
|---|---|---|---|---|
| | | | Internal | External |
| Traffic wardens | Compulsory education | Doctors | Members of Parliament | Treaties |
| **Further examples?** | | | | |

state is both part and whole', in the sense that it is both:

- **Separate** from wider society (since if it wasn't we couldn't talk about its distinctive functions) and

- **Integral** to society – 'the state' and 'the society' are not mutually exclusive entities since, as **Jessop** notes, the state is 'peculiarly charged with responsibility for maintaining the integration and cohesion of the wider society'. As **Giddens** (1985) puts it: 'The state is both part of and "over" society.'

## Ambiguity

Although this idea may be a little difficult to take on board (it's a bit like the idea that someone can be their own parent), it's important because it suggests the state may have an:

**Ambiguous role.** The question here is the extent to which we can explain the role of the state in terms of:

**Autonomy** – the idea that the state can be studied 'separately' from the rest of society, as an object in its own right. This reflects a belief that the state can, for example, act *independently* of the various political, economic and ideological interest groups in any society. In other words, explanations focus on identifying the *unique characteristics* of the role of the state 'in society'.

**Dependency**, meanwhile, reflects the position that although we can examine the various functions of the state, to explain its role we have to look at wider social processes. A classic representation of this idea, perhaps, is the Marxist argument that 'the state becomes the committee for managing the common affairs of the . . . bourgeoisie'. In

other words, the various institutions of the state are considered to be under the domination of a particular (ruling) class and, consequently, represent and favour that class.

In the next part we can develop these ideas by thinking about the distribution of power in:

- **Modernity**: Explanations here focus on some of the traditional ways sociologists have theorised the distribution of power across social groups. We can complement this analysis by suggesting how these different explanations can be applied to the role of the modern state.

- **Postmodernity**: More contemporary social theories have examined the distribution of power in slightly different ways to their traditional counterparts and we need to reflect these differences by thinking about how social processes such as *globalisation* have impacted on both explanations of the distribution of power and the role of the state.

## ✳ SYNOPTIC LINK

**Theory and methods:** Modernity and postmodernity are considered in more detail in this chapter.

We can begin, therefore, by exploring a range of positions that focus on explanations for the distribution of power and the role of the state in *modern* societies.

## ⚠ Preparing the ground: Pluralism and power

From this position, power in modern democratic societies is held by a variety of:

**Competing groups**, none of which wholly dominates all other groups because checks and balances are built into the general fabric of political life. Political parties, for example, compete for control of the law-making process, while the police and judiciary have a degree of *autonomy* over how such laws are interpreted and applied. Judges may also be able to rule on the legality of different laws. Such societies are, therefore, characterised by a *plurality* of groups with different levels of power and influence, the nature of which is theorised in terms of a:

**Zero** (or **constant**) **sum** capacity – the amount of power in any society is relatively fixed (constant), so an increase in the power of one individual or group must be at the expense of other individuals or groups (hence the idea of a zero-sum totality of power).

For example, teachers have more power than their students within a classroom by virtue of their position in a hierarchical social system (the school). However, if the students decide to disobey their teacher (shout, scream, run riot – the usual stuff) and the teacher can't stop them, this demonstrates a 'constant sum' of power. While the teacher controls the class, they have power and students do not. If, however, the class decides to take control, then they have power and the teacher has lost it.

## The potting shed

In this situation, what options does the teacher have to take back the power their students have taken? (What other sources of power can a teacher call upon if classroom control breaks down?)

Unlike *functionalist* positions, pluralists don't need to explain:

**Social order** on the basis of value or norm *consensus* (broad, society-wide agreements) because, they argue, society consists of a range of different:

**Interest groups** which ultimately pursue their own *sectional interests*. In other words, societies consist of groups which compete for power and seek to advance their interests at the expense of other groups. Although this resembles a *Marxist* form of explanation (social classes as massive interest groups, for example), the main difference is in the way interest groups are theorised in terms of:

**Vertical cleavages**. Interest groups contain individuals with characteristics that cut across categories like class, age, gender and ethnicity. As **Robinson** (2001) puts it: 'Class is a *horizontal cleavage*, while ethnicity is a *vertical cleavage* (there will be both workers and capitalists in ethnic groups).' Interest groups, therefore, do not need a common value system since they may be organised to achieve different goals.

Although this may give the appearance of society as potentially a 'war of all against all', stability within the (*pluralist*) system is generated through the role of the state.

## Digging deeper: The pluralist state

A conventional way to describe the role of the state from this position is that of an:

**Honest broker** between various sectional interests in society. Its role, like that of a *referee*, is to mediate between these interests – to balance, for example, the interests of road builders with those of environmental groups. In this respect, we can talk about the idea of a:

**Representative state** – one that, because it reflects the interests of different, competing groups in society, effectively represents the interests of 'the system as a whole'. As **Eriksen** (2004) puts it: 'The state is subordinate to society, in the sense that the character of the state is explained as an effect of the character of society.'

In this respect, the state's major role is the:

**Coordination of social resources**; in other words, the state represents the institutions and machinery of government that serve to maintain order in society in three basic ways:

- **Political order**: In a system characterised by competing groups, the state functions to oversee and maintain an orderly democratic process through, for example, the operation of free elections, an orderly system of political representation (political parties and Parliament, for example) and, where necessary, an orderly transfer of power between different political groups.

- **Legal order**: This involves the regulation of conflict. For example, through the general policy-/law-making process competition is regulated, in both individual terms (laws governing interpersonal relationships) and group terms (laws governing the role and behaviour of business corporations, trade unions, political parties, and so forth).

- **Social order**: The main objective, for the state, is to create and maintain the conditions under which interest groups can successfully compete and, in this respect, the state is characterised as:

**Neutral** in terms of how it relates to different groups. It doesn't, for example, necessarily favour one group (such as business) over another (such as trade unions). What the state does, however, is act to resolve conflicts between these groups, hence the idea of the state as a

## ⚑ Growing it yourself: Mediating the problem

In the wake of a ruthless bombing campaign, the government is under pressure to act. It convenes a policy group to take evidence from two groups to provide suggestions to combat terrorism.

- The first – Protect Liberties Act Now (PLAN) – should identify and discuss suggestions that *do not* infringe civil liberties.

- The second – Back Action Now (BAN) – should provide suggestions that *will involve curbs* on civil liberties.

Divide the class into two groups, one taking the role of PLAN, the other that of BAN. Each group should feed their ideas to the government (the teacher) who may act as an advisor to each group. The government should record each group's arguments and the class as a whole should discuss the strengths and weaknesses of each in the context of finding the best possible solution to the problem.

*mediating agency* (honest broker) between competing interests.

In general terms, therefore, pluralist perspectives see the state in *dependency terms* – as a set of politically neutral organisations (the police and judiciary, for example) that can, at various times, be *directed* – but *not directly controlled* – by politically organised parties. As **Held** (1989) puts it: 'The state becomes almost indistinguishable from the ebb and flow of bargaining [and] the competitive pressure of interests.'

## ⚠ Preparing the ground: Elite theories of power

Like pluralism, this general theory involves the idea of competition between different groups for power. However, competition here is between *elites* – powerful groups which can impose their will on the rest of society.

**Elite theory** developed in the early twentieth century through the work of **Pareto** (1916) and **Mosca** (1923), although, as writers like **Greenfield** and **Williams** (2001) have argued, it still has currency in some circles. Both **Mosca** and **Pareto** saw elite rule as:

**Desirable** – it was 'right and proper' that those best suited to rule *should* rule, and **Inevitable**, for two different reasons:

**Superior organisational ability** was, for **Mosca**, the key to elite rule because successful elites were those that, because of their superior *internal* organisational abilities, were able to develop the political support needed to take power (either democratically or non-democratically – **Mosca** recognised that the organisational qualities needed to assume power varied from society to society).

In *democratic* societies, for example, the masses could have some input into the political process through elections. However, **Mosca** considered democracy as little more than a manipulative, legitimating process whereby elites consolidated their power by co-opting the masses (who were born to be led and could be kept 'in their place' through propaganda) to support elite interests.

**Superior personal qualities** (intelligence, education, cunning, and so forth) were the key for **Pareto**, who also saw political change as based around:

**Circulating elites**. An elite group achieved power because of its superior

**Lion elites**
**Rule by force**
**Military regimes**

**Fox elites**
**Rule by cunning and manipulation**
**Democratic regimes**

abilities when compared with other elites and 'the politically disorganised masses'. Elite groups could, for **Pareto**, rise and fall at different times because, after achieving power, elites have a limited life-span – they grow decadent (*corrupt*), isolated, lose their vigour, and so forth, and are replaced by other, more vigorous elite groups, of which **Pareto** identified two basic types: lions and foxes.

## ⚠ Digging deeper: The elitist state

A basic premise of this type of explanation is that the (political and legal) machinery of the state is under the control of an elite group which is generally *not accountable* to the mass of the population, an idea we can illustrate by outlining three different forms of elite rule:

- **Absolute monarchies**: Although largely characteristic of pre-modern/early modern society, the elite group here is the monarch and his or her trusted advisors. The monarch, in effect, *is* the state in the sense that they assume absolute power and control, through either ideological (a divine right to rule, for example) or political/military means.

- **Totalitarian dictatorships**: These dictatorships (such as Hitler's Germany in the 1930s) involve a slightly different form, namely the:

  **Corporate state**: a strong, centralised state (where control of the machinery of government, from the civil service to the police, judiciary and armed forces, is concentrated in the hands of a small group which exercises absolute power) is used as an *instrument* for the

reorganisation of society along whatever lines (usually repressive) are decided by the ruling dictatorship. The general role of the state is one of promoting 'national unity' through a variety of means:

- **Political**: A ruling elite makes all the necessary political decisions. Political parties are normally banned or replaced by a single party that represents the 'will of the people/nation'.

- **Economic**: The state is directly involved in some areas of the economy (normally those deemed vital to the 'interests of the nation') and may attempt to influence and regulate the behaviour of private businesses and corporations (by force if necessary).

- **Ideological**: As with economic activity, the state may take on a direct 'information (propaganda) function' through public media ownership or it may be heavily involved in the regulation/censorship of private media.

Although this example relates to *totalitarian regimes*, a softer form of *corporate state* occasionally develops in democratic societies when governments co-opt business (and occasionally labour) leaders into the machinery of government in an attempt to solve society-wide problems (such as high levels of unemployment or low levels of consumption).

- **Oligarchies**: An oligarchy is a relatively small group, situated at the top of any organisation, which assumes control over the activities and behaviour of that organisation, a situation that translates into politics in the sense that power is invested in the hands of a small group which controls and directs the machinery of the state. **Michels** (1911) famously argued that all organisations were oligarchic ('Who says organisation, says oligarchy'), an idea that crystallised around his concept of an:

- **Iron law of oligarchy**, which states that even *democratic organisations* evolve to a point where an elite group eventually dominates and decides the policies of the organisation. **Michels** argued that a political party, for example, is always an '... organization which gives birth to the domination of the elected over the electors' – a process that occurs, he argued, for three reasons:

  - **Bureaucracy**: Large-scale organisations (such as governments) are forced to develop rules and routines governing their day-to-day administration.

  - **Use**: Elites are able to control bureaucratic procedures and organisations to consolidate their grasp on power.

  - **Specialisation**: The need for specialised staff to run bureaucratic organisations leads to the inevitable development of hierarchical power structures.

## The potting shed

Identify and briefly explain one way the British government's cabinet system might be considered an oligarchic system.

## Preparing the ground: The power elite

A different type of 'rule by elites' theory, developed by **Mills** (1956), focused on how elite groups organise and take power in democratic societies through the control of various social institutions – a process, he argued, that was neither desirable nor inevitable. Since some institutions are more powerful than others (in modern societies an economic elite is more powerful than an educational or religious elite), it follows that groups that controlled important social institutions would hold the balance of power in society. Thus, in his analysis of US society in the 1950s, **Mills** identified three major:

**Power blocs** organised to pursue elite interests:

- **The economic elite**, consisting of large-scale business and industry interests.

- **The political elite**, represented in terms of parties (both government and opposition) which hold similar *ideological beliefs* to each other. In the UK, although the three major parliamentary parties (Labour, Liberal and Conservative) have their own distinct political identities and policies, all hold similar general beliefs about the nature of our society.

- **The military elite**, consisting of the higher levels of military command.

Although each *power bloc* could pursue *separate* – and sometimes *contradictory* – interests, the necessary cooperation between them meant they formed a:

**Power elite** dedicated to the wider interest of maintaining elite status, power and rule. Cooperation between power blocs was also developed through:

**Elite membership**. Powerful individuals could be members of more than one elite at any given time – business leaders could take up political appointments in government and politicians could sit on the boards of major corporations. In this way political power becomes concentrated and political decisions (about whether to go to war, for example) are effectively taken by a small, interlocking, elite minority.

As an example here, **Chatterjee** (2002) notes Richard ('Dick') Cheney was US Defense Secretary during the first Gulf War (1990), became chief executive of Halliburton, 'the world's largest oil services company', in 1995 and took up the post of Vice President in George Bush's first government (2000), a position he still held as of 2006.

### ⚠ Digging deeper: The power elite and the state

As we've just suggested, the power blocs identified by **Mills** (sometimes called the *military-industrial complex* because of the economic, political and ideological cooperation between the various power blocs) are *autonomous* in the sense that they each have their own separate hierarchical structure and personnel. Where they come together to form a mutually beneficial *power elite*, however, is through the coordinating agency of the state. In other words, a *power elite* forms around the ability of the three major power blocs (economic, political and military) to control *key* social/government institutions. Once this occurs the machinery of the state is used to advance their sectional and communal interests.

Although, for **Mills**, a power elite forms out of the 'convergence of interests' between

different power blocs, their members are also connected by shared:

**Social backgrounds**, involving family networks and educational backgrounds (such as, in the UK, the major public schools, Oxford and Cambridge universities and the like), and by:

**Ideological outlooks** that develop from both common class backgrounds and experiences. As **Hadfield** and **Skipworth** (1994), for example, report: 'If you spend ten years of your life … in a closed society [public school] where the Cabinet and heads of the armed forces are just ahead of you – Old Boys and Girls – you identify with the powerful.'

### ✳ SYNOPTIC LINK

**Theory and methods:** The instrumental Marxist Ralph **Milliband** (1973) argues that the members of a ruling class are also connected by their 'shared cultural backgrounds'.

This connectivity is not, however, a *causal* factor in the creation of a power elite; rather, it represents a *consequence* of the convergence of interests – members of the various power blocs meet and 'do business' in the normal course of their lives, not the other way round. It is not their common class background that brings them together, but rather their common *power* positions.

This idea leads into a more contemporary take on power elite theory and the role of the state. **Domhoff** (1990), for example, develops the concept of a power elite by adding a *class dimension* to the debate. He argues that the economic power wielded by business leaders in countries like the United States gives this particular power bloc a:

**Leadership role** in government. In other words, their importance to the functioning of both government and the state means their general interests are always paramount in policy-making. Business leaders, in effect, come to resemble a:

**Governing class** in the sense that their economic interests are reflected in the way decisions are made by political leaders.

## Power networks

Although this starts to resemble a traditional Marxist interpretation, there is a major difference. Whereas Marxists generally see the role of the state as being either an:

- **Instrument** of class domination (**Milliband**, 1973, for example) or
- **Relatively autonomous** from a ruling class (**Poulantzas**, 1975, for example)

**Domhoff** (1997) argues that the state is an:

**Autonomous space** – it doesn't actually exist outside of the way different:

**Networks of power** combine, at various times in various societies. In other words, all societies develop what **Mann** (1986) terms four 'overlapping and intersecting sociospatial networks of power' (ideological, economic, military and political) – with the key idea here being *overlap*.

Thus each network represents a *semi-autonomous power bloc* with the freedom to pursue its own particular agenda. Each may, for example, try to pursue its own:

**Sectional interests** at the possible expense of the others. A political elite, for example, may woo the masses by imposing tax increases on private corporations to win votes, just as corporations may develop ways of avoiding taxation, something that may be criticised by ideological institutions such as the media.

The role of the state, according to **Mann**, is to act as a 'space' that regulates the general behaviour of the different networks. Its usefulness, according to **Domhoff**, is in 'laying down rules and adjudicating disputes in specific territories'.

## ⚠ Preparing the ground: The functions of power

**Functionalist explanations** generally take a different position in relation to the distribution of power in society. **Parsons** (1967), for example, argues that power has two major dimensions:

**Variable-sum**: First, power levels can vary within any society because power is possessed by society as a whole rather than by individuals. Thus, unlike the general Marxist position, some groups do not necessarily become powerful at the *expense* of others. This fits neatly into functionalist concepts of:

- **Social consensus** since, if power levels are *variable*, conflicts do not necessarily arise over competition for power. By cooperating, everyone can gain a share of an expanding overall level of power. Just as levels of economic resources can expand (general living standards rise over time, for example), so too can power as a social resource. Cooperation, therefore, is viewed as a *structural imperative* if a society is to develop and progress.

**Social resources**: Second, power represents the capacity to mobilise resources in society for the attainment of *social goals*. Societies have collective, developmental goals (such as eradicating unemployment); the more progress made towards these goals, the greater the levels of overall power that come into existence. For example, as the market position of formerly powerless individuals is improved (they find paid work, perhaps), they develop some measure of power over their own lives.

## Dysfunction

Power, therefore, is distributed and exercised in the *general interests of society* as a whole and, although some groups will be more powerful than others, this is necessary (*functional*) because the achievement of *collective goals* requires organisation and leadership which, in turn, is based on power. If some groups become too powerful, however, this becomes:

**Dysfunctional** since they would be tempted to pursue sectional interests at the expense of long-term social development and stability. Modern democratic societies, therefore, develop:

**Checks and balances** on the ability of groups to exercise power. These include things like democratic elections (where powerful groups can be voted out of office), a 'free press' that is able and willing to draw public attention to abuses of power, and so forth.

## Digging deeper: The functions of the state

To understand the general role of the state we need to understand that society, according to **Parsons** (1951), is a:

**Normative system**; that is, a *social system* founded on certain types of normative understanding and, of course, *integration* (people have to be socialised into the

general norms of their society). The system, if it is to function, has *needs* which can be expressed in terms of:

**Imperatives** (or commands). For example, there is a *need* for people to be socialised into both the general normative structure of society (human development) and the specific normative needs of different institutions (think about how you are expected to behave within the education system and the consequences of deviance).

As societies become more complex (*functionally differentiated*), the state also develops more complex forms. Think, for example, about the different forms of political democracy – local and general elections, universal suffrage (everyone has the right to vote), and so forth – that exist in our society now, compared with 500 years ago. This relationship between society and the state is significant because it suggests that the state plays a functional role in the:

**Coordination of system resources**. In other words, the complex machinery of the state develops as a direct reflection of general social development, in terms of:

- **Political development**: The state plays a range of roles in terms of political organisation (such as elections), legal organisation (the development and application of laws), relations with other countries and the like.

- **Economic development**: Part of this role involves enforcing various legal relationships (such as laws governing economic contracts, who you may marry, and so forth), the punishment of criminality and the like, but the state also coordinates the relationship between different economic organisations (such as employers and trade unions).

- **Cultural development**: In the UK, the state regulates the education system and from time to time attempts to regulate family relationships (by encouraging or discouraging different types of relationship, such as the introduction of civil partnerships (2004) that give, according to the government's **Women and Equality Unit** (2005), 'same-sex couples ... parity of treatment in a wide range of legal matters with those opposite-sex couples who enter into a civil marriage').

# 🏠 The potting shed

**Identify and briefly explain two ways the state currently regulates family behaviour.**

The state, in other words, handles the mechanics of social (normative) organisation – it represents the means by which the *social system* is kept in broad equilibrium. In this respect, an important role for the state is that of an *integrating mechanism* for the system as a whole. It is the means through which system adjustments are carried out, a classic example being the development of state education in England at the end of the nineteenth century. Tensions within the social system – between the needs of industrial employers (workers with basic literacy and numeracy) and the inability of the family group to perform this literacy and numeracy function – were resolved by the development of state-funded schools.

## New right

A contemporary variation on the general functionalist approach is that of the:

**New Right**, whose general position can be summarised in terms of the:

**Minimalist state.** The argument here is that economic prosperity and social cohesion are best served by the operation of 'free economic markets' – in other words, as **Hildyard** (1998) notes, for the New Right the *marketplace* is the arena in which a society's wealth is created, mainly because it encourages:

- **Entrepreneurial activity**: People strive to develop new and better ways to make money, which leads to creativity and innovation.

- **Individual freedoms**: For markets to work efficiently (and for the greatest levels of wealth creation) people need the freedom to live and behave in ways that maximise both their individual abilities and their responsibilities towards others (in terms of, for example, providing for their dependants).

- **Efficiency**: In the economic marketplace there is no room for subsidies or restrictive practices that use social resources to protect people from either the consequences of their own behaviour (inefficient production methods, for example) or the consequences of competition.

The modern state, from the New Right position, is subject to two processes:

- **Centralisation**: Decision-making is carried out by state representatives 'divorced from the realities' of the marketplace.

- **Bureaucracy**: As the state grows larger and more complex it is slow to respond to the changing economic needs of society.

The New Right objection, therefore, is to

# Discussion point: Evaluating efficiency

**Oxfam** (2004) reports: 'The UK pays around £4 billion into the Common Agricultural Policy (CAP) to subsidise British and European farming ... The average payment to seven of the wealthiest landowners in England amounts to £879 a day ... The annual food bill for an average family of four is £800 higher than it would be without the CAP.'

In small groups, identify and discuss arguments *for* and *against* the continued payment of subsidies to UK farmers. We have done the first one for you.

| Arguments for subsidy | Arguments against subsidy |
|---|---|
| Rural unemployment falls | Inefficient farming methods |
| **Further arguments?** ||

the state developing into an 'autonomous institution' with a logic and momentum of its own, and the solution is to cut back the state by stripping it of any function that could be 'better carried out' by private companies or individuals. As **Hildyard** puts it, for the New Right, 'the best government is the least government'.

This general position is related to functionalism in the sense that it recognises that the state has a role to play in society in terms of what **Sowell** (2002) characterises as 'ensuring observance of the "rules" essential to the continuance of free markets'. In other words, the *minimalist state* is limited to guaranteeing individuals the freedom to go about their daily lives (however this is actually achieved).

## ⚠ Preparing the ground: Marxism and power

**Marxism**, in all its variations, is a form of elite theory in the sense that it advances the theory that power in society resides with a:

**Ruling class**, consisting of the owners of the means of economic production (the *bourgeoisie*). In this respect:

**Economic ownership** is the most significant source of power in society – power that creates both political influence (the institutions of government and the state reflect the interests of owners) and cultural influence (through ownership of the media, for example). The distribution of power in capitalist societies has a couple of characteristics:

- **Concentration**: Power is concentrated in the hands of a relatively small number of wealthy and influential people.

- **Interests**: Power is used to further the interests of the powerful at the expense of the powerless.

**Conflict** occurs because, at root, the rich and powerful want to consolidate and expand their wealth while the poor and powerless would like a share of this wealth, an assessment that points to a:

**Constant-sum** theory of power.

Within this general position we can note a couple of variations.

## Instrumental Marxism

From this position, power flows from the 'top' of society (a ruling class) to the bottom (the subject classes) and represents 'a tool' to control the behaviour of the powerless. In this respect, control is exercised at all levels of society:

- **Economically**: Power is most obviously exercised in the workplace (such as control over people's time, wages and working conditions). In addition, wealth is a powerful instrument through which to buy or create political influence.

- **Politically**: Those with political power favour the interests of an economic elite, not only in terms of how the state machinery can be used for the economic benefit of a ruling class (tax subsidies and the like), but also in areas such as law creation, where laws are seen to favour the interests and behaviours of the ruling class.

- **Culturally**: Ideological control (over how people think about the social world) extends through areas like the mass media and the education system.

## ✷ SYNOPTIC LINK

**Education: Bowles** and **Gintis** (1976) argue that the education system is structured, in terms of knowledge, qualifications, rules and routines, in ways that reflect ideas favourable to a ruling class.

## Structural Marxists

A different approach to understanding the distribution of power in capitalist society is taken by structural Marxists. **Poulantzas** (1975), for example, argues we should see power in terms of how it pervades all aspects of a society. In other words, power is not simply a tool used by the bourgeoisie to keep the subject classes in their place; rather, it represents a way of creating a:

**World view**, a lens through which the social world is filtered. Power is used to create a 'way of life', one to which the subject classes are continually exposed through a variety of:

**Cultural institutions** (such as the media, education system and religion). This represents a *hegemonic* view of power that operates in two main ways:

- **Continuous exposure** to a familiar set of ideas reflecting capitalist views about the nature of social life. As **Bocock** (1986) argues, the effectiveness of *hegemonic power* lies in the way people from *all classes* are encouraged to 'buy into' ideas ultimately favourable to the interests of a ruling class – a simple but effective example being something like the UK National Lottery. Each week millions of people buy a lottery ticket, even though the odds of being struck by lightning (1 in 3 million) are better than their chances of winning the jackpot (1 in 10 million). The point, of course, is that people *want* to be rich (and someone, after all, *will* become rich each week).

**Strike it lucky before you're struck unluckily?**

- **Marginalisation** and **criticism** of alternative world views.

**Stratification and differentiation:** These general ideas can be used to inform your assessment of Marxist theories of social class.

## ⚠ Digging deeper: Marxism and the state

Although Marxists have put forward a range of differing interpretations about the role of the state in capitalist societies, we can note some general points of agreement within this perspective:

- **Capitalist state**: The role of the state is, ultimately, that of protecting and enhancing the economic and political interests of the ruling class.

- **Partiality**: The state, as **Eriksen** (2004) notes, is *not* a 'neutral framework for struggle and compromise'; it doesn't, in other words, reflect the interests of 'society as a whole' by balancing competing economic, political and ideological interests. It is *not* an arena where 'common social values' are created; rather, state power is directed towards promoting and maintaining values favourable to a ruling class.

The reasons for this general perception are not hard to find since, for Marxists, the state reflects the nature of class relationships and conflict in capitalist society. In a situation where the interests of one class (the *bourgeoisie*) are the opposite of those of another (the *proletariat*), it follows that the role of the state must be to promote and enhance the specific interests of the class which, almost by definition, controls it. Ultimately, the state performs this service through its 'monopoly of violence' – the power of the state, either directly (**Milliband**, 1973) or indirectly (**Poulantzas**, 1975), reflects the nature of unequal class relationships in capitalist society.

## ⚠ Weeding the path

There are, as we have seen, differences of interpretation over the specific role of the state within Marxist theory.

**Instrumentalist** positions see the machinery and institutions of the capitalist state (government and the civil service, for example) as being controlled by a ruling class, and the role of the state is viewed as a channel through which ruling-class interests are articulated (spread throughout society) and promoted. There is, therefore, a relatively direct and straightforward:

**Correspondence** between ruling-class interests and the actions of the state. Economic power is reflected in political power (the control of government and the institutions of the state) through a process of what **Glasberg** (1989) calls:

**State capture** – the idea that 'capitalists control key positions within the political structure to attain their goals and further their interests'. This occurs for a couple of reasons:

- **Economic interests**: The state both reflects and acts in the interests of a ruling class because its economic ownership and control makes it the most powerful force in society.

- **Political personnel**: Politicians are either part of the ruling class (immersed in its interests and values) or *agents* of an economic elite in the sense of identifying the interests of a ruling class with the interests of society as a whole (and acting accordingly).

## Role

Overall, from this position the role of the state is a wholly *dependent* one – the most powerful economic groups in society control how the state behaves.

**Structuralist positions** take a different approach in that they don't see the state as being somehow *separate* (or used as an *instrument* of class rule) from a ruling class. Rather, the interests of a ruling class are *automatically* reflected in the political behaviour of the state since, for someone like **Poulantzas** (1975), the idea of a capitalist state that doesn't reflect the interests of a dominant economic class is 'untenable' – there is simply no reason why a dominant economic class would not also be the dominant political class.

As **Carson** (2004) notes: 'Political leadership does not have to be subject, in any crude way, to corporate [business] control. Instead, the very structure of the corporate economy and the situations it creates compel the leadership to promote corporate interests ... policies that stabilize the corporate economy and guarantee steady ... profits are the only imaginable alternatives'. Having said this, the:

**Correspondence** between economic power and political power is neither direct nor straightforward in capitalist democracies. **Apple** (2000), for example, suggests *hegemonic control* is a:

**Reflexive process** – one subject to constant re-evaluation in the light of challenges to bourgeois ideas. Ruling-class

power, in other words, has to be sufficiently *flexible* and *adaptable* to incorporate new ideas and explanations without ever losing sight of the fundamental values of capitalist economics.

## Problems

In addition, we can note two further complicating ideas:

- **Class fractions**: A ruling class is not necessarily free of conflicts and contradictions. The particular economic interests of *manufacturers*, for example, are not necessarily the same as those of *financial* capitalists (such as banks). Although both have a *broad interest* in 'maintaining capitalism', this doesn't mean their relationship is necessarily *consensual* (banks, for example, make money through interest they charge and manufacturing capitalists are subject to these costs).

- **Class domination**: Differences within a ruling class make it difficult to see how their broad common interests can be translated into specific (*instrumental*) state actions. Rather, the state from this position acts as a necessary balancing mechanism *between* the different class fractions that make up the ruling class, such that internal conflicts do not endanger overall ruling-class cohesion and domination. In this respect, the state has a:

- **Relative autonomy** from the ruling class. It may, for example, make decisions that go against the particular, *short-term* interests of a ruling class (or some part of that class), but in the *long term* these decisions are designed to ensure the survival of the capitalist system (and if this involves making concessions to the working class – a minimum wage here, legal trade unions there – then such concessions have to be made to safeguard the stability of capitalist society).

For political domination, therefore, a ruling class needs an institution (the state) that broadly reflects its interests, while *appearing* to be neutral in its composition and decision-making – something that reflects the importance of the state's:

**Ideological role. Poulantzas** argues that since ideological domination is best served when the powerless do not appreciate or realise they are being exploited, it is unnecessary for an economically powerful class to rule 'in person' (although, of course, its representatives must rule in the general interests of the bourgeoisie) – the greater the *appearance* of a *separation* between economic and political power, the better. In this respect, the state has the *appearance* of autonomy from the ruling class (it is not directly controlled) while, in reality, being dominated by people thoroughly socialised into the ideology of capitalism.

**Offe** (1974) suggests the precise way the state operates is in terms of:

**Selective mechanisms** that **Chorev** (2004) characterises as an 'institutionalized sorting process that ensures the state will only select and consider policies corresponding to the interests ... of capital'. These operate in three main ways:

- **Negative selection** mechanisms exclude anticapitalist ideas and proposals. In the UK, for example, excluded from the political agenda are ideas such as 'employee control of industry'.

- **Positive selection**, whereby the state acts on ideas that serve the interests of a ruling class 'as a whole'. The objective is

## 🌱 Growing it yourself: The element of disguise

The Minister for Educational Security wants to introduce CCTV into every educational establishment in the UK. The plan is for cameras to be placed in every room (including lavatories). Two groups have been set up to handle this idea:

- Group 1 should identify possible objections to this scheme.

- Group 2 should identify ways to positively present this scheme to the public.

Once each group has finished its deliberations, the class as a whole should discuss the best way to present this idea so that it has the best possible chance of being accepted.

You might want to consider:

| Cost<br>Privacy issues | Possible benefits<br>Possible drawbacks | Data use, security and access |
|---|---|---|

Note: The minister was formerly a paid consultant to the company that will supply and monitor the cameras.

for the state to act in ways that best serve the general interests of 'capitalism' rather than the particular interests of class fractions.

- **Disguising selection**: To maintain the illusion of neutrality, the state disguises its *partiality* by claiming to act in an objective, even-handed way. For example, policies that limit the power of trade unions to take strike action are presented in terms of 'preventing public disorder' (since no reasonable person could be 'pro public disorder', by conflating the two ideas it is possible to limit the effectiveness of industrial action).

Finally, a slightly different way of seeing the role of the state in capitalist society is to adopt a:

**Dialectical approach** that suggests the state has a level of *actual autonomy* that allows it to act in ways that don't directly benefit the bourgeoisie – through welfare policies targeted at the poor and the unemployed, for example. While it's always possible to argue such policies *indirectly* benefit the ruling class (by preventing social unrest, for example), this type of 'left functionalist' explanation – where everything that happens can be made to fit the idea that a ruling class always benefits in some way – is not a particularly helpful type of explanation (since, of course, it can never be disproven).

The idea that the state is not simply a product of class relationships in society, but can, in some ways, act autonomously for the benefit of different social groups, leads us to consider an alternative conflict approach to power and the role of the state.

## ✳ SYNOPTIC LINK

**Crime and deviance:** The idea of 'left functionalism' has been used by New Left Realists (such as Young) to criticise radical criminology.

## ⚠ Preparing the ground: Weberian concepts of power

In general, **Weberian** theories use a: **Zero(constant)-sum** notion of power that can, at different times, result in both:

- **Extreme imbalances**, such as in a *monarchical system* where the ruler has absolute power (at least in theory; in practice power is usually devolved to other, trusted individuals and groups) and their subjects have little or no power – they may, for example, be slaves or bonded subjects (serfs) whose lives are directly controlled by the powerful.

- **Relative balance**, as in modern democratic societies, where political elites can be voted out of office or the relatively powerless can have some form of political representation.

In general, Weberian analysis focuses on the development of two types of group:

- **Status groups,** such as genders and ethnicities, and

- **Interest groups** – any group organised around a set of common goals.

These groups are engaged in constant power struggles, both *internally* (in terms of status differences, for example) and *externally* (between different groups), and the source of power is:

**Social resources**. Unlike *functionalists*, who view resources as long-term social goals and system requirements, *Weberian* notions of power are rooted in social relationships at the individual level – how people struggle to acquire resources to improve their personal social situations.

Although, like *Marxists*, economic power is significant, it is not always the most important social resource. *Social characteristics*, such as being male in a *patriarchal* society or white in a *racist* society, and *commodities*, such as skills and knowledge, are also important resources. In this respect:

**Sources** of power can be *economic*, *political/communal* or *cultural* (or a mix of all three). This fragmented view of power makes Weberian analysis a little more flexible than other *conflict perspectives* (such as Marxism or feminism) because it allows us to see how categories like class or gender – while clearly significant – are not necessarily always the most significant factor in any explanation of power and its distribution. In contemporary societies, for example, some women may be more powerful than some men, just as some sections of the *working class* may accumulate more (economic) power than some sections of the *middle class*. In addition, in a society where both ethnicity and wealth are valued, wealthy members of a subordinate ethnic group may not have the same overall levels of power and status as wealthy members of a majority ethnic group.

## ✳ SYNOPTIC LINK

**Social differentiation:** Weberian perspectives give us an alternative way of looking at social class and can be applied to assessments of Marxist, Functionalist and Feminist positions on social inequality.

## ⚠ Digging deeper: The role of the state

If we combine **Weber's** idea of power being distributed across different social groups with his definition of the state as a 'compulsory association claiming control over territories' (and the people within them), the state is characterised by two things:

- **Autonomy** (or at least the *possibility* of autonomy) from the behaviour of competing social groups. This follows, as **Held** (1989) argues, because **Weber** considered the development of the modern state to *pre-date* capitalism. Whereas, for Marxists, the capitalist state develops out of class domination, for Weberians such as **Block** (1987) the reverse is true: capitalist forms of economic behaviour are encouraged and developed by the state. This doesn't mean the state is always or necessarily autonomous from class, gender or ethnic group control; rather, there is no necessary and inevitable relationship between, for example, ownership of the means of production and 'ownership' of the state. One reason for this is the second characteristic of modern states.

- **Bureaucracy**: The argument here is that the development of regulations and procedures within the state means it develops to reflect the concerns and preoccupations of a *bureaucratic elite* – one that exists to both administer state machinery and preserve its own power base within the state. These ideas follow from **Weber's** claim that modern states are:

- **Rational/legal organisations**, staffed and led by policy specialists and professionals with the ability and capacity to promote or hinder political decision-making. This relates to **Weber's** ideas about power, in that knowledge (in this instance, *procedural knowledge* – how the state and its various departments operate) represents a significant source of (bureaucratic) power. In other words, without the active cooperation of bureaucratic leaders, political policies cannot be successfully enacted. **Block**, for example, uses the concept of:

- **State managers** to reflect the idea that bureaucrats are 'independent' of class control, in the sense that they do not necessarily and automatically carry out the wishes of a ruling class.

**Skocpol** (1979) also argues that we should consider the state as 'an organization for itself' – a subtle reference to Marxist ideas about class consciousness – with its role being related to:

In the BBC TV programme *Yes Minister* (1980–84) Nigel Hawthorne (left) played a classic civil service bureaucrat (Sir Humphrey Appleby) whose main role in life was to prevent his political masters (such as Jim Hacker, centre, played by Paul Eddington) making decisions with which he did not agree (all of them, as it happens)

**Managing change** and promoting social stability. This idea is often expressed as an:

**Interventionist role**. Because the state can act *autonomously* from *status* and *interest* groups (based on class, gender and ethnic interests, for example) it can promote a variety of political agendas, such as:

- **employment** – **Glyn** (2003) argues that all recent increases in private-sector employment have resulted from increased public (state) spending

- **gender equality** (the Sex Discrimination Act, 1975, for example)

- **globalisation** and its economic and political effects (reducing Third World debt, for instance).

**Instigating change**: **Skocpol** (1985) suggests the state can ' ... formulate and pursue goals that are not simply reflective of the ... interest of social groups, classes or societies'.

## Preparing the ground: Feminism and power

**Feminism** comes in a number of forms (**Livesey** and **Lawson**, 2005), but each, in its different way, focuses on the idea that women are subject to various forms and expressions of *male power*. For the sake of convenience we can outline two basic positions:

**Second-wave feminism** focuses on concepts of:

- **Patriarchy** and the ways male power is expressed in both:

    - **Cultural terms** – how male-dominated societies are structured to oppress and exploit women (the power source here is male domination of the highest levels of economic, political and cultural institutions) – and

- **Interpersonal terms** – the specific ways male power is exercised over women, through physical violence, for example, or exploitation within the family group.

- **Sex class** expresses a *conflict approach* to understanding gender relationships in the sense that gender represents a major **horizontal cleavage** in society – men and women as distinct social classifications with their own (gender) class interests.

## Power

As with Marxist concepts of economic class, men and women have fundamentally *opposed* lives and interests. **MacKinnon** (1987), for example, argues that 'men have power over everything of value in society – even the power to decide what has value and what does not'. Male power, therefore, is expressed in two main ways:

- **Hegemony**, involving the power to define both concepts of masculinity and femininity and, in effect, what it *means* to be male and female. A concrete example here might be the concept of a:

  - **Glass ceiling** in the workplace. Women are allowed to achieve only so much and no more compared with their male counterparts. **Stephenson** (1998) suggests a more valid representation of current hegemonic relationships is the:

  - **Glass trapdoor** – women can enter predominantly male worlds (election to Parliament, for example), but only in limited numbers. Entry also comes

at a price – women have to adopt *male* characteristics, values and attitudes to survive in male-dominated institutions and spaces.

- **Coercion**: For **Mackinnon**, *personal* forms of male power (such as superior strength, the willingness to use violence and the physical subordination of women) translate into *cultural* terms in that social institutions (from government, through education and family life, to the media) are:

  - **Gendered** – they reflect a *hierarchical organisation* that values male lives and experiences and devalues those of females. Social institutions, from this position, 'have been historically constructed in male images to suit male preoccupations, needs and interests'. In this respect, **Mackinnon** characterises women as being:

  - **Unempowered** in patriarchal society. They are not only alienated in terms of their relationship to men and other women, but also from their own bodies (women as the objects of male power).

## ❋ SYNOPTIC LINK

**Mass media:** These ideas can be related to the concept of the 'male gaze'.

## ⚠ Digging deeper: Feminism and the state

In the main, second-wave feminist thinking has developed around the concept of a:

**Patriarchal state** with a number of dimensions of *male domination*.

**Political offices** and **positions** are male-dominated – the composition of Parliament, the Cabinet (very few women are included and, where they are, this is normally in positions relating to 'women's issues') and the civil service, for example, show women are more likely to be employed at the lowest levels and less likely to fill the highest grades (**Civil Service Statistics**, 2004).

## 🏠 The potting shed

**In the 2005 UK general election, for each of the three main parties, what percentage of their elected MPs was female? (Answer at the end of the section, page 149.)**

In addition, according to **Mulholland** (2005), female civil servants earn 25% less, on average, than their male counterparts. Women are also less likely to hold full-time posts.

**Ideologically**, the state reflects and pursues male interests, agendas and concerns (ranging from gendered achievement in school, through crime, to the workplace). Areas of traditionally female concern (such as childcare or the problems associated with part-time working/family commitments) generally have a low priority for the state. As **Jessop** (2003) notes: 'Many feminists would argue that politics is dominated by the priorities of a male-based agenda.' And in a patriarchal society the role of the state is one of both reflecting and reinforcing gender inequalities.

## 🔱 Weeding the path

This *conflict view* of the state, where its composition and behaviour reflect either *class* relationships (*Marxist feminism*) or *patriarchal* relationships that pre-date the modern state (*radical feminism*), is not necessarily shared by all second-wave feminists.

**Liberal feminism**, for example, has generally adopted a more *Weberian* approach to understanding the role of the state in the sense that its potential *autonomy* from both class and patriarchal relationships means it can be used to promote policies and behaviours that both reduce gender inequalities and address feminist issues:

- **workplace equality** (equal pay, conditions and treatment)
- **sex discrimination** (making such behaviour illegal)
- **childcare provision** (for working mothers, single parents, and so forth).

In this respect, feminists such as **Brown** (1992) have argued that feminists should *engage* with the state for two main reasons: it has an important role to play (potentially) in changing women's lives and many women are *dependent* on it, either as employees or as recipients of state aid.

In the final part of this section we can examine some contemporary notions of both the distribution of power and the role of the state under the general heading of:

**Power in postmodernity**, initially in terms of *third-wave feminism* and finally in terms of late/postmodernism.

## ⚠ Preparing the ground: Post-feminism and power

**Third-wave feminism** reflects a different approach to understanding the distribution of power between the sexes, one that focuses on:

**Vertical cleavages** – gender relationships complicated by class, age and ethnicity (upper-class women, in terms of experiences and interests, may have more in common with upper-class men than with lower-class women).

Analysis of the relative distribution of power focuses more on the lives of individual men and women than on the (supposed) power differences between them as 'sex classes' – ideas that reflect a broad sense of social change and a consequent change of feminist focus. If *modernist* feminism focused on how women were *disempowered* in patriarchal society, *post-feminism* shifts the focus to an understanding of:

**Gender constructions**. The social construction of gender is not, of course, a new idea, but feminists such as **Butler** (1990) take the idea of *constructionism* much further, to talk about gender as:

**Performance** in the sense that being male or female is not something you *are* but something you *do* – there is nothing intrinsic (*essential*) to the biological categories 'male' or 'female' that determines how we think, feel or behave. Observed gender differences result from the way power shapes both our perceptions and our lives.

## 🏠 The potting shed

**Identify and briefly explain two ways socialisation shapes perceptions of gender and its associated identities.**

Similarly, **Kristiva** (1995) argues that categories like 'man' or 'woman' are too restrictive (and hence meaningless in terms of *lived realities* – although they are clearly not meaningless in terms of how they are generally used). If there are 'as many sexualities as there are individuals' it follows that to talk about power relationships in terms of social groups is similarly meaningless. **Haraway** (1991) blurs the 'gender divide' further with the idea of:

**The cyborg**: She uses this concept to explore two ideas:

- **Space**: Where people increasingly interact in *cyberspace*, through computer networks, traditional notions of gender and biology become redundant since interaction is not face to face.

The cyborg:
Part-human, part-machine

- **Networks**: How people (of whatever sex) are connected (networked) in cyberspace is more significant than how they are connected (or not) in 'the real world'.

In other words, interaction across computer networks can be:

- **Agendered**: First, you don't necessarily know whether the people you interact with are male or female, and second, they – or you – may disguise their gender (a female claiming to be male, for example). The distribution of power across *space* and *networks*, therefore, becomes less a matter of 'gender relationships' as they're traditionally conceived, and more one of exploring how *individuals* accumulate, use and distribute power.

- **Girl power**: A further dimension to post-feminist thinking about power is a version of femininity focused on female bodies, sexuality and experiences. Here, the concept of *girl power* is both *ironic* ('girl' is traditionally used to suggest a relatively powerless woman) and *empowering* (a reassertion of female identity). The 'in-your-face' aggressiveness of girl power (the *ladette*, for example) both co-opts and confronts traditional forms of male behaviour.

## ⚠ Digging deeper: Post-feminism and the state

**Third-wave feminism** has generally adopted an:

**Intersectional approach** to understanding male and female lives. In other words, it's not just a case of variables such as class, age and ethnicity being significant factors in gender development; it's also a fact that there are significant differences within artificial gender categories, identities and sexualities.

These *gender contradictions* don't just occur in society – they are also reflected in the role of the state, as **Jessop** (2003) notes when he talks about the way 'state structures and policy areas' are changing in the light of changes to the way we think about gender. On the one hand, the modernist state with its centralised bureaucracy and procedures plays an important role in:

**Defining gender categories**, in terms of what someone is or is not *legally* allowed to be (such as male *or* female). On the other hand, the state has responded to changing attitudes and behaviours by conferring legitimacy on a wider range of gendered behaviours (especially in relation to sexual identities – *civil partnerships*, for example, take a further step towards official recognition of same-sex relationships).

Unlike their predecessors who saw *patriarchy* as being 'embedded in state structures and practices', post-feminism argues that there is no logical necessity for this to be the case. On the contrary, post-feminists point to a couple of significant ideas when theorising the role of the modern state in relation to gender:

**Heterogeneity**: Mottier (2004) notes that post-feminists do not see 'the state as a homogeneous, unitary entity which pursues specific interests'. Rather, it represents a 'plurality of arenas of struggle, rather than a unified actor', in two basic ways:

- **Externally**, in the sense of differences in the way different nation states (even those of a broadly similar democratic nature) enact gender-based policies.
- **Internally**: The state is not simply a 'homogeneous, undifferentiated, mass';

rather, it consists of different departments that may or may not act in concerted ways. In other words, gendered social policies are not necessarily consistent across all parts of the state structure; the policies pursued by one department may contradict the activities of other departments. **Toynbee** (2005), for example, argues that tax credits paid by the state to low-income families 'have become a way of subsiding low-paying employers'. Part of the state encourages people (especially women) to take/keep low-paid work (thereby lowering levels of unemployment), while another part effectively encourages employers to pay low wages through the use of subsidies.

What this means, therefore, is that we should view the modern state as a:

**Fragmented** structure that is neither 'wholly patriarchal' nor 'wholly non-patriarchal' – an idea that leads post-feminism to focus on the *positive aspects* to the role of the modern state, in particular the various ways its resources have been used to both improve male and female lives and to change attitudes towards gender. As **Mottier** notes, the existence of a welfare state in the UK 'has a positive effect on gender relations in that it makes for a lessening of the financial dependency of women on men'.

## ⚠️ Preparing the ground: Postmodern power

As with their modernist counterparts, a range of ideas and explanations have been advanced by postmodern theorists for changing interpretations of both the nature and distribution of power.

**Foucault** (1980), for example, argues that explanations for the distribution of power in 'late modernity' require a different approach to the thinking we've previously outlined. Unlike traditional positions where, for example, power resides with dominant groups (the 'ruling class' of Marxism or the 'male power' of traditional feminism), power, as **Gauntlett** (1998) notes, isn't tied to 'specific groups or identities', mainly because such groups and identities are no longer (if indeed they ever were) rigid and unchanging. On the contrary, if social life and identities are:

**Fluid** and **amorphous** (having no fixed shape), it follows that power also has this characteristic; it flows through particular contexts and situations – at different times and in different situations people exercise varying levels of power. No one in this scenario is 'completely powerful' and, of course, no one is completely powerless.

## Powershift

In addition, when we looked earlier at the *nature of power* we noted the significance to **Foucault** of *discourse* and its related elements of *language* and *knowledge*. **Toffler** (1991) picks up this idea to suggest a change in the way we think about and understand power when he argues it has three basic sources:

- **violence** – something that can only be used *negatively* (punishment)

- **wealth** – something that can be used both *negatively* and *positively* (either preventing others from becoming wealthy or sharing wealth around)

- **knowledge** – something that can be *transformative* (or *shared* without necessarily diluting or diminishing the source itself – shared knowledge, for example, can be a source of increased power). In this respect, **Toffler** argues that postmodernity is characterised by a '*powershift*' in that *knowledge* is now the dominant source of power in society.

### ⚠ Digging deeper: The postmodern state

Postmodern explanations for the role of the state turn on the concept of:

**Globalisation**, in terms of how it impacts on the political, economic and cultural structures of modern societies. We can understand this idea in a variety of ways.

**Essentialism**: The types of (modernist) explanation we've outlined all (with the possible exception of **Mann's** (1986) concept of *overlapping networks*) claim the state has *essential* features that can be empirically described (such as administrative capabilities, departmental and legal structures, and so forth). Postmodernists, however, advocate an:

**Anti-essentialist position**. The 'state' is a *label* we give to a number of *processes*. As **Allen** (1990) notes in the context of (post-) feminism, analysis should focus on a range of *areas* (policing, law and medical culture, for example) and *issues* (such as sexuality, the body and bureaucratic culture). Although, in modernist terms, we're encouraged to see the state as a:

**Centre** (something that has both substance and power and functions as a stabilising force in society), **Lyotard** (1979) argues that there are 'many centres' in postmodern society (none of which is able to stabilise or 'hold society together'). Rather than see the state as a *centralised* power base, charged with giving substance to the various (conflicting or consensual) factions within

society and government, we should view 'the state' as, in **Foucault's** terms, 'a diffuse and dispersed' range of institutions and processes, many of which have little or nothing to do with conventional questions of 'government', which leads us to the question of the 'power of the state' to control and direct people.

### ⚠ Weeding the path

At the heart of postmodern analyses of the role of the state is a central *contradiction*: the external (international) processes of *globalisation* weaken the ability of the state to control:

- **economic events** – the price of oil, the investment in and physical location of jobs, corporate taxation and the like
- **political events** – where the UK, for example, is subject to European Union laws, human rights agreements, and so forth
- **cultural events** – think, for example, about how the flow of information across the internet makes it difficult for politicians and the state to 'manage news'.

However, one form of state response to this 'loss of external control' is a consequent tightening of *internal* control and surveillance. Issues of identity cards, for example, or the use of CCTV surveillance, demonstrate the attempt to control *physical space*, while laws relating to 'terror' or 'harassment' may represent similar attempts to control *psychological space*. **Giddens** (1985) suggests *surveillance* (along with industrialism, capitalism and militarism) represents one of the key:

# Discussion point: Responding to terrorism

Walter Wolfgang, an 82-year-old delegate, was ejected from the 2005 Labour Party conference for shouting, 'That's a lie and you know it', during a speech by the Foreign Secretary. He was prevented from re-entering the conference by the subsequent police use of the Terrorism Act (2000), an Act described by the **Home Office** (2001) as 'legislation containing the most vital counter-terrorism measures'.

How do you think the state should respond to the 'threat of terrorism'?

**Clusterings** in late modern society that come together in the form of 'the state'. He argues that the extension of both *covert* and *overt* surveillance is an important development for the state's role because it represents a fundamental change in the way people are controlled through modern state agencies.

## Moving on

In this section we've examined definitions and explanations of power and how they relate to the role of the state. In the next section we can develop and apply these general ideas to an understanding of different types of political party and ideology.

(Answer to 'Digging deeper': 2005 general election: Female MPs: Labour (28%); Conservative (9%); Liberal Democrat (16%).)

# 3. Different political ideologies and their relationship to different political parties

In previous sections we looked at the political process in terms of different types of social group (such as parties and movements) and related their organisation and purpose to the pursuit of political power. This section narrows the focus to look specifically at political parties and the beliefs that underpin their existence.

## Preparing the ground: Ideology and party

An *ideology* involves a number of general ideas relating to the way we think about (and behave in) the social world, and while the concept may, as **Bjørnskov** (2004) notes, be 'hotly disputed ... difficult to define and consequently difficult to measure', for our initial purpose we can think of ideologies as involving such things as norms, values and beliefs that are, in some way, connected and interrelated. In this respect ideological beliefs may be demonstrably true or demonstrably false, but the important thing, as far as *political ideologies* are concerned, is that they are:

**Collective beliefs** – ideas, in other words, shared with and supported by others in a culture, community or society. For **Jones** (2004), *political* ideologies have the same basic features as other forms of ideology, in that they involve:

- **beliefs** about the nature of the world
- **justifications** for those beliefs (and, implicitly or explicitly, beliefs about the superiority of such beliefs when compared with other ideological forms)
- **political objectives** – whatever these beliefs are designed to achieve
- **instructions** about how these objectives can be realised.

In this respect, political ideologies need to be considered in terms of both their:

**Content** (the particular beliefs they represent) and the various ways beliefs are put into:

**Practice** – *operationalised* through some form of political process.

**Mullins** (1972), for example, links these ideas when he argues that political ideologies involve 'a program of collective action for the maintenance, alteration or transformation of society', while **Gerring** (1997) suggests that 'ideologies' (a set of related beliefs and values) become *political* ideologies when they 'specify a concrete programme of action' (such as that found in a party manifesto).

**WARM-UP: THE STATE OF THE PARTIES**

To make informed choices about a political party to support, you, as either eligible or potential voters, should know what each party stands for in terms of their general policies.

In small groups, use the preceding table as

| Policy area | Labour | Conservative | Liberal |
|---|---|---|---|
| Education | | | |
| Crime | | | |
| Immigration | | | |
| The economy | | | |
| Europe | | | |
| Equal rights | | | |
| The environment | | | |

the basis for identifying your beliefs about the broad political policies put forward by each of the three main parties at the 2005 general election.

Compare your answers with the chart at www.sociology.org.uk/a24aqa.htm

What does this comparison tell us about the relationship between voters and parties?

Considering these ideas, therefore, we can initially distinguish between two basic forms of political ideology: *systemic* and *party*.

## Systemic

**Systemic forms** relate to broad (and fundamental) beliefs about the basis and general organisation of political behaviour within a society. They refer, in other words, to the idea of political *systems* which, for the sake of example, we can characterise in two broad ways (*totalitarian* and *democratic*):

## Totalitarian

**Totalitarian** political systems are characterised by a:

- **Totalist ideology**: This represents a set of fundamental ideas and practices (an 'official ideology') that is not merely the *dominant* political form in a society, but the *only* permissible form. According to **Grobman** (1990), totalist ideologies seek to establish 'complete political, social, and cultural control over their subjects'; classic twentieth-century examples here might be the Soviet Union under the control of Stalin (*communism*) or Nazi Germany under the control of Hitler (*fascism*).

- **Single-party state**: Unlike democracies, where different parties and ideologies may

be in competition (the *pluralist doctrine* we outlined in the previous section), totalitarian societies are organised around a single party. In this respect, such societies represent a form of:

- **Dictatorship**, whether this involves a single powerful figure (a *leader*) or a powerful group of people (an *oligarchy*). Whatever the precise form, party organisation is, according to **Friedrick** and **Brzezinski** (1965), strongly *hierarchical* with a high degree of centralised control and decision-making. Power, in this respect, is exercised 'from the centre, outwards' – in other words, political decisions are made by a relatively small political group at the top of the party hierarchy and are then disseminated to the mass of the party/population.

- **Social control**: This system extends control *downwards* into every area of social life (family, education, work, and so forth) and the legal system is usually under the control or influence of the party hierarchy. A common feature is the existence of a 'secret police force' whose main role is:

- **Ideological policing** – an activity designed to uphold, maintain and extend the existing political order. Such policing may involve imprisonment without trial, torture or even death.

In general terms, therefore, totalitarian societies develop a system of:

**Monopoly control** that extends across all areas of society – economic, political and ideological. This may involve, for example, the development of the type of *corporate state* structure we outlined in a previous section on the elite state, as well as party

## China steps up Web controls but investors untroubled

Lindsay Beck, www.reuters.com 23/09/05

'China's cyber police have intensified controls over the country's 100 million Internet users in the past few months but that hasn't stopped Western Web firms from pushing ever farther into the booming market.

Rather than using their clout to help push the boundaries of free speech and information in the one-party state, critics say companies like Google, Yahoo and Microsoft are at best turning a blind eye to the machinations of the cyber police. "It's too early to say that just by doing business in China and developing the Internet in China they will foster democracy and human rights," said Julien Pain, of media watchdog Reporters Without Borders. "It doesn't work that way."

## China 'blocks Google news site'

(www.bbc.co.uk: 30/11/04)

China has been accused of blocking access to Google News by the media watchdog, Reporters Without Borders. The … English-language news site had been unavailable for the past 10 days. It said the aim was to force people to use a Chinese edition of the site which, according to the watchdog, does not include critical reports.'

control of all means of communication – press, radio and television, film and the like. In some modern societies, control extends to the internet by the blocking of websites critical of the state.

## Democratic

**Democratic political systems** have a number of different characteristics:

- **Pluralist ideology**: Democratic ideologies stress that, ultimately, political authority resides with 'the people'; in other words, there exists a form of *social contract* between those who govern and those who are governed, based around a number of basic ideas:

- **Free elections** based, in contemporary democracies, on the principle of every citizen having the right to periodically vote for the party – or individual – of their choice. In the UK, for example, a number of competing political parties exists, with the governing party (Labour, as of 2005) serving for a *maximum* of five years (although the prime minister may call an election before this).

A basic principle underpinning the idea of free elections is:

- **Government accountability**. The electorate can reasonably expect, within the dictates of changing national and global circumstances, a government to carry out the policies it presented in its manifesto. Democratic accountability also involves *interest groups* (such as the media) being free to examine and criticise government ideas, policies and behaviours. Ultimately, the ruling political party *must* submit to periodic election and, if defeated, engage in an orderly and peaceful handover of power.

- **Democratic debate**: The law-making process is the result of democratic discussion and voting from within the supreme constitutional body in a democratic society, although different democracies structure their parliamentary systems differently. In the UK there is an *elected* 'Lower House' (the House of Commons) charged with originating political legislation, and an *unelected* 'Upper Chamber' (the House of Lords) whose main task is to review this legislation. In the USA, Congress (Lower) and the Senate (Upper) perform similar functions, although here both are democratically elected.

> ## 🏠 The potting shed
>
> **Identify and briefly explain one argument in favour of the UK system of an unelected Upper Chamber and one argument against.**

- **Civil** and **political rights** involving ideas related to freedom of:

  - **association** – to form and join groups which may be fundamentally opposed to government policies and practices, for example

  - **speech** – to express and debate ideas that may be contrary to government policy

  - **action** – to peacefully demonstrate and protest, for example.

  Fundamental to these ideas are further ideas such as *legal equality* – the right to a fair trial, regardless of class or ethnicity, for example – and the freedom of the media to disseminate information in ways that are not subject to party political control, influence or censorship.

Finally, we can note that there are two main forms of democratic ideology:

- **Participatory (direct) democracy**, where everyone has a direct say in the decision-making process. Modern societies tend to be too large and complex for this type, but elements of direct democracy do appear in modern societies from time to time in the shape of:

  - **National referenda** in various European countries, including Britain (the last was over the decision about whether to join the European Community in 1973). More recently (1997), referenda were held Scotland and Wales over questions of *political devolution*.

  - **State referenda** in the United States or Switzerland where, in addition to voting for political representatives, people may vote on a range of propositions (concerning local taxation, criminal law, and so forth) that, if passed, become legally binding.

- **Representative democracy** (characteristic of the UK) where government decisions are taken by the *elected representatives* of the population – once elected, politicians are assumed to have a *mandate* from the electorate to take decisions on their behalf, without the need for further consultation. A *delegatory version* of this sometimes exists, whereby elected representatives are mandated to vote in ways decided by the electorate.

**Party forms**, on the other hand, relate to the particular ways *systemic beliefs* are operationalised within a society. In the UK, for example, although each party represented in Parliament has its own unique set of policies, principles and practices, all generally subscribe to the notion of democratic political ideology we've just outlined.

| UK Parliament: May 2005 | | |
|---|---|---|
| Party | Seats | % of vote |
| Labour | 356 | 35.3% |
| Conservative | 198 | 32.4% |
| Lib Dem | 62 | 22.0% |
| Others (nationalists and independents) | 30 | 10.3% |

In other words, when we examine specific forms of political ideology we need to do so in the light of these *systemic* beliefs – something we can do by noting the general ways political ideologies can be classified in democratic societies.

The conventional way to classify political ideologies is to view them as a continuous line (the *continuum*), at one end of which are left-wing parties (communist and socialist) and at the other are right-wing parties (conservative and fascist) – see below.

## Weeding the path

Although this type of classification has some basic use in classifying political ideologies and their relationship to political parties, it is a crude typology with some serious drawbacks.

- **Complexity**: Political ideologies and parties are complex entities and this type of continuum fails to reflect this. The Labour Party, for example, is a broad organisation and some members could be classified as communist while others are much closer to New Right beliefs.

- **Fragmentation**: Ideological positions (and the parties that hold them) tend to be more fragmented in contemporary societies – Labour policies, for example, have embraced both ideas and issues (social inclusion, welfare, child poverty and the like) conventionally associated with socialism, and ideas and issues (such as increased prison funding) conventionally associated with the New Right.

- **Meaning**: It's not clear whether this type of classification has any real meaning in contemporary societies, especially if we think about how political parties may change and adapt to different political situations. The Labour Party, for example, has been transformed over the past 20 years, from one advocating policies such as the nationalisation of public services (gas, electricity and telecommunications, for instance) to one that now embraces policies (such as privatising some aspects

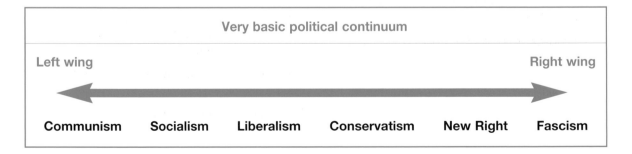

Very basic political continuum

Left wing                               Right wing

Communism      Socialism      Liberalism      Conservatism      New Right      Fascism of health care and education) traditionally associated with the Conservative Party.

The above notwithstanding, we can illustrate the idea of *ideological difference* by comparing the UK Labour and Conservative parties.

## The Labour Party

Traditionally, Labour has been viewed as what **Nilsson** (2000) terms a 'reformist socialist party'. Similarly, **Dearlove** and **Saunders** (2001) argue Labour has 'always been a reformist party dedicated to running Capitalism, as against a socialist party dedicated to the overthrow of Capitalism'. Its origins as the political wing of the trade union movement in the early twentieth

# Growing it yourself: Labour's changing ideological principles

We can demonstrate this general ideological change by comparing some current examples of Labour thinking (as presented during the successful 2005 election campaign) with that put forward during the unsuccessful 1982 election campaign (in a document memorably described by the then Shadow Environment Secretary and current Labour MP Gerald Kaufman as 'the longest suicide note in history').

Summarise the continuities and changes in Labour Party ideology between 1982 and 2005.

| 1982 | 2005 |
| --- | --- |
| Increase public spending and investment. | Increase choice over hospital and school places. |
| Renationalise privatised 'public industries'. | Increase numbers of police, community support officers and prison places; new Supreme Court. |
| Promote women's rights by strengthening the Equal Pay and Sex Discrimination Acts. | New equality commission; ban incitement to religious hatred. House of Lords = appointed chamber; more elected mayors. |
| Introduce citizenship and immigration laws which do not discriminate against women, black and Asian Britons. | Reduce asylum numbers by tougher rules on settlement and more deportations. |
| Stop further development of nuclear power, cancel the Trident nuclear missile programme and remove (American) nuclear bases from Britain. | Stand by Iraq war. New powers for government to detain terror suspects; increase defence spending. |
| Withdraw from the European Community. | Target of 60% for cutting $CO_2$ emissions by 2050. |
| | Back new EU constitution. |

century gave it a close association with the interests of the working class and, although it still retains this association, in recent times it has reinvented itself (as New Labour) in a successful attempt to both gain and hold political power. In this respect we can characterise Labour as a:

**Social democratic party**, one that no longer advocates 'worker control' of the economy, state ownership of public services and the like. In some respects, therefore, it represents a party of the 'centre ground' – one that appeals to both business and labour interests.

## Growing it yourself: Conservatism's changing ideological principles

Like its Labour counterpart, the Conservative Party has changed ideologically over the past 20 years, something we can demonstrate by comparing examples of Conservative thinking presented during the unsuccessful 2005 election campaign with examples put forward during the successful 1982 election campaign.

Summarise the continuities and changes in Conservative Party ideology between 1982 and 2005.

| 1982 | 2005 |
|---|---|
| Trade union reforms (secret ballots and restrictions over ability to strike). | Increase choice over hospital and school places; increase involvement of private sector. |
| Reform of employment law to reduce barriers to employment. | Increase police numbers and prison places. |
| Development of youth training schemes and reform of school curriculum. | Improve quality of motorways and major roads. |
| Privatisation of 'publicly owned' industries. | Encourage renewable sources of energy. Expand roads/speed up repairs. |
| Continue sale of council housing. | House of Lords = mostly elected chamber; repeal Human Rights Act. |
| Lower and simplified taxation. | Cut personal taxation. |
| Oppose racial discrimination. | Oppose banning incitement to religious hatred. |
| No withdrawal from European Community. | Annual refugee and immigrant quotas. |
| Continue development of 'safe nuclear power'. Maintain 'independent nuclear deterrent'. | Oppose EU constitution and adoption of euro. |
| | Back Iraq war but with reservations; oppose some new antiterror laws (e.g. ID cards). |
| | Increase defence spending. |

## The Conservative Party

Historically, the Conservative (or Tory) Party has had close ideological links with financial, industrial and agricultural interests. It can in this respect be characterised as the 'party of business'. In the twentieth century the party promoted a generally:

**Paternalist** ideological outlook, best characterised by the label 'One Nation Conservatism' – ideologically the party, while still favouring business interests, embraced a range of ideas and policies (the National Health Service, free state education and the like) that had previously been the preserve of the Labour Party.

In the 1980s, under the leadership of Margaret Thatcher, Conservative ideology took a distinctive turn with the adoption of a *New Right* economic agenda. See 'Conservatism's changing ideological principles' on the opposite edge.

The December 2005 election of **David Cameron** to lead the Conservative Party may signal a further ideological change given his pronouncement of the need for '... a more compassionate Conservatism' that included undoing the 'scandalous under-representation of women in the party'. He also 'promised to ... support Tony Blair's government when the Tories agreed with it'. Liberal Democrat MP Simon **Hughes** argued meanwhile (2005): 'Mr Cameron ... wrote the Conservative manifesto for the 2005 general election ... he is a convinced anti-European, a keen supporter of tuition fees and is likely to back the government on nuclear power. If that is the definition of modern Conservatism, they will continue to struggle to emerge from the political wilderness.'

## Digging deeper: Ideology and party

We can dig a little deeper into the ideas and issues we've just raised in the following way.

**Systemic forms: Wintrobe** (2002) identifies a problem with the concept of 'totalitarian ideologies' when he notes that much of the literature, especially that produced just after the Second World War, overemphasises the idea of such societies being dominated by 'dictators wielding absolute power' and 'ruling on the basis of terror and propaganda'. He argues this 'top-down' approach to understanding dictatorships (whereby a ruler or dominant group simply imposes their will on the masses) doesn't necessarily accord with the reality of life in such societies – the fact, for example, that a substantial proportion of the population may be broadly *supportive* of the actions and behaviours of elite groups.

As he argues: 'The general population may be repressed ... but other aspects of the regime may *compensate* for this as far as they are concerned ... The use of repression doesn't mean dictators aren't popular. Indeed, it sometimes appears from the historical record that the more repressive they were, the more popular they became!' He suggests, therefore, classifying dictatorships in terms of *four basic types* related to concepts of *regime repression* and *population loyalty*.

This type of fine-tuning is significant for a couple of reasons. First, it suggests that not all totalitarian ideological forms are the same, and second, that some forms of totalitarianism exist 'in the margins' of what we think of as democratic ideological forms. Some forms of *one-party state* (such as China) operate a *quasi-democratic system* of

| Types of dictatorship: Wintrobe (2002) | | |
|---|---|---|
| | Repression | Loyalty |
| Tinpot | Low | Low |
| Tyrants | High | Low |
| Totalitarian | High | High |
| Timocrats | Low | High |

government that involves, for example, elections for Communist Party officials and positions. Although this is different to pluralistic democratic systems it does, nevertheless, suggest we should avoid over-simplified distinctions between the two ideological types.

In addition, some democracies have elements of what we might term *totalising tendencies*, involving ideas like:

**Elite rule**. Different democracies exhibit this feature in different ways:

- **Family**: In India, for example, the **Nehru** family has dominated post-war politics in terms of providing political leaders and prime ministers. In the USA, different dynasties (the **Kennedy** family in the 1960s and the **Bush** family in recent times) have dominated the upper political levels.

- **Party**: This can be interpreted in a couple of ways. First, the long-term political rule of the *same party* (a characteristic of Japanese politics, for example, or, indeed, the UK, where the Conservative Party was in power for around two-thirds of the last century). Second, the long-term domination of a broadly similar set of ideological principles. **Gamble** (2005), for

example, argues: 'Labour critics complain that the Blair government has at best continued Thatcherism by other means, at worst by the same means. It has accepted the neoliberal political economy … given priority to its alliance with the US … has not renationalised industries or substantially changed Conservative union laws … the gap between rich and poor has continued to widen … '

These ideas are sometimes seen in terms of:

**Self-perpetuating elites**, a process that involves elite groups holding power over time, even in democratic societies, by a process of:

**Elite self-recruitment** whereby entry into elite groups is restricted to people from the 'right' family, social and educational background. An example of this type of 'elite rule' in our society might be the judiciary. **Malleson** (2003), for example, has shown that 90% of all judges are male and 98% are white.

## ✳ SYNOPTIC LINK

**Stratification and differentiation:** These ideas link into discussions about how something like elite self-recruitment enhances or diminishes life chances and social mobility.

## ⌂ The potting shed

Identify and briefly explain one way that education and one way that families can contribute to elite self-recruitment.

The Conservative politician **Quentin Hogg** (later Lord Hailsham) raised a further interesting idea, namely that of an:

**Elective dictatorship** – the idea that once elected and with a majority in Parliament, governments can effectively 'rule' without too much regard to opposition ideas, whether these come from other political parties or from the country at large. As **Hogg** (1976) noted: 'The powers of our own Parliament are absolute and unlimited. And in this, we are almost alone. All other free nations impose limitations on their representative assemblies. We impose none.'

Although it's important not to *understate* the fundamental differences between democratic and totalitarian forms of ideology and practice, we need to be aware that differences should not necessarily be *overstated*. While **Gamble** (2005) may characterise Labour as governing in an ' … authoritarian, centralist style, running the government through a small circle around the leader, sidelining cabinet, parliament and party', it nevertheless has to submit itself for periodic, democratic election.

## Mind maps

**Mapping ideologies**: If the difference between *systemic ideological forms* is not necessarily clear-cut and straightforward, the work we've previously completed on party ideologies (focused, for the sake of example, on the two main UK political parties) has also demonstrated the difficulty of disentangling and mapping different ideological beliefs at the:

**Party political level**, an idea we can explore further in terms of:

**Ideological maps**. Thus far we've classified different ideological positions (and their relationship to UK political parties) in terms of a relatively unsophisticated 'left wing–right wing' continuum.

## Weeding the path

This idea has a couple of fundamental problems.

**Clarity**: Categories like 'left wing' are vague in terms of their content; not only do they cover a range of ideological groups, they have no easily determined *boundaries* (where, for example does 'left wing' end and 'right wing' begin?). A further complication is added by something like *libertarian* philosophies that embrace elements of what are conventionally seen as both right-wing ideologies (low taxation, little or no government regulation of business and charitable, rather than state, welfare systems) and left-wing ideologies (personal tolerance, the freedom to choose lifestyles and the like).

**Complexity**: It's not clear that the complexity of ideological beliefs can be expressed on a *linear* (*one-dimensional*) continuum – one polarised at the extremes (communism to the left and fascism to the right) and converging in a centre occupied by a range of 'centre-left' and 'centre-right' parties and ideologies. This picture is further complicated by the idea that political parties may express a particular set of ideological beliefs and principles while operating, in practice, under a different set of principles.

Writers like **Dearlove** and **Saunders** (2001) argue that 'it is a mistake to try to map political positions on a simple "left–right" continuum' in the contemporary UK and, instead, suggest we think about party ideological principles in a slightly different way. They argue that our society is characterised by three great ideological traditions:

- **socialism**, with its concerns about social and economic inequality

- **conservatism**, with its paternalistic concerns for custom, tradition and evolutionary change

- **traditional liberalism**, with 'its commitment to private property, the free market and the liberty of the individual as against the threat posed by the modern state'.

Rather than each ideological position being separate from the other, whereby different political groups adopt each position as the ideological marker for their particular brand of politics (the left–right continuum), **Dearlove** and **Saunders** suggest we should see parties as being in a continual state of:

**Flux**, constantly shifting their positions as they 'dip into and out of' each tradition. Thus, the Conservative Party led by Margaret **Thatcher** (1979–1991) mixed both conservative and traditional liberal (or New Right, if you prefer) ideas with the emphasis on the latter. Following Thatcher's political demise, the party (led initially by John **Major**) gradually re-emphasised its 'traditional conservative' roots at the expense of New Right radicalism. The current party leader, David **Cameron**, has signalled both *modernisation* (increasing the number of female MPs, for example) and *continuity* with New Right policies of the recent past (such as cuts in personal taxation).

## ✳ SYNOPTIC LINK

**Crime and deviance:** In the 1997 election campaign Tony **Blair** repeatedly used the phrase, 'Tough on crime, tough on the causes of crime'. **Williamson** (2002) notes how this was ' . . . geared to appeal both to the law-and-order lobby and to those . . . who believe that crime takes place for a variety of complex social reasons which cannot, fundamentally, be changed simply by punishing individual perpetrators'.

Similarly, the Labour Party under Tony **Blair** has mixed elements of all three ideological traditions to produce a new ideological alignment sometimes called the:

**Third Way**, a position characterised by **Giddens** (1998, 2001) as neither wholly socialist nor wholly conservative – it combines different elements of these traditions to produce a:

**Political synthesis**. Rather than seeing politics as being a *choice* between two ideological positions (state-funded or charity-funded welfare systems, for example), *Third Way* politics argues there is a 'middle road' between these positions. Many current Labour policies reflect this idea – that it's possible to combine state-funded (education, the National Health Service, and so forth) with privately funded institutions.

## ✳ SYNOPTIC LINK

**Education:** Examples of this attempt to combine public and private funding can be found in this section, the development of academy schools being one example.

These ideas are explored in more detail in the final section when we look at *political participation*, mainly because some contemporary writers (such as **Lees-Marshment**, 2001, 2004) have characterised political parties as 'acting like businesses' that design their product (policies) 'to suit whatever the voters want'. This position suggests the conventional way of understanding ideological principles and their relationship to political parties is out-dated – it is no longer a case of parties developing an ideological position that is then presented to the electorate to accept or reject; rather, parties change and adapt their ideological positions to suit whatever their research tells them are the policies that will get them elected (or re-elected).

These ideas are reflected in the concept of:

**Branding**. Rather than seeing parties in terms of 'selling products' (such as a particular set of ideological beliefs), **Lees-Marshment** argues that they now act like brands – what they sell is still 'ideas', but these are related to 'whatever the market wants' rather than to some fundamental ideology.

 **Weeding the path**

We can look at an alternative view to the idea that it's no longer possible to think about contemporary political parties in terms of an ideological left–right continuum through the work of the **Manifesto Research Group** (as expressed by writers such as **Budge** and **Bara**, 2001) and their attempt to develop what **McLean** (2004) calls a:

**Multidimensional approach** to mapping political ideologies. According to **McLean**, 'parties try to "own" issues' (such as immigration, law and order and the like), which, once identified, can then be mapped to a general left–right continuum. The basic idea here is that the interpretation of these issues is reasonably consistent across different left–right ideological positions. As **McLean** (2004) correctly predicted, for example, 'the UK Conservative manifesto for the 2005 General Election *will* [our

emphasis] contain more sentences on asylum, and fewer sentences on the NHS, than the Labour manifesto'.

By studying a range of party manifestos, **Budge** and **Bara** were able to identify 'ideological sentences' that correlated positively with either a left-wing or a right-wing political position, as shown in the table below.

---

**Ideological phrases: Budge and Bara (2001)**

The **Manifesto Research Group** analysed party documents for specific phrases that could be grouped into general left–right ideological categories. As the following examples show, 'left-wing sentences' are qualitatively different to those produced by 'right-wing' political parties.

| Left-wing phrases | Right-wing phrases |
|---|---|
| Democracy | Free enterprise |
| Regulate capitalism | Economic incentives |
| Nationalisation | Law and order |
| Military: negative | Military: positive |

---

This type of research suggests, therefore, that it may still be possible to locate different types of political party (from extreme left wing to extreme right wing and all points in between) according to their fundamental ideological principles.

## Moving on

In this section we've looked at the relationship between political ideologies and parties, and in the final section we can apply these ideas to an understanding of political participation – how and why the electorate in contemporary British society make decisions about which political parties (if any) they support.

# 4. The nature of, and changes in, different forms of political participation, including voting behaviour

This final section looks at the concept of political participation, something we touched on previously when we examined ideas about parties, pressure groups and social movements. Although we're not going to cover the same ground again, this work does provide the basis for a more thorough and focused examination of political participation. In this respect we can look initially at participation in terms of things like membership and involvement in political groups and activities, but the main focus is on an examination of different *explanations* for a specific form of political participation – *voting behaviour*.

We can begin by noting a qualification to the general focus of this section, in the form of the idea that:

**The personal is the political**. Writers like **Hanisch** (1970) have argued *all* forms of social behaviour have a political dimension since all interaction involves power relationships and decision-making. In the classroom, for example, a variety of 'personal political relationships' bubble around just beneath the surface of everyday interaction, from questions about who has the most power in the class to decisions about the length and content of the lesson or where and with whom to sit.

## ✳ SYNOPTIC LINK

This idea can be applied to an understanding of all areas studied during the A level course.

This argument, however, is too broad an area to cover in this section and to make things manageable we've decided to focus on various forms of:

**Public political participation**, in the sense of people's membership of, or support for, political groups or activities, as well as what **Norris et al.** (2004) term 'informal political activity ... protests, social movements and, increasingly, voluntary activities in pressure groups, civic associations, charities and other associations'.

## ⚠ Preparing the ground: Nature and changes

Political participation, as we've suggested, comes in different forms. There are, as **Dahlgren** (1999) puts it, many ways of 'imagining – and doing – democracy' and we can start to think about the general nature of (and changes to) political participation in our society by noting some basic 'models of political participation' suggested by **Leach** and **Scoones** (2002).

**Liberal models** focus on the idea of individuals 'who act rationally to advance their own interests, while the State's role is to protect and enforce their rights'. Under this model, individual rights are:

**Universal** – everyone is entitled to rights, safeguarded by the state, such as legal equality, the right to own property, to vote, and so forth. Although these rights are *automatically* given (there may be *some* restrictions in terms of age, for example), individuals are also granted:

**Choice** over whether or not to exercise such rights or to participate in the political process – voting in the UK, for example, is not compulsory (unlike in countries such as Australia and Belgium).

## WARM-UP: PERSONAL AND PUBLIC PARTICIPATION

As a class, use the following table to identify examples of 'personal' and 'public' political participation in various areas of social life (we've provided some examples to get you started).

| Specification area | Personal | Public |
| --- | --- | --- |
| **Family** | | |
| **Education** | | |
| **Mass media** | | Support for political party |
| **Health** | | |
| **Wealth, poverty and welfare** | Giving to charity | |
| **Work and leisure** | | Trade union membership |
| **Power and politics** | | Voting |
| **World sociology** | Caring for the environment | Government aid |
| **Religion** | | |
| **Crime and deviance** | | |
| **Social inequality** | | |

# ⌂ The potting shed

Identify and briefly explain two ways that the rights of adults are different to the rights of children in the UK.

## Communitarian models

From the work of writers like **Etzioni** (1993) and **Putnam** (2001), this participatory model focuses on the concept of a:

**Socially embedded citizen**; in other words, the 'good of the community' has priority over the interests of the individual. This model, therefore, focuses on the ways people form and sustain local communities (such as neighbourhoods) through their general participation in the political life of that community, an idea often expressed in terms of:

**Social capital** – what **Putnam** calls 'social networks of trust and reciprocity' (people, in other words, are willing and able to help each other). **Cohen** and **Prusak** (2001) suggest social capital represents a 'social glue' that binds people in (political) networks of mutual help and cooperation.

This model of political participation is one that, after a fashion, has been adopted by Labour in the twenty-first century, with their ideas about social *inclusion* and *exclusion* reflected in attempts to create or develop local self-help communities and initiatives. On a broader scale we can note that *communitarian models* of participation are characteristic of some forms of new social movement.

## ✳ SYNOPTIC LINK

**Crime and deviance:** One example of this idea is the development of community security officers to patrol local areas and neighbourhoods.

## Civic models

These represent political participation in terms of the development of specific groups that, in turn, attempt to participate in, and influence, wider political processes. In other words, they represent the idea of:

**Sectional interests** – groups which develop around a common theme or purpose and attempt to influence the decisions made by those in power. This model can be applied to a relatively wide range of groups, from citizens banding together to oppose the development of a new road or hostel in their neighbourhood, to the general behaviour of *pressure groups*.

## Identity models

Although similar to their civic counterpart, this participation model focuses on the concept of:

**Identity politics** – the idea that certain types of *identity group* (women, ethnic groups and the like) develop *group identities* based around a common theme (such as feminist politics or religious beliefs). For this type, the distinction between personal and public political participation is generally blurred – the personal experiences and beliefs of individual members are directly transferred into public political actions. An example here might be the development, especially in US politics, of New Right ('born-again') Christian groups that attempt to impose their personal religious beliefs on the general political sphere (in terms of, for example, an anti-abortion position).

We can develop more specific ideas about the nature of (and changes to) political participation by examining ideas about membership and support relating to the categories we've used in previous sections – parties, pressure groups and social movements.

## Parties

In terms of **membership**, both the main parties in the UK have seen a decline in the post-war period:

| Party membership: 1950–2004 | | |
| --- | --- | --- |
| Year | Labour | Conservative |
| 1950 | 1 million **Rallings** and **Thrasher** (2000) | 3 million **Strafford** (1999) |
| 2004 | 280,000 **Mullard** and **Swaray** (2005) | 300,000 **White** (2005) |

Although the decline for both major parties has been *absolute*, it has not necessarily been steady. **Sparrow** (2004) notes how Labour Party membership *increased* (from around 210,000 to 410,000) in the early part (1998) of Tony **Blair's** leadership. This suggests parties attract and lose members in ways that reflect their changing electoral *support*.

## Weeding the path

It also suggests, as **Granik** (2003) notes, that party membership is not necessarily stable over time. She makes the distinction between:

- **Continuous members** – those who consistently renew their membership and have a long-term commitment to their chosen party – and

- **Discontinuous members** – people whose membership may fluctuate as they join, lapse and rejoin their chosen party. We shouldn't necessarily see this type of membership pattern as evidence of party discontent; members may forget to renew their membership or move away from the area in which their membership was based.

**Estelle Morris** (2004), however, suggests the *overall decline* in party membership is related to ideas like:

- **Globalisation**: She argues power in our society is increasingly *dispersed* across a range of social institutions (both national and international) and political parties are no longer at the centre of power, an idea echoing **Lyotard's** (1984) observation that there are 'many centres [of power in postmodern society] and none of them hold'. In other words, it's no longer possible for parties to monopolise political power – they face increasingly stiff competition from pressure groups and social movements, for example.

- **Ideological fragmentation**: In postmodern societies people no longer see 'social problems' as solvable on a grand scale. Poverty, for example, has many faces and dimensions that cannot be confronted head-on – the idea that 'poverty' can be easily eradicated is not something that features in the postmodern mindset. Rather, each *dimension* of poverty has to be addressed in different ways and from different angles. There is, in short, no longer the belief in a one-size-fits-all solution. As perceptions change, people lose faith in the ability of 'mass movements' (such as political parties) to confront and solve *micromanagement* problems (like regional and neighbourhood poverty), since mass movements are, almost by definition, organisations designed for *macromanagement* – operating, in other words, at the national and international political levels.

- **Communication**: The development of 24-hour news channels, the internet, and so forth, means parties may no longer require the type of organisational structure they had in the past. Rather than communicate with voters through party structures (local political associations, for example) they can now communicate *directly* with the electorate through the media, in a variety of ways:

  - **political broadcasts** and current affairs programmes

  - **poster** and **direct-mail campaigns** (paid political advertising is not allowed on UK TV, unlike in the USA where TV advertising is a central feature of political campaigns)

  - **media 'events'** and photo opportunities (such as party conferences)

*Newsnight* (BBC TV) is one of the main political/current affairs programmes on terrestrial UK TV.

- **email and SMS** (text) communication directly to voters and potential supporters

- **websites** – most parties have their own sites and forums through which they can communicate directly with the electorate and receive feedback. Websites have the advantage of both reaching a potentially massive audience in a relatively cheap and efficient way and giving party hierarchies a high level of control over presentation and content.

**Social change**: **Morris** (2004) argues local party structures played a more central role in individual and community life in the past. Party membership was also more likely to be seen as an important aspect of people's identity and could be used as a networking platform for social and economic contacts. In contemporary society, she argues, people have a wider range of social and political institutions from which to choose, each offering differing levels of participation and commitment.

## Growing it yourself: The state of the parties

You can find the URLs of a range of political parties at www.sociology.org.uk/a24aqa.htm (or search for a party by name using a search engine like Google or Yahoo).

Divide the class into groups. Each group should choose a party website to visit and report back to the class on their assessment of its:

- content

- presentation.

As a class, identify and discuss the advantages and disadvantages of the internet as a means of communication for political parties.

## Weeding the path

In any pluralist democracy, *support* for individual parties will, almost by definition, increase and decrease at different times (depending on a party's general popularity). Rather than look at individual party voting figures, therefore, we can note the *trend* in voter turnout at major elections is *downward* (although for European elections the recent UK trend has been upward, from a 24% turnout in 1999 to 38% in 2004). Local elections are generally decided on a very low voter turnout (41% in 1994 and 25% in 2003). General elections, therefore, offer a more *reliable* and *valid* measure of general party popularity; the trend in UK electoral turnout in the post-war period is as follows:

- 1950: 85%
- 1983: 73%
- 2001: 59%
- 2005: 60%

This type of general downward trend is not restricted to the UK. As the **Institute for Democracy and Electoral Assistance** (2000) demonstrates, declining voter turnout is a global phenomenon. We can, however, look briefly at the reasons for declining political turnout:

**Technical considerations**: These include factors such as:

- **Outdated electoral rolls** (elections occasionally occur when the list of registered voters has not been updated). The recently deceased, for example, may remain on the electoral register.
- **Failure to register**: For whatever reason, people fail to register to vote (even though required to do so by law).
- **Geographic mobility**: People may be registered in one area but, having moved, fail to update their registration (something quite common among students).

Although technical considerations account for a number of non-voters, they are unlikely to account for the 40% of the electorate who didn't vote in the 2005 general election. **Kitcat** (2002) points to further reasons for declining turnout.

- **Choice**: Where voters are offered a choice between two parties pursuing roughly the same ideological and policy agendas there is less reason to vote since, unless you are particularly committed to a party, you're likely to see little difference between them.

- **Competition**: In situations where the election is considered a 'foregone conclusion' there may be little incentive for any but the most ideologically committed to vote. In addition, the 'first past the post' electoral system can provide strong voting disincentives; in situations where a minority party candidate has no chance of winning, for example, their supporters may simply decide not to vote. The exceptions here serve to reinforce the general rule – **Richard Taylor**, for example, is the only Independent MP in the current UK parliament.

- **Perceptions**: In situations where some parts of the electorate see Parliament and/or the policies of political parties as irrelevant to their immediate needs and concerns, there is little incentive to vote.

- **Protest**: For an unknown number of the electorate the decision not to vote is a conscious statement of protest against either the voting system or the policies of the parties standing in the election.

## Pressure groups

In terms of:

**Membership**, the most recent trend appears to be downward. **Margetts** (2001) argues: 'Even the more successful pressure groups have experienced a reversal of an upward membership trend from the first half of the 1990s.' Greenpeace currently has around 200,000 members, a 50% decline over the past ten years. Having said this, accurate estimates of group membership are not always easy to discover, partly because, as **Jordan** and **Halpin** (2003) argue, the study of such groups involves three main problems:

- **Definitional**: As we've seen, our ability to define pressure/interest groups in a consistent and coherent fashion is often limited by the blurring of distinctions between pressure groups and new social movements.

- **Numerical**: Estimates of the size of different pressure groups are hampered by the lack of reliable membership data released into the public domain by such groups.

- **Normative**: An idea that relates to how we measure participation. As with political parties, 'participation' can be measured in two different ways – *active* involvement and *passive* involvement (in terms of, for example, donating money but not time and effort to a group) – and these, in turn, can be subdivided into further categories of 'participation'. Deciding what 'level of participation' actually counts as 'participation' is a *methodological problem* whose resolution has important consequences for how we view pressure groups and political participation.

We can also add that, unlike with political parties, the same person may be a member of a number of different pressure groups.

**Support**: Most pressure group participation appears to be relatively *passive*, something that is also true of party participation (where support is measured *objectively* in terms of voting behaviour). This, however, may be a quality of the nature and purpose of pressure groups – to exert influence on political parties and governments. This makes distinctions between 'membership' and 'support' redundant in the sense that they are frequently the same thing – by gathering support *through* (a relatively passive) membership, pressure groups enhance their ability to influence governments and political parties through 'weight of numbers' (they are seen to represent a substantial number of people, although this, in itself, is no guarantee of pressure group effectiveness or success).

**Jordan** and **Halpin** suggest this creates problems for the sociologist when considering questions of 'political participation', since participation is expressed through support that is then operationalised through the organisational structure of the group – the majority of members rarely, if ever, play a *direct* participatory role.

## Social movements

**Social movements** present both *external* problems of definition (how, for example, different types of movement differ from pressure groups) and *internal* problems (the distinction between OSMs and NSMs, for example). In terms of the latter:

**Membership** of OSMs is generally easier to estimate, but this applies mainly to movements, such as trade unions, that have evolved to resemble interest groups. If, for the sake of example, we look at union membership, the trend over recent years has been in two directions:

- **Decline**: According to the **Labour Force Survey** (2005), over the past 25 years both membership *numbers* and the *percentage* of the workforce who are union members have declined (from 13.2 million to 7.3

million and 55% to 28%, respectively). Having said this, we shouldn't lose sight of the fact that trade unions still have a substantial membership.

- **Conglomeration**, in the sense of fewer, but larger, unions. Unison, the largest union with around 1.3 million members, represents workers in public service industries such as the NHS, police, transport and the voluntary sector. The three largest unions now represent nearly 50% of all union members.

While there are specific reasons for the decline in union membership (the decline in traditional forms of manual manufacturing work and an increase in service employment that is less likely to be unionised, the growth of part-time working patterns that are similarly less likely to involve union membership, and so forth), a more general trend, suggested by writers such as **Putnam** (1995), is the decline in *any* kind of organised political participation.

## ⚠ Weeding the path

Although the available evidence from both parties and pressure groups does suggest a general decline in:

**Organisational participation**, considered in terms of membership, how we *interpret* this evidence is significant. The main question here, therefore, is the extent to which this evidence of decline represents a change in:

- **Individual behaviour**, in the sense of fewer people choosing to overtly participate in such organisations, or
- **Institutional behaviour**, in the sense of changes in the way political organisations operate.

For interest groups, for example, the development of bureaucratic structures and professional hierarchies reflects the environment in which many operate – that of government departments and bureaucracies where 'influential work' is done in committee rooms and offices rather than on 'the street' (through mass demonstrations, for example).

Here, 'decline' is a function of the organisations themselves; that is, they invite a *different form* of political participation, one channelled through both conventional and non-conventional organisational structures. In other words, 'political participation' has become professionalised – carried out by professional negotiators, backed by relatively passive forms of public support in the form of media coverage, donations and membership subscriptions.

This picture is further complicated when we consider:

**New social movements**. This type of political organisation doesn't, by its very nature, lend itself to easy analysis in terms of membership, mainly because NSMs are not 'conventional political organisations' in the way we generally understand the term in relation to parties and pressure groups. NSMs frequently exist 'on the boundaries' of conventional political behaviour and organisation, which makes measuring political participation difficult. There are, however, a couple of ways we can note (if not necessarily *reliably* measure) participation.

**Active participation**: **Margetts** (2001) argues for a 'dramatic upsurge in single-issue protest activity and unconventional forms of political participation' that is ' . . . not accompanied by a rise in membership.

Newer environmental groups rely on symbolic action rather than mass mobilization for their effectiveness'. As **Doherty** (1999), notes, newer forms of environmentalist groups ' . . . have no central organization and no centralized pool of resources and there is a strong ideological commitment to avoiding any institutionalization'.

The idea of 'symbolic action' can, of course, be interpreted in two ways. First, it might represent a *new form* of political action and participation, whereby a relatively small group of *activists* draws attention to a particular set of ideas or grievances by relatively small-scale – but dramatic and hence newsworthy – events. However, it might simply represent the fact that 'symbolic actions' (such as those carried out by Fathers 4 Justice in 2005) are not 'mass demonstrations' precisely *because* such organisations don't actually command very much public support or participation.

A second form of 'participation' is to think about NSMs more generally; for example, rather than concentrate on measuring or assessing participation through overt means (membership numbers, activists, supporters, and so forth), **Martin** (2000) suggests participation can be conceptualised in terms of:

**Cultural participation**; in other words, an assessment of the impact NSMs have made on the cultural life of our society – influencing perceptions, changing the nature of political debate and generally 'changing people's attitudes' to a wide range of issues. This of course either stretches the concept of participation to breaking point (since it's possible to argue that political participation has increased without any overt, measurable growth in such behaviour) or introduces a new and different way of thinking about the concept.

## Digging deeper: Nature and changes

To complete this section we're going to look at political participation in a little more depth, with the focus on:

**Voting behaviour**. Voting (or at the least the opportunity to vote) is one of the main forms of political expression and participation in our society (27 million people voted in the 2005 general election), and, for this reason alone, it's worth examining a range of theories that seeks to explain this type of participation.

When we start to think about explanations for *voting behaviour*, **Hyde** (2001) suggests there are two general models we need to consider.

### Expressive

**Expressive models** focus on the idea that voting behaviour is influenced by a range of factors (such as *primary and secondary socialisation*) that influences both party identification (the particular political perspective we choose) and how we decide to vote. This model has traditionally focused on *social class* as the basis for party identification, although in recent years ideas about the relationship between age, gender and ethnicity have also been incorporated in various ways into the general model.

### Instrumental

**Instrumental models** focus on concepts of individual:

**Self-interest** – voting for a party that promises to lower personal taxation, for example – or

**Issue selection** – such as when a party promotes an issue with which an individual strongly agrees or disagrees.

In some instances people will make calculations about what they believe are the best interests of a particular social group to which they belong (or in some cases the nation as a whole) and vote accordingly.

These models are not mutually exclusive (many of the explanations we outline here have elements of both) and their main purpose is simply to help us think about general ways to classify different models of voting. We can see this more clearly if we look at some examples of *expressive* explanations.

## Social determinist

**Social determinist models** are, somewhat confusingly, among both the earliest and latest models of voting behaviour.

Early models, for example, argued that there was a clear and relatively consistent relationship between social background, usually, but not exclusively, expressed in terms of class and political choice. An (American) example of this approach is **Lazersfeld et al.'s** (1944) argument that voting behaviour is influenced by the socialising ideas and behaviours of the people who surround us (in the family and workplace, for example), an explanation originally proposed to test the idea that the media played a direct and influencing role in people's behavioural choices. Their argument is summed up by their claim that 'social characteristics determine political preference'.

A variation on this general theme is one that introduces, according to **Andersen** and **Heath** (2000), a *two-way* element into the relationship between the social background

of the voter and the party for which they vote.

## Parts identification

**Party identification models** suggest people vote for the party that best reflects and matches their particular social background. In other words, the influence of social background (and parents in particular) leads people to associate themselves with particular ideologies and parties. This, as **Gerber** and **Green** (1998) suggest, represents a form of:

**Partisan alignment**, whereby people both see themselves as members of coherent social groups (classes, in particular, in the British context) and associate particular parties with an important component of their overall *social identity*.

In this respect, how political parties present and position themselves is significant for identification – part of a 'two-way communication' process, whereby voters identify with the party that reflects their social background, and parties, in turn, compete with each other to represent particular political constituencies. In Britain, for example, Labour has traditionally associated itself with working-class voters while the Conservative Party has traditionally been identified with middle- and upper-class voters.

## Proximity theory

**Proximity theory** is, according to **Downs** (1957), a refinement of this general model, in the sense that it involves people supporting the party they *believe* is closest to their own particular political beliefs, something that reflects an *expressive model* of voting because people vote for a party *regardless* of whether they feel it has any chance of winning. **Hope** (2004) has suggested that the concept of:

**Modified proximity voting** takes account of non-voters by demonstrating that people will not vote if no party is considered 'close enough' to their particular position (or 'dominant issue space', as he puts it).

## Weeding the path

The strength of these types of explanation, at least in the recent past, has been that, on a general level, they describe an observable process – the *correlation* between social background and voting behaviour. *Partisan loyalties*, for example, have been a reasonably consistent, general theme in British politics (and possibly even more so in Northern Irish politics where class and religion appear as influential factors in party identification). However, these models have a number of problems.

**Group identities**: The relationship between class (and other forms of identity), although strong in some respects, is not an infallible guide to voting behaviour. We can point to a range of different 'types of voter' who don't conform to this general relationship. These *deviant voters* include:

- **Deferential voters**: They 'defer to legitimate authority'. In this instance, some working-class voters (in particular) support parties (such as the Conservatives in the recent past, according to **McKenzie** and **Silver**, 1972) which they see as 'best equipped' to exercise power.

- **Contradictory voters**: Those whose socialisation gives them 'mixed messages', in the sense, for example, that those

experiencing upward or downward social mobility are more inclined to vote for parties representing their *former* social positions.

- **Affluent voters**: This idea was related, in the late 1950s, to the concept of *embourgeoisement* – the claim by **Zweig** (1961) that changes in the class structure were making notions of class identification redundant. The main idea here was that the working class was rapidly disappearing and the middle class rapidly expanding. In a situation where the 'majority of the population were middle class', the idea of party identification appeared less plausible, although this idea itself involves certain problems, not the least being a tendency to oversimplify the nature of both social classes and the class structure. Affluent workers, for example, were considered more likely to vote for parties traditionally associated with the middle classes. **Nordinger** (1967), however, found that 'working-class Tory' voters generally earned less than their Labour-voting peers.

## ✳ SYNOPTIC LINK

**Stratification and differentiation:** The concept of embourgeoisement has been used to argue that the class structure of modern societies (such as Britain and the USA) is converging ('becoming flatter'), in the sense that the 'old divisions between social classes' are no longer relevant to our understanding of social inequality.

This idea led, however, to the concept of:

- **Instrumental voters**: These people voted

for whichever party seemed to offer them the most (whether in terms of higher incomes, lower taxes, higher aspirations or whatever). This group, it was argued, voted *pragmatically* – that is, for whichever party offered the most at a particular time. Party allegiance was, consequently, weak and open to change.

## Branding

We can initially explore this idea through **Lees-Marshment's** (2004) concept of:

**Branding**, a relatively recent form of explanation that can be applied, in different ways, to both *expressive* and *instrumental* voting models. In terms of the *former*, the concept relates to the idea of *consumption patterns* – voters pick and choose their political preferences in ways that 'best fit' their current lifestyles. Thus, rather than broad *expressive* categories like class and gender being significant attachment and

**Cool Britannia?**
**In the mid-1990s the Labour Party under Tony Blair's leadership made a conscious decision to update its public perception. We'll leave you to judge how successful it was . . .**

identification factors, political parties are assessed on a range of 'lifestyle factors' (including how they are perceived in terms of confirming and enhancing a particular lifestyle).

Parties that are seen as 'fresh, modern and dynamic', for example, appeal to a certain section of the electorate, while parties seen as 'unfashionable' or 'stuck in the past' may similarly be considered 'unappealing'. In other words, voters are likely to support whichever party is best suited to their lifestyle, self-perceptions and aspirations.

Branding also has an *instrumental dimension*, according to **Lees-Marshment** (2004), in that 'British politics is consumer-led, with the main parties acting like businesses, designing their "product" to suit what voters want'. In this respect, parties 'shape their policies' to fit what they believe the electorate finds most attractive. In addition, the idea of 'brand loyalty' may apply here – just as people may buy more expensive products because they 'trust' or are attracted to the brand, the same may apply to political parties.

## Tactical voting

Brand loyalty is also a possible explanation for:

**Tactical voting** (voting for a party you do not support in situations where your favoured choice has no chance of winning, to prevent the party you least like from winning). By voting for a party they 'least dislike', people indirectly show their support for their favoured party by increasing its chances of victory at a national level.

These ideas suggest the UK may be increasingly:

**Volatile** (or constantly changing) in terms of the support people give to particular parties at particular times. If this is the case (and it's by no means certain it is), 'voter volatility' may help to explain:

**Instrumental models** of voting behaviour. These come in two distinct forms – those that focus on individual interests and those that focus on group interests – and suggest a more complex relationship between voters and parties than is generally the case with *expressive* models.

## Rational choice

In terms of *individualistic* models, therefore, we can note the idea of:

**Rational choice theory**, based on a:
**Cost-benefit analysis**. Scott (2000) defines this idea as 'the profit a person gains in interaction is measured by the rewards received minus the costs incurred'. In this respect voting choices are 'rational' because, as **Martin** (2000) puts it, 'individuals act ... to maximise their benefits and minimise their costs' which, in terms of voting behaviour, means *instrumental voting* – people vote for whatever party offers them the best (individual) deal. This *basic model*, as **Andersen** and **Heath** (2000) note, is highly *individualistic* in the sense that each voter matches 'their individual issue preferences with party platforms'.

## ✳ SYNOPTIC LINK

**Crime and deviance:** This idea is at the root of all New Right thinking across a range of social behaviours. We can, for example, use it to understand approaches to crime (as well as family life, education, wealth, poverty and welfare and more).

## ⚠ Weeding the path

The basic theory of 'rational choice' has certain attractions because it explains how people vote on the basis of individual decision-making. In basic terms, people vote 'selfishly' in that decisions to vote for a particular party or candidate are based on what they perceive to be their own best *economic* interests. The strength of the model lies, therefore, in its ability to explain people's *motivations* for the voting choices they make. However, rational choice theory (at least as it's constructed at this individual level of choice) is not without its problems.

### Why vote?

One of the central problems, as **Purdam et al.** (2002) point out, is that the individualistic cost-benefit type of analysis that underpins this version of rational choice fails to explain *why people vote*. In other words, because people cannot *individually* decide the outcome of an election, the *costs* involved, 'such as the time taken to visit the polling station', outweigh the *benefits* because there can be *no direct economic benefit* from the act of voting. This, as **Brennan** and **Hamlin** (2006) point out, has led 'some commentators within the rational actor school of politics' to argue that voting is *irrational*, for two reasons:

- **Information**: No individual voter can have all the information they need about likely benefits to make an informed rational choice about their 'best interests'.

- **Aggregated benefits**: As **Purdam et al.** argue, under this model it is actually

## ⚘ Growing it yourself: The rational choice dilemma

We can simulate the rational choice model in the following way. Split the class into groups of four. Each group member ('player') represents a different political interest. Each player has a number (1–4) and players 1–3 should also have a sheet of paper with the numbers 1, 2 and 3 written clearly on it (their ballot paper).

The group has ten minutes to discuss who should be elected by the votes of the three players. Player 4 may enter the discussion but cannot vote. At the end of the discussion each player should *secretly* select the number of the player they want to vote for by placing a cross ('X') against their number. They should fold their ballot paper and place it on the table. Player 4 then 'counts the votes' and the player with the most votes is elected.

However, each player should strive to act and vote *rationally*. In terms of their own *best interests* they should, therefore, vote for themselves but at the same time seek to convince the other players to vote for them.

If each player receives one vote (there is no clear majority), player 4 wins the election. This player should, therefore, do their best to convince the other players to 'vote rationally'.

As a class, identify and discuss the conclusions we can draw from the simulation about rational choice models of voting behaviour. Consider how this exercise could be applied to an understanding of tactical voting.

*rational* for the individual *not* to vote. If individual voters are unable to directly influence an election (and they will incur various costs by voting), their most rational decision would be to let others do the voting since anyone 'is equally able to enjoy the benefits if their preferred party wins the election'.

Although *individualistic* rational choice models have their problems, alternative versions stress the idea of 'group rationality'; that is, rather than seeing instrumental voting in terms of specific benefits to individuals, benefits are considered in more general terms at the level of social groups or classes. For example:

**Partisan alignment** is similar to the party identification model in the sense that an individual's class background, for example, influences their voting behaviour. However, the major difference is that people vote *instrumentally*; in other words, they vote for the party that best represents their economic interests *as a class* (or a *gender*, or an *ethnic group*). **Butler** and **Stokes** (1974) argued that in Britain the two main political parties have, historically, strong class associations; people understand these different interests and vote accordingly for the party that most clearly represents their class interests.

More recently, this type of analysis has been extended to include *partisan alignment* based on:

**Ethnicity**. George **Galloway**, representing the Respect Party, overturned a 10,000

Labour majority to win the Bethnal Green and Bow seat in the 2005 general election. His successful campaign targeted, and generally won, the large Muslim vote in the constituency.

## ⚠ Weeding the path

The 'problem of deviant voters' we noted earlier applies equally to this model of voting behaviour. In addition, although **Butler** and **Stokes** argued that class was 'pre-eminent among the factors used to explain party allegiance in Britain', not everyone agreed with this assessment – for many the relationship between social class and voting behaviour was by no means as clear-cut as they suggested. An alternative interpretation, therefore, might be:

**Partisan dealignment**, an explanation based on the idea that *partisan identities*, such as those based around social class, occupation and the like, have progressively broken down in such a way that **Crewe** (1984) argues: 'No form of partisan alignment theory can account for the changes in voting behaviour we have witnessed in Britain over the past 20–25 years.'

## Partisan dealignment

In basic terms, therefore, this model involves two main ideas:

- **Dealignment**: It is no longer possible to correlate ('align') voting behaviour with the kind of purely *expressive* factors we've previously discussed. As **Crewe et al.** (1977) claim: ' ... none of the major occupational groups [in Britain] now provides the same degree of solid and consistent support for one of the two

major parties as was the case in the earlier post-war period.' More recently, **Heath** (1999) has observed that 'Labour gained relatively more votes [at the 1997 general election] in the middle class than it did in the working class, leading to a marked *class dealignment*'.

- **Partisanship**: Although some form of partisan decision-making is, by definition, part and parcel of the electoral process (people have to make *choices*, after all), the argument here is that such choices are increasingly:

  - **Issue based**; in other words, electoral support for any given party at any given election is relatively *fluid* – large numbers of votes are effectively 'up for grabs' by whichever party addresses (and promises to resolve) the particular 'issues of the moment' uppermost in the electorate's collective consciousness. A classic example here might be the Conservative victory in the 1982 general election. Although trailing badly in every opinion poll leading up to the election, a crucial issue (Britain's involvement in the Falklands war against Argentina) may have proved decisive in re-electing the Conservatives by rallying national sentiment behind 'the party in power'.

## Explanations

Explanations for dealignment generally focus on the idea of:

**Fragmentation**, something that takes two basic forms:

- **Class fragmentation** involves the idea that classes, in a globalised world, are no longer coherent and effective social groupings. People, in short, have less attachment to their class in contemporary societies than they did in the past, and party identification based on class is consequently no longer a viable explanation for voting behaviour.

## ✳ SYNOPTIC LINK

**Stratification and differentiation:** Part of the reason for this (suggested) fragmentation are the changes in the class structure outlined in this chapter.

- **Political fragmentation** has developed whereby voters are no longer faced with a relatively simple choice between two distinctive political parties (something reflected in the decline in the relative number of votes each party receives). This involves both the electoral presence of a major *third party* (the Liberal Democrats) and the presence of a range of nationalist and single-issue political parties that extend voter choice.

Various explanations have been put forward for political fragmentation.

**State overload** theory, for example, argues that as political parties have increasingly promised to provide the electorate with all kinds of benefits in return for their vote, people have become sceptical about the ability of governing parties to deliver on their promises.

**Legitimation crisis** relates to the idea that, in a global political economy, national governments are unable to influence events (or 'deliver on their promises'). In this respect, where governments and parties are seen to be prisoners of events beyond their control, it matters little which party is

actually in government – something that creates a legitimation crisis that leads to voter disillusionment (and a consequent decline in political participation and the numbers voting for major parties).

As **Bromley et al.** (2004) argue: 'There has been a decline in levels of trust in government and confidence in the political system ... and confidence has fallen further since 1997.'

**Consumption politics** links to the idea of *issue-based voting* in the sense that, as **Himmelweit et al.** (1985) suggest, voting behaviour should be seen as a form of 'consumer decision'. Deciding how to vote, just like deciding which washing powder to buy, becomes a matter of weighing the alternatives and plumping for the party that seems to offer the most, an idea that links into **Lees-Marshment's** (2004) concept of 'political branding' which we discussed previously.

### ⚠ Weeding the path

Although partisan dealignment models are attractive in that they both question the idea of a simple relationship between voting and expressive attachments and offer a general explanation of 'voter volatility', they are not without criticism.

**Issues**: **Evans** and **Andersen** (2004) argue that while political issues are important in terms of voting behaviour, we need to look beneath the surface of a simple relationship between 'what parties are offering' and 'what voters want' to understand *why* people see some issues, but not others, as important. To do this, they argue, we need to see:

**Partisan orientations** as being the defining factor; in other words, people see certain issues as important (both personally and in the wider context) precisely *because* of their pre-existing political situations and influences. For a working-class voter, therefore, issues surrounding things like unemployment, the minimum wage, and so forth, are 'issues of class' precisely because class background, socialisation, and so forth, make them important (in the same way that they may be important to a rich, upper-class voter for different reasons).

## Expressive judgement

**Expressive instrumentalism**: In a related way, **Brennan** and **Hamlin** (2006) argue that *apparently instrumental* forms of voting are themselves always based on some form of *expressive* bedrock. In other words, when people vote, they do so ' . . . not to bring about an intended electoral outcome (action we term "instrumental") but simply to express a view or an evaluative judgement over the options (action we term "expressive")'.

In other words, voting behaviour (even when it *appears* instrumental and issue-based) can actually be rationally explained only in terms of how people perceive the act of voting (as a *duty*, for example), something that, ultimately, is rooted in an *expressive* understanding of their individual roles in a collective undertaking. As **Brennan** and **Hamlin** argue: 'I can satisfy my expressive desire to voice my opinion that Z should happen, without believing that doing so will actually bring Z about, and, indeed, without any expectation that Z will happen. It is, in this case, the simple expression of the opinion that matters.'

levels, poverty or living
ds) are relatively easy to identify,
and construct in an objective,
dised way. *Qualitative measures* are
roblematic (*questionable*) in the
f being more difficult to define and
dise, both within and across
s (making comparisons, for
e, more difficult).

## mic indicators

development involves clear
of operationalisation in terms of
defined and measured, it's possible
some possible *economic* and *social*
s of this process:

mic indicators: **Barbanti** (2004)
conventional way to understand
ent since the 1950s has been to see
nonym for economic growth'. In
ds, development has traditionally
sured in terms of economic
s such as:

**domestic product (GDP)** – a
re of the total value of economic
and services created by a society
specific time period, or:

**national product (GNP)** – a
re (sometimes called **gross national**
e) that includes net income from
l (such as the value of foreign
ments).

## Weeding the path

c indicators such as GDP and/or
useful in a number of ways.

ic development provides a broad
assifying different societies in terms
eneral living standards and can be
stimate the likely level of many

# World sociology

In this chapter we focus on the concept of *development* in terms of two major contexts:

- **A national context** in relation to the various ways our society has changed over time, and
- **An international context** considered in terms of how the development of our society has both influenced and been influenced by developments in other societies.

In general, this involves looking at the *process* of development (in relation to concepts like *industrialisation* and *urbanisation*), *aspects* of development (such as its impact on employment, education, health and gender) and development *strategies* (involving an understanding of the role of aid and trade). Finally, we need to consider the role of economic, political and cultural *globalisation* in a national and international context.

## 1. Different definitions and explanations of development and underdevelopment

In this opening section, the focus is on the concept of development itself – thinking initially about how it can be *operationalised* (in terms of definition and measurement) and, subsequently, about a range of possible sociological explanations for social development.

### Preparing the ground: Definitions of development and underdevelopment

Although the concept of *development* is central to this chapter (with each section looking at different aspects of this idea), the concept itself is by no means simple and straightforward to define, for two main reasons. First, there are general disagreements among social scientists about how we can *operationalise* and explain this concept; and second, there are disagreements about the meaning of the concept itself. We can illustrate this by thinking initially about social development as what **Leinbach** (2005) terms both a *process* and a *condition*:

- **Process** relates to the conventional meaning of development – that a society, for example, 'grows' or changes in some way and the developmental process is both:
- **Dynamic** – it involves *movement* or

*change* (from, for example, *undeveloped* to *developed*) and

- **Progressive** or **cumulative** – that is, 'development' also involves the idea that change produces a new form of society that is both *quantitatively* and *qualitatively* different to what has gone before.

- **Condition**: If social development is a *process*, it follows that, at various points, we can identify the extent to which a society is – or is not – 'developed', making it possible to compare the extent of a society's development in two main ways:

- **Historically** – how a particular society has changed over time (comparing, for example, Britain in the nineteenth and twenty-first centuries).

- **Cross-culturally**, in the sense of comparing different societies to measure/understand their respective developmental differences (such as comparing Britain with both broadly *similar* societies, such as France or the USA, and potentially *dissimilar* societies, such as Ethiopia or China).

In small groups, consider ea[c]
meanings in turn and apply
society (for example, identif[y]
have improved over the pas[t]

As a class, identify and brief[ly]
possible strengths and weak[ness]
meaning in terms of underst[anding]
and why our society has dev[eloped]

## Weeding the [

If we view development in t[he]
*process of social change* where
the potential, both historical
comparatively, to move from
(*undeveloped*, for example) t[o]
as *developed*), two things foll[ow]

- **Measurement**: Some sort
which to measure develop[ment]
making it possible to *cate[gorise]*
different societies on the
levels of development.

- **Linearity**: This (convent[ional]
viewing development effe[
characterises it in terms o[f]

- **Continuum** where at [one]
have 'non-developed' s[
the other we have 'full[y]
societies.

These ideas suggest develop[
two important concepts:

**Hierarchy**: If social deve[l]
*unequal* it follows that some
*stratification* will exist where
societies are grouped in ter[ms]
respective *levels* of developm[ent]
crudely, in terms of being ri[ch]
developed or underdevelope[d]
crudely, in terms of things li[ke life]
expectancy or average inco[me]

adaptation, regression, degradation and the like'. In other words, social change becomes development only when it produces 'increased likeness to some more advanced or better state of being'.

**Categorisation**: To identify changes that are meaningful in the context of development we must make *judgements* about what constitutes ideas like 'improvement' or development, and **Barbanti** (2004) notes 'there is little consensus' as to how to operationalise such concepts objectively, for two main reasons:

- **Value judgements** about what does or does not constitute *development*, as opposed to *change*.

- **Ideological debates** relating to whether development can be measured in *objective*, quantifiable ways, *subjective*, qualitative ways or some combination of both.

Development is, therefore, a:

**Contested concept** that involves debates not only about how it can be measured – if at all – but also about the meaning of the term itself.

**Measurement**: Although it's possible to measure concepts like development in a variety of ways, such measurements involve two main problems:

- **Indicators**: There are a wide variety of possible economic, political and cultural aspects to development and this involves decisions about what indicators can be used to measure it. Debates, for example, surround not only things like the choice of economic indicators, but also whether development should be measured in purely economic terms.

- **Reliability** and **validity**: *Quantifiable measures* (such as historical changes in

inc[
sta[
acc[
sta[
mo[
sen[
sta[
soc[
exa[

## Eco[

Altho[
proble[
how it[
to sug[
indica[

**Eco[
notes t[
develo[
it 'as a[
other [
been n[
indicat[

- **Gro[
mea[
goo[
ove[

- **Gro[
mea[
**inco[
abr[
inve[

Econo[
GNP a[

**Econo[
way of[
of thei[
used to[

| Gross domestic product: selected world areas, 2004 | | |
|---|---|---|
| Source: Quebec Institute of Statistics (2005) | | |
| | **Highest** | **Lowest** |
| **Africa** | 510,000 (South Africa) | 1,100 (Guinea-Bissau) |
| **Europe** | 2,300,000 (Germany) | 7,350 (Moldova) |
| **North and Central America** | 11,600,000 (USA) | 270 (Dominica) |
| **South America** | 1,480,000 (Brazil) | 24,300 (Bolivia) |
| **Asia** | 7,100,000 (China) | 5,100 (Mongolia) |

(US$ millions, adjusted for purchasing power parity (PPP) – a measure of the relative purchasing power of different currencies)

other social factors (such as education, health care, literacy and so forth).

## ✳ SYNOPTIC LINK

**Stratification and differentiation:**
Economic indicators (such as income and wealth) are frequently used as objective indicators of social class.

**Comparisons**: They allow us to make broadly reliable historical and cross-cultural comparisons (using objective, quantifiable criteria) of relative economic standing and growth.

**Classification**: Different societies can be easily ranked (*stratified*) in terms of their different levels of GNP/GDP (with the USA, for example, ranking as the most highly developed, and places like Dominica among the least developed countries).

## Classifications

In terms of classification, we can note some of the different ways societies have been conventionally grouped on a global level.

**Three worlds system**: A traditional form of classification involves dividing the globe into three distinct worlds, based on levels of both *economic wealth* and *political ideology*:

- **First world** – wealthy, industrialised, technologically developed, capitalist economies of Western Europe, North America and Japan.
- **Second world** – relatively poorer industrial and semi-industrial communist societies, such as the USSR (as was) and China.
- **Third world** – relatively impoverished pre- and semi-industrial nations with low levels of technological development in

Africa, South America and South East Asia.

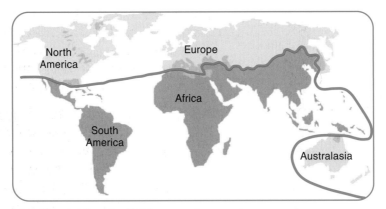

## Weeding the path

Although this classification is still occasionally used (in the media, for example), it has largely outgrown any classificatory significance it might once have had in a couple of ways:

- **Politics**: The break-up of the former USSR has made the concept of a 'second world' based around 'communist principles' largely redundant.

- **Homogeneity**: The system is too broad to *reliably* and *validly* reflect developmental differences both within and between these worlds.

**Two worlds system**: An alternative classification (proposed by the 1980 **Independent Commission on International Development Issues** – the **Brandt Report**) focused on the idea of a 'north–south' global divide. The most developed and wealthiest economies are largely found in the northern hemisphere and the poorest, least developed in the southern hemisphere.

## Weeding the path

Although this broad division arguably reflects the relative distribution of economic development across the globe (in 2005, for example, the most economically developed countries consumed around 80% of the world's economic resources, a figure that had increased from 67% 50 years previously), the 'two worlds' distinction has two main problems:

- **Geography**: The divide is not geographically perfect – Australia is an obvious anomaly.

- **Economic change**: In recent years the growth of economies in China and South East Asia (India, for example) has made a simple north–south divide invalid – in terms of GDP (2004), for example, China has the second largest economy after the USA, with India in fourth place.

**Many Worlds system**: This classification is relatively more sophisticated in terms of how development is characterised, with both a greater number of categories and a recognition that the vast majority of

The North–South divide
(Source: www.bbc.co.uk)

societies around the world have experienced some form of economic development in the post-Second World War period. Thus we can talk about:

- **MEDCs** – more economically developed countries
- **LEDCs** – less economically developed countries
- **LLEDCs** – least economically developed countries.

## Weeding the path

This classification – which can be expanded to include a range of further types (such as NICs – newly industrialising countries) – is both more sophisticated in the way it defines different levels of development and less tied to notions of geographic space. However, it still presents a couple of problems.

**Labelling**: Although the use of a 'sliding scale' reflects the dynamic nature of economic development (and avoids the rigidities inherent in both the three- and two-worlds systems), there remains a strong correlation between MEDCs and the first world/north and LLEDCs and the third world/south systems.

**Fragmentation**: The main problem here is the number of different levels of development it is potentially possible to define, without necessarily being able to agree a definitive economic definition of development. We could, for example, include relative levels of manufacturing and service industries, consumption patterns or even the price of a standardised product in different societies:

**The Hamburger Standard** (devised by *The Economist* magazine) takes a global commodity (such as a Big Mac),

manufactured to exactly the same standards worldwide, and compares its relative cost in different societies to arrive at a general estimate of economic development – the more developed a society, the greater the purchasing power of its currency. In an economically strong country, something like a Big Mac would cost relatively less than in an economically weak country.

More fundamentally, perhaps, **Thirlwall** (2002) has questioned the usefulness of *economic indicators* as measures of *development* (as opposed to *growth*), mainly because they fail to take into account factors (such as levels of health care, income distribution, literacy and the like) that impact on a society's overall development, a criticism

| Highest purchasing power (2004) | Least purchasing power (2004) |
|---|---|
| Britain | Taiwan |
| Western Europe | South Korea |
| North America | Hungary (!) |
| Australia | Indonesia |

**More bite for your buck in Britain?**

that brings into play a range of further observations.

**Income distribution**: Relatively simple economic indicators of development tell us little or nothing about how incomes are distributed throughout a society (and hence the overall level of development in that society).

**Reliability**: Indicators such as GNP/GDP are not necessarily defined or calculated in the same way in all societies.

**Quality of life**: Economic growth and prosperity may come at a price – in terms of environmental degradation, large-scale unemployment, and so forth – for large numbers of people. This suggests we shouldn't automatically assume economic indicators measure social development – economic growth, in this respect, should perhaps be seen as one possible means to one possible end.

## Social indicators

Although economic development is an important aspect to consider, it arguably doesn't tell the whole story – just as, for example, there's more to social class than income alone, the same is true of development. In this respect we can note a number of possible social indicators of development, starting with what **Badri** (1994) identifies as *political factors* such as:

**Democracy**: The basic idea here is that greater levels of social development are associated with a broad range of *political*:

- **Freedoms**, such as democratic elections, the right to free assembly and association, peaceful protest, freedom of speech and religion.
- **Rights**, such as legal representation, a fair trial, and so forth.

- **Relationships**, such as '. . . a country's level of respect of borders, of others' national sovereignty and abidance by international laws and treaties'.

The focus here is on the level of *personal control* people have over the way they live. On a wider scale, **Leinbach** (2005) notes the concept of:

**Distributive justice** – the idea that development should not be seen just in terms of political freedoms and rights, but also in terms of how 'basic human needs' are satisfied. These might include areas like the provision of and access to:

**Public goods and services** (such as health care, education and the like) as well as general measures of need relating to:

**Demographic variables** like:

- **Infant and child mortality rates**: These relate to children surviving, respectively, their first year after birth and after their fifth year.
- **Death rates** relating to the chances of people dying from both natural and non-natural causes (such as murder or suicide). These, in turn, can be related to:
- **Life expectancy**: The average age to which people in a society live can be indicative of a range of developmental factors, and although average life expectancy generally rose across the globe during the twentieth century (**Palacios** (2002) notes an average rise from 50 to 66 years), there are clear differences between societies at different stages of development. **Kinsella** and **Velkoff** (2001) note: 'On average, an individual born in an MEDC can expect to outlive his/her LEDC counterpart by 13 years.'

# The potting shed

**Moore** (1993) suggests that a range of developmental factors are responsible for rising national/global average life expectancy since the 1800s; these include medical and sanitation advances coupled with 'new modes of familial, social, economic, and political organization'.

**Badri** (1994) identifies a further range of *cultural indicators* that contributes to our understanding of levels of development:

- Levels of adult literacy and educational opportunities.
- Access to basic services (such as shelter, clean water and electricity).

She argues it would be possible to devise a continuum or ladder scale against which to measure a society's developmental progress – educationally, for example, such a scale 'could begin with the elimination of illiteracy and the enrolment of all children of school age, continuing up to quality of education in terms of the student–teacher ratio, availability of training in various skills, knowledge for all those soon to be on the labour market, and the opening up of various educational facilities to those outside the school and labour market population'.

## Weeding the path

Social indicators of development provide a different – and arguably more rounded – way to measure development. They also provide a range of:

**Development goals** against which to measure a society or region's progress in meeting certain universal life standards.

As with purely economic indicators, however, there are measurement problems:

**Reliability and validity** questions arise over how particular countries produce statistical data relating to areas like life expectancy and child mortality, which

| Average male and female life expectancy: selected world areas | | |
|---|---|---|
| | Highest | Lowest |
| **Africa** | 74 (Tunisia) | 38 (Malawi) |
| **Europe** | 80 (Sweden) | 66 (Ukraine) |
| **North and Central America** | 79 (Canada) | 66 (Guatemala) |
| **South America** | 76 (Costa Rica) | 63 (Brazil) |
| **Asia** | 81 (Japan) | 60 (Bangladesh) |

Source: US Census Bureau (2001)

# Growing it yourself: Development scales

In small groups, choose one of the following and devise a continuum/ladder scale to express different possible levels of social development.

| Shelter | Health | Politics | Economics |
|---------|--------|----------|-----------|

creates problems of comparability between different societies.

Social indicators are also subject to distortion within and between different societies – in the USA, for example, some groups have higher average life expectancy than others. Young, black, urban, working-class males have lower average life expectancies due to high homicide and suicide rates. In developing countries, average life expectancy can be lowered by high rates of infant and female mortality during childbirth (which distorts life expectancy figures for those who survive).

Given that both economic and social indicators have certain drawbacks when considered in isolation from one another, an obvious thing to do is to combine indicators to arrive at a:

**Human Development Index (HDI)**, such as that constructed by **Mahbub ul Haq** (1990) and used by the **United Nations** development programme. The index assesses and ranks countries in terms of three economic and cultural dimensions:

- **life expectancy** at birth
- **knowledge** – measured by adult literacy and educational provision
- **living standards** measured by GDP per capita.

## Weeding the path

The HDI has an obvious advantage in that it doesn't rank countries according to some form of predetermined 'development scale' (in the sense of, for example, universal standards of development/ underdevelopment). Rather, it focuses on a comparison between different societies and their relationship to each other. This type of index also redresses one of the main criticisms of development scales based on economic indicators, namely their possible:

**Ideological bias** towards Western societies with high levels of economic development. Using the HDI, it is possible for countries with high levels of economic capital but low levels of investment in human capital (through education, for example) to be ranked as 'less developed' than less wealthy societies which invest more in social and educational welfare. In this respect the HDI measures the:

**Ends** of social development (what it means in terms of raised living standards, for example) rather than the *means* to achieve such ends (*economic growth*). This type of index can also potentially measure levels of:

**Overdevelopment** – the illnesses and diseases, for example, that affect affluent societies (high levels of heart disease, obesity, and so forth, that may reduce average life expectancy).

The HDI is not, of course, without its drawbacks, some of which relate to the *reliability* and *validity* problems we've previously noted, and others to the idea it needs to be used in *combination* with other indexes (such as those measuring Human Poverty (HPI) or Gender Development (GDI) – the former introducing an element of class measurement and the latter reflecting the idea that gender differences exist in most societies in terms of how economic and cultural development is experienced).

## Digging deeper: Explanations of development and underdevelopment

**Todero** and **Smith** (2005) suggest *four main models* that explain how and why societies develop.

## Modernisation

**Modernisation theory** has its theoretical roots in classical (nineteenth and early twentieth century) sociology that involved a general (*modernist*) perception of development following a broadly:

**Linear** trend – from economically, politically and culturally *undeveloped* societies to fully *developed* social formations. As **Capitán** and **Lambie** (1994) put it: 'Modernisation is the process by which the gap between tradition and modernity (development) is progressively closed.'

We can note a couple of examples of this particular tradition in terms of:

**Classical functionalism** that theorised development in terms of different *stages* through which all societies passed. **Comte**

(1853) considered these in ideological terms; theological, metaphysical and scientific ('positive') stages represented a move from a society based on superstition to one based on scientific knowledge. The motor of change, in this respect, was:

**Institutional differentiation** – development was driven by *evolutionary* changes in social institutions; as institutions such as work developed, they forced changes in other institutions (such as education and the family), thereby creating institutional specialisation and evolutionary social development.

These general ideas were further developed in the twentieth century by **Parsons** (1951), who conceptualised development in terms of how *social systems* adapt to changing political, economic and cultural environments (such as the process of *globalisation* in recent times).

**Classical Weberian** interpretations, meanwhile, saw modernisation in terms of a change from pre-modern (traditional) society to modern (industrial) society. **Weber** (1905) argued that social development, once started, followed an inevitable process of modernisation, features of which included industrialisation, urbanisation and rationalisation (behaviour and social organisation based on scientific principles). The motor of modernisation, for **Weber**, was the ideological ideas and principles embodied in the Calvinist (Protestant) religion.

## ✳ SYNOPTIC LINK

**Religion:** Weber's ideas on the relationship between modernisation and religion are outlined in more detail in the 'Different theories of religion' section.

Contemporary modernisation theories developed initially in the post-Second World War period, the most well-known of which is associated with **Rostow** (1960) and his:

**Stages of Growth**, a development theory based around the idea that all societies pass through five separate (*discrete*) developmental stages:

1. **Traditional society**: The initial stage for all societies has three common characteristics:

   - **Technological**: Such societies are pre-scientific. Religion is generally the dominant ideological form.

   - **Economic** production is largely agricultural with no industrial development.

   - **Political**: This type tends to be 'rigidly hierarchical', with little or no social mobility. Social relationships are largely *ascriptive* (fixed at birth) and based around family/kinship structures.

## ✳ SYNOPTIC LINK

**Stratification and differentiation:**
Traditional society is often considered *pre-modern* and its general features are discussed in more detail in this chapter.

2. **Preconditions for take-off**: The second stage is characterised by a range of developments triggered, in the post-war period at least, by relationships with developed societies in the form of:

   - **trade** – goods and services are exchanged in the marketplace

   - **aid** – in the form of grants and loans from developed countries.

This type of development has three basic characteristics:

- **Technological**: Scientific ideas and practices develop, leading to either technological developments (such as inventions) or the application of technologies introduced by or from more developed societies.

- **Economic**: Industrial production develops, initially focused around labour-intensive extractive industries such as mining, although this may depend on relationships with other, developed societies (they may, for example, be instrumental in introducing different forms of manufacturing industry, such as shipbuilding or car manufacture). Agricultural production is still significant, but starts to decline gradually in economic importance.

- **Political**: Societies develop as recognisable nation states, often ruled by an elite group (such as a monarchy or military/civilian dictatorship). A key development is the emergence of a *bourgeois* (capitalist) class, with the knowledge, skills and motivation to exploit economic opportunities; they must be able and willing to invest capital and reinvest profits to lay the foundations for the next stage.

3. **Take-off** is the stage where economic growth becomes self-sustaining – levels of capital investment (from both within and outside society) and productivity reach a critical level from which economic expansion can be sustained. The general characteristics of this stage include:

**Preparing to take off or stalled on the runway?**

**Economic**: Manufacturing develops strongly and in the normal run of events one or two economic sectors develop rapidly to provide a motor for further development. In Britain during the nineteenth century, for example, shipbuilding and clothing manufacture led the developmental thrust. In this stage *indigenous* agricultural production generally declines in economic and social importance (although various forms of *agribusiness* – large-scale agricultural production run along the lines of manufacturing industry – may develop or be introduced by foreign investors).

**Political** and **cultural** institutions develop a more mature form; for the former this may involve more democratic systems of government, while for the latter education systems providing skilled, literate and numerate workers and managers start to develop.

4. **The drive to maturity** – a consolidation phase in which science and technological developments are increasingly applied across different economic sectors.

**Economic** development involves the production of a wider range of goods and services for both internal consumption and export; the economy becomes more diversified, in terms of a wider range of economic activity within both the manufacturing sectors and service industries.

**Political** reforms tend to be consolidated in this phase, with the emergence or extension of democratic processes. A range of social reforms, some of which are likely to be government sponsored (such as welfare systems), may be introduced.

5. **Maturity**: In the final phase we reach what **Rostow** termed the 'age of high mass consumption' (think about contemporary Britain as an example here), a situation characterised:

**Economically** by advanced levels of activity and development, relating not just to manufacturing and service industries, but also, in the twenty-first century, to knowledge industries (such as advanced communications).

**Politically** by an increasing range of choices to be made about all aspects of development, such as the type of society in which people want to live and also the type of society they envisage for their children. These choices are exercised at both the:

- **individual level** in terms of consumption patterns, and the
- **institutional level** in terms of, for example, *social infrastructure* (whether, for example, to develop state-sponsored welfare systems, as occurred in countries such as Britain and Germany, how the education system is

structured, developed and financed and the like).

![alt text] Weeding the path

Modernisation theory is both a *description* and an *explanation* of the development process in that it represents a way of understanding how development occurs as well as a blueprint for that process – ideas that have led to a range of criticisms.

**Process**: Modernisation is generally characterised as a *linear*, *evolutionary* process that, once started, proceeds along a set path towards a specific end. This, however, assumes modernisation is an 'inevitable historical process' (once started it cannot be stopped). However, although modernisation theory may accurately reflect the experiences of the *first societies* to modernise (in Europe and the USA), they did so under different conditions to those facing, for example, contemporary African societies – the most obvious difference being the fact that developed societies exist and may have an interest in the economic and social exploitation of less developed societies. In other words, the conditions under which development occurs have arguably *changed* and we cannot assume modernisation theory will reliably and validly *explain* the development process in, for example, Iraq or Ethiopia (if only because when Britain, for example, modernised, developed societies did not exist).

**Convergence**: If modernisation is an inevitable, linear process, it follows that all societies are 'converging' in terms of their social, economic and political structures, something ideologically convenient for developed Western societies because it holds there is only one way (the Western way)

towards development. This, in turn, can be used to justify:

- **Intervention**: A range of economic, political and cultural interventions by developed countries in the internal affairs of undeveloped countries can be justified on the basis that these are necessary for modernisation.

- **Hegemony** by developed societies in the sense of prescribing what undeveloped societies must do to modernise.

**Cultural values**: The argument here is that a Western model of development is *imposed* on the basis of both its *utility* (it worked in the past) and its *inevitability* (it is the only way to modernise). As **Coury** (1997) argues, development 'is defined in terms of very specific Western societies which are characterized as being individualistic, democratic, capitalist, scientific, secular and stable'.

**Economism**: **Capitán** and **Lambie** (1994) note how this model is based around economic factors and measures; development equates to economic change and growth, regardless of the social and political consequences for a population. As they note: 'Social and political factors are held to be less important and are simply assumed under broad concepts such as modernity and freedom.'

**Neo-modernisation** theorists like **Berger** and **Hsiao** (1988) and **Redding** (1990) have addressed this issue (mainly in relation to Japan and East Asia) by suggesting that development has a 'cultural trigger'. That is, in much the same way that **Weber** identified *Calvinism* as the crucial variable in the development of capitalism and modern society, **Borrego** (1995) notes how neo-modernisation theorists argue *Confucianism*

# ⚘ Growing it yourself: Developing development

Modernisation theory sees 'developed societies' as an ideal to which underdeveloped societies should aspire.

In small groups, identify the possible economic, political and cultural benefits and drawbacks of the type of development suggested by modernisation theory.

| Benefits of development | Drawbacks of development |
|---|---|
| Higher living standards | Environmental problems |
| **Further examples?** ||

played a similar role in East Asia – its central beliefs (a 'high value placed on education, a commitment to meritocratic personal advancement and a capacity for hard work') provided the qualities needed to exploit opportunities presented by developments in Western societies; in Japan, for example, development 'took off' once Japanese companies started to make cheap copies of US electrical goods.

## Structural change

A key criticism of modernisation theory is that it fails to recognise the idea that development is not a 'one size fits all' model. Structural change theories, however, recognise that development is a process affected by the fact that developing countries are locked into a set of *global* economic, political and cultural relationships that affect their ability to develop. In other words, we should not look for a *uniform model* of development.

The main difference between undeveloped and developed societies, from this position, is a structural one between the two types of society. Whereas the former are predominantly *agricultural* societies, the latter are predominantly *industrial* or *post-industrial* societies – a key economic fact that explains why some societies have developed and why others remain relatively undeveloped. Initially, therefore, *industrialisation* is the most important feature of development – where societies are able to industrialise they are able to create:

- **High-value economies** – a range of products is developed and traded.
- **Investment** and reinvestment opportunities that promote economic growth.
- **High-productivity** economies that create both profits for reinvestment and relatively higher wage levels to encourage domestic consumption.

The ability to produce a diverse range of goods and services, allied to making profits to be reinvested in areas such as new machinery, research and products, represents the key to understanding the development process – or, as **Todero** and **Smith** (2005) put it: 'Structural change focuses on the sequential process through which the economic, industrial, and institutional structure of an underdeveloped economy is transformed over time to permit new industries to replace traditional agriculture as the engine of economic growth.' The focus, therefore, is on how structural relationships, both *internal* and *external*, act as *constraints* on the development process.

**Internal constraints** include:

- **Geographic factors**, such as the availability of natural resources (coal, gold, diamonds, etc.) that can be exploited to develop extraction/manufacturing industries, or the physical location of a country (whether it is landlocked, for example).

- **Human capital factors**, such as the size and demographic composition (age and gender structure) of the population. Also included here would be things like levels of general education and skills.

- **Government ideologies** in terms of attitudes to foreign investment, aid and trade, as well as economic and cultural development (inward foreign investment, for example, is likely to be attracted to low-wage economies, but if this is encouraged, social inequalities may widen).

**External constraints** relate to political, economic and cultural relationships with other countries. To take an extreme example, *Cuban* economic development has been hindered because, as **Hillyard** and **Miller** (1998) note: 'The United States government has maintained an economic embargo against Cuba for some 38 years ... in 1996 the "Helms-Burton Act" extended the territorial application of the existing embargo to apply to *foreign companies* trading with Cuba.'

International constraints generally relate to things like the ability to attract foreign investment and technology as well as the nature of political relationships with neighbouring countries. Crucially, developing countries also need access to foreign economic markets for trade purposes.

## Weeding the path

One strength of structural change theory is its recognition of how international relationships – and the fact that the world consists of countries with different levels of development – impact on undeveloped countries. This general position has similarities with modernisation theory in that it sees the key to development as being industrial production (at least initially) and the idea that development is a relatively linear, evolutionary process – once a society begins to industrialise. The development process is seen as both:

- **self-generating** – as profits are created they can be reinvested, and

- **self-perpetuating** – once the industrialisation process has been kick-started it takes on a life of its own, with successive developments building cumulatively.

This situation, however, depends to a large extent on the reinvestment of capital, either from indigenous capitalist or, more crucially perhaps, foreign investors – and this may not happen because of:

**Capital flight** – the idea that foreign investors have little or no interest in the development of the country/economy in which they invest. Rather, profits are exported to an investor's home country, an observation that links to a further explanation of development.

## Dependency

Dependency theories broaden the focus to examine the relationship *between* societies, with particular emphasis on the way developed societies relate to *underdeveloped* societies. In this respect:

**Underdevelopment** denotes the process whereby a society at a certain level of development becomes *less developed* as a result of its relationships with developed societies. **Chaliand** (1977) notes: 'Underdevelopment is marked by … distorted and highly dependent economies devoted to producing primary products for the developed world and to provide markets for their finished goods … the economies of underdeveloped countries have been geared to the needs of industrialized countries … The prices of products are usually determined by large buyers in the economically dominant countries of the West.'

Although dependency theories come in a number of forms, we can briefly note two variations (*dual development* and *colonialism*) by way of providing a general overview of this position.

**Dual development**: **Capitán** and **Lambie** (1994) argue that, from this position, global development is *uneven* in the sense that developed nations represent:

**Core** or **centre** economies that dominate world trade. Their relationship with underdeveloped nations, for this perspective, is *exploitative*. Transnational corporations (TNCs), for example, from developed nations may operate within an underdeveloped nation to extract natural resources (such as coal or oil) or exploit opportunities for cheap labour.

**Periphery** economies, meanwhile, are those dependent on developed nations in three main ways:

- **Intellectual**: Ideas about economic and social development are imposed by developing countries.
- **Cultural**, whereby developing countries adopt, according to **Capitán** and **Lambie**, 'behavioural and consumption' features from developed nations – from their choice of dress, through films and magazines to fizzy drinks …
- **Technological**: Underdeveloped nations import technology from developed nations rather than developing 'indigenous technologies'.

## ⚠🏠 The potting shed

Identify and explain one behavioural and one consumption feature *our* society has adopted from the USA or the rest of Europe.

**Ferraro** (1996) identifies two 'key arguments' for this position:

- **Coexistence**: 'Powerful and wealthy industrialized nations compete with weak, impoverished peasant societies in the international economy.'

- **Persistence**: This is not a temporary situation where unequal and exploitative relationships gradually disappear. Rather, dependency is a *condition of the relationship itself*. In other words, dominant societies have an abiding interest in 'creating and maintaining underdevelopment'.

Relations of dominance and dependence are not simply reflected by the superior economic power of one nation over another. Rather, this relationship is *integral* to their dealings in that developed societies are involved in the:

**Economic penetration** of under-developed societies through, **Ferraro** (1996) suggests: the activities of transnational corporations within the dependent society; the provision of aid to develop economic and political infrastructures that facilitate the operations of such corporations; the lending practices of world banking organisations 'and any other means by which the advanced industrialized countries can represent their economic interests abroad'. In this respect the (in)ability of dependent countries to develop modern, industrialised economies is conditioned by their:

- **External** political and economic relationships (such as the ways under-developed societies are locked into international relationships with developed societies).

- **Internal** political and economic relationships and how their development is affected by external relationships.

A basic example here is the relationship between a relatively developed society such as the USA and its relatively under-developed neighbour Mexico. **Thompson** (2004) notes that '. . . about 85% of the goods and services exported by Mexicans are sold in the USA' and their relationship is one of:

**Dominance** and **dependence** – Mexico is economically dependent on the USA and the USA is 'the dominant global economic and military power'. As **Thompson** summarises this relationship: 'The USA is of great importance to Mexicans . . . but Mexico is not in the forefront of the consciousness of most Americans.'

**Colonial dependence models** originate within *Marxist* perspectives, both classical, where the focus has tended to be on the earliest periods of aggressive capitalist development and exploitation, and *neo-Marxist*, where the focus in recent years has been less on:

**Aggressive colonisation** (one country invading and ruling another, for example) and more on subtler forms, such as:

**Hegemonic colonisation**, a situation in which underdeveloped societies effectively become 'client states' for a dominant power through economic, political and cultural penetration. A classic example here might be the way US and British popular music ('Rock 'n' Roll') has, since the 1960s at least, become a global cultural phenomenon.

This type of dependency theory focuses on the way capitalist economies in the developed world (Europe and the USA in particular) have used their dominant economic position to exploit the natural resources and human capital of under-developed countries. As we've just suggested, colonial dependence models focus on the various ways (*aggressively* and/or *hegemonically*) dependent societies are kept in a state of underdevelopment. These include, by way of example:

- **Direct political rule** by dominant powers.
- **Indirect political rule** through the support of (corrupt) local elites who make political and economic decisions that favour the general interests of dominant nations.
- **Trade agreements** that give exclusive access to, for example, raw materials (such as oil) by transnational corporations.
- **Aid packages** conditional on the receiving society providing access to internal markets and the like.

**Ferraro** summarises this general position (one associated with a 'neo-Marxist, neo-colonial view of underdevelopment') by noting it '... attributes a large part of the developing world's continuing and worsening poverty to the existence and policies of the industrial capitalist countries of the Northern Hemisphere and their extensions in the form of small but powerful elite or *comprador* groups in the less developed countries'.

## Weeding the path

Dependency theories not only locate development within a global context, they also focus on the idea that international investment and trade are not necessarily mutually beneficial; on the contrary, they can be exploitative in situations where there is an imbalance (economic and/or political) between the various trading partners. **Todero** and **Smith** (2005) therefore summarise this general position in terms of:

**Power relationships**: In a global context developed societies dominate on the world stage. Historically this has led to what **Capitán** and **Lambie** (1994) characterise as 'a situation in which the economy of certain countries is conditioned by the development and expansion of another country to which it is subservient'. For Marxist dependency theories, inequalities between developed and underdeveloped societies are not simply the result of 'historical or demographic accidents'; rather, unequal development is built into the structure of global capitalism; developed societies dominate at the *expense* of underdeveloped nations. In some ways, therefore, dependency theories reflect, on a global scale, the concept of *class conflict* that is a feature of Marxist theorising; in this instance, however, conflict occurs on a vast scale, between developed and under-developed nations.

## The potting shed

Identify and briefly explain one way the relationship between developed and underdeveloped societies reflects a global form of class conflict.

There are, however, problems with this general theory.

**Persistence**: In the first place, it is difficult to see how the dominated societies ever break away from the 'vicious circle' of dependence and underdevelopment – yet some formerly underdeveloped societies (such as China and India in recent times) do manage to break away.

**Colonisation**: Although dependency theory emphasises the exploitative relationship between colonisers and those colonised, it is possible to argue that the benefits of this relationship are not totally one-sided. *Former colonies*, for example, may benefit from the development of their political and economic infrastructure, and their relationship with former colonisers may give them privileged access to technology, markets, capital investment and the like.

**Externalisation**: Dependency theory views underdevelopment in terms of the operation of factors external to the dependent society, with local elites co-opted into the exploitation process as agents of international capitalism. While this is true in many cases (elite corruption, for example, may contribute to underdevelopment), this is not always or necessarily the case – indigenous political movements, for example, have succeeded in developing the political and economic structures of formerly dependent countries while simultaneously developing a more equitable relationship with developed countries.

**Trade and aid**: It is possible to argue that some actions by developed nations to aid underdeveloped nations are not necessarily prompted by economic self-interest. The promotion of political stability, the alleviation of human suffering and the promotion of environmentalist policies are examples of a potentially *less exploitative* relationship (although, as with most things, it's possible to argue that such behaviour 'contributes to the maintenance of capitalism' as a global system of exploitation).

## World system approaches

These argue we need to understand development in the context of:

**Global systems and networks**: In other words, the focus is on understanding how nations are locked into political and economic relationships that, in the widest

sense, make them interdependent. **Frank** (1995) abandoned his previous advocacy of dependency theory to explore the various ways, both historical and contemporary, 'world systems' developed:

- **Politically**, in terms of, for example, the spread of various empires (from ancient Rome to modern Britain) and their effect on international relationships.

- **Economically**, in the modern period, whereby the spread of capitalism has encouraged the development of a global economic system within which every country has some sort of stake.

In theoretical terms a world system perspective involves, for **Capra** (1983), seeing systems as being 'integrated wholes whose properties cannot be reduced to those of smaller units ... the properties of the whole are considered greater than those of its parts'. In other words, to understand both development and underdevelopment we need to explore the complex interplay of political, ideological and economic relationships that characterise the globalised modern world.

This general perspective has a number of dimensions and arguments, but the original statement of this position comes from **Wallerstein** (1974), when he argues that, historically, we can chart the development of a world system from the:

**Pre-modern period** (the mid-fifteenth to late-seventeenth centuries) that represented a consolidation of individual Western European states (in particular) in terms of their internal political and economic cohesion. This consolidation laid the condition for the:

**Modern period**, where the development of industrial capitalism led, by the eighteenth century, to economic expansion among many European states through the search for new sources of raw materials, labour and markets. This, he argued, was the beginning of a world economic system that would eventually be characterised by the complex and interdependent nature of relationships within a globalised economic system that was:

**Interdependent** in that we cannot make sense of ideas like development and under-development except in the overall context of the relationship between nations – both their *direct* relationships (one country trading with another, for example) and their *indirect* relationships (the effect, for example, of one country choosing to trade with another to the exclusion of other nations).

## World regions

**Wallerstein**'s original formulation focused on the idea of a world economic system based around three concepts:

- **Core regions** represent the most highly developed economies in the modern world. They were the first to develop fully-fledged capitalist economies and are characterised by strong central governments, highly developed industrial bases and bureaucratic administration structures.

- **Periphery regions** represent under-developed countries defined, in this context, by their unequal relationship with the core regions. Peripheral states are characterised by weak governments under the control of indigenous elites or representatives of the core regions (where peripheral states are colonies of core societies). Peripheral regions serve as sources of raw materials, surplus labour

and captive markets for core regions, and their underdeveloped status is maintained, as **Chase-Dunn** and **Grimes** (1995) express it, by being locked into a world political and economic structure that serves to reproduce their subordinate status – to function as part of the world system, in other words, peripheral regions by and large have to accept economic practices that, in the long term, maintain their dependence on developed nations.

- **Semi-peripheral regions** occupy a space somewhere between the core and the periphery. Such regions may aspire to core membership or they may be former members of the core whose economic development has stalled or declined. Either way, such regions represent significant elements in the world system since, although they are frequently exploited by core regions, they in turn frequently attempt to exploit those on the periphery of the world economy.

In some situations (such as the former Soviet Union under communism) some societies could stand – at least temporarily – 'outside' the general world system for as long as their political and economic hegemony could be maintained over client states (those which were either under occupation or which cleaved to the dominant state).

## Weeding the path

This type of analysis locates questions of development and underdevelopment within a global context, in the sense that political and economic relationships are governed by a nation or region's position in the global marketplace. In this respect, when we think about how or why societies develop or fail to develop we need to consider the constraints and pressures that act on societies in this global context. More specifically, world systems approaches see:

**Capitalism** as a 'world economic system' in the sense that it is the *predominant* world economic system and the development of any society – core, semi-periphery or periphery – is constrained by the need to participate in this economic system.

**Dependency** and domination are features of a world system and entry into the world economic system is dependent on the adoption of capitalism. Dependency, in the contemporary world, is based on a mix of *hegemonic* factors, political and cultural as well as economic – an idea we can note in relation to a more contemporary take on this general perspective:

**Complexity theories** combine both a *Marxist realist* perspective (**Urry** (2002), for example), in terms of their understanding of social structures and systems, and the idea that, in terms of the development of global capitalism, the focus is not just on economic interdependencies but on a range of additional political and ideological factors. Dependency, for example, is not simply 'one-way' (from the periphery to the core); it has dimensions that relate to the behaviour of both semi-peripheral and periphery nations in terms of how their behaviour impacts on the behaviour of core nations (in relation to environmental policies, the consequences of rapid industrialisation in semi-peripheral regions such as China in recent times, and so forth.

## Moving on

Having outlined some general ideas about the concept of development and how it can be theorised, in the next section we can look more specifically at the related processes of industrialisation and urbanisation.

# 2. Development in relation to urbanisation, industrialisation and the environment

Although there are arguments surrounding how and why development occurs, an underlying theme of most theories (there are exceptions) is that of *industrialisation*; that is, although there are clear theoretical differences between, for example, modernisation and dependency theories, both assume that development involves some form of industrialisation process – a not unreasonable assumption in the context of global historical development. This section, therefore, explores some general ideas about industrialisation and its relationship to urbanisation and the environment.

## Preparing the ground: Industrialisation and urbanisation

**Industrialisation**, as we've suggested, is central to a range of general theories of development, from *modernisation* theories that identify the process as crucial to developmental 'take-off', through *neoliberal* theories that see industrial production as the motor of development, to *structural change* theories that pinpoint the move from rural-subsistence to urban-industrial as the key to development and *dependency/world systems* approaches, which explore the role of industrialisation in relation to both national and international forms of capitalist development. So significant is industrialisation, **Breinlich** (2004) notes, it is 'generally viewed as an essential part of a successful development strategy'. To understand how and why industrialisation occupies this relatively privileged position, we need first to think about what it involves.

At its most basic, *industrialisation* describes a process whereby:

- **Machine technology** is applied to the production of goods; this, in turn, results in the development of:
- **Factory-based** forms of economic production involving the:
- **Mass production** of consumer goods.

**Breinlich** (2004) further notes that industrialisation involves:

- **agricultural decline**, in terms of its share of *gross domestic product* (GDP), the number of people employed in farming, and so forth
- **dominance of manufacturing industry** (and, at a later point, service and knowledge industries)
- **rises** in income levels, living standards, economic consumption and the like

- **population movements** on a large scale, from rural to urban environments.

## Weeding the path

Agricultural decline doesn't necessarily mean a gradual 'withering away' of agricultural production; although agricultural and industrial production are often, for the sake of illustration, portrayed as *separate processes* (which they may be in the later stages of agricultural subsistence farming/the early stages of industrial manufacturing), contemporary forms of agricultural production are generally heavily industrialised; farming, in this respect, becomes 'just another form' of industrial (factory-type) production.

## The potting shed

Identify and briefly explain two examples of 'family-type' agricultural production in the UK.

---

**WARM-UP: ENVIRONMENTAL CHANGE**

In small groups, identify and briefly discuss as many changes to the 'human and physical environment' (both national and global) as you can (where 'environments' can be interpreted as broadly as you want).

Once you've done this, as a class, decide how many of the changes you've identified can be traced to the industrialisation process in developed and developing countries.

If you wish, you can expand this exercise into a general discussion of possible relationships between environmental changes, producer and consumer lifestyles, and so forth.

Industrialisation, therefore, represents a process of change, both:

- **Economic** (a new and different way of producing commodities) and

- **Cultural**, in the sense that wide-ranging economic changes, such as the development of factories, have a knock-on cultural effect, not only in terms of how social relationships are reorganised in the production process, but also in more general terms (such as the development and expansion of towns and cities).

We can encapsulate this process of change by noting that, *historically* (in terms of Western societies at least), the basic 'blueprint for development' appears to be that societies pass through three development phases:

- **pre-industrial society**, where the *dominant* form of production is agriculture,

- **industrial society**, where the *dominant* productive form is manufacturing, and

- **post-industrial society**, where both services and knowledge are the *dominant* productive industries.

## Weeding the path

These phases are not *discrete* – one phase doesn't simply replace the previous phase – the key idea here is *dominance*, considered in terms of productive capacity, wealth creation, levels of employment and the like.

## Urbanisation

This involves the idea that as nations *industrialise* they experience a general population movement/redistribution, away from relatively small-scale, agricultural settlements to larger-scale communities based on towns and cities. This relatively simple distinction between rural and urban areas can be firmed up by following the **US Population Reference Bureau** (2005) argument that *urban* areas have some distinctive characteristics:

- **Residents** in large numbers (although numbers alone are not necessarily a useful guide – an urban area in the USA, for example, is defined as having 2500+ inhabitants, while Botswana defines it as 5000+ and Portugal 10,000+).

- **High population density**: Canada defines an urban area as having a population density of 400+ people per square mile.

- **Industrial dependence**: Botswana defines urban areas as places where '75 per cent of the economic activity is non-agricultural'.

- **Developed infrastructure** of 'public utilities and services such as electricity and education'.

## ✳ SYNOPTIC LINK

**Theory and methods:** The **UN Demographic Yearbook** (2003) notes: 'Because of significant national differences, there is *no internationally agreed* definition of urban and rural that would be applicable to *all* countries'. The question of what counts as an 'urban area' illustrates the significance of *quantifying* concepts for comparative purposes.

## The potting shed

Identify and briefly explain two methodological problems with defining levels of urbanisation across different countries.

## ⚠ Weeding the path

Problems of comparability can be resolved, in part, by using a *standard area definition*, like the **UN-Habitat** (2004) concept of:

**Urban agglomeration** that defines urban areas as 'built-up or densely populated areas' consisting of three subdivisions:

- **city proper** (representing the major areas of economic production)

- **suburbs** (representing major areas of habitation that serve the city)

- **commuter areas with continuous settlement** (areas of established habitation that exist beyond the city's suburbs and from which people travel to work in the city).

In general the *process* of urbanisation involves a combination of two main factors:

- **Social migration** or population movement from rural to urban areas, something normally considered in terms of two types of *structural pressure*:

  - **Push factors** involve pressures that force people *away* from rural living. These include war, natural disaster, population pressures and a lack of physical resources (people find it difficult to earn a living, for example).

  - **Pull factors** *attract* people to towns and cities, usually for economic reasons. As the **World Bank** (2005) suggests, people move 'from rural areas in search of jobs and opportunities to improve their lives and create a better future for their children'.

- **Natural increase**: The second factor involves differences between birth and death rates within urban areas. If the former is higher than the latter, the population will increase, even if there is no *net social migration* (the difference between the number of people arriving and leaving urban areas) from the countryside to towns.

Urbanisation represents a significant feature of *modern, industrial societies*. Even though urban centres may exist in pre-modern, pre-industrial society (in the UK, London was an urban area throughout the pre-modern period), it is in the modern period that towns and cities become the *norm*. This suggests both a close relationship between industrialisation and urbanisation and that this relationship is not coincidental, especially given that urbanisation requires, as we've just suggested, an:

**Economic infrastructure** that supports and enhances the production and development of goods and services; factory-based production leads to the emergence of towns and cities as people are drawn from rural to urban areas to work.

In a global context, the number of people living in urban areas has now overtaken the number living in non-urban settings. According to the **World Bank** (2005), just over half the world's population – more than *3 billion people* – now live in cities. On current trends, around 70% of the world's population will be urban-dwellers by 2050 (compared with 30% in 1950 and 2% in 1800).

## ⚠ Digging deeper: Industrialisation and urbanisation

The close relationship between industrialisation and urbanisation (whereby

| Cities by selected region (2000) | |
|---|---|
| Region | Number of cities with 1 million + inhabitants |
| Asia | 206 |
| Europe | 64 |
| South America | 51 |
| Africa | 43 |
| North America | 41 |

Source: UN-Habitat (2001)

the former is the motor that drives the development of the latter) is not as straightforward as we've suggested. Although *urbanisation* is a global trend – and developed nations have a greater percentage of their population living in urban areas (around 75% compared with 40% in developing nations, according to the **US Population Reference Bureau**, 2005) – urbanisation is not a uniform process; it occurs in different ways in different societies. In developing nations, for example, the general *pattern* is one of:

**Fragmentary urbanisation**: A feature of urbanisation in developing countries is not so much the fact of urbanisation itself (even though, according to the **UK Communication and Information Management Resource Centre** (2006), around '90% of contemporary growth in urban populations' occurs in such countries), but rather *how* it occurs. For example, the **US Population Reference Bureau** (2000) notes that 90% of the population of Argentina lives in urban areas – the same

percentage of urban dwelling as the UK. However, the two countries are very different in terms of their industrial development and this apparent contradiction can be resolved by the fact that, in Argentina, around 40% of the population live in a single city (Buenos Aires).

This suggests that *patterns of urbanisation* are different for nations with different development histories; while early developers (such as the UK or the USA) have followed one pattern of development (with industrialisation producing a particular form of urbanisation), later developers have followed another, one whose development path has been influenced heavily by the presence and behaviour of developed nations. In part, this pattern of *fragmentary urbanisation* is expressed in terms of:

- **Megacities** (cities with over 5 million inhabitants) in developing nations. As the **US Population Reference Bureau** (2005) argues, 'by 2015, 59 megacities will exist, 48 in less developed countries' and, of these, '23 cities are projected to hold over 10 million people; all but four will be in less developed countries'.

The problem here is not so much the *size* of urban areas, but their *demographic relationship* to the rest of a country, whereby a *concentration* of urban development in a relatively small number of areas is indicative of:

**Fragmented industrialisation**: That is, industrial development, rather than taking root across the nation as a whole, is concentrated in a relatively small number of areas that, in turn, attract further migrants from rural areas. One consequence of this fragmentation is:

| The pace of urban change | | |
| --- | --- | --- |
| In 1950, only New York had more than 10 million inhabitants. By 2000, 19 cities in the world had achieved this status. | | |
| City | Inhabitants (Millions) | City |
| Tokyo | 26.4 | 12.3 Dhaka |
| Mexico City | 18.1 | 11.8 Karachi |
| Mumbai | 18.1 | 11.7 Delhi |
| Sao Paulo | 17.8 | 11.0 Jakarta |
| New York | 16.6 | 11.0 Osaka |
| Lagos | 13.4 | 10.9 Metro Manila |
| Los Angeles | 13.1 | 10.8 Beijing |
| Calcutta | 12.9 | 10.6 Rio de Janeiro |
| Shanghai | 12.9 | 10.6 Cairo |
| Buenos Aires | 12.6 | |

Source: UN Habitat (2001)

**Unemployment** and low-wage work for many in the population, a consequence of a limited range of manufacturing/service industries, allied to a huge urban population chasing what jobs there are in the formal employment sector. **Khosla et al.** (2002) note that, in developing nations, 'there is little evidence of growing investments in industrial infrastructure that could absorb the influx of urban population. Unlike at the time of the Industrial Revolution when the enormous rise in factory production and investment offered jobs to the urban migrants, today's developing world migrants often have few employment opportunities'. One consequence here, according to the **US Population Reference Bureau** (2005), is that migrants 'often end up not finding the opportunities they are looking for, but become part of the urban poor'.

## Discussion point: Megacities

In small groups, consider the following questions:

- What reasons can you identify for the growth of megacities in less developed countries?

- What are the social implications of rapid growth in these cities (in terms of things like disease, for example)?

As a class, what conclusions can you draw from your discussions about the impact of megacities on developing nations?

 **Weeding the path**

Of all the theories of development we outlined in the previous section, none satisfactorily explains the pattern of development we've just described, although dependency and world system approaches arguably come closest. Dependency theories, for example, highlight the importance of colonial and neocolonial political and economic legacies in developing nations, while world system approaches, using concepts like core, periphery and semi-peripheral regions, capture something of the piecemeal, patchy and fragmented nature of development in both the poor and semi-poor regions of the world.

**Khosla et al.** (2002), however, identify two key factors underpinning fragmentary industrialisation and urbanisation.

- **The post-colonial state**: The first factor, according to **Hobsbawn** (2000), involves the idea that for many developing nations the 'degree of external and internal order'

that was once imposed by a colonial power disappears in the post-colonial period, leaving a situation **Khosla et al.** (2002) pinpoint as one where developing nations 'are without effective central authority', with 'either an absence of, or the presence of weak, state structures'. The state, in other words, is not strong enough to effectively oversee planned internal development or to resist external influence from developed nations.

- **External influences**: The weakness of state structures in post-colonial developing nations opens them to external economic and political forces – either the national interests of developed nations (often, but not necessarily, using their past colonial links as leverage to gain access to things like natural resources and markets) or the international interests of global capitalism (in the shape of transnational corporations).

**Weeding the path**

The general argument here, therefore, is that fragmentary patterns of industrialisation and urbanisation are indicative of an unequal, exploitative and dependent relationship between developed and developing nations, a legacy of post-colonial political weaknesses that follow almost directly from past colonial dependence. We can develop this idea further when we look at *development strategies* and the role of international agencies and TNCs in the development process. For the moment, however, we can outline, by way of illustration, a couple of ways (*import substitution* and *export-led growth*) in which developing countries have chosen industrial development routes.

| Development routes by trade orientation | |
|---|---|
| **Strongly outward**<br>• No or low trade controls<br>• High incentives to export<br>• Low regulation of business<br>• Exchange rates neutral or undervalued to encourage international buyers<br><br>Recent example: **Singapore** | **Moderately inward**<br>• Production for domestic market favoured<br>• Relatively high protection from foreign competition for domestic market<br>• Extensive controls placed on imports<br>• Little incentive for export<br>• Overvalued exchange rate<br><br>Recent example: **Pakistan** |
| **Moderately outward**<br>• Bias towards domestic consumption, not export<br>• Low rates of domestic production<br>• Limited trade controls<br>• Limited incentives to export<br>• Exchange rate slightly higher for imports<br><br>Recent example: **Chile** | **Strongly inward**<br>• Strong incentives for domestic production and consumption<br>• High protection for home markets<br>• Strong controls on imports<br>• Exchange rate overvalued<br><br>Recent example: **India** |

Source: World Bank (1987)

## Routes

**Import substitution industrialisation** (ISI) is an example of a *strongly inward* trade orientation, whereby a developing nation *substitutes* the goods it would normally import with domestically produced alternatives. In other words, the general orientation is towards producing goods for *export* with minimal importing of foreign goods, a strategy (classically pursued by the USA in the nineteenth century as a means of limiting the effects of competition from the UK, the major industrial power of the period) which allows developing nations the opportunity to:

• **earn** foreign exchange through high exports and low imports

• **protect** *infant industries* from foreign competition, giving them time to establish a strong foothold in both national and international markets. This generally involves establishing and maintaining *trade barriers* (such as import taxes), as well as state subsidies for domestic industries.

Generally, this strategy requires a strong, centralised state structure committed to directing and overseeing the industrialisation process by:

• resisting foreign pressures to open up domestic markets to competition

• well-established and patrolled border controls for controlling imports and exports

• administrative oversight and implementation of taxation policies

• industrialisation policies that identify and encourage key domestic industries

• organisation of domestic labour policies to ensure a steady supply of industrial workers.

# ⚠ Weeding the path

Import substitution can have a range of both internal (*domestic*) and external (*international*) consequences. Domestic consequences may involve:

- **Decline in productive efficiency**: Although the strategy may encourage both industrialisation and economic growth, it runs the risk of becoming inflexible and structurally entrenched, whereby the strategy doesn't evolve to meet changing economic conditions. Where domestic industries benefit from state subsidies and the absence of foreign competition, there is little incentive for efficiency in the production process.

- **Interest groups**: This strategy encourages state involvement in the economy, either as regulators of economic behaviour or economic owners (through nationalised industries, for example), something that may create *powerful interest groups* which depend on the state for their power and influence (which opens up the possibility of collusion and corruption within and between economic and political elites).

- **Hardship** for those at the bottom of society. Pressure on domestic prices through lack of competition and choice, in addition to increases in taxation, create hardship for both the employed and unemployed workforce. Wage levels may become depressed as companies seek to raise profitability at the expense of their workforce as economic efficiency decreases.

- **Inequality increases** as the majority suffer high domestic prices and lowered wage levels, while a minority of upper income groups benefit through guaranteed state support and the development of monopoly state and private industries.

International consequences, meanwhile, may involve:

- **Retaliatory** trade barriers and protections from developed nations. As developing markets are closed off, developed nations may retaliate by introducing measures (trade quotas and tariffs, for example) designed to protect their own industries from cheaper competition.

- **Uncompetitive pricing**: Where domestic companies lose their economic efficiency their products become more costly and can be undercut on world markets.

- **Fiscal deficits**: Where export earnings fall away, governments have to increase the level of support given to domestic industry, leading to a drain on state resources (and possible cuts in areas such as health and educational services).

- **Export-led growth** represents the opposite strategy to ISI – its trade orientation is *strongly outward*, with industrialisation and economic growth fuelled by orientating trade towards exports to attract both foreign currency and investment. In this respect:

- **The role of the state** is generally *less interventionist* and its economic actions are largely directed towards encouraging exports (through taxation, subsidy and exchange-rate policies – attempting, for example, to make domestic products attractive to international buyers by lowering exchange rates).

- **Competition** between domestic producers is encouraged by governments orientating economic activity towards international markets and competing effectively in those markets. There is frequently little or no state action to protect domestic producers by restricting imports and foreign competition.

- **Specialisation**: Developing countries following this strategy normally focus on a limited range of export goods and services, the classic example, perhaps, being *Japan* in the 1950s specialising in the development of cheap, mass-produced, electronic goods (such as radios and televisions).

## Weeding the path

Export-led strategies generally lead to higher levels of development and economic growth than those associated with import substitution strategies. Japan, for example, had sustained growth in the post-Second World War period and has consolidated its position in the 21st-century world trade hierarchy through its development, production and consumption of computer goods and technologies. Export-led strategies, however, may have domestic consequences, such as:

- **Commodity shortages** as goods are directed towards international rather than national markets.

- **Rising costs** as goods and services are priced beyond the range of domestic consumers.

- **Depressed wage levels** as the need to compete in international markets leads to domestic companies cutting wage levels to increase profitability (and high levels of internal migration to cities, as we've seen, can produce a ready-made pool of domestic labourers, forced to compete against each other for employment).

## Preparing the ground: The environment

At the start of this section we suggested that an *underlying theme* of the development theories we've examined was the almost synonymous relationship between development, industrialisation and urbanisation. More recently, however, this relationship has been questioned, in terms of both whether development is *necessarily* dependent on industrialisation and the relationship between development, industrialisation and the environment. We can, therefore, examine these ideas more closely, starting with the relationship between:

**Human and physical environments**, considered in terms of the various ways people *interact* with physical environments. This relates to a number of ideas, ranging from how people use *physical space* and natural resources to ideas about environmental damage and destruction resulting from industrialisation processes. Historically, for example, industrialisation has affected the global environment, as **Lebel** and **Steffen** (1998) argue, in a range of ways:

- the **over-consumption** of natural resources (such as coal, oil and gas)

- **Pollution** in a variety of forms (air, water and land)

- **Climate change**, such as the possible effects of global warming

- **Environmental damage** to the ozone layer, deforestation and desertification (two frequently interlinked processes –

the removal of tree cover (*deforestation*) can lead to rapid soil erosion (*desertification*)

- **Population growth** and pressure on urban areas and resources
- **Death/disease** caused by natural and man-made environmental disasters and so forth.

As this suggests, we need to think about 'the environment' in terms of the various ways human and physical environments are *interconnected*, in terms of a:

**Reflexive relationship**. That is, we need to think about how one impacts on the other in a kind of circular relationship. For example, while physical environments initially impact on human behaviour (in terms of where and how people live), social environments rapidly transform the relationship through the use to which physical resources, for example, are put (the various processes and consequences we've just noted in relation to industrialisation, for example).

When we think about changes to the physical environment we tend, understandably perhaps, to focus on 'the present' and think about areas like environmental damage and destruction (the exploitation of natural resources and ideas about global warming, for example); however, we can put human relationships with the physical environment in context by noting that throughout history people have interacted with their physical environment, changing it in various ways. In prehistoric times, for example, one of the greatest environmental changes involved the development of agriculture, with natural forest cover being systematically cleared to create farmland. Similarly, industrialisation

and urbanisation in the modern period have seen massive environmental changes over the past 200 or so years.

However, as **Stern** (2000) notes: 'Only relatively recently has *environmental protection* become an important consideration in human decision making', an idea echoed by **Porritt** (2000) when he argues: 'It was only about thirty years ago that it started to dawn on people that ... To generate prosperity we were literally laying waste to the planet, tearing down forests, damming rivers, polluting the air, eroding top soil, warming the atmosphere, depleting

## The potting shed

Air pollution from factories is an example of how the human and physical environments interact.

Identify and briefly explain one further example of how the human environment can be affected by changes to the physical environment and one further example of how the physical environment can be affected by changes to the human environment.

fish stocks, and covering everything with concrete and tarmac.'

When thinking about the relationship between development and the environment, therefore, we need to recognise the changing nature of the interaction between the social and physical worlds in the context of:

**Sustainable development**, a situation defined by the **United Nations** (2000) as involving a balance between economic, social and environmental needs 'to ensure socially responsible economic development while protecting the resource base for the benefit of future generations'. This, in turn, relates to two further ideas:

- **Triple bottom line** – the idea that sustainable development involves the 'simultaneous pursuit of economic prosperity, environmental quality and social equity', and

- **Sustainable consumption/production** – 'Continuous economic and social progress that respects the limits of the Earth's ecosystems, and meets the needs and aspirations of everyone for a better quality of life, now and for future generations to come.'

## Approaches

The idea of *sustainable development*, although relatively new, has been adopted and explained in a couple of distinctive ways (*consensus* and *conflict* approaches) that reflect the kind of theoretical work we've previously examined.

**Consensus approaches** reflect both broadly functionalist and New Right positions on development 'in the post-industrial world'; that is, they propose ideas about sustainable development that attempt to marry two apparently contradictory positions, namely that 'classical development' has historically been driven by the economic processes associated with industrialisation, whereas sustainable development involves the need to include ideas about environmental protection and human development. This apparent contradiction is resolved in two main ways (*politically* and *economically*):

**Politically** – and reflecting *functionalist* approaches to conflict resolution – **Symons** (2002) argues that sustainable development should be seen in the context of:

- **International laws** and **agreements**: In other words, a global legal and moral framework needs to be established to regulate the behaviour of both developed and developing nations. Trade, for example, is regulated through the WTO, while conferences, such as the Rio Earth Summit (1992) and the Kyoto Conference (1997), have tried to establish ground rules and targets for a range of sustainable development aims. Rio produced a statement of 'eight principles' relating to the environment and development (from agreement to reduce poverty, through limiting environmental damage, to changes in production and consumption patterns). The *Kyoto Protocol*, among many other things, proposed limits on greenhouse gas emissions.

- **Engagement** between nations to produce voluntary agreements (such as *Multilateral Environmental Agreements* (MEAs) that promote controls on air pollution, the use of pesticides and the like). As **Symons** puts it, the 'essential provision is to keep everyone in touch – both those drawing up the environmental rules and those drawing up the trade rules. Better informed policy making will further add to mutual supportiveness.'

### ⚠ Weeding the path

Although international conferences and agreements are important, they largely depend on the voluntary cooperation of governments, something that is not necessarily forthcoming. The USA, for example, has repeatedly declined to ratify the *Kyoto Protocol* on the basis that, as **President Bush** (2001) argued, it '... would cause serious harm to the US economy ... it is an unfair and ineffective means of addressing global climate change concerns'.

**Economically**, reflecting *New Right* approaches that focus on the discipline of the marketplace and consumer behaviour to regulate corporate behaviour. **Browne** (2000) argues that solutions to global problems can be theorised in terms of international capitalism and the concept of:

- **Enlightened self-interest**, an idea encapsulated by the observation that 'business needs sustainable societies in order to protect its own sustainability ... very few businesses are short-term activities. Most want to do business again and again over many decades'. In other words, **Browne** argues that changes to the way companies do business represents the best way to solve global development and environmental problems, something that will be achieved through things like:

- **Technological developments** that improve the efficiency of businesses and make them more responsive to changing consumer and environmental needs.

Examples here might include the removal of lead from petrol in the UK, the development of 'emission-free power stations' and research into the use of 'clean fuel technologies' (where no harmful gases are produced) to power cars.

- **Trade liberalisation** to promote, as **Symons** (2002) argues, 'the more efficient use of natural resources and the dissemination of cleaner technology'.

- **Consumer behaviour**: How consumers behave is an important influence on businesses in that consumer choices influence how companies develop. In this respect, if consumers demand 'environmentally friendly' products and services, then businesses that provide them will flourish at the expense of those that do not.

**Conflict approaches** (and Marxist theories in particular) take a different view of the relationship between development and the environment, with the general focus being on relations of:

**Domination and exploitation**, played out within and between societies in the developed and developing worlds. In this respect, the concept of class struggle underpins Marxist conflict approaches at both the national level (*within* societies) and international level (in terms of how developed societies use their political, economic and cultural hegemony to exploit developing nations).

### ⚠ Weeding the path

A fundamental difference between consensus and conflict approaches is that for the former businesses are part of the solution to global environmental problems whereas for the latter their behaviour is part of the problem. At the heart of Marxist approaches is the argument that the destruction of physical and human environments is an integral part of:

**Capitalist production and distribution processes**: In other words, the primary concern of business corporations is the pursuit of profit – and when it comes down to decisions about environmental preservation *versus* loss of profitability, the argument here is that profitability always takes precedence. For conflict theorists, therefore, business claims about environmental responsibility and preservation should be regarded as:

**Ideological constructions**: While transnational corporations (and governments), for example, will promote sustainable development, they will do so only in contexts that preserve profitability.

Conflict positions, therefore, focus on ideas about:

**Global inequalities** and **exploitations** theorised at the levels of:

- **Class**, whereby rich, developed nations systematically exploit poorer nations (which, as we have seen, are kept in a situation of *underdevelopment* as they service the needs and requirements of developed nations).

- **Ethnicity**: Weintraub (1994) uses the term '*environmental racism*' to describe the 'intentional siting of hazardous waste sites, landfills, incinerators, and polluting industries' in both developing nations and areas within developed nations populated by minority ethnic groups.

## The potting shed

Identify and briefly explain two reasons for *Weintraub's* claim that 'minorities are particularly vulnerable' to environmental exploitation.

- **Gender**: Exploitation, for Marxist conflict theorists, takes place primarily at the level of social class (with working-class men and women suffering greater levels of exploitation than their middle-class counterparts). For *ecofeminism*, however, as **Jackson** (1997) notes, male-dominated (patriarchal) societies are held to be more environmentally destructive.

Finally, a further area of inequality relates to:

**Consumption differences** between the developed and developing worlds that fuel

## Discussion point: Where do you stand?

Thinking about the two general sets of arguments we've just noted:

1 Decide whether consensus or conflict approaches most closely match your view of 'sustainable development'.

2 If this produces two groups (one aligned to consensus and the other to conflict), each group should attempt to convince the other of the correctness of their position.

3 If the class is in complete agreement, your teacher should take responsibility for arguing the opposite position.

human and environmental exploitation. **Haub** and **Cornelius** (2000) calculate that the developed world, containing 25% of the global population, consumes 70% of the world's energy resources, and **Robbins** (2005) suggests this general pattern is repeated across all areas of consumption. He concludes that 'someone has to pay for our consumption levels, and it will either be our children or inhabitants of the periphery of the world system'.

## Weeding the path

**True** (2002) argues that the two approaches we've just outlined represent 'conventional accounts' of international relationships, whereby *consensus* accounts have 'emphasised the freedom that comes with liberalisation and marketisation', and *conflict* accounts 'have been much more pessimistic' about the behaviour of developed nations. We can complete this section, therefore, by examining a range of 'non-conventional accounts' of the relationship between development and the environment.

## Digging deeper: The environment

As regards sustainable development, consensus approaches interpret the balance between economic development and environmentalism in terms of economic behaviour that takes a more environmentally sensitive approach, whereas conflict approaches define the balance in terms of a radical reappraisal of political development, focused, for Marxists at least, on the creation of more equal societies.

There are, however, different approaches

we can consider, based around an interpretation of sustainable development that generally rejects the notion of *industrialisation* as the route to development. These approaches share the basic idea that we have to marry economic development to a concern about the environment that generally reverses conventional approaches. Where the latter focus on environmental protection as a by-product of economic growth, less conventional approaches place environmental protection at the centre of the equation, with economic production and consumption being shaped by environmental concerns. At the *softer theoretical edge* we can note ideas about:

**Counter-urbanisation**, a process involving gradual population devolution, away from urban and into rural areas. This process, somewhat ironically, perhaps, has been influenced, at least in developed nations, by the growth of communication systems, both in terms of:

- **Transport** – the widespread availability of cars, for example, makes it possible to live outside, while working in, urban areas.

- **Information technology** that allows for homeworking and lessens the need for travel to offices, thereby cutting pollution, congestion and the use of energy resources.

## The potting shed

Identify and briefly explain one environmental advantage and one environmental disadvantage to counter-urbanisation.

Alternatively, **Khosla et al.** (2002) build on the work of **Sen** (1999) to argue that we should see development in terms of the *human environment*, something that involves 'the enhancement of freedom for individuals to live the life they want to live', and to make this possible we have to rethink concepts of development – to move away from seeing it in economic terms (as a debate over 'poverty versus prosperity') and reconceptualise in a way that 'integrates economic, social and political considerations with equal weight'.

Following **Sen**, therefore, **Khosla et al.** identify five *instruments of freedom* against which '*unfreedoms*' (or constraints on freedom) can be objectively measured (see table below).

Thus, the development objective is to remove as many 'unfreedoms' as possible, in order to increase human capabilities, using a combination of public and private, market-based and communal resources.

**Ecological modernisation**: According to **Mol** and **Sonnenfeld** (2000), the aim here is 'to analyse how contemporary industrialised societies deal with environmental crises', with a particular emphasis on seeing 'environmental problems as challenges for social, technical and economic reform, rather than as immutable consequences of industrialisation'. In this respect, the focus is on:

**Transformations** of social and institutional practices as a way of adapting to changing environmental situations. For **Mol** and **Sonnenfeld** such transformations involve five clusters:

- **Science and technology**: 'Science and technology are not only judged for their role in the emergence of environmental problems but also valued for their actual and potential role in curing and preventing them.' In this respect

| Measuring unfreedoms | | |
|---|---|---|
| **Instruments of freedom** | **Example quantitative evaluators** | **Example qualitative evaluators** |
| **Political** | Persons imprisoned<br><br>Voting rights | Constraints on access to law and order services<br>Access to voting booths |
| **Economic** | Male/female employment<br>Income | Access to credit<br>Access to transport |
| **Social** | Life expectancy<br>Birth and death rates | Access to fuel<br>Exposure to pollution |
| **Transparency** | N/A | Facilities to report crime |
| **Security** | Epidemic cases<br>Catastrophic deaths | Access to emergency food programmes<br>Access to communication networks |

Source: Khosla et al. (2002)

environmental concerns and considerations need to be built into technological development, but the solution to environmental problems will not be found by marginalising science and technology.

- **Market dynamics** involve building ecological reforms into the relationship between, for example, producers, customers and consumers.

- **The role of the nation state**: The objective of this transformation is to make the state more responsive to people's needs (*political modernisation*) through *decentralising* and consensual styles of governance. The development of supranational institutions (such as the WTO or UN) is seen to 'undermine the nation state's traditional role in environmental reform'.

- **Social movements**: Both public and private movements should occupy the centre of political decision-making on the basis that they are more in touch with people's ideas and behaviours and more responsive to their needs.

- **New ideologies** involve the *reimagining* of the relationship between the environment and economic concerns, whereby 'complete neglect of the environment and the fundamental counter-positioning of economic and environmental interests are no longer accepted as legitimate positions'.

If we turn towards considering the *harder theoretical edge*, we can note approaches like: **Ecofeminism** that, as we've suggested, considers environmental destruction as the inevitable manifestation of *patriarchy*. **Jackson** (1997), however, argues its analysis is 'weakened by a failure to link empirical and historical evidence to theoretical position'. As she notes, 'Ecofeminist assertions that male-dominated societies are more environmentally destructive are not borne out by evidence from countries like India, deeply patriarchal but with very low per capita rates of resource use and abuse.'

**Deep ecology** perspectives argue that people should strive to live in harmony with their environment in terms of:

- **Biological egalitarianism** – the idea that human societies should attune themselves with nature by orientating development away from industrialisation and the exploitation of natural resources. In this respect, people and nature are not separate and discrete; rather, each depends on the other.

Different positions within this general approach emphasise different ways of developing the human/nature axis:

**Anti-consumerist positions**, for example, reject the consumption patterns of industrial, developed societies and advocate a 'return to nature' lifestyle, based on traditional forms of consumption and production that stress a *symbiotic relationship* between people and the environment.

**Post-industrial ecological** groups advance ideas about *biodiversity* (ensuring diversity in relation to ecosystems and species, for example) and the importance of developing renewable forms of energy. Some groups advocate spiritual education focused on 'nature religions' (Wicca and various forms of neo-paganism, for example), which hold that everything in the world – including people – is connected by a web of energy (sometimes called a *life force*) embodied in nature.

## ⚠ Weeding the path

Post-industrial spiritual groups *reify* the concept of 'nature'; that is, they treat an abstract concept ('nature') *as if* it were something concrete and real (references, for example, to 'Mother Nature', whereby the natural world is given human (female) qualities, are an obvious example here).

**Neo-populist positions**: **Hettne** (1995) summarises the general nature of these positions in terms of their relationship to – and differences from – traditional forms of populist politics, economics and culture. Thus, where *traditional populism* represented 'a defence of the territorial community' against the challenges and pressures created by economic growth', *neo-populism* represents an attempt to 're-create community as an offensive against the industrial system'. In this respect, the development of neo-popularist movements (in both developed and developing nations) can be seen in terms of a desire for:

- **Community-based** social relationships that reflect 'traditional' or popular beliefs about life 'in the past' (usually in some nebulous period prior to the disruptive influence of modernisation, industrialisation and urbanisation).

- **Primary production** techniques, with the focus on localised development that reflects the influence of modern industrial forms of production, consumption and culture.

- **Non-industrial civilisation** – a rejection, as it were, of Western consumerism.

Neo-populism takes a number of forms, from rejection of 'outside' (usually Western) cultural and political influences to an acceptance of some forms of aid and trade as a means of encouraging development processes. Where neo-populist movements and ideas are not *rejectionist* (that is, rejecting any involvement with the developed world), they may become incorporated into development systems through, for example, non-governmental organisations (NGOs), such as charities which provide aid and assistance in ways that build on local knowledge and skills, rather than imposing a 'one size fits all' model of development.

## Moving on

Having looked at the processes of industrialisation and urbanisation in relation to current environmental concerns we can move forward, in the next section, to think about how the various theories and processes we've outlined in the first two sections relate to concepts of *globalisation*.

# 3. The cultural, political and economic inter-relationships between societies

One of the interesting features of world sociology is that it encourages us to think about relationships in a *global context*, not only in the obvious sense – the relationship *between* different nations – but also in terms of the ways being members of a 'global community' impact on our individual experiences and the relationships *within* nations.

It is not, however, simply a case of thinking about the variety of economic, political and cultural relationships that exists between contemporary societies; it is also necessary to think about how these relationships are *changing*, and one way to do this is to put such changes into a sociological context – that of *globalisation*.

One way to start to think about globalisation is to identify 'global connections' – the various ways societies are connected economically and culturally, for example.

In small groups, identify some of the ways you are connected to other societies in terms of the things you *consume* (food, clothing, media, etc.). For example, think about the origin of various objects that surround you in the classroom (paper, pens, chairs) and expand this to objects in your home.

## ⚠ Preparing the ground: Globalisation

We can begin by noting **Sklair's** (1999) observation that contemporary relationships ' . . . cannot be adequately studied at the level of nation-states . . . they need to be conceptualized in terms of global processes'. Globalisation, therefore, provides a context for understanding the relationship between societies in the contemporary world because it represents a *process* that both reflects and contributes to *change* – the idea that how nations relate to each other is different *now* compared with even the recent past. Before we think about how globalisation can be applied to an understanding of changing relationships, however, we need to consider initially how it can be:

**Defined**: Although we can refer, in vague terms, to globalisation as 'a process', it is much harder to pin down a definition that's broadly recognised and accepted within the sociology of development (**Rosamond** and **Booth** (1995) refer to globalisation, with good reason, as a *contested concept*). **Scholte** (2000) notes that some things that are *not*, in themselves, 'globalisation', although each has *global consequences*:

- **Internationalisation** ('cross-border relations between countries').

- **Liberalisation** of political and economic relationships (such as 'removing government-imposed restrictions on movements between countries').

- **Universalisation** of cultural forms (such as television) 'in the sense of spreading various objects and experiences to people of all corners of the earth'.

- **Modernisation** involving the spread of the social structures of *modernity* (capitalism, rationalism, industrialism, and so forth) across the world.

The key to understanding globalisation, therefore, is to see it as a *process* that *facilitates other processes*, something **Virilio** (2000) expresses when he argues: 'The speed of light does not merely transform the world. It becomes the world. Globalisation is the speed of light. And it is nothing else!' In other words, globalisation is something that, through the speed of its occurrence, transforms the nature of other processes (such as the transfer of capital, physical movement and the flow of information around the globe) and, in so doing, becomes synonymous with change.

## ⚠ Digging deeper: Globalisation

We can develop these ideas in terms of the:

**Distanciation** (of time and space): **Giddens** (1990) argues that a major feature of globalisation is the separation of *time and space* – something we can illustrate in the following way: when you watch a live broadcast on TV in your living room *time* is *separated* from *space* – although the event and your viewing occur at the same time, you don't have to be physically present at the event to view it (and if you record it for later viewing, time and space are even further separated). This feature of globalisation (in this example the *speed* at which television pictures can be transmitted and received) means communication can take place instantaneously *across the globe*, 'as if' people occupied the same physical space.

For **Virilio**, globalisation makes concepts of distance and physical space *irrelevant* in the contemporary world – something that contributes to what **Harvey** (1990) considers the:

**Compression** (of time and space): The speed at which things can be done shortens the time required to do them and, effectively, shrinks distances (not literally, of course). To illustrate this, think about the time it takes to write and send an email to someone on the other side of the world as opposed to writing and sending a letter or actually visiting them.

Both *distanciation* and *compression* represent, for **Ebeltoft** (1998), 'vital preconditions' for an idea with direct consequences for our understanding of changing social relationships:

**Disembedding** – something we can understand by thinking about its opposite. If something is *embedded* it is firmly fixed in its surroundings (located in a particular context that gives it a particular meaning). *Disembedding*, therefore, means things are separated from their original surroundings and contexts. This can include:

- **objects**, such as credit cards – disembedded from their original physical context (coinage)

- **processes**, such as the electronic transfer of money into and out of a bank account, and

- **people**, in two ways. First, in the sense where global communication between strangers is both possible and takes place in *indeterminate space* (a cyberspace chat room, for example), and second, in the sense of physical and cultural disembedding – the former in terms of *territoriality* and its associated meanings (how people define themselves in terms of national/global identities, for example), and the latter in relation to the various ways cultural hybrids (the mixing of different cultures to produce something new and different) develop out of the globalisation process.

## ✳ SYNOPTIC LINK

**Theory and methods:** These ideas can be given a *postmodern* twist by linking them to **Baudrillard's** (1998) concept of:

**Simulacra** ('representations that refer to other representations' – for example, a credit card is a *simulation* of coinage which, in turn, is a simulation of something like a piece of gold). Where disembedding takes place the 'origins of the original' are lost or concealed in time and space. In other words, the simulation has the same general status as whatever it is simulating, such that both are 'as real' as each other. Thus, a credit card payment is 'as real' as paying in cash;

similarly, a telephone call or an email is 'as real' as talking to someone in the flesh.

*Disembedding* has important consequences for a range of economic, political and cultural relationships, particularly in the context of what **Scholte** (2000) terms:

**Deterritorialisation** or **supraterritoriality** – something he relates to the argument that 'globalization entails a reconfiguration of geography, so that social space is no longer wholly mapped in terms of territorial places, territorial distances and territorial borders'. In other words, social interactions are no longer limited by notions of 'territory' (places that are fixed in time and space), an example here being the internet as a place where social interaction occurs in *indeterminate space*.

In addition, *deterritorialisation* also refers to the idea that *political and cultural identities* are no longer necessarily and intimately tied to physical spaces (such as towns, counties and whole countries); for example, one can be a Muslim in a Christian country or a British citizen permanently living in Spain. It also refers to the fact that, economically, capitalist forms of production, distribution and exchange (both manufacturing and services) operate on a global scale, cutting across national and international borders.

For **Scholte**, the significant point here is that the spread of 'supraterritorial connections' between societies, cultures and individuals 'brings to an end … "territorialism", a situation where social geography is entirely territorial. Although … territory still matters very much in our globalizing world, it no longer constitutes the whole of our geography'.

## Growing it yourself: Embedded identities?

One way to think about embedding and disembedding is to link them to ideas about national identities:

- In small groups, decide how we can define 'national identity' (what, for example, are the cultural characteristics/indicators of this concept?).

- Identify the ways *your* national identity is embedded in notions of a territory (for example, does where you are born determine your national identity, and, if so, in what ways?).

- Have notions of national identity in contemporary societies become disembedded from ideas about territory, and, if so, in what ways?

A further aspect here, according to **Giddens** (1990), is 'the intensification of worldwide social relations which link distant localities in such a way that local happenings are shaped by events occurring many miles away and vice versa' – in other words, the processes of *disembedding* and *deterritorialisation* connect both nations and individuals in new and important ways; events on one side of the world can have significant – and unforeseen – consequences on the other side of the world. We can see this in terms of two examples: the *tsunami* that struck Indonesia on Boxing Day 2004 was an event that attracted worldwide publicity and aid – a local event with a global economic, political and cultural significance – and in 2005 the price of oil in the West reached an all-time high, partly as a result of increased consumption in newly industrialising societies such as China.

## ✳ SYNOPTIC LINK

**Theory and methods:** The idea of global connectedness – and even relatively small events in one part of the globe triggering much larger events elsewhere in the world – is reflected in **Lorenz's** (1972) discussion of the 'butterfly effect' in the section on the nature of science.

 ## Preparing the ground: Cultural, political and economic interrelationships

We can start to apply ideas about the impact of globalisation by identifying some of the economic, political and cultural inter-relationships between societies.

### Economic interrelationships

These are based around the idea of:
**Trade**, involving the *production*, *distribution* and *exchange* of goods and services focused around manufacturing, financial services and, increasingly, knowledge industries.

A further dimension to the inter-relationship between developed and undeveloped countries is:

**Aid**, something that may take a variety of economic forms, from loans, through development grants, to providing goods and services, and so forth.

We can outline how the general process of globalisation has impacted on – and in many respects *changed* – the nature and extent of economic interrelationships in terms of:

**Mobility**, where we can note the increasingly global nature of stock markets and trading blocs – both *capital mobility* (companies and investments moving into and out of different countries as profitability and economic policy dictates) and *labour mobility* represent significant developments in economic interrelationships.

**Transnational corporations** are companies that, while *based* in a specific territory (such as Britain or the USA), *operate* in a range of countries and markets across national borders. Although TNCs are a feature of *modern society* (first established in countries like the USA in the nineteenth century), **Smith** and **Doyle** (2002) suggest that globalisation has increased their power and status in world economic terms.

## ✳ SYNOPTIC LINK

**Stratification and differentiation:** Examples of economic globalisation involving TNCs are outlined in the section dealing with reasons for *changes in the class structure* – **Nike**, for example, 'is a global company that designs and markets footwear – but it owns no production facilities; rather, it contracts out the production of footwear across the world to smaller companies'.

**Economic trading blocs**, such as the European Union or the North and South American Trading Alliance, represent a further example of the economic inter-connections between societies. In these instances, nation states develop political agreements and alliances that involve things like preferential trading privileges for member nations.

The development of the internet has complicated the nature of economic inter-relationships in the sense that an increasing amount of economic activity takes place in:

**Virtual trading communities**: That is, communities that have no physical contact, as such, but which are connected in cyberspace. These economic networks involve the distribution and exchange of *physical products* (such as books and electrical goods in the case of **Amazon**, the world's largest online company), *financial products*, *services* and *knowledge*. The implications for the future development of virtual trading communities are enormous, given the ability for companies (both large and small) to tap into a potentially global audience and market for their goods and services.

For example, one implication is the breakdown (through the types of globalising processes we have already noted – distanciation, compression, disembedding and deterritorialisation) of distinctions between the local, national, international and global. We've seen, for example, how the process of:

**Disembedding** is both encouraged and accelerated by globalisation in areas like economic *exchange* (the development of credit cards, smart cards and the like). However, disembedding also occurs in terms of economic production and distribution. In highly developed countries, there has been a progressive *decline* in manufacturing – both *primary industrial production* (the extraction of raw materials like coal) and *secondary production* (things like car manufacture and shipbuilding, etc) and a consequent rise in service industries (such as finance and banking) and, in recent times, knowledge industries (such as computing). The production of goods hasn't stopped, of course

(people still want to buy these things); rather, manufacturing has shifted to less developed countries.

## ✳ SYNOPTIC LINK

**Stratification and differentiation:** Changes in global economic relationships can be related to changes in the class structure in modern societies.

## Political interrelationships

These conventionally operate between nation states in terms of ideas like:

**Trade**: The development of transnational trading blocs (in North/South America, Asia and Europe, for example) involves some measure of political interrelationship. In the case of Europe, *economic* inter-relationships have developed alongside a range of *political* interrelationships – the European Union has an elected parliament, bureaucratic structure and single European currency (although member countries may opt out of specific parts of political agreements – the UK, for example, is not currently part of the single European currency).

On a global level, world trade agreements relating to the movement of goods, access to markets and the like provide some form of regulatory framework for economic activity. In some instances, these agreements override national law (as in the case of the European Union, for example, and the provision for the free movement of labour across national boundaries).

**International law**: Political relationships between societies also exist at the legal level, not just in terms of trade agreements (which can be legally enforced and tested), but also in terms of areas like extradition treaties, cross-border policing (in the European Union, for example), membership of the United Nations and the like.

**Military**: How different countries relate to one another in military terms (through cooperation or antagonism, for example) also represents a political dimension to the interrelationship between societies.

## Cultural interrelationships

On this level we can note how general cultural interrelationships are related to:
**Economic** relationships that in some ways inform cultural connections and relationships, especially if we think about *culture industries* like television, film and print. In these areas reference is often made to the:

**Cultural hegemony** of Western society (and the USA in particular, post-Second World War, in the sense of the various ways this powerful country's cultural exports are received across the globe). Language is another area of cultural interrelationship, especially in terms of English representing a 'common cultural language' in many parts of the world.

### Weeding the path

**Held et al.** (1999) note that simply because we can identify instances of one society (such as the USA) being dominant in the production and distribution of cultural products doesn't necessarily mean it is possible to 'read off in any simple way the impact of those sales on other cultures and identities'. However, we can think about how cultural relationships are changed (or

not, as the case may be) through the coming together of different cultural products, considered in terms of both:

- **material culture** – exposure to a range of cultural objects (such as food and clothing), and
- **non-material culture** – the ideas and meanings embodied in cultural objects (the various ways our experience of different cultural products changes both the way we live and, to some extent, our perception of other cultures).

We can consider these ideas in terms of two concepts (*diversity* and *homogenisation*).

## Diversity

Cultural interrelationships relate to *cultural diversity* and *development* in, as **Lechner** (2001) notes, a range of ways:

- **Pluralisation**: Interactions between societies, through cultural products (such as film and television), the cultural influence of immigrants and the like can lead to the 'mixing of cultures in particular places and practices' – to create:
- **Cultural hybrids** – something new develops as the result of the meeting and mixing of different cultural ideas and behaviours.

For example, chicken tikka masala, according to the Food Service Intelligence (2001), is the most popular dish in the UK: 'Said to have originated between the 1950s and 1970s … Legend has it one obstinate diner demanded gravy on tandoori chicken. A bemused chef responded by adding tomato soup and a pinch of spices, unwittingly partaking in an early example of *fusion cookery*.'

Chicken tikka masala

## The potting shed

Chicken tikka masala (CTM) is an example of a *cultural hybrid*. Identify and briefly explain two further examples of cultural hybrids in the UK.

- **Contestation**, whereby the 'spread of ideas and images provoke reactions and resistance' within and between different cultural groups.

- **Glocalisation** (*sic*) – the meaning and impact of *global* cultural products (such as Hollywood films or McDonald's restaurants) are interpreted and used differently in different *local* contexts. In India, for example, the traditional Hollywood musical has been reinterpreted to produce a new form ('Bollywood') specific to Indian culture.

- **Institutionalisation** operates on two levels. First, the cultural products of one society are accepted and incorporated wholesale – and largely unchanged – into the culture of another society. Second, the idea of cultural diversity itself – as something to be valued and encouraged – is 'promoted through international organizations, movements and nation states' (**Lechner**, 2001).

## Homogenisation

**Lechner** cites a number of ways diversity can be *diminished*:

**Lifestyles**: The global reach of transnational corporations (such as Coca-Cola) creates a particular kind of 'consumerist culture, in which standard commodities are promoted by global marketing campaigns' to 'create similar lifestyles' – a form of *cultural hegemony* that **Lechner** calls 'Coca-Colonisation' (the idea that one culture is *colonised* by the cultural products and lifestyle of anther culture). A related example is **Ritzer**'s (1996) concept of:

**McDonaldisation**: This represents the idea that contemporary corporate cultural products are *standardised*, *homogenised* and *formulaic*; everyone who buys a McDonald's hamburger, whether in London or Singapore, gets the same basic product made to the same standard formula. When this idea is applied to cultural relationships and experiences, the argument is that homogenisation occurs because *global cultural products* are designed:

- **efficiently**, using a limited range of themes around which products are created and recreated

- **rationally** – all aspects of the production

and consumption process are measured and evaluated to produce standard products in standard settings

- **predictably** – cultural products are designed to be safe and unthreatening: there is, to use **Beck**'s (1992) idea, 'no *risk*' involved in buying and consuming a particular product – the consumer knows exactly what to expect *before* they buy it.

The consumption of cultural products is also related to:

**Identity** – the things we consume 'say something' about us and our status. If this is valid then corporations may be able to key into – or possibly create – *consumer identities* and *brand loyalties* that both increase profitability and homogenise cultural behaviours within and between societies.

**Bryman** (1999) suggests this idea involves the:

**'Disneyisation'** of cultural relationships, encompassing things like:

- **Theming** – the creation of 'consumption experiences' whereby people buy in to a general, standardised lifestyle.
- **De-differentiation** where consumers are locked in to a range of related products in ways that provide a seamless 'lifestyle experience' (a particular perfume, for example, is associated with a particular lifestyle, clothing, footwear and the like) – something closely related to:
- **Merchandising** – by consuming cultural products people take 'themed lifestyles' into their homes and social groups.

## Discussion point: Homogeneity or diversity?

In small groups, using the following table as a template, choose a category, such as film (or add your own), and identify any common cultural products for your age group that you think conform to the idea of McDonaldisation and/or Disneyfication. Once you've done this, repeat the process – but this time identify cultural products that *don't* conform to McDonaldisation and/or Disneyfication.

|  | Television | Music | Film | Magazines |
|---|---|---|---|---|
| **McDonaldisation** | **Cartoons** | **Pop** [bands are manufactured to appeal to a certain age and gender group] | **Romantic comedies** [follow standard themes and developments] | Heat FHM |
| **Disneyfication** |  |  |  |  |

- **Cultural imperialism**: a situation where a particular culture or lifestyle is held up as the ideal to which other cultures should aspire. Western lifestyles, values, customs and traditions, for example, may be introduced into non-Western societies and thus destroy traditional cultural lifestyles.

## Weeding the path

Questions of cultural diversity and/or homogenisation frequently turn on:

- **Definitions**: 'Diversity', for example, is difficult to operationalise for a couple of reasons. First, its meaning is not simple and straightforward (how different does something have to be to count as diversity, for example), and, second, diversity (like homogenisation) is not necessarily an *either/or* condition (*either* cultural diversity exists *or* it doesn't). It is possible for diversity to exist in some cultural relationships whereas others show the opposite – high levels of cultural homogenisation. In other words, diversity and homogenisation can *coexist* in the same *cultural space*.

- **Cultural homogenisation** – while we should not underestimate how global companies (like McDonald's) influence cultural development, we shouldn't *overstate* their influence. While McDonald's may have restaurants across the world, it doesn't necessarily follow that 'all cultures are converging' – mainly because *cultural production* and *reproduction* don't work in a simple *behaviourist* way (if we consume similar, standardised, cultural products we consequently become identical

consumers). Cultural development can be both *filtered* and *changed* by the social contexts within which products are used by people in different situations.

Thus, although we might find instances of *cultural homogenisation* in different towns and cities across the world (as **Peace**, 2005 puts it, 'If for instance, one was to find oneself in a high street in Sydney, Kuala Lumpur, Rio or Johannesburg we would find the same shops, selling the same products accompanied by the same background music'), we also find *diversity* in the same places – not just in the range of different shops, but also in terms of different products.

## Digging deeper: Cultural, political and economic interrelationships

We can develop ideas about economic, political and cultural interrelationships by thinking about how these have been – or are potentially – changed by globalisation.

### Economic interrelationships

**Sporer** (2000) suggests, 'Globalisation is the latest stage in the permanent process of social change that started as industrialisation and modernisation in Europe but now is spreading globally', and that, in economic terms, it 'involves the process of converting separate national economies into an integrated world economy'. We can, in this respect, follow **McMichael**'s (2004) lead by noting the idea of:

**Global commodity chains**: In an increasingly globalised economic system, networks of production, distribution and exchange are linked across national boundaries, and individual producers and consumers become locked into a global chain of economic events. The significance of this idea is not simply the various linkages involved (since trade across national boundaries can hardly be considered new), but the *network* of economic relationships that creates both:

- **Hierarchies** – whereby highly developed countries sit atop the global commodity chain, exploiting the fact that clothes or electrical goods can be manufactured using relatively cheap labour in developing countries, and

- **Dependencies**: Unequal economic relationships create a network of dependencies that is difficult to break – developing countries become a source of relatively cheap production whereas developed countries come to depend, in some respects, on the flow of (cheap) goods to maintain certain living standards. The nature of global networks, complexities and dependencies is illustrated, **McMichael** argues, by the fact that 'the Japanese eat poultry fattened in Thailand with American corn, using chopsticks made with wood from Indonesian or Chilean forests. Canadians eat strawberries grown in Mexico with American fertiliser ... The British and French eat green beans from Kenya, and cocoa from Ghana finds its way into Swiss chocolate'.

In this respect, **Held et al.** (1999) pinpoint three areas of economic globalisation and interrelationships:

- **Global trade**, involving the 'globalization of production', whereby products can be sourced from different places and assembled in whatever country is able or willing to offer the most advantageous political and/or economic incentives.

- **Global finance**: The flow of global production and distribution requires an extensive network of financial arrangements whereby capital can be moved around quickly and easily. The development of global financial institutions (such as banks) is, like international trade, not a particularly new phenomenon, but the ease and speed by which money can be moved, tracked and managed have been increased by the development of computer technology and global networks. In addition, money has itself become a commodity traded on global markets as investors (and speculators) execute deals across global networks.

## Weeding the path

The ability to speculate on the behaviour of stocks and shares is a form of gambling, albeit on a potentially massive scale. In 1995, for example, **Nick Leeson**, a 28-year-old stock market trader for Barings Bank, lost nearly £1 *billion* of his employer's money in failed share dealings. When Barings was declared insolvent, 1200 people lost their jobs and **Leeson** served four years in prison.

- **Global products**: The opening up of *global marketplaces* means companies best positioned to take advantage of such developments (transnational corporations in particular) can sell products on a world stage. Corporations not only have access to markets and populations in different countries, they can also, as **Yip** (1995)

**Nick Leeson being extradited to Singapore, where he was jailed for deception**

argues, sell the *same product* (such as a car, computer game or film) across the globe with little or no alteration to the basic product.

## ✳ SYNOPTIC LINK

**Stratification and differentiation:** Ideas about global economic interrelationships link into ideas about global Fordism and flexible specialisation. Transnational corporations are also discussed in terms of modular consortiums and agile corporations.

Although business corporations have operated around the world since the nineteenth century, **Castells** (1997) argues that the way they operate 'in a global context' has changed – a new *form* of capitalism has developed, one related to older forms of capitalism, but sufficiently different to be considered in its own right. The key features of *globalised capitalism* are:

**Information** and **knowledge**: Whereas older forms of capitalism focused on the production of *things*, newer forms focus on knowledge, information and systems. This isn't to say that companies no longer produce things (like cars) or that information wasn't significant in the past; rather, what we are seeing is a:

**Reordering** of economic production, with information being the *primary* product – something made possible by computer networks that traverse the globe ('connectivity'). As **Smith** and **Doyle** (2002) put it, for developed societies 'the balance between knowledge and resources has shifted so far towards the former that knowledge has become perhaps the most important factor determining living standards ... Today's most technologically advanced economies are truly knowledge-based'.

## ⚠ Weeding the path

Although there's an agreement that *something* is changing in terms of global economic inter-relationships, not everyone agrees about what these changes *involve*. In basic terms, therefore, we can note three *general positions* in relation to *economic globalisation*:

- **Full** involves the changes we've just outlined, with globalisation considered the motor for a new phase of capitalist economic production, distribution and exchange (one with major consequences for the way economic interrelationships are formed and maintained).

- **Partial** or regional globalisation. The world, according to **Thompson** (2000), is divided into three major *regional economic blocs* (North and Central America, Europe and Asia), within which the processes we've described may be taking place. However, each of these regional blocs is effectively *closed* to competition from the other – apart from a handful of global companies (although **Veseth** (1998) argues that **Nike** was the only truly global corporation in the twentieth century), most TNCs and nations trade predominantly and substantially within each bloc.

- **Mythical**: **Rugman** and **Hodgetts** (2000) note economic globalisation, as we've discussed, is often defined by 'the production and distribution of products and services of a homogeneous type and quality on a worldwide basis'. This, they argue, sees globalisation portrayed as encouraging the 'dominance of international business by giant, multinational enterprises (MNEs) selling uniform products from Cairo, Illinois to Cairo, Egypt and from Lima, Ohio to Lima, Peru'. **Rugman** (2001), however, argues that such economic globalisation is 'misunderstood – it does not, and has never, existed in terms of a single world market with free trade'.

His argument, backed by a range of *empirical data* relating to where and how businesses conduct international trade, both reinforces **Thompson**'s argument and expands it by arguing that attempting to trade in 'globalised markets' does not make economic sense even for transnational corporations.

## Political interrelationships

One of the main themes of globalisation theory, as **Sporer** (2000) notes, is the idea of the 'loss of power and authority of nation states', something echoed by **Smith** and **Doyle** (2002) when they note 'a decline in the power of national governments to direct and influence their economies'. This change

in the way nation states relate to one another has a number of significant features:

- **Economic**: The globalisation of trade (whether in terms of regional blocs or world systems) removes from national governments the ability to control major areas of economic policy in areas like:
  - **Employment**, where nations experience rising or declining levels of employment depending on how capital, labour and jobs move across national borders.
  - **Taxation** policies relating to businesses, especially transnational corporations. If business taxation is too high, 'capital flight' may occur – TNCs, for example, choose to locate and invest elsewhere. TNCs can also export profits, making it difficult for national governments to track what profit is being made and where.
  - **Investment**: In a global economic climate, where TNCs can potentially locate and relocate factories and businesses in the most favourable economic areas, there is increased pressure on governments to provide environments and packages to attract corporate investment.
- **Political**: Involvement in regional economic and political institutions (such as the European Union) further limits the decision-making powers of national governments, mainly because decisions are conditioned by things like international:
  - **agreements**, binding on member states and relating to areas like trading arrangements, levels of national debt, and so forth

- **laws** relating to, for example, the free movement of labour across national borders.

## 🏠 The potting shed

Identify and briefly explain one benefit and one drawback of the free movement of labour for the member states of the EU.

## ⚠ Weeding the path

Those who argue that economies are locked into a global financial system that limits the ability of national governments to act are conventionally seen as advocating:

**Hyper-globalisation**: **Reich** (1991) suggests that globalisation has created a world political, economic and cultural web that, as **Veseth** (1998) puts it, connects ' ... people and businesses without much attention to geography, government regulation, or anything else. High-tech, knowledge-intensive connections to the global web are the source of wealth and power in Reich's world and a sort of global class system arises that is based on access to the web, much as an industrial class system based on access to capital appeared to Karl Marx'.

National governments, from this position, are 'secondary players' on the world stage – if they have a role at all. **Ohmae** (1995) suggests: 'The modern nation-state itself – that artefact of the eighteenth and nineteenth centuries – has begun to crumble.'

The demise of the nation state (imminent or otherwise) has, some argue, been overstated. **Gray** (2002) is sceptical about the idea that globalisation involves 'the world becoming a true single market, in which nation-states have withered away ... supplanted by homeless multinational corporations'; he sees this – as do **Hirst** and **Thompson** (1996) when they refer to 'the political impact of 'globalization' as 'the pathology of over-diminished expectations' – as ideological wishful thinking on the part of, in the main:

**New Right/neoliberal** theorists who argue, in broad terms, that *development* is related to the presence or absence of free economic markets. In other words, for countries to maintain their developed status they must adjust, politically, to the new demands of a globalised economy, while developing nations must be opened up to the economic benefits of free market economies. In this respect, the private sector is considered the motor of development – the way to achieve economic growth is through the adoption of free-market policies and initiatives that include things like private ownership of businesses, educational and welfare provision and the like. In these terms, a lack of development is caused by, among other things:

- **corrupt government** and political leadership in developing countries
- **government** economic intervention and ownership
- **state**-controlled/financed welfare systems.

**Capitán** and **Lambie** (1994) summarise neo-liberal development theories in terms of:

- **economic inequality** 'as an important human incentive'

# Growing it yourself: Roles and relationships

In small groups, identify and briefly explain examples of political roles and inter-relationships that exist between modern states in the twenty-first century.

| Role | Examples |
| --- | --- |
| **Military** | Anti-terrorism? |
| **Economic** | Agreements/trading blocs |
| **Environmental** | Kyoto Agreement |
| **Development** | Aid |

- **non-intervention** by the state in economic markets 'will maximise efficiency and economic well-being'
- **international trade** between developed and developing countries is 'mutually beneficial'
- **a minimalist state** (in terms of welfare etc.).

## ✳ SYNOPTIC LINK

**Crime and deviance:** The basic theory behind New Right development thinking (rational choice, cost-benefit analyses and the like) can be applied to an understanding of crime.

Although *hyper-globalising* tendencies may, as **Veseth** (1998) argues, be over-exaggerated, this is not to say global economic developments have had no impact on political interrelationships; **Hirst** and **Thompson** (1996) suggest we should see nations as:

**Pivotal institutions** in terms of creating the stable political conditions under which trade and international development can continue. **Shaw** (1997), in this respect, argues we should not see nation states as being 'in opposition' to globalisation, since 'globalisation does not undermine the state but involves the transformation of state forms'.

The main problem here, therefore, is one of interpretation – where nation states play an international role (such as Britain and the USA's military involvement in countries like Iraq), do we interpret this as a changing and expanding set of political interrelationships between societies or merely the dying attempts of nation states to exert political influence in a globalised world?

## Cultural interrelationships

Globalisation, as we've suggested, is frequently considered at the *economic level*, in terms of things like the growth in world trade, the development of transnational corporations and their respective impact on nations and political/cultural inter-relationships. However, if economic and political forms of globalisation are, at best, unsubstantiated and, at worst, as **Rugman** (2001) argues, *mythical*, cultural inter-relationships promise more fruitful ground for globalisation theorists, for a couple of reasons:

- **Cultural products** (such as films, radio and television) are not necessarily physical commodities – they can, for example, be easily transmitted across physical boundaries. This is not necessarily the case, of course, but digital cultural products are increasingly packaged and sold in this way.

- **The internet** is a potentially global medium for the transmission of digital products (although satellite and cable are also significant carriers of digital information).

**Sklair** (1999) suggests the study of cultural interrelationships, focused around the global spread of the *mass media*, is an important area for globalisation theorists because of the ability to *empirically* demonstrate something like the 'global diffusion and increasingly concentrated ownership and control of the electronic mass media, particularly television'. **Sklair** notes that even in relatively poor countries there has been a huge and rapid growth in television (and the cultural products/ideas it carries).

Cultural products, in this respect, have both substantial economic value and political content – an idea we can briefly note in terms of:

**Cultural imperialism**: One argument about the relationship between politics and culture is that when we talk about something like the *globalisation of culture*, what we are actually talking about is the globalisation of *American* culture – the widespread export of US products, values and ideas around the globe. **Rice-Oxley** (2004) argues: 'America exports its culture on an unprecedented scale. From music to media, film to fast food, language to literature and sport, the American idea is spreading inexorably . . . today's technology flings culture to every corner of the globe with blinding speed. If it took two millenniums for Plato's *Republic* to reach North America, the latest hit from Justin Timberlake can be found in Greek (and Japanese) stores within days' (something that reflects back to our discussion of *cultural homogenisation*).

### Weeding the path

One problem with notions of cultural imperialism and homogenisation is that the influence is assumed to be one-way – from the producer to the consumer. This model of *cultural domination* can be questioned on two levels:

- **Consumption**: Cultural consumers are assumed to accept passively whatever cultural influences are thrown their way, but consumers may, for example, actively interpret cultural influences, customising and filtering them through their own lives and lifestyles to create new, hybrid cultural forms.

- **Production**: Technological developments like the internet are changing the way people relate to cultural influences in the sense that opportunities arise for *cultural production* as well as for consumption (the producer *is* the consumer and vice versa). This occurs in areas like chat rooms, blogs and the development of modifications ('*modding*') to computer games as well as through the exchange and sharing of online information (through photo albums, for example).

Although anecdotal evidence suggests some form of cultural homogenisation is at work (think, for example, about how American words and language use have found their way into everyday British language), there is little *empirical evidence* to support this argument. Even in the UK, where a common language arguably lowers the barriers to US cultural influence, it is debatable whether British culture – even among the young – is overly similar to US cultures. There is also the question here of whether we can simply assume American cultural influences are homogeneous in themselves – the USA is, for example, a large, culturally diverse society.

Finally, we can note that in terms of cultural interrelationships, the ideas we've outlined suggest that tensions exist between two areas:

- **the local** or **particular** – characterised as showing high levels of cultural diversity, and

- **the global** or **universal**, characterised in terms of its homogeneity.

While we've suggested the two can be separated, at least in theoretical terms, we've also suggested there are points and spaces where the local and global meet, and **Robertson** (1992) expresses this in terms of a:

**Dialectical relationship** (which involves thinking about how both the local and the global interact – each both *influences* and is *influenced* by the other). In this respect, as **Sklair** (1999) suggests, globalisation at the cultural level involves understanding two processes:

- **The particularisation of universalism** – the idea that some forms of globalised cultural features are adapted and changed by particular (local) cultural behaviours (customised and changed for local consumption, for example).

- **The universalisation of particularism** – the idea that the features of local cultures (their uniqueness, individuality, and so forth) become a feature of globalised cultures. That is, rather than seeing the globalisation of culture as a homogenising process, we should see it in reverse –

## Discussion point: Americanisation?

Thinking about your particular age group, identify some ways youth cultures have:

1 been influenced by American culture (think about music, fashion and the like)

2 adapted these cultural influences to produce new and different forms of culture.

As a class, discuss the extent to which you believe UK youth cultures are characterised by:

- cultural homogenisation

- cultural diversity.

globalisation involves the spread of diverse cultural beliefs and practices across the globe in ways that create new and diverse cultural forms.

**Appadurai** (1990) rejects the idea that cultural interrelationships flow 'from the core to the periphery' (globalised, homogeneous, cultural forms are picked up by individual cultures). Rather, we should see these interrelationships in terms of a variety of 'scapes' – imagined worlds that cut across territorial borders that can be connected in a variety of (electronic) ways:

- **Ethnoscapes** that reflect the way people of different cultures physically interact.

- **Technoscapes** that relate to the way different forms of technology (and its cultural adaptations and uses) interact.

- **Finanscapes** that refer to the interplay of economic relationships and their effect on political and social cultures.

- **Mediascapes** involving the flow of information across different societies and cultures.

- **Ideoscapes** that refer to the way people interact in terms of the exchange of images and ideas.

In this way, he argues, local cultural concepts spread across national boundaries, both influencing and being influenced by the cultural ideas and relationships they encounter.

## Moving on

Thus far we've looked at development and its associated processes – such as industrialisation and urbanisation – in fairly general terms. In the next section, however, we can look more specifically at the development process in terms of strategic factors like the respective roles of aid, trade, corporations and international agencies.

# 4. The role of aid, trade, transnational corporations and international agencies in different strategies for development

As we've seen, industrialisation brings both potential *benefits* (in the shape of improved living standards) and potential *drawbacks* (in terms of environmental damage and destruction), and, despite the arguments involved, it is still arguably seen as the main way for societies to develop in the modern world. With this in mind, therefore, we can examine some of the main strategic routes to development currently in play around the world.

## ⚠ Preparing the ground: The role of aid

Before we examine the role of aid in the development process we need to think about how it is:

**Defined** – and we can follow the **OECD** (1995) lead by considering it in terms of:

- **Development assistance**, given to promote 'economic development *and* social welfare', involving:

  - **Grants** (non-repayable).

  - **Loans** (repayable) – although to count as *aid*, loans must have *favourable interest rates* (lower than the going market rate, for example) and must also have a *grant* element – the norm is around 25% of the loan given as a grant, and

- **Non-monetary** assistance such as technological and military help, advice and training.

- **Development finance**, or aid in the form of *credit*, guaranteed by a developed nation, through which developing nations can establish trading links.

**Types of aid** can, for the sake of theoretical clarity, be divided into two broad categories (*public* and *private*).

## Public

**Public (official)** development assistance takes two main forms (direct or *bilateral* and indirect or *multilateral*).

**Bilateral (direct) aid** is given by one government to another, and its main purpose, as the American **Congressional Budget Office** (1997) puts it, is 'to encourage equitable and sustainable economic growth in developing countries'. The concept of *sustainable growth* is significant because it reflects the idea that *economic aid* should be directed towards the specific development needs of the receiving country in a way that will, in the long term, lead to the development of self-sustaining economic growth.

Other forms of aid, however, may have different objectives.

**Military** assistance, for example, can take a couple of basic forms:

- **Economic** – the provision of loans, grants and credit agreements – enables a developing country to purchase military hardware (from the country providing the assistance).

- **Political** – ranges from things like providing military advisors and trainers to a physical military presence in the developing country.

**Humanitarian** assistance includes:

- **Donations** made by a government for the alleviation of suffering (caused by war or natural disaster), usually – but not necessarily – in a developing country (many European governments, for example, offered humanitarian assistance to the USA following Hurricane Katrina in 2005 – the picture used in the *Warm-up* exercise was actually taken in New Orleans).

- **Physical aid** (food, clothing and the like) provided either directly or through non-governmental organisations such as charities.

## Weeding the path

Some forms of aid are called *tied aid* because *conditions* are attached by the donor country.

**Tied by source**, for example, means the aid can be used only to purchase specified goods and/or services from the donor country, while:

**Tied by project** means assistance can be used only for a specific purpose (such as the building of a road or hospital). Further conditions, such as the use of contractors from the donor country, may also be attached to this type of aid. **Boseley** (2006) cites a slightly different example when she notes how the USA has, since 2001, tied aid to a requirement that 'any organisation applying for US funds sign an undertaking not to counsel women on abortion – other than advising against it – or provide abortion services'.

## The potting shed

Identify and briefly explain one advantage and/or one disadvantage of tied aid to *both* the donor and receiving country.

**Multilateral (indirect) aid** involves assistance channelled to receiver countries through international agencies, such as:

**The International Monetary Fund** (IMF) and the:

**The World Bank**, both established in 1944. These are economic agencies whose primary development role is to lend money

at *concessional rates* to low-income countries (and at non-concessional rates to middle-income countries that find it difficult to raise loans in private markets). Certain political and economic conditions have to be met by the receiving country before assistance is given, and although these differ depending on specific circumstances, **Greenhill** (2004) argues: 'The World Bank is still lending money to developing country governments on condition they adopt specific economic policies such as *privatisation*' (whereby private companies must be allowed to develop/run industries like water, gas and electricity generation and supply).

**The United Nations**, through, for example, the *Development Programme*, currently (2006) operates in 166 countries, to 'help develop the capacities required to achieve the *Millennium Development Goals* (MDGs)'; these, **Clemens et al.** (2004) note, represent 'a set of quantitative, time-bound targets' (as agreed by the United Nations General Assembly in 2000), for every country to attain by 2015.

## Weeding the path

Although **Clemens et al.** doubt the Millennium Development Goals (MDGs) will be attained by every country by 2015, they argue that 'development progress has been occurring at unprecedented levels over the past thirty or more years ... halving the number of people living in poverty will probably be met globally, but for most developing countries to achieve this at the national level, the growth rates required are at the bounds of historical precedent'.

In 1970 the major developed nations committed themselves to a target of contributing 0.7% of gross national income

# Discussion point: The Millennium Development Goals

The eight targets (with an illustrative indicator included by way of example) are listed below.

How many of these targets have already been met by the UK?

| Target | Key indicator |
|---|---|
| 1. Eradicate extreme poverty and hunger | 1. Halve the number of people living on less than 60p a day |
| 2. Universal primary education | 2. Both boys and girls to complete primary school |
| 3. Promote gender equality | 3. End discrimination in primary and secondary schooling |
| 4. Reduce child mortality | 4. Reduce child mortality by two-thirds |
| 5. Improve maternal health | 5. Reduce by 75% the number of women who die in childbirth |
| 6. Combat HIV, malaria and other diseases | 6. Halt and begin to reverse the spread of HIV |
| 7. Ensure environmental sustainability | 7. Halve the number without access to safe drinking water |
| 8. Development as a global partnership | 8. Develop a fair and open trading system, providing debt relief or working for democracy |

to official development assistance. However, the number regularly meeting this target is small (only Netherlands and Luxemburg achieved it in 2003). None of the largest world economies had achieved this target by 2006.

## Private

**Private (or unofficial) development assistance** is mainly related to NGOs – charities like Oxfam, the Red Cross and Red Crescent, *Médecins sans Frontières*, and so forth. The assistance provided to developing countries ranges from specific, targeted project work to acting as channels for both government and privately donated humanitarian aid.

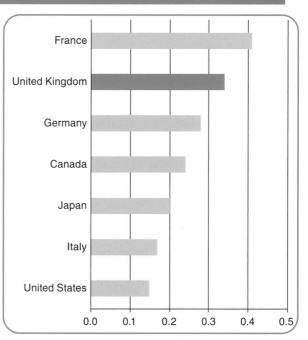

Official Development Assistance: % of GNI, 2003
(Source: *Social Trends* 35, 2005)

## Digging deeper: The purpose of aid

The broad categories of aid we've outlined only scratch the surface in terms of the range of types and forms of development and humanitarian assistance available. They are, however, sufficient for our general needs since we're more concerned with thinking about the general *purpose* of aid. In this respect we can outline some arguments about the nature of development assistance, while simultaneously relating these, where necessary, to the types of development theory we encountered in the first section. Thus, in general terms, aid may represent a crucial element for:

**Modernisation theorists** in helping developing societies achieve 'take-off'. Similarly, for:

**Structural change** theorists, carefully targeted economic aid may represent an important way for developing societies to stimulate the industrialisation process, allowing such societies to make the transition from agricultural to industrial society. For:

**World system** perspectives aid may provide one of the ways *periphery* and *semi-peripheral* societies develop their industrial and knowledge base in order to play a part in the overall development of global economic markets.

More generally, if the overall objective is to encourage developing countries to industrialise (and, in the long run, to reduce their dependence on developed countries), aid represents a way of 'easing the pain' of rapid industrialisation, while also bringing developing countries into the overall world political infrastructure – for example, aid gives donor countries a certain level of political leverage that can be used to ensure environmental targets are met. Some further arguments in favour of aid include:

- **Reconstruction**: American aid played a significant part in the post-Second World War reconstruction of Europe (under the *Marshall Plan*).

- **Disease**: Aid has contributed to both the reduction of polio and the eradication of smallpox.

- **Humanitarian aid**, in areas like Africa and South East Asia, has lessened the effects of *natural disasters*. In recent years, NGOs have also worked towards reducing the impact of drought and famine by helping indigenous populations to improve their farming methods and sanitation, increase their overall levels of education and the like.

**Public development** is also instrumental in helping to develop economic infrastructures (sanitation, waste disposal, and so on) in situations where private companies are unwilling to intervene because opportunities for profit are limited.

While these are significant ideas – and key to *official* rationales and objectives of development aid put forward by donor countries – not everyone sees aid as either unequivocally beneficial to the recipient or necessarily *altruistic* on behalf of the donor. In this respect, criticism of aid programmes falls into three main categories (*exploitation*, *inefficiency* and *ineffectiveness*).

## Exploitation

*Dependency theorists* argue development assistance contributes to the:

- **Client status** of receiving states: Developing nations can be locked into a cycle of economic development that serves to benefit companies from the donor country – as the **US Agency for International Development** (2005) puts it: 'The principal beneficiary of America's foreign assistance programs has always been the United States … 80% of Agency contracts and grants go directly to American firms.'

- **Ideological domination** of receiving states: According to the **Agency**, for example, 'US foreign assistance has always had the twofold purpose of furthering America's foreign policy interests in expanding democracy and free markets while improving the lives of the citizens of the developing world.' In this respect, US development objectives since 1961, according to the **US General Accounting Office** (2002), include things like:

  - integrating developing countries into the international (capitalist) economic system

  - assisting the development of the private sector in developing countries

  - using private and voluntary organisations to implement development activities

  - eliminating illicit narcotics production

  - demonstrating US ideas and practices in education and medicine.

## Inefficiency

*New Right/market liberal* approaches to development argue that 'trade rather than aid' represents the most efficient and cost-effective solution to the problems of development, dependency and industrialisation. Although some forms of (mainly humanitarian) aid may be useful, the only *long-term* development solution is incorporation into the global market economy. This involves, for example, transnational companies operating freely in developing countries to develop and exploit natural resources (such as coal, oil and gas), provide employment and develop indigenous economic infrastructures.

## Weeding the path

New Right approaches to aid mirror their general approach to welfare, education and heath in developed countries – private companies, rather than the state, should provide these services. **Looney** (2005), however, while noting *neoliberal theories* of aid and development were 'in vogue around 1990', argues this position is no longer the 'dominant global development paradigm', although he does suggest the US-led reconstruction of countries like Iraq and Afghanistan is based around neoliberal economic and political ideas about the role of both private companies and the state in reconstruction work.

## Ineffectiveness

The question here is whether aid is an effective way to promote political and economic development, not only in terms of achieving desired goals, but also in terms of whether aid actually creates more problems than it solves for the receiving society, relating to, for example:

- **Political environments**: **Collier** and **Dollar** (2002) argue the effectiveness of aid in stimulating economic growth is related to political environments and policies – developing nations that have, for example, stable political *superstructures*, benefit from aid, while those where the political situation is unstable do not.

## Weeding the path

This begs the question of whether aid could and should be used to assist the development of stable political structures in the first place. However, **Easterly et al.** (2003) found no significant empirical relationship 'between the amount of aid and economic growth of the recipient countries'. Similarly, **Clemens et al.** (2004) argue the relationship between aid and economic growth is empirically weak.

- **Waste**: Aid is sometimes used for schemes and activities that bring no long-term economic or cultural benefits – where, for example, the receiving country lacks the ability to develop projects once they have been completed. Building roads to develop communication systems has little or no benefit if a country doesn't have the capacity to maintain those roads.

- **Harm**: **Bauer** (1971) argues, from a *neoliberal perspective*, that where aid is given directly to governments a major historical outcome has been an increase in the political power of ruling elites, using aid to consolidate their power base through things like *patronage* and *corruption*.

## Discussion point: Ineffective aid?

Browne (2006) argues: 'Poor Africans are condemned to live in poverty so long as they and their governments are encouraged to blame the West for all their problems, rather than confronting the real causes of poor governance, corruption and poor education.'

Do you agree or disagree with this statement (and why)?

## Preparing the ground: The role of trade

All (Western) theories of development focus on the significance of trade as an integral aspect of the development process, usually in the context of a debate over *industrialisation* and its political, economic and cultural significance. Arguments surface, however, over the precise role of trade, the nature of trading relationships within and between nations and how these affect the development process – something further complicated by processes like 'globalised trading markets' and the changing relationship between trading partners.

We can begin to disentangle some of the complexities involved by focusing, initially, on the concept of:

**Sustainable development**: We can conceptualise this idea in terms of the objective of development being the promotion of long-term, self-sustaining, economic stability and progression, both in terms of developing nations and also in the wider global context of the relationship between developed and developing nations.

We can illustrate the role of trade as part of a strategy for *sustainable development* by outlining two opposed approaches: *neoliberal* (free market) and *state interventionist*.

## Neo-liberal approaches

These, as we've suggested, argue that the route to long-term sustainable development lies through free-market trading policies between nations, involving a number of fundamental principles:

**Trade liberalisation** involves opening national markets to international competition. This gives developing countries access to lucrative markets in the developed world and vice versa; corporations from the developed world gain access to markets and resources in the developing world. This, it is argued, brings significant benefits in terms of access to both capital investment and newer forms of technology.

**Protectionism**: If competition is the most effective way to encourage development (through things like the need to develop new and cost-effective ways of producing goods and providing services), the developed world must abandon protectionist policies (such as prohibitive tariffs on goods from developing nations and state subsidies to inefficient industries) and allow developing countries access to developed markets. In Europe, for example, the *Common Agricultural Policy*, which provides subsidies, guaranteed prices and markets for agricultural products, is seen as a barrier to trade liberalisation.

**Non-interventionist state**: The state ownership and control of businesses and industries distorts the workings of free markets by giving some companies an unfair competitive edge (through access to cheap loans and the like). Private companies, disciplined by the need to be competitive or face going out of business, are the essential motor of economic development.

**Light regulation**: Although the state plays a role in outlawing and policing unfair competitive practices, it should not over-regulate business behaviour. Instead, business discipline comes from the need to be competitive in free markets.

**Low taxation**: People should be allowed to keep as much as possible of their earned income and wealth since this provides both individual incentives and structural incentives for businesses to invest, innovate and the like.

## ⚠ Weeding the path

The free-market approach does have arguments in its favour, not the least being that China – a nation with the highest level of economic growth in the world over the past few years – has adopted a range of free-market initiatives. **Morrison** (2000) notes the gradual *privatisation* of many formerly state-owned enterprises (SOEs) – around one-third of industrial production remains state-owned in this communist country – and the development of 'private enterprise zones' with lower rates of business taxation, less stringent labour laws, and so on. Similarly, the relative success of the 'Asian Tiger' economies may be attributable to the adoption of free-market policies (although as **Borrego** (1995) argues, the role of *cultural factors*, such as religious values, is an alternative explanation). Critics of this approach, however, note that:

**Market restrictions** generally apply in developed countries (as well as between developing countries), and a range of protectionist policies exists even in countries like the USA.

**Free trade** policies tend to give developed nations and transnational corporations significant economic advantages; they use both their greater political influence and economic strength to overpower indigenous industrial development. Where TNCs have access to markets, resources and labour in developing countries, their behaviour may be exploitative rather than developmental.

**The state**: Governments have a role to play in ensuring the self-interested activities of businesses are regulated to limit their impact on the environment. Similarly, the ability to prohibit uncompetitive practices, corruption and the development of *cartels* (where a group of companies, for example, secretly agrees not to compete against each other to maintain high prices) are all areas where the state has a significant role.

## Interventionist approaches

These generally argue a *balance* between state involvement in economic activity and the behaviour of private corporations is *necessary* in the context of global economic activity. Action at government level is seen as the way the economic power of developed nations can be both *channelled* and *restricted* to provide a coherent development strategy that takes into account and balances the needs of all nations. As **Justino** (2001) puts it, a significant interventionist role of the state is as 'conflict manager'.

Interventionist approaches, like their free-market counterpart, also focus on the importance of:

**Trade**: The ability of developing nations to participate equally in a global trading system is the cornerstone of any development strategy, for two main reasons. First, international trade encourages the development of indigenous industry and sustained self-development; it represents the means through which the world's poorest countries can be weaned away from aid dependence. Second, trade represents a standard development model followed by the world's richest nations; it has, in other words, been shown to work as a development strategy.

## Weeding the path

Although these ideas have a basic similarity to their free-market counterparts (the significance of trade and the stigma of aid), the main *epistemological break* between the two approaches can be found in two areas:

- **The role of the state**: For interventionists, governments have a significant political and economic role to play in any development strategy, in areas like:

  - **Trade agreements** that give developing countries access to developed markets.

  - **Regulation** of economic activity to encourage competitive business practices.

  - **Aid** to encourage both economic diversity, by helping developing countries move away from monocultural production (over-dependence on the production of a single product like coffee or bananas that can make it vulnerable to price collapses on world markets), and the development of indigenous industries.

**Economic self-interest**: Nations start from different development points – something that makes it difficult for newly industrialising nations to gain a competitive foothold in established world markets, since developed nations have a certain self-interest in protecting their own markets and industries from the effects of international competition. This, for interventionists, makes the idea of 'free markets' in world trade something of an ideological illusion, since developed nations develop various (self-interested) ways to limit global competition (through trade agreements, economic quotas for goods from developing countries, taxation policies, subsidies, etc.).

Interventionist approaches argue, therefore, that international economic inequalities will not disappear without state intervention, both as a means of 'kick-starting' economic development and regulating the (potentially anti-competitive) activities of TNCs.

## ⚠ Weeding the path

*Dependency theorists* have been critical of free-market approaches in terms of the idea that it is possible (and desirable) to leave economic development (and, by implication, political and cultural development) to both the 'hidden hand' of market forces and the activities of large business corporations. As evidence of the problems created they point to various experiments in free-market liberalisations in South America in the 1990s – countries like Chile, Brazil and Argentina were encouraged to follow the neoliberal economic policies (popularly characterised as *monetarism*) of writers like **Friedman** (1962) and **von Hayek** (1973), with, dependency theorists argue,

problematic economic and social outcomes (in terms of development, poverty and social unrest).

Both free-market and interventionist polices may also, as **Short** (2001) notes, act more in the interests of developed countries and TNCs than those of developing nations: 'Trade liberalisation can harm the low-skilled and hit the poor disproportionately hard … and where privatization is undertaken it needs to be properly managed to ensure access of services to the poorest.'

## ⚠ Digging deeper: The role of trade

Although arguments surround the precise and most effective role of trade in global development strategies, more recent thinking locates it within a second meaning of:

**Sustainable development** – one that reflects a general recognition among developed nations that trade and/or aid need to be located within a developmental context that, as the **Brundtland Commission** (1987) put it, 'meets the needs of the present without compromising the ability of future generations to meet their own needs'. What this involves, according to the **European Commission** (2005), is the ability to reconcile 'economic development, social cohesion, north/south equity and protection of the environment'. In this respect, sustainable development – in both developed and developing societies – involves what **von Stokar** and **Steinemann** (2004) term a:

**Three-dimensional approach**, involving 'economic, social and environmental processes', plus an indication of both time and region.

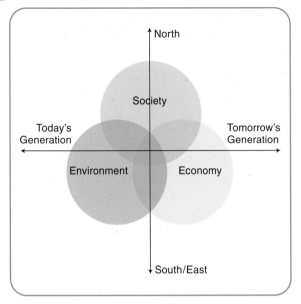

**Sustainable development: The 3D Approach (Source: von Stokar and Steinemann, 2004)**

As **von Stokar** and **Steinemann** suggest, different regions and generations face different but interlinked problems. For developing countries in the South, for example, the overriding need is to develop trade while protecting the environment. For the developed North, meanwhile, strong economies and some measure of environmental protection already exist. The main problem in this region is the adjustment to *cultural lifestyles* (society) that both encourage better environmental protection (producing less waste, using fuel-efficient transport and the like) that will benefit *future generations* and offer greater opportunities for economic development in the South.

As **von Stokar** and **Steinemann** (2004) put it: 'Sustainable development calls for long-term structural change in economic and social systems, with the aim of reducing the consumption of the environment and resources to a permanently affordable level, while maintaining economic output potential and social cohesion.'

# Discussion point: Aid or trade?

In two groups, use the following table as a template to identify the advantages and disadvantages of aid and trade (one group should cover developed nations, the other developing nations).

As a class, discuss whether or not you believe aid, trade or a combination of both provides the best strategy for development.

|  | Aid | | Trade | |
|---|---|---|---|---|
|  | Advantages | Disadvantages | Advantages | Disadvantages |
| **Economic** |  |  |  |  |
| **Political** |  |  |  |  |
| **Cultural** |  |  |  |  |

## Preparing the ground: The role of international agencies

Although international agencies are too numerous – and diverse – to examine individually here, we can illustrate their general role in development strategies in terms of their broadly economic, political or cultural focus.

## Economic agencies

The two most significant international agencies we can examine are arguably the:

**International Monetary Fund** (IMF): In 2006 this had a global membership of around 180 countries, each paying a subscription based on its relative economic size (the USA is the largest net contributor). In general terms, the IMF plays two main roles in the world economic system:

- **Lending** to members to address and correct economic problems.

- **Crisis prevention** that involves providing advice, as well as funding, to encourage members to adopt 'sound economic policies'.

In this respect the IMF functions to promote the:

- **balanced development** of global trade, and the

- **stability** of world exchange rates.

- In other words, its main (*official*) objective is to promote an orderly system of world trade within which member nations can develop their economic capabilities.

**World Bank**: This has the primary objectives of *poverty reduction* and the *improvement of living standards* among its member states. To this end the Bank provides:

- **Educational services** relating to both economic (such as debt management, repayment and relief) and cultural concerns (such as health issues).

- **Economic services**, such as 'low-interest loans, interest-free credit and grants' to developing countries for education, health and infrastructure/ communications development.

## Political agencies

Although agencies like the IMF and World Bank play an *implicit political role* in world affairs, through the provision of economic advice, there are international agencies with a more explicit political role. These include:

**The United Nations** (UN), an organisation with a complex membership structure covering a range of:

- **Political institutions**, such as the General Assembly (a forum for political debate), the Security Council, which focuses on issues relating to international peace and security, and the International Court of Justice.

- **Economic institutions**, focused on development issues (such as international trade, finance and sustainable development).

- **Cultural institutions** that relate to social issues associated with development – areas like gender discrimination and health issues, for example.

The UN's *official aims* include international:

- **peace and security**

- **cooperation** to resolve economic, political and cultural problems
- **dispute resolution**
- **promotion** of human rights and freedoms.

We can also note, by way of illustration, another major international political institution:

**The World Trade Organisation** (WTO) was established in 1995 with the primary aim of regulating world trade, something it attempts to achieve through:

- **negotiation** at government level
- **agreements**
- **rules**
- **dispute settlement**.

It attempts, in other words, to establish and enforce *political rules* relating to international trade.

## Cultural agencies

A range of international agencies focuses on areas of social development, the majority of which have been established and funded through the UN. Examples here include the Office on Drugs and Crime, the International Research and Training Institute for the Advancement of Women, the Children's Fund (UNICEF) and the World Health Organization (WHO).

**Non-government organisations**, as we've suggested, represent a form of international agency (one frequently referred to as *civil society organisations* (CSOs), to reflect the separation between this type of agency and the state), although one important difference between NGOs and agencies like the IMF, UN or WTO is that they represent, as **Malena** (1995) notes, 'private

organizations that pursue activities to relieve suffering, promote the interests of the poor, protect the environment, provide basic social services or undertake community development'. This general definition, as **Shah** (2005) argues, covers a wide range of different groups, with different forms of funding, organisation and objectives, from 'corporate-funded think tanks', through 'community groups and development and research organizations', to charities and relief agencies.

Although a defining characteristic of NGOs is their economic and political independence from government, the diversity of these organisations makes them difficult to classify in any meaningful way; some, for example, work openly with national governments, but many others do not, and yet others, **Schuh** (2005) argues, work *covertly* with national governments to promote certain economic and political aims.

In the past 50 years NGOs have increased rapidly in type and number – the World Bank estimates there are upwards of 30,000 NGOs operating in developed countries – and **Robbins** (2005) suggests a number of reasons for this increase:

- **Communications**: New forms of communication (such as the internet) have made it easier for NGOs to create international communities of like-minded individuals and organisations.

- **Public awareness** of development issues is much greater now, as the mass media, for example, publicise humanitarian issues.

- **Ideological developments**: Changes to the way national governments view economic and political development have resulted in a transfer of resources away from state-sponsored initiatives and assistance towards NGOs, partly because of their:

- **Responsiveness** to development problems. Many NGOs have developed networks *within* developing countries that allow them to respond quickly to issues and direct assistance to where it is immediately needed.

## Weeding the path

A further dimension here is an *ideological shift* towards *neoliberal* ideas about the relationship between, for example, aid and trade as development strategies – this has involved a shift away from *bilateral* forms of assistance (seen as being ineffective, economically destabilising and open to corruption) and towards greater private (NGO) involvement.

## Digging deeper: The role of international agencies

The political and economic roles of some international agencies have, in recent times, become a matter for debate and dispute; in particular, the focus has been on how such agencies *interpret* their roles as part of a general development strategy, an idea we can illustrate using the example of:

**International debt**: The development role of agencies like the IMF and World Bank has come under the critical spotlight in terms of the idea that such agencies have imposed a particular – and highly partial – model of economic reform (*monetarism*) on developing countries as a condition of both aid and trade. A classic illustration is the 'debt crisis' among developing nations that arose in the 1980s (beginning with Mexico announcing, in 1982, that it was unable to meet its debt repayments). The World Bank's response was the:

**Structural Adjustment Programme** (SAP), designed to bring developing economies into line with developed nations and, by so doing, stimulate economic recovery. The programme focused on two strategies: powering economic growth through the private sector and encouraging foreign investment through high rates of interest. Structural economic adjustments in developing countries were encouraged by tying aid and debt repayment to a country's willingness to adopt a range of political and economic measures related to *neoliberal free-market* principles. **Hong** (2000) notes that these measures included:

- **deregulation** of private industry and ending restrictions on foreign investment
- **privatisation** of state-owned industries and services
- **currency devaluation** (that increased the costs of domestic production and goods)
- **cutting government expenditure** on *social spending* (areas like health and education), food subsidies and the like
- **lower corporate taxation**
- **export-led strategic growth** that involved producing goods for foreign markets (to increase national income). This resulted, **Hong** argues, in agricultural changes that abandoned crop diversity for domestic consumption in favour of producing cash crops, such as coffee and cotton, that could be sold in developed markets.

The overall result of the SAP strategy, according to **Hong**, was that developing nations suffered:

- **Increased poverty**.

- **Corruption**: **Hawley** (2000) argues: 'Western businesses pay huge amounts of money in bribes to win friends, influence and contracts ... conservatively estimated to run to £50 billion a year – roughly the amount the UN believes is needed to eradicate global poverty.' **Hanlon** (2004) argues that corruption flourishes in developing countries precisely because of the 'economic liberalisation policies required of Southern countries by Northern donors'.

- **Deteriorating social conditions**, including the 'collapse of both preventive and curative care due to the lack of medical equipment, supplies, poor working conditions and low pay of medical personnel'.

- **Altered ecosystems**: The environmental impact of changes in land use and the introduction of *monoculture* farming (the widespread growing of a single crop) have resulted in more intensive farming methods, the increased use of pesticides and herbicides and the introduction of genetically modified (GM) crops. Illegal logging in areas like the Amazon Basin has resulted in *deforestation*, land deterioration and increased carbon dioxide emissions from burning woodland.

- **Social dislocation and unrest**: **Hanlon** (2005) argues: 'The World Bank stresses the free market, small government, and fiscal austerity' that, in countries like Sierra Leone have contributed to – if not caused – social unrest. He argues, for example, that cuts to education budgets meant many young people received no schooling, leading to both social

grievances and social exclusion, two contributing factors, he claims, to civil war during the 1990s.

## Weeding the path

Although initiatives such as the SAP have raised questions about the strategic role of international agencies, **Dalmiya** and **Schultink** (2003) argue that agencies like the World Bank and WHO have 'played a significant role in' helping to raise nutritional standards and combat disease in developing countries. A couple of more recent initiatives are also worth noting.

**Debt relief**: In 2005 the G8 summit (a meeting of the finance ministers of the United States, Canada, Britain, France, Germany, Italy, Japan and Russia) agreed to write off the debts of 18 countries (at a cost of around £22 billion), saving them around £1 billion in interest payments each year. A proposal currently (2006) exists to extend debt relief to nine more countries.

**International Finance Initiative** (IFI): Britain's proposal to raise around £27 billion in extra financial assistance for developing countries by selling government bonds on world capital markets has, thus far, been rejected by both the USA and Japan (France has proposed an alternative plan, involving an international aviation tax to raise further aid funds).

## Preparing the ground: The role of transnational corporations

TNCs play an important role in world trade and, while it's difficult to measure their overall size and revenues with any great precision, both **Raghavan** (1996) and **Gray**

**Comparing nation states and TNCs**
In terms of size (measured by gross domestic product for nations and revenue for TNCs), Wal-Mart, the US supermarket chain, ranks 35th in world economic terms (with greater revenues than countries like Ireland).

| 5 largest nations | 5 largest TNCs | Wal-Mart larger than: |
|---|---|---|
| 1. USA | 35. Wal-Mart | Switzerland |
| 2. China | 36. BP | Portugal |
| 3. Japan | 37. Exxon Mobil | Chile |
| 4. India | 39. Royal Dutch/Shell | Ireland |
| 5. Germany | 45. General Motors | Luxembourg |
| | | Nicaragua |

Sources: TNCs: Fortune Magazine (2005)/Nations: World Factbook (2005)

(1999) estimate that they account for around one-third of *total* world economic output.

**Anderson** and **Cavanagh** (2000) give a flavour of the immense size and economic scope of TNCs when they note:

- **Economies**: In terms of revenue, of the 100 largest economies in the world 51 are TNCs.
- **Sales**: The top 200 TNCs account for around 25% of the world's *daily* economic activity.
- **Trade**: Around 30% of world trade involves 'economic transactions among various units of the *same corporation*'.

The strategic role of TNCs in relation to economic development has attracted a range of criticism, mainly focused on the *negative impact* their presence and behaviour has had on both world trade and economic development. **ActionAid** (2005) identifies 'six reasons to regulate global food corporations':

- **Abuse of market power** that involves forcing down prices paid to producers in developing countries.

- **Profiteering**: Despite forcing down prices for producers of, for example, coffee, rice and tea, (Western) consumers do not pay lower retail prices.

- **Marginalisation**: Producers who fail to comply with the economic terms laid down by corporations are 'forced out of the supply chain' – their produce remains unsold.

- **Human rights and the environment**: In developing countries TNCs 'operate in a "regulatory void" where they can weaken labour, environmental and public health laws'. **ActionAid** argues that TNCs 'behave more responsibly in countries with tighter regulation'.

- **Corporate social responsibility** (CSR) refers to 'voluntary efforts by companies to improve their social and environmental performance'. **ActionAid**, however, argues that such forms of self-regulation are ineffective, unworkable and rarely observed in developing countries.

- **Social harm**: It is difficult, if not impossible, for the poorest sections of the global economy to seek redress for harms caused by the activities of TNCs. Weak national laws in developing countries and the difficulties of applying international laws contribute to this sense of injustice.

## 🏠 The potting shed

**Identify and briefly explain two problems governments in developing countries might face when trying to regulate the behaviour of TNCs.**

## ⚠ Digging deeper: The role of transnational corporations

Given **Madeley's** (2003) conclusion that TNCs have 'used their money, size and power to influence international negotiations and taken full advantage of the move towards privatisation to influence the policies of governments ... they have especially used their power to cause hardship for millions of the poor in developing countries', you might be forgiven for thinking TNCs *simply* occupy a hugely destructive strategic position in the global economy. This, however, may not necessarily be the case.

**Aisbett** (2003) argues that although in the public consciousness 'benefit to transnational corporations ... implies loss to everyone else, particularly the most poor and marginalized groups', this is not necessarily borne out by the empirical evidence. She does, however, suggest that the various economic benefits of international trade are not always shared equitably between TNCs and the countries in which they operate – but this, it can be argued, is more a matter for national governments, international law and consumer behaviour in developed countries than an inevitable consequence of capitalist corporate behaviour.

### Benefits

In this respect, we can note a number of benefits to developing countries that derive from TNC activities.

**Trade and investment**: These can be generally related to both growth and poverty reduction and, more specifically as **Contreras** (1987) argues, to benefits like:

- **Employment and income increases**.
- **Educational development**: Corporations need local workers with knowledge and skills.
- **Capital income** that develops from 'rents, dividends and other capital income for shareholders'. Indirectly, capital incomes also increase through the development of supplier and service industries linked to the primary economic activities of TNCs.
- **Taxation**: Increased levels of government income (for infrastructure development, welfare, health and educational services) result from economic activity stimulated by TNCs.

**Technological developments**, whose specific benefits, according to **Contreras**, include:

- **Regional development**, whereby economically isolated and underdeveloped regions can realise their productive capabilities.
- **Industrial growth**, as technological

developments provide a 'short cut' to economic development.

- **Technology transfer** that gives increased access to knowledge and skills.

**International markets**: Through TNCs, developing countries gain access to markets for domestic produce from which, ordinarily, they may be excluded. The technological benefits of TNC activity also include the ability to compete successfully in such markets. This, in turn, brings both foreign exchange and investment into host countries.

**Breaking the cycle**: The involvement of TNCs provides the 'industrial and technological spark' that modernisation and free-market theorists see as essential to escape from subsistence agriculture and poverty.

**Consumption benefits**: Western consumers benefit from the supply of goods from developing nations.

In general, **Contreras** (1987) argues, 'Transnational corporations have had a decisive influence in the development of Africa, Latin America and Asia ... particularly in those countries where rapid economic growth and industrialization have high priority and where sophisticated technology and massive capital investments are needed.'

## Weeding the path

The overall argument about the role of TNCs in any development strategy is that their undoubted economic power has to be *regulated* – and since developing nations find this difficult, regulation has to come from both developed countries and international agencies. In other words, if TNCs engage in

exploitative economic and political behaviour it falls mainly on developed countries to ensure trade is fair and equitable. The regulation and oversight of TNCs therefore, needs to be included as part of a wider regulatory and behavioural framework involving aid and trade.

## Moving on

In the final section we can apply some of the ideas we've discussed in this section to a number of different aspects of development (such as health, education and employment).

# 5. Employment, education, health, demographic change and gender as aspects of development

In this final section the focus is on a range of *quantifiable* aspects of development that outlines and explores a number of substantive developmental differences (in relation to areas like health, education and employment) between nations.

## Preparing the ground: Development and demographic change

We can begin this section with the idea of: **Demographic change**, something that involves a statistical analysis of the *structure* of a population, in terms of *variables* like *geographic distribution*, levels of *disease, birth and death rates, age and sex distributions*, and so forth. In other words, it involves understanding populations in terms of *objective, quantifiable* characteristics and,

**WARM-UP: THINKING ABOUT DEMOGRAPHIC CHANGE**

In small groups, use the following table to identify and explain some of the ways our society has changed demographically.

| How have the following changed and what has been the social impact of such changes? | |
| --- | --- |
| **Geographic distribution of the population** | |
| **Diseases** | |
| **Birth and death rates** | |
| **Age structure** | |
| **Gender relationships** | |

using a *comparative analysis* of differences within and between populations, it allows us to build up a picture of demographic difference and, most importantly, *change*.

## ⚠ Weeding the path

The ability to establish statistical patterns and regularities in demographic data is significant because if we can demonstrate regular demographic differences across both:

- **time** – the historical analysis of change *within* a society, and

- **space** – considered in terms of a comparison *between* different societies,

this will demonstrate the *empirical validity* of development itself (as a real process with consequences for human behaviour).

## Demographic difference

On the principle that we need to understand demographic differences *before* we can explain both their causality and significance, we can outline some broad features of developed societies in terms of:

**Age and sex structures**: The population structure of developed nations (as reflected in the UK population *age–sex pyramid* – see opposite) has a number of classic features.

**Slow population growth**: This type of age–sex pyramid reflects a steady population growth, something the **US Population Reference Bureau** (2006) links to development: 'Pyramids where the proportions of the population are fairly evenly distributed among all age groups are representative of many highly industrialized societies.' This general shape is indicative of:

- **Birth rates** generally falling: It also tells us that average family size and fertility rates are falling and suggests that average

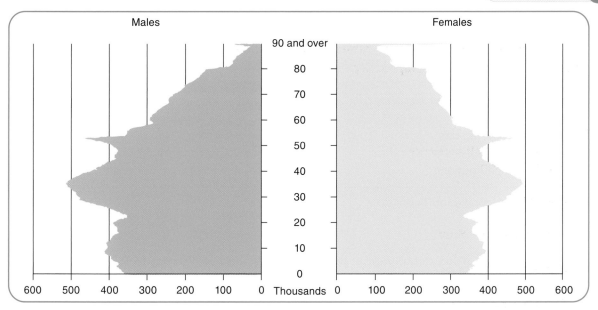

UK Age–Sex Population Pyramid, 2000
(Source: Matheson and Babb, 2002)

child and infant mortality rates are relatively low (more children survive into adulthood and old age).

- **Death rates** falling (or not rising) and average life expectancy increasing (as shown by the number of people aged 90+).

Total fertility rates (TFR) are defined by the OECD as 'the average number of babies born to women during their reproductive years'. For a population to *replace itself*, an annual TFR of 2.1 is needed.

| Selected total fertility rates (TFR) | |
|---|---|
| **More developed countries** | **1.6** |
| **Less developed countries** | **3.2** |
| Europe | 1.5 |
| United States | 2.0 |
| Asia | 2.7 |
| India | 3.2 |
| China | 1.8 |

Source: d'Addio and d'Ercole (OECD, 2005)

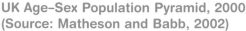 **The potting shed**

The TFR for *developed nations* is indicative of both an *ageing population* (an increasing proportion of the elderly in the population) and a fall in the overall population size, while for *developing nations* the opposite is true – population increase and a younger demographic profile. One exception is China. Identify and briefly explain one reason for this.

**The potting shed**

Identify and briefly explain one reason for the 'population bulge' in the UK pyramid around the 35–55 age group (a similar bulge is found in countries like Germany and the USA).

| Migrants residing in major regions 1990–2000 (millions) | | |
|---|---|---|
| Region | 1990 | 2000 |
| **More** developed regions | 82 | 104 |
| **Less** developed regions | 72 | 71 |
| **Least** developed regions | 11 | 10 |

Source: UN International Migration Report, 2002

**Migration** is a further demographic factor that links to population change, in terms of developed nations generally experiencing higher levels of *net inward migration* (more people enter the country to live and work than leave).

In the case of the UK, **Summerfield** and **Babb** (2005) note that 'since 1983 there has generally been net migration into the UK' – something that explains the discrepancy between a TFR *lower* than required for zero population growth (the number being born exactly matching the number dying) and the fact the UK population is increasing (56 million in 1971, for example, and 60.5 million in 2005).

A significant pattern, linked as we've seen to both *industrialisation* and *urbanisation*, is the migration of people towards towns and cities. Population movements are, however, dynamic; **Summerfield** and **Babb** report a net population *loss* of 100,000+ from London in 2003, with the majority (around 60%) moving to the East and South-East – within relatively easy commuting distance of the capital.

We can contrast the above with some broad demographic features of *developing nations*.

**Age and sex structures**: The population structure, as reflected in the example of the India age–sex pyramid – see page 255), is significantly different in terms of both its overall shape (a classic pyramid) and characteristics.

**Rapid population growth**: This population shape is indicative of a young population:

- **Birth rates**, for example, are generally much higher than in developed nations. Although this is no guarantee, in *absolute* terms, of an expanding population, fertility rates (as we've seen) and average family size are generally higher in developing nations.

- **Death rates**: Average life expectancy in developing countries is lower, for a combination of reasons (disease, lower living standards, poorer working conditions and the like). Child and infant mortality rates are also much higher (as is the number of women dying during childbirth). However, high levels of childbirth represent a classic pattern of 'adaptation to poverty' – the birth rate rises to compensate for anticipated higher child and infant mortality rates.

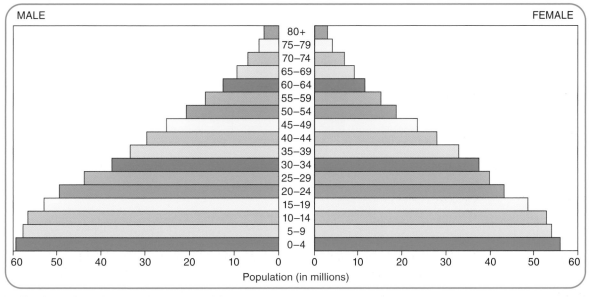

India Age–Sex Population Pyramid, 2000
(Source: US Census Bureau, 2005)

## ⚠ Weeding the path

One way of testing possible differences between the population structure of developed and developing nations is to use a:

**Historical comparison** of the same society – in other words, to examine the historical age–sex pyramid for currently developed nations. Although the precise national data we need is unavailable, we can look at an *area* of the UK which shows a similar age–sex pyramid to present-day population demographics in developing countries (see the figure on page 256).

## ✳ SYNOPTIC LINK

**Theory and methods:** How would you assess the reliability and validity of this data?

**Migration**: Developing regions in the modern world generally experience higher levels of *net outward migration* (more people leave the country to live and work). In addition, the majority of the population live in rural rather than urban areas. See the table of net migration flows on page 256.

## ⚠ Digging deeper: Aspects of development

We can dig a little deeper by examining aspects of development that link into concepts of demographic change.

### Health

**Health** and ill-health can be linked to a range of demographic factors, and, while it's tempting to see illness in terms of *chance factors* (the idea that illness may strike anybody, anywhere, at any time), this is not the complete story – ill-health can be *quantitatively* and *qualitatively correlated* with a range of structural factors closely related to economic development, ranging from extremes of wealth and poverty to lifestyle factors and choices.

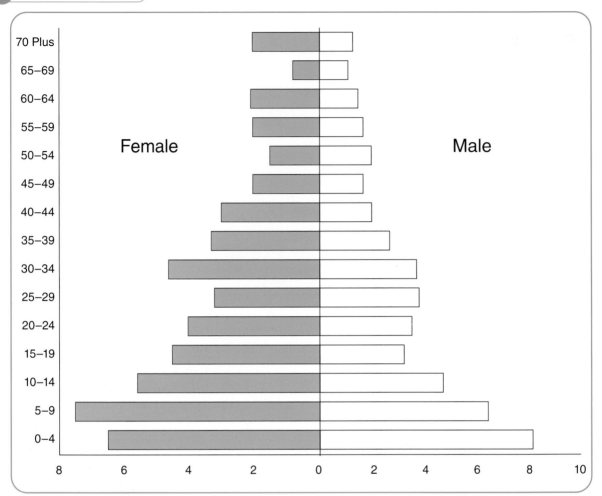

Age–Sex Pyramid for Stoke-upon-Trent (UK), 1701
(Source: Gatley, 2001)

| Net migration flows: selected regions 1995–2000 | |
| --- | --- |
| Region | Average annual net flow of migrants |
| North America | 1,394,000 |
| Europe | 769,000 |
| Africa | −447,000 |
| Asia | −1,311,000 |

Source: UN International Migration Report, 2002

# Growing it yourself: Applying theories of development to demographic change

Divide the class into four groups. Each group should choose one of the following:

- modernisation theory
- dependency theory
- world system analysis
- neoliberal market theory.

Identify and apply the main features of each theory to an understanding of demographic change. (How, for example, does each interpret and explain the significance of demographic change?)

Each group should present its analysis to the other groups.

## ✳ SYNOPTIC LINK

**Stratification and differentiation:** Social differences in health and ill-health can be related to the concept of *life chances*.

To locate health and ill-health specifically within a development context we initially need to establish two things:

- **Structural relationships: Robbins** (2005) argues that 'the fact each historical period has its characteristic illnesses clearly reveals that how we live … largely defines the kinds and frequencies of diseases to which human beings are susceptible'. In other words, the association between lifestyles and health can be demonstrated empirically. For example, some forms of illness (such as lung diseases like asbestosis and silicosis) can be related to industrial processes, while others (such as obesity leading to heart disease) can be related to *post-industrial* consumption patterns.

- **Risk**: Ill-health has two main dimensions:
  - **Individual**: This relates to the idea that anyone can potentially fall victim to disease and ill-health.
  - **Social**: The fact that ill-health is *not* randomly distributed across and within populations (the chances of contracting typhoid, for example, increase under conditions of poor sanitation) means we have to take account of social factors that impact on levels of health within and across developing and developed nations.

The idea that risk involves the relationship between both *social factors* (like different chances of exposure to disease) and *individual factors* (like lifestyle choices) can be applied to an understanding of ill-health in both the developing and developed worlds.

## The developing world

One obvious relationship here is with ill-health and:

**Poverty**: **Braveman** and **Gruskin** (2003) note universally 'strong and pervasive links between poverty and health ... For centuries, powerful associations have been noted between health and an absolute lack of economic resources'. This, in turn, is linked to different levels of:

**Health spending** in developing and developed nations. This occurs on two levels:

- **Individual levels** of personal spending on health care: The **British Medical Association** (2005) notes: 'Roughly 1.2 billion people survive on less than 60p a day and have access to little or no healthcare ... Poverty also causes an increased susceptibility to disease through malnutrition and lack of access to life-saving treatment.'

- **Cultural levels** of societal spending: The **World Health Organization** (2003) reports that although Africa 'accounts for about 25% of the global burden of disease', it involves 'only about 2% of global health spending'.

Government health spending is also a significant factor in health care, given that a large proportion relates to:

**Public infrastructure** – the ownership or financing of things like hospital buildings and equipment, the employment of doctors, nurses, administrators, and so on. As the **OECD** (2005) notes: 'The public sector is the main source of health funding in all OECD countries, except for the United States, Mexico and Korea.'

## Weeding the path

The figures in the table below hide wide spending disparities within each category. **Smith et al.** (2006) note that the US average yearly health spend in 2004 was £5300 (four times the average for HICs). Within specific countries, variables like *class* and *gender* also distort average spending (the wealthy, for example, spend more on health care than the poor, in both developing *and* developed countries).

| Yearly health spending per capita (£GB) | | |
|---|---|---|
| Level of development | Total | Government |
| Least developed countries [LDCs] | 7.70 | 4.20 |
| Other low income countries [OLICs] | 17.50 | 9.10 |
| Lower middle income countries [LMICs] | 65.10 | 35.7 |
| Upper middle income countries [UMICs] | 168.70 | 87.50 |
| High income countries [HICs] | 1,330 | 945 |

Source: Mathews (2001)

## ✴ SYNOPTIC LINK

**Theory and methods:** When we think about health spending we need to keep in mind issues of:

- **Reliability**: 'Average spending', for example, hides widespread differences *within* societies and may also be defined differently in different countries (for example, spending on vitamins, supplements, cosmetic surgery and the like in developed countries all contribute to health spending).
- **Validity**: There is no *absolute* relationship between health spending and health. The USA, for example, spends most on health, but is not necessarily 'healthier' than other developed countries. A significant proportion of spending may go on expensive technology designed to treat relatively small numbers. This isn't to say that levels of health spending are insignificant, but rather that there may be diminishing investment returns. For example, some forms of spending (on sanitation, for example, or preventive medicine) produce significant improvements in overall health levels, while other forms do not.

**Living conditions/standards** can increase or decrease the risk of ill-health. **World Health Organization** (2003) research shows that communicable diseases (such as measles or HIV/AIDS) 'represent seven out of the ten major causes of child deaths' in developing countries. In other areas, such as child and infant mortality rates, lower standards of living contribute to the fact that, as **Haub** and **Cornelius** (2000) note, infant mortality rates in Japan run at 3.5 per year, compared with 116 in Ethiopia.

**Robbins** (2005) notes the impact HIV/AIDS has had on both the populations and economies of developing countries – he terms it 'the signature disease of the latter quarter of the twentieth century, serving as a marker for the increasing disparities in wealth between core and periphery ... 98% of deaths from communicable disease (16.3 million a year) occur in the periphery ... infectious disease is responsible for 42% of all deaths [in developing countries], compared to 1% in industrial countries'.

### ⚠ Weeding the path

The **US Population Reference Bureau** (2005) argues that in both the developing world and, to a lesser degree, the developed world, 'Poverty is both a cause and an outcome of disease'; that is, the poor suffer more from disease, while those who suffer from disease generally suffer higher levels of poverty (through both an inability to work and a lack of state-supported welfare systems) than those who do not.

## Discussion point: Causes of health

In small groups, identify as many causes of health *and* ill-health as you can (ranging from structural factors like poverty to lifestyle choices relating to diet) and then consider the following:

Are concepts of health and ill-health related to social factors or can illness be explained as a random condition that can strike at any time?

## The developed world

While disease and ill-health are not, of course, confined to developing countries, there is a range of quantitative and qualitative health differences between developing and developed nations. These include:

- higher levels of health care spending (both private and public)
- greater access to care and medical provision
- highly trained medical staff
- greater knowledge of disease transmission
- higher levels of sanitation and clean water
- higher levels of nutrition and better balanced diets.

In addition we can note differences in:

- **Types of disease**: As the **British Medical Association** (2005) notes: 'Poverty ... is intertwined with major communicable diseases including TB and malaria.'
- **Effect**: We've noted, for example, that a communicable disease like measles kills very few children in developed countries, partly because of *immunisation programmes* (the recent rise in measles-related deaths in the UK, following a decline in the number of children being immunised, supports this idea). HIV/AIDS, although affecting large numbers in developed nations, has not had the same devastating impact as in Central Africa, for example, where it has caused an overall decline in life expectancy; **WHO** (2005) statistics also show that while 2.4 million have died from AIDS-related illnesses, European deaths number around 12,000.

Another way of looking at health differences is to think in terms of what **Gardner et al.** (2004) term:

**Consumption diseases**: Certain forms of ill-health are related to people's consumption *practices* and, in developed societies especially, *choices*. Where consumption is generally much higher in developed countries, it follows that certain types of ill-health are both unique (in their type and effect) or more prevalent. **Freund** and **Martin** (2005) argue that 'contemporary capitalism' has created:

**Hyper-consumption**, an important feature of which is:

**Overeating** – not just in terms of the personal consumption of food, but also in terms of how food is processed. **Meadows** (1999) notes that Americans consume '700 kilos of grain per person per year', most of which is fed to pigs and chickens to produce meat. She also notes (2000) that nearly 40% of the world grain crop is fed to animals.

Her argument is that 'contemporary capitalism with its hyperintensive modes of consumption ... contributes to unhealthy environments and people'. In particular, according to the **WHO** (2003):

**Obesity** 'has reached epidemic proportions globally, with more than *1 billion* adults overweight – at least 300 million of them clinically obese ... Obesity and overweight pose a major risk for chronic diseases, including type 2 diabetes, cardiovascular disease, hypertension and stroke, and certain forms of cancer'.

## Weeding the path

Over-consumption in developed nations is linked to under-consumption in developing nations, not just in terms of food and diet,

# Growing it yourself: Applying theories of development to health

Divide the class into four groups. Each group should choose one of the following:

- modernisation theory
- dependency theory
- world system analysis
- neoliberal market theory.

Identify and apply the main features of each theory to an understanding of health. (How, for example, does each interpret and explain the significance of health?)

Each group should present its analysis to the class for discussion.

but also in terms of areas like developed nations recruiting doctors and nurses from developing nations.

## Employment

If, as we've suggested, poverty is a major fact in ill-health in developing countries and developed countries suffer from problems associated with over-consumption, a related aspect of development we can examine is:

**Employment**, mainly because work is a major source of income that influences both lifestyles and life chances.

## Weeding the path

Although the **International Labour Office** (2003) argues that 'employment is the way out of (absolute) poverty' in developing nations, this is not necessarily the case, either in terms of absolute poverty (common in developing nations) or relative poverty. What is more important here is whether work provides a:

**Living wage** that enables individuals and families to exist above any notional poverty line. The **International Labour Organization** (2005) notes that 'in 1997 around 25% of the employed labour force in developing countries were working poor'. In addition, it notes (2006) that half the world's workers 'did not earn enough to lift themselves and their families above the $2 a day poverty line – just as many as ten years ago. Among these working poor, 520 million lived with their families . . . on less than $1 a day'.

In terms of general employment patterns and trends, we can briefly examine some major areas of difference between developing and developed nations.

**Types**: Global employment patterns are becoming increasingly complex under the influence of economic globalisation. For most of the twentieth century, for example, one of the major areas of difference has been the distinction between:

- **Industrialised**, developed nations, where the majority of employment has been in manufacturing industry (both *primary*, in terms of extractive industries such as coal mining, and *secondary*, in terms of areas like car production), with a growing service sector throughout this period, and

- **Non-industrialised**, developing nations where the main source of employment has been agriculture (and, in the case of the least developed nations, subsistence farming).

In the latter part of the twentieth century changing economic conditions in the developed world have seen a gradual switch from manufacturing towards service and knowledge-based employment that has led to a couple of significant developments. First, changing employment patterns in developed nations have seen an increasing number of women entering the full-time workforce. Second, manufacturing that was once the staple form of employment for developed nations has increasingly moved to middle-income developing nations. In this respect, the impact of globalised economic processes on employment patterns and trends across the globe has, for **Polaski** (2004), crystallised around two major areas:

**Global labour market supply**: There is 'currently a global surplus of workers', with China, for example, having around 200 million unemployed or underemployed workers (to put this into context, the UK currently has a *total* employed workforce of around 30 million).

**Integrated labour markets** involve seeing labour markets in global (*integrated*) rather than national (*segmented*) terms. Where there was once only competition *within* nations for work, now there is competition *between* nations for labour. The globalisation of labour markets relates to:

- **Employment emigration**: This involves workers in *different nations* competing for a limited number of jobs – a process called 'off-shoring'; work that was once done in a developed nation (such as call-

centre monitoring or financial services) is moved to a developing nation (such as India) where employment regulations are weaker, benefits and wages lower and governments offer a range of incentives for the relocation of jobs. At present this is generally occurring between highly developed and lesser developed nations (those, like India, with the economic, political and cultural infrastructure to compete for service and knowledge-based work).

## ✳ SYNOPTIC LINK

**Stratification and differentiation:** The changing nature of employment can be related to changes in the class structure in developed nations.

- **Labour mobility**: This occurs in two ways: labour movements largely between developed nations (such as increasingly occurs in the EU) and the recruitment of labour from developing countries to fill gaps in the employment situations of developed nations. Although this may involve work at the lower end of the economic spectrum (immigrants doing work the indigenous labour force doesn't want to perform, for example), it also involves work in the middle and upper employment ranges (such as doctors from developing countries working in the UK Health Service).

- **Unemployment** in lesser developed countries, resulting from the economic practices of developed nations. For example, **Polaski** notes farmers in developing countries find it impossible to compete in world markets because of 'agricultural subsidies to high-income

# ⚘ Growing it yourself: Applying theories of development to employment

Divide the class into four groups. Each group should choose one of the following:

- modernisation theory
- dependency theory
- world system analysis
- neoliberal market theory.

Identify and apply the main features of each theory to an understanding of employment. (How, for example, does each interpret and explain the significance of employment?)

Each group should present its analysis to the other groups.

farmers in the United States and Europe'.

## ⚒ Weeding the path

Labour mobility between nations, as **Ghose** (2000) argues, is restricted by a range of political, economic and cultural factors: 'Outside the United States, the share of migrant workers in the labour force showed generally insignificant growth and actually declined in several countries. More importantly, annual immigration flows were declining'. Given the current world labour surplus, developed nations are able to 'pick and choose' the labour they require from developing nations, something that **Ghose** argues contributes to a:

'**Brain drain**', whereby 'the average skill level of the migrants from developing to industrialised countries tends to be much higher than that of the population of their home countries'. This, in turn, alters the balance of:

**Human capital** in both developed and developing nations, in favour of the former.

**Barro** and **Lee** (1994) consider human capital an 'integral aspect of economic growth', the loss of which seriously hinders development prospects.

Overall, the development company **GTZ** (2004) argues: 'Increasing numbers . . . in developing countries are sliding into poverty because of economic and social conditions – a situation characterized by:

- lack of economic competitiveness
- unemployment
- unstable financial systems
- lack of access to economic resources such as capital, education, land, and information.'

## Education

**Peet** and **Hartwick** (1999) suggest that 'Development theories differ according to the political positions of their adherents . . . their place and time of construction . . . and their scientific orientation', and while all development theories refer, in some way, to education in the development process they

263

generally offer different interpretations of the significance of its role.

**Modernisation theories**, for example, generally view education as an integral and broadly functional aspect of the development process. For **Rostow** (1960), basic literacy and numeracy in early industrialisation (the 'pre-conditions for take-off' phase) are functional requirements, whereas the 'take-off' stage requires a more highly educated general population if economic development is to be sustained and expanded.

## Weeding the path

A classic example here is UK development from the late nineteenth century, when we start to see the emergence of a state-sponsored mass education system, to the present where a government aim is to have 50% of the workforce educated to undergraduate level.

**Neo-modernisation theories** focus on the social aspects of economic development, in terms of:

**Human capital** formation and education: **Fonseca** (2001) points to the work of **Schultz** (1960) and his emphasis on 'education and training as pre-requisites of growth'. More recently, **Fonseca** notes a move away from linking education specifically to economic growth and towards seeing it in terms of its potential contribution to a wider range of social environmental concerns (such as health education).

## ✳ SYNOPTIC LINK

**Stratification and differentiation:** These ideas can be located in wider debates about

*embodied capitals* (**Gershuny**, 2002a) and their relationship to human capital and *life chances* (**Gershuny**, 2002b).

**Neoliberal theories**: Although education systems are fundamental to development and economic growth, the focus here is on the role of 'rational economic actors' within a market-based, private-sector-led social system. Educational development is considered an *automatic* consequence of economic growth in that, to maximise their economic potential, individuals act in their own 'best interests', and this means that to compete in international markets people appreciate the need for personal educational development. A classic example here might be India, where, as the Labour Party's **National Policy Forum** (2003) noted, ' . . . its increasingly well-educated, English-speaking workforce is becoming a significant competitor'.

## Weeding the path

**Tooley**'s (2005) study of 'low-income areas' in India, Ghana, Nigeria and Kenya found that 'private, unaided schools', when compared with government schools, generally had better:

- pupil-teacher ratios
- teacher commitment and satisfaction
- facilities
- educational achievement.

**Tooley** concludes that the 'private unaided sector is . . . a dynamic demonstration of how the entrepreneurial talents of people in Africa and India can forcefully contribute to the improvement of education, even for the poor'.

**Dependency theories** focus on education as a *cultural institution* – part of, for Marxists, the *ideological superstructure* of capitalist societies. In this respect, while education per se is viewed as something valuable and desirable, their general issues are with the organisation, content and focus of educational development. In particular, building on concepts of *cultural capital, hegemony* and *imperialism*, **Noah** and **Eckstein** (1988) argue that education in (developing) capitalist societies reflects the interests, needs and preoccupations of the core/centre economies of developed nations that dominate world trade.

## 🏠 The potting shed

Identify and briefly explain one way education in developing countries 'may reflect the interests' of the developed world.

## 🛠 Weeding the path

It's important to keep in mind a couple of general problems with the kind of broad characterisations we've just made:

- **Positions change and develop**: Classical modernisation theory is, for example, different to neo-modernisation. They share the same basic premises, but involve different emphases and interpretations.

- **Empirical exceptions**: The broader the generalisation involved, the more likely that exceptions to the general rule occur. For example, although it is *broadly true*

that developing nations are either *pre-literate* (in the sense that the vast majority of the population have little or no general literacy) or *semi-literate* (people have a basic level of literacy), whereas developed nations exhibit high levels of literacy (a large proportion of university undergraduates in the general population, for example), there are exceptions. **Zachariah** (1998) notes that, by 1951, in Kerala (a state in India), 'nearly half the population ... were literate. By 1991, Kerala was a 100% literate state'. The cultural reasons for this included 'the importance given to education in Kerala culture' and 'the efforts of European missionaries, who finding Kerala already had a high proportion of Christians, turned their attention to education and health'.

Although theoretical positions are important for understanding the *general role* of education in the development process, it's useful to look more closely at some of the ways education potentially contributes to development, in terms of areas like gender relationships, health and employment. **Psacharapoulos** and **Patrinos** (2002) argue that education represents an 'important economic asset' for both individuals and nations, and **Archer** (2006) identifies various 'practical reasons' for government educational investment:

- **Participation** in decision-making processes, in both the *private* and *public* spheres, is increased, something particularly important for gendered involvement; female participation in community life, for example, increases by level of education.

- **Health**: Educational participation is strongly correlated with a decline in infant mortality and improved child health. In addition, child and adult educational programmes play a part in both responding to and reducing 'the spread of HIV/AIDS'. **The Global Campaign for Education** (2004), for example, argues: 'If all children received a complete primary education, the economic impact of HIV/AIDS could be greatly reduced and around 700,000 cases of HIV in young adults could be prevented each year.' In addition, HIV/AIDS 'is spreading fastest among young women (aged 15–24), not only because their physiology puts them at risk but also because they have little access to knowledge, economic resources and decision-making power'.

- **Education**: **Smith** and **Haddad** (2001) note that 'young women with a primary education are twice as likely to stay safe from AIDS'. They also link education to the 'empowerment of families to break the cycle of poverty' – female earnings, for example are '10–20% higher for every year of schooling completed'. In addition, 'educating women is the single most powerful weapon against malnutrition – even more effective than improving food supply'.

## ⌂ The potting shed

**Identify and briefly explain one reason why 'educating women' helps prevent malnutrition.**

- **Economic development**: **Cameron** and **Cameron** (2006) argue child and adult education (the latter in terms of literacy) produces significant *micro* (individual) and *macro* (structural) economic benefits. In terms of the former, 'people who had completed literacy courses tended to be more confident and more willing to take initiatives in developing their livelihoods'. In this respect, **Archer** argues that educational provision represents both a safety net for AIDS orphans (by providing the skills they will need to survive in adult life) and a way of reversing the economic exploitation of child labour (by keeping them out of the workplace and in the school).

### Gender

**Peace**'s (2005) interesting observation – 'Pick a signifier of development . . . and it's almost guaranteed that the experience of women will be notably worse than their male counterparts' – captures something of the general nature of gendered differences in relation to economic, political and cultural development, an impression we can firm up by looking at a couple of widely used *empirical measures* of gender inequality introduced by the UN in 1995:

- **The Gender-related Development Index** (GDI) was designed, as **Oxaal** and **Baden** (1997) note, to measure 'inequalities in achievement between women and men . . . Countries with greater gender disparity in basic capabilities (life expectancy, educational attainment and income) will have low GDIs compared to their Human Development Index'.

**The Gender Empowerment Measure** (GEM) represents a 'composite indicator

| The Gender Empowerment Measure: selected countries (2000) | | | | |
|---|---|---|---|---|
| HDI rank | GEM rank | Female seats in parliament (%) | Female administrators and managers (%) | Female professional and technical workers (%) |
| 1. Canada | 8 | 23 | 37 | 52 |
| 2. Norway | 1 | 36 | 31 | 58 |
| 3. USA | 13 | 13 | 44 | 53 |
| 10. UK | 15 | 17 | 33 | 45 |
| 50. Trinidad and Tobago | 22 | 19 | 40 | 51 |
| 84. Sri Lanka | 66 | 5 | 17 | 27 |
| 146. Bangladesh | 67 | 9 | 5 | 37 |

Source: United Nations (2001)

which looks at women's representation' in areas like parliament, workforce participation and roles and their share of national income. It represents, as **Oxaal** and **Baden** note, a statistical measure of male and female participation 'in economic and political life and . . . decision making'.

## The potting shed

**Seers** (1983) argues: 'We cannot, with our own eyes and ears, perceive more than a minute sample of human affairs, even in our own country . . . So we rely on statistics to build and maintain our own model of the world. The data that are available mould our perceptions.' Identify and briefly explain one advantage of statistics and one disadvantage of statistics in terms of understanding global gender inequalities.

## Weeding the path

The two measures are complementary in that while the GDI focuses on a comparison, across different countries, of gendered inequalities, the GEM focuses specifically on areas of power and political/economic decision-making. **Anand** and **Sen** (1995) welcome this as an attempt to 'shift the focus of attention . . . onto indicators that come closer to reflecting the well-being and freedoms actually enjoyed by populations . . . [in addition to] inequalities in the opportunities of women and men'.

**Jahan** (2001) argues that the GEM is a useful way of reflecting the 'distributional aspect of development, particularly the issue of inequality', or, as **Kodoth** and **Eapen** (2005) put it, 'the extent to which women are able to use their basic capabilities to acquire economic and political voice'. For **Oxaal** and **Baden**, 'the GEM shows that access to basic needs, education and health, does not in itself automatically mean empowerment for women'. In other words, although many countries (the UK included) do not have *legal barriers* to male and female equality, they do not necessarily have high levels of female participation and representation.

> ## ⚠ The potting shed
>
> **Outline, in your own words, the meaning of 'empowerment'. Give one example of male *or* female empowerment to support your definition.**

## Explaining inequality

We can apply a range of concepts to explain the nature and level of gendered inequalities in both developing and developed nations:

**Patriarchy** and **patriarchal ideologies**: These reflect 'traditional attitudes' to gender, expressed in a variety of ways through traditional power structures, filtered through institutions such as the family, education and work. These may involve a combination of both *explicit* (patriarchal) discriminations and *implicit* discriminations based around traditional forms of gender relationship and practice. The **World Bank Gender and Development Group** (2003) has identified a range of global gendered inequalities based on patriarchal principles:

- **Legal, social** and **economic rights**: 'In no region of the developing world are women equal to men' in all three areas.

- **Access to resources**: 'In most countries, women continue to have less access to social services and productive resources than men'.

- **Representation**: 'Women remain vastly under-represented in national and local assemblies'.

- **Education**: 'In most low-income countries, girls are less likely to attend school than boys' and are 'more likely to drop out (in many cases after getting pregnant, often due to lack of access to reproductive health services)'.

- **Earnings**: Women earn on average 77% of male earnings in developed countries; in developing nations they average 73% – about 'one-fifth of the wage gap can be explained by gender differences in education, work experience, or job characteristics'.

**Family life**: The size of individual families impacts on both male and female lives in situations where traditional forms of gender relationship apply. In the case of the former, larger families means more mouths to feed and places stresses and strains on the breadwinner role; in the latter, both pregnancy and child care (especially, but not exclusively, in situations of poverty) place severe restrictions on the ability of women to participate in the public sphere, not least in terms of educational and paid work. In this respect:

**Fertility rates** impact on female participation in the public sphere. According to the **US Demographic and Health Surveys** (1991–99) there is a strong correlation between fertility rates (average births per woman) and educational levels. In Niger, for example, the fertility rate for women with no education was 7.8 in 1998, whereas for those completing secondary education it was 4.6. The surveys also note that 'within countries, rural women tend to marry earlier than urban women and … have larger families. Access to contraception is an important contributor to the differences in the fertility rates among countries, but culture and socioeconomics weigh heavily as well'.

## Socioeconomic factors

**Education**: As the **US Population Reference Bureau** (2006) suggests, education is a key variable in improving the general status of women in developing countries (and, by extension, in developed nations). This follows because 'educated women are more likely to know what social, community, and health services, including family planning, are available and to have the confidence to use them'. Education, in this respect, has some subsidiary effects:

- **Opportunities** outside the home, in terms of work/career development, are increased.

- **Status levels** are increased for women (and their families).

- **Family size** is reduced, leading to both *economic benefits* (income can be concentrated on fewer family members) and *health benefits* (the chances of dying in childbirth are reduced).

- **Life chances** are raised for both male and female children where the benefits of parental education can be passed on through the primary socialisation process.

## ⚒ Weeding the path

Although improvements in educational provision have been made in many developing countries, the rate of progress remains relatively slow. The **US Population Reference Bureau** estimates: 'It will take more than 100 years before all girls in Africa go to primary school and hundreds more before they get a chance at secondary education.'

In addition, although education has certain gender ramifications (in terms of women working, for example), it doesn't represent a panacea for gender inequality, since 'women … face embedded disadvantage in labour markets, property ownership and sexual and reproductive choices', related, broadly, to both *patriarchal practices* and *behaviours*. However, to relate female inequality *only* to these ideas is both simplistic and mistaken, an idea we can illustrate in relation to:

**Work**: **Connelly et al.** (2000) note, for example, a number of economic processes that have contributed to gendered inequality:

**The feminisation of labour**: For **Standing** (1999) this describes the idea that modern labour markets have become increasingly 'flexible' over the past 20 or so years, such that many forms of employment now mirror the conditions of what was once, in developed nations, called the 'secondary labour market' – a market dominated by women in part-time, low-skill, low-wage, low-status work. **Standing** argues these conditions are characteristic of work in developing nations (and, arguably, in some developed nations) that involves 'sub-contracting, part-time and home-based work

... with low rates of unionization'. The 'feminised' aspect of this work, as **Connelly et al.** note, is that 'insecure, low-paying jobs with few prospects for advancement' are largely rejected by men and so are performed mainly by women. In addition, where some developing countries have pursued:

**Export-led industrialisation**, this has resulted in the creation of large numbers of relatively low-skill, factory-type jobs, performed mainly by women. **Gladwin** (1993) suggests one reason for this is that women have greater 'patience, dexterity and are more prepared to do tedious and monotonous jobs'.

Finally, although most of this section has focused on the general situation of women in developing countries, we can note that poverty is a general problem that affects both males and females (although even here we find gender differences, with the condition of women being generally worse). The **World Bank** (2002) has summarised some dimensions of poverty in the following terms:

| Gender equality and its links to poverty | |
|---|---|
| **Dimensions of poverty** | **Gender differentiated barriers** |
| **Opportunity** | Women suffer more in economic downturns (more likely to lose their job)<br>Gendered access to labour markets<br>Pay discrimination favours men |
| **Capacity** | Unequal access to education<br>Unequal access to health<br>Time poverty (large amounts of female time spent securing daily necessities like water) |
| **Security** | Vulnerable to natural disasters<br>Vulnerable to civic and domestic violence<br>Vulnerable to environmental risks |
| **Empowerment** | Institutions not accessible to poor men and women<br>Lack of voice in local and national politics<br>Lack of voice in community decision-making |

Source: World Bank (2002)

# Growing it yourself: Applying theories of development to gender

Divide the class into four groups. Each group should choose one of the following:

- modernisation theory
- dependency theory
- world system analysis
- neoliberal market theory.

Identify and apply the main features of each theory to an understanding of gender. (How, for example, does each interpret and explain the significance of gendered relationships, behaviours and practices?)

Each group should present its analysis to the class.

# CHAPTER 4

# Theory and methods

This chapter examines a number of ideas related to sociological *methodology*; how, in short, we can produce *reliable* and *valid* knowledge about the social world, both in theoretical terms, such as different sociological theories, and in practical terms when, for example, we explore the relationship between sociological theory and *social policy*.

This chapter, therefore, is designed to enhance and complement the work you did on sociological *methods* at AS level.

## 1. Concepts of modernity and postmodernity in relation to sociological theory – consensus, conflict, structural and social action theories

### Preparing the ground: Sociology and modernity

'Sociology', according to **Peter Taylor** (2000), 'is a product of modernity' – by which he means it has its origins, as an academic discipline, in the development of 'modern society'. To understand why this is significant, we can initially classify our society in terms of three broad historical periods:

- **Pre-modern**, considered (very roughly) as a type of society existing before the late sixteenth century.

- **Modern**, a type that developed out of the pre-modern period and (arguably) stretches to the late twentieth century.

- **Postmodern** – a type considered by some sociologists (others, such as **Giddens** (1998) or **Habermas** (1992) refer to this period as 'high' or 'late' modernity) to be characteristic of our society in the twenty-first century.

This, as we stress, is a very *basic classification* used primarily to sensitise you to the concept of different types of society. Its secondary purpose is to allow us to identify some *key features* (economic, political and cultural) of modern society that arguably differentiate it from both its pre- and postmodern counterparts.

### WARM-UP: SOCIETIES AS SHOPS

In this exercise we can use an analogy to understand the difference between types of society. Think of:

- pre-modern society as a corner shop
- modern society as a supermarket
- postmodern society as shopping on the internet.

In small groups, identify some of the features that characterise the different types of shops (a mall, for example, is much larger than a corner shop, it has more choice and involves different types of relationship between customer and staff).

As a class, discuss how these differences can be applied to different types of society.

## Economic characteristics

*Modernity* differs from *pre-modernity* in a number of ways:

**Technology**: The invention of machines – and the gradual discovery/invention of new sources of power (gas, electricity and, eventually, nuclear, for example) – opened up the potential for:

- **Industrialisation** – the application of machine technology to the production of things (*commodities*). People working with machines (*mechanisation*) led to the development of factories that allowed large quantities of goods to be produced quickly, cheaply and to the same general standard (*mass production*). Further developments included *automation* (machines controlling other machines, with little or no direct human involvement) and, most recently, the *computerisation* of some production processes.

Alongside these developments, modern society is characterised by:

**Capitalist** economic relationships ('employer–employee', for example) that involve a process of:

**Rationalisation**, in the sense of ideas about organisation and efficiency being applied to the production process. As **Sarup**

(1993) puts it, modernity involves ' ... the progressive economic and administrative rationalisation ... of the social world'. For **Weber** (1905), rationalisation involved *institutions* (such as work) and *practices* becoming increasingly well organised and efficient. Examples of different types of economic rationalisation include:

- **Fordism**: Named after the production-line technique developed by the US car manufacturer Henry Ford at the beginning of the twentieth century. With this technique a complex task, such as assembling a car, is broken down into a number of smaller, relatively simple tasks.

## 🏠 The potting shed

Modern supermarkets are contemporary examples of rationally organised institutions. Identify and briefly explain two ways 'selling food' is broken down into highly specialised roles.

- **Global Fordism**: Where *Fordism* involves production-line principles applied *within* a factory, this version involves different parts of a product being created in different countries (where labour and parts may be relatively inexpensive) and assembled in yet another country.

- **Just-in-time** (JIT): Involves bringing together the parts needed to create a product 'just in time' to sell the completed product (thereby saving on things like storage costs).

For **Weber**, a further feature that developed alongside *rationalisation* was:

**Bureaucracy**, which **Ritzer** (1996) describes as 'a large-scale organisation composed of a hierarchy of offices ... people have certain responsibilities and must act in accord with rules, written regulations, and ... compulsion exercised by those who occupy higher-level positions'.

A final characteristic we can add (with the proviso that there is some dispute as to whether this is characteristic of *modernity* or *postmodernity*) is:

**Globalisation**, considered in terms of ideas such as:

- **Global Fordism.**
- **Transnational corporations** that operate and trade on a global scale. Areas such as *telecommunications* (BT, for example) and *computer software* (think Microsoft – which sounds a bit like subliminal advertising) are contemporary examples of global marketplaces for transnational companies.

## Political characteristics

Modernity involves ideas like:

- **Nation states**: Although 'a nation' may exist in some pre-modern societies, a *nation state* is a feature of modernity – the basic idea being that *states* develop systems of national government with some form of political representation (a parliament, for example), legal system, civil service and fixed geographic borders.

- **Representation**: This doesn't have to be *democratic* – many early-modern nation states involved monarchies, and even into the twentieth century a range of totalitarian societies have existed (Germany, Italy, Spain and the USSR, for example), but political democracy is a feature of most Western societies in the twenty-first century.

## ✳ SYNOPTIC LINK

**Power and politics:** Note how the above ideas about the origin and nature of the state underpin discussion of the role of the state in modern society.

If we turn the focus slightly to the idea of *modernity* itself (as a way of thinking about and understanding the social and natural worlds), we can explore the:

**Cultural** characteristics of modern society, mainly because modernity involved major changes in the way people experience and interpret the world (something that led to the development of both sociology and many other forms of intellectual endeavour).

## Cultural characteristics

The obvious place to start, in this respect, is with the concept of:

**Belief systems** which, for our current purpose, we can examine in terms of:

**The Enlightenment: Harvey** (1990) argues that the origins of *modernity* as a belief are in the explosion of creative thinking and practice that began in late seventeenth-century Europe. As **Scambler** and **Higgs** (1998) argue: 'Modernity refers to Western society over the past 200 years, with its triumphs of medicine and science, beliefs in social progress and improvement, and the emergence of mass institutions such as hospitals, schools, and the nation state, as well as mass production. Social theory ... has its roots in the project of modernity.'

The philosopher and social reformer Thomas **Paine** (1795) called the Enlightenment the 'Age of Reason', with good reason (pun intended) because it involved rejecting the 'ignorance and superstition' of pre-modernity and embracing a rational understanding of the natural and social worlds – an idea that introduces a major defining feature of modernity:

**Science**: For **O'Donnell** (1997) modernity is: ' . . . a period during which science and reason become the main means by which human beings seek to understand the world and solve problems . . . modernity is driven by a belief in the power of human reason to understand and change, in short, to master the world'; and the impact of scientific thought was – and continues to be – felt in terms of:

**Objectivity**: Scientific beliefs involve the idea that it's possible to both discover and create knowledge through objective observations. In other words, both the natural world (the object of study) and the scientific method are based on:

**Foundational principles** or assumptions. In the former, the world is subject to 'laws' governing behaviour and in the latter, objective science can be used to discover these laws (based, for example, on the foundational principle of 'cause and effect').

Science, therefore, is a very powerful method of explaining the world, for two reasons:

- **Truth** can be separated from fallacy (*fiction*). A classic example is the religious suppression of Galileo's argument that the Earth revolved around the Sun (and not the other way around, as the Catholic Church hierarchy believed). For a time this idea was successfully suppressed, but its *demonstrable truth* was simply too powerful to deny. Under modernity, therefore, *objective truths* replace *subjective faiths* as the primary form of explanation.

- **Instrumental utility**: **Keat** and **Urry** (1975) note that one of the most powerful features of science is that 'it works' – scientific thinking and principles have a use in the 'real world' of cars, computers and compact disks.

From this, it's only a short step to the concept of:

**Progress** – the idea that, as we understand more and more about the natural world, modern society is constantly 'moving

## Discussion point: Can things only get better?

Split into two groups. One group should identify the *benefits* of science and the other should identify its *drawbacks*.

As a class, discuss the benefits/drawbacks you've identified (some, you'll find, have *both*).

| Benefits | Drawbacks |
| --- | --- |
| Longer life expectancy<br>The eradication of disease (such as smallpox) | Nuclear war?<br>Genetic modifications |
| **Further examples?** | |

forward' – from superstition to science, ignorance to knowledge and, finally, from subservience to mastery of nature.

Once the natural world has been 'mastered' (or at least its foundational principles understood), it's but a small step to the idea of mastery of the social world; if the inanimate world of 'things' is governed by natural laws, perhaps the same is true of the animated world of people?

### ⚠ Digging deeper: Modernity and sociological theory

Given sociology's origins in 'the modern period', it's not surprising that the founders of the discipline (writers such as **Saint-Simon**, **Comte** and **Durkheim** in France, **Weber** and **Marx** in Germany and **Spencer** in England) were immersed in the general philosophies and principles of modernist social thought. **Lechner** (1998) notes: 'Modernity is the central concern of sociology as a discipline ... In its early period, sociology aimed to illuminate ... the changes that were remaking Europe and America ... it dealt with the consequences of industrialization and urbanization in leading nation-states ... [as] part of a broader debate about the meaning of social change.'

Sociology in the early modern period (from **Saint-Simon** onwards) was concerned with the description and explanation of modernity and its associated processes. To paraphrase **O'Donnell** (1997), sociology was initially driven by a belief in the power of human reason to understand, change and – possibly – master the social world. In this section, therefore, we're going to explore a couple of areas:

- **Themes**: involves relating some of the basic concepts of 'modernist sociology' to the cultural themes of modernity we outlined above.

- **Perspectives**: we can examine *consensus*, *conflict* and *social action* theories and their relationship to both *modernity* and *postmodernity*.

## Themes

In terms of the first of these ideas, therefore, in many of the classic texts of 'modernist sociology' we can see the basic themes of eighteenth/nineteenth-century thought:

**Science** represents one of the key ideas for classical sociology, since sociology, as the 'science of society', was founded on a number of assumptions that dovetailed neatly with modernity:

**Structure** over **action**: Just as behaviour in the natural world was subject to certain *objective forces* (laws of gravity, for example), social behaviour was subject to 'social forces' that pushed people into *action*. Different sociologists did, of course, have different views about the nature and extent of these forces:

- **Consensus** theorists (such as **Comte** and **Durkheim**) focused on forces of *order* and *stability* – in the case of the former, the attempt to isolate the laws governing social behaviour; in the latter case, laws governing *social statics* (order) and *dynamics* (change).

- **Conflict** theorists (such as **Marx**) focused on forces of *conflict* and *change* (such as the idea of class struggle).

Whatever their difference of emphasis and approach, the underlying belief was similar: these forces could be discovered using

*The X-Files*
**A modernist preoccupation with 'truth' and 'certainty' in a mixed-up postmodern world? Or just a daft TV programme about aliens?**

scientific methods (such as detailed *observation*, *theory* development and *objective testing*) – a belief that reflected an underlying modernist certainty that 'the truth', to coin a phrase, was 'Out There Somewhere'. The task of *any* scientist was to find it.

Thus, if behaviour was subject to 'underlying forces', this presupposed:

**Regularity**: There was a *logic* to behaviour based on the various ways cultural behaviour was structured by 'unseen forces' that could be both *theorised* and *observed*:

**Theorised**: If behaviour isn't random, unstructured and meaningless, it follows that we can speculate about its causes.

**Observed** in terms of its effects (using various indicators). In dealing with objective forces, observation had to be similarly objective, structured and free from subjective judgements, in other words:

**Empirical**: *Objectivity* and *value freedom* are, for modernist theory, non-negotiable; if the aim is to find undiscovered or obscured truth, scientists must be objective in their theory and practice since, if they were not,

we could not be certain a truth had really been discovered.

## ✳ SYNOPTIC LINK

**Religion:** 'Secularisation' (a decline in religious belief and behaviour) is, for some sociologists, a 'hidden process' that cannot be directly observed; its existence, however, can be theorised by studying observable indicators of its effect.

**Essentialism**: All varieties of early modern sociology contained a belief in human behaviour/societies having fundamental (*essential*) organisational features, an idea reflected in the concept of:

**Progress**: For both consensus and conflict sociology the idea of a progressive revelation of 'scientific truths' was a fundamental goal. In this respect, the concept of *progress* is found in much of classical sociology – from writers as diverse as **Saint-Simon** (*Fonseca* and *Ussher* (1999) point to his call, in the early eighteenth century, for a 'science of society' having parity with the natural sciences), **Comte** (and his vision of society governed by a 'scientific priesthood' based on their understanding and mastery of the 'laws of human behaviour'), **Marx** (with his scientific critique of nineteenth-century capitalism and the vision of a future, communist society) and **Weber** (who saw the rational ordering of society as an achievable goal).

Finally, we can note how classical sociology gave rise to two forms of scientific *methodology*:

- **positivism**, mainly associated with *consensus* sociology, and

- **realism**, mainly associated with *conflict* sociology.

# Perspectives

**Modernist** sociology, as we've suggested, has historically been dominated by *structuralist perspectives*, the basic themes of which we can review next, beginning with:

**Consensus structuralism**, which involves, for **Giddens** (2001), a focus on the way agreement over ' . . . basic social values by the members of a group, community or society' is both socially constructed and a fundamental characteristic of social behaviour. The persistence of society, therefore, is based around a:

**Common value system** involving 'consensual beliefs held by the majority of the population'. Value systems are organised around:

**Social institutions** – patterns of shared, stable behaviour that persist over time and around which modern societies are structured in terms of:

- **economic** institutions (work, for example)
- **political** institutions (government, police, judiciary, and so forth)
- **cultural** institutions (such as religion, education and the media).

Each institution (or set of related institutions) is *functional* for society because they are connected by their:

- **Purpose** – what each institution exists to do (the function of economic institutions is to provide the physical means to survive; the function of the family is primary socialisation, and so forth).
- **Needs** – what each institution takes from other institutions in order to function. Work, for example, needs the family to produce socialised individuals and, in return, provides the means of family group survival.

# Themes

This perspective is related to a couple of the main themes of modernism:

**Foundationalism**: The concept of *function* – the basic *foundation* on which consensus theory rests – takes a number of forms, an example of which is:

- **Functional imperative** (a command that must be obeyed): Each social institution is functionally connected to other, related institutions on the basis of the functions they must perform if a society is to survive and prosper (*purpose* and *needs*, in other words).

- **Structure**: Because institutions are *functionally linked*, we experience society in terms of pressures and constraints on our behaviour (the pressure to work, form a family, and so forth). In this respect, society is a *hidden hand* pushing people to perform the roles required for the reproduction of social order. **Durkheim** (1895) identified two significant aspects of order:

  - **Social solidarity** – the feeling we both belong to a society and have certain basic things in common: culture, socialisation, values and the like.

  - **Collective conscience** – the 'external expression' of the will of the people. This is the force that binds people to each other as a society (to integrate them into collective forms of behaviour).

- **Essentialism**: **Parsons** (1951) argued that every institution needs to solve four *essential problems* if it is to exist and function:

  - **Goal attainment** involves the need to

# Growing it yourself: Fun with GAIL

Although functional imperatives apply to any institution, Parsons (1959) explicitly identified the functional imperatives for an *education system*. Using the following table as a template (we've given you some examples to get you started), how do schools perform the following essential functions?

| Goal attainment | Adaptation | Integration | Latency |
|---|---|---|---|
| Qualifications | The school | Uniforms | School rules |
| **Further examples?** | | | |

set behavioural goals and to specify the means through which they can be achieved.

- **Adaptation** involves *creating* the means to achieve valued goals. This may, for example, involve the ability to provide the *physical necessities* of institutional life.

- **Integration**: People need to feel a part of any institution and one way to achieve this is to provide something they have in common (norms and values, for example). The ability of an institution to successfully integrate people is crucial for its internal harmony and reproduction.

- **Latency** (or pattern maintenance) refers to the development of *social control* mechanisms to manage tensions, motivate people, resolve interpersonal conflicts, and so forth.

## Perspectives

**Conflict structuralism** focuses, according to **Bilton et al.** (1996) on 'the notion that society is based on an unequal distribution of advantage and is characterised by a conflict of interests between the advantaged and the disadvantaged'. It encompasses perspectives such as *Marxism* (conflict between social *classes*) and *feminism* (gender conflicts) and can be related to the main themes of modernism in terms of:

**Foundationalism**: Conflicts of interest, as we've just noted, are central to this perspective. For Marxists, a key term is:

**Social class**, where class conflict creates social change through the opposition of classes as they pursue their different *collective* interests. For Marxists, classes are defined in terms of their relationship to the:

**Means of production** – the social process whereby goods are created. For *traditional* Marxism, capitalist society consists of two great classes:

- **the bourgeoisie** – those who own and control the means of production

- **the proletariat** – those who sell their labour in the economic marketplace.

Modern forms of Marxism, however, tend to note the existence of:

**Class fractions** (subdivisions of each main class). For example, the bourgeoisie (or ruling class) might be subdivided into the:

- **bourgeoisie** (owners of large companies)

- **petit (small) bourgeoisie** (owners of small businesses) and

- **professionals** (such as academics or managers who control the day-to-day running of companies).

**Essentialism**: Different forms of conflict theory have slightly different essential features. Marxism, for example, focuses on areas such as the economic structure of society as the key to understanding human behaviour and development. Radical feminists, meanwhile, focus on the essential features of males and females in terms of, for example, their different psychologies.

---

## ✳ SYNOPTIC LINK

**Stratification and differentiation:** These ideas are developed in more detail in relation to ideas about – and consequences of – the changing class structure.

---

## ⚠ Preparing the ground: Sociology and postmodernity

The idea of postmodern society is a *contested concept* within sociology in that, although economic and cultural changes are clearly occurring, there are arguments about whether these changes relate to a *new type* of (postmodern) society or are simply a *different form* of modern society – what **Giddens** (1998) calls *late modernity* or 'modernisation happening under different conditions from the past'. Whatever your position on this argument, we've split this section into a discussion of:

- **Late modernity** – considered, for theoretical convenience, to include sociological theories (such as interactionist sociology) from the mid- to late twentieth century and

- **Postmodernity** – considered in terms of the late twentieth/early twenty-first centuries, where we look at some possible characteristics of postmodern society.

We can identify some of the main features of late/postmodernity in the following terms.

## Economic characteristics

Writers such as **Bell** (1973) suggest that a major economic change in the late twentieth century was the development of:

**Post-industrial society**, with an emphasis on the *provision of services* (banking, insurance, etc.) rather than the *production of goods* (a feature of modern society) – something that involves an increasing emphasis on *knowledge* (ideas about how to do things) as a saleable commodity. For **Bell**, post-industrial society was based on three main characteristics:

- **Service**: Most people would be employed in service industries, from the low-level, poorly paid and insecure (shopworking, call centres and the like) to the high-level, handsomely rewarded and relatively secure (information technology, computing, finance, and so forth).

- **Science**: The development of computer technology, applied to the production of *goods* and *services*, that would revolutionise how things were made and distributed.

- **Consumption**: In modernity, *producers* of goods and services, rather than consumers, were the dominant economic force; in postmodernity, the reverse is true. Through information technology (such as the internet) the consumer exercises *choice* that exposes producers to such fierce competition that the consumer becomes the main focus of economic activity.

## ✳ SYNOPTIC LINK

**Stratification and differentiation:** This type of economic change has had important consequences for both the way we define and measure social class (traditionally involving occupation as a crucial indicator) and the significance of concepts like class in the construction of individual identities. **Bauman** (1997), for example, questions the importance of class as a source of identity in postmodernity.

Post-industrial society, **Bell** argued, developed in the heavily industrialised societies of the USA and Western Europe and would, eventually, spread across the world. The UK, for example, saw a steady decline throughout the twentieth century in the economic significance of, first,

## 🔺 Growing it yourself: Can you do it?

**Read the following:**

# You can do it, if you B&Q it

Source: Heather Stewart, *The Guardian* 06/12/03

'Manton Colliery – Sharing Success' reads the blue crest on the pit wheel of what was once one of the most productive coal mines in the country. Silent since the pit was shut almost 10 years ago, the wheel now sits embedded in the grass – a monument to an economy which has disappeared.

Stacked on top of those memories, though, will soon be pallets of bathroom tiles, power tools and six-inch nails – and 1,000 new jobs … There could be few better symbols of the changing shape of Britain's economy over the last decade than a once-mighty coal mine levelled off to make room for a giant distribution centre for DIY bits and bobs.

In 1996, the claimant count in Bassetlaw was close to 4,000; the latest figures show that has fallen to just over 1,000, many of whom should be swept up by B&Q with its on-site gym and its crèche to help mums get into work. The firm says it wants to have more women, and more part-time workers, than at its average distribution centre.

**Split into two groups and use the following table as the basis for:**

- **Group 1 identifying positive aspects of this economic change**
- **Group 2 identifying negative aspects of this economic change.**

**As a class, consider the conclusions that can be drawn from these changes.**

| Positive | Negative |
| --- | --- |
| New forms of employment? | Job insecurity? |

agriculture (which now accounts for about 3% of all employment) and, second, manufacturing (now roughly 20% of all employment). The past 30 years have seen a sharp decline in heavy industry (such as coal-mining and steel production) and a rapid rise in computer-based, service technologies – something that's partly accounted for by the increasing *rationality* of economic production. Economic decisions, in this respect, are made in *global*, rather than national, contexts, partly because of the behaviour and influence of:

**Transnational corporations**: Where corporations are able to operate freely across national borders (moving capital, production and even people from one country to the next) it becomes difficult for *national governments* to control the behaviour of such corporations. To take one example, the development of cheap international communications has meant call-centre jobs once based in the UK can now just as easily be based in countries such as India, where labour costs are lower.

## ✳ SYNOPTIC LINK

**Power and politics:** The behaviour and influence of transnational companies has a significant impact on the role of the state in modern societies.

 Weeding the path

Not everyone necessarily subscribes to the idea of a post-industrial society. **Harvey** (1990) argues that there has simply been a gradual change in the nature of economic production, away from:

**Fordist** models of accumulation based around what **Postero** (2005) characterises as mass production, rigid labour relationships and centralised production processes, towards:

**Flexible accumulation** involving the combination of a range of ideas **Harvey** characterises as:

- **Flexibility** across all areas – from the way goods and services are produced (products created in different countries and assembled in their 'home markets', for example), through *labour markets* (people employed on short-term contracts and being prepared to seek work across national frontiers), to *consumption patterns* (where people are encouraged to seek out new products and experiences).

- **New production sectors**: The constant development and refinement of services, the seeking out of new markets and ' … above all, greatly intensified rates of commercial, technological, and organisational innovation'.

- **Time** and **space compression**: With computer technology making global communication quicker (instantaneous at times), the world appears 'smaller', enabling transnational corporations to coordinate the manufacture of goods and the provision of services in a wide range of countries. Examples here might be the development of internet-based companies such as the book retailer Amazon.

Flexible accumulation, therefore, involves a complex interplay of ideas and activities, from the:

**Global Fordism** of car manufacturers where **Harvey** notes ' … production is spread out, complexly intertwining across the globe like a spider web – Japanese cars are made with Korean parts in the United States', to the behaviour of:

**Cyberspace companies** such as **eBay**, a company that hardly exists in the physical sense of buildings and factories.

These ideas reflect what **Goldman et al.** (1995) argue is a significant development, unique to postmodern society:

**Agile corporations** – a 'new type of transnational corporation' that developed at the end of the twentieth century. These operate globally (coordinating production, distribution and exchange across a number of markets, countries and continents) and are alert to economic and cultural developments and changes.

## ✳ SYNOPTIC LINK

**Stratification and differentiation:** We can link these ideas into Sabel's (1991) concept of unbounded networks (economic networks that have no boundaries).

## Political characteristics

The political characteristics of late/postmodernity are many and varied, but some significant ideas we can note are:

**Nation states** that came into being in the modern period steadily *decline* in significance, gradually being replaced by one – or both – of the following:

- **International states** that take two potential forms:

  - **Real**, as in something like the European Union where nation states (Britain, Germany, France, and so forth) form a much larger, international, political bloc. The EU, for example, has its own elected parliament, and individual member states abide by a range of common political and legal agreements.

  - **Virtual**: In this situation people transcend national boundaries through communication systems like the internet. Virtual communities of like-minded individuals and groups can 'meet' and interact in cyberspace.

- **Local states**: As nation states dissolve, local or regional communities (and identities) become more important to people. **Chiu et al.** (1997) argue that places like Hong Kong resemble the 'walled city states' of pre-modern societies.

These ideas have implications for concepts of identity; the global movement of people, commodities and knowledge, for example, makes the idea of 'a nation' increasingly difficult to sustain in postmodern society and also impacts on ideas about:

**Community**: This is an important concept for both sociology in general and modernist sociology (especially conflict and consensus perspectives) in particular, since it represents a significant source of *personal* and *social identity*. **Bellah** (1985) suggests that a community consists of people who:

- are socially **interdependent**
- **participate** in discussion and decision-making
- **share practices** that define and nurture a sense of community.

The concept of community, in modernist social theory, is frequently used to underscore the idea of categories such as class, age, gender, ethnicity and region (both local and national) as sources of identity. In other words, a clearly defined sense of community provides support for identities based around these categories, since they are:

**Solid referents**: Within *modernist theory*, gender, for example, has a relatively clear meaning in that it refers to both *biological* categories (male and female) and *social* categories (masculine and feminine) that reflect this basic biological division.

*Postmodern social theory*, however, questions this notion of community and, by extension, the kinds of theory on which it's based – within postmodernity, for example, the usefulness of concepts like class and gender as the basis for analysing behaviour is questioned. We can understand this by thinking in terms of what **Hudgins** and **Richards** (2000) call 'traditional approaches to understanding community' that stress, as in the **Bellah** example, things like:

* **physical proximity**
* **face-to-face interaction**
* **primary social relationships**
* **commitment** to shared meanings and beliefs
* **centred identities**.

## Community

**Hudgins** and **Richards** suggest that, in postmodern society, concepts of community based on 'shared social spaces' (physically interacting with people) and 'community as a source of meaning and identity' may change. As they put it: 'What happens to the spatial sense of community, for example, in an era of hyperspace in which our modern concepts of space are meaningless; in which space has been annihilated and spatial barriers have disappeared?'

**Rosenau** (1992) further argues that, in postmodern society, the concept of

community changes (she refers to the notion of 'community without unity' – the idea that we still look to 'the community' for a sense of meaning and identity, but this 'community' may exist only in a *virtual world* of people with whom we interact but never meet). In terms of social theory, therefore, postmodern explanations of behaviour are radically different to modernist explanations, if for no other reason than the fact that they view the concept of 'society' (and, by extension, concepts of community and identity) in radically different ways – an idea that leads us to consider the cultural characteristics of postmodern society.

## Cultural characteristics

**Belief systems**: Postmodern societies are characterised by multiple belief systems – in terms of differences *between* economic, political and cultural systems and *within* such systems. **Lyotard** (1984) argues that one consequence of this:

**Diversity** of belief systems is an 'incredulity towards grand narratives'; people are increasingly *unlikely* to believe 'all-encompassing explanations' that claim to explain 'everything about something'. This includes explanations produced by *religions* (Christianity, Islam), *politicians* (conservativism, socialism), *philosophers* (Marxism, fascism) and – of particular interest here – *scientists*. This sense of 'incredulity' represents a form of:

**Anti-essentialism** – the idea that it is impossible to reduce complex systems (such as societies) to their 'essential features' – for example, that 'gendered behaviour' can be explained in terms of the 'essential qualities' of males and females (their genetic, biological or psychological differences, for example). The 'search for essence' is, for postmodernists, a peculiarly *modernist* quest, one related to the concept of:

**Truth**: In modernist theory 'truth' is an essence; it represents the idea that it is possible to distinguish *objectively* between truth and falsity such that we can demonstrate that something is 'true for all time'. Postmodern *anti-essentialism*, however, sees 'truth' as a socially constructed category – nothing in the social world 'exists' outside of ideology and social construction. In other words, 'truth' is both *ideological* (defined from a particular viewpoint) and *relative*; my truth may not necessarily be your truth – and even if it is, this truth may not survive into the future.

## Relativity

These ideas have important consequences for how we understand concepts of sociological theory and science (discussed in the following section) – mainly because 'The Truth' is not 'Out There' waiting to be discovered in some objective way. Rather, 'truth' is *always* a *relative* concept, constructed from the subjective ways people experience and understand their world. If we accept this idea, it follows that a concept such as:

**Progress** is a subjective concept that cannot be measured quantitatively. It is simply one more form of ideological construction (or *discourse*, as postmodernists describe it).

In the above we've outlined some basic ideas relating to the idea of late/postmodern society, and it was in the light of such changes throughout the twentieth century that sociology took a distinctive turn, away from a preoccupation with *structure* and towards thinking about *agency*. We can examine this idea by thinking, first, about *interactionist* perspectives, and second, *postmodern* perspectives.

**Interactionism** is a generic name we give to a range of positions (symbolic interaction, phenomenology and ethnomethodology, for example) that 'reversed the theoretical gaze' – away from a preoccupation with *structures* and onto a consideration of human *agency*. In this respect, we can begin by noting that, for interactionists, the theoretical focus is on:

**Action over structure**: Interactionist perspectives focus on the individual – rather than 'society' or 'social structure' – as the primary unit of analysis. Understanding how and why people construct and reconstruct the world on a daily basis is, therefore, the main object of interest for this type of sociology. As **Heise** (1996) puts it: 'Interactionism emphasizes the force of shared culture and individual agency in human interaction [and offers] a view of society as constantly reinvented by individual people applying their shared culture to solve immediate problems'. This, he argues, leads to:

**Society** representing the ' . . . net outcome of active individuals dealing with daily challenges'. In other words, when we talk about 'society' we can do so only 'as if' it were a real force; from this perspective society is something we create, in our minds and through our behaviours, to express a sense of social solidarity and belonging.

## Micro sociology

To explain human behaviour, therefore, we need to study social interaction at the *micro* level – that of people going about their daily lives. From this perspective neither *society* nor *reality* are things that can be studied separately from people because they are:

**Negotiated abstractions**: **Schutz** (1962) argued that 'subjective meanings give rise to an apparently objective social world'. In

# ⚠ Growing it yourself: Creating the world

For this exercise you need to split into groups and each take a particular area of the social world to analyse (obvious choices might be education, which we've used as an illustration, family, crime, religion, and so forth).

Each group should identify the 'things we do to create' education (or whatever) and also the various ways our creation 'reflects back' on us to be experienced as a 'structural force'.

| Things we do to create [education] | How our creation reflects back on behaviour |
|---|---|
| Attend<br>Create authority structures<br>Obey norms | Organisational rules<br>Classroom norms |
| **Further examples?** ||

other words, our individual (subjective) behaviours give rise to *apparently* objective social structures (*abstractions*) that 'reflect back' on the behaviour we originally created.

The concept of *negotiated reality* brings into question the idea of 'objectivity'; if a world we experience objectively (such as going to school) is actually the result of the subjective behaviour and intentions of many individuals, we can similarly understand 'education' only subjectively, in terms of how people experience this elaborate 'structural fiction'. **Wilson** (2002) expresses this in terms of:

**Intersubjectivity**, where 'we experience the world with and through others. Whatever meaning we create has its roots in human actions'. In other words, the social world – its 'social artefacts and cultural objects' – consists of *phenomena* whose meaning is both *negotiated* and *interpreted* through social interaction. For example, we may learn something through personal

experience ('fire burns') that we pass on to others who may then incorporate it in to their own belief system. In school, for example, you build on the work done by previous human beings – as **Wilson** argues, in geography you don't have to sail around the globe to 'map countries of the world (although someone once did have to do just that'), just as in PE you don't have to invent football before you can play it.

In terms of sociological theory, these ideas run *counter* to early modernist notions that social behaviour can be theoretically isolated and empirically studied (the idea of *essentialism* . . . ); such ideas and research techniques are simply not going to work in the kind of world described by interactionists, governed by subjective beliefs and processes like:

**Categorisation**: To help us keep track of our lives and interact successfully in wider society, we 'group related phenomena' by developing stereotypical categories that help maintain a sense of order and stability in a potentially chaotic world. This gives rise to the concept of:

**Labelling**: The labels we devise ('mother', 'criminal' and the like) define the nature of the social categories we create. In late/postmodern societies people increasingly behave towards each other on the basis of the labels each attracts from others, mainly because face-to-face interaction may be limited (or, as in the virtual world, non-existent). Some labels can be considered:

**Master labels** because they are so powerful they condition *every* aspect of our behaviour towards the person so labelled (think about the consequences of being labelled a 'terrorist', for example). The labels we attract, either through choice (*achievement*) or through imposition (*ascription*), are important because knowledge of a label serves to unlock the assumptions we hold about particular social categories and, of course, conditions the way we feel it appropriate to behave towards someone.

## ✳ SYNOPTIC LINK

**Crime and deviance:** Labelling theory is an important explanation of both crime and deviance.

## ⚠ Digging deeper: Postmodernity and sociological theory

We can dig a little deeper into late/postmodern social theory by, first, developing some ideas about:

## Interactionist sociology

Like the structuralist (consensus and conflict) theories we've discussed previously, Interactionist sociology is rooted in modernist ideas about the possibility of explaining the social world in ways that are both *reliable* and *valid* – although, as we've discussed, its theoretical focus is very different. The main question we need to address, however, is, to paraphrase **Heise** (1996), how do the 'minute-by-minute behaviour inventions of millions of individuals culminate in the machine-like daily order' that, to take only one example, educates us in schools and colleges across the country? How, in other words, is social order possible if 'society' consists of people 'going about their individual lives'?

## Networks

The answer, **Heise** suggests, is ' ... society emerges from the creative activities of enculturated individuals'. In other words, patterns of behaviour – how they originate and develop in terms of social groups – can be understood in terms of:

**Social networks** based, according to **Cook** (2001), on two features:

- **Nodes** – defined as people (individuals or groups) in a particular network. 'The only requirement for a node,' according to **Cook**, 'is that it must be able to relate in some manner to other nodes' – something that leads to the concept of:

- **Ties** – or the relationships between two *nodes* (that can be many and varied – think about the range of relationships within your sociology class, for example). *Ties* (a relationship people recognise) are generated through *shared meanings* based around role-play – for example, the tie between a teacher and a student in an educational network. Group networks are also *not* self-contained; they involve links to other social networks, which leads to the development of larger networks and, ultimately, a sense of *social structure*.

**Cook** refers to the connections *between* networks as:

**Bridging ties** – a relationship that 'connects two otherwise distant portions of a network'. Continuing the educational theme, a class teacher plays a bridging role here because they link a specific class into the wider structure of the educational network. Individual students may also represent bridging ties by, for example, linking a school into a parental network. In this way we can see how, according to **Heise** and **Durig** (1997):

- **Micro-actions** – the actions of individuals – lead to:
- **Macro-actions** – routines that shape the behaviour and structure of large organisational networks.

Before we move on to consider a different approach to understanding the construction of social systems, we can note that, in **Heise's** (1996) formulation, *network theory* – what he terms:

**Affect control theory** – can be used to explain how 'the majestic order of society emerges from repetitive application of evolved cultural resources to frame and solve recurrent problems' – social structures result from people's repeated, meaningful actions within social networks.

## Weeding the path

Although this is one way contemporary modernist theory examines and explains the development of social structures, we can explore an *alternative explanation* that reflects a more *structuralist* preoccupation with social order, namely **Luhmann's** (1995) concept of:

## Growing it yourself: The ties that bind

This concept of social networks is one based on the idea of a **role set** (a group of related roles). In this exercise, you're required to construct a social network diagram for your class, showing the relationships that exist within this network.

To help you, we've constructed a simple network example (five students focused on one teacher).

In your example, you should not only show the ties within the network; you should also indicate how this particular network (the school class) links to additional networks both within and outside education.

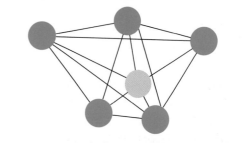

**Simple social network showing nodes and indicating ties**

# Systems theory

Where something like *affect control theory* argues that *complex systems* are created through the purposeful actions of individuals, **Luhmann's** *systems theory* argues the reverse; he begins from the idea of a 'world system' (all societies in the modern world are in some way connected) and, effectively, *works backwards* to an explanation of individual social action. To understand how this works we need to think about societies as:

**Complex systems**: **Luhmann** assumes human behaviour is generally characterised by complexity, considered in terms, for example, of the number and range of possible relational combinations across the social world. In addition, this level of complexity introduces the idea of:

**Chaos**: If social life is (essentially) based on conscious individuals making behavioural choices across a range of groups and social networks, it's difficult to see how social order can be created and maintained; in other words, if we focus on the idea that networks are built *upwards* – from individuals at the bottom to systems at the top – it's difficult to explain how individual behaviours (in terms of the possible behavioural choices people can make in any given situation) can produce a relatively orderly and predictable social system.

**Luhmann** suggest this is possible only if we think in terms of systems *imposing* an order and stability on individual behaviour that is, in turn, sufficiently flexible to accommodate individual choice and deviation. The question here, according to **Vandenberghe** (1998), is how 'the social ordering of chaos' comes about, and the answer involves:

**Autopoiesis** ('auto-poe-ee-sis'): According to **Maturana** and **Varela** (1980), autopoiesis involves an organisation (such as a social system) being *self-reproductive*; in other words, **Luhmann** sees social systems as both:

- **Autonomous** – systems effectively operate 'independently' of people. They are able to do this, for **Luhmann**, because societies are not 'things' or 'structures', as such, but *communication networks*.

- **Self-maintaining** – through their involvement 'in' and use of 'the system', people effectively contribute to its reproduction.

According to **Krippendorff** (1986), an *autopoietic system* ' . . . produces its own organisation and maintains and constitutes itself .. for example, a living organism . . . a corporation or a society as a whole'. To put this in less abstract terms, think about society as, in **Maturana** and **Varela's** evocative description, 'living machines' (or, if it makes it easier, something like the *internet*).

---

## ✳ SYNOPTIC LINK

**Stratification and differentiation:** **Luhmann's** ideas about autopoietic networks link into modernist theories of stratification.

---

We can clarify these ideas through the following example.

Every Sociology A2 class in England is structured by a range of *exterior* factors – some *formal* and *direct* (the Specification, for example), others *informal* and *indirect* – your personal reasons for being in class perhaps.

On a *systems level* the behaviour is much the same. Each class is a *network* contributing to the continued functioning of the educational system without the *conscious* efforts of the people involved. In other words, when you arrive for your sociology class you don't think, 'How does this behaviour help to reproduce social relationships at the structural level of society?' And even if you did you'd have no way of knowing exactly what behaviour is required to 'reproduce the education system'.

Structure, therefore, is imposed (from *outside*) and reproduced *within* (the class), which effectively means structure is the most significant variable involved in understanding human behaviour, since, without the initial sense of structure, a social network could not form.

This type of analysis provides a bridge between *modernist* and *postmodernist* social theory – the former in terms of, to paraphrase **Vandenberghe** (1998), systems theory being an attempt to 'explain everything' about the construction of the social world (a *metanarrative*, in other words), and the latter in terms of the conclusion that the social world 'is like a ship adrift from its moorings and without the possibility of a captain on board'. In other words, for postmodernists social life can be understood only through *descriptions* of social encounters; the world is too large, diverse and fragmented to be understood as some sort of coherent, unified system in the way it's generally understood by modernist sociology.

## Postmodern

**Postmodern perspectives**, therefore, focus on the concept of:

**Narrative** as a way of conceptualising the different ways people have of describing their situation. These 'stories' relate to both sociologists and non-sociologists alike – while sociological stories are of a different order they are, from this position, no more and no less 'true'. Narratives alone, however, don't adequately explain how social life hangs together. For this we need the concept of:

**Discourse**, something that refers, according to writers like **Foucault** (1972), to a system of ideas, organised in terms of a specific vocabulary. Both sociology and psychology, for example, are social science *discourses* (which is itself a further discourse). A discourse, therefore, involves a set of related narratives that both define something and, consequently, shape the way we interpret and understand its meaning. The same thing can, of course, be the subject of a number of different discourses – homosexuality, for example, may be the subject of different discourses depending on how you view this behaviour.

## 🏠 The potting shed

Identify and briefly explain one discourse on human sexuality (for example, think about what some people class as 'normal' or 'abnormal' sexuality).

**Fiske** (1987) notes how the meaning of something both depends on the discourse that surrounds it and 'serves the interests of' the social group from which it arises. The term 'queer', for example, has a different meaning for gay men than it does for the British National Party.

291

## ✳ SYNOPTIC LINK

We can find examples of discourse and
narrative right across the Specification – from
politics (conservative and socialist
discourses), through religion (such as
Christianity and Islam), to education
(selective or comprehensive schooling).

If discourses are part of everyday life,
surrounding and shaping our perception of
both people and the world, it follows that all
knowledge must be *subjective* (or ideological,
if you prefer), which has important
ramifications for how sociologists can study
the world, since it seems to negate the
concept of:

**Truth**: We suggested earlier that
postmodernists consider all forms of
knowledge to be *relative*; one form can never
be objectively proven to be superior to
another form. This characterisation is,
however, true(?) only up to a point.
Questions of truth are *not wholly* relative;
rather, they are *partially* relative – a nice
distinction, perhaps, but one that has
considerable relevance for sociology since it
suggests something may be 'true in
principle', but not universally true for all
time. In other words, the concept of truth is:

**Context-bound**: Something may be true
(or false) within a given set of specified
parameters and under certain conditions.
Thus, 'truth' itself is *not* a relative concept;
the *contexts* within which truths can be
established are, however, relative in time
and space. If this is a little unclear, an
example should clarify it.

### Example

It is true that I have the status 'husband';
however, the validity (or truth) of this
statement is *context-bound* in the sense that
it depends on how the concept of 'husband'
is defined. For example, if we define it as 'a
man who is married to a woman', then I am
a husband. If, however, 'husband' is defined
as 'a man married to a lamp post', then I am
*not* a husband. In this particular context, of
course, we would also raise questions about
how things like 'man', 'woman' and 'lamp
post' were defined (but that only goes to
show how complicated things can get).

### ⚠ Weeding the path

In terms of *social theory*, the idea of truth
being context-bound has implications for
sociology, science and, perhaps, the question
of whether or not sociology is scientific. If
questions of truth are necessarily bound up
with both narratives and discourses, it
follows that we are effectively defining them
from a particular, partial and subjective
viewpoint – which raises the question of
how it is possible to generate reliable and
valid knowledge, not just about the *social*
world, but about the *natural* world as well.

## Characteristics

To complete this section we can draw on
**Rosenau's** (1991) ideas about the general
characteristics of postmodernity and their
implications for social science:

- **Objectivity**: All knowledge is *inherently
  subjective* in terms of the assumptions
  made about how it is possible to study and
  understand the world (both natural and
  social). This follows, for postmodernists,
  because knowledge is created and
  validated within the context of specific
  discourses; thus, for natural scientists
  knowledge is validated by a belief in
  *empirical* principles (such as the existence

of facts, causality, and so forth). If we buy into a natural scientific discourse we *must* accept its ability to produce reliable and valid knowledge; if we *reject* that discourse we also, of course, reject its assumptions about reliability and validity.

- **Transgression**: Postmodernists raise important questions about *how* we can study the social world. In particular, they question the idea that knowledge can be neatly compartmentalised (in terms of categories like 'science' and 'non-science' or 'sociology' and 'physics'). They question, therefore, the idea of *rigid* (modernist) *boundaries* in all areas of social life (from the distinction between 'men and women' to that between 'truth and falsity').

- **Diversity**: Knowledge is always tentative, partial and incomplete; what we believe we know is always open to challenge and, in this respect, consists of 'competing stories' that are evaluated in terms of prevailing cultural orthodoxies. There is not – and can never be – a universal truth.

Finally, **Hudgins** and **Richards** (2000) summarise quite neatly the different perspectives we've examined in this section when they note: 'Postmodernism ... may be seen as a completely new social science paradigm and a complete overthrow of modernism, or as the most recent stage of modernism itself. It may be seen as a force undermining social order leading to chaos and anarchy, or as the freedom from the repressive systems of thought of the past. Some fear the radical relativism of postmodernism, and some see it as the promise of a new and better society ... One thing is certain, however, we are moving toward a new way of understanding the social world ... '

## Moving on

In this section we've looked at the ideas of modernity and postmodernity and how they relate, in very broad terms, to different forms of sociological theorising. In so doing we've raised questions about the methodological concepts of reliability and validity along the way, and in the next section we're going to focus on this area by examining questions about the nature of 'science' and the status of sociological knowledge.

# 2. The nature of 'science' and the extent to which sociology may be regarded as scientific

In the previous section we raised some methodological questions relating to the production of knowledge about the social world which, in this section, we can develop in the context of how we define 'science' and the question of whether or not sociology can be classified as 'scientific' in both its approach and the knowledge it produces. Initially, however, we can note a couple of reasons for wanting to explore these ideas, both related to the concept of *status*:

- **Knowledge status**: Scientific knowledge is generally considered, in modern societies, to be the most reliable, valid and (perhaps) superior form of knowledge it's possible to generate. In short, we associate (rightly or wrongly) scientific knowledge with *truth* – which is probably reason enough to think about this particular assumption in more detail.

- **Subject status**: If scientific knowledge is

## WARM-UP: WHAT IS SCIENCE?

'Science' is a familiar idea in our society and you should, therefore, have a reasonable idea about the concept and be able to visualise various characteristics (and, by extension, the characteristics of non-science) when you hear the word itself.

In small groups, use the following table to identify and categorise your thoughts about science. Once you've exhausted all possibilities, as a class decide what constitutes science and non-science (and, of course, why).

| Science is: | Science is not: |
| --- | --- |
| Factual | Opinion |
| Physics | Theatre studies |

generally considered to be a *superior* form of knowledge, it's hardly surprising that sociologists would like a piece of the action – like anyone else, sociologists want their ideas to be taken seriously and one way for this to happen is if sociological knowledge has a similar status to natural scientific knowledge.

## ⚠ Preparing the ground: The nature of science

When we think about the concept of science, two initial ideas need to be clear:

**Knowledge**: 'Science' is *not* a 'body of knowledge' – it isn't, for example, the preserve of particular subject areas (such as chemistry or physics). Rather, *science* is a way of producing a particular *kind* of knowledge. As **Popper** (1934) classically puts it: 'Science is … a method of approaching and studying phenomena. It involves identifying a problem to study, collecting information about it and eventually offering an explanation for it. All this is done as systematically as possible.'

In this respect, therefore, we can think about science as a:

**Methodology** – a way of producing *reliable* and *valid* knowledge. Scientific knowledge has, in this respect, been *tested* against available evidence and not been *disproven*, something that, at the very least, gives such knowledge greater *plausibility* than non-scientific knowledge – ideas that are consolidated around the ability to make:

**Predictive statements** based on scientific knowledge: Predictive ability means the scientist is in a position to say with *complete certainty* that something *will* happen in the

'Science is best defined as a careful, disciplined, logical search for knowledge about any and all aspects of the universe, obtained by examination of the best available evidence and always subject to correction and improvement upon the discovery of better evidence. What's left is magic, and it doesn't work'
**James Randi (1993), magician**

future – perhaps the most powerful form of knowledge statement we can make.

## ⚠ Weeding the path

Although the power of science is bound up with its ability to make predictive statements, **Carpi** (2003) identifies a common misconception about science (that it somehow defines 'truth'): 'Science does not define truth; rather, it defines a way of thought. It is a process in which experiments are used to answer questions' – an important distinction because scientific knowledge (despite the claims of some postmodernists) doesn't claim to be 'true' in the sense that it can never be questioned.

Rather, it involves the idea that scientific knowledge, properly tested and evidenced, represents the *most plausible* explanation we currently have for something and it retains this status only until some other scientist produces a *more plausible* explanation.

---

## ✳ SYNOPTIC LINK

**Religion/Power and politics:** We can note that different definitions of 'truth' may apply in different contexts. For example, in terms of *religion* people may accept the truth of something (such as the existence of God) on the basis of *faith* (an unquestioning – and untestable – belief). Alternatively, *politicians* often ask their followers to accept the truth of something 'on *trust*' – which, unlike science, once again reflects an *unquestioning* attitude to truth.

---

If science is a methodology, it follows it must involve a set of *rules* applied by the scientist in the research process, and these, for our purpose, fall into two categories (*procedures* and *ethos*).

## Procedures

Scientists must follow an agreed set of *methodological procedures* governing how data can be collected and analysed. One of the most influential examples here comes from **Popper's** (1934) notion of a:

**Hypothetico-deductive model**, involving a number of phases, starting with:

**Phenomena**: Scientists choose – and think about – 'a problem' requiring explanation. They then:

**Generate ideas** about how to study 'the problem'. This involves observations, both personal and of any work that may previously have been done in the area of interest. This eventually leads to the formation of a:

**Testable hypothesis**: To clarify 'the problem', a hypothesis is stated that must be capable of being tested through the collection and analysis of evidence. In **Popper's** formulation, a hypothesis must be *capable* of being disproven through:

**Systematic observation**: Hypothesis testing involves collecting data in a reliable way. In the natural sciences, for example, *experimentation* is widely used because the scientist can control the conditions under which data are generated and, in theory at least, maintain an objective position that avoids personal interference in the data-collection process. After collection, data are:

**Systematically analysed** – the data have to be objectively interpreted so that:

**Conclusions** can be drawn from them. On the basis of the evidence, the hypothesis is *either*:

- **Refuted** (shown to be false) – in which case the scientist might develop a new testable hypothesis – or
- **Confirmed** – shown to be 'not false', an important distinction because **Popper**

argues scientific knowledge can never be conclusively shown to be 'true'. A 'confirmed hypothesis' then becomes part of a:

- **Theory** – an explanatory statement (usually) consisting of a series of linked, confirmed hypotheses that allow the scientist to make *predictive statements* about the behaviour initially observed.

## Ethos

**Ethos** refers to rules governing the general conditions 'science' must satisfy if it is to both attain and maintain scientific status. In other words, the process of 'doing science' is located in a *community* that specifies:

- **standards** for the overall conduct of scientists and scientific forms of research, and
- **policies** for scientific practice, to ensure rules of procedure, such as the ones we've just noted, are obeyed.

**Merton** (1942) identified four areas of *research ethics* that, in combination, make up what he termed a:

**Scientific ethos** – a set of *normative guidelines* related to the practice of science:

- **Universalism**: The scientific community must evaluate knowledge only on the basis of objective, universally agreed criteria. Personal values – either those of the scientific community or of society as a whole – play no part in the evaluation process and criticism of a scientist's work should focus on refuting ('falsifying') their conclusions, identifying weaknesses in the research process, and so forth. In technical terms, scientists must avoid what **Labossiere** (1995) calls the:

**Ad hominem fallacy** – a situation in which an argument is rejected ' ... on the basis of some irrelevant fact about the author of or the person presenting the claim or argument' (whether this rejection is based on personal factors – their character, for example – or social factors such as gender, nationality, class, age and the like).

---

## ✳ SYNOPTIC LINK

**Stratification and differentiation:**
**Etzkowitz et al.** (2000) argue that, despite this ethos of universalism, female scientists frequently find their work and careers hampered by the 'hidden barriers, subtle exclusions and unwritten rules of the scientific workplace'.

---

- **Communality**: Scientific knowledge is 'public knowledge' shared, initially, within the scientific community for a number of reasons:

  - **Progression**: Scientists must be able to build on the work done by other scientists. This not only saves time and effort (scientists are not continually 'reinventing the wheel'), but also encourages the 'leaps of faith' (where one scientist, for example, is inspired to develop new ideas by understanding the work of other scientists) through which scientific understanding advances on a *cumulative* basis.

  - **Evaluation**: If scientific knowledge cannot be accepted 'on trust', it follows that scientists must make their work, including details of research methodology, available for peer review and criticism.

  - **Replication**: An important aspect of

scholarly criticism is the ability to repeat ('replicate') a piece of research to see whether the same results are attained. Such replication is normally done by other scientists who, therefore, require detailed knowledge of the original research. In recent times one of the most famous examples of 'peer review' in the natural sciences is **Fleischmann** and **Pons'** (1989) claim to have created energy through a process called 'cold fusion' – subsequent attempts by other scientists to repeat the experiment failed to confirm **Fleischmann** and **Pons'** findings.

- **Disinterestedness** has two basic meanings here:

  - **Institutional**: The main responsibility of the scientist is the pursuit of knowledge. This is not to say scientists should not be recognised for their achievements (or rewarded for their efforts), but they should not have a stake in the 'success' of their research since this risks introducing personal bias into the research process.

  - **Detachment**: The use to which research is put is not the responsibility of the scientist who produced it. Scientists, in other words, cannot be held accountable for how others (such as politicians) use their research.

- **Organised scepticism**: One of the guiding principles of science is that nothing is beyond criticism, a significant idea for two main reasons:

  - **Critical reflection**: The scientific community must continually evaluate knowledge (rather than simply taking it for granted) since this 'process of questioning' contributes to the development of human understanding.

## ⚠ Growing it yourself: Functional science

The scientific ethos is rooted in **Merton**'s Functionalist outlook on social behaviour – an ethos develops and is maintained because it's in the interests of both scientists and non-scientists to ensure its normative principles and procedures are obeyed.

In this respect, we could also note how such an ethos reflects **Luhmann**'s ideas about autopoiesis – the scientific community resembles a self-reproducing organisation that exists independently of its individual members.

As a class, identify as many *functions* (both personal and organisational) as possible of a scientific ethos (we've given you some ideas to start you off).

| For scientists | For society |
|---|---|
| Preserves the personal and institutional credibility of science and scientists | Trust – we know research has been checked and rechecked |

- **Inherency**: Knowledge is never 'inherently true' (an article of faith). This 'sceptical attitude' represented, for **Merton**, the main way scientific knowledge differed from other forms of knowledge (such as religious faith); the former is 'true' only because it has not, *as yet*, been disproved. The latter, however, is considered by its adherents to be *self-evidently true* (it cannot be refuted).

The idea of a scientific ethos, to which all scientists – by choice, peer pressure or institutional imperative – are forced to subscribe, enables us to understand the way scientific research is both organised and validated according to a set of institutionalised norms and values concerning what does and does not constitute science.

### Weeding the path

**Prelli** (1989) notes that four types of 'oppositional counter norms' have been suggested to set against **Merton's** moral norms:

- **Particularism**, whereby the personal status, ability and experience of a scientist leads others to uncritically accept their arguments and findings.

- **Solitariness**: Scientists are increasingly claiming 'property rights' to the commercial exploitation of their work, thereby preventing scientific scrutiny under the guise of 'commercial confidentiality'.

- **Interestedness**: With commercial employment and exploitation scientists

are under increasing pressure to ensure their work 'produces the desired results'.

- **Organised dogmatism** involving scientists fervently defending their research and findings against external criticism, while 'doubting the findings of others'.

### Digging deeper: The nature of science

**Prelli's** identification of 'oppositional norms' suggests we need to look more critically at both the theory and practice of science, not only in terms of a *scientific ethos* but also in terms of the logic and procedures of a scientific methodology (such as the hypothetico-deductive model proposed by **Popper**).

In thinking about the conduct of science, therefore, we can begin by noting **Kaplan's** (1964) distinction between two types of logic:

- **Logics-in-use**: Solomon (2000) describes this as 'what people actually do' – and how they go about doing it – when they carry out research.

- **Reconstructed logics** refer to how a piece of research is presented to the world, for both peer review within the scientific community and public consumption.

Ideally, the two logics should be the same since the scientist is simply recording and presenting a description of their research, but research 'in the real world' is rarely, if ever, the smooth, uncluttered process described by **Popper's** (idealised) research procedure.

## ⚠ Weeding the path

Although these two ideas express possible differences between what scientists 'say they do' (a *reconstructed logic* that presents a polished narrative for peer and public consumption) and what they 'actually do' (*logic-in-use*), this is not to say scientists deliberately cheat or falsify their procedures and results. As **Medawar** (1963) argues, scientific papers describing the research process are 'fraudulent' only in the sense that they ' . . . give a totally misleading narrative of the processes of thought that go into the making of scientific discoveries'.

However, it does suggest that if reconstructions are the norm, it is difficult for scientific research to be reliably and validly *replicated* since what is being retested is a *narrative* that *describes* a research process, not the actual process itself – something **Kaplan** (1964) calls an 'idealisation of scientific practice' rather than an objective description of such practice. This distinction raises an important question for the sociology of science (and, by extension, the question of whether or not sociology can be considered scientific), namely the extent to which the ability of natural scientists to produce highly reliable and valid knowledge is based on a:

- **Scientific methodology** that guarantees the production of such knowledge or a:

- **Subject matter** that, because it does not have *consciousness*, allows the natural scientist to produce reliable and valid knowledge 'regardless' of the exact form of methodology used to generate it.

These questions are crucial to both an understanding of science and, by implication, the question of whether or not sociology can

be a science in the same way that physics, for example, is a science. If 'scientific knowledge' is the product of a *methodology*, it's theoretically possible for social scientists to use a similar methodology to study human behaviour. If, however, such knowledge is a quality of the *subject matter* of natural science (inanimate objects rather than thinking subjects), it will be impossible to reliably and validly use such a methodology in the social sciences.

## Systems

We can develop these ideas further by thinking about the difference between two types of system:

- **Closed systems** allow researchers to tightly control variables that potentially affect the behaviour being studied (as in a laboratory, for example). Such systems are 'closed' because they can be isolated from wider environments (the 'outside world').

- **Open systems** involve the opposite idea – they represent situations where the possible range of influences on behaviour cannot be completely controlled by the researcher. In the social world, 'society' is the ultimate *open system*, but open systems are also found in the natural world – in the study of global weather systems, for example – and this makes for an interesting observation.

For both types of system:
**Laws of cause and effect** operate, making it theoretically possible to predict how something will behave. However, the inability to fully control all possible variables in *open systems* makes *predictions* about observed behaviour difficult – if not impossible. In this respect:

# 🌷 Growing it yourself: Open and closed systems

Using the following table as a template, we can relate ideas about open and closed systems to research methods by identifying the advantages and disadvantages of studying people's behaviour in a laboratory as opposed to their natural environment (society).

| Laboratory (closed system) | | In society (open system) | |
| --- | --- | --- | --- |
| *Advantages* | *Disadvantages* | *Advantages* | *Disadvantages* |
| Control of variables | Unnatural environment | Natural environment | Difficult to control variables |

**Chaos theory** provides an example of how open systems work and the problems they hold for scientific research methodology in that it argues that small variations in behaviour can produce very large differences in outcome, sometimes referred to as the:

**Butterfly effect: Lorenz** (1972) posed the question 'Does the flap of a butterfly's wings in Brazil set off a tornado in Texas?' to demonstrate the idea of *random variation* – something illustrated quite neatly in the film *Jurassic Park*, where the 'chaos mathematician' Ian Malcolm argues that the plan to cage dinosaurs in a *closed system* (an isolated theme park) is doomed to failure because 'nature always finds a way'. In other words, although open systems are relatively stable and in some measure predictable, there are times when minute changes lead to random (or unpredictable) outcomes – and since we have no way of knowing what change will produce what outcome, the ability to predict behaviour in open systems with any certainty is impossible.

## 🛠 Weeding the path

Both *chaos theory* and the nature of *open systems* suggest two things:

- **Science** is a methodology sensitive to the subject matter it is designed to study.
- **Societies** – and the behaviour of people within them – are open, chaotic systems that cannot necessarily be studied in the same way we study behaviour in closed systems.

In addition, thus far we've failed to question the idea of a 'single scientific methodology' (that proposed, for example, by **Popper**). However, we can correct this by suggesting there may be different ways of 'doing science' both *within* natural sciences such as chemistry and biology and *between* different areas of science (such as biology and sociology). **Feyerabend** (1975), for example, contributes a couple of interesting ideas here:

- **Complexity**: The natural world is a

*complex space* that cannot be easily contained within simple categories of thought; developments in *chaos theory* (and *quantum physics*), for example, call into question a 'one size fits all' methodology based around *falsification* (the hypothetico-deductive model). For **Feyerabend** this methodological straightjacket of a 'single prescriptive scientific method' was too restrictive and led to a:

- **Rigidity of thinking**: Natural scientists become locked into the need to defend '*the* scientific method' against both internal and external attack and, by so doing, close themselves off to alternative arguments and methodologies.

 **Weeding the path**

**Feyerabend's** arguments are sometimes interpreted as an 'attack on science' (he has been accused of being 'antiscience' and the advocate of an 'anything goes' view of scientific methodology). However, **Feyerabend** can also be seen as contributing to a debate about the nature of science designed to *strengthen* science by making it more responsive to new ideas.

More recently, the question of objective forms of knowledge and practice has been attacked by postmodernists in two related ways.

## Theoretical critiques

**Theoretical critiques** focus on the idea that science is simply another:

**Discourse** that explains something about the world and, as such, it competes against other discourses (religion, mysticism, magic, and so forth). Science has no special claim to truth because, from this viewpoint, concepts like 'truth' are, as we've suggested, inherently subjective. The argument, for example, that 'scientific explanations' are *superior* to religious explanations (because scientific knowledge is based on objective testing and proof while religious knowledge is based on faith) is rejected by postmodernists because tests of 'superiority' are inherently based on *subjective criteria*; certain groups (such as scientists or priests), for example, have the *power* to define the criteria against which something is judged. In this way, therefore, science (like religion) represents a:

**Metanarrative** – just another grand narrative that seeks, by whatever means, to establish its *hegemony* over all other possible narratives. Postmodernist theoretical critiques tend, in this respect, to focus around ideas like:

- **Objectivity**: Taking a lead from **Polyani's** (1958) observation that 'all observation is theory-dependent' (to understand what we are seeing we must, by definition, already know what it is – we must have already formulated a *theory* that describes what we're seeing *before* we see it), postmodernists have argued that the concept of 'objectivity' (the ability to observe something dispassionately without influencing the behaviour being observed) is not possible.

- **Midwifery**: Natural science argues that 'reality' (and by extension *knowledge*) is something that 'exists to be discovered' (*heurism*). The scientist, therefore, is like a midwife – someone charged with the delivery of knowledge rather than its actual creation (which is how scientists are able to claim objectivity). For postmodernists this involves what

**Polyani** (1967) termed '*tacit knowledge*', a fundamental conviction about the nature of things in the natural world – in this case, the *subjective belief* (one based on the cultural values of the scientist) that reality and knowledge take the form they claim.

## ⚠ Weeding the path

**Craig** (2005) notes: 'Science bases its pursuit of and claim to truth on *objective* enquiry. Denials of the possibility of objectivity therefore attack science 'at its root' and, as you might expect, scientists have responded to the criticisms put forward by postmodernists in a variety of ways:

- **Reality**: The natural world really is different to the social world and the two should not be confused. *Causal relationships* between inanimate objects are *real* – they occur whatever the political and ideological outlook of the observer. Partly this is the result of the *heuristic* nature of the natural world (things exist and can be discovered), but it is also due to the skill and knowledge of the scientist. **Feyerabend** (1992) – although, as we've suggested, sometimes seen as a critic of modern science – makes a significant supporting point when he notes: 'Movements that view quantum mechanics as a turning point in thought – and that includes fly-by-night mystics, prophets of a New Age, and relativists of all sorts – get aroused by the cultural component and forget predictions and technology'.

- **Misinformation**: Critics of postmodernism, such as **Sokal** (1994), have argued that a great deal of

postmodern writing on science is generally misinformed, lacking in depth and misunderstands what scientists attempt to do. An example here is the concept of:

- **Truth** – scientists, according to **Sokal**, are well aware that any claim to 'truth' must, as **Popper** (1934) argues, '...remain tentative for ever'.

## Practical critiques

**Practical critiques**, meanwhile, focus on the uses to which scientific knowledge is put, an idea bound up in the concept of:

**Progress**: Postmodernists have been critical of the association between scientific knowledge and 'progress' – the idea that science has practical uses in terms of *improving* our lives. **Campbell** (1996) captures the general flavour of this criticism when he notes: 'Science is viewed as the vanguard of European exploitation, a discipline run amok, the instigators of nuclear and other weapons systems, the handmaiden of big business and as the defilers of nature.'

The charge here, in effect, is that science is not necessarily the 'dispassionate, objective 'search for truth' that scientists would like us to believe, and **Malik** (1998) articulates this general situation quite neatly: 'Whereas once science stood as a metaphor for human advancement, today it stands more as a metaphor for human debasement. That is why with every technological advance – from cloning to genetically modified food – there is a tendency for people to stress the *problems* it may cause rather than the promise that it holds. *Fear of science* has become the vehicle through which wider social insecurities are given vent.'

# Discussion point: What have scientists ever done for us?

Whether or not you see this type of criticism as valid, it's clear that people no longer (if indeed they ever did) view science and scientists as necessarily being beneficial bringers of progress.

To explore this idea as a class, identify some positive and negative aspects of science and scientific knowledge.

Use these ideas to discuss the extent to which you see science as a broadly beneficial or broadly harmful enterprise.

Further questions develop, with a practical focus, from the idea of **Prelli's** (1989) 'oppositional norms' which we noted earlier, and the extent to which scientists actually conform to a 'community of values' represented by a *scientific ethos*. We could, for example, note the problem of:

**Scientific fraud**: Although both **Martin** (1992) and **Jones** (2002), among others, have documented examples of scientific fraud, the fact that it is routinely detected tells us that either the policing of science is relatively successful or, as with other forms of deception, 'revealed deviance' is merely the tip of a very large iceberg. Although we can't know with any certainty the extent of fraud within various branches of science, **Martinson et al.** (2005) discovered 33% of 3200 US scientists 'confessed to various kinds of misconduct – such as claiming credit for someone else's work, or changing results because of pressure from a study's sponsor'. They suggest, however, that the real area of concern is the ' … wider range of questionable research practices', such as:

**Misrepresentations**: **Martin** (1992) suggests: 'In the routine practice of scientific research, there are many types of misrepresentation and bias which could be considered dubious. However, only a few narrowly defined behaviours are singled out

and castigated as scientific fraud.' This characterisation has two major consequences:

- **Routinisation**: A variety of 'dubious practices', **Martin** (1992) suggests, permeate the research process. These 'routine deviations' are technically misrepresentations but are rarely, if ever, punished. Included in this general category are behaviours such as:

  - **Reconstructed logics** – as we've seen, publications detailing a research process may bear only a passing resemblance to the *actual* process.

  - **Referencing**: A failure to adequately reference all sources. **Simkin** and **Roychowdhury** (2002) found 80% of citations in research papers were simply copied – spelling mistakes included – from other reference lists.

  - **Intellectual exploitation**: Making use of the work of others without giving them the credit/recognition they deserve.

  - **Unrealistic assessments** of the research's importance (in order to achieve higher levels of funding).

- **Function**: **Martin** argues: 'A narrow

definition of scientific fraud is convenient to the groups in society – scientific elites and powerful government and corporate interests – that have the dominant influence on priorities in science.' He notes that one function of 'the denunciation of fraud' is that it 'helps to paint the rest of scientific behaviour as blameless'.

## Preparing the ground: Is sociology scientific?

When we start to consider the question of whether sociology can – or cannot – be considered scientific, an initial problem we face is one of:

**Definition**: The extent to which anything can be considered scientific depends on how science is defined; however, for the sake of argument, we can think of science in the way we've outlined it at the start of this section and focus our efforts on the question of the extent to which sociology is scientific in the way something like physics is considered scientific. We can do this by examining a number of theoretical and practical ideas surrounding the theory and practice of science and the extent to which sociology meets these scientific criteria.

## Principles

We can, therefore, examine the general methodological principles of science, starting with the idea that it is:

**Theoretical**: This idea works on two levels. First, science, as we've suggested, operates on the principle of testable hypotheses. Second, it represents a body of reliable and valid theoretical knowledge that can be used to inform our judgements about – and interpretations of – future behaviour.

In the natural sciences both these levels are attainable; within sociology, however, although the first is achievable, the second is more questionable ('*problematic*').

## Weeding the path

Predicting individual behaviour is, for reasons we'll explore in a moment, either methodologically unattainable (the social world does not conform to *simple* cause-and-effect relationships, for example) or unattainable given our present levels of technology (the development of computerised mathematical modelling, for example, may change this). We need to remember, however, that not all forms of behaviour in the natural world are 'individually predictable' – weather systems being a case in point (scientists have never been able to *precisely predict* weather patterns).

At the level of social groups it's possible, in some ways, to make theoretical sociological statements that have 'law-like' qualities. **Parsons'** concept of *functional imperative* might be a case in point and, on a more general level, we could note the fact that all social groups involve roles, socialisation, values, beliefs and norms (although we can't, unlike with natural science, necessarily predict with any certainty their precise content).

## ✳ SYNOPTIC LINK

Crime and deviance: **Durkheim's** analysis and explanation for different types of suicide could fit this category of theoretical statements with law-like qualities.

**Empiricism** involves specifying what constitutes an acceptable form of data. In a simple sense, empirical data is information collected 'through the use of our senses' (sight, touch, smell, hearing, taste) – in other words, it involves generating data through our *observations* and *experiences*, and although 'empirical' is often confused with the idea that something is 'factual' or 'scientific', this is not necessarily the case. For example, your *description* of your reasons for doing something (in an interview or questionnaire, for example) represents *empirical data* – it doesn't have to be true (you could be making it up) and it is not scientific because it hasn't been verified, which means an important quality of science is:

**Testing**: This is an important quality, according to **Popper**, because it opens up the possibility of:

**Falsification**: Although a hypothesis may be sufficiently robust to resist all (past and current) attempts to disprove it, scientific theories *always* contain the *possibility* of falsification through testing. This 'test of testability', as it were, is frequently cited as a crucial element in the distinction between scientific and non-scientific knowledge.

## Weeding the path

In terms of something like **Popper's** hypothetico-deductive model, sociology can be considered, at best, as being:

- **Pre-theoretical**: Although it is capable of developing testable hypotheses, it hasn't made the necessary leap to the development of a body of theoretical knowledge that can be used as the basis for predictions (in the way that natural sciences like physics and chemistry have made such a leap). Sociological theories,

in this respect, are sometimes criticised for being ideological statements whose truth or falsity is *assumed* rather than tested. However, in relation to the idea of:

- **Empiricism**, not all sociologists subscribe to empirical testing as the basis for the generation of reliable and valid knowledge, for a couple of reasons. First, as we've suggested, some have questioned the definition of science employed in the natural sciences as an *ideological imposition*, whereby a powerful interest group (natural scientists) imposes its definition of science on other, competing groups to its own advantage. Second, some forms of sociology (such as **Luhmann's** systems theory) focus on large-scale group behaviour that can only be theorised, not empirically tested.

This objection is also significant because in the natural world non-empirical testing (and falsification) is not unknown – **Youngson** (1998) argues that *quantum physics* cannot be studied using **Popper's** model of science (for complicated reasons we don't need to concern ourselves with here).

## The potting shed

From any area of the Specification, identify and briefly explain one tested sociological hypothesis with which you are familiar.

**Accumulation** expresses the idea that a scientific body of knowledge is built up from previous (tested) knowledge. In one general respect sociology satisfies this criterion since sociologists have accumulated a stock of knowledge that informs the work of other sociologists. In another respect, the idea of cumulative knowledge is open to question if it is taken to mean a:

**Linear progression** – one confirmed theory forming the basis for other theories, and so forth. As **Kuhn** (1962) suggests (albeit in a slightly different context), the variety of sociological perspectives and interpretations used to explain much the same sort of thing (human social behaviour) suggests there is no great sense of 'cumulative unity' within sociology.

**Objectivity**: As we've noted earlier, this idea works on two basic levels of meaning:

- **Personal**: On this level we need to consider the extent to which individual scientists (natural or social) can remain detached from whatever they're studying. In this respect, questions of *personal bias*, *influence* and, in some cases, *fraud* enter the equation and, while it's probably easier to maintain an emotional detachment from bacteria in a Petri dish than it is from, say, a starving child,

Say hello to my little friends . . .

distressed mother or suicidal teenager, there's no real evidence to suggest sociologists are any more – or any less – personally biased in their work than physicists (indeed, as we've seen, with the latter the 'pressure from sponsors' to produce desired results may put more temptation in the way of natural scientists).

- **Institutional** objectivity, meanwhile, is a slightly different question. Here we're concerned with the status of knowledge itself and the question of whether it is possible to collect *objective* knowledge about human behaviour. This idea goes to the heart of the distinction between the inanimate subject matter of natural science (which simply *reacts* to stimulation) and the animate (self-conscious) subject matter of sociology. The question here is whether it's possible to study human behaviour without changing that behaviour. In addition, institutional objectivity needs to consider whether it is possible – or for some sociologists desirable – to keep values and beliefs separate from the things being researched.

**Ethics**: Sociologists, like their natural science counterparts, produce work within a community that both regulates and scrutinises their work.

### ⚠ Digging deeper: Is sociology scientific?

In this final part, we can address the second of the ideas noted above – the *practical principles* involved in 'doing science' – and we can begin by suggesting that, whatever the *theoretical* claims to scientific status

# Discussion point: Big Brother is watching?

A simple way to grasp the idea of self-awareness (and its relationship to sociological research) is in terms of the *Big Brother* TV show where contestants are fully observed by cameras 24/7.

**BIG BROTHER**

- How might the knowledge of being observed by a hidden TV audience affect the contestants' behaviour?
- How might behaviour be affected by the lure of possible 'celebrity status' if they 'perform well' in the show?

A criticism which *Big Brother* contestants frequently make about each other is that they are not 'being themselves' and are, in consequence, somehow 'false' (people are 'playing to the cameras').

To what extent do you think social interaction involves 'giving a performance' (and how might this relate to the question of whether it's possible for sociology to be scientific)?

advanced by sociologists, it would be naive to pretend sociological data can match the general precision, reliability and validity of everyday examples of natural scientific research. It is impossible, it could be argued, for sociology to match the consistency of natural science in terms of predicting behaviour at the individual level, for two related reasons:

**Self-awareness**: People have a consciousness that gives them the ability to both act and react; we can both respond to social stimulation *and* initiate social action.

**Complexity**: People are not just thinking, reasoning, self-aware beings (one layer of complexity), they are also part of a complex web of social interactions and meanings – a further layer of complexity. The constant, dynamic interplay between these two levels makes it difficult for sociologists to control the conditions under which research takes place. As **How** (2005) puts it: 'The

Sociologist has to undertake two acts of interpretation: one involves the concepts and ideas that she or he has about the subject matter, the other involves the concepts and ideas the people involved in the social situation being investigated have about themselves.'

We could also add that in many forms of research (from interviews to overt participant observation) a third layer of complexity is added by the fact that research subjects may also interpret the presence and behaviour of sociologists in ways that affect the 'naturalness' of the behaviour being observed.

## Weeding the path

This is not a situation unique to sociology. Some areas of natural science involve complex systems that make precise levels of predication impossible – think, for example, about the behaviour of viruses (such as the common cold) that constantly *mutate*. It is not possible to predict accurately who will catch a cold (although it is possible to predict the *conditions* under which you are likely to catch a cold).

Although ideas about consciousness and complexity are significant, they are not the whole story. An important area of doubt surrounding the 'scientific status' of sociology relates to the nature of the subject itself and a key concept here is:

## Diversity

Although it's clear that, within the natural sciences, there are demarcation lines between different categories of science – physics and chemistry, for example, are different disciplines – there is also a sense that they are in some way generally *unified* around a common methodology. Within sociology, divisions are also apparent, but when **Dawe** (1970) refers to the idea of '... two sociologies; a sociology of the social system and a sociology of social action', this is something more than a simple divergence of focus or interest, since the rider to **Dawe's** 'two sociologies' is that 'at every level, they are in conflict'.

Notwithstanding something like **Giddens'** (1991) attempt to forge a sense of theoretical unity between structural and action approaches through *structuration theory*, the 'two sociologies' occupy different positions in relation to the extent to which 'sociology in practice' can lay claim to scientific status.

**Interactionist sociologies** suggest the concept of science can be redefined in relation to understanding the behaviour of human subjects. There is, for example, little or no interest in the type of elaborate and wide-ranging, theory-building characteristic of the natural sciences for the deceptively simple reason that action theorists generally recognise that the attempt to replicate the success of natural science in the context of social science is unlikely to succeed. Rather, the 'redefinition of science' is carried out through the idea that a different order of phenomena (*subjects* who are capable of reflection and action as opposed to *objects* that are incapable of either) requires a different form of methodology – one that concentrates on *descriptive explanation* rather than hypothesis testing and theory building.

**Structuralist sociologies**, meanwhile, suggest sociology can aspire to a form of scientific status, but only at the expense of eliminating human consciousness from the equation. In this respect, if we remove the source of the problem (the subject/object distinction noted above) we can examine structural phenomena (large-group behaviours, for example) *as if* they were objects without consciousness. This idea goes back to **Durkheim's** (1895) concept of:

**Social facts** involving the claim that certain classes of phenomena, such as language, are essentially *external* to the individual; they exist *prior* to the individual and will continue *after* the individual. Social facts, therefore, exist outside individual consciousness – people internalise these facts as and when necessary, but their status nevertheless remains one of separation from individual behaviour. To communicate verbally, for example, we have to learn a 'common language' that, in effect, acts as a constraint on behaviour. For **Durkheim**, therefore, *social facts* could be studied 'as things' – a belief that, in some respects taken to its logical conclusion by writers such as **Luhmann**, revolves around the concept of:

**Objectification**: This relates to the idea

that sociologists should concentrate their efforts on the behaviour of social groups and, by extension, how the necessity of group living creates objective, observable phenomena. By adopting this view, sociology can come closer to matching the *practical utility* of the natural sciences, albeit at the expense of reducing the complexities of individual human behaviours to an interesting – but relatively inconsequential – status.

If we throw postmodernism into the mix, the situation becomes further complicated, since this general way of seeing the world doesn't recognise the 'special status' afforded to science. From this position it is a matter of supreme indifference as to whether sociology is 'scientific' since the question could be asked – with equal validity and consequence – to what extent is sociology a religion, a sport or a lifestyle choice (or, indeed, to what extent is science a sociology)? Such questions matter, postmodernists argue, only in the context of:

**Status discourses**, and since these are inherently subjective, such an 'evaluation of worth' can be played out only in the context of power struggles between different status groups.

## Normal science

In more conventional terms, perhaps, the inability of sociology to present a 'united theoretical front' is, for **Kuhn** (1962), a fundamental weakness – one that prevents it being considered in terms of:

**Normal science**, which he identifies as:

**Paradigmatic**: A scientific paradigm, according to **Ritzer** (2000), represents a consensual image, shared by all practitioners, of its subject matter. 'It serves to define what should be studied, what questions should be

asked, how they should be asked, and what rules should be followed in interpreting the answers obtained.' For **Kuhn**, normal science involves a clearly defined, uncontested paradigmatic structure. Scientists are socialised into the paradigm and, as such, adopt the basic assumptions involved about how to theorise, test and establish scientific relationships. Disciplines such as physics, chemistry, mathematics and the like would be included in this characterisation of science. For **Kuhn** sociology is:

**Pre-scientific** because it hasn't, as yet, attained the features and status of normal science. Pre-scientific disciplines are characterised by:

- **Disorganisation** in terms of the different ways practitioners define and understand the discipline, with a range of diverse – frequently non-complementary – perspectives and activities.
- **Debates** over – and questioning of – fundamental principles.
- **Diversity**, in the sense of little or no agreement over basic methodological principles.

## ⚠ The potting shed

From any area of the Specification, identify and explain one example to support or reject the idea that sociology has a pre-scientific status.

Finally, we can return to the idea that debates about what constitutes 'science' revolve around questions of *definition* – are we, **Lee** (1992) argues, ' . . . too easily seduced by a particular view of scientific knowledge – the so-called "positivist"

# Discussion point: Reading sociology and science

The following table (adapted from **Fuller**, 1998) forms the basis of this individual essay-writing exercise.

Take *each* idea in Column A in turn and write a paragraph with the following format:

- Briefly state the idea and explain what it means from a sociological viewpoint.

- Add to this the *adjacent* idea in Column B by explaining 'how scientists read' the sociological explanation.

- Complete the paragraph by explaining how scientists have, according to **Fuller**, misrepresented sociological ideas about the nature of science.

| A. When sociology says . . . | B. Scientists read . . . |
| --- | --- |
| Science is socially constructed | Science is whatever enough people think it is |
| Sociology has its own aims and methods | Sociology wilfully ignores the aims and methods of science |
| Science is only one possible way of interpreting experience | Science is merely an interpretation that distorts experience |
| Gravity is a concept scientists use to explain why we fall down, not up – there are other explanations | Gravity exists only in our minds and, if we wanted, we could fall up, not down |
| Scientists' accounts of their activities are not necessarily the best explanation for those activities | Scientists' accounts of their activities can be disregarded when explaining those activities |

conception – which identifies science with certainty (**Keat** and **Urry**, 1975). To possess this certainty, it is said, knowledge must take the form of an agreed body of theory expressed as objective general laws; these laws in turn, must have been established through the detached observation of "facts".'

In other words, do the characteristics we've blithely assigned to the natural sciences (positivistic, objective, predictive and the like) owe more to the success of scientific interest groups and elites in projecting a particular view of 'science' and 'the scientist' on to Western societies than to any real description of natural science?

## Moving on

In this section we've examined ideas about the nature of scientific methodology and drawn some tentative conclusions about the extent to which sociology can be considered a science. In doing this, we've raised further questions about the nature and status of sociological theory and method that we can examine further in the next section.

# 3. The relationship between theory and methods

This section explores in more detail the nature of the relationship between theory and methods by thinking about how they are linked through different types of sociological methodology. In this respect we need to note:

**Theory** is something we use all the time in everyday life. Whenever we *speculate* about why people do things (such as marry, commit criminal acts or vote for particular political parties) we are using theory to guide our explanations – and although the development of sociological theory is a bit more sophisticated than our everyday theories, the basic principle underpinning both is very similar.

To start with, we can think about two types of theory – *descriptive* and *causal*. The former is usually designed to provide *qualitative* explanations while the latter seeks to establish (*quantitative*) cause-and-effect relationships.

## ⚠ Preparing the ground: Theory and method

When we think about the relationship between theory and methods we are actually thinking about the nature of the sociological research process – a common-sense description of which might involve a researcher thinking about what they want to study, coming up with a few speculative ideas (theory) and then testing them with whatever method seems most appropriate. This, however, obscures a more sophisticated set of ideas and processes – something we can begin to appreciate by thinking about the research process as being like a game; it

### WARM-UP: THINKING THEORETICALLY

In small groups, choose an issue related to education – it can be as large ('why do boys achieve less than girls in our educational system?') or as small ('why can't I concentrate in class?') as you like. Using the following activities as a guide:

- Brainstorm some possible explanations for your chosen issue.
- Choose one explanation and write either a research question or research hypothesis to guide your research.
- Choose the most appropriate method for your research.

| | |
|---|---|
| Issue to explain: | |
| Possible explanations? | |
| Research question [descriptive research]? | |
| Research hypothesis [causal research]? | |
| What research method (and why) would you choose for this research? | |

involves certain rules and procedures that need to be obeyed and it can be played on different levels: some play it for fun in their back garden (such as when you speculate about the reasons for someone's behaviour) and others play it professionally – something that involves moving away from the 'everyday' or common-sense understanding of 'theory' to develop a more sociological level of understanding.

## Theory

In this respect, we can begin by noting that 'a theory' is a:

**Model** or **framework** consisting of tested and confirmed hypotheses that can be used to explain something. In this sense, therefore, rather than seeing 'theory' as a form of speculation about behaviour (something more correctly seen as a *hypothesis*), we should think of it as representing a body of tried-and-tested knowledge, from which we can make:

**Generalisations** about people's behaviour. **Thio** (1991) notes that a theory represents 'a set of logically-related hypotheses that explains the relationship among various phenomena' and we can add a couple of ideas to this formulation. First, behaviour models are:

**Tentative** – there is always the possibility that they can be falsified or that some other theory will be developed that explains more than the original theory.

Second, the distinction between 'theory' and 'practice' used in everyday conversation is misleading since it confuses 'theory' with 'hypothesis'. If an explanation works 'in practice' it must also, by definition, work 'in theory'; the two ideas are part of the same, interrelated process.

At this point we can introduce 'methods'

into the equation since, as you will be aware, some theories achieve greater acceptance than others. This is because the strongest theories – those that have not, as yet, been falsified – have been:

**Tested** and supported by *evidence* collected using *research methods*.

In this respect, theory and methods are initially linked (at a basic level) by the fact that they have a:

**Symbiotic relationship** – the one, in other words, needs the other:

- **Theories without evidence** to support them provide no way of knowing which, if any, particular explanation is true (or at least not false), whereas:

- **Evidence without theory** means we would have no way of telling what, if anything, it was evidence *of*.

## Guide

**Theory**, therefore, *guides* data collection, telling us *where* and *how* to look for evidence.

**Methods**, meanwhile, are the 'nuts and bolts' of research in the sense that evidence is used to refute or confirm a particular theory.

Sociologists, as you've discovered at AS level, have a wide range of methods at their disposal – something that reflects a diversity of different sociological interests and beliefs about how it is possible to study social behaviour. Some methods (such as questionnaires) lend themselves to large-scale, quantitative macroanalysis, whereas others (such as covert participant observation) are better adapted to small-scale, qualitative microanalysis.

## Digging deeper: Theory and method

Just as we can identify different research

methods, we can also talk about different kinds of theory:

- **Low-level theories** involve explaining or describing a specific (low-level) aspect of social behaviour – why, for example, are some individuals more likely to commit crimes than others?

- **Mid-range theories** are broader in scope and focus on explaining or describing a general class of social behaviour (such as why girls achieve higher educational qualifications in the UK than boys).

- **High-level theories** are the broadest kind of theory and focus on the development of a general picture of society itself – when we talk about sociological perspectives, for example, we're generally referring to this type of theory.

## ⚠ The potting shed

**From any area of the Specification, identify and briefly explain one example of each of the above types of theory.**

The three types we've just delineated for the sake of conceptual clarity are, in the real world of sociological research, necessarily *interconnected*. The general picture of society held by the sociologist, for example, influences the type of mid-range (and possibly low-level) theories developed to explain social behaviour. In other words, high-level theories represent perspectives (or paradigms, if you prefer) that reflect fundamental beliefs about the nature of human society, how behaviour can be studied and explained, and so forth. As **Blunt** (1994) puts it: 'Researchers approach inquiry from a particular philosophical stance or world view, which determines the purpose, design, methods used and the interpretation of results.'

Given the significance of high-level theories, therefore, we can examine how different perspectives involve different interpretations of both the nature of society and, most importantly for our purpose, the relationship between theory and method. In order to draw out this relationship, therefore, we need to organise our observations in some way – and the most obvious way to do this is to think in terms of the following categories.

## Organising categories

**Ontological**: The most fundamental area of belief is to ask the question '*What do you believe exists?*' which translates here into beliefs about the nature of the social world (do we, for example, see it as socially constructed or biologically programmed? Do we take a systems or a non-systems approach? and so forth). How we answer these fundamental questions determines:

**Epistemological** beliefs relating to the kinds of:

**Proof** we will accept to justify our ontological beliefs. In the natural sciences, for example, *ontological beliefs* about the world (that it is governed by causal relationships that form the basis for the discovery of laws of physical behaviour) influence *epistemological beliefs* about how to go about the task of establishing these relationships (through experimentation, for example).

For the study of social behaviour the range of possible proofs may be greater, but the general principle holds. If, for example, you believe proof should be built around the development of reliable data that can be replicated exactly, participant observation is unlikely to figure highly in your choice of research methods – which leads to a further aspect of belief:

**Methodology** is concerned with ideas focused on the *reliability* and *validity* of both knowledge and the methods used to generate it. Methodology, therefore, provides a link between *theory* and *method* because it specifies how to generate data to test a particular hypothesis or research question. The final area of belief, therefore, involves:

**Research methods**: Although there is no simple, hard-and-fast relationship between different types of sociological theory and different types of method, some methods are more closely aligned with some perspectives than with others, as we will see in a moment.

These ideas form the basic structure for an outline of different types of high-level sociological theory that broadly specify how it is both possible and/or desirable to study the social world. Conventionally, debates surrounding the different theoretical models we can apply to sociological research revolve around two 'opposing' positions:

- **Positivist** sociology, where the focus is on procedures and research methods that mirror those found in the natural sciences, and

- **Interpretivist** (sometimes called '**anti-positivist**') sociology, where the focus is on a different set of procedures and methods 'more applicable' to the different nature of the sociological subject.

## Weeding the path

Although convention dictates that we examine these two basic positions, we need to note two ideas. First, sociological theory is frequently presented as some sort of battleground between these two, absolutely opposed, positions. Second, where theory is represented in this oppositional way it's easy to fall into the trap of seeing 'positivists' as 'the Bad Guys' and 'anti-positivists' as 'the Good Guys' (or vice versa, of course).

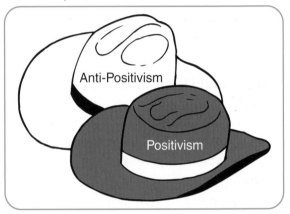

This type of *Disneyfication* of theory – where complex ideas are reduced to simple black-and-white oversimplifications – is something we want to avoid by both presenting a range of different positions here and, more importantly, stressing that our observations should not be misinterpreted as being definitive statements about 'positivists', 'interpretivists' or whoever. In this respect, what follows can be broadly characterised as a series of:

**Ideal types** where we emphasise a range of *ideal* features of a high-level theory (such as positivism) and hold them up as 'perfect examples' against which to measure the reality of a situation. In other words, although 'positivist theory' *ideally* involves certain ontological, epistemological and methodological ideas, it doesn't necessarily follow that there are actually sociological researchers who can be clearly and unequivocally labelled 'positivists'.

## Preparing the ground: Methodologies

The first 'ideal type' of sociological methodology we can outline is the classic one of:

## Positivist principles

**Positivist ontology**, characterised in terms of two major ideas:

- **Laws** and law-like relationships: The social world is similar to the natural world; both involve *patterned behaviour* (which, in the social world, resembles law-like relationships) capable of being discovered through careful observation.

- **Objectivism**: The social world, governed by causal relationships, has an objective existence over and above the control of individuals.

Human society, therefore, consists of identifiable patterns of behaviour (we go to school, work, form families, and so forth) that must have *social causes* and such causality, from this position, resides in:

**Social structures**: Although the social and natural worlds are different (people have consciousness and are aware of themselves and their surroundings in a way that rocks, for example, are not), this 'problem of difference' is resolved by arguing that social behaviour is a:

**Reaction to stimulation** (deriving from structural imperatives such as socialisation, for example). In other words, behaviour can be studied and explained by understanding the *cause* of the reaction (structural pressures) rather than the effect (individual actions).

**Positivist epistemology** rests on objective forms of knowledge – the idea that proof must be based on empirical evidence. Reliable and valid knowledge, for positivist science, doesn't rest on the idea that something is true or false on the basis of things like faith, trust, personal conviction or prejudice. Ideally, truth or falsity rests on:

**Replication**: For something to be considered true (or 'not false') it has to be *repeatedly* shown to be true, which has clear implications for the direction of:

**Positivist methodology**: An important concept here is *reliability*, considered in terms of:

- **Input**: This refers to how sociologists organise their research, in terms of both the overall methodological procedures (**Popper's** hypothetico-deductive model would, for example, be appropriate here) and the specific methods used.

- **Output**: The research data produced should, *in principle*, be capable of *replication* by other researchers as a way of both producing reliable knowledge and checking that previous researchers actually followed the methodological principles they claimed to follow.

## Weeding the path

In methodological terms, it's both *possible* and *desirable* to *quantify* human behaviour for a couple of reasons:

- **Comparison**: *Quantification* establishes an objective platform from which to compare behavioural changes (such as marriage rates). Quantification, therefore,

plausibly documenting people's experiences, beliefs, meanings, and so forth, while proof of valid data is based on the ability to experience the world as others experience it. **Weber**, for example, used the term *Verstehen* ('deeper understanding') to suggest that the sociologist can collect valid data by *empathising* with their subject matter – experiencing the world as their subject matter experiences it and, by so doing, arrive at a deeper understanding of social behaviour.

## Weeding the path

The 'search for validity' generally has a certain trade-off in terms of data *reliability* – this is more difficult to achieve. Observed behaviour, for example, has to be recorded systematically, methodically and accurately if it is to be considered reliable.

In general, therefore, interpretivist methodology reflects the idea that the most significant aspect of social behaviour is the creation of:

**Meanings** – and it follows that the task of the sociologist is to reveal and understand the meanings people bring to and take from social interaction. If people actively (if not always consciously or deliberately) create their world, any attempt to establish cause-and-effect relationships is unlikely to yield a great deal of useful information. In this respect, we can think of social behaviour as resembling a:

**Chaotic system**: Behaviour – although not totally unpredictable – is subject to random variations at the individual level studied by interactionist sociologists. The task of *science*, from this position, is quite different to conventional definitions of both science and the role of the scientist; the scientific role here is one of *understanding*

(which may or may not lead to explanation), *not* prediction.

**Interpretivist methods**: Where data validity is preferred to reliability, research methods that help the sociologist understand social situations from the participant's viewpoint are favoured. *Qualitative* methods, such as unstructured interviews and participant observation, are frequently used by interpretivists because the research objective is to explore and understand behaviour in all its depth and detail – something that's difficult to do using a closed questionnaire.

This is not to say that other types of research method have no place in interpretivist methodology – interpretivism, as we've suggested, is not purely and exclusively concerned with creating qualitative data. Experimental methods, for example, have been used to demonstrate certain features of the social world. For example, **Garfinkel's** (1967):

**Breaching experiments** show how to demonstrate both the existence of unobservable features of the social world (norms, for example) and the various ways people 'construct reality' by deliberately 'breaching social expectations' and observing the outcome. **Garfinkel** sent student researchers into restaurants where they were instructed to deliberately 'mistake' customers for waiters while the latter's reactions were observed secretly.

A contemporary example here is **Mann et al.'s** (2003) 'sousveillance' breaching experiments, one of which involved going into shops that had security cameras (surveillance of customers) and 'reversing this gaze' by filming the shop assistants as they served customers and recording their reactions.

One objective of this experiment was to demonstrate how surveillance has become an accepted, everyday, *uncontested* part of life in modern societies.

 **Digging deeper: Methodologies**

Thus far we've looked at methodology in terms of positivism and interpretivism and suggested the conventional way of viewing them in terms of what postmodernists call:

**Binary oppositions**: 'Binary' means something can be one of two states – 'off' or 'on', for example – and their relationship is one of exclusion (if something is 'on', it can't be 'off' at the same time). This idea is a familiar one in Western society, as the example on the following page demonstrates.

## Realist principles

With this in mind we can dig a little deeper by looking, first, at an alternative explanation for the relationship between theory and method in terms of a:

# Growing it yourself: Breaching experiments

Breaching experiments can be both fun and informative (although you have to be careful for *ethical* reasons that any disruption that occurs doesn't cause the 'victim' emotional pain or distress). In small groups, try some of the following (or invent your own ways of disrupting norms):

- Ask directions from someone in the street and, once they've explained which direction to go, walk off the opposite way.

- 'Tip' someone – 10p for example – for information (as in the above situation). This could also be done in another teacher's classroom – ask a question and then tip the teacher.

- Two students stand talking in a narrow hallway, leaving roughly 4 feet between them, but with space behind each student and the wall.

- Test 'window-shopping' norms. How far away from a shop window can someone stand before their presence is ignored by passers-by?

- In a public space (like a library or classroom), place a coat over the back of any empty chair.

- Go into McDonald's and ask for a product from another fast-food chain, such as a Whopper (Burger King) – be persistent and insist they serve you.

During the experiment all behaviour should be systematically and accurately recorded (this will involve some preparation and the allocation of different roles).

Report your findings (and conclusions you can draw about social behaviour) to the class.

If you don't have the time and/or inclination to perform any of these breaching experiments, identify and briefly explain some possible ethical considerations involved in such experiments.

**Binary oppositions: Ridgeway (1997)**

| Culture | Reason | Mind | Public | Society | → | Civilised |
| ↕ | ↕ | ↕ | ↕ | ↕ | | ↕ |
| Nature | Emotion | Body | Private | Individual | → | Primitive |

**Realist** conception of science:

**Realist ontology**: Although realism is sometimes called '*post-positivism*' (**Trochim**, 2002), this is not entirely accurate since we find examples of realism in the work of writers like **Marx** and **Durkheim**, but we find features of *positivism* in their work too, with one point of convergence between the two methodologies being that both accept the social world has:

**Objective features** (or **structures**) that can be studied scientifically since, as we've suggested, social structures have an independent existence from people. Structures, in this respect, are 'real forces' in our everyday lives of work, family, culture and so forth and although the social and natural worlds are different, the basic principles involved in the study of each are similar. The 'real' features of social systems, for example, make it possible to establish causal relationships. Realists, however, add the proviso here that causality will be *limited* in time and space (what is true in one context may not be true in another).

**Realist epistemology**: Empirical evidence through direct observation is *desirable*, but not in itself sufficient. Realists suggest the structures we experience 'as real' (and which positivists, for example, argue are what must be studied) are the product of 'hidden mechanisms and forces' that may *not* be directly observable. For example, **Durkheim's** (1897) analysis of suicide involves the idea that it can be explained in terms of how the individual is socially *regulated* and *integrated* and since these are 'unobservable mechanisms' acting on people's behaviour, it follows that they cannot be directly observed. Their *effects*, however, can be measured through the use of various *indicators*.

## ✳ SYNOPTIC LINK

**Crime and deviance:** Explanations of suicide – and how different methodological principles have been applied to the understanding of this behaviour – are considered in more detail in this chapter.

Realist epistemology, therefore, goes beyond 'simple descriptions' of causal relationships to discover how such relationships are initially created. The social world 'as we see and experience it' is, from this position, governed by the operation of *social processes* we need to understand if we are to explain the observable world (something, realists suggest, that is true for *both* the social and natural sciences).

## Example

An example should help to clarify this basic idea. **Soothill** and **Grover** (1995) argue that the concept of 'sex crime' (such as rape, paedophilia and the like) is *socially constructed* through the media; in other words, 'sex crime' is real, in that it's possible to empirically identify people who are both 'criminals' and 'victims':

- **Positivist explanations** of rape, for example, focus on the observable features of a situation – the relationship between the rapist and their victim, their social backgrounds and characteristics, and so forth – in the attempt to explain why such a crime occurs.

- **Realist explanations,** while recognising these things are important, spread the net further to dig deeper into areas that might, on the face of things, seem to have no direct relevance to a sex crime. A realist, for example, would want to examine ideological factors (such as cultural attitudes to gender – do we live in a sexist society, for example) that surround – and contribute to the creation of – a particular social act.

In other words, a 'real explanation' of sex crime is more likely to be found by examining the *unobservable* aspects of social life (power and gender relationships, for example) than by simply focusing on directly observable aspects of behaviour.

**Realist methodology**: These ideas have significant consequences for how we can generate reliable and valid knowledge – the social world, for example, has to be understood in its *totality*. While it's possible to study particular 'events' (such as a crime),

to validly explain *why* people commit crimes we have to think more widely in terms of how the interconnected parts of a social system impact on each other. If you think about this for a moment, two things are apparent:

- **Complexity**: Social research becomes very complicated; for every situation we study we have to understand the social context of the behaviour involved to make sense of it.

- **Science**: Realism reflects the way natural scientists understand and study the world; all phenomena are connected to each other in some way because they are all governed by natural laws. When you repeatedly drop a pen and it falls to the floor, the 'unobservable mechanism' that explains this regularity is gravity.

## Triangulate

Given the above, realists see reliability and validity in terms of constructing both an overall ('in depth') view of social behaviour in different contexts (something shared with *interpretivists*) and, at the same time, producing specific, causal-type explanations for behaviour (something they share with *positivists*). We can use the concept of:

**Triangulation** to illustrate a realist methodological approach. Different research methods have different strengths and weaknesses; questionnaires, for example, may produce reliable data, but with low validity, while the reverse is true for covert participant observation. For realists this reflects the nature of the social world – no single method can capture its complexity; since all have weaknesses, the obvious thing to do is to *combine* different methods so that the weaknesses of one can be offset by the strengths of another.

Methodological triangulation: Harvey and MacDonald (1993)
1. Two or more researchers using same research technique
2. One researcher using two or more research techniques
3. Two or more researchers using two or more research techniques

As **Trochim** (2002) argues, if all research methods contain the capacity for *error*, the only sensible thing is to combine methods so that one type of error cancels out another, an idea called *methodological triangulation*.

This type of triangulation has a range of uses in terms of:

- **collecting** different types of data (qualitative and quantitative, primary and secondary)

- **checking** data reliability and validity

- **comparison**: different researchers using the same method can compare data for similarities and differences

- **confirmation**: verifying the accuracy of different types of data.

Just as research methods are *inherently error prone*, so too, for realists, are theoretical positions – and the way to resolve this is through:

**Theoretical triangulation**: Different theoretical perspectives have their strengths and their weaknesses that, again, can be used to the researcher's advantage. The argument here is that by looking at the social world in terms of *both* structure *and* action we can arrive at the best possible representation and explanation of social behaviour.

## ✳ SYNOPTIC LINK

**Crime and deviance:** *The New Criminology* (**Taylor, Walton** and **Young**, 1973) is an example of an attempt to apply a realist methodology to an understanding of deviance.

**Realist methods** focus on gaining a mix of quantitative and qualitative data to get the fullest possible research picture. Primary sources such as questionnaires and interviews and secondary sources such as official statistics may be used to develop empirical indicators of underlying, non-observable causalities, while observational methods may similarly be used to reveal, for example, people's underlying beliefs and assumptions.

## Postmodern principles

The final methodological position we can examine is:

**Postmodernism**: Although this position involves a range of ideas that makes it difficult to explain in terms of traditional forms of sociological perspective, we can identify some general features of postmodernism in the following ways:

**Postmodern ontology**: This involves thinking about two distinctive definitional strands – one that focuses on what postmodernism *is not* and the other that focuses on the fundamental principles of postmodernism. In terms of the first idea, postmodernism represents a:

**Critique of modernism**: This involves, as we've suggested, the idea that concepts like 'truth' and 'objectivity' are inherently *subjective* constructions that need to be considered as narratives within a scientific discourse. In other words, such ideas represent *stories* that describe the social world from a particular position of power, rather than unequivocal, objective features of that world.

In terms of the second idea, postmodernism is:

**Constructivist**, in the sense of seeking to describe how narratives and discourses develop and disappear – a preoccupation that involves ideas about *subjective experiences*, considered in two main ways:

- **Personal subjectivities** – how people experience and reflect on the social world in terms of their particular beliefs, values, norms, identities, and so forth.
- **Social subjectivities**: Personal experience is grounded in the experiences and activities of others. Traditionally, for example, one way of expressing this idea is to think about areas like primary and secondary socialisation and how the behaviour of others (such as parents,

friends and the media) impacts on how we see both ourselves and the social world.

## ✳ SYNOPTIC LINK

**Mass media:** This idea reflects the notion that each individual is both the *producer* and *product* of society, something that can be illustrated by the idea of weblogs – information systems that bypass 'traditional' media organisation and practice. We can also think in terms of how the internet is evolving in more cooperative ways. (See 'Growing it yourself' on the next page.)

**Relative**: in a subjective world it follows that all explanations are relative, something **Troest** (1999) identifies as the claim that we have no way of objectively distinguishing that which is true from that which is false. Is it possible, for example, to objectively demonstrate the superiority of one set of beliefs over another?

In this respect, concepts of reliability and validity are social constructs inherently relative in time and space, an idea **Curran** and **Takata** (2004) take to its logical conclusion by observing that, for postmodernists, there is no possibility of 'a unifying overall truth' or 'unifying overall metanarrative that could tell the ultimate "truth" for humans'.

**Postmodern epistemology** would, on the face of things, seem to be a contradiction in terms, since the *relativity* of knowledge makes questions of proof redundant – **Lyon** (1994) suggests 'postmodern philosophy claims there can be no ultimate epistemology upon which to base our search for knowledge'.

In this respect, postmodernists argue we need to redefine the role of the sociologist; rather than seeing sociology as being a quest

## 🌱 Growing it yourself: Write here, write now

WIKIPEDIA
*The Free Encyclopedia*

An interesting illustration of this idea is the **Wikipedia** (http://en.wikipedia.org), a 'free encyclopaedia written collaboratively by people from around the world'. The English version currently has around 600,000 articles.

Start at the main sociology page (http://en.wikipedia.org/wiki/Sociology) and explore what it has to say about this topic. You are not, however, restricted to a *consumer* role. Once you get a feel for the interface (have a look at the Help page if necessary), you can develop a *producer* role by creating and adding material to the Wikipedia for the world to see (and, of course, to criticise and edit).

Class exercise: Add information about 'A level sociology' to the Wikipedia.

You should plan what you want to say, keeping in mind that if others disagree they can edit your words, just as you can edit theirs.

You can either submit your contribution as a class or, if you prefer, once you've discussed the general areas you want to cover, divide into groups and assign each group a topic to research and write.

**navigation**
- Main Page
- Community Portal
- Current events
- Recent changes
- Random article
- Help
- Contact us
- Donations

**search**

[ Go ] [ Search ]

**toolbox**
- What links here
- Related changes
- Upload file
- Special pages
- Printable version
- Permanent link
- Cite this article

for 'truth' (by attempting to evaluate the differing 'claims' put forward by, for example, scientific and religious discourses), the *epistemological* role of the sociologist becomes one of *describing* competing claims to truth. This involves, according to **Yeatman** (1994), a rejection of the assumption that knowledge about the world somehow 'stands outside' the individual in a way 'free of the power regimes in which it is constructed'. In other words, a sociological epistemology should focus on understanding and describing the power relationships that give rise to knowledge, rather than seeking to distinguish between different forms of knowledge in terms of concepts like reliability and validity (which are themselves just one more form of subjective categorisation).

In the context of postmodern epistemology, therefore, knowledge is not just individually and culturally relative, it is also the outcome of historical and cultural *power struggles*. The role of sociology, in this respect, becomes one of understanding *why* some forms of knowledge are considered 'more reliable' or 'more valid' than others in different cultures and at different times.

**Postmodern methodology**: These epistemological arguments can be related to methodology in two general ways:

### Discourse

The world consists, at different times and in different places, of competing discourses. At times, one discourse may become the dominant mode of explanation and at other times no single discourse is able to dominate.

The key point, however, is that we are simply talking about different interpretations of the world between which we have no objective way of discriminating. The 'search for objectivity', therefore, is a symptom of the way knowledge is organised by powerful interest groups – something is true *not* because it has some inherent quality of truth, but because powerful groups are able to define it as true. As **Crebbin** (2000) puts it: 'Knowledge and meanings are . . . culturally and historically situated, and saturated with previous power contests. Knowledge is therefore understood to be political, contested, and diverse.'

## Deconstruction

As befits a term originated by postmodernists (the concept is usually attributed to **Derrida**), **Rorty** (1995) suggests its meaning has changed and developed over the last 40 years in ways, somewhat ironically, unintended by its author. For our purpose, however, we can think of this idea in a relatively simple way: **Marling** (2001) suggests a 'loose definition' involves the idea of 'taking something apart' (a narrative or discourse, for example) to show how it has been socially constructed – to lay bare, in effect, the various elements by which a particular, 'taken-for-granted' set of meanings has certain ideological characteristics. **Boles** (2003), therefore, suggests deconstruction involves 'the process by which the audience identifies the elements that make up the construction of meaning within a text'.

An important aspect of postmodern methodology, therefore, is the ability to 'deconstruct texts' (anything that involves language), something linked to our previous observations about *epistemology* – the best we

can do is understand how people construct their beliefs. In this respect, **Neuman** (2000) suggests postmodern methodology has the following characteristics:

- **Subjectivity**: Rather than seeking the impossible (objectivity), postmodernists combine 'intuition, imagination, personal experience, and emotion' to produce descriptive interpretations.

- **Relativity**: The postmodern world consists of 'infinite interpretations', none of which is (objectively) superior or inferior.

- **Representation**: All forms of research are representations of whatever is being studied. Research, therefore, consists of different 'representations of truth' (as conceived by the researcher, the researched, the reader, and so forth) rather than 'truth' itself. **Usher** (1996) argues that academic texts are always partial in the sense that they are subjective narratives that must conform to the 'rules and language games' of academic discourse. **Coffey** (2000) captures the idea of both postmodern research and the role of the researcher when he notes, 'I am not an innocent bystander' – all research, in other words, is necessarily partial (in the sense of being constructed from a particular viewpoint).

These ideas do, of course, make it difficult to discuss:

**Postmodern methods** in the way we conventionally discuss research methods. This follows for a couple of reasons:

- **Society**: **Coffey** (2000) suggests postmodern perceptions of 'society' lean towards seeing it, in **Deleuze** and **Guattari's** (1987) terms, as a:

- **Rhizomatic structure**: This involves 'a system without a trunk that has no pattern and expands endlessly from any of its points in all directions' – the internet being a classic example of this idea. It has no clearly defined structure and is constantly being made and remade through the interaction of its users – just like 'society'. The question here, of course, is, how is it possible to study such a phenomenon?

- **Research**: In the above sense, trying to study 'society' is like trying to step into a river in the same place twice; each time you step off the bank (even if it's exactly the same spot), the water you step into is not the same water.

## ⌂ The potting shed

Identify and briefly explain one implication of this idea for *each* of the concepts of reliability and validity.

For these reasons, postmodern research tends not to focus on conventional or traditional research techniques. There is, after all, little apparent point in trying to quantify something (human behaviour) that's both changing as you measure it and changed in unknown ways by your presence – a postmodern researcher would probably find it more interesting and fruitful to understand the researcher's reasons for

## Discussion point: The meaning of love

Each member of the class should reflect for a few minutes on the meaning of the word 'love'. Make a few notes about what – if anything – this idea means to you.

As a class, share the meanings you've identified (write them on the board for all to see). The authors of each idea should then briefly elaborate on the meanings they attribute to 'love'.

Once you start to think about it (to 'deconstruct' or 'unpack' this simple word), things start to get rather complicated rather quickly. Think about and briefly discuss, for example, the following:

- How do you know when you are 'in love' (what are the indicators and, more importantly, how do you know these are indicators?)

- How can you describe 'love' – both the idea and the (emotional) feeling?

- Is it possible to be 'in love' with more than one person at the same time? Do you have to fall 'out of love' with someone you previously loved before you can fall 'in love' with someone else, and if so, why?

- How is 'the meaning of love' specified through language (what words, for example, give expression to love and is it possible to express the 'meaning of love' in words)?

- How does our culture restrict or expand the meaning of love (think, for example, about ideas such as heterosexual and homosexual love, monogamous and polygamous love)?

- Is love 'natural' or just the meaning we give to sexual attraction?

wanting to carry out such research. Research methods, therefore, generally reflect ideas about *discourse analysis* and *deconstruction*, applied in various ways to an understanding of both:

- **Living texts** (people). The objective here is to 'read' how people construct and reconstruct personal narratives by understanding the rules on which such constructions are built. **Bowker** (2001) studied 'identity exploration within an online community', through the use of internet relay chat (IRC) because she was interested in the cultural dynamics of the interaction involved in this medium.

- **Dead texts** – books, film, newspapers and the like. These are only 'dead' in the sense that the researcher is trying to deconstruct, for example, the meanings inherent in a particular text.

## Moving on

In this section, the discussion of possible relationships between theory and method has, at times, raised questions about concepts such as subjectivity, objectivity and value-freedom, and we can examine these ideas in more depth and detail in the next section.

# 4. Debates about subjectivity, objectivity and value-freedom

Debates about concepts like value-freedom help us to both firm up the ideas about science and the scientific status of sociology we've previously discussed and lay the framework for subsequent discussion, in the final section, about the relationship between sociology and social policy.

## ⚠ Preparing the ground: Value-freedom

The term 'value-freedom' is a little misleading since it implies human behaviour (in this instance, sociological research) can somehow be 'free from the influence of values'. This, of course, is not possible since all human behaviour is guided by values. An alternative way of thinking about this idea, therefore, is in terms of:

## Value-neutrality

If it's not possible to 'act without values', the best we can do is recognise the various points at which values potentially (or actually) intrude into the research process and adjust our research strategy accordingly. For example, a researcher needs to ensure any conclusions they draw from their research are not influenced by personal prejudices. **Dentler** (2002) suggests debates surrounding concepts of value-neutrality fall into two main camps – is value-neutrality:

- **Possible**? Can sociologists control the intrusion of their values into the research process?

- **Desirable**? Not all sociologists believe sociology can – or should – adopt a value-neutral approach. Writers as diverse in their approach as **Marx** (1845) and **Gouldner** (1962), for example, have variously argued that sociology (and sociological research) should reflect a:

  - **Committed approach** to identifying and promoting social change. **Marx's** famous (1845) statement that 'philosophers have only interpreted the world … the point is to change it' gives a flavour of this approach.

In small groups:

1   Identify some examples of possible research that fit the following categories:

| Always unethical | Sometimes unethical | Never unethical |
|---|---|---|
| Threatening someone with a gun 'to see how they react' | Secretly observing people | Content analysis? |

2   Each group should share their examples with the other groups and briefly justify their categorisation of each research example.

3   Identify research examples where value-neutrality is not an option for sociologists.

4   What conclusions can be drawn about the role of values in sociological research?

Whatever your commitment to these positions, the debate is complicated by:

- **Practical research considerations**, relating to the *choices* a sociologist must make in order to carry out research, which involve issues such as:

- **Choice of topic**: Decisions about what, or who, to study are influenced by values in many ways, such as whether you intend to study the activities of:

  - The **powerful**, as in, for example, **Pearce's** (1998) study of corporate criminality in the chemical industry

  - The **powerless**, where the choice is almost endless – **Davis'** (1967) study of the social processes involved in 'becoming a prostitute' is one example among many – or

  - The **powerful** *and* the **powerless** in combination – **Chambliss** (1978) compared the different experiences of school students from privileged and less privileged social backgrounds.

*Choice of topic* may also be influenced by:

- **Funding**: This idea relates not only to *what* is studied but also to *how* it is studied and *why* it is studied – an idea related to a further (ethical) issue:

- **Purpose**: The question of whether a researcher should be held accountable for the purpose to which their research is put is something that can be argued over. However, there are instances where researchers have set out to implement government social policies that are ethically questionable. 'Project Camelot', for example, was a research project funded in the early 1960s by the US government and military, designed to influence the internal politics and development of nation states (in this instance, Chile) (**Horowitz**, 1967; **Solovey**, 2001).

- **Choice of method**: In many ways the research method(s) chosen by, or forced on, the researcher reflects beliefs about how it's possible to study social behaviour (quantitatively or qualitatively, for

# The potting shed

**Building a better mousetrap?**

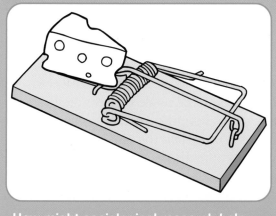

**How might sociological research help the powerful control the activities of the powerless?**

example) and, indeed, about the nature of the social world itself (whether it can – or should – be studied objectively, for example).

## Digging deeper: Value-freedom

**Theoretical issues** are an important consideration relating to the values held by sociologists:

- **Ontological beliefs** influence the general perspective a researcher adopts when making decisions about how to study behaviour. Postmodern and interactionist ontologies, for example, focus on the more subjective aspects of knowledge, whereas positivist and realist perspectives adopt a more objective general attitude and orientation.

- **Epistemological beliefs** also come into play here because these types of values affect how a sociologist approaches questions such as how to collect data, the different levels of proof required in the research process or even, in the case of some postmodernists, whether concepts of proof are inherently subjective (and, therefore, out of the question entirely).

- **Methodological beliefs** influence perceptions of *reliability* and *validity* and, in turn, our choice of research method.

## Ethics

Surrounding these ideas are:

**Ethical questions**: At various points in the research process these questions assume different levels of significance. At a fundamental level sociologists have to confront their beliefs about their subject matter – whether people are seen, for example, as 'equal participants' in a research process in which their active involvement is encouraged, or as 'research objects' to be questioned and observed in whatever way the researcher deems appropriate. On another level, natural scientists don't have to address the problem of a rock protesting vehemently if they throw it into a tank of water to see whether it sinks or floats (although this is *not* to say there are no ethical problems in the natural sciences). A sociologist attempting the same 'experiment' with a person would, rightly, be considered to be acting unethically.

## Weeding the path

This example raises the question of whether 'value-neutrality' is automatically desirable in sociological research. There are situations where sociologists are encouraged to act on

**329**

their values (or those of the communities in which they live and work) and, rather than seeing this as a weakness of the social-scientific approach, it may represent a strength in terms of its responsiveness to people's beliefs and feelings.

Before we turn to discussing concepts of objectivity and subjectivity, it's important that we don't confuse these ideas: value-neutrality, for example, is *not* the same as objectivity, just as value-commitment is *not* the same as subjectivity. This separation is particularly important in terms of the relationship between:

**Theory and methods** in the sense that value-neutrality isn't a concept (in which you either believe or you don't) that's somehow attached to particular theoretical positions – most obviously and conventionally, in terms of the idea that 'positivists' use objective methods and *therefore* their methodology is value-neutral, whereas 'anti-positivists' use subjective methods, *therefore* their methodology is value-committed. It is, however, possible to show a commitment to value-neutrality and objectivity in terms of research methods, while simultaneously employing a subjective methodology, an idea we can briefly explore in the following way:

**Methods**: All forms of science have to address and resolve the 'problem of values' – although there is a difference in kind between the biologist who studies the behaviour of human cells and the sociologist who studies the behaviour of humans in cells, the fundamental point is that a *choice* has to be made: does the biologist try to develop a cure for AIDS or a new anti-ageing cream? Does the sociologist research ways to keep people out of prison or more effective ways to put people in prison?

## Limiting effects

**Coser** (1977) argues that choice is always 'value relevant' and can never be wholly value-neutral. However, once choices have been made (what to study and how to study it, for example), value-neutrality (or at least this interpretation of the term) involves the scientist *recognising* their values and, by so doing, not imposing them on the research process. Once we accept there is a distinction to be made between 'relevance' and 'neutrality', the main question becomes one of how to *limit* the effect of values and, in terms of methods, this involves adopting, as we've suggested, an objective approach that operates on two levels (reflecting a general form of scientific ethos):

- **Practices**: On this level all researchers should be objective in terms of how they carry out their research – apply research methods impartially and ethically, don't falsify data, and so forth.

- **Assumptions**: On a second level, sociologists, like their natural scientist counterparts, should clearly state any value-relevant *assumptions*. In other words, they should make *explicit* the values they hold relating to their research so that these assumptions may be questioned, challenged or changed by other researchers. We can note, in passing, a distinction here between:

- **Epistemic values** that relate to the fundamental values of a science. These represent implicit scientific values (such as, in natural science, the concept of cause and effect) that are so ingrained in the value system of the science, they are *assumed* rather than always explicitly stated.

- **Non-epistemic values** (ethical, political, and so forth) that *do* need to be made explicit by the researcher since these may introduce *uncontrolled* forms of bias into the research process. A sociologist with strong religious views researching atheism would need to acknowledge clearly their values, since this information would be relevant to the audience's ability to evaluate the research produced.

## ⚠ Preparing the ground: Objectivity and subjectivity

Objectivity has three distinctive, but interrelated, meanings:

### Ethics

- **Ethical** objectivity refers to the way a sociologist behaves when conducting, analysing and presenting their research. This is something to which all sociologists (at least in principle) aspire, in the sense that they are honest and accurate in their work, whether this involves recording answers given during an interview, observing the behaviour of people during an experiment or detailing the researcher's experiences while living with a group as part of a participant observation study.

### Conduct

- **Research conduct**: Although general ethical questions surrounding social research are important, they represent *epistemic* values in the sense one would *trust* that no sociologist embarks on a piece of research with the explicit intention of producing something

inaccurate or deceitful. However, a second meaning to objectivity refers to how the researcher actually studies behaviour and involves choices surrounding personal demeanour, in terms of, for example:

- **Personal detachment** – the researcher does not become 'personally involved' with the people they are studying and, therefore, attempts to maintain a:
- **Social distance** from the object of their research.

In this respect, 'objective' research methods reflect the idea that, as far as humanly possible, the researcher *doesn't* interact with their research subjects in ways that influence how these subjects behave. 'Subjective' research methods, however, involve the researcher participating, with varying levels of interaction, in the research process: unstructured interviews, for example, involve little or no personal interaction (the researcher simply records what they are told), whereas covert participant observation involves high levels of interaction. For this type of method the purpose, of course, is to get as close as possible to understanding the reasons for people's behaviour (either through allowing them to talk or by observing and experiencing their behaviour). The key idea here, therefore, is:

- **Objective knowledge** – the idea that it is possible to get at some idea (or version) of 'truth' – whether this version is one generated by maintaining a *social distance* and *emotional detachment* or by becoming so intimately involved in the research process that the researcher becomes, in effect, a crucial part of the research itself.

We need to note here that the concept of

*objective knowledge* is an elastic one that can be stretched in various ways – from the idea of knowledge that is 'reliable, valid and capable of generalisation', to knowledge that simply describes some aspect of social behaviour.

Whatever your particular methodological take on the status of knowledge, the basic idea here is that we can generate some form of objective knowledge about subjective states and behaviours. To take a simple example, if I tell you a joke and you laugh, then it's probably reasonable to assume that, even though the data were produced by our subjective interaction (you wouldn't have laughed if I hadn't told you the joke), you are laughing because you found the joke funny (objective knowledge about your sense of humour).

## Reality

These ideas are closely related to a *third meaning* of objectivity and subjectivity:

**Social reality**: If sociologists have different beliefs about how to collect and interpret research data, it follows that these beliefs are based on different ways of seeing both the nature of the social world and how sociologists should research it. In other words, this relates to how different sociologists see the nature of the thing (social behaviour) they are studying; in basic terms, there are two main ways to understand this idea:

- **Objective** sociology, as **Mulder** (2004) notes, involves the idea that the object of study (whether it be people or inanimate objects) ' ... exists independent of the researcher's perception of it ... the object would "be there," as it is, even if no-one perceived it'. This meaning of objectivity,

he argues, is 'typically associated with ideas such as reality, truth and reliability'.

- **Subjective** sociology involves the idea that human behaviour is something that cannot be validly studied independently of the people who create it. In this respect, we can talk about:

- **'Hard' subjectivity**, a position associated with *postmodernists*, for example, that argues it's impossible to separate the influence of the researcher from the people or things being researched.

- **'Soft' subjectivity**, a position we could associate with *interactionism*, that argues that the researcher can distance themselves sufficiently from their research object in order to describe social behaviour. Such descriptions will be *representations* of behaviour only at a particular moment, but they do have greater validity than the observations of non-sociologists.

A couple of general points are worth noting before we explore the ramifications of these ideas:

**Theoretical preferences**: What we believe about the social world determines what we collect evidence about and, of course, how we go about the task of collecting evidence. At a minimum, theoretical preferences will influence what we believe, as **Weber** argues, 'is worthy of being known' (and, by extension, how it is possible or permissible to know it).

**Values determine preferences**: Complete value-freedom is impossible since values inform everything we do; just as they influence how we see the world, they also influence decisions about the worth of different types of knowledge.

## Digging deeper: Objectivism and subjectivism

We can develop our thoughts about the meaning – and consequences – of different ways of understanding social behaviour in terms of two positions:

- **Objectivism** refers to looking at the social world in terms of it having an independent existence from the people who make up that world. In other words, this general position holds that sociologists can study objective features of the social world – whether in broadly *positivist* or broadly *realist* terms – that have some form of permanence and solidity (institutions such as families, educational systems, and so forth).

- **Subjectivism**: From this position social behaviour is qualitatively different to the behaviour of non-conscious matter. If, therefore, the social world is created through subjective behaviours, sociological theories and methods – from both interactionist and postmodern positions, for example – must reflect this difference. In this respect there can be no theoretical or practical separation between the subject (the researcher) and the object of study ('society'). What may be considered valid knowledge 'yesterday' may not constitute valid knowledge 'today' or 'tomorrow'.

Although the above is a simplified *dichotomy* that ignores differences *within* these categories (between interactionist and postmodern positions, for example) and similarities *between* categories (realism may have more in common with interactionism than it does with positivism), we can examine these two broad positions in more detail:

**Objectivism** involves a range of further ideas:

**Reality**: At root, there is something 'real' that exists independently of the observer. Although people may, at various times, believe in multiple realities, only one is *actually* real and it can, ultimately, be:

**Experienced** directly or indirectly. By applying a scientific methodology (theory building, careful observation, and so forth) we can identify various elements from which reality is constructed. In other words, scientific procedures eventually lead the researcher to some form of:

**Discovery**: Just as natural scientists have progressively uncovered the rules, laws and procedures on which the physical world is based, so too, in their different ways, can social scientists discover the objective basis of social behaviour – an idea that works on two levels:

- **System-wide**, where the objective is to uncover the principles on which whole societies (or systems) are based, and

- **System-specific**, where we see the operation of these principles, as in, for example, **Durkheim's** explanation of suicide or **Michels'** (1911) *iron law of oligarchy*.

## ✳ SYNOPTIC LINK

**Power and politics:** The iron law of oligarchy is discussed in more detail in relation to elite theories of power.

**Value-neutrality** is possible in that the fundamental principles on which behaviour is based (the 'social laws' of some forms of *positivism*, for example) can be identified and studied independently of a researcher's value-commitment. Such principles would remain true regardless of whether the researcher wanted them to be true. The guarantor of value-neutrality is ethical and methodological objectivity.

**Cumulation**: The idea that knowledge is cumulative is important for:

**Knowledge-building**: The development of theories and explanations of ever greater complexity and explanatory power is possible once factual knowledge is established.

These ideas give sociology a *structural* focus since they make assumptions about both the nature of the social world and, by extension, the subject matter of sociology – in particular, an overwhelming concern with the:

**Problem of order**: From this position, if we can establish patterns and regularities in human behaviour (such as suicide) this would suggest some form of external constraint on individual actions and behaviours.

## Social facts

In terms of this example, **Durkheim** (1897) theorised the existence of social structures in terms of a *collective consciousness* – a general set of beliefs about what is good, proper, right, and so forth – that arises from the interaction process within society. The *collective conscience* is rooted in individual behaviour, but takes on an *externalised* form because people's relationships produce norms, values, routines and responsibilities that appear (to all intents and purposes) to exist over and above the individual's personal beliefs, desires and actions. In this respect, therefore, we experience the world as an *external reality* that constrains our choices of action. Thus:

**Social facts** exist which, **Durkheim** (1895) argues, we can consider as 'things' that can be studied sociologically. Just as there are facts we can discover about the natural world, facts associated with human behaviour can also be discovered and explained. **Dawe** (1970) expresses this idea thus: 'Since individuals cannot of their own volition ("unaided") create and maintain order, constraint is necessary for society to exist at all; without it, the only possibility is the war of all against all. Accordingly, society must define the social meanings, relationships and actions of its members for them. And, because it is thus assigned priority over them, it must in some sense be self-generating and self-maintaining.'

## Stimulus – response

The basis of the objectivist argument, therefore, is that subjective states (the meanings and interpretations that guide individual behaviours) are the product of relationships operating at the structural level of society. Human behaviour, in this respect, is considered, as **Dawe** suggests, to be the result of some form of:

**External stimulation**: Just as in the natural world where the behaviour of matter – such as an apple falling to the ground – is determined by the operation of *physical forces*, human behaviour is theorised as the result of a complex interplay of *social forces* (whatever these may actually turn out to be – the socialisation process, the workings of economic markets or whatever).

In this respect – to continue the analogy – if a natural scientist wants to understand why apples always fall to the ground rather than float into the air, they do not ask the apple; they study the forces that propel apples to behave as they do. Similarly, from this position, to understand people's behaviour there's little or no point studying and questioning the individuals involved; rather, we need to understand the *social forces* that compel people to behave in particular ways. If, on this basis, individual action is a product of external social stimuli, it follows that such stimuli can be isolated, researched and explained in an objective, scientific way – an argument that, if valid, resolves two main problems:

- **Subjective meanings** cease to be a variable in the explanation of human behaviour because they are theorised as an 'effect' of structural 'causes'.

- **Objective analysis** is possible because we have removed the element of subjective interpretation (and uncertainty) from the equation.

## Weeding the path

We can note some critical ideas relating to this position in terms of:

**Facts**: An important aspect of objectivity is the ability to weigh evidence carefully – to accept that which is true and reject that which is false. This deceptively simple statement does, however, have a sharp sting in the tail, namely on what basis is it possible to distinguish truth from falsity in the social world? In other words, how do we recognise a fact when we see it? In the natural sciences, facts are established by repeated observations and confirmations – every apple that's ever been seen to fall from a tree has always fallen to the ground. In the social world, facts are less clear-cut; if you fall out of a tree, how you react will differ depending on the context of the behaviour (you might laugh, swear, cry, scream or whatever, depending on a range of factors – who you are, where you are, who you're with, what you were doing in the tree).

**Measurement**: Even if we assume that 'social facts' exist, a couple of further questions need to be asked. First, do social facts have the same qualities as facts in the natural world? Are facts 'waiting to be discovered' by the social scientist or are they, as interpretivists argue, socially constructed?

## Criteria

Second, how can we measure facts? In the natural sciences this is possible because the measuring criterion can be standardised and tested 'against reality'. We know, for example, that 'time' exists for a couple of reasons – things change and time itself changes the further away from the Earth one goes. The problem in the social sciences is that the criteria we use to 'measure facts' are themselves social constructions – which leaves us in the position of trying to measure something objectively on the basis of what are ultimately subjective criteria. This leads us to consider:

**Epistemology**: In order to verify something is a fact we have to establish criteria against which it can be measured; however, to establish such criteria we have to know what it is we're measuring in the first place. This raises the question of whether we have to know something is 'a fact' before we identify it as such. If this is the case, how can the social world be measured objectively?

**Interpretations**: If facts are not 'self-evident things', it follows that they have to be interpreted (or recognised) as facts – and this, of course, can only be done subjectively. As **Kharkhordin** (1991) puts it: 'Facts without interpretation are impossible, even in natural sciences (the standard of objectivity) a discovery of data is affected by the measurement process.'

If we accept the argument that the social world is not only *quantitatively* different to the natural world, but is also *qualitatively* different, we need to consider an alternative position.

## Subjectivism

**Subjectivism** embodies a number of ideas about the nature of the social world and, by extension, how it's both possible and desirable to study it. We can look first at some basic ideas before widening the debate slightly to consider questions of subjectivity and value-neutrality.

**Realities**: A central feature of this position is that 'reality' is defined from the position of different social groups, and we need to think, therefore, in terms of 'multiple realities' rather than a single 'reality'. Although this still involves a concept of 'society', in the sense that structural relationships (such as *socialisation* processes) affect individual behaviour, it is a different conception to that held by objectivists and means we need to

understand how individuals construct realities that then *reflect back* on their behaviour.

## Death of the author

If this is unclear, think about 'society' (defined in terms of the structure of our social relationships) as being like the author of a book. The author constructs a reality (a story or narrative) we enter as we read. However, whatever the ultimate intentions of the author, each reader *interprets* the narrative in different ways, some of which are intended by the author, but many of which are different for each reader. Thus, when **Barthes** (1968) talks about 'the death of the author', he's suggesting there is no single author of a text because each reader reconstructs it in different ways through the meanings they give to the narrative. As he puts it: 'The death of the author is the birth of the reader.'

If we think of this in terms of the relationship between 'society' and the 'individual', the former is not 'the author' of the latter – people are not simply blank pages on which the author (society) writes. On the contrary, from a subjectivist position it is 'society' that is the book (something that has a particular historical structure) and people who are the authors of their own narratives or, to paraphrase **Keep et al.**

## 🌱 Growing it yourself: The structure of groups

Split into small groups, each choosing a different social group (family, school class, gender, ethnic group, etc.).

Identify and briefly explain examples of 'structural demands' made by group membership on the individuals involved.

(2000): 'The author ("society") is not simply a 'person' ("thing") but a socially and historically constituted subject.'

Whenever you join (through choice or *ascription*) a group, therefore, you become subject to a range of 'structural pressures' – people within the group 'make demands' on your behaviour. However, you also help maintain group structure – by conforming and contributing to demands.

**Values**: Although, as **Williams** (2005) suggests, the researcher must strive for objectivity in their work, ' … values are ever present in investigation'. However, rather than see objectivity and subjectivity as 'either/or' categories, he argues they are part of a:

**Continuum** – a line with 'pure objectivity' at one extreme and 'pure subjectivity' at the other. Thus, although sociological research is *more* value-laden than natural scientific research, this doesn't automatically render it unreliable and invalid, for two main reasons. First, 'pure objectivity' is an *ideal* which some scientists aspire to but can never attain because *all* research involves some degree of value-commitment. Second, if sociologists recognise how values impact on their work (by, as we've suggested, identifying the assumptions involved), this research is less value-laden, more reliable and valid than, for example, the opinions of the 'person in the street'.

## ✳ SYNOPTIC LINK

**Power and politics:** A continuum can be used to (crudely) represent different political ideologies (from 'left wing' to 'right wing').

From the above, we can note a couple of ideas:

**Empathy**: Rather than seeing the 'ability to identify with the feelings of others to see events from their viewpoint' as something to *avoid*, sociologists should take advantage of the fact that they have something in common with their object of study (social behaviour) by using such knowledge to inform their research. **Murphy** (1988) argues that if we get rid of the 'objective/subjective' *binary opposition* and recognise that how we *see* something (in terms of our values) can't be separated from how we *interpret* what we see, we arrive at a more coherent understanding of human behaviour. From this position:

'**Value freedom** may pervert data, rather than assure sociologists access to truth' since it's (unattainable) pursuit stops the researcher *questioning* how and why their values are part of the research process. Sociologists should, according to **Murphy** ' … strive to understand the value base of data, rather than searching for ways to purge values from research'.

## Interpretations

**Facts:** In the pursuit of 'objective knowledge', facts are given a *special status* as things that are true regardless of whether we want or believe them to be true. From a *subjectivist* position, if social facts are not 'things waiting to be discovered', but rather 'interpretations waiting to be made', it follows, as **Murphy** suggests, that the objective of social research should not be to follow a natural scientific methodology (*positivism* or *realism*) with the (unattainable) goal of producing 'objective knowledge' about behaviour that is inherently subjective; rather, it should be

' ... to capture the social meaning of facts' – something that can be achieved using research methods that encourage 'communicative competence'. In this respect, **Francis** and **Hestler** (2004) suggest sociological research should focus on understanding and explaining the social processes involved in the construction of what people believe – or don't believe – to be factual information.

## Weeding the path

We can note a number of evaluative points relating to subjectivism in terms of:

**Relativism**: Subjectivist arguments tread a fine line between the idea that 'all knowledge is relative' and 'all knowledge is relative to all other knowledge'. In other words, the first position holds there is no objective way of distinguishing between competing knowledge claims (sociological knowledge has as much – or as little – validity as the opinions of anyone else), whereas the second suggests some forms of knowledge may have greater reliability and validity than others.

**Objectivity**: Where *ethnographic* research methods (such as participant observation) are used we can never know whether a researcher 'observed what they claimed to see'; in other words, their *validity* rests on *trust* (and their *reliability* is invariably low because such methods can never be exactly repeated).

**Science**: From an objectivist viewpoint, a major criticism of subjectivism is that it misrepresents the nature of a scientific methodology. **Popper** (1966) argues that objectivity should be considered *not* at 'the level of individual researchers', but at the 'communal level of critical reflection, argument and assessment'. This suggests that *reliable* and *valid* knowledge is something more than a 'simple social construction' in the sense that it is not merely the result of a 'consensus of the crowd' (valid knowledge is whatever people believe it to be) for two reasons: people may be coerced or tricked into believing something and, more significantly perhaps, scientific knowledge is the product of repeated critical testing.

**Trochim** (2002) further suggests it's possible to argue that a 'scientific consensus' about the status of knowledge is based on the idea of a 'natural selection theory' that argues that ' ... ideas have "survival value" and knowledge evolves through a process of variation, selection and retention. These have adaptive value and are probably as close as our species can come to being objective and understanding reality'.

## New Right

A couple of broader criticisms of 'subjectivism', from a *New Right* perspective, come from:

**Moore** (1993), who suggests: 'It is unlikely many people have ever taken subjectivism completely seriously as far as their own personal lives are concerned, because a consistent subjectivist would not survive very long in the real world.'

**Marsland** (1995), meanwhile, is highly critical of *postmodern* approaches (or 'fashionable gibberish' as he calls them): 'This French pseudo-philosophy has been stirred in with the absurd fantasies of German socialism to render sociology almost entirely immune to the careful, commonsensical sifting of evidence which is fundamental to the traditional British approach to the advance of knowledge. Now anything, or almost anything, goes.'

## Moving on

The work we've done so far suggests the relationship between value-freedom, objectivity and subjectivity is a complex one, operating on a number of levels – from a researcher's personal beliefs (and how they might influence the research process) at one extreme, to questions of how we should view the social world (as an object to be studied or a subject to be created) at the other. Although these issues and debates may, at times, appear to be somewhat academic, in the final section we're going to look at some of their 'practical applications and implications' in terms of the relationship between sociology and social policy.

## 5. The relationship between sociology and social policy

This final section explores the various ways theoretical and applied forms of sociology meet in the area of *social policy* – something that initially involves thinking about the way sociologists view the relationship between:

- social problems
- sociological problems and
- social policy.

### ⚠ Preparing the ground: Social and sociological problems

We can begin by thinking about the difference between two types of 'problem':

### Social

**Social problems**, as **Stanley** (2004) suggests, refer to social behaviour that 'causes public friction and/or private misery' and involves some form of 'public outcry or call for action' to resolve the problem. **Carter** (2001) further notes that a *social problem* is considered harmful ' . . . according to the beliefs and values of some influential or dominant group in the society', and comes to be defined as a problem ' . . . when it persists over time and is not solved because there are a number of competing proposed solutions on which people do not agree'.

### Sociological

**Sociological problems**: The study of social

---

**WARM-UP: PROBLEMS, PROBLEMS**

As a class, identify as many 'social problems' as possible. Once you've done this, identify equivalent examples of sociological problems (we've given you a couple to get you started).

| Social problems | Sociological problems |
|---|---|
| Crime | Why are some forms of behaviour identified as criminal but not others? |
| Single-parent families | How does poverty affect single-parent family life? |
| **Further examples?** ||

problems has traditionally involved examining questions such as how and why behaviour comes to be defined as a social problem. In other words, sociologists have rarely been concerned with trying to produce 'solutions to social problems'; rather, the focus has generally been on understanding how behaviour is constructed as 'a problem' in the first place.

An example of this distinction (and relationship) is provided by the concept of 'disability'. **Adomaitiene** (1999) notes how 'the disabled' face a number of *social problems* – discrimination, lack of facilities, unsuitable building environments, and so forth. In addition, 'the disabled' are frequently defined, by politicians and the media, for example, as a social problem in themselves. *Sociological problems*, in this respect, relate to understanding the nature of the problems presented by disability – such as why discrimination occurs, or why (and by whom) disability is constructed as a social problem.

## Social policy

The previous exercise should have started you thinking about possible relationships between social and sociological problems, and the point where they often meet is:

**Social policy**: **Calvert** and **Calvert** (1992) define this as ' ... the main principles under which the government of the day directs economic resources to meet specific social needs'. **Susannah Morris** (2004) develops this by suggesting it involves the government identifying and regulating:

- **social problems** – such as how to deal with terrorism
- **social needs** – such as those of the elderly
- **social conditions** – such as planning regulations.

## ✳ SYNOPTIC LINK

**Wealth, poverty and welfare:** Ideas about social policy are explored in greater depth in this module.

In terms of the relationship between sociology and social policy, the former, in the post-Second World War period in the UK, has not had a great deal of:

**Direct (explicit)** input into social policies. Governments, for example, rarely seek the advice and guidance of sociologists when formulating policies to tackle some perceived social problem or need. There are reasons for this – partly relating to the perception of sociological knowledge (which links back to questions of objectivity and subjectivity and the different levels of reliability and validity these presuppose), and partly relating to the interests and preoccupations of sociologists (as we've suggested, sociologists and governments frequently have different views about what constitutes 'a problem'). However, even if we accept the above characterisation, sociology has made:

**Indirect (implicit)** contributions to social policy; sociological theories and research have, for example, influenced both the *development* and *direction* of social policy, for a range of reasons:

**Sociality**: Sociological ways of looking at and explaining social behaviour have helped shape the way people view both human behaviour and the possible causes of that behaviour. For example:

- **Holism** involves the idea that to understand something we need to consider all possible influences and causes (the 'bigger picture', if you like). In other words, when we look at behaviour we are able to see beyond its *immediate causality* to locate it within a wider system of ideas and events (as with subcultural theories of crime, for example).

## ✳ SYNOPTIC LINK

**Crime and deviance:** A central feature of sociological theories in this area is their focus on the social causes of deviance. This places them in direct opposition to individualistic/biological theories of deviant behaviour.

- **Structure and action**: Sociology moves the policy focus away from locating behavioural causes and explanations 'wholly within the individual' (by reference to individual psychology or biology) and into a *social context* where membership of social groups ('sociality') is a crucial aspect of any behavioural explanation. In policy terms, the recognition that an individual's *social environment* has an important part to play in explaining their behaviour has helped frame policies such as those associated with current (2006) government ideas about *social inclusion* and *exclusion*.

## ✳ SYNOPTIC LINK

**Wealth, poverty and welfare:** Social inclusion is a good example of how recent social policy in Britain has been partly framed against a background of sociological theories of community (in particular **Etzioni's** (1993) communitarian ideas and **Putnam's** (2001) concept of social capital).

**Research**: Throughout your sociology course you've examined different areas of society

(such as family life and education) where social policy has been *informed* by sociological research and evidence on a couple of levels:

- **Direct inputs** involve research into particular areas and concerns, commissioned, for example, by government departments and agencies.

- **Indirect inputs**: Sociological research also serves to highlight particular *social issues*. **Townsend** and **Abel-Smith's** (1965) work on poverty in the UK in the late 1950s, for example, challenged the accepted wisdom that poverty had been largely eradicated. This 'policing role', as it were, draws attention to the need for social policies to address particular areas of public concern.

Further dimensions involve the use of sociological research for:

**Testing** social policies to evaluate their success in tackling particular social issues. David **Blunkett** (2000), when Secretary of State for Education and Employment, expressed this idea when he noted: 'We need to be able to rely on . . . social scientists to tell us what works and why and what types of policy initiatives are likely to be most effective.'

**Comparative** purposes when *formulating* social policy. **Stephens** (1999) has compared the UK and Nordic (Scandinavian) welfare models to explore ideas about social inclusion and exclusion that can be used to inform social policy.

**Evaluation and monitoring**: In the UK the development of social policy is surrounded by a range of competing ideas and explanations relating to areas like the direction, scope, focus and extent of such policies. At different times – and depending to some extent on prevailing political ideologies – different types of policy are put in place and it's important that their success or failure is monitored and evaluated through research (carried out by a range of social scientists – economists and psychologists, for example, as well as sociologists). One idea sociology brings to the evaluation process is an understanding of both the:

**Intended and unintended** consequences of social policy. **Stephens**, for example, argues that *intended* consequences of recent developments in the UK welfare model have been to use *means-testing* to 'exclude' the middle classes and target help where it is most needed, and lower direct taxation by moving the middle classes towards *private insurance* welfare provision. However, an *unintended* consequence here, **Stephens** argues, has been to increase feelings of social

exclusion among both the very poor *and* the middle classes by lessening the contact between such groups.

## ✳ SYNOPTIC LINK

**Crime and deviance:** The idea of manifest (intended) and latent (unintended) functions developed by **Merton** can be applied across a range of Specification areas (education, welfare and deviance, for example) and issues.

A further example – **Tilley** and **Laycock's** (2002) research into the relationship between CCTV surveillance and 'crime displacement' (the question of whether criminals simply move their activities to areas not covered by cameras) – has shown how sociological research is useful for identifying the ways social policies can be 'fine-tuned'. The issue of CCTV and its role

## ⚠ Growing it yourself: Evaluating research

This exercise focuses on your ability to select, interpret and evaluate sociological research.

In groups no larger than three people, choose a different area of the Specification and:

1 Identify three pieces of research that have contributed to the development of social policy within that area (for example, social exclusion in welfare and poverty).

2 Each member of the group should choose one piece of research and write:

- 100 words outlining how it has contributed to our understanding of an issue.

- 100 words explaining how it has directly or indirectly contributed to social policy on this issue.

- 50–75 words assessing the contribution the research has made to our understanding of the issue.

At the end of the exercise each individual summary can be photocopied so that every student has access to a range of research examples.

in crime reduction, for example, has been shown to be a complex, three-dimensional one: some forms of crime are *deterred*, some *discovered* and some *displaced*.

## ⚠ Digging deeper: Problems and policies

We can look at the relationship between sociology and social policy in more depth by observing that the distinction we made earlier between *social* problems and *sociological* problems has – in recent times perhaps – been more observed in the breach. This isn't to say sociology has, in the past, ignored social policy – we can, for example, point to a selection of writers over the past 200 years whose work, often highly theoretical and speculative, has nevertheless been focused on practical issues and policies. Examples from classical sociology include:

- **Marx** (1867) and his work on forms of economic and social exploitation in the nineteenth century.
- **Durkheim** (1893) and his analysis of the relationship between anomie and the dysfunctions of crime.

In more recent times we could point to the work of second-wave feminists in highlighting the effects of *patriarchy* on gender relationships (as well as their influence on the development of social policies such as the Sex Discrimination and Equal Pay Acts in the 1970s). In addition, we could note:

- **Townsend's** poverty research as instrumental in drawing attention to both the continued existence of poverty and the development of poverty definitions (such as *relative deprivation*) that updated

such definitions in the light of changing cultural circumstances.

- **Becker** (1963) and his work on labelling theory and **Wilkins'** (1964) concept of deviancy amplification, which have also been influential in the development of policies directed at criminal behaviour.

There are more examples we could note, both in *general* terms (criticism of the validity of official crime and employment statistics, for example, has led to the development of measures with greater validity, such as the **British Crime Surveys**) and in *specific* terms, such as **Clarke** and **Mayhew's** (1980) work on the relationship between crime and the physical environment.

## Social and sociological

As the above suggests, there is a frequent meeting point between social problems and sociological problems – which is not too surprising, perhaps, given sociology's focus on the examination and exploration of social relationships. However, sociologists generally tend to be wary of forging *too close* an association between sociological and social problems for a number of reasons:

**Objectivity**: The term 'social problem' begs the question of to whom social behaviour is 'a problem'. For sociologists to think only in terms of *social* – as opposed to *sociological* – problems poses the risk of *overidentification* with a particular social group, something that impacts on the idea of personal objectivity. A social problem is, by definition, defined as such by a powerful social group. If sociologists simply accept the 'definitions of the powerful' they run the risk of failing to investigate the possible role of such groups in 'creating the problem' in the first place. In addition, identification with the powerful calls into question the sociologist's:

**Role**, in the sense that the sociologist effectively becomes an *agent of social control* – a role defined in terms of helping to ensure the smooth, orderly running of society. This, in effect, reduces the study of human behaviour to a narrow, 'problem-based' perspective and raises questions about the:

**Scope** of sociological research: **Mills** (1959) argued that an 'unimaginative view' of sociology as 'problem solving' reduces its power and scope to 'the accumulation of facts for the purpose of facilitating administrative decisions'.

Sociologists, therefore, need to be constantly aware of both their relationship to powerful (and powerless) social groups and the potential uses to which their research may be put – a position that treads a fine line between:

- **Co-option** into the general social control process, whereby sociological research focuses on finding better, more efficient ways of making people conform to dominant social norms.
- **Marginalisation**, whereby sociological research is seen as largely irrelevant to the lives of the people who are the subject of that research.

## Application

Ideas about value-neutrality, objectivity and subjectivity are relevant in this context because they can be applied in ways that allow sociologists to define what **Stanley** (2004) expresses as the idea that 'sociological problems' relate to all forms of behaviour ' ... be they defined as "normal" or "deviant".' Thus:

- **Value-neutrality** relates to the idea that *all* social behaviour is of interest to sociologists – there are no areas sociologists should not study.

- **Objectivity**, in this context, refers to the idea that sociologists should be able to 'stand apart' from non-sociological behavioural definitions in order to study all aspects of that behaviour (and not just the parts defined as 'problems' by powerful groups).

- **Subjectivity** involves sociologists making conscious, committed choices about what to study and how to study it. For some this involves applying their research efforts to the illumination of what may be defined as 'social problems'; for others effort may be directed towards exploring neglected areas of social behaviour (such as the experiences of differently abled social groups); yet others may simply be interested in exploring the theoretical issues involved in the way social problems are constructed 'as problems'.

## Issues

In this respect, **Mills** (1959) considered the focus of sociological research to be:

**Public issues** rather than public *problems* or, indeed, 'private troubles' (things that affect the lives of individuals, such as being the victim of a crime or becoming unemployed, but which, in the normal course of events, do not have a society-wide impact). We can illustrate these distinctions in terms of how something like *unemployment* takes on a different character depending on whether it's seen as a:

- **Private trouble**, in terms of how it affects the individual and their family.

- **Social problem**, in terms of suggesting ways to modify the individual and social problems created by unemployment (although **Mills** considered the concept of 'social problem' on a much grander scale, such as perceived threats to human freedom, for example).

- **Public issue** that looks at all possible aspects of the (sociological) problem, from the impact of unemployment on individual lives, through to the possible structural causes and consequences of large-scale unemployment on a society.

**Stanley** (2004) argues that this distinction is important because 'it may affect both the location of blame for social problems in ways which de-politicises the understanding of them, and it may produce inappropriate social policy. The implication here is that not only may people in different social positions perceive different social problems, they may also perceive the "same" social problem in different ways'.

In this respect, the process whereby some forms of behaviour come to be defined as 'a problem' is, according to **Jamrozik** and **Nocella** (1998), one that needs to be examined in terms of:

- **causal links** between various social behaviours that, in combination, create social problems

- **social actors** – their motives and motivations in identifying and promoting problems

- **those primarily affected** by the problem – how they view it, for example

- **'methods of intervention'** intended to resolve the problem.

We've started to suggest here that the relationship between sociology and social policy is a complex one, not just in terms of how official policy-makers view and use sociological research, but also in terms of how sociologists themselves see their research and its potential uses and applications. This does, of course, reflect a basic tension both:

- **between** sociologists and policy-makers, since the two do not necessarily share similar ideas about the purpose of sociological research, and

- **within** sociology, concerning the relationship between research, problems and policy.

On the one hand, sociologists generally want their work to be recognised as a useful contribution to any understanding of social behaviour, but on the other they're aware of the potential for such research to be used in different ways, for different purposes, by different groups. In this respect, therefore, we can briefly outline how different sociologists have interpreted their general role.

## Feminism

**Redressing bias**: For some, 'objectivity' involves thinking clearly about the nature of society, understanding its biases and injustices and researching possible solutions to these questions that can, in some circumstances, be translated into social policy. An example here is feminist sociology, especially from the 1960s onwards. Generally speaking, feminist writers were particularly concerned to address the 'malestream' bias in both:

- **Sociology**, where accounts of the lives and experiences of women were either ignored or interpreted in terms of their relationship to men – the sociology of deviance being a good example.

- **Society** – in the 1970s, for example, feminist research contributed to the development of 'equal opportunities' policies (and laws) that sought to redress gender discrimination in the workplace (the Equal Pay Act, for example) and society (the Sex Discrimination Act).

Feminist research, in recent times, has focused on a range of policy issues and practices. In terms of the former, for example, **Pascall** (1997) charts how policy changes in the 'UK welfare dynamic' in recent years have resulted in an increasing dependence on 'women's unpaid work' as carers. **Hanmer** and **Statham** (1999) have examined ways that social work can develop ' . . . a genuinely woman-centred practice' by exploring the common ground between female social workers and their clients and the development of non-sexist codes of practice.

**Misra** (2000) highlights how, in the USA, social policies (including those relating to employment, poverty reduction and reproduction) have been both influenced by 'women's activism' and, perhaps more significantly, *connected* to show how policy in one area of women's lives (such as the development of 'family-friendly' employment policies) relates to policies in another area (such as poverty, where single parents have been largely unable to share in the benefits created by the former). In the UK, **Blackburn** (1995) has noted how ' . . . feminist work has been significant in exposing the gendered aspects of the welfare state'.

**Addressing disadvantage**: Although a significant part of the 'feminist project' has been to identify and address disadvantages experienced specifically by women, other sociologists have pointed to the ways 'disadvantaged groups' are either the target for social policies (the 'social problem' approach) or politically marginalised. **Becker** (1967) argues that value-neutrality over social issues is impossible and sociologists should make a choice about how and why their research is used – to promote the interests of the disadvantaged or to support the activities of the state (although the two positions are not mutually exclusive). One expression of this idea is **Young's** (1971) application of:

**Labelling theory** to users of illegal drugs to demonstrate how the policy of labelling deviant behaviour may lead to an increase in the very behaviour official agencies try to resolve.

## Ethnicity

Another application is in the perception and explanation of black male underachievement in UK schools, something that's variously seen as a:

- **Problem** of (and for) British society: **Gillborn** and **Youdell** (2000), for example, suggest *institutionalised racism* is an integral part of the debate.
- **Problem** for black youth and their families: **Sewell** and **Majors** (2001) focus on an 'anti-school peer-group culture' being at the root of the problem.
- **Problem** for both: As **Gewirtz** (2004) puts it: 'Whilst **Sewell** writes about racism in schools, his analysis focuses particularly on the need to tackle an anti-school peer-group culture. Whilst, for **Gillborn**, the solution lies in eradicating racist practices in schools, for **Sewell**, the

solution lies ... in helping boys who are anti-school to change their attitudes and behaviour and in helping them to successfully navigate the mainstream culture.'

A further development we could note is how some sociologists focus on:

**Promoting social change**: **Tombs** and **Whyte** (2003), for example, argue that sociological research should go 'beyond value-freedom' to adopt a 'partisan objectivity' that involves sociologists 'being answerable to the relatively powerless ... we should neither conduct research exclusively in league with powerful groups, but neither should we communicate our research exclusively to powerful groups'.

Thus, rather than engaging in research to inform social policy, the role of the sociologist is transformed into someone able to empower the powerless by providing the information needed to challenge the interpretations and policies of the powerful. The main difference between this position and that of someone like **Becker** is, according to **Tombs** and **Whyte**, that 'radical sociologists ... take the standpoint of the *underdog* [and] apply it to the study of the *overdogs*'.

## ⚠ Weeding the path

There are a number of points we can make relating to value-committed sociology:

**Slumming**: **Gouldner** (1973), while generally advocating a *value-committed* approach, suggests the underlying ideology of 'underdog' approaches owes more to the desire of some sociologists to appear 'radical' than to any real sense of identification with 'the poor and the powerless'. **Gouldner**

views this type of 'underdog posturing' as an example of romanticism and the search for the exotic.

**The underdog**: It's unclear as to who these people are in any society. While interactionist sociology, for example, has portrayed some deviants as 'victims' of social forces and processes, there is – ironically, perhaps – no way of objectively identifying such people. This 'lack of objective focus' can, at times, lead to difficult theoretical positions – in a racist society, for example, 'the underdog' could just as easily be seen to be the perpetrator of racist violence (since they are 'victims of ideological manipulation') as the actual victim of such violence.

**Partisan objectivity** involves the idea that although the sociologist is committed to a particular political viewpoint, they carry out their research in an 'objective' fashion, but exactly what this involves is unclear: **Tombs** and **Whyte** variously refer to it as involving 'openness, accountability, rigour, and honesty'. In some ways, *partisan objectivity* resembles little more than a reworking of **Weber's** ideas about value-neutrality, which we noted earlier, whereby, according to **Tombs** and **Whyte**, 'researchers recognise, describe and are open about the perspective from which their research commitments, [and] questions ... originate'.

## New right

Although these ideas represent general criticisms of a value-committed approach to the relationship between sociology and social policy, a more concentrated attack on 'underdog sociology' has come, in recent times, from a:

**New Right perspective** that, in its own

way, advocates a form of *partisan objectivity*. For **Marsland** (1994), the starting point for analysis is the idea that, all things considered, British society is by no means as exploitative, unequal, racist and sexist as some forms of sociology suggest. On the contrary, for **Marsland**, we live in a society that, while imperfect, is one where people generally enjoy relatively high levels of income, security and longevity.

**Marsland** argues that ' ... the last twenty years have seen relatively few sociologists ... apply sociological techniques and insights to the solution of social problems', and suggests that the task of sociology is to address 'social problems' as they are defined and identified by the political consensus in democratic societies. He further argues that at a time when 'governments are open to influence by empirical social research and argument', the dominant mood in sociology has been 'anti-establishment and anti-empirical'.

Rather than engage in irrelevant – as far as the rest of society is concerned – debates over the epistemological status of sociological research, **Marsland** argues that 'systematic empirical sociological research has a necessary, important, and constructive role to play in relation to policy formulation, implementation, and evaluation'. He uses two further arguments to support his claim that a 'fully engaged' sociology is one that takes a commitment to social policy (and the empirical research it necessarily involves) seriously:

- **Control agency**: The 'Project Camelot' example we noted earlier is, according to **Marsland**, a good example of just how rare the 'corrupt incorporation of weak sociologists' as agents of government

actually is – the fact that it's noted in so many textbooks (including, of course, this one) suggests **Marsland's** observation is justified.

- **Disengagement**: A sociology that refuses to become involved in social policy, at all levels, is one that effectively leaves the field open to other social sciences (such as psychology) and, more importantly perhaps, *vested-interest groups*. Although sociologists are aware of the practical, methodological and ethical problems and pitfalls of aligning social research to social policy, a *failure to engage* in policy research doesn't mean it won't be carried out. If sociologists leave the field open, two things potentially occur:

  - **Marginalisation**: Sociology is pushed towards the political margins by disciplines, such as psychology, history and economics, willing and able to engage in social research that, in effect, promotes their particular view on social behaviour.

  - **Vested interests**: Policy-making is less well informed and not subject to checks and balances, leaving it open to co-option by powerful groups, able to impose their ideas and opinions – unsupported and unchecked by objective research.

## Complexity

The above suggests the relationship between sociology and social policy is not an easy one to define, and the situation is further complicated by the existence of various theoretical positions relating to the different ways sociologists see both the purpose of social policy and their particular value-orientation towards the conceptualisation of social behaviour in terms of 'problems' or 'issues'. This situation is rendered more complex by disagreements over what, exactly, constitutes social policy and how it can be defined. To complete this section, therefore, we can note a couple of further ideas about how social policy can be defined and, by extension, possible roles for the sociologist in the formulation and creation of policy.

**Definitions**: **Susannah Morris** (2004) suggests 'social policy problems are constructed from a mixture of economic, social and political circumstances' – an idea that reflects **Marshall's** (1950) classic argument that social policy involves 'the use of political power to supersede, supplant, supplement, or modify operations of the economic system in order to achieve results which the economic system would not achieve on its own'.

These ideas, therefore, point towards thinking about social policy as reflecting a political desire (or need) to correct 'social problems', mainly defined at the level of economic relationships. Unequal economic relationships impact on a wide range of political and cultural behaviours, from relationships within the family and the education system, to questions of crime, welfare and poverty, for example.

## ✳ SYNOPTIC LINK

**Stratification and differentiation: Davis** (2000) draws our attention to the way the above types of definition '… attempt to understand the dynamic relationship between social policies and social stratification'. In this respect, UK social policies have aimed not only at limiting the effects of economic inequality, but also at ways of limiting social exclusion.

**Scope**: Although social policy potentially covers a wide range of ideas, we can narrow the focus to manageable proportions by adopting **Davis'** (2000) formulation that social policy needs to be considered in terms of:

- **Intentional actions**, originating within or focused on the public sphere and designed to achieve:
- **Welfare goals**, in the sense of involving some 'positive conception of human well-being' (which itself can be interpreted widely to include ideas like equality of opportunity, social justice and social inclusion). These goals are put into practice through:
- **Policy instruments**, involving a variety of programmes aimed at areas such as family life, the workplace, education, poverty, and so forth.

# Growing it yourself: Sociology and social policy

A useful revision (and synoptic) exercise is to identify areas of social policy in your A level course and relate them to sociological research.

**Susannah Morris** (2004) has suggested a number of areas where sociological research has, in the recent past, provided an input into social policy formulation. These include:

- wealth distribution and redistribution

- living standards (in relation to the elderly and the sick)

- social disadvantage (involving help for the unemployed, the poor and single parents)

- safety net (the idea of government ensuring a minimum standard of living)

- social inclusion (in terms of family life, education, religion, and so forth)

- social exclusion (as above).

In small groups, each should examine any *one* of the above areas and:

- Identify social policies relating to this area.

- Identify at least *two pieces of sociological research* you believe have contributed to the development of social policy in that area.

Each group should then, in turn, outline their findings to the class.

# CHAPTER 5

# Crime and deviance

This chapter examines concepts of crime and deviance by applying them to issues (such as criminal and non-criminal deviance) and *situations* (how deviance occurs in areas such as family life and the like).

## 1. Different explanations of crime, deviance, social order and social control

### ⚠ Preparing the ground: Defining deviance

The concept of deviance, at its most basic, refers to 'rule-breaking' behaviour; actions, in other words, that violate (or 'deviate from') a *social norm* or rule, of which we can identify two main types.

- **Formal norms** include *laws* and *organisational rules* and they represent

A 'No Smoking' policy in a workplace is an example of a formal organisational rule

official standards that apply in a given situation. Punishment ('negative sanction') for deviance is specified as part of the rule.

- **Informal norms** vary from group to group and there are no formal punishments for deviation – smoking with a group of friends, for example, may be considered deviant or non-deviant depending on their particular attitudes towards such behaviour.

the other groups (briefly discussing anything that needs clarification).

What does this work tell us about deviance and deviant behaviour? Think about:

- Who makes rules (and why)?
- Are rules selectively policed and punished?
- If the same behaviour can be seen as both deviant and non-deviant, what does this tell us?

In everyday use, 'deviance' has certain *pejorative* (negative) overtones, but sociologically we can think about different types of deviance as involving ideas such as:

- **'good'** (admired) behaviour, such as heroism (or *altruistic* behaviour – putting the needs of others before your own)
- **'odd'** behaviour, such as eccentricity – the person who shares their house with 50 cats, for example
- **'bad'** behaviour, examples of which range from a misbehaving child to murder.

These general behavioural categories give us a flavour of the complexity of deviance, but they're not very useful in terms of thinking about deviance 'in the real world', mainly because of the relationship they presuppose between:

**Interpretation** and **classification**: To classify behaviour as 'good' or 'bad' involves taking a *moral* standpoint – to judge, in other words, different forms of behaviour *before* classifying them. This means deviance has two important characteristics:

- **Subjectivity**: If decisions about deviance are based on judgements about behavioural norms, all behavioural

classifications are based on subjective understandings and interpretations – an idea that raises questions about whether any behaviour can be 'inherently' (always) deviant (in all societies and at all times). It also raises questions about 'who decides' whether behaviour is classified as deviant or non-deviant – something that involves:

- **Power**: This relates not only to how deviance is defined by social groups, but also to how it's explained. We can, for example, explain deviance in terms of ideas such as the qualities possessed by the deviant, the social processes by which rules are created (as **Becker**, 1963, puts it: 'Social groups create deviance by making the rules whose infraction constitutes deviance'), or a combination of the two.

## 🏠 The potting shed

Identify and briefly explain one example of behaviour that is deviant but not criminal, and one example of criminal behaviour that's not always seen as particularly deviant.

## 🔯 Digging deeper: Defining deviance

Deviance has some further dimensions we need to note.

- **Absolute** conceptions have two main dimensions. First, the idea that some forms of behaviour are *proscribed* (considered deviant) and negatively *sanctioned* in all known societies at all times. Second, particular types of individual are inherently (genetically, socially or psychologically) predisposed to

## ◢ Growing it yourself: Definitely deviant?

In small groups, identify as many examples as possible of behaviour that:

- is deviant in our society now but wasn't deviant in the past
- is not deviant in our society now but was deviant in the past
- is deviant in our society but not in other societies
- is deviant in another society but not in our society.

As a class, consider what these examples tell us about deviance as an absolute or relative concept.

deviance – in other words, they can't help breaking social rules.

## ✳ SYNOPTIC LINK

Think about how the examples you've identified in the 'Definitely deviant' exercise can be related to different areas of the Specification.

- **Relative** concepts also have two dimensions. First, the idea that *no* behaviour has always been considered deviant in all societies (a *cross-cultural* dimension) and at all times (a *historical* dimension). Second, that deviance, according to **Becker** (1963), is not a quality of what someone does but rather a quality of how someone *reacts* to that behaviour; the relative dimension here is the idea that the same behaviour can, for example, be seen as deviant in some societies but not in others.

The previous exercise suggests two further ideas – what **Plummer** (1979) considers to be the distinction between:

- **Societal** deviance, where there's a broad consensus in a society that behaviour is morally wrong, illegal, and so forth, and

- **Situational** deviance, where a group defines its behaviour as non-deviant, even though such behaviour is considered societally deviant.

**Roberts** (2003), for example, argues that 'swinging' ('an increasingly popular leisure choice for married and courting couples') fits this particular category – an idea that suggests deviance can be a matter of personal choice (if I don't want to 'swing' then I don't go to swinger parties).

In this respect, deviant behaviour carried out with an *awareness* of its deviant nature is:

- **Culpable** deviance – behaviour for which the offender is held personally accountable, something that differentiates it from
- **Non-culpable** deviance – acts for which the offender is *not* held personally accountable (such as crimes committed by the mentally ill, for example).

## ◢ The potting shed

Identify and briefly explain one example of societal, situational, culpable and non-culpable deviance from any area of the Specification.

In terms of the above, therefore, deviance is not necessarily as clear-cut and straightforward as we initially suggested – an idea reflected in the range of sociological explanations for deviant behaviour.

## Preparing the ground: Functionalist perspectives

Functionalist perspectives involve the explanation of crime and deviance in terms of three basic ideas:

- **Consensus**: A basic level of general agreement exists in any society over shared norms and values.

- **Conformity** to social norms is not automatic (people are not naturally law-abiding or naturally deviant). Social controls exist to promote normative conformity.

- **Control**: Deviant behaviour is explained in terms of the breakdown (for a variety of reasons) of social controls.

Functionalist explanations, therefore, share the common theme that by discovering the *characteristics of conformity* we can also discover the *causes of deviance*. The classical expression of this perspective is the work of writers such as **Durkheim** (1895), who argued that all societies faced two major problems – how to achieve:

- **Social order** and maintain:
- **Social stability** in a situation (a vast range of possible individual beliefs, behaviours and actions) that appeared inherently unstable and disorderly.

The answer, **Durkheim** suggested, could be found in the concept of a:

**Collective consciousness**: society, from this position, is an *emergent entity* (it emerges from – and reflects back on – the behaviour of individuals) and social interaction is possible only if it's based on shared understandings and meanings; once these are established they 'take on a life of their own', existing outside the consciousness of *individual* actors (but deeply embedded in each individual through primary and secondary socialisation processes).

The collective consciousness is a mental construct and, as such, has no physical form; it needs, therefore, to be consistently reinforced if order and stability are to be maintained. For **Durkheim**, one way to reinforce the collective conscience was to repeatedly challenge and test its most fundamental beliefs through deviant behaviour. Deviance, therefore, was:

- **Normal** – it represents a mechanism through which the collective conscience is both recognised and affirmed – and

- **Functional** because it serves such essential purposes as:

  - **boundary setting**: as societies become more complex in their range of social relationships, *control mechanisms*, such as a legal system, must develop (society as a self-regulating (*autopoietic*) mechanism) to codify moral behaviour in terms of laws marking the boundaries of acceptable and unacceptable behaviour

  - **public boundary marking**: legal boundaries are 'given substance' by 'ceremonies' such as public courts and media reporting of crimes.

## ✳ SYNOPTIC LINK

**Religion:** Note the similarity between this 'public function' of crime and law and the distinction Durkheim makes between 'the sacred' and 'the profane'. In this instance, the collective conscience parallels the sacred – it is something special that requires veneration and respect and is separated from the profane through public markers and ceremonies.

- **social change**: deviant behaviour is a functional mechanism for change because it tests the boundaries of public tolerance and morality. It is a *social dynamic* that forces people to assess and reassess the nature of *social statics* (such as written laws). Laws banning male homosexuality in our society, for example, have gradually been abandoned as public tolerance has grown – an example of what **Durkheim** argued was the role of deviance in promoting things like freedom of thought and intellectual development. Challenges to the prevailing orthodoxy, he argued, are signs of a healthy society.

- **social solidarity**: deviance promotes *integration* and solidarity through its 'public naming and shaming' function. Popular alarm and outrage at criminal acts, for example, serve to draw people closer together 'against a common enemy'.

### ⚠ Weeding the path

This type of traditional functionalist perspective has been subjected to a number of significant criticisms:

- **Collective conscience**: Conflict theorists, among others, have challenged the idea that social behaviour is based on a broad social consensus. They argue such 'consensus' is manufactured by powerful interest groups (such as the media).

- **Social dynamics**: Powerful groups in society can use the existence of deviance (such as *terrorism* in recent times) to curtail civil liberties and freedoms, thereby inhibiting social change.

- **Anomie**: Not all crime is functional. Although **Durkheim** noted that 'too much crime' damaged the collective conscience (by creating 'normative confusion' or *anomie*), we have no *objective* way of knowing when crime might become *dysfunctional*.

### ⚠ Digging deeper: Strain theory

This development in functionalist theory was pioneered by **Merton** (1938) when he used the concept of anomie to explain crime and deviance as an *individual response* to problems at the *structural level* of society – an explanation, as **Featherstone** and **Deflem** (2003) note, based around two concepts:

- **Structural tensions**: For societies to function, people have to be given incentives to perform certain roles (the cultural *goals* – or *ends* – of *social action*). **Merton** argued that, for societies like Britain and America, a fundamental goal was 'success' and, as part of the *collective consciousness*, such goals become incorporated into the general socialisation process – people are encouraged to want success. However, when societies set *goals* they must also set the structural *means* towards their achievement and the blocking or unavailability of the means to achieve desired goals results in:

- **Anomie**: For **Merton**, this represented a situation in which, although behavioural norms existed, people were unable – or unwilling – to obey them, a situation that would result in a (psychological) *confusion* over how they were expected, by others, to behave. If societies failed to provide the means towards desired ends, people would resolve the resulting *anomic situation* by developing new and different norms to guide them towards these ends. A classic expression of this idea is that:

**Success** (however it may actually be defined) is a universal goal in our society, learnt through the:

**Socialisation** process: As **Akers** and **Sellers** (2004) put it: 'Everyone is socialised to aspire toward high achievement and success. Competitiveness and success are ... taught in schools, glamorised in the media, and encouraged by the values passed from generation to generation. Worth is judged by material and monetary success.' Socialisation, therefore, stresses:

**Socially approved** (legitimate) means to achieve this goal. As **Akers** and **Sellers** suggest: 'Success is supposed to be achieved by an honest effort in legitimate educational, occupational, and economic endeavors. Societal norms regulate the approved ways of attaining this success, distinguishing them from illegitimate avenues to the same goal.' However:

**Strains** occur at the *structural level* when people are denied opportunities to realise their success goal through legitimate means (such as work). Thus, although everyone 'wants success', only a limited number can actually achieve it through legitimate means. The *tension* between 'socialised desires' and society's inability to satisfy those desires through legitimate means results, for **Merton**, in anomie – something, in turn, manifested in a number of general individual responses, as shown in the table below.

| Responses to strain: Merton (1938) | | | |
|---|---|---|---|
| | **Structural means** | **Cultural ends** | **Example** |
| Conformity (law-abiding) | ✓ | ✓ | Shop assistant |
| Innovation | ✗ | ✓ | Entrepreneur Bank robber |
| Ritualism | ✓ | ✗ | Bureaucrat |
| Retreatism | ✗ | ✗ | Drug addict |
| Rebellion | Deny legitimacy of both ends and means | | Terrorist |
| ✓ = accepts and ✗ = rejects | | | |

## ⚠ Weeding the path

Strain theory combines *macro* theories of structure (tensions) and *micro* theories of action (how individuals respond to anomie) to produce a *reactive theory* of deviance that has been criticised in terms of:

- **Scope**: Although the theory may, arguably, explain 'purposeful crime' (such as theft, an 'alternative' way of achieving economic success), it's less convincing when dealing with what **Cohen** (1955) calls 'purposeless crime' (such as juvenile delinquency).

- **Cultural values**: The idea of 'shared values' is difficult to demonstrate empirically in culturally diverse societies such as Britain in the twenty-first century – 'success', for example, may mean different things to different people. In addition, cultural diversity exposes people to different, frequently contradictory, socialising influences. If goal diversity exists, then how are people socialised into the same general kind of 'success values'?

- **Choice**: There is little or no conception of people making rational decisions about whether to conform or deviate.

- **Conformity**: People are either conformists or deviants, but the question here is the extent to which there is always an easy distinction between 'deviants' and 'non-deviants'. **Clarke** (1980) argues that even those heavily involved in criminal behaviour actually spend a large proportion of their time conforming to conventional (non-criminal) social norms and values.

- **Operationalisation**: **Agnew** (2000) has noted the difficulties involved in measuring concepts such as social strain, cultural goals and individual aspirations, whether using *subjective* measures (exploring how respondents feel about how they have been treated by society), or *objective* approaches that involve identifying causes of strain (such as divorce or unemployment) and measuring their relationship to criminal involvement.

# Discussion point: A virtue of vileness

Imagine a society consisting of three groups which vary in their susceptibility to social pressures:

- The Virtuous – a minority who never do anything bad.
- The Vile – a minority who never do anything good.
- The Vacillators – a majority who are neither of the above.

A change in society initiated by The Vile – an increase in unemployment and poverty, for example – results in greater numbers of Vacillators becoming Vile. Who is responsible for this 'decline in virtue'?

- The individual Vacillator who chooses to become vile?
- The Vile who created the change in society?
- The Virtuous who did nothing to prevent the change?

## ⚠ Preparing the ground: Ecological theories

The main focus of ecological theories is the relationship between the individual and their physical and social ('demographic') environment. As **Wilcox** and **Augustine** (2001) note, *human ecologists* examine how the '... social and physical characteristics of a community affect crime by altering the administration of resident-based social control'. In other words, this perspective examines how (mainly) informal social controls are enhanced or disrupted by the way a community is *physically* and *socially* organised.

**Physical environments**, for example, affect the conditions under which informal social controls apply and **Wilcox** and **Augustine** suggest a number of factors affecting the way people think about and relate to their physical environment:

- **Territoriality**: who 'owns and controls' physical and social space?

- **Surveillance**: the extent to which offenders move freely and unseen through a community.

- **Milieu**: the level of 'civic pride and possession' people feel about where they live, for example.

These ideas are, in turn, affected by aspects of the physical environment. Poor street lighting, for instance, may make community surveillance difficult and consequently make it easier for offenders to control certain social spaces (the classic 'street-corner gangs of youths', for example).

## 🏠 The potting shed

Are you aware of areas controlled by 'deviant groups'? If so, how do you feel when you have to pass through such spaces?

**Social environments** and organisations relate, **Wilcox** and **Augustine** note, to questions about 'poverty, ethnic heterogeneity ... and residential mobility' in terms of how these 'enhance or diminish the cohesiveness among neighbours, thereby affecting their supervision and intervention behaviour'. Social environments, in other words, relate to the development – or otherwise – of community bonds, a theme previously noted by **Shaw** and **McKay** (1932) in terms of:

**Social disorganisation** theory, based on the idea that if people develop a sense of communal living, rights and responsibilities, they also develop attachments to an area and its members (they care, in other words, about what happens in that area).

## Concentric zones

From this initial proposition **Shaw** and **McKay** sought to explain how and why some areas of a city (in this instance, Chicago in the USA) had higher levels of crime than others. In particular they noted that *inner-city areas* consistently had the highest rates of crime, an observation they developed into a:

**Concentric zone** theory (based on the work of **Park** and **Burgess** that linked physical environments to social environments). The basic idea here is that every city consists of *zones*, radiating from

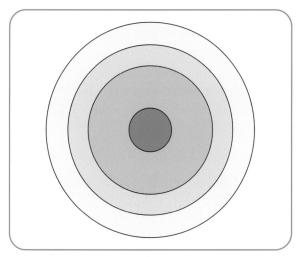

The 'central business district' is in the centre, surrounded by the inner-city 'zone of transition' or 'interstitial zone'

the centre (think about an archery target, with the bullseye being Zone 1 – the central business district – and each radiating ring being named successively).

Zone 2 (the 'zone of transition' or inner-city area) – characterised by cheap housing that attracted successive waves of immigrants – had a consistently higher rate of crime than any other zone, regardless of which ethnic group dominated the cultural life of the area. This led **Shaw** and **McKay** to argue that high crime rates were *not* a consequence of the behaviour of any particular group. Rather, the *transient* nature of people's lives meant that no settled community developed in the inner-city zone. Immigrants, for example, who initially settled there, moved to the outer residential areas as they became established in the city, to be replaced by a further wave of immigrants. High population turnover (including people temporarily entering the transition zone from the outer, residential zones, looking for excitement and entertainment) resulted in a 'socially

disorganised area' where informal social controls were either absent or ineffective.

## ✳ SYNOPTIC LINK

**Wealth, poverty and welfare: Bottoms** and **Wiles** (1992) note how the idea of 'social disorganisation' has re-emerged in contemporary New Right theories of the underclass. 'Welfare dependency', for example, is blamed on the disorganised behaviour of this 'class'.

## Weeding the path

Although the empirical demonstration of the relationship between conformity and the development of strong communal relationships is impressive, a major problem with this particular theory derives from the idea of:

**Disorganised behaviour**: Although this has echoes of *anomie theory* (subsequently developed to greater effect by **Merton**), it is theoretically inadequate because no form of social behaviour is ever 'disorganised' (in the sense of *chaotic*), although it may *appear* to have such characteristics to the outsider.

**Tautology**: 'Social disorganisation' is both a cause and an effect of crime – disorganisation creates high crime rates which, in turn, create disorganisation. The problem here, of course, is that we have no logical way of knowing which is the cause and which the effect.

A response to such criticism saw the development of:

**Cultural transmission** theory, where the focus moved from disorganisation to how groups became *criminally organised* in the zone of transition (where opportunities for crime were greater and criminals could move 'anonymously'). When criminal behaviour becomes established it represents 'normal behaviour' for some groups and, once this occurs, criminal norms and values (culture) are transmitted, through the socialisation process, from one generation to the next.

## Weeding the path

Although cultural transmission is a logical development in ecological theory, a major problem remains: if cultural transmission is such a powerful form of socialisation for some people, why doesn't it apply to others in similar social positions? Why do some people commit crime because they have been socialised to see it as normal, while others do not? Statistically, for example, young males are far more heavily involved in crime than older males or females, yet each group would, presumably, have been subject to similar socialising tendencies when living in the interstitial zone.

## Differential association

One way of resolving this problem is to adopt **Sutherland** and **Cressey's** (1939) theory of:

**Differential association**: This holds that an individual is likely to develop criminal tendencies if they '... receive an excess of definitions favourable to violation of the law over definitions unfavourable to violation'. Differential association, therefore, uses concepts of *socialisation* and *social learning* to locate behaviour within a cultural framework of rules and responsibilities – who you associate with influences the likelihood of conforming or deviant behaviour.

However, this wasn't simply a case of 'if you associate with criminals you will become a criminal', since it was possible for individuals to receive:

**Contradictory socialisation**: An individual's family, for example, might stress non-criminal behaviour whereas the peer group sends out another message entirely. **Sutherland** and **Cressey** suggested, therefore, that *four main variables* influenced individual decisions about behaviour:

- **Frequency**: The number of times criminal definitions occur (for example, the belief that crime is acceptable) influences how people see deviant behaviour.

- **Length**: The longer the exposure to definitions (criminal or conforming), the more likely they are to be accepted and acted on.

- **Intensity**: The prestige/status of the person making the definition is important; we are more receptive to the ideas of people we respect.

- **Priority**: The importance we attach to socialising messages from different sources. A child, for example, may prioritise the views of their parents as more important than the views received from television programmes.

## The potting shed

Identify and briefly explain two examples, from different areas of the Specification, of contradictory socialisation.

## Weeding the path

A major advantage of this analysis is that it *isn't*:

**Culture** or **class specific**: Anyone, from any social background, is liable to offend if sufficient definitions encourage such behaviour, an idea that encouraged the recognition and study of middle-class forms of criminality ('*white-collar crime*'). However, potential problems relate to:

- **Operationalisation**: The complex relationship between the variables (how does *priority* relate empirically to *frequency*, for example) and the difficulty of actually measuring ideas like 'frequency of definitions' make it a difficult theory to test.

- **Differential involvement**: Crime data suggest some groups are more involved in crime than others. If differential association is significant, why don't those close to offenders (such as marriage partners) display similar levels of criminality?

- **Distinctions**: There is, once again, a separation between 'criminals' and 'non-criminals', something that, as **Clarke** (1980) has argued, may not be as clear-cut as this theory suggests.

## Subcultures

We can develop these general ideas by noting ecological analyses have been influential in relation to:

**Functionalist subcultural theories**, which distinguish between two basic forms of subculture.

**Reactive (or oppositional) subcultures**: These involve group members developing norms and values as a *response* to and *opposition* against the prevailing norms and values of a wider culture. **Cohen** (1955) argued that male delinquent subcultures developed on the basis of:

**Status deprivation/frustration**: People joined subcultural groups to achieve a desired social commodity (status or respect) denied to them by wider society (note how this develops **Merton's** strain theory). **Hargreaves** (1967) showed how status denial in school led the boys he studied to develop oppositional subcultures.

**Cloward** and **Ohlin** (1960) also noted a different form of reactive subculture that developed in terms of:

**Opportunity structures**: Like **Merton**, they noted the significance of 'legitimate opportunity structures' (such as work) as a way of achieving success. However, these were paralleled by 'illegitimate opportunity structures' that provided an 'alternative career structure' for deviants. They suggested three types of subcultural development:

- **Criminal**, that developed in stable (usually working-class) communities with successful criminal *role models* ('crime pays') and a *career structure* for aspiring criminals.

- **Conflict**: Without (structural) community support mechanisms, self-contained *gang cultures* developed by providing 'services', such as prostitution and drug dealing.

- **Retreatist**: Those unable to join criminal or conflict subcultures (failures, as it were, in both legitimate and illegitimate structures) retreated into 'individualistic' subcultures based around drug abuse, alcoholism, vagrancy, and so forth.

**Independent subcultures**: The second basic form identified by functionalist subcultural theorists involves individuals holding norms and values that developed out of their experiences within a particular cultural setting. Subcultural development is an 'independent' product of – and solution to – the problems faced by people in their everyday lives. A classic example here is provided by **Miller** (1958) in his analysis of gang development in the USA, when he argues that the:

**Focal concerns** of lower-class subcultures (acting tough, being prepared for 'trouble', a desire for fun and excitement) bring such groups into conflict with the values of wider culture, leading to their perception and labelling as deviant. In a British context, **Parker** (1974) observed the same phenomenon in his study of Liverpool gang behaviour.

## Weeding the path

Although these subcultural theories identify the ways membership is functional to its participants (reflecting **Plummer's** (1979) notion of *situational deviance*), this general theory is not without its critics. **Costello** (1997), for example, suggests that two crucial problems are left unanswered by subcultural theories (including those based around differential association):

- **Existence**: Are subcultures simply an assumption that similar behaviour patterns are indicative of some form of organised group? **Cohen** (1971) suggests a similar criticism when he argues that 'subcultural groups' represent a *labelling process* by outside groups (especially the media) which impose a sense of organisation and meaning on behaviour that has little or no collective meaning for those involved.

## ✳ SYNOPTIC LINK

**Mass media:** Examples of media labelling can be found in areas like sexuality and disability.

- **Cultural transmission**: Subcultural groups lack mechanisms for cultural transmission (socialising new and potential members, for example). This suggests they are not particularly coherent social groups.

**Neo-tribes**: **Bennett** (1999) has argued that the concept of subculture has become a 'catch-all' category that has outlived whatever sociological use it may once have had. He suggests, instead, that the concept of neo-tribes has more meaning and use in the analysis of subcultural behaviour, since it reflects a (postmodern) emphasis on the way cultural identities are 'constructed rather than given' and 'fluid rather than fixed'.

## Preparing the ground: Critical theories

This section explores critical perspectives (in the Marxist tradition) that focus on the various ways deviant behaviour is constructed and criminalised in capitalist societies. In this respect, we can start by outlining some of the basic ideas underpinning:

**Orthodox Marxist theories** of crime: These take as their starting point the standard sociological line (from *functionalism* through *action theory*) that no form of human behaviour is inherently deviant – behaviour becomes deviant only through the creation and application of rules.

In this respect, therefore:

**Rule creation** is a function of capitalist economic organisation and behaviour. In other words, to understand how and why criminal forms of deviance occur we must study the social and economic conditions that give rise to certain types of rule. In this respect, rule creation at the structural level (*laws*) reflects two things:

- **Power**: Laws are created by the powerful and reflect their basic interests, either in a *relatively simple* way for instrumental Marxists like **Milliband** (1973), or in a more complex way for hegemonic Marxists like **Gramsci** (Hoare and Nowell-Smith, 1971) or **Poulantzas** (1975). In terms of the latter, all societies require laws governing:

  - **Social order** – relating to things like the legality or otherwise of killing people, violent behaviour and the like. On the other hand, laws of:

  - **Property/contract** are structurally related to the requirements of capitalism and include areas such as private property ownership, theft, inheritance rules and the like.

- **Social inequality**: Decision-making processes are dominated by those who hold economic and political power, and the exact form of law creation reflects the interests of those with the most to lose if the social and economic order is threatened. If the *economic* dimension sets the underlying parameters of social control and the *political* dimension specifies the shape and policing of legal rules, a third cultural dimension is important in terms of 'selling' these ideas to the wider population.

For powerful social classes, the problem of how to control the behaviour of other classes has two basic dimensions:

- **Force** – considered in terms of *hard policing* (the police and armed forces as *agents* of social control) and *soft policing* (social workers and welfare agencies 'policing' the behaviour of the lower classes) – may be effective in the *short term*, but it also creates *conflicts* between the policed and those doing the policing.

- **Socialisation** – a form of ideological manipulation (in terms of values, norms and so forth) that seeks to either convince people that the interests of the ruling class are really the interests of everyone or to present society as 'impossible for the individual to influence or change' (except through legitimate means such as the ballot box, where, for orthodox Marxists, political representatives of the ruling class achieve legitimacy for their political power). Socialisation may be more effective in the *long term* because people incorporate the basic ideology of capitalism into their personal value system, but it also involves making economic and political concessions to the lower classes to ensure their cooperation.

## ⚠ The potting shed

You can apply these ideas by thinking about how education involves a mix of force and socialisation. What is the role played by each in controlling behaviour and how effective – in the short and long term – are these strategies?

We can examine various ways these ideas relate to crime and deviance by looking at:

**Critical subcultural perspectives** that link orthodox Marxist preoccupations with law creation and, as we will examine in a moment, a *radical criminology* that explores structural and (sub)cultural relationships. For Marxists, the development of subcultures is initially explained in terms of:

**Meaningful behaviour**: Although not a particularly novel observation, **Downes** (1966) argues that deviant behaviour, from a subcultural perspective, involves groups and individuals attempting to solve particular social problems in meaningful ways.

Marxist subcultural perspectives have chiselled out a unique take on deviant subcultural development by focusing on two ideas:

- **Hegemony** – considered in terms of how a ruling class exercises its leadership (*hegemony*) through cultural values. Although *cultural hegemony* is an effective long-term control strategy, it also involves the idea of:

- **Relative autonomy**: People enjoy a level of freedom (*autonomy*) to make decisions about their behaviour, albeit heavily influenced by structural factors (wealth, power, and so forth). Although the vast majority choose broadly conformist behaviour (partly because they're 'locked in' to capitalist society through, for example, family and work responsibilities), others (mainly young, working-class males) resist 'bourgeois hegemony'. The focus on *youth subcultures* develops from preoccupations with:

**Social change**, especially at the economic and political level of society.

**Cultural resistance** as 'pre-revolutionary consciousness' and behaviour. Youth subcultures demonstrate how social groups in capitalist society can both absorb and counteract bourgeois hegemony and the various ways the lower classes develop cultural styles as 'alternatives to capitalist forms of control and domination' (think, for example, about the 'counter-culture' lives of

travellers, environmentalist groups, peace-camp protesters and the like).

## Youth and resistance

Historically, critical subcultural theorists have interpreted the *resistance* of subcultural groups in terms of two 'solutions' (*real* and *symbolic*) to problems.

**Real solutions**: This approach is characterised by the **Centre for Contemporary Cultural Studies** (CCCS), with research focused on how working-class subcultures develop as a response to – and attempt to resist – economic and political change. For example, we can note how deviant subcultures developed as a reaction to changes in areas like:

**Social space**: This refers to both:

- **Literal space** – the 'loss of community' thesis put forward by writers such as **Cohen** (1972), where urban renewal in working-class communities created a subcultural (frequently violent and ill-directed) reaction among young, working-class males, and

- **Symbolic space** – a 'loss of identity' thesis to explain the emergence and behaviour of skinhead subcultures (**Cohen**, 1972), with their violent response to the loss of a traditional 'British' identity – anger directed towards immigrants ('Paki-bashing') and 'deviant sexualities' ('queer-bashing').

Subcultural behaviour, therefore, represents a collective attempt to both deal with a sense of loss and, in some respects, reclaim spaces through the fear and revulsion of 'normal society'.

Writers such as **Hall et al.** (1978) linked subcultural theory to structural tension and upheaval by suggesting that increases in deviant behaviour (real or imaginary) were linked to periodic 'crises in capitalism' (high levels of unemployment, poverty and social unrest, for example).

Classical studies of white, working-class male education from writers like **Willis** (1977) and **Corrigan** (1979) transfer the focus of 'class struggle' away from the streets and into the classroom. **Young** (2001) notes how, in the case of the former, subcultural development among lower-stream, lower-class 'lads' was an attempt to 'solve the problem of failure' (in the middle-class terms perpetuated through the school) by 'playing up in the classroom, rejecting the teacher's discipline' and giving 'high status to manliness and physical toughness' (ideas that have echoes of **Cohen's** (1955) concept of *status frustration*).

**Symbolic solutions**: Although all forms of subcultural behaviour have symbolic elements (the skinhead 'uniform' of bovver boots and Ben Sherman shirts ape 'respectable', working-class work clothing), the emphasis is shifted further into the cultural realm by focusing on how subcultures represent *symbolic* forms of *resistance* to bourgeois hegemony. **Hall** and **Jefferson** (1976) and **Hebdidge** (1979) characterised youth subcultures as ritualistic or 'magical' attempts at resistance by consciously adopting behaviour that appeared threatening to the 'establishment', thereby giving the powerless a feeling of power. This behaviour is, however, 'symbolic' because it doesn't address or resolve the problems that bring subcultures into existence in the first place.

## ⚙ Weeding the path

Although this type of subcultural theorising avoids reducing complex forms of group interaction to individual *pathologies* (such as predispositions to 'bad' behaviour), this doesn't mean they are without their problems (and the observations we made about functionalist subcultural theories can also be applied here).

**Spectacular subcultures**: In the 1960s and 1970s a number of highly visible, deviant subcultures developed (such as mods, skinheads, punks and hippies) that have not been replicated over the past 20 or so years. If subcultures are symptomatic of 'structural problems', why has their visibility declined? At best we can suggest some form of evolution in subcultural behaviour (using concepts like *subcultural capital*, proposed by writers like **Thornton** (1996), for example); at worst we may have to discard the notion of subculture as a useful concept.

**Symbolism**: One problem with ideas like 'symbolic resistance' is a reliance on *semiological analysis* for their explanatory power. Although semiology can reveal underlying (hidden) patterns in people's behaviour, the danger is that such analyses lack supporting evidence.

When **Hebdidge**, for example, writes about 'the meaning of style', the problem is that it's *his* meaning filtered through *his* perception. As **Young** (2001) points out, **Hebdidge's** assertion that some punks wore Nazi swastikas in an 'ironic way' is unsupported by any evidence (not the least from the people who wore them).

# The potting shed: Rorschach testing

## What do you see in the picture?

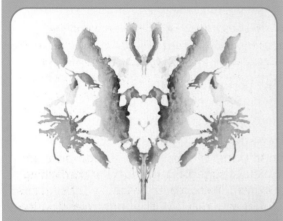

**Semiological analysis**
'There is a danger groups become sub-cultural Rorschach blobs onto which the theorist projects his or her own private definitions' (Young, 2001)

**'The Other'**: **Stahl** (1999) argues that Marxist subcultural theory implicitly sets up 'the subculture' in opposition to some real or imagined 'outside group or agency' (the school, media, and so forth); however, by so doing they neglect 'the role each plays in the sub-culture's own *internal* construction'. That is, they neglect the idea that subcultures may simply be a reflection of how they are seen by such agencies – as social constructions of the media, for example. **Grossberg** (1997) also argues that 'oppositional influences' (such as 'loss of community'), against which subcultures supposedly develop, are little more than convenient *ciphers* that stand for whatever a

theorist claims they stand for in order to substantiate their theories.

**Identities**: The focus on *class* as the key explanatory concept neglects a range of other possible factors (gender and ethnicity in particular – the majority of subcultural studies, both functionalist and Marxist, focus on the behaviour of white, working-class men).

## Digging deeper: Critical criminology

The final theory in this section is one that represents a major development in terms of explanations for deviance.

**Critical** (or, as it's sometimes known, the **New/Radical**) criminology builds on concepts of hegemony and subculture (especially the idea of *resistance*) to develop what **Taylor, Walton** and **Young** (1973, 1975) term a:

**Fully social theory of deviance**:

- **Methodologically** critical criminology was based around a Marxist *realist methodology*. This involved thinking about all possible inputs into the creation of criminal behaviour (*structural* as well as *action based*).

- **Critically, Taylor, Walton** and **Young** identified the main strengths and weaknesses of both conventional and interactionist forms of criminology. Both, they argued, represented entrenched ideological positions that suffered from the problem of:

- **Overidentification**: Conventional (*correctional*) criminology was seen to identify too closely with the aims and objectives of *control agencies* such as the police (how to catch and process

| The Seven Dimensions of a 'Fully Social Theory of Deviance': Taylor, Walton and Young (1973) | |
| --- | --- |
| **Wider Origins of the Deviant Act**<br><br>(A theory of culture) | To understand deviance we must understand how structures of inequality, power and ideology operate in capitalist society, whereby concepts of deviance are shaped at a very general level. For example, 250 years ago to own black slaves in England was a sign of success; in contemporary Britain slave ownership is illegal. |
| **Immediate Origins of the Deviant Act**<br><br>(A sense of subculture) | This involves understanding the specific relationship between the people involved in a particular act. An individual's cultural background is, for example, a significant factor in explaining their conformity or deviance. We must, therefore, understand how people are socialised – someone whose family background is steeped in racist ideology may be more likely to commit race-hate crimes than someone who has no such family background. |
| **The Actual Act** | What people do is as important as what they believe. It's possible, for example, to believe in white racial superiority without ever committing an act of racial violence. We need, therefore, to understand the factors surrounding any decision to deviate, which involves understanding the rational choices an offender makes. |
| **Immediate Origins of a Social Reaction**<br><br>(Subcultural reactions) | How people react to what someone does is crucial, both in terms of physical reaction (revulsion, disgust, congratulation) and how they label the behaviour (deviant or non-deviant) in terms of particular (sub-cultural) standards. The reaction of control agencies such as the media and the police will also be significant. |
| **Wider Origins of the Deviant Reaction**<br><br>(Society's reaction) | This examines how the (labelled) deviant 'reacts to the reaction of others'. Do they accept or reject the deviant label? Do they have the power to deflect any social reaction (something related to the individual's structural location in society, conditioned by factors such as class, gender, age and mental competence)? |
| **Outcome of the Social Reaction to a Deviant's Further Action** | How the deviant 'reacts to the social reaction' is significant on both a psychological (contempt, remorse and so forth) and a social level, such as the ability or otherwise to mobilise forces (like favourable articles in the press or the best lawyers) to defend/rationalise the original behaviour. |
| **The Nature of the Deviant Process as a Whole**<br>We must look at the 'process as a whole' (as outlined above) and the connections between each of the dimensions. | |

criminals more efficiently – the 'official' view of crime as a 'social problem'), while interactionist theories were criticised for their overidentification with the 'victims' of labelling processes.

## Structure and action

Essentially, critical criminology located deviance in a:

**Structural setting** – deviance is not random or arbitrary. On the contrary, critical criminology argued concepts of crime and law were based on the ability of powerful classes to impose their definitions of normality on all other classes. Crime and deviance, therefore, had to ultimately be understood in terms of *power relationships* that derived from ownership/non-ownership of the means of production in capitalist society. As **Scaton** and **Chadwick** (1991) argue, criminologists need to understand both how some acts come to be labelled criminal, and the power relationships that underpin such labelling processes.

Critical criminologists argued, however, that it was not just a matter of looking at class positions and relationships and 'reading off' criminal/conforming behaviour (the working classes are 'more criminal' than the middle classes, for example) for the deceptively simple reason (informed by interactionist sociology) that:

**Decisions** about deviance/conformity were played out at the individual level of *social interaction*. Critical criminology, therefore, wanted to understand not just *why* some forms of behaviour and groups (but not others) were criminalised and *why* some people (but not others) chose crime over conformity; it also added a political dimension by seeing crime as having wider significance for both capitalist society and the relationship between different social classes.

Although critical criminology is *suggestive* of what needs to be done to understand deviance – rather than a theory of deviance that can be operationalised – we can note a couple of studies 'in the critical tradition' that give a flavour of the general approach.

**Hall et al.** (1978) explain the 'moral panic' surrounding 'black muggers' in the early 1970s as a way of *scapegoating* a section of society (young black males) and, by so doing, deflecting attention and criticism away from the political and economic crises of this period.

**Schwendinger** and **Schwendinger** (1975) questioned the role of the state in criminal activity and characterised government in capitalist society as *agents of a ruling class*. A contemporary equivalent might be to question the role of government in promoting genetically modified crops, the curtailment of civil liberties and the like.

In addition, **Chambliss'** (1974) observational study demonstrated a *symbiotic* (mutually beneficial) relationship between law enforcement agencies (police, judiciary and politicians) and the criminals controlling gambling and prostitution in Seattle, USA.

## Weeding the path

*The New Criminology*, as originally formulated by **Taylor**, **Walton** and **Young**, represented less a 'theory of deviance' as such (as we've suggested, it cannot be tested empirically in the conventional sense) and more a way of thinking about how any sociology of deviance should be constructed. Much of *The New Criminology*, for example, focuses on 'reassessing' (to put it politely) previous theories of deviance – only 8 out of

282 pages actually discussed this new formulation.

**Critical reactions**: This technique drew a strong reaction from defenders of these positions. **Cohen** (1977), from an interactionist position, suggested critical criminology was neither 'new' nor, in an important respect, 'critical' (in that, he argued, it romanticised criminals as somehow being at the vanguard of 'opposition to capitalism').

**Hirst** (1975), from an orthodox Marxist position, criticised the whole 'new criminology' project, both in terms of 'romanticising criminals' (the *lumpenproletariat*, or 'social scum', as **Marx** described them) and for its application of a Marxist methodology which, he claimed, could not be applied to 'sociologies of . . .' anything.

**Left idealism**: Later, in the development of *New Left realism*, **Young** was to argue along the same lines in terms of critical criminology being both *idealistic* in its representation of crime and criminals (the latter being considered in almost 'Robin Hood' terms) and a form of 'left functionalism', where the interests of a 'ruling class' replaced the 'interests of society as a whole'.

## Moving on

Despite the heavy criticism of critical criminology, one point in its favour, perhaps, was the idea that some form of theoretical:

**Synthesis** – between looking at the *structural* aspects of crime (who makes rules) and the *action* aspects that have traditionally focused on ideas about labelling and social reaction – was required in order to fully understand deviant behaviour.

Having looked in the main at structural theories, the next section focuses on exploring *social constructionist* explanations.

# 2. The social construction of and social reactions to crime and deviance, including the role of the mass media

In the previous section we examined a number of structuralist explanations for crime and deviance, so, to redress the balance somewhat, this section focuses on both interactionist and postmodern forms of explanation.

### Preparing the ground: Interactionist perspectives

At the start of this chapter we made a distinction between *absolute* and *relative* concepts of deviance and, in so doing, left open the question of whether some people may be inherently deviant (predisposed, for whatever reason, to deviance). Interactionist sociology answers this question by arguing that deviance is:

**Socially constructed**, a concept that has two main dimensions:

- **Deviance**: Every society makes rules governing deviant behaviour and applies them in different ways.

- **Deviants**: If the same behaviour can be deviant in one context (or society) but non-deviant in another, it suggests, as **Becker** (1963) puts it, '. . . deviance is not a quality of the act the person commits, but rather a consequence of the application by others of rules and sanctions to an "offender"'.

From this position, therefore, deviance is 'behaviour that people so label', and although this *relative concept of deviance* is not unique (**Durkheim** (1895), for example, noted: 'What confers (criminal) character . . . is not some intrinsic quality of a given act but the definition which the collective conscience lends it'), a further dimension does confer this quality.

**Social reaction**: The quality of deviance is not found, to paraphrase **Becker**, in some kinds of behaviour and not others, just as it doesn't reside in different *types* of people (those supposedly 'predisposed to crime'). Rather, the *essence of deviance* is in the *interaction process*; only when people interact – to make and break rules, to name and shame (maybe) offenders – does deviance arise as a quality of how people *react* to what someone does.

If people don't react to criminal behaviour – no one is pursued, processed or punished – the offender is, to all intents and purposes, law-abiding. 'Criminals', therefore, are different to 'non-criminals' only when they are *publicly labelled* as such by a control agency, an idea that leads into:

**Labelling theory**: 'Labels' are names we give to phenomena ('football', for example) that identify what we're seeing. Labels, however, aren't *just* names – they have further, important, qualities:

- **Meanings** – what we understand something to be.
- **Interpretations** – how we are encouraged (through socialisation processes) to understand meanings based on:
- **Characteristics** attached to the label.

Think of a label attached to a closed box. Inside the box are different (personal and social) characteristics associated with the label. If we understand the meaning of the label, we also understand the characteristics associated with the label.

## ⚠🏠 The potting shed

What characteristics are associated with the label 'student':

- In our culture?
- By you personally?

For labelling theorists, the application of labels to human behaviour is significant because they impact on:

**Identity** (how we see ourselves and our relationship to others). Labels, here, have two main dimensions:

- **Social identities** relate to the general characteristics assigned to a label by a particular culture. Think about the different characteristics our society assigns to the label 'man' or 'woman' (how each is supposed to behave, for example).

- **Personal identities** relate to the different ways individuals (with their different cultural histories) *interpret* a label. For example, when I think about myself as 'a man' this label carries certain cultural characteristics, some of which I may include as part of my personal identity, others of which I may (perhaps) reject, something **Thomas** (1923) relates to '... the ability to make decisions from *within* instead of having them imposed from *without*'.

## Master labels

These ideas are significant for labelling theories of deviance because they suggest two things:

**Cultural expectations**: When a deviant label is successfully applied to someone, their subsequent behaviour may be interpreted in the light of this label – depending, of course, on the nature of the deviance. If you are given the label 'murderer' or 'paedophile', this is likely to have more serious consequences than if you attract the label 'speeding motorist', an idea related to:

**Master labels**. **Becker** (1963) suggests these are such powerful labels that

everything about a person is interpreted in the light of the label.

**Individual behaviours**: The outcome of a labelling process is not certain. Just because someone tries to label you in some way doesn't necessarily mean they will be successful. You may, for example:

- **Reject** the label by demonstrating you do not deserve it.

- **Negate** the label by, for example, questioning their right (or ability) to impose it.

Interactionism questions the assumption that ideas such as 'crime' and 'deviance' are clear and unambiguous (many of us 'break the rules' but suffer no consequences for our offending because no one reacts to our behaviour). Instead, it stresses that any explanation of deviance must consider:

- **power** and **social control** in terms of the ability to make rules and apply them to people's behaviour, and

- **ideology** in terms of decisions about what forms of behaviour (and why) are considered deviant, criminal, both or neither.

## Social contexts

*Labelling theory*, therefore, switches the focus away from searching for the 'causes of crime' in people's social/psychological background, to understanding how 'deviant situations' are created. This involves understanding how behaviour is put into *social contexts* – both deviant/non-deviant – through a:

**Definition of a situation**: In terms of crime, **Thomas** (1923) argues that societies provide 'ready-made' *definitions of situations* that allow people to both 'understand what's going on' and, more significantly, know how to respond to this behaviour.

Interpretations within situations can, of course, be subtle – making behavioural distinctions between, for example, a private motorist running through a red traffic light and a fire engine doing the same. Both are 'deviant' (illegal), but the reaction to the latter is mitigated and transformed by knowledge of a 'higher moral purpose' (the law is being broken in order to save lives).

## ✳ SYNOPTIC LINK

We can apply the idea that others 'define situations' for us to a range of Specification areas, such as education (where the meaning of education is defined by governments, teachers, and so forth) and family life (where the meaning of different types of family is socially defined).

An example of an interactionist explanation for deviance is represented by the concept of a:

**Deviancy Amplification Spiral**: As originally formulated by **Wilkins** (1964), deviancy amplification (or a 'positive feedback loop') built on ideas developed by **Lemert** (1951) based on the distinction between two types of deviation:

- **Primary deviation** is deviant behaviour in its 'pure form'; it represents some form of rule breaking (real or imagined). **Lemert**, however, argued that unless and until attention is drawn – and *sanctions* applied – to primary deviation, it has little or no impact on the 'psychological structure of the individual' (they may not, for example, see themselves as deviant).

- **Secondary deviation** refers to how someone responds to being labelled as

'deviant'. For **Lemert**, this involves the offender interpreting their behaviour in the light of the labelling process, where repeated deviance becomes 'a means of defence, attack or adaptation' to the problems created by being so labelled.

## ⚠ 🏠 The potting shed

Identify and briefly explain one example of your own primary deviation in the family, school or workplace.

We can outline the amplification process diagrammatically (including some indication of the role of the mass media in this general process).

The basic idea here is that deviancy amplification represents a:

**Positive feedback loop** involving a number of ideas.

**Primary deviance** is identified and condemned, which leads to the deviant group becoming:

**Socially isolated** and resentful of the attention they're receiving. This behaviour leads, through a general labelling process, to an:

**Increased social reaction** on the part of the media, politicians and formal control agencies (less toleration of deviant behaviour, for example).

This develops into:

**Secondary deviation** if the deviant group recreates itself in the image portrayed by these agencies. Once this happens the:

**Reaction** from 'the authorities' is likely to increase, leading to new laws (criminalisation of deviants) or increased police resources to deal with 'the problem'.

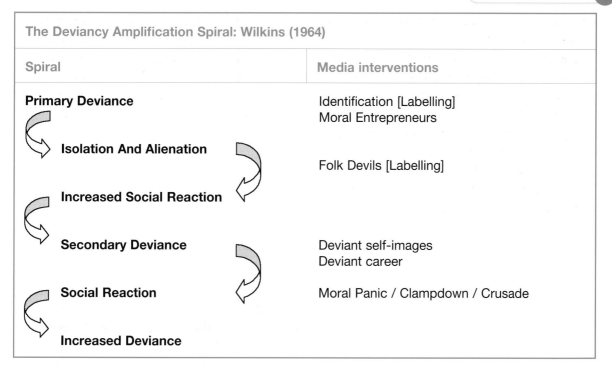

**The Deviancy Amplification Spiral: Wilkins (1964)**

| Spiral | Media interventions |
| --- | --- |
| **Primary Deviance** | Identification [Labelling]<br>Moral Entrepreneurs |
| **Isolation And Alienation** | Folk Devils [Labelling] |
| **Increased Social Reaction** | |
| **Secondary Deviance** | Deviant self-images<br>Deviant career |
| **Social Reaction** | Moral Panic / Clampdown / Crusade |
| **Increased Deviance** | |

In other words, after the initial identification and condemnation of deviant behaviour, each group – deviant and control – feeds off the actions of the other to create a 'spiral of deviance'.

## Role of the media

In complex modern societies where people rely, to some extent, on the media for information about their world, its role in any amplification spiral can be crucial. We can identify the various points the media may intervene in the process in the following way.

**Identification** involves bringing primary deviance to the attention of a wider audience through:

**Moral entrepreneurs** – people who take it upon themselves to patrol society's 'moral standards'. They may be individuals (politicians, for example) or organisations (such as newspapers). Entrepreneurs add a *moral* dimension to primary deviance by

reacting to and condemning behaviour, something that's part of a wider labelling process.

**Folk devils**: If entrepreneurial activity is successful (and there's no guarantee it will be), the media may create what **Cohen** (1972) calls *folk devils* – people who, in **Fowler's** (1991) words, are 'outside the pale of consensus' and can be:

- **represented** – as threats to 'decent society', for example
- **labelled** – as 'subversive', 'perverted' and the like
- **scapegoated** (blamed for social problems).

The media have the opportunity and the power to represent groups in this way and may also have a significant role to play in:

**Deviant self-image**. This refers to how the deviant group, as part of secondary deviation, comes to define itself in reasonably coherent terms (they may, for example, accept the 'deviant label' as a form of *resistance*). A possible role for the media here is in areas like:

- **Publicising** deviant behaviour to a wider audience (some of whom may, ironically, decide they want to participate in the 'deviant subculture').

- **Labelling** deviant groups ('chavs', 'goths', 'predatory paedophiles') and suggesting they represent a coherent social grouping (rather than, perhaps, a disparate group of individuals).

**Moral panic**: **Cohen** (1972) suggests that this is a situation where a group is 'defined as a threat to societal values' and is presented in a 'stereotypical fashion by the mass media' as a prelude to the demand for 'something to be done' about their behaviour. Moral panics have attendant attributes of a:

**Moral crusade**, where 'the media' take up arms against a particular type of offender – paedophiles being an obvious example – and demand a:

**Moral clampdown** on the deviant and their behaviour.

These ideas and processes, **Miller** and **Reilly** (1994) argue, reflect *ideological social control* as a prelude to political action. In other words, a moral panic represents a way of 'softening up' public opinion so that people are prepared to accept repressive social controls (new laws, for example) as 'solutions to a particular problem'.

## 🏠 The potting shed

**Identify further examples of the way public opinion has been 'ideologically softened up' through the media in recent times.**

Finally, an idea that arises from the above discussion, and has implications for *social policies* designed to limit and control deviance, is a:

**Deviant career**: **Becker** (1963) argued that the successful application of a label

## 🌷 Growing it yourself: Subcultures or media creations?

# Media student 'expert on chavs'

Alison Smith, news.bbc.co.uk 14/06/05

'Verity Jennings considered two theories – that chav is a subculture which differentiates itself from the rest of society and that it is a term describing undesirable features picked upon by the media ... [She] looked at 890 newspaper stories featuring the word "chav" ... the label "chav" was in part a product of media concerns about anti-social behaviour.'

If 'chavs' are not a **subculture** (something you could check against your knowledge of functionalist and Marxist subcultural theory), identify and explain some of the ways the media might 'socially produce chavs'.

frequently has the effect of 'confirming the individual' as deviant, both to themselves and others around them (teachers, employers and the like). This may block off participation in 'normal society' (a criminal, for example, may be unable to find work), which, in turn, means the deviant seeks out the company of similar deviants, resulting in increased involvement in deviant behaviour. The public *stigmatisation* ('naming and shaming') of paedophiles in the UK media, for example, may illustrate this process; paedophiles are shunned by 'normal society' and so start to move in organised groups whose development, arguably, increases the likelihood of deviance.

## Weeding the path

Although *deviancy amplification* demonstrates how the behaviour of control agencies may have 'unintended consequences' in terms of creating a class of deviant behaviour (such as crime) out of a situation that was only a minor social problem, it's not without its problems or critics.

- **Prediction**: Although the concept uses a range of constructionist ideas (labelling, for example), it was originally presented by **Wilkins** (1964) as a model for *predicting* the development of social behaviour. However, the general *unpredictability* of the amplification process – sometimes a spiral develops, but at other times it doesn't – means its strength is in *descriptive* analyses of behaviour 'after the event'. **Young's** (1971) classic analysis of drug takers is a case in point, as is **Critcher's** (2000) explanation for the development of moral panics surrounding 'rave culture' and its use of Ecstasy.

- **Moral panics**: McRobbie (1994) argues that this concept has become such *common currency* in our society that its meaning and use have changed in ways that reflect a certain 'knowingness' on the part of the media and, in some respects, well-organised political targets (such as environmentalist groups). In this respect, **McRobbie** suggests we should neither automatically assume 'the media', in every instance, is part of the overall control structure in society (slavishly following whatever moral line the political authorities would like people to believe), nor should we ignore the ability of some groups to use the media to defuse moral crusades.

**McRobbie** and **Thornton** (1995) also contend that the media has become so sophisticated in its understanding of how amplification and moral panics work that 'moral panics, once the unintended outcome of journalistic practice, seem to have become a goal'. **Miller** and **Reilly** (1994) also point out the problem of understanding how and why moral panics ever end.

**Power**: Although interactionist sociology clearly sees power as a significant variable in the creation (and possible negation) of labels, there's no clear idea about where such power may originate. In addition, the power of:

**The state** to commit various forms of crime (against humanity, for example) doesn't fit easily into constructionist concepts of deviance.

## ⚠ Digging deeper: Postmodern criminology

So far we've looked at 'classic constructionist' ways of seeing crime and deviance and we can bring these ideas up to date by focusing on some postmodern-influenced ideas about the nature of crime and control in contemporary societies. Given that postmodernism gives media analysis a central role, we can begin by exploring the concept of:

**Discourse**: The role of the media here is twofold. First, media are important because they propagate and, in some senses, control, organise, criticise, promote and demote (marginalise) a variety of competing *narratives*. Second, none of these is especially important *in itself* (teachers and students, for example, probably do most of these things); they become important, however, in the context of *power* and the ability to represent the interests of powerful voices in society.

In a situation where knowledge, as **Sarup** (1989) argues, is 'fragmented, partial and contingent' ('relative' or dependent on your particular viewpoint), and **Milovanovic** (1997) contends 'there are many truths and no over-encompassing Truth is possible', the role of the media assumes crucial significance in relation to perceptions of crime and deviance in contemporary societies. In this respect, media organisation takes two forms:

- **Media discourses** (generalised characterisations such as crime as 'a social problem') and
- **Media narratives** – particular 'supporting stories' that contribute to the overall construction of a 'deviance discourse' – instances, for example, where deviance is portrayed in terms of how it represents a 'social problem'.

## Perceptions

The main point here is not whether media discourses are 'true or false', nor whether they 'accurately or inaccurately' reflect the 'reality of crime'; rather, it's how media discourses affect our *perception* of these things. The difference is subtle but significant since it changes the way we understand and explain concepts like 'crime' and 'deviance'. Examples of media deviance discourses take a number of forms:

- **Domination discourses** involve the media mapping out its role as part of the overall 'locus of social control' in society. In other words, the 'media machine' is closely and tightly integrated into society's overall mechanisms of formal and informal social control.

  In this respect, the media is both a witting and unwitting mouthpiece for control expression, in both calling for new, *tougher* punishments and criticising 'soft on crime, soft on the causes of crime' approaches. This particular discourse weaves a variety of narratives that draw on both traditional forms of punishment (prisons, for example) and newer forms of technological surveillance (CCTV, biometric identity cards and the like) to create a discourse that locates 'criminals' and 'non-criminals' in different physical and moral universes.

- **Democratic discourses** involve the media acting as a *watchdog* on the activities of the powerful – the ability to expose political and economic corruption, for example, or, as in the case of the Iraq war in 2003, to act as a focal point for oppositional ideas.

- **Danger discourses**: However we view the

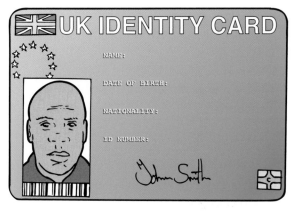

Biometric identity cards can store personal details (medical and criminal history, for example) and can be set up for fingerprint, facial and iris recognition

role of the media, a range of narratives are woven into the general fabric of media presentation and representation of crime. In particular, two main themes are evident within this type of discourse:

- **Fear**: Crime and deviance are represented in terms of *threat* – 'the criminal', for example, as a cultural icon of fear (both in personal terms and more general social terms). Part of this narrative involves:

- **Warnings** about behaviour, the extent of crime, its consequences and

- **Risk** assessments, in terms of the likelihood of becoming a victim of crime, for example.

- **Fascination**: Crime and deviance represent 'media staples' used to sell newspapers, encourage us to watch TV programmes (factual and fictional), and so forth.

## Postmodern spectacle

These two narratives (*fear* and *fascination*) come together when postmodernists such as

**Kidd-Hewitt** and **Osborne** (1995) discuss deviance in terms of:

**Spectacle** – crime is interesting (and sells media products) because of the powerful combination of fear and fascination. An example of 'postmodern spectacle' is the attack on the World Trade Center in 2001, not only because of the 'fear aspect', but also because of the way the attack seemed to key into – and mimic – a Hollywood disaster film. The attack demonstrated an acute understanding of both fear and fascination – by 'making real' that which had hitherto been merely 'make-believe' – that both *repelled* (in terms of the terrible loss of life) and *fascinated* (drawing the viewer into an appalling disaster-movie world of death and destruction).

Although this is an extreme example, the basic argument here is that 'spectacles' are an integral part of the 'crime and deviance' narrative in postmodern society, not just in terms of the 'reality of crime', but also crime as 'entertainment', whether this be the 'reality crime' version (reconstructions and real-life crime videos, for example) or the 'fantasy crime' version (television cop shows

Crime as postmodern spectacle?
The destruction of the Twin Towers in New York, 11 September 2001

377

and the like). For postmodernism, this is expressed in terms of:

**Intertextuality**: Both 'reality' and 'fiction' are interwoven to construct an almost seamless web of 'fear and fascination', where the viewer is no longer sure whether what they are seeing is real or reconstruction. **Kooistra** and **Mahoney** (1999) argue that tabloid journalism is now the dominant force in the representation of crime and deviance. Presentation techniques once the preserve of tabloid newspapers, for example, have been co-opted into the general mainstream of news production and presentation (where 'entertainment and sensationalism' are essential components for any news organisation trying to break into particular economic markets or preserve and enhance market share in those markets).

---

## ✳ SYNOPTIC LINK

**Mass media:** Think about how this analysis cuts into the debates we encountered in the study of media effects and representations.

---

We can outline an example of a postmodern criminology in the shape of:

**Constitutive criminology**: The basic idea here is to adopt what **Henry** and **Milovanovic** (1999) call a **holistic** approach, involving a 'duality of blame' that moves the debate away from thinking about the 'causes of crime' and the 'obsession with a crime and punishment cycle', towards a 'different criminology' theorised around what **Muncie** (2000) terms:

• **Social harm**: To understand crime we have to 'move beyond' notions centred around 'legalistic definitions'. We have to include a range of ideas (poverty,

pollution, corporate corruption and the like) in any definition of harm and, more importantly, crime (which, as **Henry** and **Milovanovic** put it, involves 'the exercise of the power to deny others their own humanity').

## Redefining crime

In this respect, a *constitutive criminology* 'redefines crime as the harm resulting from investing energy in relations of power that involves pain, conflict and injury'. In other words, some people (criminals) invest a great deal of their time and effort in activities (crime) that harm others physically, psychologically, economically, and so forth. In this respect, **Henry** and **Milovanovic** characterise such people as:

**Excessive investors** in the power to harm others – and the way to diminish their excessive investment in such activities is to empower their victims. Thus, rather than seeing punishment in traditional terms (imprisonment, for example, that does little or nothing for the victim), we should see it in terms of:

**Redistributive justice**, something that **De Haan** (1990) suggests involves redefining 'punishment', away from hurting the offender (which perpetuates the 'cycle of harm'), to *redressing* the offence by 'compensating the victim'. This form of *peacemaking criminology* focuses on reconnecting offenders and their victims in ways that actively seek to redress the balance of harm.

## Weeding the path

Constitutive criminology moves the focus on to an assessment of 'harm' caused to the victims of crime and, by extension, the

# Discussion point: Is making up hard to do?

One aspect of redistributive justice is that the perpetrator of a crime 'makes good' the harm they have caused to their victim. This might involve, for example, offender and victim meeting, under supervision, to discuss the effect the crime has had on the victim. In addition, the offender will be required to recompense their victim in some agreed way – by doing something for the victim, for instance, rather than in monetary terms.

Thinking about this idea, identify and discuss some ways redistributive justice might operate in places like the workplace, the home and the school (for example, a disruptive student having to spend their lunchtime helping children lower down the school to read).

What advantages and disadvantages of this type of justice come out of this discussion?

social relationship between offender and victim. It draws on a range of sociological ideas, both *theoretical* (holistic approaches to understanding deviance, for example) and *practical* (such as the concept of 'redress'), to argue for a *less punitive* approach to deviance and a more consensual approach to understanding the complex relationship between crime, deviance, social control and punishment. There are, however, a couple of points we need to consider here.

- **Harm**: As **Henry** and **Milovanovic** (1999) define it, 'harm' results 'from any attempt to reduce or suppress another's position or potential standing through the use of power'. The danger here, however, is that it *broadens* the definition of crime and deviance in ways that redefine these concepts out of existence (which may, of course, be the intention). Such a definition could, for example, apply equally to a teacher in the classroom or an employer in the workplace.

- **Crime**: Extending the notion of crime to include, for example, 'linguistic hate crimes' (such as racism and sexism) may

not cause too much of a problem; however it does raise questions of where such a definition should begin and end (it may, for example, have the unintended consequence of criminalising large areas of social behaviour that are currently not criminalised).

- **Redress**: Without a radical rethink/overhaul of the way we see and deal with crime and deviance as a society, 'redistributive justice' may simply be incorporated into conventional forms of crime control. In this respect we might characterise this type of criminology as:

  **Idealistic**, in the sense that, rather than providing an alternative to conventional forms of 'crime and punishment', ideas about redistributive justice simply provide another link in the chain of social control.

## Moving on

With these ideas in mind, the next section examines and develops the concept of power, in terms of its relationship to both social control and deviance.

# 3. The relationship between deviance, power and social control

In the two previous sections we have necessarily touched on some aspects of the relationship between deviance, power and social control (in terms, for example, of thinking about who makes rules and how they are enforced). In this section we're going to develop these ideas by looking more explicitly at concepts of power and control, beginning with an outline of how these two concepts are related.

## ⚠ Preparing the ground: Power and control

**Power** is an important concept in the sociology of deviance given that most sociological explanations for crime and deviance (from functional consensus, through critical criminology, to social constructionism) draw on the concept at some point as a way of explaining rule creation, rule enforcement and, occasionally, rule-breaking.

## ❋ SYNOPTIC LINK

**Power and politics:** The concept of power has been extensively discussed in this chapter, so rather than simply repeating this information, it would be helpful to review this material if you haven't already studied it.

**Social control:** Sociologically, deviance is both a product of social interaction and something that cannot exist without the power to proscribe and control social behaviour; concepts of *power*, *control* and *deviance* are, in this respect, *symbiotic*. In other words, for deviance to be identified, someone has to establish where the normative behavioural line should be drawn (power) and then take action to defend that line (control).

**Pfohl** (1998) expresses this idea neatly: 'Imagine *deviance* as noise – a cacophony of subversions disrupting the harmony of a given social order. *Social control* is the opposite. It labours to silence the resistive sounds of deviance ... to transform the noisy challenge of difference into the music of *conformity*.'

On this note (pun intended), we can identify two basic types of control:

- **Formal controls** relate to legal/organisational codes of behaviour, operate at the overt, usually written, level and involve a formal *enforcement mechanism* – a police or security force, for example. Formal control systems involve formal prosecution procedures. In the case of crime these may entail arrest, charge and trial, whereas in an organisation such as a school or business some sort of disciplinary procedure will be in place.

- **Informal controls** operate between people in their everyday, informal, settings (the family or school, for example) and don't involve written rules and procedures. Consequently, these controls work through *informal enforcement mechanisms*, the object of such controls being the type of informal normative behaviour we might find going on between family members, friends or indeed strangers (such as the normative behaviour that occurs when you buy something from a shop).

Both types of control have a couple of things in common: They can, for example, operate:

- **Directly**: Here, the objective is to regulate a rule (normative standard). If you break the rule, you lay yourself open to punishment (or *sanction*). If you break the law, you might be fined or imprisoned; if you're cheeky to a teacher you might be given detention.

- **Indirectly**: As socialised individuals we don't need to be told constantly where boundaries lie because we learn (from personal experience or from others) the nature of norms and what might happen if we break them.

## ⚠ The potting shed

**Identify two examples of social control that operate within peer groups.**

For example, if you continually skip your sociology class you may be asked to leave the course and, since you don't want this to happen, you (indirectly) control your behaviour to obey the norm. **Blalock** (1967) suggests two further forms of control:

- **Coercive** involves the attempt to make people obey through the exercise of some form of *punishment* (imprisonment, for example).

- **Placative** involves control through some form of *reward* (giving a child a sweet, for example, to stop it crying).

Finally, both formal and informal social control involve the concept of:

**Sanctions**: These, as we've suggested, may be *positive* (rewarding people for conformity) or *negative* (punishments for deviance).

- **Time**: Different parts of the day are divided into different time periods during which we are expected to do different

---

**WARM-UP: FEELING THE FORCE**

Using the following table as a guide, identify as many examples as possible of different types of social control across a range of sociological areas:

| | Formal | Informal | Coercive | Placative |
|---|---|---|---|---|
| Family life<br>Education<br>Welfare<br>Work<br>Health<br>Politics<br>Mass media<br>Religion | | | | |

Although it's tempting to think about dimensions of control solely in terms of *sanctions*, there are other, less obvious ways it is exercised.

things (travel, work, eat, play, sleep). **Shaw et al.** (1996) noted how the 'free time' of young people (especially young women) was 'controlled or structured by the dominant adult culture'.

- **Mind**: While 'mind control' is probably too strong a term to use (although experiments have been conducted in clinical psychiatry into 'behaviour modification' through both chemical means and brain surgery), one way control reaches into the realm of thought is through:

  - **Language**: The use of language (in everyday talk, for example) is significant in terms of how we classify people. Think, for example, about the way different accents are taken to indicate different levels of sophistication, intelligence and class. Language, therefore, involves the power to both shape how we think about something and influence how we react to it. Language, for example, is linked to sexuality and social control through concepts like 'stud' and 'slag' (something that reflects the power of language to glorify or stigmatise).

## ✳ SYNOPTIC LINK

**Mass media:** In terms of deviance we could note how the 'language of crime' may influence how we see this behaviour. The media frequently use the language of violence to describe crime when they talk about 'crime fighting' or 'the war on crime'.

## Types of space

The *patrol* and *control* of different types of space is an interesting aspect of power and social control:

- **Private space**, for example, represents areas of individual control, such as the private spaces in your home.

- **Public space**, meanwhile, signifies areas where access and activities are socially controlled. In other words, when someone enters these spaces they become liable to a range of control mechanisms (CCTV observation being a simple example). The power to control public space is significant because it involves the ability to define the deviant use of space. An employer owns and controls the space occupied by their workforce and is consequently able to specify behaviour in such space. **White (1993)**, among others, has noted how conflict between the police and youth is frequently based on differing interpretations of the purpose and use of public space (such as shopping precincts and malls).

- **Controlled space** involves the idea that institutions (prisons, mental asylums and hospitals, for example) regulate space in ways that relate to the control of things like body and language. In terms of the latter, for example, a relatively modern development is the concept of **medicalisation**, a situation in which deviant behaviour is defined and treated as a physical or mental illness.

## ✳ SYNOPTIC LINK

**Wealth, poverty and welfare:** The idea of physically controlled spaces links to the concept of 'gated communities'.

# ⚘ Growing it yourself: Changing rooms

Technological developments change the way we see and use public spaces. For each of the following (and any others that come to mind) briefly explain how they have the potential to change the way public space is used and controlled.

| Technology | Use | Control |
| --- | --- | --- |
| **The internet (cyberspace)** | Access to information | Dangerous spaces? |
| **Mobile phone** | Public space redefined as private space? | |
| **Wireless laptop computers** | Changes to the way work is organised | The distinction between work and leisure is increasingly blurred |
| **Further examples?** | | |

**Body**: The relationship between bodies and social control works in a number of ways:

- **Personal control** relates, in part, to what we do with our bodies in terms of individual adornment, display, and so forth (although these choices will be conditioned by social norms governing such things as nudity).

- **Public control** relates to ideas about gender and sexuality (the social meaning of being male or female, for example, and decisions about different types of sexuality) that are, in no small measure, governed by social norms and controls. Our society, for example, generally views monogamous, heterosexual attraction as the norm. Public control also extends into areas such as:

- **Body image** – what size and shape the body should be, for example – and

- **Attitudes** to areas like physical disability and less tangible notions of patriarchal ideas and practices.

**Morcillo** (2005) suggests public controls extend into areas such as attitudes to youth and ageing, reproduction and *cyberbodies* (the idea that computer technology allows us to create private and public images in the relative anonymity of cyberspace).

A further dimension here is the question of physical public control over both body and space involved in ideas like *incarceration* (prisons, mental institutions and, in some respects, schools) and the various forms of punishment that can be (legally and, in some instances, illegally) directed against the body.

## Digging deeper: Power and control

We can apply some of the ideas we've just explored to an understanding of crime control in contemporary societies in a range of ways. According to **Cohen** (1979), contemporary systems of deviancy control in our society developed at the end of the eighteenth century around three basic ideas:

* **The state** as a centralised, coordinating structure (considered in terms of definitions of crime, law creation and the construction of law-enforcement agencies).

* **Differentiation** between *criminal deviance* (involving punishment) and *dependent deviance* (such as mental illness) that involved care.

* **Institutionalisation** – the separation of deviants from non-deviants in prisons, asylums and hospitals.

In conventional terms, therefore, societal control has been underpinned by two ideas that we can loosely term '*traditional penology*' (to differentiate it from contemporary penology):

* **Reactive control**: Social controls are applied 'after the event' – following a crime, the offender is identified and processed through the judicial system on the basis of 'what they've done'.

* **Difference**: This involves the idea that 'deviants are different to non-deviants', something expressed in terms of:

**Identification** – the objective ways

deviants differ from non-deviants in terms of, for example, their:

* **Biology**: **Lombrosso** and **Ferrero** (1895) attempted to identify the physical signs of criminality – 'a comparison of the criminal skull with the skulls of normal women reveals the fact that female criminals approximate more to males'.

* **Psychology**: Traditional forms of analysis focused on the idea of crime as *pathological* (mental disturbance) or, as **Lagassé** (2005) notes, the result of 'emotional disorders, often stemming from childhood experience and personality disorders'.

* **Sociology**: **Box** (1983) notes how social factors (such as poverty) have traditionally been *correlated* with official crime statistics to produce a composite picture of 'the criminal offender'.

* **Quantification** – the idea that once the specific origins of deviance are established we can quantify *causality* (whether in terms of chemical imbalances in the brain, family upbringing, social conditions or whatever) that serves as the basis for:

**Treatment**, considered in terms of punishment and/or care.

## Traditional penology

As an example of traditional penology we can note how different control roles are played out at the institutional level of society.

**The state**, for example, has played a traditionally reactive role in terms of both the way laws are created (largely 'after the event') and applied.

The police role was also traditionally interpreted as a reactive one ('catching offenders'). This involved different styles of policing, traditionally interpreted in three (idealised) forms:

- **Consensus** policing involves formal control agents being integrated into the community they police. Their role, in effect, is one of policing with the cooperation and consent of the community.

- **Patrol** policing involves the use of technology (fast cars, mobile communications and the like) to patrol areas in a *semi-consensual* way. There is little day-to-day interaction between the police and the community, but relations between the two are not necessarily antagonistic.

- **Military** (or occupation) policing involves the police playing an occupying and pacifying role, one that involves imposing order on a population, usually through a physical show of strength. In this type of policing the 'consent' of the community is neither sought nor freely given.

## The courts

Punishment is:

- **based** on what someone has done rather than who they are
- **objective** – following agreed procedures and practices
- **delivered** according to certain rules and tariffs (the penalty for murder in the UK is greater than the penalty for theft)
- **impartial** – regardless of social characteristics (such as class or gender).

If the above represents a basic outline of 'traditional penology', what **Feely** and **Simon** (1992) call the:

# Discussion point: The three faces of policing

- In three groups, each focusing on one type of policing, identify (using examples) the advantages and disadvantages of your chosen type of policing and present your ideas to the class.

As a class, consider which of the three types of policing is most likely to be effective in the control of crime.

|  | Consensus | Patrol | Military |
|---|---|---|---|
| **Advantages** | Police get reliable information from the public about crime | Quick and efficient response to crime | Order can be re-established in a situation of civil unrest |
| **Disadvantages** | Slow to react to crime | Police may seem remote from the people they police | No cooperation from those being policed |

**New penology** involves subtle changes of emphasis in the roles played by control agencies in contemporary societies. We can outline these in terms of three related categories:

- **Extent of control: Cohen** (1979) suggests three ways to think about how social controls have gradually been extended in modern societies:

  - **Blurring the boundaries**: The development of 'segregated institutions of incarceration' (prisons and asylums, for example) had one virtue, according to **Cohen** – they clearly defined the boundary between the deviant and non-deviant. Modern forms of penology blur these boundaries, through various programmes and treatments, to create a '*continuum of control*', involving a range of preventative, diagnostic and screening initiatives, from 'pre-delinquents' (those who haven't 'as yet' committed an offence) at one extreme, to high-risk populations (persistent offenders) at the other.

  - **Thinning the mesh** involves the idea of 'interventions to combat crime' by catching deviance *before* it develops and treating offenders *before* they develop deviant careers. We can think in terms of crime control being a net – the larger the holes, the more fish (deviants) escape; by making the holes smaller (thinning the mesh), more people are brought into the overall crime control programme. One effect of this is to:

  - **Widen the net** by increasing the total number of people processed through various programmes (including prison). New forms of offence and the increased application of current laws also draw more and more people into the social control net.

## Surveillance

- **Nature of control: Foucault** (1983) argued that the *panoptic prison* (an architectural design that allowed warders to constantly monitor prisoners without the latter knowing exactly when they were being watched) represented 'the essence of power' because it was based on differential access to knowledge. Surveillance was also, he argued (1980), both 'global and individual' (warders could view both the whole prison and individual prisoners). **Shearing** and **Stenning** (1985) develop this idea in the context of the kind of processes described by **Cohen** when they describe postmodern forms of surveillance in terms of:

  - **Disneyfication**: Disney World, they argue, is a clever system of social control (what you can do, where you

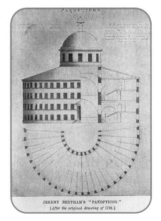

The panopticon prison: A central column gave warders visual access to all parts of the prison building
Source: Barton and Barton (1993)

can do it), designed to keep people moving through the theme park without an awareness of being controlled. Control, in this respect, is disguised as being 'for the safety of the consumer'. In other words, controls in postmodern society, like those in Disney World, are:

- **pervasive** – covering all areas of life

- **invisible** – there is little awareness of being controlled

- **embedded** – in 'other, less alarming, structures' (such as safety issues)

- **seamless** – they have no beginning or end.

**Shearing** and **Stenning** argue that this creates a situation where control is *apparently consensual* because people willingly participate in their own control (as with, for example, the use of CCTV cameras in shops and arcades). This type of surveillance is, they argue, indicative of:

- **Changes in control** expressed, on one level, by *proactive* procedures designed to prevent crime by taking action *before* an offence is committed, which leads **Feely** and **Simon** (1992) to suggest another level, the idea of:

- **'At risk' populations** – people who, on the basis of known probabilities, are the most likely to commit offences 'at some time in the future'.

## 🏠 The potting shed

Identify and briefly explain two possible social characteristics that might allow control agencies to identify 'pre-delinquents'.

## Economic approach

This position, **Feely** and **Simon** argue, represents a 'new discourse' surrounding how we view crime, one that replaces 'traditional' moral or medical descriptions of the individual with an:

**Actuarial approach** 'of probabilistic calculations and statistical distributions applied to populations' (actuaries calculate things like 'early death' probabilities for life insurance companies – they mathematically calculate levels of *risk*). This 'economic approach' to crime and social control involves:

- **Identifying** and **managing** 'unruly groups' with high probabilities of criminal involvement.

- **'Low-cost'** forms of control (such as electronic tagging).

- **Managing** criminal activity through risk assessments (identifying possible situations and areas that require additional surveillance or police resources).

- **Resource targeting**: Some groups, such as young, working-class men, are statistically more likely to offend than others, and by concentrating police resources in the areas where these groups live, offending can be reduced.

- **Sentencing according to risk**: Incarceration in prisons doesn't reform offenders, but when people are in prison they can't commit further crimes. Rather than sentencing offenders for what they've done, therefore, sentencing should reflect the 'risk of reoffending'; habitual offenders, a high-risk category, should be given longer sentences than low-risk offenders.

## ✳ SYNOPTIC LINK

**Wealth, poverty and welfare:** Note how this approach keys into concepts of an underclass that needs to be controlled and punished.

We can complete this section by looking at a couple of different theories of crime and deviance that illustrate the relationship between power and social control. The first type (**administrative criminology** and **New Right realism**) is related to *ecological theories*, while the second (**New Left realism**) has a connection to the strain and subcultural theories we outlined earlier.

**Administrative criminology** is an umbrella term for a range of theories that draw on *ecological* ideas about people's relationship to their immediate environment and its impact on their behaviour. Although there are a number of different strands to this form of analysis, we can note that, as with its *human ecology* predecessor, administrative criminology focuses on the relationship between two areas, cultural and physical environments.

**Cultural environment**: This focuses on the development of general theoretical ideas about the 'nature of criminal behaviour' in terms of thinking about *why* people offend (a theoretical analysis of crime and its causes) and *how* to prevent offending (a practical analysis that forms the basis of the type of *situational analysis* of crime prevention discussed below). In this respect, **Clarke** (1980) argues that crime theory should focus on a:

**Realistic approach** to crime prevention and management that *rejects* traditional ways of viewing criminal behaviour as:

- **Dispositional**: Crime has traditionally, according to **Clarke**, been theorised in terms of 'criminal dispositions'; the idea, in short, that some people are predisposed to crime for biogenetic, psychological or sociological reasons (boredom, poverty, social exclusion and the like).

## ⚠ Weeding the path

These ideas have been questioned in various ways.

## 🏠 The potting shed: Criminal interventions

Which, if any, of the following 'criminal interventions' are likely to result in a *decrease* in criminal activity? (Answers at the end of this section.)

| | |
|---|---|
| Increasing police numbers | Targeting known offenders |
| More police on random patrol | Protecting repeat victims |
| Charging more suspects | Patrolling 'hot spots' |
| Corporal punishment | Targeting risk factors (poor parenting, etc.) |
| Diversion to leisure and recreation facilities | Family interventions |
| Fear arousal (e.g. 'scare them straight') | Instant punishment (on-the-spot fines) |

**Genetic** predispositional theories, for example, ignore the weight of evidence suggesting that the behaviour of offenders changes over time. Most crime in the UK is committed by young males, which suggests that, as they get older and take on a range of personal and family commitments, their behaviour is modified by social factors.

**Sociological** explanations focusing on areas like poverty as 'causes of crime' are also questioned because people from similar social environments behave in different ways – some choose to offend whereas others do not.

**Clarke** argues, therefore: 'Theoretical difficulties can be avoided by seeing crime … as the outcome of immediate choices and decisions made by the offender' – something that leads neatly into a range of 'preventative options' to either limit the possible choices available to 'potential offenders' or make the consequences of 'choosing to offend' outweigh the possible benefits.

## ✳ SYNOPTIC LINK

**Theory and methods/social policy:** This idea reflects a cost-benefit form of analysis that argues that potential offenders make decisions about their behaviour on the basis of what they are likely to gain from a crime (the benefits) as against any likely costs (such as being caught and punished). This, as we will see, has clear implications for the effectiveness of crime prevention policies.

Part of the 'realistic approach' advocated by writers such as **Clarke** stems from the observation that 'crime' is *not* a:

**Homogeneous category:** Criminal behaviour comes in many shapes and sizes – property theft, for example, is very different to rape – and it makes little sense to assume that just because they share a common label (*crime*) they have similar causes or outcomes. **Clarke** argues that just as we don't view 'illness' in an *undifferentiated* way (a doctor would see a heart attack and a cold as having different causalities), we should similarly see crime as being *differentiated*. If this is the case, different types of crime respond to different forms of 'treatment'. In particular, there are two basic characteristics of crimes, both of which fit neatly with the idea of *rational choice*, that make them amenable to various forms of prevention:

- **Opportunity:** The majority of crimes in our society are those of *opportunity* – as **Felson** and **Clarke** (1998) argue, 'no crime can occur without the physical opportunities to carry it out' – and *opportunism*. In other words, many crimes are unplanned; offenders don't particularly look to commit crimes, but if an opportunity occurs (a purse left unattended, for example) they may be tempted to offend if the chances of being detected are less than the likely benefits.

- **Territoriality:** Most crime, according to **Wiles** and **Costello** (2000), is *local* to the offender. Their research showed the 'average distance travelled to commit domestic burglary was 1.8 miles', which confirmed **Forrester et al.'s** (1988) research into patterns of burglary in Rochdale.

These ideas are linked, within administrative criminology, in two ways. First, offences committed *outside* the offender's local area are mainly related, as **Wiles** and **Costello** argue, to opportunities presenting themselves 'during normal routines', rather than being consciously planned. Second, if measures can be taken to reduce opportunities for crime in a particular area, crime rates will fall, since the denial of opportunity, allied to territoriality, means the majority of crimes will *not* be *displaced* to other areas (there are exceptions – activities like drug smuggling and prostitution, for example, are sensitive to displacement).

## Physical environment

Where administrative criminology rejects the idea that there is anything unique about offenders – just about anyone, given the right conditions, is capable of offending – crime can be limited by a variety of measures designed to make it more difficult, less attractive and ultimately more costly for the potential offender. Examples of crime prevention strategies include:

- **Crime awareness** – making people more aware of opportunities for (mainly low-level) crime. Advertising campaigns, for example, focus attention on simple ways people can protect their property ('Lock It or Lose It') or be more aware of crime ('Look Out – there's a thief about').

- **Community involvement** includes initiatives to promote both 'self-policing' strategies such as Neighbourhood Watch or Crimestoppers (providing cash rewards to people for informing on offenders) and closer relations between the police and the community. The development of community safety officers in the 1990s was designed to help the police develop community linkages (although **Gilling** (1999) has doubted their effectiveness in this role).

- **Built environment**: A central (ecological) idea behind administrative criminology is the management of

physical space, examples of which we noted earlier in **Wilcox** and **Augustine's** (2001) ideas about how people think about and relate to their physical environment (levels of street lighting, for example). A significant idea here is:

- **Defensible space**, which involves 'structuring the physical layout of communities to allow residents to control the areas around their homes' (**Newman**, 1996). The objective here is 'to bring an environment under the control of its residents' using a mix of 'real and symbolic barriers, strongly defined areas of influence, and improved opportunities for surveillance'. 'Alleygate' projects, for example, have been developed around the UK as a means of limiting access to 'outsiders' on housing estates – gates prevent potential offenders both gaining access to houses and making their escape through a maze of alleyways. A further example is the use of CCTV surveillance.

On another level (quite literally) writers such as **Coleman** (1985) have criticised the replacement of 'the traditional street of houses-with-gardens by estates of flats'. The result, she argues, was not the 'instant communities' envisaged by government planners, but rather the reverse – 'problem estates'. She identified two main reasons for this:

- **Lack of community ownership** of 'common space' (no one took responsibility for corridors, for example) and:

- **Freedom**: The ability of non-residents to move freely – and anonymously – through blocks of flats (something Alleygate projects seek to prevent).

# Discussion point: Designing out deviance?

Divide into three groups and identify an area familiar to everyone in the group (your school/college or somewhere reasonably close, perhaps) where you know deviant behaviour takes place. Each group should choose a different *one* of the following to discuss:

- **Awareness:** Ideas for a poster campaign to raise community awareness of deviance and its consequences.

- **Involvement:** Ways to encourage people to become more involved in the policing of their community.

- **Built environment:** Changes you would make to the physical environment to deter deviant behaviour.

Each group should present their ideas to the class.

In terms of the impact of the physical environment on crime (and crime prevention) **Power** and **Tunstall's** (1995) longitudinal study of 'twenty of the most unpopular council estates in the country' confirms that changes suggested by writers such as **Newman** and **Coleman** do have the effect of reducing many forms of offending behaviour.

## New Right realism

Administrative criminology is, in some ways, related to a further general variation on ecological theories, namely **New Right realism**, a perspective that has a number of core themes:

- **Rational choice**: This involves a general 'cost/benefit' explanation which we have outlined previously. Although some of the cruder applications of this concept suggest individuals are fundamentally *rational* in their behaviour (people *always* weigh the likely costs of crime against possible benefits), **Wilson** (1983) notes that, at the:

- **Individual level**, this is not always possible or likely. Try calculating, for example, *your* chances of being arrested should you decide to embark on a career of crime and it's probable you'll have little idea what these chances might be, which suggests rational choice can operate only at a:

- **General level**, where beliefs about chances of arrest are propagated through the media, family and peer group – people whom, **Wilson** suggests, 'supply a *crudely accurate* estimate of the current risks of arrest, prosecution, and sentencing'. In this situation – where knowledge is, at best, rudimentary – potential offenders are unlikely to be deterred by things like length and type of possible punishment; they are, however, likely to have a good working knowledge of one thing:

- **Situational variables**: That is, the best places and times to commit crimes with the least possible chances of being detected or caught. **Wiles** and **Costello's**

(2000) research supports this idea when they note *convicted offenders* gave three main reasons for their choice of place to burgle:

- poor security
- unoccupied
- isolated/quiet.

## Risk

The key idea here, therefore, is:

- **Risk**: For **Wilson**, the way to combat crime is to increase the risk for potential offenders, something related to ideas about **deterrence**. If a community puts in place measures to deter crime, the associated risks rise. These measures are many and varied, but all ultimately devolve to another core idea, the importance of:

- **Community** and **informal social control**, involving a number of crime prevention strategies:

  - **Maintaining order**: Although not the first to suggest it, **Wilson** (1982) observed the *broken window* effect. If a neighbourhood is allowed to physically deteriorate it becomes a breeding ground for unchecked criminal activities. This follows because urban decay indicates the breakdown of *informal social controls* that keep crime in check – 'one unrepaired broken window is a signal that no one cares ...' This, in turn, is related to the:

  - **Fear of crime** within a community. As **Kleiman** (2000) argues, where people fear crime they take steps to avoid it – to the detriment of community life (the streets, for example, become the preserve of lawbreakers).

  - **Low-level regulation** involves maintaining 'community defences' against non-conformity. These include things like community surveillance, such as Neighbourhood Watch in the UK, or:

  - **Zero-tolerance policing**: Every deviant or illegal act, no matter how trivial, needs to be acted on by the police and community because it sets clear behavioural markers and boundaries for potential offenders and the law-abiding alike.

  - **Self-regulation**: If the people of a community take pride in their neighbourhood, they learn how to protect it. If criminal behaviour is not tolerated

## Discussion point: We know who you are

Imagine you are in complete charge of policing strategies for your local community and the residents tell you that:

- street/low-level criminality is their major concern
- 'everyone knows' who the local criminals are.

You decide to arrest these 'known criminals' and send them for 'rehabilitation' against their will. The crime rate drops, but some innocent people are imprisoned and their families fall into poverty.

Analyse and debate the pros and cons of this strategy.

at any level the potential offender learns that the costs of offending become greater than the benefits.

※ **SYNOPTIC LINK**

**Family:** Wilson (1983) suggests informal social controls are more significant than formal controls in preventing deviant behaviour – and the most important institution for 'socialising out crime' is the family group and the values learnt within it.

**Community policing:** The police must be fully integrated into and trusted by the community. This means a strong local presence 'on the ground', with foot officers building relationships with law-abiding citizens.

 **Weeding the path**

*Administrative criminology* and *New Right realism* share some related problems:

- **Displacement:** While some writers (**Town**, 2001) suggest measures to combat crime (such as CCTV) do *not* result in offenders moving their activities to areas where such measures are absent, **Osborn** and **Shaftoe** (1995) argue that the evidence is not clear cut; improvements in crime rates tend to be:

  - **ineffective** – physical measures reduce the *fear* of crime rather than crime itself – and

  - **misplaced** – concentrating on areas like business and property thefts rather than areas, such as violence, that cause greater concern.

- **Interventions:** **Osborn** and **Shaftoe** conclude that policy interventions in

'traditional areas of concern' – relieving poverty, eliminating economic inequality and supporting family life – give more effective *long-term* returns in terms of reducing crime and offending.

- **Self-fulfilling prophecies:** Strategies such as *criminal profiling* (where the police build up a picture of *typical criminals*) result in some groups and individuals being targeted as 'potential criminals'. When the police target such groups they discover more crime (especially if a *zero-tolerance* policy is being pursued), which 'confirms' their initial profiling and feeds into continued profiling.

## 🏠 The potting shed

After the London bombings in 2005, the British Transport Police Chief Constable Ian Johnston said his officers would concentrate their efforts on 'particular racial groups' and wouldn't 'waste time searching old white ladies'. Identify two possible problems with this approach to crime prevention.

## New Left realism

**New Left realism** uses a three-cornered approach (see diagram below) to understand deviant behaviour and its relationship to social control. As **Young** (2003) puts it: 'The job of realism is to tackle all three sides of the deviancy process.' In other words, where *administrative criminology*, for example, focuses on one or other of these areas, left realism focuses on both the content of each area and, more importantly perhaps, the *interaction* between them. This represents a 'realistic approach' in two senses:

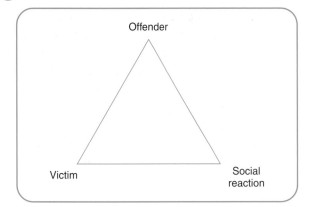

**The 'three-cornered approach'**

First, 'the problem of crime' is not an academic one in that, to use **Mills'** (1959) formulation, crime is both a:

- **private problem**, in the sense of its social and psychological effects on victims, and a

- **public issue**, in the sense of the cultural impact it has on the quality of people's lives and experiences.

Second, it addresses the *multidimensional nature* of crime in terms of the relationship between *offender*, *victim* and *social reaction* – something we can understand more easily by considering each dimension in turn.

## Offender profiles

These suggest the majority of crime in our society is committed by young, working-class males. Although there may be areas of *over-representation* (black youths, for example, figure disproportionately in official crime statistics) and *under-representation* (the extent of middle-class or female criminality, for example), the statistical picture is, for left realists, *broadly accurate* – there is not, for example, a vast reservoir of undetected 'crimes of the elderly'.

## Explaining crime

**Lea** and **Young** (1984) suggest that *three related factors* explain why people choose or reject criminal behaviour:

**Relative deprivation**: Concepts like poverty and wealth are subjective categories *relative* to what someone feels they should have when compared with others (a *reference group* such as 'society', peers or whatever). **Lea** and **Young** use this concept for two reasons:

- **Deprivation** alone cannot 'cause criminality'; many poor people do not commit crimes.

- **Relativity** allows them to include the 'well-off' in any explanation of offending. An *objectively* rich individual may, for example, feel *relatively deprived* when they compare their situation to a reference group that has greater income and wealth.

**Marginalisation** relates to social status. As writers such as **Willis** (1977) have shown, young, working-class men are frequently 'pushed to the margins of society' through educational failure and low-pay, low-status work. A further aspect of (political) marginalisation is the idea that, where deviant individuals see themselves as facing problems and need to resolve grievances, 'no one is listening'. Criminal activity, therefore, becomes the social expression of marginalisation, especially when it combines with:

**Subculture** (although the concept of *neo-tribes* would probably fit just as neatly – loose conglomerations of people who have something in common). The ability to form and move around in groups is seen as a *collective response* to a particular social situation. In this instance, the form of the subcultural/tribal group is determined by feelings of *relative deprivation* and *marginalisation*. Specific subcultural values, in this respect, are not independent of the culture in which they arise and, for **Lea** and **Young**, it is precisely because working-class youths, for example, *accept* the general values of capitalist society that they indulge in criminal behaviour – the pursuit of desired ends by illegitimate means.

 Weeding the path

Once again, the strength of this general theory is that 'subcultural-type groupings' are not restricted to the young and the working class – middle-class company directors who deal illegally in shares or fix prices to defraud the public may have their behaviour supported by a (sub)culture that sees such behaviour as permissible.

## Victim profiles

As **Burke** (1999) notes, left realism tries to bring *victims* into the picture in a number of ways:

**Problematising crime**: In this respect **Burke** notes 'crime is a problem for ordinary people that must be addressed' by criminologists, especially the 'plight of working class victims of predatory crime' whose views have been variously *ignored* (by radical criminologists, for example) or *marginalised* (by administrative criminology and the New Right).

In this respect, left realists argue the:

**Lived experiences** of crime victims (or those who live in high-crime areas) need to be considered and addressed. In other words, we need to understand how 'fear of crime', for example, is related to 'lived crime rates'. That is, how the experience of crime is *localised* in

the sense of affecting different individuals and groups in different ways – the chances of being a victim differ in terms of factors such as class, age, gender, ethnicity and region.

As **Burke** notes, official crime statistics suggest women are less likely to be murdered than men, but *black* women have a greater chance of being murdered than *white* men. Victim impact is similarly *fragmented*; men tend to feel anger, whereas women are more likely to report shock and fear, and such impact, **Burke** suggests, 'cannot be measured in absolute terms: £50 from a middle class home will have less effect than the same sum stolen from a poor household'.

In addition, someone living on a *council* estate is more likely to experience crime than someone who owns a *country* estate, and, in a similar way to their New Right counterparts, left realists argue that part of the process of understanding and combating the effects of crime is to work with local communities to build safer environments.

**Relationships**: Many forms of criminology, as we've suggested, *over-determine* the relationship between offender and victim. In other words, the two are seen as practically, and therefore theoretically, distinct and separate. Some forms of criminology *under-determine* the relationship; everyone is seen as a 'potential offender', an idea reflected in increasingly restrictive forms of social control and surveillance in the school, workplace and community. For left realists the offender–victim relationship, for many types of everyday crime, is more complex in two ways:

- **Personal**: Offenders may be well known to their victims.
- **Cultural**: People may be, at different times, both offenders *and* victims.

# The potting shed

The ideas we've just noted concerning offenders and victims impact on the third corner of the left realist approach in terms of:

## Social reactions

Unlike interactionist sociology, which has been concerned largely with demonstrating how different forms of public reaction contribute to the 'problem of crime', left realism focuses on how different types of social relationship (between police and public, offender and victim, and so forth) create different social reactions and, more importantly, different (policy) solutions to the problem of crime.

**Young** (1997) sketches the broad relationships involved in the understanding of social reactions in terms of what he calls the 'square of crime'. In this respect, social reactions are mediated through a range of different reciprocal relationships, such as that between the police and offenders – how, for example, the police view 'potential

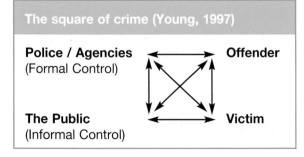

**The square of crime (Young, 1997)**

Police / Agencies (Formal Control)    Offender

The Public (Informal Control)    Victim

and actual offenders' and, of course, the reverse view, how potential offenders view their relationship with control agencies.

This general relationship, and different levels of social reaction, is:

**Multidimensional**, in the sense that the relationship between formal control agencies and offenders will be mediated further by things like how the general public (informal control agencies) views both offenders and their victims. For example, where an offender or victim can't be easily identified, public reactions may be muted (or uncooperative), which, in turn, may hinder formal police attempts to control a particular type of offending (as may occur with complicated and opaque forms of white-collar/business crime). Similarly, in relation to 'victimless crimes' (such as illegal drug use) 'offender' and 'victim' may be the same person.

## Interventions

For left realism, therefore, policy solutions to crime are framed in terms of different 'forms and points of intervention' in the deviancy creation process, and such interventions occur at all levels of society. For **Young** (1997), therefore, the concept of social reaction involves reacting to 'crime' as a general behavioural category rather than simply reacting to criminal behaviour at particular moments (such as when a crime is committed). Reactions, therefore, shouldn't just focus on what to do *after* an offence; rather, *interventions* (or reacting prior to an offence) need to occur at all levels of society:

- **Cultural/ideological** in terms of improving our understanding of the causes of offending, the role and relationship of the police and public, and so forth.

- **Economic** in terms of things like

educational provision and prospects, support for families, job creation and training.

- **Political** in terms of both *punitive* aspects of control (a variety of ways of dealing with different offenders) and the general climate within which offenders and victims operate (levels of tolerance over crime, for example).

Although we've isolated these ideas for theoretical convenience, they are, of course, interrelated; economic interventions (such as providing education and training) are mediated through ideological interventions (how we view different types of offender and victim, for example) and political interventions (the practical measures developed to control crime, for instance).

## Weeding the path

Left realism suggests the relationship between crime, deviance and social control is a complex one that, in consequence, requires complex theorising and solutions. The problem of crime is not one (as history shows) that can be solved by relatively simplistic 'solutions' (the idea that imprisonment is both appropriate for all forms of crime and that 'it works' as a deterrent rather than simply as a form of punishment, for example). 'Solutions to crime' require complex analyses that involve thinking about the genesis of deviant behaviour in terms of offenders – the social and psychological conditions that give rise to such behaviour – and control agencies (the role of the public, police and courts, etc.). We can, however, identify two problematic areas:

- **Operationalisation**: The complexity of the left realist position makes it difficult to operationalise in its totality, and although complexity is not a criticism, it does mean that certain forms of intervention are more likely to be pursued than others. These include, for example, the types of intervention we've previously discussed in relation to both administrative criminology and New Right realism, which in some circumstances makes it practically impossible to disentangle these different types of theory. On a practical level it's difficult to see how specific concepts like relative deprivation and political marginalisation can be measured, and if we can't quantify something like 'marginalisation', how do we know it has occurred for an offender?

- **Common sense**: **Mugford** and **O'Malley** (1990) argue that a significant problem with left realism is the 'over-determination of the real'; in other words, it makes what people *believe* about crime (in terms of its causes and explanations) a central theoretical consideration. The experiences of 'ordinary people', in this respect, are considered 'more real' than explanations produced by social scientists, and this leads to the idea that the police concentrate on working-class forms of crime because 'that is what people want'. Although this may reflect the idea that street crime, for example, is a cause for concern for people, it neglects the idea that less visible, more subtle forms of white-collar crime may have greater long-term impact on the general quality of people's lives.

## Moving on

Although the precise relationship between deviance, power and control is a complex one, it is evident that certain groups in our society have greater and lesser involvement in offending behaviour. In the next section, therefore, we can examine a variety of ways in which criminal behaviour is socially distributed by looking at the relationship between crime and the social categories of class, age, gender, ethnicity and locality.

('Criminal interventions' answer: According to the Home Office (1998), the measures in the right-hand column are effective in reducing crime.)

# 4. Different explanations of the social distribution of crime and deviance by age, social class, ethnicity, gender and locality

In previous sections we've examined some of the more theoretical aspects of crime and deviance, and while this section contains its fair share of theoretical conundrums (over how we can operationalise the concept of crime, for example), the primary focus is on identifying and explaining patterns of crime (its *social distribution*, in other words).

## Preparing the ground: Operationalising crime

**Young** (2001) suggests *four main ways* to calculate and quantify the amount of crime in our society:

1 **Official crime statistics** record crimes *reported to the police*. These twice-yearly government statistics include a variety of categories (robbery, fraud, violent and sexual offences, for example) that constitute:

- **Officially recorded crimes**: That is, those crimes reported to, or discovered by, the police that appear in the official crime statistics.

## Weeding the path

We need to note that not all crimes actually make it into the official crime statistics, for a couple of reasons.

First, as **Simmons** (2000) notes, crime statistics record *notifiable offences* – crimes 'tried by jury in the crown court that include the more serious offences'. *Summary offences* (such as some motoring offences) are generally excluded from the statistics.

Second, the police can exercise *discretion* over *how*, *why* and *if* a notified offence is actually recorded. As **Simmons** notes, although some UK police forces record 'every apparent criminal event that comes to their attention', the majority do not – an offence may be classified as 'an incident' which does not appear in the crime statistics.

### WARM-UP: CRIMINAL KNOWLEDGE

| | 2004 | 1994 | 1950 |
|---|---|---|---|
| How many crimes do you think were officially recorded by the police in England and Wales in: | | | |

Keep these estimates safe for the moment – we'll return to them shortly.

## 🏠 The potting shed

**From any area of your personal experience, identify an example of criminal behaviour you didn't report to the police and briefly explain why you didn't report it.**

2 **Victim surveys** record crimes people have experienced, but not necessarily reported to the police. This is often achieved, as with the government-sponsored *British Crime Surveys* (BCS), by interviewing people about either their personal experience of victimisation or their general awareness of criminal behaviour in an area. The BCS covers crime in England and Wales (biennually between 1982 and 2000 and annually since) and now involves interviewing around 50,000 people aged 16 or over. Victim surveys' use in understanding criminal behaviour lies in two main areas:

- **Unreported crimes**: They provide information about crimes that may not, for a variety of reasons, have been officially recorded.

- **Risk**: They can tell us something about people *at risk of* different types of crime, their attitudes to crime and the measures they take to reduce their chances of victimisation.

Alongside such surveys, a range of *local crime surveys*, focused on particular areas, are carried out by sociologists from time to time. The **Islington Crime Surveys** (**Jones et al.** 1986, 1990) and **Policing the Streets** (**Young**, 1994, 1999) are probably the most well known, and such surveys use similar techniques to their national counterparts – **Policing the Streets** surveyed 1000 people in the Finsbury Park region of London. According to **British Crime Surveys** data (2005), approximately 12 million crimes occurred in 2004 (compared with a peak of nearly 20 million in 1995).

3 **Self-report surveys**: These are usually based around interviews or anonymous questionnaires and ask people to admit to crimes they've committed in any given time period. Such surveys provide us with data about the social characteristics of *offenders* (their class and ethnic background, for example) that may be excluded from other survey methods.

4 **Other agencies**: As **Maguire** (2002) notes, sources of 'systematic information about unreported crime' (from hospitals, for example) have been explored by government departments such as the Home Office, although these are not widely used by sociologists (as yet, perhaps).

## ✳ SYNOPTIC LINK

**Theory and methods:** The collection of crime data illustrates the different ways both quantitative and qualitative research methods can be applied to an understanding of the social world.

## 🛠 Digging deeper: Operationalising crime

We can think about some of the respective advantages and disadvantages of different crime survey methods in the following terms.

**Official crime statistics**: Crime statistics involve practical and methodological problems (in terms of both *reliability* and *validity*) relating, in particular, to:

**Under-reporting**: The British Crime Surveys tell us two interesting things in this respect. First, crimes reported by the public account for around 90% of all recorded crime (the police, in other words, are responsible for discovering around 10% of recorded crime). Second, around 50% of all crime is not reported to, or recorded by, the police, and the reasons for non-reporting are many and varied:

- **Minor crimes**: The victim suffers minor inconvenience and doesn't want the trouble of reporting the offence.

- **Personal**: The victim chooses to personally resolve the issue (by confronting the offender, for example). This is likely to occur within families or close-knit communities where informal social controls are strong (a school or business, for example, may choose to deal with an offender through internal forms of discipline).

- **Fear**: Victims may fear possible reprisals from the offender if they involve the police (something that may, for example, apply to child abuse as well as more obvious forms of personal attack). Alternatively, witnesses may fail to come forward to identify offenders – in London, for example, Operation Trident was set up in 1998 to 'tackle gun crime in London's black communities', a type of crime hard to investigate 'because of the unwillingness of witnesses to come forward through fear of reprisals from the criminals involved'.

- **Trauma**: With sexual offences like rape (both male and female) the victim may decide not to prolong the memory of an attack; alternatively, they may feel the authorities will not treat them with consideration and sympathy. **Simmons** (2000) notes that sexual offences are the least likely of all crimes to be reported.

- **Confidence**: Unless a victim is insured, for example, there is little incentive to report crimes such as burglary if the victim has little confidence in the ability of the police to catch the offender.

- **Ignorance**: In areas such as fraud, over-charging and the like, the victim may not be aware of the crime. Many businesses, for example, are victims of crimes (such as petty theft) that are defined by offenders and witnesses as 'perks'. Alternatively, as **Simmons** notes, 'only half of detected frauds are reported to the police', one reason being that businesses may want to avoid bad publicity from a police prosecution.

- **Services**: Offences such as prostitution and drug dealing involve a 'conspiracy of silence' between those involved – someone buying illegal drugs from a drug dealer has little incentive to report the offence (a type of crime sometimes referred to as 'victimless').

- **Over-reporting**: This occurs when the police, by committing more resources to tackling a particular form of crime (such as burglary), discover 'more crime' and, in consequence, the crime statistics increase. One reason for this is the:

  - **Iceberg effect**: A large number of crimes take place each year and those notified and recorded represent the 'tip of the iceberg' (the true extent of crime is effectively hidden from view).

When control agencies target certain types of crime they dig into the '*dark figure*' of submerged crime – it's not necessarily that more crime is being committed, only that more committed crimes are discovered. This may mean crime statistics tell us *more* about the activities of control agencies than about crime and offenders.

## Crime surveys

**Victim surveys** potentially give us a more *valid* picture of crime in that they include an overall estimate of *unreported crime*. They suggest crime is widespread throughout the population (although it needs to be remembered that many offenders commit multiple crimes), which may have implications for a simple 'criminal'/'law-abiding' dichotomy. They are not, however, without their problems. **Mason** (1997) highlights three specific issues:

- **Selective memory**: People are required to remember events, sometimes many months after they happened, and their recall may be limited.

- **Values**: **Young** (1994) notes that the 'differential interpretation respondents give to questions' (such as the meaning of 'being hit' in cases of violent behaviour) creates problems of *comparison* for victim surveys. Interpretations of 'crime', and different tolerance levels of criminal behaviour, may vary in terms of things like class and gender.

- **Emotions**: Just as people may be reluctant to report crimes to the police, they may be similarly unwilling to talk about their victimisation to 'middle-class interviewers'. A frequent criticism of British Crime Surveys in the past has been that the extent of family-related crime (such as domestic violence) was underestimated because the victim was reluctant to admit to victimisation in the presence of the offender (their partner, for example). Recent refinements in interviewing technique have gone some way to resolving this particular problem.

A further issue to include is:

**Knowledge**: This extends from knowing about a criminal offence (such as vandalism) but not considering yourself 'a victim', to areas like corporate crime where 'victims' are *unaware* of their victimisation. The BCS, for example, tells us little or nothing about complex, sophisticated forms of criminality carried out by the middle and upper classes, thereby reinforcing the idea of crime as a working-class phenomenon.

**Self-report surveys** are significant for three main reasons:

- **Foundation**: The researcher can get as close as possible to the 'source of criminal behaviour', thereby increasing the *validity* of the information gained, something that, **Thornberry** and **Krohn** (2000) argue, encourages 'increased reporting of many sensitive topics'.

- **Characteristics**: Such surveys are one of the few ways available for sociologists to systematically gather information about the social characteristics of *offenders*.

- **Data**: These surveys can collect information about the frequency and seriousness of different forms of offending.

## Weeding the path

Despite these advantages, **Young** (1994) suggests the general *reliability and validity* of such surveys can be criticised in terms of:

- **Representativeness**: The majority of self-report surveys focus on the behaviour of *young people* (with some exceptions – **Thornberry** (1997) and **Jessor** (1998) for example). Although this tells us something about their behaviour (offending in terms of class, gender and ethnicity, for instance), it's difficult to see how findings can be *generalised*.

- **Delinquency**: Self-report surveys discover a mass of relatively trivial delinquent behaviour, but miss a vast range of offending that's more usually associated with adults (**Weitekamp**, 1989). This includes, of course, 'crimes of the powerful' (such as corporate crime).

- **Participation**: There is evidence (**Jurgen-Tas et al.**, 1994) that 'prior contacts with the juvenile justice system' make offenders less likely to participate in self-report surveys. In addition, the setting of many studies ('a middle-class interviewer, often in the official setting of the school') creates what **Young** calls 'an optimum socially structured situation for fabrication'. In other words, respondents consciously and unconsciously *lie*. **Jupp** (1989) further suggests that respondents tend to admit fully to trivial offences and

display an unwillingness to admit to serious offences.

### ⚠ Preparing the ground: Explaining crime patterns

Although there are problems and arguments surrounding the operationalisation of crime, this doesn't necessarily mean the data produced are meaningless. In this respect, we can identify a range of patterns and explanations for the social distribution of crime, starting with:

**Social class**: Although, as **Young** (1994) notes, self-report studies question the (simple) association between class and crime (partly because they tend to pick up on a wide range of relatively trivial forms of deviance), the general thrust of sociological research shows a number of correlations between class and more serious forms of offending. The majority of convicted offenders are drawn from the working class, for example, and different classes tend to commit different types of offence (crimes such as fraud are mainly middle-class). One reason for this is:

**Opportunity structures**: Where people

## Discussion point: Criminal knowledge revisited

According to the Home Office Crime Reduction & Community Safety Group (2005), officially recorded crime in England and Wales was just under 6 million in 2004, around 5.25 million in 1994 and 461,000 in 1950. How close were your estimates to the actual figures?

What do the estimates produced by the class as a whole tell us about our understanding of crime?

What reasons can you identify for the changes in recorded crime over the past 50 years?

are differently placed (in the workforce, for example) they have greater or lesser criminal opportunities. Corporate crime is largely carried out by the higher classes (the working class are not, by definition, in positions of sufficient power and trust to carry out elaborate frauds). However, all classes have the same basic **opportunities** to commit a wide variety of offences (from street violence and theft to armed robbery). This suggests we need alternative ways to explain the predominantly working-class nature of these offences, such as:

**Lifestyle** and **socialisation**: Given that crime statistics show young people have the highest rates of offending, middle-class youths are less likely to be involved in 'lifestyle offending' that relates to various forms of street crime, partly for:

- **status reasons** – a criminal record is likely to affect potential career opportunities, and partly for
- **economic reasons** – middle-class youths are less likely to pursue crime as a source of income.

## Theories

We could also include here a range of sociological theories concerning the relationship between crime and primary/secondary socialisation (from **Merton's** strain theory, through differential association and subcultural theory, to New Right and administrative criminological explanations). However, an alternative explanation involves changing the focus from the social characteristics of *offenders* to the activities of:

**Social control agencies** and their perception and treatment of different social classes. *Policing strategies*, for example, covers a number of related areas:

- **Spatial targeting** focuses police resources on areas and individuals where crime rates have, historically, been highest (which, in effect, usually means spaces mainly occupied by the working classes – clubs, pubs, estates or designated 'crime hotspots').
- **Stereotyping**: There is an element of *self-fulfilling prophecy* in this type of targeting ('high-crime' areas are policed, therefore more people are arrested, which creates 'high-crime' areas …) which spills over into:
- **Labelling theory**: **Young** and **Mooney** (1999), for example, note how working-class ethnic groups are likely to be targeted on the basis of *institutional police racism* as well as the sort of routine police practices just noted.

## Crime visibility

A further aspect to labelling is that some forms of crime may not be defined as crimes at all. These include forms of petty theft (using the company's photocopier for personal work), as well as more complex and serious forms of (middle-class) crime. Computer crime, for example, tends to be underestimated in crime statistics because, as we've seen, even when it is detected a company may prefer to sack the offender than involve the police.

**Social visibility** is also a factor here. Working-class crime, for example, tends towards high visibility – in situations with clear victims, witnesses and little attempt to hide criminal behaviour, detection and conviction rates are likely to be higher.

Some crimes (such as insider share dealing) are *less visible* to the police and public. Corporate and middle-class forms of criminality may also be *highly complex* and *diffuse* in terms of criminal *responsibility* (as with the Hatfield rail crash) and *victimisation* (there may be no clear and identifiable victims).

---

## Network Rail guilty over Hatfield

news.bbc.co.uk 06/09/05

'Network Rail has been found guilty of breaching health and safety legislation in the run-up to the Hatfield crash.

But three … managers, and two former employees of Balfour Beatty, the firm that maintained the line, were cleared at the Old Bailey. Four people died when a London to Leeds express train hit a cracked rail and left the tracks on 17 October 2000. Prosecutors said the crash resulted from a "cavalier approach" to safety.'

---

**Hale et al.** (2005) also point to the way the media 'reinforce dominant stereotypes of crime and the criminal' in ways that downplay and marginalise corporate forms of criminal behaviour and emphasise the types of crime mainly carried out by the working classes.

**Age**: A consistent finding of statistical and survey methods is the correlation between age and deviant behaviour; young people (the 10–24 age group in the UK) are more involved in crime and deviance than their older counterparts. **Social Trends** (2005) puts the peak age for offending at 18 for males and 15 for females, which suggests criminal behaviour declines with age.

**Hirschi** and **Gottfredson** (1983) argue that 'the relationship between age and crime is invariant [constant] across all social and cultural conditions at all times', while **Kanazawa** and **Still** (2000) suggest 'crime and other risk-taking behaviour … peaks in late adolescence and early adulthood, rapidly decreases throughout the 20s and 30s, and levels off during middle age'.

According to **Social Trends** (2005), for all types of *notifiable offence* the highest offending age group in 2003 was 16–24 year olds. A range of explanations exists for this relationship.

## Explanations

**Socialisation and social control** can be used to explain both the relationship between youth and class (different social classes experience different forms of socialisation and control) and the relationship between declining criminal activity and age. In terms of the former, for example, the *relative* lack of middle-class youth criminality can be explained by their primary involvement in education and their focus on career development. In terms of the latter, **Maruna** (1997) notes:

**Sociogenic** explanations focus on the idea of *informal social controls* (such as family responsibilities) that increasingly operate with age. In other words, where young people generally have fewer social responsibilities and ties than older people they experience looser informal social control, which results in a greater likelihood of *risk-taking* behaviour. Fewer responsibilities for others, as **Matza** (1964) noted, make young people more likely to indulge in 'self-centred' (deviant) behaviour, an idea sometimes expressed in terms of:

**Social distance theory**: As **Maruna** notes, things like:

- finding **employment**

- staying in **education**
- getting **married** and
- starting a **family**

*distance* people from (public) situations in which opportunistic criminality occurs. Complementing this, we could note how:

**Peer-group pressure** among the young may promote deviant behaviour (something that links to **Sutherland's** notion of *differential association*). Given that, as **Matza** argues (and statistics seem to confirm), there is no strong, long-term commitment to crime among young people, this may contribute to explanations about why deviance declines with age. A further dimension here is that for some youth, crime represents a source of:

**Social status** within a peer or family group. The ability to commit skilful crimes or be the 'hardest' person in a group, for example, may confer status that is denied to many working-class youths in society.

## Lifestyle

These types of explanation link into:

**Lifestyle** factors which focus, to some extent, on the difference between the *public* and *private* domains:

- **Public** domain explanations involve the idea that young people are more likely to have a lifestyle that creates opportunities for (relatively petty, in the majority of cases) deviance – in situations where large numbers of young people congregate and socialise there are greater *opportunities* for relatively unplanned, opportunistic criminality. In this respect, **FitzGerald et al.** (2003) noted the interplay of two factors in youth criminal activity:

  - **Cultural factors**: 'Image-conscious'

youth not only had to maintain a certain sense of image and style (clothes, mobiles, and so forth), they also needed to constantly update and change this image, something that links to:

- **Economic factors** – the need for money to finance their image. Where family financial support was absent, crime provided a source of funding.

- **Private** domain explanations relate to the way greater forms of individual responsibility develop 'with age', effectively taking people out of the situations in which the majority of crime takes place. The least criminal in our society, the elderly, are also the least likely to be involved in *public domain* activities (most elderly people do not, for example, have a 'pubbing and clubbing' lifestyle).

## Alternatives

Although these types of explanation focus on the personal/cultural characteristics of 'age groups', alternative explanations focus on the activities of:

- **Social control agencies**: As with class, gender and ethnicity, *policing strategies* make an important contribution to our understanding of age and crime:

- **Spatial targeting** focuses on spaces occupied by youth and, as we've seen, involves elements of *stereotyping* and *self-fulfilling prophecy*. Part of the ability to police the young in this way comes from their lower social status and lack of power to resist police control and surveillance strategies.

- **Social visibility** is also a factor in spatial

targeting since policing strategies reflect beliefs about the places and situations in which crime is 'likely to occur'. In addition, adults are more likely to commit low-visibility crimes whereas the young are more likely to display:

- **Status deviance**. Many crimes are not committed for economic reasons alone; some relate to power and prestige within a social group and involve a combination of *risk-taking* and the idea of 'thumbing your nose' at authority. **Smith et al.** (2005) suggest young people's contact with the police is more likely to be *adversarial* (conflict-based). Interestingly, this has a class dimension; the higher the class, the *less likely* that police contact would be adversarial.

## Gender

Higher male involvement in crime is, according to **Maguire** (2002), a 'universal feature ... of all modern countries'. Statistically, UK men and women commit much the same *types* of crime (**Social Trends**, 2005), with theft, drug offences and personal violence being the main offences for *both* sexes. Men, however, commit more crime and a wider range of offences (from robbery, through burglary, to sex offences). Explanations for this difference focus on a range of ideas:

- **Socialisation** is a traditional place to

begin when discussing gender differences, mainly because males and females are subject to different forms of socialisation and levels of social control. Traditional sociological discourses, for example, contrast the active, instrumental nature of male socialisation with the passive, affective nature of female socialisation, and while this may or may not be an accurate reflection of current realities, it forms the basis of different attitudes to:

- **Risk**: Males and females develop different attitudes to 'risk-taking' which, in turn, explains greater or lesser involvement in crime. Contemporary takes on this idea, **Davies** (1997) suggests, focus on:

- **Identity formation**, where gender is 'viewed as a *situated accomplishment*'; in other words, deviance and conformity represent cultural resources for 'doing masculinity and femininity'. What this means, in effect, is that concepts of masculinity and femininity in our culture are bound up in different attitudes to risk – men display greater risk-taking attitudes than women because 'taking risks' is associated with 'being male'. **McIvor** (1998), in this respect, argues greater male involvement in youth crime is 'linked to a range of other risk-taking behaviours which in turn are associated with the search for [masculine] identity in the transition from adolescence to

# Discussion point: Risky business?

Do men have different attitudes to risk than women?

As a class, identify and discuss some of the ways you think men do – or do not – display a greater willingness to take risks in their behaviour. (You could, for example, think about behaviour in the school/classroom – are boys, for example, more demanding and disruptive?)

adulthood' – something that reflects, for example, functionalist forms of subcultural theory.

Socialisation, social control and identity differences also find expression in the idea of:

**Opportunity structures** which reflect different forms of participation in the *public* and *private* domains. **Davies** (1997) notes how greater female participation in the private sphere of home and family demonstrates how the relative lack of female criminality 'reflects their place in society' – restrictions imposed by family responsibilities and a lesser participation in the public sphere result in fewer *opportunities* for crime.

Although social changes (such as higher levels of female participation in the workplace) have blurred this general 'private/public' distinction, where men and women have *similar* opportunity structures, their respective patterns of crimes appear broadly similar. Shoplifting, for example, is one area in the UK, according to **McMillan** (2004), 'where women almost equal men in the official statistics'. 'Middle-class crime', such as fraud, is predominantly committed by men, which reflects their relatively higher positions in the workplace.

## Alternatives

As with class and age, an alternative way to see gender differences in criminality is to focus on the perceptions and activities of:

**Social control agencies**: Men and women, in this respect, are viewed differently by control agents (from parents, through teachers to the media, police and courts) and, consequently, are treated differently. This difference may be expressed in terms of a couple of ideas.

**Overestimation** of male criminality: Control agents are more likely to recognise and respond to male offending, which is related to the:

**Underestimation** of female criminality: One (contested) argument is that the police and judiciary have *stereotyped* views about male and female criminality that, in basic terms, see the former as 'real criminals', which means the police are less likely to suspect or arrest female offenders. In addition, the courts may deal more leniently with female offenders, an idea called the:

**Chivalry effect**: **Klein** (1996) notes how writers such as **Pollack** (1950) have perpetuated the above ideas about police and judicial behaviour. While **Carlen et al.** (1985) argue that such an effect is overstated, they note that where strong stereotypes of masculinity and femininity pervade the criminal justice system, *both* women and men who do not fit neatly into gendered assumptions about male and female roles and responsibilities are likely to receive *harsher* treatment than those who do.

Although ideas about over- and underestimation are open to some dispute, one aspect of gendered treatment is the:

**Medicalisation** of female crime. While *pathological* concepts of crime and deviance (explanations that focus on some essential (inherent) biological or psychological quality of males and females) are, as **Conrad** and **Schneider** (1992) show, nothing particularly new, the medicalisation of *female deviance* (in particular) sees offending behaviour redefined as *illness*; female offending, in other words, is more likely to be interpreted as a 'psychological cry for help', or as having a medical rather than criminal causality. This *redefinition process*, therefore, helps to explain lower (apparent) levels of female criminality.

# The potting shed

**Identify and briefly explain two ways that female deviance may be explained in medical rather than criminal terms.**

**Easteal** (1991) documents a number of instances in both the UK and the USA where *premenstrual tension* has been used as an explanation for different types of female criminality, something that **Klein** (1996) argues represents an extension of the way 'femaleness' has a long cultural association with 'nature' and 'biology'. **Easteal** notes, however, that many feminists have objected to this medicalisation process because it 'reinforces the view of women as slaves to their hormones'.

An alternative take on the possible underestimation of female criminality is the idea of:

**Social visibility**. Female crime is underestimated because it is 'less visible' to the police, either because women are more successful in hiding their criminal behaviour or because formal control agencies are less likely to police female behaviour. **Maguire**

(2002), however, argues that the weight of research evidence suggests there is no great reservoir of 'undiscovered female crime' – there is, he suggests '. . . little or no evidence of a vast shadowy underworld of female deviance hidden in our midst like the sewers below the city streets'.

**Ethnicity**: While it's important not to lose sight of the fact that, in the UK, the 'white majority' represents a significant ethnic group, the focus here is mainly on *ethnic minority groups* and crime (since previous sections have tended to focus on ethnic majority forms of criminality). In this respect, the **Commission for Racial Equality** (2004) suggests *ethnic minorities* are more likely to be:

- **victims** of household, car and racially motivated crimes
- **arrested** for notifiable offences ('arrest levels from stop-and-searches were eight times higher for black and three times higher for Asian than for white groups')
- **remanded** in prison (refused bail)
- **represented** disproportionately in the prison population.

Just as experiences of crime differ *within* majority ethnic groups (in terms of class, age and gender), the same is true of minority groups. We also need to recognise that different minorities have broadly different experiences; Asians, for example, have a higher risk of being victims of household crime, whereas black minorities are at greater risk of personal crimes such as assault. Although there is little significant difference in *offending* rates between ethnic minority groups, the past few years have seen an increase in gun crime and murder rates (as both victims and offenders) among young Afro-Caribbean males.

When thinking about explanations for ethnic minority crime we need to recognise two important demographic characteristics of the general minority population:

- **Social class**: Ethnic minority group members are more likely to be working class.
- **Age**: Black minority groups generally have a younger age profile than both the white majority and the UK population as a whole.

## Explanations

These characteristics are significant because of the relationship we've previously discussed between class, age and crime. If we control for *social class*, for example, all ethnicities show *similar* levels of 'street crime' activity in their populations. Crime rates for ethnic minorities living in low-crime, 'white majority' communities are not significantly different and the same is true of whites living in 'black majority' areas. This suggests, perhaps, that we should not overstate the relationship between ethnicity and offending. With this in mind, explanations for ethnic minority criminality can be constructed around concepts like:

- **Opportunity structures**: The class and age demographics for ethnic minority groups suggest that a general lack of involvement in 'middle-class' forms of offending can be explained in terms of such groups not generally being in a position to carry out this type of crime.
- **Social control**: The relatively low levels of female Asian offending can be partly explained by higher levels of surveillance

and social control experienced within the family. Similarly, black minority youth are more likely to be raised in single-parent families than their white peers, and this type of family profile is *statistically* associated with higher rates of juvenile offending.

- **Over-representation**: One set of explanations for black over-representation in prison focuses on the greater likelihood of black youth being:

  - **Targeted** by the police as potential/actual offenders (an idea that relates to police *stereotypes* of class, age and ethnicity). **Clancy et al.** (2001) note that when all demographic factors are controlled, 'being young, male and *black* increased a person's likelihood of being stopped and searched'.

  - **Prosecuted** and convicted through the legal system. **Home Office** (2004) statistics show that although arrests for notifiable offences were predominantly white (85% as against 15% from non-white minority groups), blacks overall were three times more likely to be arrested than whites, although arrest rates varied significantly by locality. *Urban* areas (such as London and Manchester) generally had a *lower* ratio of black/white arrest rates than *rural* areas (such as Norfolk, where blacks were eight times more likely to be arrested than whites). Significantly perhaps, black suspects were also proportionately more likely to be *acquitted* in both magistrate and Crown courts.

One explanation for over-representation might be:

**Institutional racism**: The **Macpherson Report** (1999) into the murder of the black teenager **Stephen Lawrence** suggested police cultures and organisations were institutionally biased against black offenders and suspects. Lower rates of offending and arrest for Asian minorities, however, suggest this may not paint a complete picture. **Skidelsky** (2000) argues that *social class* also plays a significant part in any explanation since 'poor people, or neighbourhoods, get poor [police] service, whatever their race'. **Young** and **Mooney** (1999) argue that much the same is true for the general policing process in the UK – 'If . . . institutionalised racism were removed the disproportionate class focus (of the police) would still result . . . but at a substantially reduced level'.

## The courts

Finally, in any explanation of ethnic minority criminality we need to note the role of the:

**Judiciary**, in terms of thinking about those who are actually found guilty and punished. **Home Office** (2004) statistics show that around 25% of the male and 31% of the female prison population was from an ethnic minority group (ethnic minorities currently make up around 8% of the UK population). Either ethnic minority groups display far higher levels of offending or some other process is at work, distorting the relative figures. One such factor is that black minority prisoners tend to serve longer prison sentences (for whatever reason) than other ethnic groups (something that might partly be explained in terms of their greater involvement in gun crime).

Thirty-seven per cent of black prisoners were serving sentences for drug offences (compared with 13% for white prisoners); although this may (or may not) reflect different levels of drug use, the fact that this single form of criminality accounts for such a large proportion of black inmates tells us something about the nature of black criminality in the UK.

## Locality

As we suggested when we looked at ecological theories, crime can be related to locality/area in a couple of ways:

- **Cultural environments**: This involves thinking about variables such as class, age and ethnicity, in the sense that area differences in crime and victimisation rates will clearly be related to the cultural composition of an area. We know, from **Clarke et al.** (2004), that working-class areas have higher crime rates than middle-class areas – the question, however, is the extent to which this difference is a function of class, locality or, perhaps, both.

- **Physical environments**: Ideas about how people interact with their environment have been outlined previously in relation to both administrative criminology and New Right realism, so we don't need to cover the same ground here. However, as **Clarke et al.** (2004) note: 'The highest crime rates are in city centre areas, with the lowest in the most rural. Different types of crime tend to occur in different types of areas.'

## Explanations

Although it's difficult to disentangle cultural and physical correlations, a number of factors can be suggested to explain the rural/urban variation:

- **Opportunities**: A relatively simple observation perhaps, but urban areas contain more people (especially young people, the peak offenders as we've seen) and places (shops, offices, factories and houses) in which to commit crime. Urban areas also contain more 'lifestyle resources' (clubs and pubs, for example) where large numbers of people (especially young people) gather and socialise, which in turn creates more opportunities for offending. **Zaki** (2003) expresses these ideas in terms of urban areas having 'higher densities of population and premises, and greater mixes of use, and therefore higher crime opportunities. They also tend to have less advantaged populations who are known to be more vulnerable to crime in general'.

- **Socialisation**: **Parsons** (1937) has argued that urban life involves a wider range of impersonal, *instrumental* relationships, something that encourages offenders to distance themselves from the consequences of their behaviour. This 'social distancing' makes people more likely to commit crime in urban areas because they are less likely to have close personal ties to their victims. The reverse holds true in rural areas where *affective relationships* are more likely; this increases the probability of a potential offender knowing their victim and acts to prevent many forms of criminal behaviour. This idea links into:

- **Social control**: **Tonnies** (1887) suggested rural areas are more likely to be characterised by community (*Gemeinschaft*) type relationships that encourage people to take an interest in the behaviour of their neighbours. Small, tight-knit communities (where everyone knows everyone else) make it easier to exercise informal types of social control. In urban areas where relationships are more impersonal (*Gesellschaft*), informal social controls do not operate as effectively.

In addition, close-knit communities may deal with offenders in ways that do not necessarily involve the police; alternatively, the police themselves (because of their closer personal ties with a community) are less likely to invoke the criminal law over minor infractions.

## The potting shed

Identify and briefly explain *two* examples of informal social controls for any *two* areas of the Specification.

- **Police resources and strategies**: Greater numbers and concentrations of police in urban areas increase the likelihood of crime being detected and reported. In addition, the police are able to target 'crime hotspots' – places where offending is either known, or more likely, to take place.

- **Social visibility**: Recent technological developments, such as CCTV, are more likely to be deployed in urban areas (especially city centres or targeted crime hotspots), making it easier to both identify and deter offenders by increasing their social visibility. Conversely, the relative size and social differentiation of urban areas make it easier for offenders to move around 'anonymously' – there are fewer chances of being recognised by victims, for example.

- **Lifestyle factors**: A range of explanations apply in this context, relating to things like:

  - **Age**: rural communities tend to have an older age demographic and the elderly are the least likely group to offend.

  - **'Lifestyle crimes'**: Involving drug use and dealing, theft of personal items, such as mobile phones and personal MP3 players, prostitution and the like.

  - **Risk avoidance**: Middle- and upper-class areas (both rural and urban) are more likely to employ a range of crime prevention strategies (such as burglar alarms).

## Digging deeper: Explanations for crime

To complete this section we can note a number of concluding comments.

**Transgression**: When we think, for theoretical convenience and clarity, about the social distribution of crime in terms of categories like class, age, gender, ethnicity and locality, we need to keep in mind the fact that these are not *discrete* categories. In other words, each individual in our society has all these characteristics – and this means, of course, that we must take account of this when thinking about how and why crime is socially distributed.

**Age** has a couple of significant dimensions we need to consider briefly. First, it can reasonably be argued that age is not, in itself, a useful indicator of criminality; this follows, as we've suggested, because there may be nothing intrinsic to the concept of age that promotes offending (young people don't simply offend because they are young). In this respect, therefore,

we need to explore factors such as lifestyle and identity formation as they relate to different age groups – the young, in particular, are more likely to lead active, public lifestyles which bring them into contact with offending behaviour and, of course, social control agencies. Similarly, if youth identities are more fluid than adult identities (they are not so tightly secured by family, work and individual responsibilities, for example), it may follow that the young are more likely to indulge in risky forms of behaviour, some of which involve crime.

Second, while **Gottfredson and Hirschi** (1990) argue that crime is inversely correlated with age (as people get older their offending declines), **Blumstein et al.** (1986) argue that age and crime do not have this characteristic in terms of *individual offenders*. In other words, crime *declines* at the general population level of society because there are fewer active offenders – where crime declines, therefore, it's because the number of offenders in society declines, not because of a decline in offending at the individual level.

This interpretation, if valid, has profound consequences for the way we examine and explain the social distribution of crime, not just in terms of age, but also in terms of removing offenders from society through imprisonment (part of a general debate about the effectiveness of prison as a crime control measure).

**Definitions**: A further complication is the fact that, although we have 'taken for granted' the definition of crime in this section, such concepts are neither neutral nor self-evident.

**Box** (1983) makes the point that even with a crime such as 'murder': 'The criminal law defines only some types of avoidable killing as murder; it excludes, for example, deaths resulting from acts of negligence, such as employers' failure to maintain safe working conditions; or deaths which result from governmental agencies giving environmental health risks a low priority . . .'.

This point is particularly relevant, as we've seen, in relation to black criminality and imprisonment, given the fact that nearly 40% of the current black prison population has been found guilty of drug offences; if drug-taking were decriminalised, for example, the consequences for our perception of this particular ethnic minority could well change dramatically.

## Moving on

In the final section of this chapter we're going to use the example of suicide to bring together a range of ideas and issues relating to the sociological study of crime and deviance.

# 5. The sociological issues arising from the study of suicide

To complete this chapter we can use the study of suicide to examine issues, both methodological and practical, of fundamental importance to our understanding of sociology.

## WARM-UP: YOU THE JURY

Read the following report:

Deborah Neill was a popular actress in the 1960s, when she appeared in over 25 films. An apparently wealthy woman, she lived alone (she was recently divorced and had no children) in a luxurious apartment in a fashionable part of the city. It was in the garage of her apartment on May 15, 2006 that she was found in her car, poisoned by carbon monoxide from the running exhaust.

The investigation into her death found spots of blood on – and in – the car and on Neill's mouth, prompting one theory she may have been knocked unconscious and then put into the car, although no suspicious people or noises were witnessed by her neighbours. Tests for blood alcohol showed a high enough level to suggest she would not have been completely conscious of her actions. To reach her car Neill had to walk down a steep flight of outdoor steps. Her high-heeled sandals, however, were free of dirt. An unidentified handprint was discovered on the driver-side door handle.

Neill had recently been the victim of a blackmail attempt, about which the police had few details. Her divorce had, moreover, been acrimonious, with suggestions of violent rows. Witness statements from neighbours suggested Neill had suffered recent bouts of depression (for which she had not sought medical help) and on occasions she had talked about 'ending it all'. At the time of her death Neill was being investigated by the Inland Revenue for unpaid taxes and was near to bankruptcy.

1 Was this a 'suicide' or some other form of death?
2 What evidence led you to your verdict?

**3** Identify, briefly explain and discuss with the class some of the sociological issues thrown up by your deliberations.

The official verdict is at the end of this section.

## ✳ SYNOPTIC LINK

**Theory and methods:** All the issues explored in this section can be related in various ways to theoretical or methodological questions. You should also note opportunities to consider these issues in relation to other parts of the Specification.

### ⚠ Preparing the ground: Sociological issues

This exercise highlights a number of sociological issues illustrated by the concept of suicide, starting with a perennial issue.

**Definitions**: The 'problem of definition' is frequently a sociological issue whenever we study social behaviour – the idea of a *contested concept*, for example, is one you've come across a number of times during the course. In this instance, however, definitional problems relate not so much to how suicide can be defined (it has a straightforward, universally agreed definition); rather, the issue here is how we recognise 'a suicide'. In other words, while we know exactly how suicide is defined, it can be difficult to decide whether or not a particular form of death is actually a suicide (as opposed to a murder, for example).

### ⌂ The potting shed

Identify two 'contested concepts' from any area of the Specification and briefly explain how and why each has more than one possible interpretation.

The issue here, therefore, is one of:

**Classification**: If we want, for example, to explain something like the social causes of suicidal behaviour, our ability to classify clearly some forms of behaviour as suicide (and others as non-suicide) is a crucial issue, one that may be neither straightforward nor simple. This relates, in turn, to a further sociological issue:

**Constructionism**: One reason for problems of classification within sociology is the idea of human behaviour as *socially constructed*; in other words, the extent to which social behaviour has different:

**Meanings** and **interpretations** for different individuals and cultures. In this instance, 'causes of death' in our culture have many possible interpretations and the same is true when we broaden the scope to include the behaviour of people in other societies and cultures. A couple of examples should clarify this issue:

- **Crime**: Until 1961, suicide was a criminal offence in the UK. Euthanasia (killing someone at their request) remains a criminal offence, although in countries such as Holland it has been legal since 1984.

- **Deviance**: In the UK, suicide is seen as a deviant act. In traditional Hindu cultures in India, however, a form of *ritual suicide* (*suttee*) was practised (and in some cases still is, even though it was made illegal in 1829) – a widow commits suicide by throwing herself on her husband's funeral pyre. To *not* commit suicide, in this instance, would be considered a deviant act.

Concepts of *construction* and *classification* suggest a further issue:

- **Typologies** (a systematic classification into different types, based on shared qualities): Here, the question is whether we can *type* 'suicide' as a prelude to explaining it; in other words, if we can identify different types of behaviour (suicide, voting, family groups or whatever) it follows that something must *cause* individuals to behave in communal ways. Whether these causes are found in areas like genetics, psychology or sociology (or some combination of each), the key point is that human group behaviour has a *causality* (a further significant general issue within sociology) that can be identified and explained using typologies, in **Tatz's** (1999) evocative phrase, as 'frameworks for speculation'.

## ✳ SYNOPTIC LINK

**Theory and methods:** Issues of causality are discussed in greater detail in relation to modernity and postmodernity.

For the moment, we can consider the issue of typologies in terms of two ideas:

- **Suicide**: Here, suicide has a relatively clear, standardised meaning deriving from the physical act itself. Once we establish the concept of 'a suicide', therefore, we can move towards identifying different possible types. **Durkheim** (1897), for example, identified four broad types (see below, page 422), whereas **Wekstein** (1979) suggests a ten-point typology, one of which involves the idea of 'suicide by murder' – attacking someone to bring about one's own death. This position sees

suicide as *unproblematic* (not open to interpretation) and, from this, the task of sociology is to explore different possible causal explanations.

- **Suicides**: An alternative interpretation is to make suicide *problematic* by thinking about the meaning people who kill themselves give to their actions. Rather than talk about 'suicide' as if it had a simple, clear and uncontested meaning, therefore, we should, according to **Douglas** (1967), see this act as involving a wide range of possible meanings and interpretations – one 'suicide' is never the same as any other.

## Objectivity and subjectivity

**Berard** (2005) argues that we should see suicide as an '*evaluative category*', one whose particular meaning is decided by 'persons, actions, institutions [and] social contexts'. In other words, 'suicide' is a socially constructed category whose meaning depends (as writers such as **Atkinson** (1978) have argued) on how the act itself is *interpreted by others*, especially those with the power (such as coroners) to decide whether an act is classified as suicide.

These two basic positions illustrate a further sociological issue, namely the distinction between two ideas:

- **Objective knowledge**: The idea here is that we can produce sociological knowledge with the status of objectivity; we can, in other words, produce factual knowledge that proves or disproves certain ideas and explanations based on the use of objective forms of evidence. **Durkheim** (1895) classically expressed this idea as, 'consider social facts as things', something that has a real, objective existence.

- **Subjective knowledge**: This position suggests all knowledge is both partial (one-sided) and incomplete. In relation to suicide, **Berard** argues that a crucial consideration in any understanding and explanation of social behaviour has to be '... the question of *how* the relevant data is identified and assembled'. In other words, the types of official (statistical) data on which supposedly objective knowledge about suicide is based are, in reality, themselves the product of choices and decisions made by social actors (something we replicated in the opening exercise by asking you to judge whether the observed behaviour should be defined as a 'suicide').

## ✳ SYNOPTIC LINK

**Theory and methods:** These ideas can be used as criticisms of statistical research data and processes.

We can highlight a further range of issues related to *how* and *why* we collect different forms of data in terms of:

- **Methodology**: The study of suicide brings into sharp relief a number of issues relating to both theory and method, some of which we can simply note and others of which we can develop. We can start by thinking about the issue of:

- **Data collection**, mainly because the problems associated with the study of suicide, while unique (in the sense that perpetrator and victim are the same and the victim can't, for obvious reasons, be personally questioned), can be related to many other areas of social life. On the face of things, given the problems just noted, the obvious way to study suicide is to use:

- **Quantitative methods**, such as official

## ⚠ Growing it yourself: Making an issue of it

Take any *two* of the following issues:

- definitions
- classification
- meanings and interpretations
- typologies
- objective knowledge
- subjective knowledge.

Apply them to any area of the social world/social behaviour you've studied during your course.

For example, identify and explain problems associated with defining 'a family' or 'intelligence'.

You should aim to write around 120 words for *each* issue.

suicide statistics. This was the route originally taken by **Durkheim** (1897), for example. His technique was to compare different rates of suicide in different societies (hence the idea of a *comparative methodology*) in order to identify possible *patterns* of suicide, which he could then explain in terms of social forces and pressures acting on individuals that 'propel them into suicidal behaviour'.

## ⌂ The potting shed

**Identify and briefly explain one reason for seeing Durkheim's approach as structuralist rather than constructionist.**

Alternatively, it's possible to compare different sets of data to search for *correlations*; for example, comparing suicide rates with factors such as levels of unemployment, poverty and family breakdown. This can be done on both regional (**Congdon**, 1996) and national (**Diekstra**, 1989) levels. The main problem with this approach, however, is that of demonstrating that successful suicides actually had the correlated characteristics.

To overcome this, a common statistical method is to work at the individual level, correlating known data about *successful* suicides to identify possible patterns in their behaviour, an approach taken by **Charlton** (1995) among others. Such data might include a mix of both *objective features* of an individual's life (employment and family status, age, gender, and so forth) and *subjective features* (mental health, for example). A problem here, however, is that

the latter type of data are open to different interpretations, especially if data about a suicidal individual's 'state of mind' is gathered from 'unqualified sources' (colleagues, friends and the like).

## ⚒ Weeding the path

Quantitative methods, as writers such as **Douglas** and **Berard** have suggested, may be *problematic* because suicide statistics are, at root, the considered opinions of powerful definers (such as coroners). Decisions about how to define a 'suspicious death' are open to different influences since, as **Berard** notes, 'categorisations of suicide can ... raise profoundly important questions of a religious, financial, moral or legal nature'. Classification decisions are, therefore, both:

- **Evaluative**, in that they take account of subjective factors and interpretations – for example, was the victim depressed? – and

- **Consequential** – a suicide verdict may have consequences for the living, such as the denial of an insurance payout, stigma attached to friends and family or blame attached to official guardians.

**Qualitative methods** share certain similarities with at least some of their quantitative counterparts in the sense that they produce:

**Reconstructed profiles** of individual suicides using a variety of techniques based, by and large, around different forms of *witness testimony*. These include, of course, the testimony of the successful suicide in the form of:

**Suicide notes**, analysis of which may tell us why someone decided to commit suicide.

While this technique may produce high-validity data, it suffers from a range of potential problems, not the least being that the majority of suicides *don't* leave a note. In those instances where notes are left, problems remain – they may, for example, be removed from the scene *deliberately* (by friends or family) or *accidentally* (blown away by the wind, for example, if the location for suicide is a cliff top).

Alternatively, reconstructions involve things like:

- **physical evidence** at the scene, such as empty pill bottles or the mode of death
- **eyewitness accounts**, such as evidence of someone jumping from a cliff top
- **testimonies** from friends, medical staff and the like concerning the deceased's 'state of mind'.

## 🏠 The potting shed

Identify and briefly explain two *ethical* problems that might arise with qualitative methods of studying suicide.

A slightly unusual method of reconstruction involves the use of:

**Observation** over a specified period to complete what **Bose et al.** (2004) has termed a '*verbal autopsy*'. **Bose** monitored 100,000 people in an area of India over an eight-year period, and suspected suicides were investigated in the light of personal observations, life histories and witness testimonies about the victim.

## Attempted suicides

A further source of evidence comes from those who have tried and *failed* to commit suicide, since they can, of course, be questioned. A couple of issues are involved here, however. First, ethical issues surround the idea of asking failed suicides to revisit a painful period in their life, and, second, there is a possible qualitative difference between those who succeed and those who fail – was the failure evidence of a *real desire* to die that simply did not work or was it a:

**Parasuicide** – an 'attempt' to commit suicide that was not, ultimately, designed to succeed? Evidence here is further complicated by what **Baechler** (1979) calls:

**Ludic suicide,** a situation in which the individual effectively *gambles* with their life (if they survive, for example, this may be

## 🌷 Growing it yourself: Master labels

'A suicide' is a master label, one that may lead people to reinterpret the behaviour of a successful suicide in the light of the label.

Identify and briefly explain possible ways this reinterpretation process may impact on qualitative approaches to suicide in terms of:

- data reliability
- data validity.

taken as evidence that they are meant to continue living).

## Digging deeper: Perspective issues

We've identified a range of sociological issues relating to suicide that we can now bring together by exploring sociological perspectives that offer explanations for suicidal behaviour.

**Positivist approaches**, for example, are based around the idea that knowledge of suicide can be informed by collecting and making sense of empirical evidence. In other words, the focus of these general approaches is the attempt to:

- **Isolate** possible factors in the decision to commit suicide.

- **Correlate** these known factors with incidents of suicide in a variety of ways (on both an individual and cultural level).

## Processes

We can illustrate this focus by thinking about a number of related processes.

**Statistical** analysis of *known suicides* involves the collection and documentation of data that identify suicide patterns and trends. This allows us to make certain statements about the nature of suicidal behaviour and, more importantly perhaps, to *correlate* suicide with different *social characteristics* (age, gender and ethnicity, for example) and *situations* (the effects of unemployment, divorce and the like). **Sale** (2003) notes differences in suicide rates in the UK based on:

- **Gender**: Around 75% of suicides are male.

- **Age**: Rates vary between different age groups (for men, the 25–44 age group consistently has the highest rates).

- **Ethnicity**: South Asian women are three times more likely to kill themselves than other women.

## Correlations

We should also, of course, note possible relationships between different characteristics. **Røn** and **Scourfield** (2005) note: 'Young people struggling with issues of sexuality and gender identity face an increased likelihood of attempting suicide.' The identification of *statistical associations* between suicide and social characteristics allows *positivists* to specify a range of:

**Correlations** between suicide and associated factors (such as age). **Field** (2000) notes how suicide can be correlated with a number of:

- **Long-term factors**, including:

  - **social isolation** (relationship problems with parents, for example)

  - **loss of parents**, through death or divorce

  - **sexual abuse**: In **Van Egmond et al.'s** (1993) research, 50% of sexually abused young women had attempted suicide (although the sample of 158 women was relatively small).

- **Short-term factors** that, when occurring in combination with long-term factors, are likely to push people into suicidal behaviour. These include:

  - **unemployment** (especially long term)

  - **substance abuse** (alcohol or illegal drugs)

  - **financial problems**.

In turn, the identification of correlations can be linked to two further areas:

- **Risk**: One spin-off from this type of analysis is the possibility of creating *risk assessments* for various social groups and categories. By identifying those groups most 'at risk' and correlating these with known short-/long-term risk factors, we can develop *intervention strategies* to identify, support and help individuals 'at risk' of suicide.

## ✳ SYNOPTIC LINK

**Social policy:** The ideas of risk and risk assessment have implications for the development of social policies, not just in the area of suicide but across a range of social behaviours.

- **Explanations**: These can be tailored to particular correlations. For example, explanations for the lower rate of female suicide in the UK involve ideas such as:

  - **Emotional differences**: Women are more likely to seek help with their problems before they get to the stage of suicide.

  - **Methods**: Men use more violent methods (hanging, jumping from a high building) that have a greater certainty of death.

Another way to explain suicide from this general perspective is to think in:

**Algorithmic terms** – a general set of *rules* that can be applied variously to all forms of suicide. **Field** (2000) suggests certain 'life events' (such as abuse and divorce) create two basic types of state:

- **Stable states** represent things 'that won't go away' (such as feelings of pain or remorse).

- **Global states** represent things that affect all areas of someone's life (such as continual depression stemming from feelings of remorse).

**Triggers**: A small, relatively trivial trigger, related to the stable state in some way, may then produce a much larger reaction in the individual and push them into a suicidal frame of mind, a general idea we can develop in the following way.

## Realist approaches

Although similar to their positivist counterparts (in the sense that there are 'real features' of social behaviour to be explained), this approach makes reference to social processes that are not directly observable. Reality, from this position, is:

**Multi-layered: Searle** (1995) argues that social reality consists of two main facts:

- **brute facts** or what we experience as *real* and

- **mental facts** that represent the *meaning* of brute facts.

In terms of suicide, a *brute fact* is that someone kills themselves and a *mental fact* is the meaning we give to this action. In other words, *mental facts* represent a layer of meaning that underpins our interpretation of *brute facts*.

However, a further layer can be added when we reflect on the idea that mental facts are, by definition, socially constructed (people have to agree on the meaning of mental facts). In other words, just as brute facts are significant in terms of how they're interpreted, mental production is itself based on a further, underlying layer. We can apply this to understand suicide in the following way.

The 'top layer' is an observable act, such as someone taking their own life. Since, from statistical analysis, we know this act is not random (there are clear patterns to suicide – in the UK, for example, the majority of suicides are clustered around December and January), there must be something that causes non-random distribution.

The layer underpinning this patterned behaviour, therefore, involves identifying a range of factors 'underlying the fact of suicide' that correlates with the act (for example, social isolation resulting from divorce that leads to 'depression' and hence suicide).

## Causality

For *positivists*, the hunt for causality begins and ends with observable and measurable relationships (for example, when a long-time partner dies and the remaining individual is

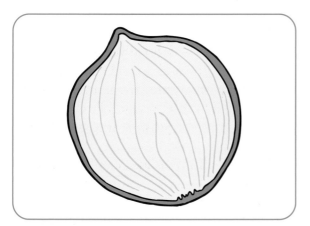

**Realist approaches**
**Think about social reality as being layered –
like an onion.**

over the age of 60 and they have no friends or family, suicide is likely).

Realists, however, want to dig deeper into a further 'layer of reality' to answer the question of what *causes* these *observable relationships*. In other words, although we know that under a certain combination of conditions individuals have an 'increased risk' of suicide, why do these conditions (social isolation, for example) give rise to increased risk? We can answer this question using **Durkheim's** (1897) classic explanation for suicide.

For **Durkheim**, social order was underpinned by two types of organisational pressure:

- **social regulation**, or the general rules that governed individual and cultural behaviour, and

- **social integration**, or the extent to which regulated individuals felt they belonged to a social group.

Regulation and integration, therefore, represent two important *forces* acting on the individual. When these are 'in balance' (the individual is 'normally regulated and integrated') there is no prospect of suicide. **Neeleman et al.** (1998) suggest lower rates of suicide among African-Americans were 'mostly attributable to their relatively high levels of orthodox religious beliefs and devotion' – in other words, they were normally integrated into a belief system that effectively decreased the likelihood of suicide.

However, if these forces are imbalanced (the individual is under-regulated or over-integrated, for example), the *risk* of suicide is increased (an idea expressed in the table on the following page).

| Emile Durkheim: Types of suicide | | | |
|---|---|---|---|
| Social order | Normal form | Pathological form | Type of suicide |
| **Integration** | When 'in balance' the individual is 'protected' from the likelihood of committing suicide | Under-integration | Egoistic |
| | | Over-integration | Altruistic |
| **Regulation** | | Under-regulation | Anomic |
| | | Over-regulation | Fatalistic |

Thus, from this perspective we can note four basic types of suicide:

- **Egoistic** results from a failure (within a social group whose membership the individual values) of group members to return the intense feelings of belonging held by the individual. Suicide derives from a weakening of the social ties that bind the individual to the group. When people become detached from group values and expectations they suffer what **Durkheim** termed an 'excess of individualism', resulting in suicide becoming a strong behavioural response.

- **Altruistic**: Individuals so closely associate themselves with a particular social group that their identity is submerged into that of the group itself. Thus, someone who feels they have shamed or disgraced the group may see suicide as a means of atonement.

- **Anomic**: **Nisbet** (1967) suggests this type of suicide is caused '... by the sudden dislocation of normative systems – the breakdown of values by which one may have lived for a lifetime'. In other words, where an individual becomes confused or uncertain about their world (through sudden, life-changing events, for example), the risk of suicide is increased.

- **Fatalistic**: Suicide results when the individual sees no possibility of relief from 'oppressive social discipline and

## ⌂ The potting shed: Types of suicide

Identify some additional examples of **Durkheim's** different types of suicide – we've done the first ones for you.

| Egoistic | Altruistic | Anomic | Fatalistic |
|---|---|---|---|
| Death of long-time partner | Suicide bomber | Bankrupt | Political prisoner held without trial |

regulation'. Suicide, in effect, becomes a means of escape.

Realist and positivist methodologies are not incompatible (as **Durkheim's** work demonstrates); whereas realist perspectives may highlight a range of general, underlying factors that increases the risk of suicide (such as anomie/lack of social regulation), positivist/empiricist studies can, in some instances, build on this insight to 'fine-tune' particular forms of explanation – for example, to examine empirically a range of anomic factors (such as periods of severe economic depression) and their particular relationship to suicide.

 Weeding the path

To complete this section we can briefly note how:

**Interpretivist approaches** have contributed to our understanding of suicide in a couple of ways:

- **Problematics**: As we've suggested, interpretivist sociology has questioned the extent to which we can take suicide data (mainly, but not exclusively, in the form of *official statistics*) at face value – in terms of the idea that statistics represent 'social facts' independent of the (subjective) decision-making processes by which they're created. **Payne** and **Lart** (1998) identify a couple of problematic features of both:

  - **Completed suicides** and
  - **Incomplete suicides** (*parasuicides*) – situations where an individual has engaged in some form of life-threatening, *self-harming* behaviour.

This distinction is important because any discussion of suicide must take into account both those who are successful and those who are not.

- **Recording**: Just as not all 'suicides' are necessarily classified as such (a range of *misclassifications* will affect the reliability of suicide data), the same is undoubtedly true for parasuicide. As **Platt** (1992) suggests, our (partial) knowledge of parasuicide is limited by the way it may (or may not) be reported. By and large our knowledge comes from hospital/medical records and this raises two main problems of *data validity*.

First, not all parasuicides are brought to the attention of the medical profession. Second, if our knowledge of parasuicides is based on partial records, and we use this knowledge to inform possible theoretical explanations of suicide (by assuming that parasuicides are simply 'unsuccessful suicides'), we run the risk of generalising from incomplete data. As **Platt** notes, the majority of parasuicides that come to official attention involve self-poisoning – and the majority of these are female. This, if we're not careful, leads to the *erroneous* (unjustified) conclusion that women are more likely than men to survive suicide attempts and that female attempts at suicide are not a 'real attempt' but rather a 'cry for help'.

## Objectivity and subjectivity

As we've seen, attempting to correlate various objective factors (employment status and age, for example) to suicide is relatively straightforward. Subjective factors (the individual's 'state of mind', for example) are much less straightforward and subject to revisionism from a variety of sources, both official (coroners, for example) and unofficial (such as family or friends). Even when dealing with parasuicide, where the victim may be willing to talk about their behaviour, it's by no means certain that a researcher can get at 'the truth' (either because the parasuicide is unwilling to give it or, more likely perhaps, because there is the danger that accounts are simply *revisions* (reconstructions and reinterpretations) of a mass of confusing and possibly contradictory feelings and actions.

(Answer to 'You the Jury': A verdict of suicide was given in the real case from which this question was constructed.)

# CHAPTER 6

# Stratification and differentiation

This chapter examines concepts of *social stratification* and *differentiation* through a range of ideas, from definitions of stratification and the measurement of social class, through the impact of stratification on *life chances* and *social mobility,* to an assessment of how and why the class structure in contemporary British society is changing.

We can begin, however, by thinking initially about the meaning of differentiation and stratification before exploring both class- and status-based theories in more detail.

## 1. Different theories of stratification

### Preparing the ground: Differentiation and stratification

To say there are many ways that people are 'different' is an interesting (if not particularly profound) observation, the validity of which is evidenced by simply looking around – something we can do in the warm-up exercise below.

When we talk about 'difference', therefore, we're making a fairly *neutral comparison* between 'things that are not the same' in the sense that all we're effectively saying is that differences exist (in much the same way as we might observe that 'daylight' is different to 'darkness'). The fact of human difference is not, in itself, particularly significant. What is significant, however, is the:

**Meaning** of these differences. A teacher, for example, is different to the students he or she teaches. However, if a teacher can direct and control the behaviour of their students *because* of this difference, this becomes something of greater significance because it involves:

- **Social differentiation**: When we *socially differentiate* between, say, a teacher and their students, we make a *judgement* about

---

**WARM-UP: SPOTTING THE DIFFERENCE**

In small groups, make two lists of 'differences between people', based on the following categories (we've given you a couple of examples to get you started):

| Physical/Biological differences | Social differences |
| --- | --- |
| Hair colour | Level of income |

As a class, combine your ideas to produce an overall list of these differences.

---

their relative worth (or *status*). We are saying, in effect, that these people are not merely 'different', but that the difference is significant because it's rooted in the nature of their relationship, considered, for example, in terms of:

- **Inequality**: A teacher has a different social status to their students, one that allows them to do things (such as direct the behaviour of the class) that students are not allowed to do. This, in turn, is related to concepts of:

- **Ideology** because social differentiation involves ideas about how teachers and students should behave in terms of:

  - **Values** relating to the teacher and student roles, and

  - **Norms** that operate within the classroom.

- **Power**: Social differentiation involves the idea that people of different statuses have differential access to power. A teacher may, within reason, punish a student, but the student has no such power.

## The potting shed

From any *two* areas of the Specification (except education), give *one* example from *each* area of inequality based on social differentiation.

If social differentiation relates to the idea that some forms of difference have a higher level of social significance (*status*) than others, it's a short step to think about their *relative status* in *hierarchical* terms, which is where we can start to talk about:

**Social stratification**: This represents a process whereby different social groups are ranked higher or lower on some form of scale, usually, but not exclusively, in terms of categories such as *class*, *age*, *gender* and *ethnicity*. Sociologically, **Giddens** (2001) defines stratification as 'structured inequalities between different groupings' while **Crompton** (1993) argues it involves 'a hierarchical system of inequality (material and symbolic), always supported by a meaning system that seeks to justify inequality'.

Historically there have been a number of different:

**Types of** stratification, involving major forms such as:

- **slave** systems that have appeared throughout human history (from Ancient Greece and Rome to eighteenth/nineteenth-century Britain and the USA)

- **caste** systems (characteristic of some parts of South East Asia)

- **estates** systems (characteristic of feudal or early modern societies) and, of course,

- **class** systems, which characterise stratification in modern societies such as Britain. In this respect, class stratification *in our society* is conventionally considered a:

**Primary** system of stratification (with stratification based around age, gender and ethnicity being *secondary* forms), on the basis that economic rankings (and their associated inequalities) have greater impact on people's lives than inequalities associated with non-economic differences in *status* (which may, of course, develop alongside primary systems – upper-class men, for

# ⚠ Growing it yourself: Who goes? Who stays? You decide

This exercise requires students, initially in small groups, to both differentiate (or assess the relative worth of) and stratify (divide into categories) a group of people with varying social characteristics.

Following a devastating shipwreck, 15 survivors have managed to scramble into a small lifeboat. Unfortunately, with no hope of immediate rescue and sufficient provisions to support only 9 survivors until they reach landfall, you have to decide which 6 of the following must be thrown overboard:

Prostitute (36): Both parents are dead. A paramedic nurse.
Multimillionaire industrialist (57). Will give you £1 million to stay in the lifeboat.
Catholic priest (64): History of mental illness and depression.
Muslim cleric (46): Has extensive knowledge of the area in which you are now travelling.
Shoe salesman (33): Divorced. Has some navigation skills.
Young child (5): Parents still alive but both HIV positive.
Black male (29): Married with three young children.
Research biologist (69): Unmarried, with adult daughter. On the boat has worked out how to produce cheap, effective AIDS vaccine.
Married couple (23 and 25): She is an alcoholic. Two young sons at home.
Male (43): Suspected child abuser (unproven). Unmarried. A sail-maker.
White male (28): Has history of drug abuse and petty crime. Good fisherman.
Senior diplomat (59): Returning home with agreement to avert war between two countries.
Cabaret artist (32): Transvestite. Excellent storyteller and singer.
Olympic rower (20): Studying medicine at Oxford and recently diagnosed as typhoid carrier.

Once the choices have been made, each group should report back to the class, justifying why they chose some people to survive and some to be sacrificed.

example, may have a different social status to upper-class women).

Scott (1999), for example, argues *social stratification* '... emphasises the idea that individuals are distributed among the levels or *layers* of a social hierarchy because of their *economic* relationships'. For **Scott**, social stratification is a *particular form* of **social division** that differs from other types of division on the basis that it is 'solidly based in *economic relations*'.

## ⚠ Digging deeper: Types of stratification

We can outline the general characteristics of the different types of stratification we've just identified in the following terms.

## Slave systems

**Slavery** is one of the oldest (and most persistent) forms of stratification that involves, according to **Mazur** (1996), a situation in which one group claims *ownership* over another, such that the former take upon themselves 'the right to use, abuse and take the fruits of the latter's labour'. The slave, therefore, is the:

- **Property** of their owner. Slave systems arguably reached their height in Europe and the USA between the seventeenth and nineteenth centuries, when the capture and shipment of slaves from Africa (in particular) took on a global dimension. Perhaps the most familiar example of a slave-based modern society is that of the US southern states in the nineteenth century, a tightly regulated system supported by a variety of laws governing the behaviour of the *enslaved* (whether they could marry, where they could live, when and if they could travel and so forth).

Although opinions differ as to whether slaves can be considered a 'class' in the same way that slave owners were a class – **Gingrich** (2002), for example, suggests slaves are a *status group* because, in **Weberian** terms, 'they have nothing to sell' and hence have no *market situation* – it's clear that, in status terms, slaves were always at the very bottom of society, or even outside it. Slave status was also:

**Ascribed** – children born to slave parents also became slaves. Slaves could, however, be given their freedom by their owners.

The basic belief system (ideology) underpinning slavery, at least in early modern society, was usually one of *biological superiority* – slaves were 'naturally inferior' to their owners.

## Feudal (estate) systems

**Estate systems** characterise *pre-modern, pre-industrial, agrarian* (agricultural) societies,

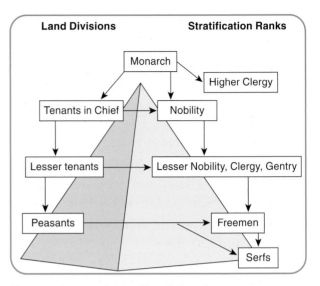

The estates system (feudalism)

such as Britain in the sixteenth century, and are based around:

- **Land ownership**: In agricultural (or *feudal*) societies, where there are no factories or machines to produce goods, farming is the main economic activity, which makes land the single most important commodity. To own land, therefore, is to be powerful, since you control something vital to the lives of thousands, if not millions, of people. Land ownership was not distributed fairly or equally and, in feudal Britain, land could not be *legally owned*; it was considered the property of God and, as such, was held 'in trust' by the monarch, as God's earthly representative. Land was delegated, initially by the monarch, in a:
- **Pyramid structure** of land divisions and stratification ranks.

## ✳ SYNOPTIC LINK

**Power and politics:** The feudal (estates) system links into elite theories of the state.

The system was based on a strong structure of *rights and duties*, underpinned by:

- **A religious belief system** that stressed its 'divine nature'. The Church taught that God had created the world in His image and, since God was all-powerful, it was not for mere mortals to question or challenge the social order.
- **Military might**, consolidated in the hands of the nobility and their knight-retainers.
- **Legal sanctions**: different levels in the structure had different legal rights – serfs, for example, although not slaves, were under the control and patronage of their feudal lord, who could impose restrictions on their behaviour: whom they could marry, where they could live and so forth.

## Caste systems

The caste system has existed for around 3000 years, mainly in India, where the influence of the *Hindu religion* has been traditionally strong (although, as **Kane** (2004) notes, variations have appeared in countries such as Brazil). The system involves the division of society into five major caste groups (*varna*), each traditionally associated with a particular form of work. Each major caste is sub-divided into thousands of different sub-castes (*jatis*).

| The caste (varna) system | |
|---|---|
| Major castes | Example caste occupations |
| **Brahmin** | Priest, teacher |
| **Kshatriya** | Soldier, landowner |
| **Vaishya** | Businessman, farmer |
| **Shudra** | Manual worker, servant |
| **Harijan** ('**Untouchables**') | Roadsweeper |

Conventionally, the caste system is portrayed as a:

**Closed system** of stratification (no individual movement up or down the class structure), with a couple of exceptions:

- **Sub-castes** (*jatis*) can improve their social status in the hierarchy (they can move up or down within the major caste categories).
- **Individuals** can lose their caste position by breaking caste law (such as marrying outside their caste). When this occurs, they become 'out-caste' – in effect, relegated to the lowest position in the caste hierarchy (*harijan* or, as it was formerly known in the West, '*Untouchable*').

## ✷ SYNOPTIC LINK

**Stratification and differentiation:** Caste systems are examples of absolute social mobility.

**Ascribed**: Caste positions are given at birth, based on parental caste position. Each caste is, therefore, *endogamous* – self-contained and allowing marriage only between members of the same caste.

## ✷ SYNOPTIC LINK

**Families and households:** Note the association between religious beliefs (Hinduism) and the concept of the arranged marriage.

The system, although based around *occupational groupings*, is underpinned by a Hindu religious belief system that stresses two important concepts:

- **Reincarnation** (*kharma*) – the belief that once someone dies they are reborn.

therefore, represent *necessary* motivations and rewards that lead to the development of inequalities and social hierarchies. For **Davis** and **Moore**, these represent 'an unconsciously evolved device by which societies ensure the most important positions are conscientiously filled by the most qualified people'.

## Weeding the path

Support for classical functionalism has, in recent times, come from writers such as **Lenski** (1994), whose analysis of 'Marxist social systems' (such as China and North Korea) suggested that social stratification, developed along classical functionalist lines, was inevitable, necessary and functional – 'incentive systems' are required to motivate and reward the 'best qualified people' for occupying the 'most important positions' within a social system. Conventional criticisms of this general approach, however, have focused on two main areas:

- **Empirical**: **Tumin** (1953) questions the idea that we can measure differences in the 'functional importance' of different roles.

- **Subjectivity**: Concepts of 'functional importance' are, at root, value judgements about the relative worth of different roles (is a well-paid company director a more 'functionally important' role than that of a nurse?).

More fundamental criticisms of this approach can be examined through the work of (neo-functionalist) writers such as **Alexander** (1995) and **Luhmann** (1997). However, since these apply equally to other types of 'modernist theories of stratification' we can examine them in a moment, after

we've outlined a couple of alternative explanations.

## Marxism

**Marxist theories:** Social stratification from this position is an:

**Inevitable** feature of contemporary capitalist societies, based around *economic* relationships and inequalities related to *social classes* – broad groups that share a common economic, political and ideological background. We can identify a range of ideas generally characteristic of Marxist analysis in the following terms:

**Economic behaviour** is the most significant activity in any society because, as we've previously suggested, it is through work that people produce the means of survival on which all other forms of behaviour (politics and culture, for example) are dependent.

## ✳ SYNOPTIC LINK

**Religion:** This idea is related to the *'economic base/political and ideological superstructure'* distinction we outlined in relation to exclusive approaches to religion.

Different types of society (such as *feudalism* and *capitalism*) organise economic behaviour in significantly different ways, but all are characterised by a specific:

**Mode of production** that, for our purposes, consists of two broad ideas:

- **Means of production** refers to the things (such as land, machinery, buildings and investment capital) used to produce commodities. People are not part of the means of production, since their role is played out in terms of:

- **Social relations to production**: This refers to the relationships that exist *within* a mode of production. In capitalist societies, for example, the main social relationship is 'employer–employee' and it derives from the important distinction between two ideas:

  - **ownership** of the means of production (the sphere of *capital*), and

  - **non-ownership**, a sphere consisting of people who sell their ability to work (their *labour power* – in capitalist societies people are neither *slaves* nor *serfs*; they are 'free' economic actors in the sense that they can 'choose' to whom they sell their labour power for the best possible wage).

Social stratification is based around the economic system (into which people are born and socialised), structured in terms of these relationships to the means of production. In *classical Marxism*, the economic structure gives rise to *two basic classes* (owners and non-owners, or the *bourgeoisie* and the *proletariat*); for neo-Marxists the *growth* of a 'third class' in modern capitalism (the 'middle' or 'petit bourgeoisie') – consisting of intellectuals, knowledge workers, professionals and managers at the higher levels and the self-employed at the lower – complicates the general class picture since this class involves people who *neither* wholly own the means of production *nor* are simply 'waged workers'. Writers like **Poulantzas** (1974) generally refer to this class as occupying a *contradictory* class position.

## ⚠ Weeding the path

Marxism offers a way of understanding stratification and differentiation in a way that is both:

- **objective**, in the sense that class positions in a stratification system can be 'read off' from people's economic relationships, and

- **empirical**, in the sense that social class can be linked objectively to social inequalities that derive from different class positions.

However, a major criticism relates to ideas about alternative forms of stratification/inequality based around:

**Gender** and **ethnicity**: **Dahrendorf** (1959), among others, argues that economic and political power are not necessarily the same thing. In other words, the question arises as to whether economic divisions are the only (or main) basis for social stratification in modern societies. As in the example of the *caste system*, Marxists generally explain ideas like *sexual* and *racial discrimination* in *economic* terms – as developments from the unequal distribution of power in society based ultimately (or 'in the last instance', as neo-Marxists such as **Poulantzas** (1974) like to put it) on unequal economic positions. Other *conflict theorists* have argued this is a mistaken interpretation.

## Weberian

**Weberian theories** of stratification are based on two fundamental ideas:

- **Social resources** (anything that is valued in a society). Where competition exists in any society, some people will have greater access to, ownership of and control over social resources, which **Weber** (1922) classified as belonging to three main types:

  - **class** (or **economic**) resources, such as income, wealth, possessions and so forth

... use to get along with the dominant groups about them'.

## Ethnicity

**Ethnic group stratification**: An initial problem we face is how to define reliably and validly the concept of 'an ethnic group', where 'ethnicity' conventionally refers to:

**Cultural differences** between groups (such as religion, family structures and organisations, ideological beliefs, values and norms). Part of the reason for this approach is to distinguish ethnicity from:

**Race** – an academically discredited concept that refers to supposed *genetic* or *biological* differences between 'racial types' (white, black, Asian and so forth). Although there is a general sociological consensus that ethnicity is more useful than race in the differentiation of social groups, problems with the concept of ethnicity relate to ideas like:

- **Categorisations**: In particular, differences between the way sociologists conceptualise ethnic groups and the way these groups label both themselves and each other.

- **Heterogeneity**: As with any classification system, it's easy to assume that ethnic groups are homogeneous categories – something that's rarely the case. Just as groups like 'working class' or 'men' have a wide range of differences within them, the same is true for ethnic groups. Clear, precise and unambiguous culture-based definitions of ethnic groups are, in reality, extraordinarily difficult to construct. This difficulty also makes it hard to distinguish in meaningful ways between different 'ethnic groups'.

- **Boundaries**: Two problems present

### ⚜ Growing it yourself: Defining ethnicity

Think about how to define the idea of an 'English' ethnic group:

- **What are the unique cultural characteristics of this group that clearly distinguish it from other ethnic groups?**

- **What problems are involved in creating a precise definition of this group that clearly marks it as a coherent group, different from other ethnic groups in our society?**

themselves here. First, how do we define the boundaries *between* different ethnic groups (and is it possible for people to belong to *different* ethnic groups at the same time)? Second, to what level of depth do we go when classifying ethnicities – do they, for example, exist as international, national or local forms?

## Types

Notwithstanding the difficulties of differentiation, stratification systems involving ethnic hierarchies can be divided, historically, into two main types:

- **Biological** systems where things like skin colour have been used to determine an individual's stratification position. A recent example here is the South African *apartheid* system where three classifications were used (white, coloured and black).

- **Ethnic systems** that involve the use of *cultural characteristics* (such as religion) to discriminate against individuals or groups, such that they are denied equality of status, income, opportunity and the like. These take two basic forms: societies where discrimination is overt and legally tolerated (such as the treatment of Jews in Nazi Germany or the practice of 'ethnic cleansing' in Bosnia in the 1990s) and societies where racist ideas and practices contribute to minority ethnic groups being in the lowest positions in the stratification system.

## ⚠️ Digging deeper: Age, gender and ethnic stratification

We can dig a little deeper into this area by thinking about possible theoretical explanations for status-based stratification:

## Age

Theoretical explanations for the presence, persistence and general form of age stratification in contemporary societies fall into three broad categories:

**Modernisation theory** suggests that the significance – or otherwise – of age stratification varies in relation to *social change* and, in particular, the transition from pre-industrial (pre-modern) to industrial (modern) society. In the former, where class-based forms of stratification are absent, some type of:

- **Age-grading** system tends to develop. This involves peer groups forming *age-sets*, where, as **Giddens** (2001) notes, each generation has certain rights and responsibilities that change with age. In the modern period age-setting is still common in some *traditional societies*, such as the Maasai in modern Kenya,

according to **Johnson** and **Tumanka** (2004), but *rigid* age-grading is not the norm in modern societies. This isn't to say age-grading doesn't occur in modern societies, but its general form is different – it is, for example, not as *systematic* as an *age-set* system.

Within modernisation theory, economic changes produce cultural changes; for example, the need for trained labour produces an education system that, in turn, creates age-stratified concepts (such as 'youth'). Similarly, at the opposite end of the age scale, longer life expectancies and the idea of 'retirement' produce concepts of old age. In this respect, age boundaries are marked by:

- **Rites of passage** that include, for instance, an eighteenth birthday party as formally marking the transition from 'youth' to 'adult' status, just as retirement marks the passage into formal old age.

## ⚠️ Weeding the path

Modernisation theory is strongest when it focuses on areas like the elderly as a distinctive status group in modern societies since 'old age' is marked by a relatively strong *rite of passage* (retirement). **Avramov** and **Maskova** (2003) argue that modernisation theory has successfully identified '. . . changes in society that are likely to reduce the status of older people', such as those suggested by **Cowgill** (1974) – the elderly as 'underemployed, untrained in the latest technologies and separated from family/community webs of relationships'. However, it's arguable this boundary has grown fuzzier in recent times and **Kiemo** (2004) also suggests that social and economic changes do not impact uniformly on this age group, which makes it difficult to see 'the elderly' as a distinctive stratum in modern societies in any but the broadest sense.

**Cohort (age stratification)** theory focuses on societies having what **Marshall** (1996) terms an 'age structure associated with different roles and statuses'. In this respect 'age' is considered as a *group*, rather than an individual, construct; the relative status of whole groups (cohorts) changes with age – think, for example, in terms of broad categories like child, youth, adult and elderly (with a range of subdivisions within each category – youth can involve subdivisions like 'teen', for example) and the different statuses they attract. Age stratification by *cohort*, therefore, is a flexible interpretation of structural differences in age groups; as each cohort ages (biologically/chronologically) they attract a range of socially produced roles, self-concepts and identity changes in the form of:

- **Normative expectations** associated with age. **Zhou** (1997) suggests 'age is a basis for acquiring roles, status, and deference from others in society. When people become old, they exit roles as workers and take on roles as retirees'. In addition, **Riley** (1994) argues that people born into the same cohort have similar '… experiences in time and may share meanings, ideologies, orientations, attitudes and values'.

## Weeding the path

One strength of this interpretation is that cohort theory reflects the way social changes impact on different cohorts in different ways at different times. As **Riley** suggests, the life experiences of a young adult today are very different to those of a young adult a century ago.

## The potting shed

Identify and briefly explain two possible differences between the lives of a 15-year-old in your society and someone of the same age 100 years ago.

**Life course theory:** Although related to cohort theory, life course perspectives suggest the concept of:

- **Chronological age** is increasingly fuzzy and unhelpful in modern societies (for the sorts of reasons **Riley** (1994) suggests) and has developed the concept of:

- **Social age** – the idea that, over an individual's lifetime, certain structured 'life events' mark the transition to different life phases and experiences. **Mitchell's** (2003) summary of life course theory suggests three related areas of interest:

- **Transitions:** The study of major 'life events' (starting and leaving school, marriage, starting work, retirement and so forth) and their impact on individual identities.

- **Norms,** in the sense of both general social perceptions of 'age-related appropriate or inappropriate' behaviour and the specific sense of how individuals interpret, incorporate or reject these norms.

- **Perceptions:** Societies not only develop ideas about normative rules associated *with* age categories, but they also develop ideas *about* age categories – the point at which youth changes to adulthood and so forth.

In general, therefore, this position synthesises concepts of individual age identities (how they develop and change) within the general structure of a (loose) age-related stratification system based around normative and status considerations and expectations.

## Weeding the path

While there is evidence of age-related grading systems in modern societies, there are doubts about whether this relates specifically to *social stratification*, as opposed to age-based *social inequalities* – the fact that some, but not all, elderly people in our society live in poverty illustrates this idea. The situation is further complicated by age-grading being both subtle and flexible – there are few, if any, rigid normative/status associations in our society wholly related to age. More specifically, however, problems with conceptualising age stratification revolve around:

- **Boundary marking** – where does one 'age group' begin and end, for example, and to what extent are age boundaries subjectively constructed?
- **Group composition and definition**: Age groups, however defined, invariably encompass a wide variety of behaviours.

- **Fragmentation**: Although we can identify general normative expectations relating to age as a status system ('big boys don't cry'), policing and enforcement are rudimentary and largely informal, even in terms of rites of passage – does adulthood begin at 16, 18 or 21? This suggests that age stratification, at least in modern societies, is not a particularly consistent concept.

## Gender

**Gender stratification**: Although gender in contemporary societies is, as **Ferree et al.** (2005) argue, '... recognised as a major social force ... a core institution of all societies and the location of significant structural inequality', a key question is the extent to which *gender inequalities* are based on *gender stratification* – the answer to which involves considering a variety of theoretical positions:

**Traditional approaches** to gender stratification have generally taken two forms:

- **Marginalisation**: Characteristic of neo-functionalist approaches, this position

## Growing it yourself: Normative expectations

In small groups, identify as many different normative expectations as you can for the following age statuses in our society.

| Baby Child | Teenager Youth | Young adult Middle-aged | Elderly |
|---|---|---|---|
| | | | |

As a class, consider how these expectations may vary in terms of gender and over time.

divided male and female roles into 'expressive and instrumental functions' that relegated women to a 'supporting role' within the family.

• **Conflation**: This position focuses on stratification as a *group* phenomenon in the sense that individual status positions are mediated by social relationships. Stratification, in this respect, is theorized in terms of partnerships – based, for example, on the concept of 'a family group' sharing the same general status regardless of the individual statuses of its members. **Goldthorpe** (1983) argues this is not unreasonable given such groups are likely to share broadly similar social/market situations. **Parkin** (1971) supports this general approach when he argues that, although 'female status carries with it many disadvantages ... inequalities associated with sex differences are not usefully thought of as components of stratification. This is because for the great majority of women the allocation of social and economic rewards is determined primarily by the position of their families and, in particular, that of the male head'. Conversely, **Ferree et al.** argue that this approach ignores marked male and female status differences (even within the same general class position).

**Cross-difference models** reflect a more contemporary approach to gender stratification. **Eichler** (1980) argues that gender stratification tends to be obscured by class stratification and 'female exploitation' within the home is not the same as 'employee exploitation'. Women, in particular, suffer dual forms of stratification:

• **class-based** in the workplace as they increasingly occupy paid work roles

• **quasi-feudal** within the home where men and women take on a form of 'master–serf' relationship – each partner has certain rights and responsibilities towards the other, but ultimately it is men who gain most benefit.

## Intersections

This approach, therefore, suggests we need to understand stratification in terms of the way class and gender intersect.

**Individual models**, as **Stanworth** (1984) has argued, see *social* stratification as involving more than a 'simple economic relationship'; that is, we need to think about how every individual in a society is open to a range of defining memberships of different stratifying forms – from economic class, through gender and ethnicity, to age. This, as **Ferree** and **Hall** (1996) argue, would avoid the still common sociological practice of placing 'gender as a micro-level issue ... ethnicity as a mid-level problem and only class as a macro-level structure relevant for organizing a whole society'.

**Class accentuation models**, as developed by writers such as **Bonney** (1988), focus on the decline in the 'male breadwinner' in our society (**Creighton**, 1999) and suggest that dual-earner families have a distorted (*accentuated*) position in any stratification structure. The position of family partners (male or female) may be *accentuated* or *devalued* by the fact of their association – individual social statuses, therefore, are affected not just by 'who they are' and 'what they do', but also by 'whom they are with'. Theories of stratification, therefore, must take into account the different ways concepts like class, gender and ethnicity intersect and interact.

## Weeding the path

Although it's not difficult to find evidence of gender inequalities, both male and female, in contemporary societies, the question remains one of whether these are structured in ways that mean men and women occupy different hierarchical positions in society on the basis of gender alone. Although the picture is complicated by variables like social class, there is evidence at least to suggest gender stratification exists in two spheres:

- **The public**, illustrated by **Husmo** (1999) in relation to Norwegian fish processing, where the 'division of labour . . . is based on an idea of gender-related characteristics which make men and women suitable for different tasks'. This idea of 'biological difference' leading to different gender capabilities still resonates in modern societies and arguably forms the basis for gendered (horizontal and vertical) stratification within the workplace.

- **The private** (mainly the home) where stratification based on patriarchal ideologies is evidenced by the fact that women generally play a *service role* (subservient to the requirements of male partners) within the family.

## ✳ SYNOPTIC LINK

**Family:** This sphere provides numerous examples of a gendered division of labour in modern society (involving ideas such as women's double/triple shift).

## Ethnicity

**Ethnic stratification**: Two initial concepts are useful here:

- **Institutionalised racism** involves the idea of ethnic status differences being built into the structure of society (such as the *apartheid* system in South Africa) or organisations (such as the police).

## ✳ SYNOPTIC LINK

**Power and politics:** The **Macpherson Report** (1999) into the police handling of the murder of Stephen Lawrence identified 'institutional racism' as a factor in the unsolved killing.

- **Disproportionate representation** involves an ethnic (usually minority) group being over-represented at the bottom of the stratification system as the result of a complex interplay of factors involving class, status and power.

## Perspectives

These ideas are not mutually exclusive, of course, and we can explore them in more detail through a range of different perspectives on ethnic stratification:

**Marxist perspectives**: Although **Hall** (1980) has argued that ethnicity is a significant dimension of stratification in capitalist societies, it is generally seen by Marxists as a secondary form – one that exists within (and because of) class stratification. As **Leonardo** (2004) puts it, ethnicity in 'orthodox class analysis is significant but secondary at best'. This follows because ethnic distinctions (like those of the concept of race it replaced) are created from the exercise of power. That is, for *status* discrimination to occur – to place, in **Hall's** terms, *social distance* between hierarchically arranged groups – a discriminating group has to be initially more powerful, and the source of such power is economic organisation and relationships. Thus, although:

**Ethnic inequality** reflects status differences manufactured within a stratification system, the concept of *ethnic stratification* itself is relatively meaningless. As **Leonardo** notes: 'The racial experiences of African-Americans, Latinos, Whites, and Asian Americans determined by the economy' are reduced to a:

**Reflex status**: Ethnic discrimination and secondary stratification occur, in other words, as a consequence of economic factors, something evidenced by the:

**Fragmented** nature of ethnic stratification in contemporary societies. The status position of individuals within different ethnic groups is, first, determined by their class relationships and *then* by their ethnicity – the emergence of a 'black middle class' in countries like Britain and the USA is instructive in this respect.

## ✳ SYNOPTIC LINK

**Education:** From this position, ethnic group success or failure is explained mainly in terms of their relative class positions.

**Hall** (1996) summarises this general position when he argues: 'Race is a mode of how class is lived.' In other words, ethnic minority experience of discrimination and inequality is a manifest expression of latent *class inequality*.

## Functionalist/New Right

**Functionalist perspectives** generally – and neo-functionalist forms of **New Right** theorising in particular – focus on the problem of:

**Integration** in relation to ethnic forms of stratification, conventionally in ways relating to the failure or inability of minority groups to become fully integrated into the value and normative system of the *dominant culture*. This is particularly apparent in relation to New Right theories of the:

**Underclass** advanced by writers like **Murray and Phillips** (2001) in the USA and **Saunders** (1990) in the UK. The 'disproportionate representation' of ethnic minorities in the underclass is related to failures in their:

**Cultural organisation** – the argument that some ethnic minorities 'disadvantage themselves' through things like:

- **Family organisation**: Some groups adopt (through choice or necessity) a family form (single parenthood) that disadvantages them in the labour market. This disadvantaged *market situation* is reflected, for the New Right, in a couple of ways:

- **Welfare dependency**, a situation where the 'cultural choices' of some minority groups (the source, it's argued, of their low social status) are supported by the welfare state, leading to a situation that *reinforces*, rather than improves, their status.

- **Cycle of deprivation**: For **Saunders**, *dependency cultures* involve a passive and fatalistic acceptance of low status that is, in turn, transmitted through different generations (from parents to children) in the form of low educational and work expectations. This, in turn, leads to minorities taking on an:

- **Outsider status**: A failure to *integrate* with a dominant culture by taking advantage of opportunities for status advancement (through education, for example) inevitably places such groups in a weak market situation, where their failure to compete successfully leads to cultural separation – different ethnic groups move in different economic and cultural spheres.

## ✳ SYNOPTIC LINK

**Family/wealth, poverty and welfare:**
New Right ideas about the underclass can be related to family organisation and diversity as well as to explanations of poverty based around ideas such as cultures of poverty.

## ⚠ Weeding the path

New Right explanations focus on how different ethnic groups (and groups within these groups) are differently placed in stratification systems. Asian Indians in the UK, for example, achieve higher than average educational qualifications and are proportionately over-represented in professional occupations; yet this group also has higher than average levels of educational underachievement. These observations suggest, for the New Right, that explanations for status positions are to be found mainly within the social organisation of minority groups themselves – a position that does involve a number of problems.

**Blaming the victim**: By starting from the assumption that stratification is both *functional* and *inevitable*, this form of explanation is forced to focus on the *cultural attributes* of those groups within the stratification system. Thus, if those at the top have different attributes to those at the bottom, it simply becomes a matter of identifying cultural characteristics that are:

**Structurally functional** and **dysfunctional** and attributing causality accordingly. By focusing on the (supposed) dysfunctional qualities of those at the lowest levels of any stratification system, this process effectively 'blames the victims' for their subordinate position and ignores the role of economic, political and ideological forms of discrimination in the creation of such characteristics.

**Integration**: This idea raises two main questions. First, is there a *dominant culture* into which subordinate groups can *integrate?* And second, is the stratification system open to *assimilation* – do dominant ethnic groups, for example, attempt to enhance their status at the expense of subordinate ethnic groups?

**Social closure**: In this respect we need to consider how dominant groups may operate in terms of closing off entry; rather than, for example, 'blaming minorities' for their failure to integrate, it might be more fruitful to investigate how dominant groups prevent integration through their individual and collective behaviours.

## Weberian

This general perspective, as we've suggested, examines the interplay between concepts of class, status and power and how they impact on the social standing of ethnic groups in a number of ways:

- **Class**: Ethnic minorities are concentrated in low-pay, low-skill, non-unionised work, as well as having a disproportionate presence among the unemployed.
- **Status**: Racial discrimination is a form of *status discrimination*, since an individual is considered to have a lower social status if they are part of a 'despised/hated' social group. In this respect, discrimination

lowers the status of ethnic minorities and contributes towards their differential treatment in all areas of society (especially employment) as well as preventing integration by forcing such groups to find status within their own particular cultural settings.

- **Power**: Partly as a result of their lower class and status positions, ethnic groups are:

  - **Politically marginalised**: Trade unions, for example, find it difficult to recruit among ethnic minorities because the nature of their employment tends to be in small, non-unionised companies, while in Britain, for example, no major political party *directly* represents the interests of ethnic minorities.

Ethnic groups, therefore, generally occupy a weak market position; on the one hand, they may lack the technical skills and qualifications required to improve this situation, while on the other they suffer higher levels of implicit and explicit racial discrimination that reinforces this weak position.

# The potting shed

**Identify and briefly explain two ways ethnic minorities in our society are portrayed as 'a social problem'.**

## Moving on

In this section we've suggested that the main form of social stratification in our society is based on social class. In the next section we can examine this position in more detail by looking first at how we define class in modern societies, and second at the relationship between occupation and class position.

# 2. Different ways of measuring social class and the relationship between occupation and social class

This section examines the concept of social class as an important dimension of stratification in modern societies, something that involves thinking about how that class can be defined (both objectively and subjectively) and measured using a range of classification scales.

## Preparing the ground: Measuring social class

In the previous section we suggested that social classes can be seen as relatively permanent, homogeneous, social divisions to which individuals sharing similar values, lifestyles, interests and behaviours can be assigned. There are, however, two immediate problems we face:

**Defining classes**: We need to develop a practical definition that can be applied to the problem of:

**Measuring class**: It would be useful, when talking about social stratification, to clearly identify different class positions and the characteristics of the individuals and groups that occupy them.

In this respect, we can begin by suggesting three related dimensions to class:

- **Economic**: Scott (1999) argues this is a *primary dimension* of class and can be measured by indicators such as wealth, income and occupation.

- **Political**: This *secondary dimension* of class can be measured by indicators of status and power on the basis that economically successful groups tend, in the main, to have higher levels of associated status and to command greater levels of power.

- **Cultural**: This is a further secondary dimension that can be measured by indicators relating to lifestyle, values, beliefs, norms and level of education. Economic position influences this aspect through the development of cultural lifestyles (associated with the type of status symbols people acquire, their leisure pursuits and so forth).

These dimensions – and how they interrelate – are important here because, as **Barratt** (2005) puts it: 'Economic capital alone does not make one upper class ... it provides experiences and opportunities that enhance cultural, social, and academic capital.' In other words, social class is 'something more' than a level of income or wealth and, if this is the case, how we measure class must reflect this idea.

## ⚠ Digging deeper: Measuring social class

The concept of class can't, in itself, be measured empirically because there's nothing concrete in the social world we can clearly identify as 'social class'. This is not, of course, a problem unique to class (many sociological concepts cannot be measured directly) and to solve it we need to refer to:

**Indicators** of class (such as occupation).

### WARM-UP: THE STATUS OF SYMBOLS

Many of the cultural aspects of class we are familiar with in everyday life are more correctly considered to be indicators of *social status* (although, as we've argued, status can be an important *indicator* of class).

As a class, consider the following categories (or develop your own if you prefer):

- cars
- houses
- alcohol
- clothing
- holidays
- television programmes

and for each identify some different types (for example, different types of car = Lada, Range Rover and Porsche 911).

In small groups, discuss the following: Do you associate the types you've identified in each category with any specific social class (for example, is a Porsche 911 'upper class')?

If the answer to this question is 'yes', briefly explain why you have made this association.

As a class, discuss your findings about the relationship between status symbols and social class.

Initially we can note two basic types of indicator (*objective* and *subjective*).

**Objective** indicators involve identifying things common to the whole population being classified, normally but not necessarily, with the proviso that they can be *quantified*. This potentially includes a range of *indicators* (occupation, income, education, housing, language and so forth) either considered:

- **individually**, such as occupation, or
- **relationally** – combining different objective indicators (such as occupation, education and income) to create a more rounded picture.

From this position, class is an *objective category* because it exists *independently* of individual social actors; people can be assigned to class positions regardless of their personal feelings about such things – and while a subjective sense of class position may be important (it will affect the way people behave), this is more properly related to *status* (a dimension of class) rather than class itself.

## ✳ SYNOPTIC LINK

**Theory and method:** Objectivity can be linked to questions of whether or not sociology can be considered scientific and to different sociological methodologies (such as positivism and realism).

 Weeding the path

Objective class measurements have a number of distinct sociological advantages:

- **Consistency**: Once the measurement indicators/criteria have been selected they can be applied consistently in terms of:
- **Definition**: Because class is defined by the

person measuring it, there is no inconsistency of definition – it will mean the same thing however and whenever it is applied (as with using occupation as a class indicator, for example).

- **Data collection**: With a consistent, objective definition, control over how and when data are collected can be effectively determined – something that allows:
- **Comparisons** to be made over time. We could, for example, track:

  - **Class patterns** – the relative size of different classes, for example.
  - **Class positions** – such as changes to the way different classes relate to one another hierarchically as the class structure changes.

- **Exteriority**: If the way people are assigned class positions is outside the control of (exterior *to*) those being classified, class represents something you *are* – whether or not you realise or accept your class position. This can be demonstrated empirically in terms of:

**Correlations** between, for example, class *position* and class *effects* – we can, for example, empirically demonstrate a strong and consistent relationship between social class and areas like crime, health, life expectancy and so forth.

## 🏠 The potting shed

**For any two areas of the Specification, identify one way for each that class position has a demonstrable effect on an individual's life.**

A second type of indicator, as we've suggested, involves:

**Subjective** definitions and measures of class, something **Bulmer** (1975) characterises as people's '. . . own conceptions of the class structure and their position in it'. In other words, subjective measure uses class indicators that, by and large, develop out of how people define both their own class position and, by extension, their class relationship to others – or, as **Liu** (2004) puts it, subjective class conceptions involve 'a personal perception of available resources and opportunities'.

Although subjective measures allow people to both define class and locate themselves on a class scale (or not, as the case may be), we need to avoid thinking that simply because social class is defined subjectively (by people themselves) it cannot be *objectively* measured using these criteria.

## ✳ SYNOPTIC LINK

**Theory and methods:** The idea of 'objectively measuring' subjective criteria relates to ideas about *personal objectivity* and a *scientific ethos* developed in this chapter.

We can illustrate this idea by noting three basic 'subjective class' indicators:

- **Class consciousness** involves ideas about people's *awareness* of belonging to a particular class. In terms of *measuring* class consciousness, **Evans** (1993) points to the idea of measuring:
  - **Attitudes and beliefs** about a range of 'class-typical ideas' (such as opinions about welfare provision, the distribution of wealth and income and so forth).

## ✳ SYNOPTIC LINK

**Religion: Bruce** (1994), for example, found that working-class Protestants in Northern Ireland had a well-developed level of awareness about their class position, both in relation to other religious groups and, as **Duffy** and **Evans** (1997) argue, 'relative to their own middle class'.

- **Class identification** relates to how closely people associate themselves to particular social classes, and such identification may involve a range of levels, from a fairly basic identification with a 'lower-' or 'upper-class' position to more sophisticated understandings of specific classes and their relationship.

## ✳ SYNOPTIC LINK

**Religion: Duffy** and **Evans** (1997), in a study of class and religious affiliation in Northern Ireland, found that 80% of Catholic males identified themselves with the working class.

- **Oppositional consciousness** involves an awareness of class *conflict* – the idea that different classes can have different (opposed) interests. This type of awareness ranges from a simple 'us and them' dichotomy to more sophisticated understanding of the association between, for example, different economic (Marx) or market situations (Weber) and different types of class.

## ✳ SYNOPTIC LINK

**Theory and methods:** Note how even when subjective indicators are used it is possible for the sociologist, as an outside observer/researcher, to maintain an objective research position. It is, for example, possible to objectively categorise how people (subjectively) view their class position.

## Weeding the path

Although not always as straightforward as objective measures, measuring and categorising social class subjectively adds a different dimension to our understanding of class in a number of ways:

- **Consciousness**: People's class perceptions are important since how they think and feel about class will affect their behaviour (and that of others) in a variety of ways – from how people vote, through the schools they choose to where they want to live.

## ✳ SYNOPTIC LINK

**Power and politics:** What people understand about class, in terms of awareness, identification and opposition, for example, may have consequences for voting behaviour. *Expressive* theories, for instance, link social class background to how people vote, as do some *instrumental* theories (such as *partisan alignment*) of voting behaviour.

- **Meaning**: A potential drawback of objective class measures is that they tell us little or nothing about what class *means* to people. Class, in this respect, runs the risk of being reduced to relatively simple *statistical categories* (such as 'middle class' or 'working class'), something that reflects what **Mills** (1959) called:

  - **Abstracted empiricism** – 'belabouring

irrelevant minutiae', as he put it, or the classification of the social world for no good reason or purpose. For example, you might want to count the number of cracks on a pavement and at the end of the exercise you will know precisely how many cracks there are; however, the key question is how significant or useful will this knowledge be?

## Problems

Subjective categorisations do, however have significant disadvantages:

- **Understanding**: 'Social class' may have different meanings to people, making it difficult to arrive at any real understanding of the concept, beyond the idea that its meanings are many and varied. This 'confusion' is not simply sociological, but is also rooted in the public consciousness. The polling organisation **MORI** (2003) found that, in 1999, 65% of respondents agreed with the statement, 'I don't feel that I belong to any particular social class'. In 2000, however, 76% disagreed with the statement, 'Britain is now a classless society'. These types of contradictions and confusions make it difficult to draw:

**Comparisons** between social classes since, if there are many different (personal) meanings to class it is difficult to compare 'like with like'. For some (postmodern) theorists this situation simply reflects the 'reality of class' in contemporary societies – a fragmented concept that holds a variety of meanings. Yet it is clearly possible to *correlate* objective social class with a range of class-based *life chances* (such as levels of income and wealth).

- **Categorisation**: As we've suggested, when people are asked to think about 'social class' they tend to see it in *status* terms (class and status are frequently confused). While status may be an important *indicator* of class, it is *not* class itself (in a similar way to the idea that while occupation can be used as an indicator of class, individual occupations are not themselves social classes).

⚠️ **Preparing the ground: Occupation and social class**

Although there are different ways of defining and measuring social class, over the past 100 years in the UK one of the most common forms of classification has been to use occupation as a:

**Single proxy measure** that allows *statistical quantification* of class groups. In other words, occupation has generally been considered a *reliable* indicator of social class for a range of reasons:

- **Objectivity**: Class groups can be created using criteria that do not rely on either *individual self-assessment* or *self-assignment* of class position. The ability to *quantify* class through occupation is a significant basis for sociological *comparisons*, both *historical* (changing class structures and identities) and *cross-cultural* (different forms of class structure in different societies).

- **Life chances**: Occupation is related to other aspects of an individual's life and, as such, allows us to make *informed guesses* about income, wealth, education and the like. In addition, *empirical correlations* can be made between occupation-based classes and individual/group life chances.

- **Identity**: Although ideas about gender, ethnicity, age and so forth all contribute to individual identities, occupation arguably remains the single most important source of identity over an individual's lifetime.

## Occupational scales

We can examine a range of 'occupation-based class scales', focusing initially on official government categorisations before exploring a selection of alternative ('unofficial' or non-governmental) class scales. We can begin, therefore, by noting an occupational scale used in the UK for most of the twentieth century (from 1911 until 1980), namely:

**Social class based on occupation** (more commonly known as the *Registrar General's Social Class scale*). A relatively simple occupational measure of class, this scale divided the population into five basic classes (with class 3 split into two subcategories).

This scale was developed around two forms of measurement:

- **Skill**: Each class consisted of occupations with similar levels of skill, such as professional workers (class 1), skilled manual workers (class 3 manual) and the like.

- **Status** – an important dimension because it introduced an:

  - **Ordinal** element into a *nominal* scale. *Nominal* refers to the idea of grouping similar occupations without making any *judgement* as to their relative worth, whereas *ordinal* refers to the

| Registrar General's classification (social class based on occupation) | | |
|---|---|---|
| **Social class** | | **Example occupations** |
| Non-manual [middle class] | 1. Professional | Accountant, doctor, clergyman, university teacher |
| | 2. Intermediate | Pilot, farmer, manager, police officer, teacher |
| | 3N. Non-manual skilled | Clerical worker, sales rep., shop assistant |
| Manual [working class] | 3M. Manual skilled | Butcher, bus driver, electrician, miner |
| | 4. Semi-skilled | Bar worker, postal worker, packer |
| | 5. Unskilled | Labourer, office cleaner, window cleaner |

idea that skill groups can be placed in some sort of *rank order*.

The scale explicitly ranked different class groups *hierarchically* on the basis of 'their standing within the community' – in other words, a *judgement* was made about the relative *status* of each group (class 1 being occupations with the highest social status). In addition, the scale explicitly divided the class structure into two groups:

- **middle-class** occupations involved non-manual work

- **working-class** occupations involved manual work.

## Weeding the path

When assessing this type of scale we need to remember that, at the time of its original development, British society was *qualitatively* different from our contemporary experience. Concepts of class, for example, were more rigidly embedded at the start of the twentieth century and ranking different occupations in terms of their manual/non-manual components was considered more plausible than perhaps it is now (due to the way the occupational structure has changed

– something we discuss in more detail in relation to the changing class structure). This type of classification, however, does have some distinct advantages:

- **Simplicity**: The scale was relatively easy to understand and, more importantly perhaps, apply. It also reflected a 'common-sense view' of social class based on occupational status differences.

- **Comparison**: As a widely used scale it was possible to compare both occupational changes over time and changes in class-related life chances (in areas such as health and family life).

Despite the fact this scale was used extensively for many years in official studies, it had a significant range of weaknesses that led, eventually, to its replacement.

**Categorisation**: For individuals to be classified they required, by definition, an occupation, and this effectively excluded parts of the population, including the:

- **wealthy** who live off investments rather than income

- **unemployed/never employed,** such as

those excluded because of age (the very young and the elderly) and disability

- **non-employed** (in the sense of paid work): This excluded, at different times, substantial numbers (mainly women) who worked within the home and who were dependent on their partner's income.

To bring categories like 'unemployed' into the general occupational scheme a range of assumptions was built into the model – the retired, for example, were classified on the basis of their 'final occupation' and 'dependent partners' were classified on the basis of their *partner's* occupation. This assumption may have been reasonable at a time when only one partner was usually in paid employment (and reflected the idea that everyone in a household shared the same general class), but, in the latter part of the twentieth century, the increasing number of:

**Dual-earner families** led to a marked decrease in the validity of the scale.

**Subjectivity**: Although the scale had a certain logic (splitting occupations into manual/non-manual categories), two problems are apparent. First, assigning specific occupations to a class owed more to the *subjective judgements* of civil servants. Second, as **Rose et al.** (2005) argued: 'The manual/non-manual divide is simply not a meaningful distinction given the nature of work and occupations in 21st-century market economies.'

**Intra-occupational status**: The simplicity of the scale was a weakness because it failed to take account of status differences *within* occupations – a probationary teacher, for example, was classified as having the same general class status as a fully qualified teacher. In addition, although income is an important dimension of individual life chances, the same occupational group could include people with widely differing incomes (accountants and the clergy, for example).

Partly as a response to internal criticisms and partly as a response to the changing nature of work, occupations and the class structure generally, a new scale (the **National Statistics Socio-Economic Classification**) was developed for use in the 2001 census. It was based on the work done by sociologist John **Goldthorpe** (see below) and represented the culmination of a radical reappraisal of the purpose and use of official statistical class scales.

We can note, in passing, that two different types of 'occupational scale' were originally developed to replace the Registrar General scale. In 1990 the **Standard Occupational Classification** (SOC) was introduced as a way of reclassifying occupations on the basis of both their *skill* element and the *educational qualifications* they generally entailed. The **SOC** underwent a number of revisions over a 10-year period.

Although interesting for the way it classifies different broad occupational groups, this was intended to be a *nominal* scale (occupations were not meant to be ranked hierarchically), and is used by government departments for research involving the need for an extensive occupational classification (the nine major categories are subdivided to cover the majority of UK occupations).

The most recent official occupational class scale is the **National Statistics Socio-Economic Classification** (NS-SEC) which has three versions (8, 5 and 3 classes respectively), something that makes it:

**Collapsible** – although the eight-class version is a *nominal* scale, it can be 'collapsed'

| Standard Occupational Classification (SOC) | |
|---|---|
| 1990 | 2000 |
| 1. Managers/Administrators<br>2. Professional<br>3. Associate professional/technical<br>4. Clerical and secretarial<br>5. Craft and related<br>6. Personal and protective services<br>7. Sales<br>8. Plant and machine operative<br>9. Other | 1. Managers and senior officials<br>2. Professional<br>3. Associate professional and technical<br>4. Administrative and secretarial<br>5. Skilled trades<br>6. Personal service<br>7. Sales and customer service<br>8. Process, plant and machine operatives<br>9. Elementary |

into a three-class scale that, according to **Rose et al.**, 'has a hierarchical element'.

## Weeding the path

A major difference between the **NS-SEC** and traditional forms of government class/occupational measurement scale is its:

**Relational** basis: As **Rose et al.** (2005) note, it's designed to measure 'employment relationships' and reflects a **Weberian**

approach to classification by combining two ideas:

- **Labour market situation** includes assessments, for each occupational group, of income levels, relative levels of work security and promotion/career development prospects, and is linked to:

- **Work situations** that involve ideas about different levels of power, authority and control within the workplace (the extent

| NS-SEC classes and collapses (source: Rose et al., 2005) | | |
|---|---|---|
| 8 classes | 5 classes | 3 classes |
| 1. Large employers, higher managerial and higher professional<br>2. Lower managerial and professional<br>3. Intermediate<br>4. Small employers/self-employed<br>5. Lower supervisory and technical<br>6. Semi-routine<br>7. Routine<br>8. Never worked and long-term unemployed | 1. Managerial and professional<br>2. Intermediate<br>3. Small employers/self-employed<br>4. Lower supervisory and technical<br>5. Semi-routine and routine | 1. Managerial and professional<br>2. Intermediate<br>3. Routine and manual |

to which workers in each occupational category are autonomous, for example).

The scale also reflects contemporary workplace relationships with regard to how work is contractually regulated in terms of:

- **Service relationships**: *Typical* of class 1, an employee provides a service for an employer and, in return, receives a range of short-term (salary) and long-term benefits (promotion opportunities, for example).

- **Labour contracts**: *Typical* of classes 5–7, the employee receives a wage in return for completing a certain amount of work or by working a certain number of hours.

- **Intermediate** contracts involve employment regulation that combines both of the above and is *typical* of relationships in class 3.

## Problems

This scale, while avoiding some of the problems of previous occupational scales and reflecting the various ways work and occupational structure have developed in recent times, is not without its problems:

**Class structure**: The underlying logic of the scale is a familiar one, in that it reflects the distinction between:

- **employers** – those who buy the labour power of others

- **employees** – those who sell their ability to work

- **self-employed** – those who sit 'between' these two groups.

However, the former exist only within the scale 'by implication', in the sense that the very wealthy, who do not have a conventional occupation, are excluded. This highlights a further problem in terms of the

'never worked' category – presumably representing a residual, *underclass* category, that groups a range of people who may have little in common, such as those who:

- have no intention of working

- cannot work (the long-term sick)

- want to work but cannot find employment.

As with all occupational scales there are a number of generic problems:

**Paid employment**: Because occupation is defined in terms of paid employment, a 'class' of unpaid workers (domestic labourers, for example) is excluded.

**Intra-occupational differences** are not adequately theorised. This relates not only to the type of problem we identified in relation to the *Registrar General* scale, but also to the status of:

**Service workers**: Changes in the organisation of work (and the effects of globalised competition) means some service workers (such as management consultants) can be characterised as 'short-term, self-employed, contract workers', but their pay and conditions are very different from those of, for example, service workers in the catering industry. This idea reflects a:

**Class boundary problem,** both in terms of thinking about where one class ends and another begins and, more importantly perhaps, the idea that social classes cannot be neatly encapsulated in occupational scales.

## ⚠ Digging deeper: Occupation and social class

Official class categorisations, although useful, are not the only way class can be measured

| Erikson–Goldthorpe Class Scheme (1992) | | |
|---|---|---|
| Service class | 1. Service class (higher grade) | Company director, senior manager |
| | 2. Service class (lower grade) | Manager small business, supervisor |
| | 3. Routine non-manual | Clerical, sales |
| Intermediate class | 4. Small proprietor/self-employed | Small farmers, electrician, plumber |
| | 5. Lower technician/supervisor | Lower-level supervisor |
| | 6. Skilled manual | Electrician, butcher |
| | 7. Semi-unskilled manual | Farm labourer |

and we can identify a number of occupational class scales, beginning with the:

**Goldthorpe Schema**: Although this has undergone a number of developments over the years, beginning with the **Hope-Goldthorpe** scale for the **Oxford Mobility Study** (1972), the most widely used variant is the **Erikson–Goldthorpe** Class Scheme (1992).

 **Weeding the path**

The scale has a number of versions (12, 9, 7, 5 and 3 classes, for example) and takes a **Weberian** *relational* approach to understanding class through occupation by including both work and market situations in its assignment of class positions.

**Market situation** takes into account ideas about:

- **self-employment/employment** – an important distinction in terms of skilled manual occupations, such as electrician and plumber

- **income** levels from different occupations

- **promotion prospects** and **career progression** – the higher up the scale, the greater the likelihood of promotions, increased levels of income and work benefits ('perks' such as share options).

**Work situation** refers to power and status in both the workplace and society – the higher up the scale, the greater levels of *personal autonomy* (freedom of action and decision-making) and power over the working lives of others.

A further interesting feature is the development of a:

**Dual-structure model**, involving a distinction between a *service* and an *intermediate* class, reflecting the changing nature of the organisation of work in contemporary Western societies. Some versions of the **Erikson–Goldthorpe** scale include a third class (*working*) to characterise classes 6 and 7.

**Status**: The scale recognises the significance of different types of workplace/occupational status:

- **Cross-category**: Self-employed skilled manual workers, for example, generally have a higher social status than those who are not self-employed.

| Wright and Perrone's class schema (1977) | | | | |
|---|---|---|---|---|
| | Class position criteria | | | |
| Class | Own means of production | Buy labour of others | Control of others | Sell own labour |
| Capitalist | ✓ | ✓ | ✓ | ✗ |
| Higher middle class | ✗ | ✗ | ✓ | ✓ |
| Self-employed/small proprietors | ✓ | ✗ | ✗ | ✗ |
| Labour | ✗ | ✗ | ✗ | ✓ |

Source: Adapted from **Persell** (2000): www.nyu.edu/classes/persell/Table93.html

- **Supervisory**: Occupations with supervisory functions (however minor) are qualitatively different to those that do not have this element of power and control.

Some potential weaknesses in this occupational schema involve:

- **Terminology**: Despite the use of terms like 'service' and 'intermediate' classes, the schema still reflects a 'traditional' model of class – a basic 'middle/working class' split by another name. In addition, potentially significant class groupings (the very wealthy or the unemployed) are excluded.

- **Situations**: Although the 'work/market situation' basis of the scheme reflects important class/occupational differences, some groupings reflect a 'manual/non-manual' split (such as the placing of 'routine non-manual' in the service class) that is difficult to justify if the scale is used hierarchically. In addition, the status of 'routine clerical work' has declined significantly in recent times, with the stripping away of any supervisory functions it may once have had.

- **Gender**: This type of occupational scale does not accurately reflect the lives and experiences of women (who are either ignored or lumped together under their (male) partner's occupational class). **Goldthorpe** has argued, however, that in dual-worker families, women by and large adopt the class identity of their male partner.

## Alternative

An alternative class scale, constructed from a *neo-Marxist* perspective, is provided by **Wright** and **Perrone** (1977), in terms of a basic *four-class model* which is constructed around the concept of:

**Social relations to production**: Individual positions in the class structure are based on things like ownership and control of the means of production, and the most important variable is represented by the social relationships that surround the production process (the major class groupings – whether you buy, control or sell labour, for example), with occupation being a relatively subsidiary category.

## ⚠ Weeding the path

Although **Wright** later added a further set of criteria to the schema (to include ideas like *decision-making* and level of *authority* over others), these represent refinements to the basic model rather than substantive changes. This model suggests a different way to measure social class, one that establishes a general set of *class relationships and processes* around which a range of occupations can be slotted.

This basic idea, albeit developed from a theoretically different position, is reflected in the work of **Hutton** (1996), an economist who uses the concept of:

**Dual labour markets** to develop an occupational schema, based around occupational changes in contemporary economies, reflected in the development of two distinct sectors:

- A **primary** or **core** sector consisting of full-time, well-paid employees with high levels of job security and job status.
- A **secondary** or **peripheral** sector consisting of part-time/casual employees, with low pay, little or no job security and low job status.

**Young** (2000) characterises the above in terms of a 'shift from *Fordism* to *Post-Fordism* ... where the primary labour market of secure employment and "safe" careers shrinks, the secondary labour market of short-term contracts, flexibility and insecurity increases as does the growth of an underclass of the structurally

unemployed'. **Hutton** argues that all modern economies (partly under the influence of *globalisation*) are *converging* around what he terms a '**40–30–30**' occupational model.

In the UK, as **Young** (2000) argues, post-Fordism crystallised in the 1980s around the *New Right* (Thatcherite) government policies that helped create what **Hutton** argued were 'deep, long-lasting and profound changes' in the economic and class structure. These policies involved, for example, legal changes to:

- **employment** that made it easier for employers to dismiss workers. Levels of unemployment also rose significantly in the early 1980s
- **workplace organisation and representation** that made it difficult for trade unions to organise employees and take effective industrial action. Legal limits were placed on actions that could be taken against an employer, secret ballots for strikes were introduced, individuals were given the right to sue unions – backed up with massive fines for 'illegal' industrial action
- **taxation** that reduced the top rate of income tax to 40%.

## ✳ SYNOPTIC LINK

**Power and politics: Hutton's** argument had a significant input into the development of Labour Party thinking in the mid-1990s, especially in terms of ideas about social inclusion and exclusion.

| The 40–30–30 Society: Hutton (1995) | |
| --- | --- |
| Top 40% | **The Advantaged:**<br>Full-time/self-employed – held their job for two years<br>Part-time workers – held their job for five years<br>Strong/effective unions/professional associations<br>Range of work-related benefits<br>Mainly male workers |
| Intermediate 30% | **The Newly Insecure:**<br>Part-time/casual workers<br>Declining employment protection/few benefits<br>Large numbers of female workers<br>Self-employed (especially manual workers)<br>Fixed-term contract workers |
| Bottom 30% | **The Disadvantaged**<br>Unemployed (especially long-term)<br>Families caught in poverty trap (e.g. single parents)<br>Zero-hours contract workers<br>People on government employment schemes<br>Casual part-time workers |

## Weeding the path

**Hutton's** slightly unconventional method of measuring class is interesting for the way it attempts to relate class to:

**Occupational security** rather than status. The schema does, implicitly, have a *hierarchical element* (the *Advantaged* are, for example, better placed than the *Disadvantaged*) but this is seen in *relational* rather than *absolute* terms. The schema reflects a broadly *Weberian* approach by empirically identifying individual market and work situations to describe the class structure of modern Britain – although this is limited because of its relatively simple, descriptive, format.

The schema has some clear advantages in that it is:

- **Not occupation-specific**: This avoids some (if not all) of the problems associated with trying to locate specific occupations on a class scale.

- **Multidimensional**: It incorporates inequalities based around *age*, *gender* and *ethnicity* in a way that many other scales do not. It recognises, for example, that the young and elderly, women and ethnic minorities are more likely to be found in the *secondary labour market*.

The schema does, however, have some limitations we should note:

- **Breadth**: The three groupings are too broad in their scope – each contains a wide range of people who may have little, if anything, in common. The 'Advantaged', for example, could include everyone from the super-rich (people like Richard Branson or Roman Abramovich) to relatively minor civil servants, teachers and the like.

- **Ownership**: The scale doesn't really address issues of ownership, power and so forth, mainly because it focuses on *individual market situations*.

## The potting shed

What, if anything, does Phillip Green (current wealth: £5 billion) have in common with someone like your teacher?

**Status**: It's debatable whether the schema measures *class*, as opposed to *market*, status. The latter is a significant aspect of class, but **Hutton** presents it as the *only* aspect of any importance. However, it could be argued that **Hutton's** schema represents a different way of looking at class relationships in contemporary societies.

**Individuals**: The focus on individual occupational positions tells us little about class positions based around family groups. Someone in part-time/casual employment

with a partner in secure, full-time employment is considered to be 'disadvantaged' – yet this may not be the case. Given a significant proportion of the workforce consists of married/cohabiting partners, this should be an important consideration.

### Moving on

In this section we've looked at examples of how governments and sociologists have tried to define and measure class in occupational terms, using a variety of class schema. In the next section, however, we can examine how changes in the class structure impact on both our understanding of class and, by extension, our ability to define and measure this concept.

## 3. Different explanations of changes in the class structure and the implications of these changes

In the previous section we identified the different ways social class has been operationalised in our society over the past 100 years – something that reflects the changing ways we think about class and how it can be defined and measured. This section continues the theme of change, this time through an examination of how political, economic and cultural changes have contributed to changes in the class structure.

### Preparing the ground: Explaining change

We can begin by thinking about how we can both identify and understand the implications of change:

## WARM-UP: REPRESENTING CLASS STRUCTURES

These graphics are different visual representations of the class structure (if none represents your idea of class, create your own representation). In small groups decide:

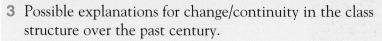

Class no longer significant

Upper / middle / working class

Small upper class with expanded middle class

Overclass, expanded middle class and underclass

1 Which, if any, in your opinion best represents the class structure in our society:

- now
- 100 years ago.

2 Your reasons for choosing a particular representation.

3 Possible explanations for change/continuity in the class structure over the past century.

**Identification**: When thinking about changes in the class structure over the past century we need to think about organisational changes within capitalism (the *dominant* mode of production in this period), on the basis that changes to the way work and the workplace are organised will produce adjustments – and possibly wholesale changes – in the nature of the class structure. In this respect we can identify the following broad changes to the way goods and services have been produced:

- **Industrial society**: For the first part of the twentieth century in England, manufacturing industry was the dominant form of employment in terms of numbers. This period saw the development of *mass production* techniques (*Fordism*), automation (machines controlling machines) and, in the latter part of the century, *post-Fordist* forms of industrial organisation based around computer technology.

## ✳ SYNOPTIC LINK

**Theory and methods:** The discussion of modernity and postmodernity includes an explanation of concepts like Fordism, post-Fordism and global Fordism in the context of globalisation.

- **Post-industrial society**: Although *service industries* were significant in employment terms in the early twentieth century, the latter part of the century saw a marked increase in this type of work, especially in areas like financial services (banking and insurance) and, of course, information technology. **Hicks** and **Allen** (1999) summarise these general changes when they note: 'The most significant occupational changes have gone hand in hand with a decline in traditional industries and growth in new areas, especially services.' The **Office for National Statistics** (2002) puts figures to this change: financial and business services now account for 20% of UK employment, compared with 10% in 1981 – 'This sector saw the largest increase in jobs between 1981 and 2001, part of the post-war growth in the service industries and the decline in manufacturing.'

| Manufacturing and service employment: percentages | | |
|---|---|---|
| | 1911 | 2004 |
| Manufacturing | 55 | 11 |
| Services | 35 | 75 |

Source: Department of Enterprise, Trade and Investment (2005)

## ✳ SYNOPTIC LINK

**Theory and methods:** This chapter provides an extended analysis of the concept of post-industrial society.

- **Knowledge society**: A late-twentieth-century development, closely related to both the decline of manufacturing and the rise of service occupations. The **Economic and Social Research Council** (2005) characterises this type of society in the following terms: 'In today's global, information-driven society, economic success is increasingly based upon ... intangible assets such as knowledge, skills and innovative potential ... The term "knowledge economy" ... describes this emerging economic structure and represents the marked departure ... from [the economic structure] of the twentieth century industrial era.'

## Trends

**Implications**: The above ideas convey a *broad picture* of the type of occupational changes in our society over the past century and, as such, provide a basis for thinking about two ideas, namely how the class structure of our society has evolved and the implications of these changes over this period (as **Nyíri** (2002), for example, argues, the '... transition from industrial to knowledge-based societies is characterised by major changes in working conditions and labour-market requirements'). We can start by noting some general trends at each level of the class structure.

- **Upper levels**: There has been a general decline in numbers at this level, partly because of greater ownership diversity through wider share holding (that is, whereas in the past shareholding was concentrated in the upper levels, it is increasingly a feature of the middle levels). However, this group has become increasingly influential on a global level.

- **Middle levels**: One feature of a service/knowledge economy is the expansion of middle-ranking occupations (managerial, technical and intellectual). While there has been an increase in higher-level (well-paid, high-status) service work associated with activity in the 'knowledge economy', there has also been an expansion of routine service work (call centres, McDonald's and the like) that is little different to the routine types of manual work this has replaced. Thus, while some see middle-class expansion as a fundamental change in the class structure, others see it as a simple redefinition of existing class relationships (what were once working-class

**The decline of UK mining**

1920 – 1,250,000 miners
1998 – 9000 miners
Source: Hicks and Allen (1999)

occupations have been redefined as middle class).

- **Lower levels**: The decline in manufacturing has led to a general contraction at this level, although there are debates in two main areas: whether routine service jobs are part of a 'new working class' or 'old middle class' and the existence or otherwise of an underclass.

In this respect, therefore, we need to consider not only the *nature* of the changes to the class structure of modern Britain, but also the *meaning* of such changes.

## ⚠ Digging deeper: Explaining change

We can look more closely at explanations for change at each of the levels we've just noted.

### Upper levels

We can pinpoint two key changes here:

- **Ownership** and **control**: From a *pluralist* perspective a major change has been a blurring of ownership and control, partly due to the rise of the:

- **Joint stock company** – a company owned by *shareholders* rather than single individuals. This, it can be argued, has spread the ownership net and effectively *fragmented* the upper levels because ownership extends across the class structure in two ways:

  - **Pension funds** that invest the pension payments of a wide variety of workers (both public and private sector)
  - **Middle-class** managers and professionals increasingly own part of the company for which they work.

## ✳ SYNOPTIC LINK

**Mass media:** Debates over the relationship between ownership and control are discussed in greater depth in relation to the media.

On a day-to-day level, control of businesses is increasingly in the hands of managers rather than owners, the argument here being that the 'upper class' is effectively disappearing from the class structure, to be replaced by a *managerial elite* who, however well remunerated, remain employees rather than employers – an idea we can examine in terms of key changes like the:

**Managerial revolution**, a *pluralist* concept developed by **Burnham** (1941), who located the 'rise of managerial control' in the idea that, in a competitive world, the consumer exercises a huge (collective) influence over organisational behaviour – if prospective buyers don't like what's on offer then an organisation must either reassess its business strategy to become more responsive to consumer demands or risk being driven out of business by other companies. **Burnham** argued that 'modern capitalism' was a *cooperative process* – managers were indispensable to modern corporations, whereas 'individual owners' were not (a corporation could function effectively without 'identifiable owners', but not without a wide range of managerial expertise, from the highest levels of decision-making to the lowest supervisory levels). On a more contemporary note, **Galbraith's** (1967) concept of:

**Technostructure** developed these ideas by arguing that modern corporations develop a 'technocratic structure' whereby effective control is in the hands of a managerial/scientific/technological elite, ultimately responsible to shareholders but, in effect, making all the important decisions about the running of a company. In the context of modern media corporations, for example, **Demers et al.** (2000) argue that, while 'corporate news organizations tend to be more profitable than entrepreneurial news organizations', they '. . . place less emphasis on profits and more on product quality and other non-profit goals' – a tendency that's sometimes called the development of *soulful corporations*.

## Weeding the path

**Davis** and **McAdam** (2000) summarise the change to the class structure suggested by *managerialism* in terms of a change from a 'Marxian society-wide conflict of workers versus owners to a Weberian conflict of workers versus managers'.

**Globalisation**: The second key change relates to the organisation and behaviour of modern corporations – what **Davis** and **McAdam** term a 'new economic shift'; the gradual replacement of organisations based around mass production (and the type of class structure and composition this has traditionally entailed) with:

**Network structures** operating across national boundaries and maintaining a fluid organisational structure that makes them responsive to new technological developments. These organisations normally have shareholders, but rarely have individual owners. As **Davis** and **McAdam** put it: 'Owners are not wealthy individuals but financial institutions', such as banks and pension funds, and they argue that modern corporations are structured and behave less like 'traditional companies' and more like:

**Social movements** – loose conglomerations with multiple internal and external structures, rather than a relatively simple internal hierarchical structure – a complex idea that an example should clarify. **Nike** is a global company that designs and markets footwear, but it owns no production facilities; rather, it contracts out the production of footwear across the world to smaller companies. In this way **Nike** both 'buys its own products' cheaply (by manufacturing in countries such as China and India, where labour costs are low) and encourages competition *between* producers by being able to source products from different countries – if companies in India can't manufacture the footwear cheaply enough Nike can switch production to a cheaper country/supplier.

## ✳ SYNOPTIC LINK

**Power and politics:** The characteristics of social movements are discussed in more detail in this chapter.

Increasingly, therefore, major global corporations own:

**Intellectual property rights** – the design of a trainer or computer software. **Sabel** (1991) refers to such organisations as belonging to:

**Unbounded networks**: Unlike traditional, national organisations, global corporations are neither bound by national borders nor constrained by traditional forms of manufacturing. *Unbounded networks* take a number of forms:

- **Global Fordism**: Instead of mass production taking place in a single space, the manufacturing process can be distributed across the world – a factory in Germany makes one thing, a factory in Peru another and the final product is assembled in France for export to the USA.

- **Flexible specialisation** reflects the type of process adopted by companies like **Nike** – sourcing completed products from wherever is cheapest.

- **Modular consortiums**: **Volkswagen's** assembly plant in Brazil was the first to be run entirely by *multinational subcontractors*. Cars marketed and sold by Volkswagen are produced by 20+ transnational companies in a single assembly plant.

---

## ✳ SYNOPTIC LINK

**Theory and methods:** A further example, discussed in relation to postmodernity, is the idea of agile corporations.

---

These ideas have a number of possible consequences for our understanding of class structures in late/postmodern society:

**Transnational class structures**: Super-rich company directors, for example, are technically employees and hence part of the traditionally defined *middle class*. However, they occupy an ambivalent class position in the sense that they function as owners (and usually own shares in the company for which they work), but, in occupational terms, are members of an (elite) middle class.

**Fragmentation**: At the upper levels of the class structure there are considerable differences between people who, nominally at least, are in a similar class position. There is also, in terms of global forms of capitalism, a blurring of the boundaries between owners and controllers.

## Middle levels

One of the most striking changes in the class structure over the past century has been the relative growth of the middle classes at the expense of both the working and upper classes, although, as we've seen, how we define and interpret 'middle class' is significant – something that suggests the:

**Fragmentation** of middle class *identities*: **Draper** (1978) compared the 'new middle class' to a 'dish of herring and strawberries', by which he meant the various groups occupying this class position had very little cohesion or things in common – and it's not too difficult to see why. At one extreme, perhaps, we have the kind of 'super-rich elite middle class' we've just described and, at the other, a whole range of low-level, routine occupational positions that, although defined as middle class, are difficult to distinguish from their working-class counterparts in terms of things like *income*, *status* and general *life chances*. It may be possible to find a dividing line in terms of attitudes, values and *lifestyles* (in the way

**Goldthorpe** and **Lockwood et al.** (1968) found lines of demarcation between the *affluent working classes* and the lower middle classes in 1960s Britain), but even this source of difference is becoming increasingly difficult to sustain in twenty-first-century Britain.

## Weeding the path

Although the idea of a fragmentation appears to usefully describe contemporary class structures, the concept has two major problems:

- **Lifestyle structures**: If, for example, 'the middle class' in late/postmodern society is defined by a wide variety of lifestyles, it calls into question two things: first, the idea of classifying them as 'middle class' (rather than class categories in their own right), and second, the basis for operationalising the concept of class – if 'lifestyle differences' classify people, we could delineate hundreds – if not thousands – of different 'lifestyles' (the ultimate logic here being that since everyone lives their own unique lifestyle, everyone is their own class).

- **Class is dead**: If lifestyles are so different and unique, the concept of a 'class' – a group who share certain economic, political and cultural characteristics – no longer has any significance (as writers like **Pakulski** and **Waters** (1996) argue). There are two general problems here. First, using different criteria to classify people (such as lifestyle over occupation/income) still involves *classifying* people. Second, it may be possible to identify broad 'lifestyle groupings' and shape them into *classes*;

this follows because lifestyles are responsive to things like occupation and income – I can't, for example, adopt a similar 'celebrity lifestyle' to **David Beckham** because I don't have his income to support that lifestyle – the best I could do is *simulate* such a lifestyle, but that's hardly the same as *living* that lifestyle.

## ✳ SYNOPTIC LINK

**Mass media:** This links into **Baudrillard's** (1998) concept of *simulacra* – 'representations that refer to other representations'.

Debates about the significance (and implications) of *class fragmentation* are important, but possibly *overstated*. While we may have to change our thinking about classes (crude upper/middle/lower distinctions may no longer be much use) it doesn't necessarily follow that there are no differences between, say, middle-class and lower-class lifestyles, especially when we think in terms of something like:

**Resource control** as an indicator of class. Class position is not simply a question of how you choose (or are forced through lack of choice) to live; rather, it reflects the different economic, political and cultural resources different groups are able to command.

## ✳ SYNOPTIC LINK

**Education: Vincent et al.** (2000) have noted how middle-class parents bring higher levels of capital – 'material (goods and finances), social (networks and relationships) and cultural (knowledge and skills)' – to bear on their children's schooling than their lower-class counterparts.

Two related concepts impact on our understanding of changes in the middle/lower-class structure:

**Proletarianisation** involves the idea that many 'middle-class occupations' are no longer easily distinguishable from 'working-class occupations' in terms of pay and working conditions. One aspect of this, as **Whitehead** (1997) notes, is that the 'job security' that was once a feature of middle-class occupational life 'has now virtually disappeared, if not forever, then certainly for immediate future generations'. Associated with this process is:

**Deskilling**: On a basic level, deskilling relates to skills being lost, for whatever reason (such as lack of practice or use). For our purpose, however, it suggests certain skills (such as those possessed by craftspeople) lose their economic value when the work to which they once applied can be performed more easily and cheaply by machines.

## Example

An extreme but illustrative example is car manufacture; where once it involved numerous skilled craftspeople, the automation of factories has *deskilled* such workers by replacing them with robots.

From a Marxist perspective, **Braverman** (1974) argued that the introduction of new technology into the workplace has been felt in two main ways:

- **Inter-class boundaries**: The occupational distinction between manual and non-manual progressively breaks down for two reasons. First, the industrial skills that distinguished the upper working class are made redundant by technology. Second, various forms of middle-class work

## ⚠ The potting shed

**The human input into making cars has been largely replaced by machines. Identify and briefly explain two other examples of deskilling in our society.**

(clerical, financial and the like) are also deskilled through computer technology. Typing, for example, was once a valuable skill now largely deskilled through the development of word processors.

- **Intra-class boundaries**: Within the working class, deskilling takes away the thing (skill) that separates the relatively highly paid, affluent worker from their low- and no-skill counterparts.

## ⚠ Weeding the path

**Neville** (1998) is critical of this interpretation when he argues that 'class struggle is both out of date and, in many cases, merely fictional, an ideology to be learnt off by heart but not a picture of reality' – mainly because, he maintains, 'the traditional proletariat ... is almost dead or more properly solely male ... except on British TV soaps such as *EastEnders*'.

## Lower levels

For **Braverman,** *deskilling* produces an *expansion* of the working class as routine white-collar workers are *proletarianised* and distinctions *within* the working class break down. Other writers, however, have interpreted economic/technological change in a different way to emphasise a process of:

**Embourgeoisement** – a concept introduced by **Zweig** (1961) to represent the idea that the class structure was becoming *increasingly middle class* as the working classes took on similar income, status and lifestyle characteristics – a picture successfully demolished by **Goldthorpe et al.** (1968) with their 'Affluent Worker' research. They did, however, suggest that a 'new form of working class' was emerging, one where affluent, home-centred (*privatised*) workers displayed different lifestyles to their less affluent, working-class peers.

## ✳ SYNOPTIC LINK

**Power and politics:** Embourgeoisement has been used (with limited success) to explain some forms of class-based voting behaviour.

More recently this general concept has been revived in a different and more sophisticated form, focused around:

**Reskilling**: Service and knowledge economies need workers with different skill sets – hence the idea of reskilling; the sons and daughters of manual workers who at one time, would have similarly gone into manual work can no longer do so. Instead, they enter the service economy at a variety of

points – most at the low level of physical services (shop workers, for example), others in the higher level of knowledge services.

This interpretation suggests a massive contraction in the working class and a massive expansion of the middle class that, as **Hauknes** (1996) notes, involves '... a shift towards higher skilled white collar employment in most industries, away from low and unskilled blue collar employment. This is accompanied by an increase in flexible, service-like production methods in several manufacturing industries, the evolution of "post-Fordist" production'.

Finally, we can note a further example of possible change in the class structure at its lower levels involving the idea of an:

**Underclass** – a group who are, at best, the very bottom of the class structure and, at worst, entirely outside it.

## ✳ SYNOPTIC LINK

**Wealth, poverty and welfare/education/ stratification and differentiation:** The concept of an underclass – usually associated with New Right perspectives – is a theme running through these areas of the Specification. In terms of welfare, for example, we can note ideas about dependency cultures and social exclusion.

## ⚠ Preparing the ground: Implications of changes

In the final part of this section we can consider the implications of changes in the class structure in two ways:

**Structural change** perspectives focus on understanding and explaining 'how and why' the class structure has changed and the

# Discussion point: Representing class structures

At the start of this section we asked you to think about representations of class; based on this work:

1 Has your opinion about the shape of the class structure in our society changed (and, if so, in what way)?

2 Thinking again about the idea of change/continuity in the class structure over the past century, has the class structure changed (and, if so, rank the reasons for any change in order of their importance)?

significance or otherwise of such changes. If the middle class, for example, is expanding, we need to understand what this means in terms of both class positions and *processes* (how the members of different classes relate to one another).

## The death of class

For writers like **Waters** (1997), the question of class structure changes has become, in the early twenty-first century, a relatively unimportant issue because class as a unit of social analysis is largely rejected. The 'implications for change' here are that class has lost whatever meaning it once had and this makes arguments over 'how and why' it has changed largely redundant.

If we assume, for the sake of argument, that social class still has some meaning and significance to people (as opinion polls continue to show – **ICM** (1998), for example, found a 98% class identification), one major change over the past century has been what **Mortimore** and **Robinson** (2003)

pinpoint as the 'loss of a rigidly-structured class basis to British society'. In other words, one general implication we can draw is that class divisions have:

**Weakened** – in the respect that an *overt* sense of class structure and position is no longer as strong as it once was. This is not to say, however, that class and class relationships have necessarily ceased being significant – a weakening of overt class differences isn't the same as saying class, per se, has lost its influence on both individual and cultural relationships. What has changed, as **Mortimore** and **Robinson** suggest, is that 'the old sense of a structured class system – in which there was a definite right or wrong answer to which class you belonged to – has disappeared'.

## Erosion

**Ainley** (2004) suggests that not only has the '. . . previously clear-cut distinction between the non-manual middle class and the manual working class been eroded', but occupational changes have resulted in a '. . . much more fluid social situation that has eroded the old clearly differentiated "upper", "middle" and "working" classes'. This idea has implications for our understanding of a changing class structure – on a theoretical level, for example, we encounter problems of:

**Boundary-marking**: The question of where one class ends and another begins has always been a problem for sociologists. Traditionally, a manual/non-manual distinction has been used with some success, but even in a society with relatively clear distinctions between these two types of work, some forms of *boundary-blurring* still existed (as reflected in something like the Registrar General's class scale where class 3 – skilled manual and routine non-manual –

was categorised as both 'separate' and occupying the same general class position). In contemporary societies, as we've suggested, this simple distinction can no longer be supported.

More generally, class structure changes have involved:

**Realignments** that run in three possible directions:

- **Convergence**, whereby the class structure is gradually 'flattening' (the vast majority of people in our society fill the 'middle-class' band).

- **Polarisation**, whereby, the class structure is increasingly 'stretched' between two extremes: those fully included in the normal, day-to-day functioning of the society in which they live and those who are fully excluded from such participation.

- **Polarised convergence** whereby, although there is a general class *convergence*, *polarisation* is in evidence 'at the edges'; there are, in other words, 'spikes' at either extreme of the class structure – with the super-rich at one end and the underclass at the other. **Ainley** (2004) expresses this idea when he notes that partly as a result of new technology, 'a new respectable "middle-working class" is no longer divided in employment between mental and manual labour but now finds itself insecurely between the super-rich of large employers and their direct agents (a so-called "service class") above and a "socially excluded", unemployed, or "unemployable", so-called "underclass" beneath'.

## Digging deeper: Implications of change

We can explore a couple of the themes we touched on earlier in terms of two basic positions relating to changes in the class structure.

**Modernism**: Although there is a broad agreement among what we might term modernist sociologists that the class structure has undergone a range of changes over the past century, there are differences of interpretation as to the extent and significance of such change.

**Persistence**: For neo-Marxists such as **Poulantzas** (1974) or **Wright and Perrone** (1977), the question is not so much whether these changes have rendered class a redundant concept, as how to theorise the growth of the 'middle classes' in late capitalism. The problem, therefore, is how to both account for and theorise class structure changes.

## Postmodernism

For non-Marxists, class structure changes are significant in terms of the way class has generally:

**Declined** in significance in terms of how it impacts on people's lives and behaviour. In this respect, the study of class and class relationships has shifted from attempts to understand the significance of class in *objective* terms (how class position impacts on life chances) to thinking about class as a:

**Subjective** concept – in the sense of focusing on how people perceive class both individually and culturally.

**Postmodernism**, however, involves two broad positions relating to class:

**Class is dead**: The relevance of class as either an explanatory concept for sociologists or to people generally in terms of their attitudes and behaviours is questioned in a couple of forms:

- **The end of history**: **Fukuyama** (1989) argues that 'class analysis' has lost whatever meaning it may once have had because 'class contradictions and struggles' no longer exist (**Marx** argued that 'all history is the history of class struggle' – hence **Fukuyama's** ironic reference). The failure of alternative political ideologies (such as communism) to effectively challenge the political hegemony of social democracy has, in this view, put an end to class struggles and, thus, to class forms of analysis.

- **Identities**: This position, while not proclaiming the death of class, as such, removes it from its privileged position in much sociological analysis by, at best, relegating it to the position of 'one more source of identity' in postmodern society (competing for attention with concepts like culture, age, gender and sexuality).

For both these positions the 'decline of class analysis' is not synonymous with social equality; inequalities still exist in contemporary societies, but how we think about them has changed – it is no longer possible to talk about social inequality in any meaningful way at a general 'group level'. This follows because class is shot through with different meanings and interpretations that make it, for postmodernists, an interesting but largely irrelevant concept.

### ⚠ Weeding the path

**Parenti** (1997) has been critical of the above position, something he labels:

'**ABC**' **theory**: He argues that some versions of postmodernism 'avoid the concept of class' by simply *relabelling* 'class processes'. As he puts it: 'They'll tell you that culture is important, group identity politics is important, personal psychology is important – *Anything But Class*'.

**Hendricks** and **Vale** (2004) develop this idea by arguing that class is still a significant concept, albeit one that raises important questions in contemporary societies, such as how to incorporate the idea of *lifestyle pluralities* (the multitude of lifestyle choices people are able to make) and *identity politics* – the idea that other forms of identity are important – into the overall concept of class.

## Identity

This reflects a second postmodernist position on class, that of:

**Identities**: Postmodernists who see class as having a significant part to play in identity politics generally reject traditional ways of defining class in terms of it being:

**Centred**: In other words, they argue it is impossible to anchor the concept on a set of slowly evolving social *characteristics*, such as occupation, or *attributes*, such as income. Class, like any form of identity, is a fluid, ever-changing concept that, for the vast majority, reflects a:

**Decentred** lifestyle: In other words, the 'lack of rigidity' in the class structure observed by **Mortimore** and **Robinson** (2003) is a feature of postmodern society – there are no 'absolute structures' (such as those of class, gender, age, ethnicity or whatever). There are, however, constantly shifting sands of identity – of which perceptions of class are, at any given time, more or less important to people. Class and class structures, therefore, can't be conceived in *objective* terms; rather, class is an inherently *subjective* concept that means different things to different people at different times and in different situations.

Savage et al. (2001) capture the flavour of this idea when they talk about the 'ambivalent nature of contemporary class identities' and suggest we 'should not assume that there is any necessary significance in how respondents define their class identity in surveys'. This follows, they argue, because people understand class in different ways; it's frequently seen less as an *attribute* and more as 'a marker by which people relate their life histories'. In other words, people in contemporary society have an awareness of the concept and terminologies associated with class that leads them to see it as a political concept loaded with cultural baggage; defining oneself in class terms, in this respect, is seen as a political statement most people are unwilling to make, for a variety of reasons.

## Moving on

In this section we've noted a range of changes, both national and global, in the economic organisation of our society over the past century – changes that have prompted debates not just about the changing nature of class and class structures, but also about the continued utility of these concepts.

In the next section, therefore, we can develop these ideas and debates by relating them to the concepts of *life chances* and *life choices* as a way of assessing how class and class structures affect people's behaviour.

# 4. Differences in life chances by social class, gender, ethnicity and age

In previous sections we've drawn a careful distinction between social *inequality* (defined as differences in the distribution of social resources between individuals and groups) and social *stratification* (the idea that inequalities are built into the social and economic structure of different societies).

This distinction is important because how we theorise the relationship between inequality and stratification has significant implications for how we study and explain social behaviour. The question here, therefore, is deceptively simple: is social stratification a cause of inequality or is it merely a *statistical exercise* that 'represents difference' in the way that classifying people by eye colour or height 'reflects difference'?

One way to resolve this question is to examine the relationship between social stratification in modern societies – both *primary* (in the sense of social class) and *secondary* (in terms of categories like age, gender and ethnicity) – and social inequality, something we can do using the concepts of *life chances* and *life choices*.

## ⚠ Preparing the ground: Chances or choices

**Life chances**: At their most basic, life chances represent, according to **Dahrendorf** (1979), an individual's 'long-term prospects' in any society; that is, their *relative chances* of gaining the kinds of things a society considers *desirable* (such as a high standard of living) and avoiding those things a society

## WARM-UP: PERSONAL AND CULTURAL VALUES

We can think about life chances by identifying some of the things our society considers both desirable and undesirable (and since, in some respects, individual value systems are important in this context, we can also identify the things you value and find undesirable).

Use the following table as a template for your ideas.

| Society | | You | |
|---|---|---|---|
| Desirable? | Undesirable? | Desirable? | Undesirable? |
| Money Loads of money | Ill health | ? | ? |
| **Further examples?** | | | |

considers *undesirable* (such as going to prison).

For **Mills** (1951), *life chances* include 'everything from the chance to stay alive during the first year after birth to the chance to view fine art; the chance to remain healthy and if sick to get well again quickly; the chance to avoid becoming a juvenile delinquent; and very crucially, the chance to complete an intermediary or higher educational grade' – social inequalities he explicitly relates to social stratification when he argues: 'These are among the chances that are crucially influenced by one's position in the class structure of a modern society.'

**Gershuny** (2002) suggests that life chances is a wide-ranging concept we can use to relate stratification explicitly to inequality and to measure in an *empirically verifiable* way (such as through levels of income, health and life expectancy) the effects of this relationship. This concept, therefore, is generally favoured by sociologists who argue that stratification is both a causal factor in the relative distribution of life chances (those at the top of a stratification system generally possess more of the desirable things society has to offer and avoid the majority of the undesirable things) and something more than just a statistical description of inequality.

## Choices

**Life choices** reflects a different take on the relationship between the two and is generally associated with sociologists who dispute the causal connection between the two. In this respect inequality is *not* the outcome of structural factors, but rather the result of the *choices* people make about their life. This concept, therefore, symbolises the dynamic range of choices that circulate around the general:

**Lifestyles** available in Western societies – ways of living and behaving that free people from traditional (or modernist) associations of class, gender, age and ethnicity.

# ⌂ The potting shed

Identify and briefly explain two different types of lifestyle in our society.

## ⚒ Weeding the path

Before we examine these positions further, we can note a couple of qualifying points:

- **Life chances**: Although this approach focuses on how social inequality is structured, life choices may still play a part in some areas of social behaviour. An obvious example here might be the *choices* we make relating to health, such as whether or not to smoke, that affect things like illness and longevity.

- **Life choices**: Although the emphasis is on understanding how and why people in contemporary societies make behavioural choices, in some circumstances, as **Gauntlett** (2002) argues, such choices may be constrained or limited. For example, an individual with a low level of income will have a lesser range of choices in relation to areas like education (those on low incomes will not be able to afford the fees charged by public schools, for example), housing and lifestyle.

---

## ✳ SYNOPTIC LINK

**Family:** The idea of life choices can be applied to the way people are able to choose different forms of sexuality in our society.

---

## ⚒ Digging deeper: Choices or chances

**Grusky** (1996) suggests three general ways it's possible to theorise the concepts of life chances and choices:

- **Structuralism** focuses, as we've suggested, on life chances, based on the assumption that social categories like class are relatively coherent groupings based around things like:

  - **endowments** – such as the level of people's education

  - **working conditions**, involving assessments of *physical environment* (the actual condition of the workplace, for example) and *political environment* (such as levels of control over others and personal autonomy)

  - **reward packages**, relating not only to income but also to other work-related benefits.

From this position, life chances combine *market situation* (or class, in *Weberian* terms), *status* and *power* – ideas that can be fairly easily translated to life chances based on gender, age or ethnicity as well as class. In this respect, the structural aspect of social inequality relates to what **Grusky** terms:

**Inequality space**: That is, the idea that people with similar life chances can actually be *mapped* to similar positions ('spaces') in any stratification system. This position argues that stratification is a *causal factor* in inequality, since if inequality simply resulted from individual life choices it is unlikely that people with similar life chances would occupy the same general social space.

- **Culturalism**: Although related to structuralist positions, culturalist perspectives add a further dimension by seeing stratified groups as not only sharing a similar structural location (in class terms, for example, upper, middle and working), but also a general set of cultural beliefs and assumptions. In other words, something like a middle class not only has things like similar levels of income, personal autonomy in the workplace and educational qualifications in common, they also share a similar:

**World view,** involving broadly similar attitudes, behaviours, values and norms. Class-specific *cultures* are, therefore, 'a defining feature of inequality systems'. In addition, the cultural dimension of stratification filters through to life chances in numerous ways – **Bourdieu's** (1986) concept of:

**Cultural capital**, for example, demonstrates a causal relationship between stratification and inequality in the sense that it provides a mechanism for explaining how each successive generation is advantaged or disadvantaged by their inherited cultural capital.

## Postmodernity

**Postmodernism**, meanwhile, questions the supposedly static, coherent nature of social stratification; writers like **Pakulski** and **Waters** (1996) argue that both class and status groupings (and, by extension, stratification based around these concepts) are little more than convenient assumptions made by (modernist) sociologists to support their particular interpretation of the relationship between sociocultural structures and inequality. As we've noted, from this position a significant variable is:

**Lifestyle**, which **Harrison** and **Davies**

(1998) define as 'patterns of actions that differentiate people', in the sense that 'lifestyles are sets of practices and attitudes that make sense in particular contexts'. Lifestyle, in this respect, reflects:

**Identity choices** in postmodern society, relating to 'how individuals wish to be, and be seen by others'. For **Gauntlett** (2002), our identity choices are made on the basis of broad:

**Lifestyle templates** that provide individuals with a set of *narrative guidelines* telling them what they have to do – and how they have to do it – to live out a particular lifestyle. These templates, although similar to the concept of role, differ in that the adoption of any given 'lifestyle template' does not force the individual into any specific forms of 'expected behaviours'. **Gauntlett** likens these templates to *film genres*: 'Whilst movie directors can choose to make a romance, or a western, or a horror story, we – as "directors" of our own life narratives – can choose a metropolitan or a rural lifestyle, a lifestyle focused on success in work, or one centred on clubbing, sport, romance, or sexual conquests.'

Lifestyles and identities are, in many respects, unique to the individuals who construct them and, consequently, defy easy classification. As **Harrison** and **Davies** argue, although lifestyles can be 'mapped onto conventional social categories of class, income, age, gender and ethnicity', they also 'transcend them'. Thus, while social inequalities exist (the resources I have at my disposal to play the role of 'film star', for example, are far fewer than someone like Brad Pitt), it doesn't mean I can't act out my interpretation of a 'film-star lifestyle'. While it is possible, as with film genres, to classify people in terms of general lifestyle, these are the result of *life choices* rather than different life chances.

## Weeding the path

We can summarise the difference between the two approaches to understanding inequality in terms of the idea that:

- **Life chances** operate at a structural level and determine individual experiences. An individual's position in a stratification system determines their life chances.

- **Life choices** operate at the individual level and determine structural experiences. Our individual life choices, therefore, determine our structural location in society.

## The potting shed

Identify and briefly explain two differences in people's life chances from any two areas of the Specification.

In the remainder of this section we can explore in more depth ideas about life chances and life choices in relation to concepts of class, age, gender and ethnicity.

## Preparing the ground: Social class

Inequalities relating to social class are many and varied in our society, but we can note some examples across a range of selected categories – see the table on the following page.

These examples show a clear relationship between class and a range of social inequalities. The main question, however, is

whether this relationship is best explained in terms of life chances or life choices.

## Digging deeper: Social class

**Life chances**: The explicit relationship between class and inequality (across just about every indicator) seems to be clear evidence of differential life chances. As **Savage** (2002) expresses it: 'Class – in terms of economic position – matters greatly for people's life chances. Measured by any material category – health, wealth, income, social mobility, morbidity, education – class represents a continuing and fundamental social division.' We can identify a number of reasons for this:

**Wealth and income** inequalities are obvious reasons for a class-based disparity in life chances, mainly because they impact on a range of social categories (from the ability to buy educational advantage, through private health care to buying protection against crime). Their importance is not

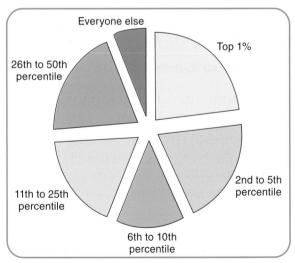

Distribution of wealth in the UK, 2002
Source: Economic and Social Research Council

| Class inequality: Selected examples | |
| --- | --- |
| | The higher the class, the more likely you are to: |
| **Family** | Inherit substantial amounts of money<br>Access significant social and financial networks |
| **Health** | Live longer<br>Have lower levels of illness, child and infant mortality rates |
| **Wealth and income** | Own significant quantity of shares, savings and disposable income<br>Have higher levels of pay/rising income |
| **Welfare** | Avoid living on state benefits<br>Avoid poverty |
| **Work** | Have higher status/control over others<br>Be employed/avoid unemployment |
| **Crime** | Avoid a criminal record<br>Avoid victimisation |
| **Politics** | Have access to the powerful<br>Participate in electoral processes |
| **Education** | Complete your schooling (less risk of exclusion)<br>Leave school at 18<br>Achieve higher-level qualifications (GCSE, A level, degree) |
| **Housing** | Live in better-quality housing<br>Have greater privacy |

Source: National Statistics Online (2005)

simply restricted to economic life chances, however, since we can characterise them as being central pillars in:

**Regimes of privilege**: A high class position has ramifications across other areas, such as status and power. High status, for example, confers access to top-level social networks (the most powerful business people, high-ranking politicians, civil servants and so forth), and once connected to such networks, a range of power possibilities flow freely – ideas that link into the:

**Cultural components** of class privilege: These operate on a number of levels, but some examples we can note include:

**Cultural capital**: In the same way different classes have different access to financial resources (such as income and wealth), **Bourdieu** (1977) argues they have access to different cultural resources that include both *material resources* (various types of consumer goods) and *non-material resources* (such as higher education). As

Heath (2002) notes, cultural capital reflects the idea that class backgrounds confer certain advantages and disadvantages in terms of life chances.

## ✳ SYNOPTIC LINK

**Education:** Numerous writers have used a version of cultural capital to explain educational differences between, for example, working-class and middle-class children. **Farkas** and **Beron** (2001) claim that linguistic and vocabulary differences confer educational disadvantages on lower-class children.

## Weeding the path

**Sullivan's** (2001) testing of the concept of cultural capital in an educational context (the possible effect on GCSE performance) concluded that cultural capital (such as families providing books and educational support materials, cultural activities – such as theatre-going – and discussions) '... is transmitted within the home and does have a significant effect on performance'. However, she also concluded that *cultural capital* itself may have a lesser influence on attainment and life chances than other class factors (such as high or low income).

**Social capital**: For **Cohen** and **Prusak** (2001), social capital relates to how individuals are connected through social networks in that it '... consists of the stock of active connections among people: the trust, mutual understanding, shared values and behaviours that bind the members of human networks'. In terms of life chances it works on a couple of levels. **Coleman** (1988) argues that middle-class parents develop cooperative *educational networks* with their children (supporting them in both material and non-material ways). In addition, *business networks* develop within companies, with the middle and upper classes better positioned to exploit their connections.

The general idea here is that cultural and social capitals promote both:

- **inclusion** among a particular class that, in turn, promotes
- **exclusion** through:

**Social closure**: **Heath** (2001) argues that workplace interaction is a major source of social closure. Higher social classes can enhance their life chances by restricting and closing access to networks of mutual self-interest (economic and political).

**Life choices**: The idea that inequalities result from the choices people make is, at first sight, *counter-intuitive*, given the seemingly self-evident relationship between inequality and life chances. However, theories of life choices fall into two main camps:

## New Right

**New Right** theories rest on the (familiar) idea of:

**Rational choice** – people act in what they see as their own best interests, weighing up the relative costs and benefits of their behaviour. People therefore make *choices* and, as a consequence, live with the outcome. **Murphy** (1990) argues that where an education system provides *equality of opportunity* (everyone has the chance to participate), differences in achievement are the result of unsuccessful students (based on categories such as class, ethnicity and gender) *choosing* not to participate in the way successful students participate. A related idea here is:

**Meritocracy**: **Miliband** (2005) argues that life *choices* refer to the ability of people to make informed decisions in the context of 'equality of opportunity'. In other words, this position sees the role of the state as one of helping to maintain a 'level playing field' by creating the conditions under which individual life chances relate to choice – people, in other words, accepting or declining opportunities for 'self-improvement' on the basis of their individual merits (hard work, positive attitudes and the like) rather than ascribed characteristics (such as family background or gender).

---

## ✳ SYNOPTIC LINK

**Education:** Evidence for this interpretation, in terms of class, might be the fact that in 2002, 50% of children of skilled manual workers gained five or more GCSE grades A*–C (**Department for Education and Skills**, 2004) and, as **Summerfield** and **Babb** (2004) note, 20% of working-class children participate in HE.

---

## Postmodernism

**Postmodern** explanations also focus on the idea that contemporary societies are

---

## Discussion point: Do people get what they deserve?

In small groups, identify arguments for and against the idea that, in our society, people receive rewards (high incomes and status, for example) on the basis of their individual merits rather than their class, gender or ethnic background.

As a class, discuss your arguments in the context of the concept of meritocracy.

---

constructed around the choices made at the individual level – something we can illustrate by noting the difference between modernist and postmodernist concepts of class and lifestyle classifications. For the former, as we've seen previously, class is generally defined in terms of:

**Production**: Class positions are based around work relationships (what people do) and how these involve differences of status, power and, in this context, life chances. For postmodernists, however, lifestyles can be classified in terms of:

**Consumption**: Social positions are related to what people *do* with what they *have*, an idea based around the different ways people perceive and pursue their life choices. There are numerous lifestyle scales in existence, an example of which is the Insight Value Group: Lifestyle Classification (2004) (see the chart on the following page).

**Grusky** (1996) notes the postmodern focus on consumption is based on the argument that 'class-based identities become ever weaker', for a couple of reasons:

- **economic** – a gradual decline in workplace conflicts
- **political** – a move away from class-based politics to identity politics (political representation based around 'values and lifestyles'). In this situation, social inequality becomes:

**Individualised**: Where people increasingly exercise choice (ranging from whether – and when – to have children, to sexuality) they construct different types of (personalised) lifestyles. The weakening of traditional ties of class, for example, contributes to this process by breaking down conventional barriers, a process further promoted by:

**Cultural globalisation**: People are

| The Insight Value Group: Lifestyle Classification (2004) | |
| --- | --- |
| Lifestyle group | Example traits |
| **Self-Actualisers** | Individualistic and creative, enthusiastically exploring and embracing change |
| **Innovators** | Self-confident risk-takers, constantly seeking new experiences |
| **Esteem Seekers** | Motivated by success and prestige |
| **Strivers** | See image and status as important while also holding traditional values |
| **Contented Conformers** | Content to establish secure lifestyle that generally reflects the behaviour and tastes of 'normal society' |
| **Traditionalists** | Risk-averse, with behaviour-guided traditional norms and values |
| **Disconnected** | Socially detached, resentful, embittered and apathetic |

increasingly exposed to different cultures and ideas, some of which they accept and others of which they adapt to create *cultural hybrids* (identities that form out of a mixing of different cultural styles).

## The potting shed

**Identify and briefly explain two examples of *cultural hybrids* in our society.**

## Weeding the path

One way of understanding the difference between life chance and life choice positions is to relate them to concepts of:

**Risk**: Life chance theorists (both structural and cultural) view this in terms of:

**Unconscious risk** – the extent to which individuals are exposed to risk without necessarily being aware of such exposure. For example, such risks relate to things like infant mortality rates – the lower your social class, the higher the level of risk of infant death. However, since some forms of unconscious risk can be identified (as with infant mortality), we need to refine the concept by noting that even where we are aware of this type of risk there is little or nothing we can consciously do, as individuals, to lessen the risk – it can only be reduced at the group level (in this instance by improvements in hygiene, welfare provision and the like).

For postmodernists, however, all forms of risk are in theory *calculable*, hence life choices involve:

**Conscious risk**: Examples here relating to health might include knowledge of the health risks associated with smoking or those associated with particular sexual lifestyles (for example, the risk of HIV or a sexually

**Growing it yourself: Constructing age**

A simple piece of sociological research might involve asking people in your school/college when they believe categories like 'childhood', 'youth', 'adulthood' and 'old age' begin and end (answers could also be correlated to categories like age, gender and ethnicity).

transmitted disease). It doesn't necessarily follow that people take steps to limit risk – there may be reasons why they trade increased levels of risk for some sort of pay-off, an idea related to:

**Risk management**: This relates to both the *choices* people make and their perception of the levels of *risk* (and consequent costs and potential benefits) involved. For example, some people choose to remain in education whereas others choose not to – choices that have consequences for future lifestyles. Similarly, some choose to risk starting their own business, whereas others choose to pursue careers, or not, as the case may be – just as some people choose criminal behaviour over conforming behaviour.

△ **Preparing the ground: Age**

There are a couple of problems to note when identifying examples of age inequality:

**Social construction**: Age has different meanings in different societies at different times, which makes comparisons difficult. **Abrams** (2005), found 'massive differences in perceptions of when youth ends and old age

begins' and that, 'on average, people felt that youth ended at 49 and old age began at 65'.

**Blurred boundaries**: Currently (2006), aside from a couple of relatively strong age boundaries (16–18 when a range of 'adult' privileges are granted and 65+ when retirement comes into effect), most age boundaries in our society are fairly fluid – something that, once again, makes it difficult to identify precise forms of age-related inequality.

There are, however, some examples of specific age inequalities we can note – see the table on the following page.

△ **Digging deeper: Age**

**Life chances**: Explanations for age-related inequalities focus on how societies are structured to reflect:

**Ageism**: It is not illegal to discriminate by age in our society (although it will be from October 2006) and **Abrams** (2005) argues that 'age prejudice between the generations' is more common than sex or race discrimination, something that holds true across both gender and ethnic boundaries. Age discrimination in our society takes two major forms:

- **Childhood**: Children are treated differently in a variety of ways (although their general life chances are influenced by factors such as class, gender and ethnicity), not the least being their compulsory attendance in education between 5 and 16. They are also prohibited from a range of activities (such as drinking alcohol) permissible in adulthood. In the period of transition from childhood to adulthood (youth),

| Age inequality: selected examples | |
|---|---|
| | **The older you are the more likely you are to:** |
| **Family** | Provide unpaid family care<br>Own family home<br>Live alone |
| **Health** | Suffer serious, life-threatening, illness/long-term illness or disability |
| **Wealth and income** | Have accumulated wealth<br>Have higher income up to retirement<br>See income decline after retirement |
| **Welfare Work** | Live in poverty after retirement<br>Have higher work-related status<br>Work part-time/be self-employed |
| **Crime** | Avoid being a victim of crime<br>Commit fewer crimes |
| **Politics** | Vote<br>Participate in electoral processes |
| **Education** | Have fewer qualifications |
| **Housing** | Live in substandard accommodation |

Source: National Statistics Online (2005)

## Discussion point: R U ageist?

In small groups: when you hear the following words, what thoughts do you immediately associate with them?

| Baby | Child | Youth | Adult | Elderly | Pensioner |
|---|---|---|---|---|---|

As a class: what do your word associations tell us about perceptions/labelling of age groups?

young people are accorded a slightly different status to adults, something reflected in their lower earning power, ineligibility for state welfare payments and lower work-related status.

- **The elderly**: 'Old age' is increasingly difficult to define in modern societies – improvements in life expectancies, for example, have increased the length of time people can expect to be labelled as 'old'; medical developments have also increased the period during which the elderly can expect to be physically and mentally active.

**Meadows** (2003) argues that job performance doesn't significantly deteriorate with age and 'there is no evidence to support the view older workers are inherently less productive than younger workers, except in a limited range of jobs requiring rapid reactions or physical strength, and people tend to move out of these as they become harder for them'. She notes, however, that older workers don't always receive the same levels of workplace investment and training as younger colleagues – where they do receive training they 'reach the same skill standards'.

A key marker – and *rite of passage* – for the elderly in our society is the official retirement age (currently 65 for men and 60 for women – although, as **Ahmed** (2002) notes, the European Union has put forward proposals to scrap compulsory retirement ages across the board). This idea leads us into a set of explanations based around *status* and control over:

**Social resources**: The argument here is that life chances in modern societies are based not so much around age, but rather the different levels of resources controlled by different age groups. Thus, two people of the same age can have different life chances based around their differential access to social resources.

## Political economy

**Political economy** theory relates age to work – the generally lower status of the elderly, for example, comes, **Townsend** (1986) argues, from their 'progressive removal from the workplace' – something, **Hockey** and **James** (1993) note, that denies them social resources such as an earned income. Lower status levels among the young fits into this general theory because they have failed, as yet, to develop work-related status resources. These ideas can be related to:

**Cultural capital** in the sense that lower-status age groups lack the general social resources to improve their life chances.

**Exchange theory**: **Turner** (1989) argues the *marginalisation* of different age groups can be related to a general failure to control a variety of social resources, not just those relating to work. The stigmatisation of 'young, unmarried, mothers' is a case in point here.

## Choice

**Life choice** perspectives flow, to paraphrase **Mae West**, from the idea that 'you're only as old as the person you feel'. In other words, although certain *age markers* still exist, the meaning of age in late/postmodern society is increasingly fluid – people are no longer restricted to rigid, age-categorised role behaviours since, as **Grusky** (1996) suggests, concepts of age – like those of gender and ethnicity – no longer have a 'privileged position'. Postmodern positions, for example, argue that individuals are:

**Congeries** of **situationally invoked statutes**: In other words, identity is an aggregation of many different ideas and statuses that shift and change depending on the situation – you may, for example, define yourself as a student in the classroom, a friend outside the classroom, a consumer when you go to the shops and so forth. This means *identity* (who and what we believe we are) is not fixed and unchanging (*centred*) in postmodern society; rather, different identities are invoked at different times and in different places – in short, we exercise choice over how age-specific identities are constructed.

### Weeding the path

This idea *contrasts* with *life chance* interpretations whereby various age-categories are seen as:

**Master statuses** that define how others both see us in terms of age and interpret our behaviour as appropriate or inappropriate to the master status.

From a life choice position, ideas about age-related characteristics and statuses are more fluid in contemporary societies because traditional ideas and associations are gradually broken down by, for example:

**Cultural globalisation** – the idea that we are exposed to alternative lifestyles relating to age. As traditional notions of age-related roles and statuses break down and fragment, changing lifestyle choices come to the fore and open up new:

**Social spaces** – 'non-traditional behaviours', for example, that different cultural/age groups claim as their own. This is illustrated by the changing appearance of *youth subcultures*; the well-documented 'spectacular subcultures' of the recent past (mods, rockers, punks and hippies, for

example) have given way to less spectacular, more individualised subcultural groupings that develop around particular forms of music, dress and lifestyle – an idea we can briefly outline in relation to three theories of ageing:

## Disengagement

**Disengagement theory** suggests that as people age biologically they progressively disengage from social relationships, both:

- **consciously**, in the sense of a gradual withdrawal from extended social networks (work being the most obvious, perhaps), and

- **unconsciously**, in the sense that the older one becomes, the greater the likelihood of family and friends disengaging through death.

Disengagement is a two-way process. The individual progressively disengages from their general involvement with society (through retirement, for example) and society disengages from the individual (people interact with the elderly on increasingly fewer occasions).

## Activity

**Activity theory** focuses on the way people learn and choose to play age-related roles (such as 'youth' or 'elderly'). From this position, *disengagement* from social relationships occurs continuously as we make different choices about our behaviour and the groups to which we belong. This process represents 'active reengagements' in social interactions as we leave some groups and join or develop others.

## ⚠ Weeding the path

While *disengagement* theory suggests that the gradual *decoupling* of the individual from social groups is a progressive experience, *reengagement* theory takes a more flexible approach to understanding how and why we form and disengage from social groups.

## Generational

**Social generational theory** examines the impact the biological ageing process has on individual self-perceptions and identities; in particular, it suggests our behavioural choices are conditioned by values that fail to adapt to social and technological changes; the elderly, for example, become, in **Dowd's** (1986) phrase, 'immigrants in time' – they are different because their life experiences are rooted in the values, norms and customs of the *past*. As society moves on, they remain trapped in the identity conferred by their past experiences (both in their own eyes and those of others). Cultural separation between age groups occurs and is mirrored by a *social distance* between those 'from the past' and 'those in the present', something that, in turn, reinforces cultural differences.

## ⚠ Preparing the ground: Gender

Historically our society has seen marked gender inequalities, with the emphasis, by and large, being on the different ways women have suffered various forms of:

**Patriarchal discrimination** across a range of areas and activities (from family life, through education, to the workplace).

As the following table suggests, women still experience a range of inequalities in modern Britain, but it's also important to point out that inequality is not simply one-way; in some areas – such as *health*, where women generally have a longer life expectancy, and *education*, where, as **Office for National Statistics** (2005) data demonstrate, 'girls outperform boys at GCSE and A level' – men have lower life chances than women.

## Inequalities

Gendered inequalities are also affected by concepts of class, age and ethnicity – upper-class boys generally achieve higher educational qualifications than lower-class girls, for example.

Conventional explanations of gender inequality in our society focus on concepts of:

**Sex discrimination** as a relatively straightforward process involving both conscious and unconscious levels of discrimination, directed, in the main, towards women and based around:

**Patriarchy** that has taken a number of related forms, from outright discrimination at one extreme to more subtle forms of ideological control through which women 'collude' in their own inequality – such as the idea that in a *patriarchal society* men consistently exploit women in areas like:

**Family life**, where female responsibility for childcare and domestic labour has served to limit economic participation. Housework and childcare have historically had lower status in our society and such work is unpaid, ideas which in combination define female lives in terms of their *service role* and lower their general life chances.

| Gender inequality: selected examples | |
|---|---|
| | Women are more likely to: |
| **Family** | Have childcare/domestic labour responsibilities (dual/triple role)<br>Marry/divorce/be widowed<br>Be a lone parent |
| **Health** | Live longer<br>Drink less alcohol/not be overweight |
| **Wealth and income** | Have lower levels of wealth while partner still alive<br>Have lower average income (currently 18% less) |
| **Welfare** | Depend on welfare payments<br>Experience poverty in adulthood/old age |
| **Work** | Have lower occupational status/not be managers<br>Work part-time |
| **Crime** | Avoid criminal record/prison<br>Avoid victimisation (except for sex crimes) |
| **Education** | Have higher educational qualifications<br>Not be excluded from school |

Source: National Statistics Online (2005)

## ❋ SYNOPTIC LINK

**Family life:** Feminist explanations for differing levels of male/female status are discussed in more detail in this chapter.

**The workplace:** Men and women have traditionally accessed and controlled different types of resources in our society; men, for example, have traditionally controlled economic resources, whereas women, to some extent, have traditionally controlled domestic resources. Both forms of resource control confer status, but at different levels. The increased involvement of women in paid work over the past 25 years has, to some extent, increased both female status and life chances through the control of economic resources, but the main question here is why female life chances have not improved significantly relative to those of their male counterparts. An answer is found in a number of different explanations:

**Workplace stratification**: Concepts of *vertical* and *horizontal* workplace stratification have been applied to explain greater male status and income. In relation to the former, the concept of a:

**Glass ceiling** has been used to explain lower female life chances, although this idea is gradually giving way to the idea of a:

**Glass trapdoor**: Some women are able to progress to higher levels in the workplace, particularly in areas (such as human resource departments) dominated by women. The majority of women, however, are 'left behind', for a couple of reasons:

- **Disrupted career development**: Where women periodically have to leave employment through pregnancy (and, in many cases, care for a family), they are placed at a disadvantage to their male peers in terms of career advancement.

- **Part-time work**: Women are more likely to work part-time, combining work with family and childcare duties. This, once again, puts them at a relative disadvantage to their male peers.

These ideas, in combination, have frequently been expressed in terms of a:

**Double shift** – women as both paid employees and unpaid domestic workers, or even, as **Duncombe and Marsden** (1993) argue, a:

**Triple shift** – the third aspect being emotional labour (the investment of time and effort in the psychological well-being of family members).

 Weeding the path

Traditional explanations for gendered life chance inequalities tend to focus on various forms of overt and covert discrimination, and although these explanations have some currency (gender inequality and discrimination clearly does exist, as the previous table demonstrates), they suffer from a couple of major problems:

**Homogeneity**: They generally treat men and women as coherent groups, such that gender inequalities are translated equally to 'all men' and 'all women'. This, however, is

clearly not the case – all women, for example, are not the same in terms of their market situation – a single, well-educated woman has very different life chances to a female single parent with low or no educational qualifications.

**Social class**: Although class is traditionally seen as a factor in differential gender life chances, it is frequently difficult to operationalise the precise extent of its influence in situations where women do not fit clearly and neatly into economic categories (either because they do no paid work or because paid work is part of a double or triple shift).

## Digging deeper: Gender

**Life chances**: One major problem with explanations for gendered inequalities that focus on ideas like patriarchy and discrimination in a relatively simple and straightforward way is that they have difficulty explaining why discrimination seems to be selective – if 'patriarchal practices and ideologies' were sufficient forms of explanation for inequality we would reasonably expect *all women* to have lesser life chances than their male counterparts (which is evidently not the case). One way to resolve this problem – while still working within a general life chances perspective – is to use the concept of:

**Embodied capitals** – a generic term for a range of forms of capital (*human*, *cultural* and *social*). **Gershuny** (2002a) suggests *embodied capitals* reflect 'personal skills, knowledge and experience, which give individuals access to participation in the activities of specific social institutions', and he uses this concept to explain and account for subtle,

## The potting shed

**Identify and briefly explain two examples of embodied capitals you employed to achieve your current level of educational participation.**

but significant, differences in the 'gendered lives' of men and women of different class, age and ethnic groups.

In this respect, **Gershuny** (2002b) focuses on the idea of:

**Human capital** – a term he defines as the economically relevant skills that give people access to different kinds of paid employment; the '... personal resources that give people material advantages or disadvantages, now and in their futures – those skills and experiences that determine their earning capacity'. These include level of education, employment and unemployment records and, most significantly, the level of jobs people can manage effectively after taking into consideration their other social responsibilities (such as childcare).
**Gershuny** relates gender inequalities to life chances in two ways:

First, women as a *group* in contemporary Britain have comparatively *fewer* life chances than either men or, most significantly, their parents' generation; and, second, on an *individual* level, *some* women have better life chances than other women, or, indeed, many men.

 Weeding the path

**Gershuny** presents a:

**Fragmented picture** of relative life

chances based on both *historical* (generational) and *contemporary* (within the same generation) evidence.

*Human capital* represents a way of determining an estimate of 'the hourly wage respondents receive or would receive if they had jobs'. Thus, by focusing on 'marketable skills' (such as level of education), it's possible to overcome one of the general problems of static class scales – the fact that many people (especially women) either do not have paid employment or, where they do, work at a level (part-time, for example) that doesn't reflect their true economic worth.

For **Gershuny**, one of the major reasons for lower (if fragmentary) female life chances is marital instability. When contemporary married/cohabiting women enter the paid workforce they do so on two levels: those with relatively low and those with relatively high human capital.

For the first (majority) group childbirth and childcare result in one partner (generally the mother) either dropping out of the workforce or participating at a lower level (since childcare costs are generally too prohibitive for this group to afford). This reduction in human capital places her at a relative disadvantage, in terms of life chances, to marriage partnerships where the mother can afford to pay others for childcare while she continues to work (and the family draws two incomes).

### Generation

However, increasing family instability and breakdown creates a *generational decline* in comparative female life chances (a female child compared with her mother, for example), because when a family splits the female partner generally takes custody of any children. The male partner is free to continue working while the female partner cannot because of childcare responsibilities and this leaves her reliant on state benefits. Compared with her mother's generation – where women normally stopped work to look after children and consequently relied on the partner's income – contemporary women have fewer life chances as a result of family breakdown.

**Gershuny** argues that we have a situation where the *majority* of women have lower life chances than their mother's generation. At the same time, a significant *minority* of women have improved life chances because educational and workplace opportunities have opened up for women who can display similar levels of commitment and motivation to their male counterparts. As **Gershuny** puts it: 'From a mid-20th century position in which most people lived in single-earner households, we move to a present with at one extreme, more high-skilled two-earner households from privileged backgrounds and at the other, more no-earner female-headed households from disadvantaged backgrounds.'

## ✳ SYNOPTIC LINK

**Stratification and differentiation:** The processes **Gershuny** describes can be related to questions of both social class and social mobility. Embodied capital explanations, he suggests, '. . . are very closely related to the operations of what was once thought of as social class'.

**Cultural capital**: **Scott** (2004) adds a further dimension to arguments about human capital by suggesting this concept is increasingly significant for women in terms of:

**Linked lives**: That is, how female life chances are enhanced or inhibited by their relationship to – and responsibilities for – *significant others* (such as children, partners, the sick and the elderly). The main argument here is that the 'linked lives' of male and female partners are subtly different; primary responsibility for the care of others still falls predominantly on women (even more so when families break down). These linkages, **Scott** argues, help to explain how female life chances are affected by:

**Asynchronies** – the idea that female family linkages restrict opportunities for the synchronisation of one's life with the requirements of wider society and, in particular, work. Childcare, for example, doesn't synchronise easily with full-time work; it also restricts opportunities to develop the social networks that ease many men through the various promotion and career ladders in the workplace – an idea related to:

**Social capital**, in the sense of the various networks in modern societies that promote or inhibit life chances. In the workplace, for example, male social networks often involve work-related leisure (such as the 'golf club network'). Family networks rarely promote the life chances of those who play a central role in them – women, in the vast majority of cases.

### Choices

**Life choices**: For **Hakim** (2000) the gender inequalities that exist in contemporary Western societies result from the *choices* people make – an idea she expresses as:

**Preference theory**: **Hakim** argues that a neglected area in the study of gender inequality are the *conscious choices* men and women make, especially in relation to two crucial areas: family life and the workplace (or 'market work and family work' as she puts it). As the building blocks of preference theory, **Hakim** (2000) identified five:

**Historical changes** 'in society and the labour market' (cumalative in their effect) that resulted in women in Britain, for example, gaining an unprecedented range of life choices:

- **contraception**: The birth-control pill gave women 'reliable control over their own fertility for the first time in history'

- **equal opportunities laws** that opened up all aspects of the labour market to women

- **occupational change**: The decline of (male-dominated) manufacturing industries and the rise of service industries gave women greater economic opportunities

- **service industries** also provided 'secondary earners' (traditionally women who supplemented the *primary earnings* of their male partner) with a range of part-time employment that fitted around their 'other life interests'

- **choice**, reflected in the changing 'attitudes, values and personal preferences of affluent modern societies' that focuses on concepts of lifestyle based on a balance between work and family life.

**Hakim** identified three broad (*ideal type*) responses to these historical changes in terms of women's work–lifestyle preferences.

For **Hakim**, life chance inequalities are the result of different groups of women (across all class and age categories) making choices in relation to work and family – those women who choose a career are able to compete equally and successfully with men and, in consequence, experience similar life chances. Those women who choose not to be economically competitive (home-centred) have fewer life chances than their male counterparts because, for whatever reason, they have excluded themselves from a major source (work) of life opportunities.

## Weeding the path

The strengths of **Hakim's** argument involve:

- **Preference**: Her focus on the *choices* people make in relation to a work–life balance is a significant attempt to redress a conventional sociological imbalance in the analysis of gender inequalities – an

| Hakim's (2000) classification of women's work–lifestyle preferences in the 21st century | | |
|---|---|---|
| Home-centred (20%) | Adaptive (60%) | Work-centred (20%) |
| Family life and children are the main priorities | Diverse group: includes women combining work and family | Childless women concentrated here. Main priority is career |
| Prefer *not* to work | Want to work, but *not* totally committed to career | Committed to work |
| Qualifications obtained for intellectual dowry | Qualifications obtained with the intention of working | Large investment in qualifications/training |

uncritical acceptance that social inequalities are *automatically* the result of structural forces and, as such, cast women in the role of *victims* of such forces.

- **Opportunities**: The focus on historical changes and how they affect individual lives is important, given that much sociological literature and analysis ignores the real changes in both society and economic behaviour that have occurred over the past generation.

- **Heterogeneity**: Women, for **Hakim**, represent a mixed group in contemporary society, with a range of preferences and commitments relating to economic activity. This contrasts with the generally *homogeneous* work preference of men that, **Hakim** argues, gives them certain economic advantages (something she interprets as a *cause*, not an *effect*, of *patriarchy*).

## Problems

**Hakim's** arguments have not been received uncritically, however. **Man Yee Kan** (2005) has 'examined the major claims' of **Hakim's** theory and, while she generally supports the idea of reintroducing the concept of *choice* into the sociological analysis of inequality (rather than relegating it to an effect of structural/ideological forces), she suggests two potential weaknesses:

- **Constraints**: While choice is an important factor in determining life chances, **Man Yee Kan** argues that choice is always exercised within certain limitations. She disputes, for example, the idea that the labour market is 'gender blind' in the sense of imposing few, if any, barriers to female advancement. On the contrary, she argues, female awareness of

sex segregation, glass ceilings and so forth act as 'disincentives to work'; in other words, *knowledge* of patriarchal ideas and practices may influence women's decisions to focus on family, as opposed to career.

- **Reciprocity**: **Hakim** assumes female preferences determine their attitudes towards and participation in different areas (such as family and work). In other words, choice is unidirectional (one-way). **Man Yee Kan**, however, argues the relationship is frequently reciprocal (two-way); that is, female work orientations are influenced by *experiences* in the workplace that, in turn, reflect back on their attitudes to work and family.

## ⚠ Preparing the ground: Ethnicity

When we consider ethnicity-related social inequalities we need to keep in mind a range of ideas:

**Definitions**: Ethnicity is not easy to define, mainly because there is a range of possible criteria we can use, from *country of origin* (English, Afro-Caribbean ... ), through *colour* (white, black ... ), to *cultural characteristics* (such as religion). In addition, official agencies may define ethnic groups in ways not recognised by those they are designed to define (the label 'Asian', for example, covers a wide range of different ethnic groupings).

**Heterogeneity**: We need to avoid the assumption of cultural homogeneity when examining ethnic inequalities; ethnic groups, like any other social group, are shot through with cultural differences related to class, age, gender and region. We need, therefore, to be aware of:

**Intersections** – differences *within* ethnic groups (*intra-group* differences) as well as differences *between* ethnic groups (inter-group differences). One of the problems we face is separating inequalities that stem from the fact of a particular ethnicity from those that stem from class or age differences. As **Westergaard** and **Resler** (1976) argue: 'Preoccupied with the disabilities that attach to colour ... research workers have been busy rediscovering what in fact are common disabilities of class.'

We can, however, identify a range of social and economic inequalities relating to *minority ethnic groups* in our society.

### ⚠ Digging deeper: Ethnicity

**Life chances**: Explanations for different forms of ethnic inequalities in this section focus on *structural factors* affecting minority life chances – the first, and probably most obvious, being:

**Racial discrimination**: Following the lead of writers like **Modood et al.** (1997), **Moriarty**

| Ethnic inequality: selected examples | |
|---|---|
| **Family** | Indians/white British most likely to provide informal, unpaid family care, black Africans and the Chinese least likely to provide such care |
| **Health** | Risk-taking behaviours: Bangladeshi men most likely/Chinese men least likely to smoke. White Irish/black Caribbean men most likely to drink above government recommendations<br>Pakistani and Bangladeshi reported highest rates of ill health, Chinese men and women reported the lowest rates |
| **Income** | Minorities on average earn lower incomes<br>Asian Indians have similar incomes to white majority |
| **Work** | Unemployment rates for minorities generally higher than for white majority (Bangladeshis have highest levels of unemployment at 18%). Indian men have similar level of unemployment to white men (7%)<br>Horizontal occupational stratification: Bangladeshi men/women (66/40%) and Chinese men/women (40/40%) work in distribution, hotel and restaurant industry<br>Chinese and white Irish have highest rates of professional employment.<br>White women have higher rate of part-time working |
| **Crime** | Minorities more likely to be victims/arrested/remanded/imprisoned<br>Young more likely to be victims across all ethnic groups<br>Fear of crime greater among minority groups |
| **Education** | Boys: Chinese and Indian highest/black Caribbean lowest achievers at GCSE<br>Girls: Highest achievers at GCSE within each ethnic group<br>Black Caribbean had highest/Chinese and Indian lowest rates of school exclusion<br>No qualifications: white Irish (19%), Chinese (20%), and Indian (19%) |

Source: National Statistics Online (2005)

and **Butt** (2004) suggest racism '. . . is an important element of the processes that lead to typically poorer life chances for minority ethnic groups'. As an explanation, however, racism involves, as **Karlsen** and **Nazroo** (2002) suggest, a number of problems:

- **Interpretation**: The meaning of 'racist behaviour' varies considerably within and between groups and individuals.
- **Identification**: **Barker** (1981) makes a distinction between:
  - **old racism**, based on biological distinctions, that frequently involved overt forms of violent behaviour ('paki-bashing') and language, and a
  - **new racism**, based on cultural distinctions (ethnic minorities having different cultural attitudes and behaviours to the ethnic majority). This contemporary form, **Barker** argues, has evolved in subtle ways – partly because racism has become less acceptable in everyday life and partly as the result of legal proscriptions. Forms of cultural and institutional racism, for example, are especially difficult to prove.
- **Reporting**: Victims of racist behaviour are frequently reluctant to report their victimisation.

## The potting shed

Identify and briefly explain two reasons why victims may not report racist behaviour to the *police*.

We can note two further points here:

- **Underestimation**: These problems make

it impossible to determine the actual extent of racism in our society. **Modood et al.'s** (1997) research reported around 12% of their sample had experienced some form of racist behaviour in the previous year, whereas **Moriarty** and **Butt** (2004) reported 50% of their ethnic minority sample had 'experienced racism'.

- **Contexts**: A further problem is the extent to which experience of racist behaviour has different consequences in different contexts; for example, an employer's racist behaviour is likely to have a different impact on ethnic minority life chances than, for example, a casual racist remark.

## Class

In addition, **Moriarty** and **Butt** (2004) found that, in relation to a range of life chances, '. . . ethnicity proved to be less important than socio-economic status'; in other words, differential life chances, although influenced in some way by racist behaviour and attitudes, are far more likely to be influenced by:

**Social class**: In relation to health, for example, they found the lowest social classes suffered similar levels of poor health – regardless of ethnic background. In terms of income they also reported wide differences in ethnic life chances, with 'Asian-Indians over-represented in managerial and professional occupations' and Asian-Pakistani and black Caribbeans 'clustering . . . in routine and semi-routine occupations'. The implication here is that income distribution differences may be more easily explained by class profiles than by ethnicity. In addition:

**Human capital** explanations, based on market capabilities, show clear correlations between ethnic minority educational achievement (Asian Indians are above average and black Caribbeans below average) and future employment status. While this doesn't, of course, remove the possibility of racial discrimination in the education system being a factor in life chances, it's difficult to see why racism should be *selective* (black Caribbeans, but *not* Asian Indians, for example). Even more difficult to explain would be racism that targeted Asian *Pakistanis* but not Asian *Indians*.

**Social capital**: **Platt's** (2003) research found class background to be a significant factor in ethnic minority life chances, operating through social networks relating to family organisation and support. As she notes: 'Family background remains important in achieving occupational success and avoiding unemployment.' However, she also found differences across ethnic groups, with religion being a significant qualifying factor – Jewish and Hindu children, for example, had greater life chances than either their parents or their Christian counterparts, while the reverse was true for Muslim and Sikh children.

The significance of social capital for life chances is further evidenced by **Platt's** observation that many ethnic minority groups (Caribbean, black African, Indian and Chinese) achieved higher rates of social mobility (children, for example, moving from their parents' class to a higher class) than their white British counterparts. In a *cross-cultural context*, **Shapiro** (2004) has shown how 'racial inequality is passed down from generation to generation through the use of private family wealth' in the USA – with the white middle classes, in particular,

being best placed to provide their children with social, economic and educational supports that give them a range of advantages over other ethnic groups.

## Choices

**Life choices**: We can subdivide this area into two main types:

- **Rational choice** approaches focus on the ways ethnic minorities enhance or erode their general life chances through a range of choices.

- **Assimilation** arguments focus on ethnic minorities as 'outsider' and 'insider' groups. The former, through a failure, for whatever reason, to assimilate with the dominant (white, in the case of our society) culture place themselves at a cultural disadvantage by a failure to adopt norms, values and behaviours that would allow them to compete successfully in educational and economic markets. The latter, meanwhile, successfully integrate into the dominant culture and, in consequence, improve their general life chances to a level of, or in some cases beyond, those of the dominant culture.

## Underclass

**Underclass** arguments suggest those at the very bottom of society (or, in some cases, actually outside the class structure) are in such a position through the general choices their members make about family life and structure, educational qualifications and achievement, crime, work and so forth. Writers such as **Murray and Phillips** (2001) and **Saunders** (1990) variously suggest the lifestyle choices of some – but crucially not all – ethnic minorities place them at a severe economic disadvantage that, in turn, is passed on from one generation to the next. Thus, among Afro-Caribbeans, **Murray** argues, 'weak and unstable family structures' produce large numbers of single-parent families that lack the resources – or aptitude – to successfully control and motivate their offspring. This, in turn, leads to lower aspirations, educational failure, low work status and income that, in turn, perpetuate a *cycle of deprivation*.

Among Asian Indians, however, strong, extended family structures support offspring, instil a strong 'work ethic' and value educational qualifications as the means to improved social mobility and life chances. Thus, 'disproportionately lower life chances' among ethnic minority groups are not evidence of exploitation, discrimination and the like, but rather of cultural and family failings among such groups.

## Labour markets

**Labour market** approaches focus on the various ways economic markets operate in terms of, for example:

- **primary labour markets** consisting of relatively secure, well-paid, long-term employment that has some kind of career structure, and
- **secondary labour markets** consisting of low wages, poor conditions, no job security, training or promotion prospects.

The over-representation of some ethnic minorities in the latter – with its consequent lower life chances – reflects a range of choices (some of which are the result of structural factors, others the result of agency) made by different individuals. The availability of free, compulsory education free from overt discrimination, for example, represents a:

**Structure of choice** in the sense that educational qualifications offer a potential way out of poverty, for example – a route taken by some ethnic minority and majority children, but not others.

## Weeding the path

In relation to both of the above types of argument, **Heath** and **Payne's** (1999) analysis of government Labour Force Survey data suggests 'ethnic minorities have been able and willing to take advantage of the educational opportunities that Britain affords. The persistence of discrimination in the lower levels of the labour market looks on the current evidence to be the most likely explanation for the persistence of ethnic penalties'.

## Moving on

In the final section we can relate the ideas in this section to a more generalised discussion of the concept of social mobility, mainly because movement up or down the class structure is indicative of improving or declining life chances.

## 5. The nature, extent and significance of patterns of mobility

*Social mobility*, according to **Aldridge** (2001), 'describes the movement or opportunities for movement between different social groups, and the advantages and disadvantages that go with this in terms of income, security of employment, opportunities for advancement etc', and in this respect links neatly to the work we've previously done in this chapter, in a number of ways:

- **Stratification**: To talk about social

## WARM-UP: ARE YOU MOBILE?

We can construct a crude approximation of social mobility in the following way. Select one of the class scales (with sample occupations) we looked at in the section on measuring social class and complete the following table.

|  | Occupation | Class position |
|---|---|---|
| Your grandparents |  |  |
| Your parents |  |  |
| Your intended occupation |  |  |

Assuming you achieve your intended occupation:

1  Will you experience upward/downward mobility compared with your parents/grandparents?

2  As a class, is the general generational trend for upward/downward mobility/no change?

mobility makes sense only in the context of a system that ranks individuals and groups in some way.

- **Measuring class**: We need class scales against which to measure mobility.

- **Changing class structures**: If social movement is possible in class-based systems of stratification it helps us to visualise class structures as relatively fluid systems.

- **Life chances**: Mobility is a tangible measure of life chances in that where people experience upward mobility we might expect their life chances to improve (with the reverse being true, of course).

## Preparing the ground: The nature of social mobility

To understand the nature of social mobility in our society we need to think about how it can be:

**Operationalised**: This involves understanding how it is both defined and measured. In this respect, *social* mobility (as opposed to other types, such as *income* mobility – the extent to which income rises or falls over a given period) is a measure of changing:

**Status** – in basic terms, the 'social standing' of an individual or group in a given society. More specifically, mobility studies focus on the idea of occupational status as the basic unit of measurement/comparison and in this respect social mobility has two major dimensions:

- **Absolute mobility**, according to **Lawson** and **Garrod** (2003), is a measure of the 'total number of movements up or down a class structure within a given period'. In other words, as **Chattoe** and **Heath** (2001) put it, 'absolute social mobility simply looks at the number of people moving from one class to another'.

---

**Examples of absolute and relative mobility**

We can use the example of **income differences and changes** to illustrate these ideas – Jill, who earns £200 per week, and Jack, who earns £100 per week.

Both receive a 10% pay increase (Jill now earns £220 and Jack now earns £110).

**Absolute (income) mobility**: *Both* Jack and Jill have experienced upward mobility.

**Relative (income) mobility**: Jill has experienced *upward* mobility compared with Jack, whereas Jack has experienced *downward* mobility compared with Jill.

Although we have used income for illustrative purposes (because it's easier to demonstrate mobility differences if we *quantify* changes), the basic *principle*, in terms of status differences, remains the same.

---

- **Relative mobility**, according to **Aldridge** (2001), '. . . is concerned with the *chances* people from different backgrounds have of attaining different social positions'. That is, a measure of the ways mobility varies according to someone's starting position in the class structure.

## ⚠ Weeding the path

The distinction between *absolute* and *relative* forms of social mobility is important for sociological analysis because we will arrive at different estimates of social mobility depending on how we measure it. It is, for example, possible for *absolute* forms of social mobility to increase in a society while *relative* mobility does not increase – an idea we can illustrate using the example of a:

**Caste system** where an individual cannot, during their lifetime, move upwards from one caste position to another – there is *no relative mobility* in this system. It is, however, possible for whole positions in the system to move up or down in status terms. A particular *occupation* can improve its caste position – *absolute* forms of social mobility *are* possible within this system.

In terms of actually *measuring* social mobility, we can note two different types of measurement:

- **Intergenerational** mobility refers to movement *between* generations (such as the difference between a parent's and a child's occupational position). For example, a manual worker's child who becomes a bank manager would experience upward social mobility, whereas a bank manager's child who became a bricklayer would experience downward social mobility.

- **Intragenerational** measures explore the progress made by an individual up – or down – the class structure over a *single generation*. This might involve, for example, comparing someone's *starting* occupation with their occupation on *retirement* (although a study of such length is quite rare – most mobility studies of this type tend to cover a period of 10–15 years).

---

## ✳ SYNOPTIC LINK

**Theory and methods:** Mobility studies, by definition, are *longitudinal studies*; they compare changes in social mobility over a given time period.

---

# 🌱 Growing it yourself: Ascribing achievement

Even in relatively open, class-type systems mobility chances are not based purely on achievement – ascribed factors (such as family background) also play a part.

Using the following table as a guide, identify examples of different achieved/ascribed factors that potentially affect levels of social mobility in our society.

| | Achieved factors | Ascribed factors |
|---|---|---|
| **Family** | Single parenthood | Parents' social class |
| **Education** | Qualifications | |
| **Politics** | | |
| **Work** | Promotion | |
| **Health** | | Illness |
| **Wealth and poverty** | | Inheritance |

## ⚠️ Digging deeper: The nature of social mobility

We can note a range of factors that enhance or inhibit our ability to measure social mobility:

**Stratification systems**: Some systems have greater openness or closure than others; open systems (such as those based around social class) allow greater general levels of social mobility than closed systems (such as those based on caste or feudal principles). In this respect we can note two concepts affecting levels of mobility:

- **Ascription**: In societies and stratification systems based on ascribed characteristics (such as gender, age or ethnicity), *relative* social mobility will be difficult at best and impossible at worst. *Absolute* mobility does, however, remain a possibility (the status of one ethnic group, for example, may improve while the status of another declines).

- **Achievement**: In societies and stratification systems based on achieved characteristics (such as educational qualifications), both *relative* and *absolute* forms of social mobility will be possible.

## Absolute

**Absolute mobility** is sometimes called *structural mobility* because it relates to changes in, for example, the class structure of modern societies. When we discussed explanations of changes in the class structure we saw how the development of a *service economy* has led to an expansion of middle-class occupations at the expense of working-class (industrial) occupations. In this respect, therefore, we would expect to see an *increase* in structural social mobility over the past century simply because there are now more middle-class occupations in the economy. We would, on this basis, expect to see further (although perhaps smaller) increases in absolute mobility with the development of a knowledge economy.

## Relative

**Relative mobility** is sometimes called *exchange mobility* because individuals 'exchange relative positions' in the class structure – as some people experience upward social mobility, others experience downward mobility. In some respects this type is related to *achieved* characteristics such as educational qualifications. As people become better qualified, for example, we might expect them to take higher positions to replace those with lower qualifications (a *meritocratic* explanation for exchange

mobility). An example we could note is that of:

**Demographic changes** in society: Where women come into the workforce in increasing numbers (as has happened in our society over the past century) this creates, at various times, *exchange mobility*. A woman who in the past might have stayed in the home to care for her family now comes into the workforce to compete on equal terms.

## ⚠ Preparing the ground: The extent of social mobility

We can summarise some of the broad patterns of mobility that have emerged from a range of studies in the following terms:

- **Absolute (structural) mobility**: One of the major trends in our society over the past century has been the increase in absolute social mobility resulting from structural changes in economic organisation. **Gallie** (2001) cites the decline in manual occupations (from around 75% of the workforce in 1911 to around 35% in 2000) and the increase in

**Absolute social mobility: diagrammatic representation**

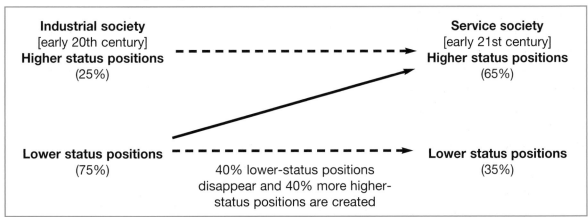

Source: Based on Gallie (2001)

managerial/professional occupations (from around 7% to 35%) over the same period. In other words, at the beginning of the twentieth century around three-quarters of the class structure consisted of jobs defined broadly as working class, whereas at the start of the twenty-first century the picture was reversed – around three-quarters of all occupations can be defined as middle class.

Within this general trend, **Heath** and **Payne's** (1999) review of mobility studies in the twentieth century – from the early work of **Chapman** and **Abbott** (1913), through **Glass** and **Hall's** (1954) mobility studies of Britain in the 1940s, to **Goldthorpe et al.'s** (1980) studies of male mobility in England and Wales of the early 1970s and beyond (using data from the British Election Surveys) – found that:

**Intergenerational mobility** 'rose during the course of the century for both men and women'. In the latter part of the twentieth century, for example, around 40% of men and 36% of women experienced upward mobility (compared with their fathers) and 13% and 27% respectively experienced downward mobility.

### ⚠ Weeding the path

Figures for female mobility are likely to be biased by the fact that the majority of mobility studies have, as **Heath** and **Payne** note, 'regarded the family as the unit of class stratification and have taken the father's position to be the best guide to the social class of the household as a whole'. A more reliable measure of female mobility would be to compare 'like with like' by relating female children to their mother's occupation,

although since women, for the majority of the twentieth century at least, were unlikely to have full-time paid occupations this would also produce biased results in this particular context.

**Paterson** and **Iannelli** (2004) confirm these conclusions about absolute mobility in the UK and, interestingly, extend it to include 'all developed societies' – something that suggests changes to the UK class structure are a trend extending across Western societies. As they suggest, experience of intergenerational mobility is something of a norm in the sense that 'it is normal for people to occupy a different class to that in which they were brought up'.

One interesting feature of structural mobility, however, is the distinction between:

* **short-range social mobility**, usually defined in terms of moving one adjacent position up or down the class structure – using the **National Statistics Socio-Economic Classification** (NS-SEC), this might involve moving from class 2 (lower managerial) to class 1 (higher managerial) – and

* **long-range social mobility**, usually defined as moving two or more positions up or down the class structure – using the NS-SEC, this might involve moving from class 6 (semi-routine occupations) to class 2 (lower managerial).

**Heath** and **Payne** found little evidence of *long-range social mobility* in Britain during the twentieth century – the majority of intergenerational mobility was short-range and **Yaqub** (2000) estimates around 'two-thirds of all mobility' in the UK (and the majority of Western societies) is short-range. What long-range mobility there was in the

UK (**Heath** and **Payne** estimate around 10% of working-class males move from the working class into the service class, with the reverse being true for service-class males) reflects:

**Relative (exchange) mobility: Paterson** and **Iannelli** (2004) note the available evidence suggests relative mobility in Britain was both small in scale and relatively unchanging throughout the 20th century. As they conclude: 'Between different classes of origin, the relative chances of being in one destination class rather than another have hardly changed at all.' In other words, the chances of an individual moving from the working class to the service class, for example, are extremely low. **Erikson** and **Goldthorpe** (1992) similarly conclude that exchange mobility in Western societies is both low and constant (when compared with *structural mobility*).

## Weeding the path

This observation suggests Britain is *not* a particularly:

**Socially fluid** society: Outside of major structural changes in the class structure, the chances of both upward and downward social mobility are fairly small. In this respect, our society (in common, **Aldridge** (2004) argues, with countries like France, Germany and the USA) seems to exhibit:

**Social closure** in terms of occupational mobility: **Powell** (2002) defines closure in terms of 'restrictions placed on people's ability to engage in certain occupational endeavours' that are reflected by 'rules and criteria restricting entry into the practice of all but the most menial and unrewarding of occupations'. This results, he argues, in 'collective entry requirements for practising

various occupations and professions that effectively work to limit social mobility'. In other words, one explanation for the lack of relative mobility is that it is restricted by the way certain occupational groups act to close off entry to 'outsiders'. In terms of professional work (such as dentistry or accountancy) this idea is sometimes expressed as:

**Elite self-recruitment** – the ability of elites to ensure their sons (and increasingly daughters) are recruited into the same, or higher, occupational levels as their parents. Recent evidence generally supports this argument. **Stanworth** and **Giddens** (1974) found clear evidence of elite recruitment among company chairmen in large corporations from 1900 onwards. Similarly, **Jeremy** (1998) observed that 'the typical 20th century business leader is upper- or upper middle-class by social origin, rising through the public schools and Oxbridge into the higher echelons of the business community', while **Nicholas's** (1999) survey of the social origins of business leaders from 1850 to the present concluded that his findings 'reinforce the majority case that British business is dominated by elite sub-groups of the population ... the interconnected socio-economic characteristics of family wealth and a high status education precipitated unequal access to leading business positions'.

## The potting shed

Identify and briefly explain two ways parents occupying elite occupational positions try to ensure the recruitment of their children into a similar class position.

Gallie (2001) identifies a further problem in relation to relative mobility when he notes differences in terms of 'opportunities for skill development ... a majority of semi- and non-skilled employees are excluded from the broad process of rising skill requirements at work'. He uses the term:

Skill entrapment to suggest that where people receive little in the way of workplace training there are few opportunities to develop new or improved skills, something that, in turn, reduces the possibilities for relative (upward) social mobility (although, as he notes, the chances of downward mobility – through an increased likelihood of long-term unemployment among low-skill workers – is actually increased).

## Intergenerational mobility

Aldridge (2004), like Heath and Payne, suggests this type of mobility has been the most common in our society over the past century and, similarly, suggests mobility has mainly been:

Structural, since 'economic and social change has increased employment opportunities in the professional classes'. This has not only increased the intergenerational mobility of former members of the working class, but also, Aldridge argues, 'allowed an increasing proportion of children whose parents were in the higher social classes to remain there'. If this is the case we would expect to see a slowdown in upward intergenerational mobility, as realignments in the class structure start to settle down and close off this particular avenue. In this respect we can note the influence of:

Globalisation in relation to structural mobility: At present economic globalisation in Western societies has had greater impact on the relationship between industrial-type and service-type economies (in terms of, for example, the relocation of (manual) manufacturing employment to developing societies with less government regulation, lower taxation and lower labour costs). However, we are already starting to see a further change with the relocation of mainly routine forms of service employment (such as call centres) to developing countries such as India, Burma and China. If this process continues (with the development of increasingly sophisticated forms of telecommunications and software, for example) it's possible to envisage a situation in which some higher forms of service employment (computer programming, management consultancy, accountancy and the like) are similarly relocated – a situation that may result in an increase in downward (structural) mobility as some parts of the service sector in Western economies contract.

## Intergenerational mobility

Aldridge (2001) argues *economic mobility* (defined broadly in terms of income and earnings) has shown a great deal of fluctuation – both upward and downward – in recent years and although it's a narrower measure of mobility than its social counterpart, it still represents a useful indicator of general mobility trends at the *intragenerational* level. In this respect, economic mobility confirms the general trend of social mobility in Britain in that it is generally short-range – incomes tend to rise and fall (in relative terms) across a relatively narrow range. Aldridge also argues that upward intragenerational mobility – 'from manual occupations to higher status professional and technical occupations' – has *declined* in recent years through a process of:

**Professional** (social) **closure**: A tightening of entry requirements across 'higher-status occupations' has effectively meant they are 'closed from below': in other words, it is impossible to enter these professions without having been through a certain level of education (from A levels, through an undergraduate degree) to professional entrance exams). Where outside entry is not possible, long-range intragenerational mobility across the class structure is curtailed – as indeed are certain forms of short-range mobility from within the middle classes, since transfers from lower status to higher status professions are similarly difficult (**Rajamanickam** (2004) notes the 'territorial struggle between the upstart, clinical psychology, and the established authority of psychiatry over the last three decades').

available. Social mobility, therefore, represents an important mechanism through which people are encouraged to develop and use their talents since it rewards their efforts in various ways (through higher incomes, status and so forth).

- **Political**: Social mobility represents a form of social control for two reasons. At an *individual level* people appreciate their abilities and merits will be recognised and appropriately rewarded – the idea that promotions, for example, are based on merit as opposed to 'who you know' (*nepotism*). On a group level, if a particular section of society, such as ethnic minorities, finds its chances of advancement artificially blocked (through discrimination for instance), such people may develop behaviours that are both socially and economically disruptive.

## ⚠ Digging deeper: The significance of social mobility

We can assess the significance of social mobility on a number of levels, the first of which being whether mobility does or doesn't exist within a society. In this respect, **Chattoe** and **Heath** (2001) argue mobility is important for two main reasons:

- **Pragmatic**: Modern societies require people with the skills and abilities to ensure economic systems function efficiently and this means that economies, if they are to develop and expand, have to make the best use of the talents

## ⌂ The potting shed

Apart from rioting, identify and briefly explain one other form of 'social or economic disruption'.

Similarly, **Aldridge** (2001) suggests mobility is a significant concept in terms of what it tells us about:

**Equality of opportunity**: A lack of mobility in society 'implies inequality of opportunity'.

**Social cohesion**: This is more likely to be achieved in a situation where people believe they can 'improve the quality of life they and their children enjoy through their abilities, talents and efforts'.

In these terms, therefore, social mobility is both *culturally* and *individually* significant in terms of an ideology of:

**Merit** – the general idea that people should be rewarded for their efforts and abilities. This concept raises questions about the significance of mobility in terms of whether it is based on structural changes or meritocratic factors.

## Disputes

As we've seen, there is no dispute that, over the past century, social mobility has occurred – and continues to occur – in our society. The nature and causes of mobility, and hence its cultural and individual significance, however, are a matter of dispute we can summarise in the following terms:

**Absolute mobility**: Over the past 25 years or so writers like **Goldthorpe** (1980), **Halsey et al.** (1980), **Marshall** and **Swift** (1996) and **Breen** and **Goldthorpe** (1999) have argued that social mobility has been predominantly *structural* in nature; in other words, mobility that resulted from changes in the economic and cultural organisation of our society (such as the change from a predominantly industrial to a predominantly service economy). In this respect, mobility has occurred almost 'by default' in the sense that it originates from a decline in (mainly working-class) manufacturing jobs and an increase in (mainly middle-class) service jobs – not to put too fine a point on it, there are more jobs defined as middle class in contemporary Britain than in the past.

**Relative mobility**: Goldthorpe et al. (1980) argue this has been both minimal and relatively unchanging (both nationally over the past 50–100 years and internationally among Western societies) – a significant claim because relative mobility is more likely to occur in meritocratic societies; if people are given the opportunity through their abilities, efforts and personal sacrifices to achieve upward mobility we should expect to see high levels of relative mobility (some members of the working class will, for example, work hard to achieve mobility, 'lazier' members of the middle class will experience downward mobility and the like).

## Weeding the path

The relationship between absolute and relative mobility is significant for a couple of reasons:

- **Limited mobility**: At a time of rapid structural change mobility will increase; however, once an economy 'settles down' (for example, the change from an industrial to a post-industrial society is complete), levels of absolute mobility will necessarily fall.

- **Social closure**: For **Goldthorpe et al.** (1980) levels of relative mobility are more significant 'in the long run' because they tell us something about the nature of:

  - **society** – such as the extent to which it can be characterised as meritocratic

- **class structure** – the extent to which it is characterised by social closure, for example, and
- **life chances** – in terms of the relation between these and social mobility.

In other words, the significance of **Goldthorpe et al.'s** claim to have found little or no evidence of *relative mobility* is that it suggests that various forms of *social closure* are powerful mechanisms in our society that limit opportunities for mobility.

## ⚠ Weeding the path

**Saunders** (1995, 1997, 2002) has taken issue with the general body of research we've just outlined, and although the overall arguments about mobility are *very complicated* and *highly technical*; these relate to different ways of *reliably* and *validly* measuring mobility – the 'odds ratios' favoured by **Goldthorpe et al.** that calculate the chances of a child remaining in the class into which they were born as against 'disparity ratios' favoured by **Saunders** that calculate the relative chances of upward or downward mobility for children of various classes. However, interpretations of what constitutes 'merit' and how it can be calculated need not overly concern us here, and we can summarise **Saunders'** main arguments in terms of:

**Absolute mobility: Saunders** argues we shouldn't dismiss 'lightly' the extensive evidence for this type of mobility since it is indicative of a general rise in both living standards and life chances across the class structure. The implication here is that **Goldthorpe et al.** underplay the significance of structural mobility because it doesn't fit neatly with their general argument that

mobility is heavily restricted by social closure.

**Relative mobility, Saunders** argues, is far more extensive than **Goldthorpe et al.** suggest, for two reasons. First, it is more difficult to define and measure than absolute mobility, and second, as we've just noted, different types of measurement produce different levels of mobility. A crucial difference here, between the two basic positions, is the assumptions each makes about the causes of mobility.

**Goldthorpe et al.** assume there are *no innate differences* in intelligence and aptitude between the members of different social classes; given the same levels of opportunity and social development, a working-class child *should* have the same relative mobility chances as a middle-class child, 'all things being equal' – that is, without the intervention of cultural factors, such as schooling differences, that give the latter certain 'mobility inhibitors' (things that prevent downward mobility). On the basis of this assumption (which **Marshall** and **Swift** (1996) argue is justified by the sociological literature surrounding the nature of intelligence and its distribution within the population), the argument here is that:

**Educational achievement** is a valid measure of 'intelligence and aptitude' as it is mediated through various social factors, such as class, parental income, type of schooling and so forth.

**Saunders,** however, argues that:

**Intelligence,** as historically measured through IQ tests, is both a significant variable and one that differs between social classes. Although stopping short of claiming IQ is determined at birth, **Saunders** argues that *social* and *developmental* factors effectively produce the *same* results –

middle-class children are, in general, more intelligent than their working-class peers. On this basis, therefore, **Saunders** claims two things. First, that relative social mobility would be higher in our society if it wasn't inhibited by variables such as class differences in intelligence (*social closure*, in effect, based on 'natural class differences').

Second, because on average middle-class children are more intelligent (and have more intelligent parents), it's not surprising that relative mobility (no pun intended) is not greater. Middle-class children and parents, for example, can insure against downward mobility through educational qualifications (and the fact they generally do better than their working-class peers), while the majority of working-class children are unable to achieve the levels of qualification they need to compete against their middle-class counterparts in the mobility stakes.

## Weeding the path

In this situation we are faced with two different interpretations of the relationship between relative mobility and meritocracy. For **Breen** (1997) the absence of relative mobility represents evidence of a *non-meritocratic* society – there is little or no relative mobility *because* of various forms of social closure. For **Saunders**, meanwhile, the absence of large-scale relative mobility is taken as *evidence of* meritocracy – those who are 'most able' in society can, at the very least, insulate themselves against individual forms of downward mobility.

Although arguments about the nature, extent and types of mobility in our society are significant, it should be evident from the

above that broad levels of agreement exist over the fact of mobility itself – Britain is, in this respect, a relatively *open system* in which social mobility is seen as both possible and, in many respects, desirable. Although debates over the significance of different *types* of mobility – and how they can be reliably and validly measured – are important, we can complete this section with a number of concluding observations about the *meaning* of social mobility in terms of what it does – and does not – tell us about the nature of our society.

## Meaning

**Social mobility**: One of the problems we have is that mobility can be considered in terms of both the individual and society; in individual terms, for example, upward mobility is generally considered 'good and desirable', and downward mobility generally seen as being 'bad and undesirable'. However, as **Miles** (1996) notes: 'The significance of social mobility extends beyond the personal concerns of particular individuals and their families; for it is the *overall pattern of mobility* which gives shape and structure to society as a whole'. This idea relates, in part, to questions of:

**Social cohesion**: **Miles** suggests that while 'too little mobility is disruptive because it encourages distinct and potentially antagonist social identities', the opposite may also be true – *too much mobility* can be socially destabilising because it may result in 'disorientation and alienation' and thereby damage social stability.

**Life chances and choices**: Upward and downward mobilities impact on individual and group life chances both historically (in the sense of intergenerational differences in wealth, for example) and in terms of intragenerational mobility; those who experience downward social mobility, for example, generally also experience a fall in their general life chances (and vice versa).

**Meritocracy** and **social closure**: The relationship between these ideas is a complex one – the two are not mutually exclusive in the sense that a 'meritocratic society' is not automatically one where individual life chances are free from various forms of social closure (such as sexual and racial discrimination). **Saunders** (2005) has noted that social closure remains 'a problem' in meritocratic societies in terms of the idea that 'the true test of the openness of a society is not the rate of upward mobility but downward mobility. The real question is whether successful people can help their kids cling on to their status, particularly if those kids are not very bright'. The fact that both merit and closure operate in our society suggests the class and mobility structure is not smoothly tapering but rather a:

**Segmented structure**: That is, some parts of the class structure are relatively more open (or closed) than others. Both **Marshall** and **Swift** (1996) and **Saunders** (2002) recognise the highest levels of the UK class structure are effectively *closed systems*; it is very difficult, if not impossible, for people from lower down the class structure to break into these higher levels since admission is not simply about wealth – it also involves a sense of culture and history.

Lower down the class structure merit becomes more important – a university education, for example, represents a *ladder* up which it is possible for working-class children to climb and gain entry to professional occupations.

## ⌂ The potting shed

Identify and briefly explain two advantages enjoyed by middle-class parents that can be used to explain the relative success of middle-class children in our education system.

The concept of *segmentation*, although similar to that of *fragmentation*, differs in the way it is possible to talk about relatively coherent structures of class, gender, ethnicity and so forth. Within each of these structures different groups experience different levels of mobility based around concepts of *openness* (merit) and *closure* – but the important point is that, taken as a whole, each structure (whether it be middle class and working class, males and females or majority and minority ethnic groups) offers broadly similar experiences to its members. The idea of segmented mobilities, in this respect, can be illustrated by reference to areas like:

**Gender**, where, as we've seen, various forms of closure (such as glass trapdoors) operate. Nevertheless, new technologies and service industries have, to some extent, acted as *mobility facilitators* by not only opening up a range of occupations to women, but also opening up ways of working (part-time, home office and so forth) that fit with the various choices women make about their lives.

**Ethnicity**: Although it's possible to see:

**Racial discrimination** as a form of social closure that blocks off certain occupational levels for ethnic minorities, it's evident that segmented mobility is an increasingly significant concept in the explanation of different forms and levels of mobility among

**507**

different ethnic groups. This works in two ways:

First, different ethnic groups experience different levels of mobility, and second, *within* ethnic groups factors such as class, gender and age play a part in the explanation for different mobility rates and experiences. **Platt's** (2003, 2005) research into the relationship between ethnic migration and social mobility reveals a range of interesting facts about segmental mobility.

In terms of *migration, first-generation immigrants* from most ethnic groups frequently experienced high initial rates of *downward mobility* – leaving, for example, white-collar employment in their country of origin for manual work in their country of destination. However, the picture is reversed for subsequent generations, with increased levels of upward mobility. Both Indians and Caribbeans in **Platt's** study 'show distinctive patterns of intergenerational mobility' – much of it upward. She also argues that once structural changes have been taken into account, many ethnic minority groups show greater than expected levels of relative mobility.

# References

## Chapter 1: Religion

Abrams, Mark, Gerard, David and Timms, Noel (eds), 1985, *Values and Social Change in Britain*: Macmillan

Adams, Bert and Sydie, R.A., 2001, *Sociological Theory:* Pine Forge Press

Adler, Margot, 1979, *Drawing Down the Moon*: Viking Press

Alexander, Jeffrey, 1985, 'Neofunctionalism: An Introduction' in Jeffrey Alexander (ed.), *Neofunctionalism*: Sage Publications

Alexander, Jeffrey, 1995, 'Modern, Anti, Post, Neo': *New Left Review*, No. 210, March/April

Alpert, Harry, 1939, *Emile Durkheim and His Sociology*: Columbia University Press

Althusser, Louis, 1972, *Ideology and Ideological State Apparatuses*: David McKay Company Inc.

Ammerman, Nancy, 1997, 'Organized Religion in a Voluntaristic Society': *Sociology of Religion*, Vol. 58, No. 3

Archbishop of Canterbury's Commission on Urban Priority Areas, 1985, 'Faith in the City. A Call to Action by Church and Nation'

Azad, Ali, 1995, 'Imperialism and Struggle in Iran': *Workers World*, March

Bader, Christopher, 2003, 'Supernatural Support Groups: Who Are the UFO Abductees and Ritual-Abuse Survivors?': *Journal for the Scientific Study of Religion*, Vol. 42, Issue 4

Balibar, Étienne and Althusser, Louis, 1970, *Reading Capital*: New Left Books

Barker, Eileen, 1999, *New Religious Movements: A Practical Introduction* (2nd edition): HMSO

Barley, Revd Lynda (Head of Research and Statistics for the Archbishops' Council), 2005, quoted in: 'Attendance figures for 2003 published': http://www.cofe.anglican.org/news/pr0106.html

Barna, George, 1996, *Index of Leading Spiritual Indicators*: Word Publishing

Barrett, David, Kurian, George and Johnson, Todd (eds), 2001, *World Christian Encyclopedia: A comparative survey of churches and religions in the modern world*: Oxford University Press

Bartkowski, John, 2000, 'Breaking Walls, Raising Fences: Masculinity, Intimacy, and Accountability among the Promise Keepers': *Sociology of Religion*, Vol. 61, No. 1

Bates, Stephen, 2005, 'Church sees rise in Sunday worship': *The Guardian*, January 8

Baudrillard, Jean, 2001, *Impossible Exchange* (Chris Turner, trans.): Verso

Baudrillard, Jean, 1998, 'Simulacra and Simulations' in 'Mark Poster (ed.), *Selected Writings*: Stanford University Press

Bauman, Zygmunt, 1997, *Postmodernity and its Discontents*: Polity Press

Bauman, Zygmunt, 1992, *Intimations of Postmodernity*: Routledge

Beck, Ulrich, 1992, *Risk Society – Towards a New Modernity*: Sage

Beckford, James, 1994, 'The Mass Media and New Religious Movements': Conference Paper, International Conference on Religion and Conflict

Beckford, James, 2004, 'Religion and Postmodernity': *Sociology Review*, Philip Allen Publishers, November

Beckford, James, 1980, 'Scientology, Social Science and the Definition of Religion', http://www.neuereligion.de/ENG/Beckford/0a.htm

Bellah, Robert, 1967, 'Civil Religion in America': *Daedalus* (journal of the American Academy of Arts and Sciences), 96

Bental, Brian, 2004, *Sociological Theory*: East Central University

Berer, Marge and Sundari Ravindran, T.K., 1996, 'Fundamentalism, Women's Empowerment and Reproductive Rights': Global Reproductive Health Forum: http://www.hsph.harvard.edu/Organizations/ healthnet/index. html

Berger, Peter (ed.), 1999, *The Desecularization of the World*: Ethics and Public Policy Center, Washington

Berger, Peter, 1973, *The Social Reality of Religion*: Penguin

Berger, Peter, 1967, *The Sacred Canopy: Elements of a Sociological Theory of Religion*: Doubleday

Berthoud, Richard, 1998, *Incomes of Ethnic Minorities*: Institute for Social and Economic Research

Bettinger, Robert, 1996, 'Neofunctionalism' in David Levinson and Melvin Ember (eds), *The Encyclopedia of Cultural Anthropology*: Henry Holt

Bežovan, Gojko, 2004, *Luhmann's Understanding of the Function of Religion*: Institute of Social Sciences

Bilton, Tony, Bonnett, Kevin, Jones, Pip, Skinner, David, Stanworth, Michelle and Webster, Andrew, 1996, *Introductory Sociology* (3rd edition): Macmillan

Björkqvist, Kaj, 1990, 'World-rejection, world-affirmation, and goal displacement: some aspects of change in three new religious movements of Hindu origin' in Nils Holm (ed.), *Encounter with India: studies in Neohinduism*: Åbo Akademi University Press

Blasi, Anthony, 1998, 'Definition of Religion' in William Swatos, Jr (ed.), *Encyclopedia of Religion and Society*: Hartford Institute for Religion Research

Boff, Leonardo and Boff, Clodovis, 1987, *Introducing Liberation Theology*: Pantheon Books

Boronski, Tomas, 1987, *Knowledge*: Longman

Brierley, Peter (ed.), 1999, *UK Christian Handbook: Religious Trends 1999/2000*: Christian Research Association

British Social Attitudes Survey: Belonging to a religion, Great Britain, 2001

British Social Attitudes Survey: National Centre for Social Research, November 2000

British Social Attitudes Survey: National Centre for Social Research, 1983–1999

Brown, Callum, 2001, *The Death of Christian Britain*: Routledge

Brown, Michael, 2004, 'American spirits: the Neopagan and New Age movements have now been put under the microscope of anthropology': *Natural History*, November

Bruce, Steve, 2002, *God is Dead: Secularization in the West*: Blackwell

Bruce, Steve, 2001, 'Christianity in Britain, R.I.P.': *Sociology of Religion*, Summer

Bruce, Steve, 1995, *Religion in Modern Britain*: Oxford University Press

Bruneau, Thomas and Hewitt, W.E., 1992, 'Catholicism and Political Action in Brazil: Limitations and Prospects' in Edward Cleary and Hannah Stewart-Gambino (eds), *Conflict and Competition: The Latin American Church in a Changing Environment*: Lynne Rienner Publishers, Inc.

Callinicos, Alex, 1991, *Against Postmodernism: a Marxist critique*: Polity Press

Canin, Eric, 2001, *Minguito, Managua's Little Saint: Christian Base Communities and Popular Religion in Urban Nicaragua*: California State University

Casanova, Jose, 1994, *Public Religions in the Modern World*: University of Chicago Press

Castells, Manuel, 1997, 'The Power of Identity' in *The Information Age: Economy, Society and Culture*, Vol. 2: Blackwell

Census 2001: Office for National Statistics, 2003; General Register Office for Scotland, 2003

Chryssides, George, 2000, 'Defining the New Spirituality': CESNUR Conference Paper, August

Cimino, Richard and Lattin, Don, 2002, *Shopping for Faith: American Religion in the New Millennium*: Jossey-Bass Inc.

Cline, Austin, 2005, 'What Is Religion?': http://atheism.about.com/mbiopage.htm

Cody, David, 1988, 'Methodism': The Victorian Web, http://www.victorianweb.org/religion/ methodist.html

Cohen, Daniel and Prusak, Laurence, 2001, *In Good Company. How social capital makes organizations work*: Harvard Business School Press

Coleman, Bruce, 1980, 'Religion in the Victorian City': *History Today*, Vol. 30, 8 August

Colls, Robert, 2005, 'When We Lived In Communities' in Robert Colls and Richard Rodger (eds), *Cities of Ideas. Governance and Citizenship in Urban Britain 1800–2000*: Ashgate

Cook, Len (National Statistician), 2003, 'Ethnic group statistics: A guide for the collection and classification of ethnicity data': Office for National Statistics

Cooke, Rachel, 2003, 'The sleek shall inherit the Church': *The Observer*, December 21

Cowan, Douglas, 2003, 'Health as the Integrating Core of New Age': Religious Movements Home Page Project, http://religiousmovements.lib.virginia.edu/

Crockett, Alasdair and Voas, David, 2004, 'Generations of decline: Religious change in twentieth-century Britain': *Journal for the Scientific Study of Religion*

Cumming, Elaine and Henry, William, 1961, *Growing Old: The process of disengagement*: Basic Books

Daly, Mary, 1986, *The Church and the Second Sex*: Beacon Press (first published 1968)

Daly, Mary, 1973, *Beyond God the Father*: Beacon Press

Daschke, Dereck and Ashcraft, W. Michael (eds), 2005, *New Religious Movements: A Documentary Reader*: NYU Press

Davie, Grace, 2002, 'Praying Alone? Church-going in Britain and the Putnam Thesis: A Reply to Steve Bruce': *Journal of Contemporary Religion*, 17 (3)

Davie, Grace, 2001, 'From Obligation to Consumption: Patterns of Religion in Northern Europe': Seminar Paper on European Secularity in Berlin

Davie, Grace, 1994, *Religion in Britain Since 1945: Believing without Belonging*: Blackwell

de Geest, Gwendolyn, 2002, 'Spirituality: The Older Adults' Search for Meaning': Symposium on Aging, International Conference on Personal Meaning

Dobbelaere, Karel, 1981, *Secularization*: Sage

Dobbelaere, Karel and Jagodzinski, Wolfgang, 1995, 'Religious and Ethical Pluralism' in Jan van Deth and Elinor Scarbrough (eds), *Beliefs in Government: The impact of values*: Oxford University Press

Dogan, Mattei, 2004, 'From Social Class and Religious Identity to Status Incongruence in Post-Industrial Societies': *Comparative Sociology*, Vol. 3, No. 2: Brill Academic Publishers

Dorsett, Richard, 1998, *Ethnic Minorities in the Inner City*: The Policy Press

Durkheim, Emile, 1995, *Elementary Forms of the Religious Life* (Karen Fields, trans.): The Free Press (first published 1912)

Durkheim, Emile, 1951, *Suicide: A Study in Sociology*: Free Press (first published 1897)

Eliade, Mircea (ed.), 1987, *Encyclopedia of Religion*: Macmillan

Eliade, Mircea, 1969, *The Quest; History and Meaning in Religion*: University of Chicago Press

Engs, Ruth, 2002, *The Hilty Pneuman Religious Inventory*: Indiana University

Enroth, Ronald, 1994, *Recovering From Churches That Abuse*: Zondervan

Enroth, Ronald, 1993, *Churches That Abuse*: Zondervan

Evans, David and Campany, Richard, 1985, 'Iran-Iraq: Bloody Tomorrows': Naval Institute Proceedings, January

Eyre, Anne, 1996, 'Religious cults in twentieth century America':

American Studies Today Online, http://www.americansc.org.uk/Online/cults.htm

Faith in the UK (Mori opinion poll for the BBC), August 2003, http://www.bbc.co.uk/religion/programmes/heavenandearth/mori_data.shtml

Fanfani, Amintore, 2003, *Catholicism, Protestantism, and Capitalism*: HIS Press

Farley, John, 1990, *Sociology*: Prentice Hall

Finke, Roger and Stark, Rodney, 2004, 'The Dynamics of Religious Economies' in Michele Dillon (ed.), *Handbook of the Sociology of Religion*: Cambridge University Press

Flew, Antony, 1971, 'Theology and Falsification: A Symposium' in Basil Mitchell (ed.), *The Philosophy of Religion*: Oxford University Press

Foucault, Michel, 1983, quoted in Hubert Dreyfus and Paul Rabinow, *Michel Foucault: Beyond Structuralism and Hermeneutics* (2nd edition): University of Chicago Press

Francis, David and Hester, Stephen, 2004, *An Invitation to Ethnomethodology*: Sage Publications

Francis, Lesley and Robbins, Mandy, 2004, 'Belonging without believing: a study in the social significance of Anglican identity and empirical religion among 13–15 year old males': *Implicit Religion*, Vol. 7, Issue 1

Fraser, Giles, 2005, 'God's Been Mugged': *The Guardian*, June 6

Furlong, Monica, 2002, *C of E: The State It's In*: Stoughton

Galper, Marvin, 1982, 'The cult phenomenon: behavioral science perspectives applied to therapy' in Florence Kaslow and Marvin Sussman (eds), 'Cults and the family': *Marriage & Family Review*, Vol. 4, No. 3: Haworth Press

Gans, Herbert, 1971, 'The Uses of Poverty: The Poor Pay All': *Social Policy*, July/August

Giddens, Anthony, 2001, *Sociology* (4th edition): Polity

Giroux, Henry, 2004, 'The Passion of the Right: Religious Fundamentalism and the Growing Threat to Democracy': www.dissidentvoice.org

Gish, Duane, 1985, *Evolution: The Challenge of the Fossil Record*: Creation-Life Publishers

Glasner, Peter, 1977, *A Sociology of Secularisation: Critique of a Concept*: Routledge and Kegan Paul

Glock, Charles and Stark, Rodney, 1965, *Religion and Society in Tension*: Rand McNally

Goffman, Erving, 1961, *Asylums. Essays on the Social Situation of Mental Patients and Other Inmates*: Doubleday Anchor

Grassie, William, 1997, 'Postmodernism: What One Needs to Know': *Journal of Religion and Science*, March

Greeley, Andrew and Jagodzinski, Wolfgang, 1997, 'The Demand for Religion: Hard Core Atheism and "Supply Side" Theory': www.agreeley.com

Hadaway, Kirk and Marler, Penny, 1998, 'Did You Really Go To Church This Week? Behind the Poll Data': The Christian Century Foundation

Hadaway, Kirk and Marler, Penny, 1998, 'Is religious belief declining in Britain?': *Journal for the Scientific Study of Religion*, 37

Hadden, Jeffrey, 2001, 'Secularization and Modernization':

University of Virginia, http://religiousmovements.lib.virginia.edu/lectures/secular.html

Hadden, Jeffrey, 1987, 'Toward Desacralizing Secularization Theory': *Social Forces*, March

Hagan, John, Simpson, John and Gillis, A.R., 1988, 'Feminist Scholarship, Relational and Instrumental Control, and a Power-Control Theory of Gender and Delinquency': *British Journal of Sociology*, 39

Hak, Durk, 1998, 'Rational Choice Theory' in William Swatos, Jr (ed.), *Encyclopedia of Religion and Society*: Hartford Institute for Religion Research

Harper, Charles and LeBeau, Bryan, 1999, 'Social Change and Religion in America: Thinking Beyond Secularisation': The American Religious Experience (West Virginia University), http://are.as.wvu.edu/index.html

Haviland, William, Fedorak, Shirley, Crawford, Gary and Lee, Richard, 2005, *Cultural Anthropology* (2nd edition): Nelson

Hume, Lynne, 1996, 'A Reappraisal of the Term "Cult" and Consideration of "Danger Markers" in Charismatic Religious Groups': Colloquium 28/1, University of Queensland

Hunsberger, Bruce, 1985, 'Religion, age, life satisfaction, and perceived sources of religiousness: A study of older persons': *Journal of Gerontology*, Vol. 40

Hunt, Stephen, 2002, *Religion in Western Society*: Palgrave

Hutchinson, John, 1981, *Paths of Faith*: McGraw-Hill

Iannaccone, Laurence, 1994, 'Why Strict Churches Are Strong': *American Journal of Sociology*, Vol. 99, No. 5

Jarvis, Peter, 1995, *Adult and Continuing Education: Theory and Practice* (2nd edition): Routledge

Jencks, Charles, 1996, *What is Post-Modernism?* (4th edition): Academy Editions

Jowell, Roger and Park, Alison, 1998, 'Young People, Politics and Citizenship: a Disengaged Generation?': CREST Paper No. 67

Kanazawa, Satoshi and Still, Mary, 2000, 'Why Men Commit Crimes (and Why They Desist)': *Sociological Theory*, 18

Kelley, Dean, 1972, *Why Conservative Churches Are Growing. Consumer Versus Commitment Based Congregations*: Harper & Row

Kelly, Aidan, 1992, 'An Update on Neopagan Witchcraft in America' in James Lewis and Gordon Melton (eds), *Perspectives on the New Age*: State University of New York Press

Kung, Hans, 1990, *Theology for the Third Millennium: An Ecumenical View*: Anchor

Langone, Michael, 1993, 'What Is New Age?': *Cult Observer*, Vol. 10, No. 1

Lea, John and Young, Jock, 1984, *What Is To Be Done About Law and Order – Crisis in the Eighties*: Penguin

Leming, Michael, 1998, 'The relationship between the sociology of knowledge and the sociology of religion', http://www.stolaf.edu/people/leming/soc265rel/questions/chBerger.html

Levinson, David, 1998, *Religion: A cross-cultural dictionary*: Oxford University Press

Lewis, James (ed.), 1998, *The Encyclopedia of Cults, Sects and New Religions*: Prometheus Books

Lizardo, Omar and Collett, Jessica, 2005, *Why Biology is not (Religious) Destiny: A Second Look at Gender Differences in Religiosity*: University of Arizona

Luckmann, Thomas, 1967, *The Invisible Religion*: Macmillan

Luhmann, Niklas, 1977, *Funktion der Religion*: Suhrkamp

Lyman, Edward, 1986, *Political Deliverance: The Mormon Quest for Utah Statehood*: University of Illinois Press

Lyotard, Jean François, 1984, *The Postmodern Condition*: Manchester University Press (first published 1979)

MacCulloch, Robert and Pezzini, Silvia, 2002, *The Role of Freedom, Growth and Religion in the Taste for Revolution*: London School of Economics

Maguire, Daniel, 2001, *Sacred Choices: The Right to Contraception and Abortion in Ten World Religions*, Fortress Press

Malinowski, Bronislaw, 1948, *Magic, Science and Religion*: Doubleday (first published 1925)

Malinowski, Bronislaw, 1926, *Crime and Custom in Savage Society*: Routledge

Malmgreen, Gail, 1987, 'Domestic Discords: Women and the Family in East Cheshire Methodism, 1750–1830' in Jim Obelkevich, Lyndal Roper and Raphael Samuel (eds), *Disciplines of Faith: Studies in Religion, Patriarchy and Politics*: Routledge and Kegan Paul

Marczewska-Rytko, Maria, 2003, 'Religious Communities as Interest Groups': Centre for Studies on New Religions (CESNUR) Conference Paper

Marshall, David, 1994, 'Canadian Historians, Secularization and the Problem of the Nineteenth Century': CCHA, *Historical Studies*, 60

Marshall, Gordon, 1982, *In Search of the Spirit of Capitalism*: Columbia University Press

Marx, Karl, 1844, *Contribution to the Critique of Hegel's 'Philosophy of Right'*: Deutsch-Französische Jahrbücher

Marx, Karl and Engels, Friedrich, 1955, *On Religion*: Moscow Foreign Languages Publishing House (first published 1844)

Maslow, Abraham, 1943, 'A Theory of Human Motivation': *Psychological Review*, 50

Matheson, Jill and Summerfield, Carol (eds), 2000, 'Social Trends 31': The Stationery Office

McGuire, Meredith, 2002, *Religion – The Social Context* (5th edition): Wadsworth

McLeod, Hugh, 1997, *Religion and the People of Western Europe 1789–1989* (2nd edition): Oxford University Press

McLeod, Hugh, 1993, *Religion and Irreligion in Victorian England: How secular was the working class?*: Bangor

Mead, George Herbert, 1934, *Mind, Self and Society*: University of Chicago Press

Melton, Gordon, 1993 'Another Look at New Religions': *Annals of the American Academy of Political and Social Science*, 527

Melton, Gordon, 2001, *New Age Transformed*: Institute for the Study of American Religion

Merton, Robert K., 1957, *Social Theory and Social Structure*: Free Press of Glencoe

Miller, Alan and Stark, Rodney, 2002, 'Gender and Religiousness: Can Socialization Explanations Be Saved?': *American Journal of Sociology*, Vol. 107

Miller, Timothy (ed.), 1995, *America's Alternative Religions*: State University of New York Press

Nason-Clark, Nancy, 1998, 'Feminist Theology' in William Swatos, Jr (ed.), *Encyclopedia of Religion and Society*: Hartford Institute for Religion Research

Neitz, Mary Jo, 1998, 'Feminist Research and Theory' in William Swatos, Jr (ed.), *Encyclopedia of Religion and Society*: Hartford Institute for Religion Research

Niebuhr, H. Richard, 1929, *The Social Sources of Denominationalism*: Holt

Norris, Pippa and Inglehart, Ronald, 2004, 'Sacred and Secular: Religion and Politics Worldwide': Cambridge Studies in Social Theory, Religion and Politics, University of Cambridge Press

O'Beirne, Maria, 2004, 'Religion in England and Wales: findings from the 2001 Home Office Citizenship Survey': Home Office Research, Development and Statistics Directorate

Office for National Statistics 'Population Trends': The Stationery Office, 2001

Palmer, Susan, 1994, *Moon Sisters, Krishna Mothers, Rajneesh Lovers: Women's Roles in New Religions*: Syracuse University Press

Pals, Daniel, 1996, *Seven Theories of Religion*: Oxford University Press

Park, Alison, Phillips, Miranda and Johnson, Mark, 2004, 'Young People in Britain: The Attitudes and Experiences of 12 to 19 Year Olds': National Centre for Social Research

Parsons, Talcott, 1951, *The Social System*: RKP

Parsons, Talcott, 1937, *The Structure of Social Action*: McGraw Hill

Perry, John and Perry, Erna, 1973, *The Social Web*: Canfield Press

Petre, Jonathon, 1999, 'Christianity "in crisis" as pews empty': *Sunday Telegraph*, November 28

Phillips, Rick, 2004, 'Can rising rates of church participation be a consequence of secularization?': *Sociology of Religion*, Summer

Pierotti, Sandra, 2003, *The Protestant Ethic and the Spirit of Capitalism: Criticisms of Weber's Thesis*: California State University

Poulantzas, Nicos, 1978, *Classes in Contemporary Capitalism*: Verso (first published 1974)

Poulantzas, Nicos, 1973, *Political Power and Social Classes*: New Left Books

Price, Maeve, 1979, 'The Divine Light Mission as a social organization': *Sociological Review*, 27

Putnam, Robert, 2000, *Bowling Alone*: Simon and Schuster

Pyle, Ralph and Davidson, James, 1998, 'Stratification' in William Swatos, Jr (ed.), *Encyclopedia of Religion and Society*: Hartford Institute for Religion Research

Report of the Special Commission on Review and Reform, 'A Church without Walls': The General Assembly of the Church of Scotland, 2001, http://www.churchwithoutwalls.org.uk/

Richardson, James and Ginsburg, Gerald, 1998, 'A critique of "brainwashing" evidence in light of Daubert: Science and unpopular religions': *Law and Science: Current Legal Issues*, Vol. 1, Oxford University Press

Ricoeur, Paul, 1974, *The Conflict of Interpretations*: Northwestern University Press

Ritzer, George, 1992, *Sociological Theory* (3rd edition): McGraw-Hill

Robbins, Thomas and Anthony, Dick, 1982, 'Cults, culture, and community' in Florence Kaslow and Marvin Sussman (eds), 'Cults and the family': *Marriage & Family Review*, Vol. 4, No. 3: Haworth Press

Robins, Tessa, Choudhury, Saarah and Matthews, Jenny, 2002, 'Turning from God': *Young Minds* magazine, http://www.youngminds.org.uk, September 2

Robinson, Leland, 2001, 'When Will Revolutionary Movements Use Religion?' in Susanne Monahan, William Mirola and Michael Emerson (eds), *Sociology of Religion: A Reader*: Prentice Hall (first published 1987)

Root, Wade Clark, 1996, 'God is in the details: Reflections on religion's public presence in the United States in the mid-1990s': *Sociology of Religion*, 57

Roozen, David, 1996, 'Empty Nest; Empty Pew: The Boomers Continue Through the Family Cycle': Hartford Institute

Sachs, April, 2004, 'Negating Religion: Meaning, Nihilism, and the Possibility of the Unreligious': unpublished dissertation

Sahgal, Gita and Yuval-Davis, Nira, 1994, 'The Uses of Fundamentalism': *WAF Journal*, No. 5

Sahgal, Gita and Yuval-Davis, Nira, 1992, 'Introduction: Fundamentalism, Multiculturalism and Women in Britain' in Gita Sahgal and Nira Yuval-Davis (eds), *Refusing Holy Orders: Women and Fundamentalism in Britain*: Virago

Sedgwick, Colin, 2004, 'Gimme that organised religion': *The Guardian*, June 12

Seiler, Robert, 2004, 'Human Communication in the Critical Theory Tradition': http://www.ucalgary.ca/ ~rseiler/critical.htm

Shiner, Larry, 1967, 'The Concept of Secularisation in Empirical Research': *Journal for the Scientific Study of Religion*, Vol. 6

Singer, Margaret, Lalich, Janja and Lifton, Robert Jay, 1996, *Cults in Our Midst*: Jossey-Bass

Smith, Greg, 1996, 'The Unsecular City: The Revival Of Religion In East London' in Mike Rustin and Tim Butler (eds), *Rising in the East*: Lawrence & Wishart

Smith, Pete, 2005, *Sects and the City*: Chartist Publications

Sommerville, John, 1998, 'Secular society/religious population: Our tacit rules for using the term "secularization"': *Journal for the Scientific Study of Religion*, 37 (2)

Spickard, James, 2003, 'What Is Happening to Religion: Six Sociological Narratives': University of Redlands

Spretnak, Charlene, 1982, *The Politics of Women's Spirituality*: New York

Staples, Peter, 1998, 'Protestantism, Protestants' in William Swatos, Jr (ed.), *Encyclopedia of Religion and Society*: Hartford Institute for Religion Research

Stark, Rodney, 2002, 'Physiology and Faith: Addressing the "Universal" Gender Difference in Religious Commitment': *Journal for the Scientific Study of Religion*, Vol. 41, No. 3

Stark, Rodney, 1999, 'Secularization RIP': *Sociology of Religion*, 60

Stark, Rodney and Bainbridge, William, 1987, *A Theory of Religion*: Rutgers University

Stark, Rodney and Finke, Roger, 2000, *Acts of Faith: Explaining the Human Side of Religion*: University of California Press

Steggerda, Moniek, 1993, 'Religion and Social Positions of Women and Men': *Social Compass*, No. 40/1

Strinati, Dominic, 1995, *An Introduction to Theories of Popular Culture*: Routledge

Stuckey, Jon, 1997, 'A community of friends: The Sunday school class as a conduit for social contacts and social support among older women': *Journal of Religious Gerontology*, 10

Swatos Jr, William, 1998, 'Religiosity' in William Swatos, Jr (ed.), *Encyclopedia of Religion and Society*: Hartford Institute for Religion Research

Swyngedouw, Jan, 1973, *Dictionary of Religious Studies*: Daigaku Shuppankai

Tawney, R.H., 1926, *Religion and the Rise of Capitalism*: Harcourt, Brace & World, Inc.

Taylor, Jenny, 2000, 'Prophets and Predictions: Religion in the 21st Century': Sociology of Religion Study Group, British Sociological Association Annual Conference

Taylor, Mark, 1987, *Erring: A Postmodern Theology*: University of Chicago Press

Thompson, Ian, 1986, *Religion*: Longman

Tschannen, Olivier, 1991, 'The secularization Paradigm': *Journal for the Scientific Study of Religion*, 30

Turner, Bryan, 1983, *Religion and Social Theory*: Humanities Press

Vaillancourt-Rosenau, Pauline, 1992, *Post-modernism and the Social Sciences: Insights, Inroads, and Intrusions*: Princeton University Press

van Leen, Adrian, 2004, 'The Nature of Cults': Concerned Christians Growth Ministries, http://www.ccgm.org.au/articles/ARTICLE-0052.htm

Viner, Jacob, 1978, *Religious Thought and Economic Society*: Duke University Press

Wallis, Roy, 1984, *The Elementary Forms of New Religious Life*: Routledge and Kegan Paul

Walter, Tony and Davie, Grace, 1998, 'The religiosity of women in the modern West': *British Journal of Sociology*, Vol. 49, Issue No. 4

Warner, Stephen, 1993, 'Works in Progress Toward a New Paradigm for the Sociology of Religion in the United States': *American Journal of Sociology*, Vol. 98, No. 5

Watchtower: http://www.watchtower.org

Weber, Max, 2001, *The Protestant Ethic and the Spirit of Capitalism*: Routledge (first published 1905)

Weber, Max, 1954, *Economy and Society* (edited by Max Rheinstein): Simon and Schuster (first published 1922)

Wilson, Bryan, 1982, *Religion in Sociological Perspective*: Oxford University Press

Wilson, Bryan, 1966, *Religion in Secular Society*: Penguin

Wimberley, Ronald and Swatos, William, 1998, 'Civil Religion' in William Swatos (ed.), *Encyclopedia of Religion and Society*: Hartford Institute for Religion Research

Winter, Therese, Lummis, Adair and Stokes, Allison, 1994,

*Defecting in Place: Women Claiming Responsibility for Their Own Spiritual Lives*: Crossroad

Wuthnow, Robert, 1992, *Rediscovering the Sacred: Perspectives on Religion in Contemporary Society*: Eerdmans Publishing Company

Wuthnow, Robert, 1986, 'Religious Movements and Counter-Movements in North America'; James Beckford and Martine Levasseur, 'New Religious Movements in Western Europe'; Said Amir Arjomand, 'Social Change and Movements of Revitalization in Contemporary Islam' in James Beckford (ed.), *New Religious Movements and Rapid Social Change*: Sage

Yeats, W.B., 1920, *The Second Coming*: The Nation (London)

Yinger, J. Milton, 1957, *Religion, Society and the Individual*: The MacMillan Company

Yip, Andrew, 2002, 'The Persistence of Faith Among Nonheterosexual Christians: Evidence for the Neosecularization Thesis of Religious Transformation': *Journal for the Scientific Study of Religion*, Vol. 41, No. 2: Blackwell

Zimbardo, Philip, 1997, 'What messages are behind today's cults?': *American Psychological Association Monitor*, May 1997

Zmerli, Sonja, 2003, 'Applying the concepts of bonding and bridging social capital to empirical research': European Consortium for Political Research (University of Essex)

## Chapter 2: Power and politics

Allen, Judith, 1990, 'Does Feminism Need a Theory of the State?' in Sophie Watson (ed.), *Playing the State: Australian Feminist Intervention*: Verso

Andersen, Robert and Heath, Anthony, 2000, 'Social Cleavages, Attitudes and Voting Patterns: A Comparison of Canada and Great Britain': CREST Working Paper No. 81

Anspach, Renee, 1979, 'From stigma to identity politics: Political activism among the physically disabled and former mental patients': *Social Science and Medicine*, 13A

Apple, Michael, 2000, 'Away With All Teachers: the cultural politics of home schooling': *International Studies in Sociology of Education*, 10

Arendt, Hannah, 1970, *On Violence*: Harvest, Harcourt Brace

Barnartt, Sharon and Scotch, Richard, 2002, *Disability Protests Contentious Politics, 1970–1999*: Gallaudet University Press.

Besley, Timothy, Burgess, Robin and Prat, Andrea, 2002, *Mass Media and Political Accountability*: London School of Economics and Political Science

Block, Fred, 1987, *Revising State Theory*: Temple University

Bjørnskov, Christian, 2004, *Political Ideology and Economic Freedom*: Aarhus School of Business

Blumenthal, Sidney, 6 October 2005, 'Republican Tremors', http://www.opendemocracy.net

Bocock, Robert, 1986, *Hegemony*: Tavistock

Bottomore, Tom, 1991, *Classes in Modern Society* (2nd edition): HarperCollins

Boulding, Kenneth, 1989, *Three Faces of Power*: Sage Publications

Brennan, Geoffrey and Hamlin, Alan, 2006, 'Constitutions as Expressive Documents' in Barry Weingast and Donald Witman

(eds), *The Oxford Handbook of Political Economy*: Oxford University Press

Bromley, Catherine, Curtice, John and Seyd, Ben, 2004, 'Is Britain Facing a Crisis of Democracy?': Centre for Research into Elections and Social Trends, Working Paper No. 106

Budge, Ian and Bara, Judith, 2001, 'Content analysis and political texts' in Ian Budge, Hans-Dieter Klingemann, Andrea Volkens and Eric Tanenbaum (eds), *Mapping Policy Preferences – Estimates for Parties, Electors, and Governments 1945–1998*: Oxford University Press

Butler, David and Stokes, Donald, 1974, *Political Change in Britain: The Evolution of Electoral Choice* (2nd edition): Macmillan

Butler, Judith, 1990, *Gender Trouble*: Routledge

Carroll, William (ed.), 1992, *Organizing Dissent – Contemporary Social Movements in Theory and Practice*: Garamond Press

Carson, Kevin, 2004 'Studies in Mutualist Political Economy': Fayetteville, http://www.mutualist.org

Chatterjee, Pratap, 2002, 'Dick Cheney: Soldier of Fortune': Corpwatch, http://www.corpwatch.org

Chorev, Nitsan, 2004, 'Institutionalizing Global Neo-Liberalism: The Structural Transformation of the WTO and Its Inherent Contradictions': Global Studies Association Conference Paper, Brandeis University

Civil Service Statistics: Cabinet Office, 2004, http://www.civilservice.gov.uk

Cohen, Daniel and Prusak, Laurence, 2001, *In Good Company. How social capital makes organizations work*: Harvard Business School Press

Cox, Laurence, 1996, 'From social movements to counter cultures' in Barker, Colin and Tyldesley, Mike (eds), *Alternative Futures and Popular Protest II*: Manchester Metropolitan University

Crewe, Ivor, Sarlvik, Bo and Alt, James, 1977, 'Partisan Dealignment in Britain 1964–1974': *British Journal of Political Science*, Vol. 7, No. 2

Dahlgren, Peter, 1999, *Imagining – and Doing – Democracy: Citizens, civic culture and the media*: Lund University (Sweden)

Dearlove, John and Saunders, Peter, 2001, *Introduction to British Politics*: Blackwell

Della Porta, Donatella and Diani, Mario, 1999, *Social Movements: An Introduction*: Blackwell

Doherty, Brian, 1999, 'Paving the Way: The rise of direct action against road-building and the changing character of British environmentalism': *Political Studies*, 47

Domhoff, William, 1997, *Who Rules America Now?*: Waveland Press

Domhoff, William, 1990, *The Power Elite and the State: How Policy is Made in America*: Aldine de Gruyter

Downs, Anthony, 1957, *An Economic Theory of Democracy*: Harper and Row

Dugan, Máire, 2003, 'Understanding Power' in Guy Burgess and Heidi Burgess (eds), 'Beyond Intractability': Conflict Research Consortium, University of Colorado, http://www.beyondintractability.org/m/development_conflict_theory.jsp

Eriksen, Stein Sundstøl, 2004, *The State in Africa: Theoretical*

*Perspectives and Empirical Cases*: Norwegian Institute of International Affairs

Etzioni, Amitai, 1993, *The Spirit of Community*: Crown Books

Evans, Geoffrey and Andersen, Robert, 2004, 'Do Issues Decide?': Centre for Research into Elections and Social Trends, Working Paper No. 105

Foucault, Michel, 1983, *Beyond Structuralism and Hermeneutics* (2nd edition): University of Chicago Press

Foucault, Michel, 1980, *Power/Knowledge: Selected Interviews and Other Writings, 1972–1977*: Pantheon

Friedrick, Carl and Brzezinski, Zbigniew, 1965, *Totalitarian Dictatorship and Autocracy*: Harvard University Press (first published 1956)

Galipeau, Claude, 1989, 'Political Parties, Interest Groups and New Social Movements' in Alain Gagnon and Brian Tanguay (eds), *Canadian Parties in Transition*: Thomson Ltd

Gamble, Andrew, 2005, 'Eclipsing Thatcherism': *The Guardian*, 14 October

Gerber, Alan and Green, Donald, 1998, 'Rational Learning and Partisan Attitudes': *American Journal of Political Science*, 42

Gerring, John, 1997, 'Ideology: A Definitional Analysis': *Political Research Quarterly*, Vol. 50, No. 4

Giddens, Anthony, 2001, *Sociology* (4th edition): Polity

Giddens, Anthony, 1998, 'How leading sociologists evaluate the contribution of postmodernism': *Sociology Review*, Vol. 8, No. 2: Philip Allan, November

Giddens, Anthony, 1985, *The Nation-State and Violence*: Polity Press

Glasberg, Davita Silfen, 1989, *The Power of Collective Purse Strings: The Effect of Bank Hegemony on Corporations and the State*: University of California Press

Gläser, Jochen, 2003, *Social Movements as Communities*: Research School of Social Sciences, The Australian National University

Glyn, Andrew, 2003, 'Labour Market Deregulation and Europe's Employment Problems': AEA/URPE Conference Paper, http://www.economics.ox.ac.uk/Members/andrew.glyn

Granik, Sue, 2003, 'Part of the Party: continuity and discontinuity amongst political party memberships': PSA Annual Conference Paper

Greenfield, Cathy and Williams, Peter, 2001, '"Battlers" vs "Elites"': *Southern Review: Communication, Politics & Culture*, Vol. 34, No. 1

Grobman, Gary, 1990, 'Nazi Fascism and the Modern Totalitarian State': http://www.remember.org/guide/index.html

Hadfield, Greg and Skipworth, Mark, 1994, *Class, Where Do You Stand?*: Bloomsbury

Hanisch, Carol, 1970, 'The Personal is Political: Notes from the Second Year': *Radical Feminism*

Haraway, Donna, 1991, 'A Cyborg Manifesto: Science, Technology, and Socialist-Feminism in the Late Twentieth Century' in *Simians, Cyborgs and Women: The Reinvention of Nature*: Routledge

Heath, Anthony, McMahon, Dorren and Roberts, Jane, 1999, 'Ethnic Differences in the Labour Market: a comparison of the

SARs and LFS': Centre for Research into Elections and Social Trends, Working Paper No. 71

Held, David, 1989, Political Theory and the Modern State: Polity Press

Hildyard, Nicholas, 1998, 'The Myth of the Minimalist State: Free Market Ambiguities': Corner House Briefing 05, http://www.thecornerhouse.org.uk

Himmelweit, Hilde, Humphreys, Patrick and Jaeger, Marianne, 1985, *How Voters Decide: A Model of Vote Choice Based on a Special Longitudinal Study Extending over Fifteen Years and the British Election Surveys of 1970*: McGraw-Hill

Hogg, Quentin (Lord Hailsham), 1976, 'Elective Dictatorship: The Richard Dimbleby Lecture': *The Listener*

Hope, Chris, 2004, 'The Cost of Conviction in British Politics: What Happens to Labour's Majority if the Party Moves Back to the Left?': Judge Institute of Management, WP 15, University of Cambridge

Hyde, Sarah, 2001, 'Changing partisan support patterns and the rise of the Mutōhasō during the 1990s': Postgraduate Research Seminar in Japanese Studies, Oxford Brookes University Research Centre

Institute for Democracy and Electoral Assistance, 2000, 'Turnout over time: Advances and retreats in electoral participation', http://www.idea.int/vt/survey/voter_turnout1.cfm

Jessop, Bob, 2003, 'Bringing the State Back in (Yet Again): Reviews, Revisions, Rejections, and Redirections': Department of Sociology, Lancaster University, http://www.comp.lancs.ac.uk/sociology/ papers/Jessop-Bringing-the-State-Back-In.pdf

Jessop, Bob, 1990, *State Theory: Putting Capitalist States in Their Place*: Polity

Jones, William, 2004, *Politics UK* (5th edition): Longman

Jordan, Grant and Halpin, Darren, 2003, 'Cultivating small business influence in the UK: The Federation of Small Businesses' journey from outsider to insider': *Journal of Public Affairs*, Vol. 3, No. 4

Kitcat, Jason, 2002, 'Turning Around Turnout', http://www.j-dom.org/h/n/WRITING/edemocracy/ ALL/43/

Kristeva, Julia, 1985, *New Maladies of the Soul* (translated by Ross Guberman): Columbia University Press (first published 1979)

Lazarsfeld, Paul, Berelson, Bemald and Gaudet, Hazl, 1944, *The People's Choice: How the Voter Makes up his Mind in a Presidential Campaign*: Columbia University Press

Leach, Melissa and Scoones, Ian, 2002, 'Science and Citizenship in a Global Context': 'Science and Citizenship in a Global Context' Conference Paper: Institute of Development Studies

Lees-Marshment, Jennifer, 2004, *The Political Marketing Revolution*: Manchester University Press

Lees-Marshment, Jennifer, 2001, *Political Marketing and British Political Parties*: Manchester University Press

Livesey, Chris and Lawson, Tony, 2005, *AS Sociology for AQA*: Hodder Arnold

Lukes, Stephen (ed.), 1990, *Power*: New York University Press

Lyotard, Jean François, 1984, *The Postmodern Condition*: Manchester University Press (first published 1979)

MacKinnon, Catherine, 1987, *Feminism Unmodified: Discourses on Life and Law*: Harvard University Press

Malleson, Kate, 2003, 'Judging Judicial Review: Criteria for Judicial Appointment' in Richard Gordon (ed.), *Judicial Review in the New Millennium*: Sweet & Maxwell

Mann, Michael, 1986, *The Sources of Social Power: Vol. 1: A History of Power from the Beginning to A.D. 1760*: Cambridge University Press

March, Scott, 1995, 'Community Organizing on the Internet: Implications for Social Work Practitioners': New Social Movement and Community Organizing Conference Paper

Margetts, Helen, 2001, 'The Cyber Party': ECPR Workshop Paper, Grenoble

Martin, Greg, 2000, 'New Social Movements, Welfare and Social Policy: A Critical Assessment': CAVA, University of Leeds

McKay, David, 2005, *American Politics and Society*: Blackwell

McKenzie, Robert and Silver, Allan, 1968, *Angels in Marble: Working Class Conservatives in Urban England*: Heinemann

McLean, Iain, 2004, 'The Dimensionality of Party Ideologies': Nuffield College Politics Working Paper, University of Oxford

Melucci, Alberto, 1996 *Challenging Codes*: Cambridge University Press

Michels, Robert, 1962, *Political Parties*: Crowell-Collier Publishing (first published 1911)

Milliband, Ralph, 1973, *The State in Capitalist Society*: Quartet (first published 1969)

Mills, C. Wright, 1956, *The Power Elite*: Oxford Press

Morris, Estelle, 2004, 'Progressive Party Politics', www.policy-network.net

Mosca, Gaetano, 1939, *The Ruling Class* (Arthur Livingston, ed.): New York (first published 1923)

Mottier, Véronique, 2004, 'Gender Theory and the State' in Gerald Gaus and Chandran Kukathas, *The Sage Handbook of Political Theory*: Sage

Mulholland, Hélène, 2005, 'Women civil servants earn 25% less – and gap is growing': *The Guardian*, 8 February

Mullard, Maurice and Swaray, Raymond, 2005, *The Politics of Public Expenditure in the United Kingdom*: University of Hull

Mullins, Willard, 1972, 'On the Concept of Ideology in Political Science': *American Political Science Review*, Vol. 66, No. 2

New Social Movements Network, http://www.interweb-tech.com/nsmnet/docs.htm

Nilsson, Tomas, 2000, 'All the Colours of the Rainbow, or Red with a Green Halo? Is there a "Green" ideology and how is it being realised?': Nordic Studies Policy Centre, University of Aberdeen

Nordlinger, Eric, 1967, *The Working Class Tories*: MacGibbon and Kee

Norris, Pippa, Lovenduski, Joni and Campbell, Rosie, 'Gender and political participation': Electoral Commission, http://www.electoralcommission.org.uk

Offe, Claus, 1974, 'Structural Problems of the Capitalist State: Class Rule and the Political System. On the Selectiveness of Political Institutions': *German Political Studies*, 1

Pareto, Vilfredo, 1935, *Mind & Society*: Dover (first published 1916)

Parsons, Talcott, 1967, *Sociological Theory and Modern Society*: Free Press

Parsons, Talcott, 1951, *The Social System*: RKP

Parsons, Talcott, 1937, *The Structure of Social Action*: McGraw Hill

Patten, Steve, 2000, 'Parties versus Social Movements: The Politics of Representation', http://www.arts.ualberta.ca/~spatten/POLS%20391%20Reading%20(Parties%20vs%20Social%20Movements).htm

Poulantzas, Nicos, 1975, *Classes in Contemporary Capitalism*: New Left Books

Purdam, Kingsley, Fieldhouse, Ed, Kalra, Virinder and Russell, Andrew, 2002, *Voter engagement among black and minority ethnic communities*: Electoral Commission, 2002

Putnam, Robert, 2001, *Bowling Alone: The Collapse and Revival of American Community*: Simon & Schuster

Putnam, Robert, 1995, 'Tuning In, Tuning Out: The strange disappearance of social capital in America': *PS: Political Science and Politics*, 28

Rallings, Colin and Thrasher, Michael, 2000, *British Electoral Facts: 1832–1999*: Ashgate

Robinson, James, 2001, *Social Identity, Inequality and Conflict*: University of California at Berkeley

Schweingruber, David, 2005, 'Demography/Social Movements', http://www.public.iastate.edu/~s2005.soc.134/134lecture42(apr25).pdf

Scott, John, 2000, 'Rational Choice Theory' in Gary Browning, Abigail Halcli and Frank Webster (eds), *Understanding Contemporary Society: Theories of The Present*: Sage Publications

Shearing, Clifford and Stenning, Philip, 1985, 'From Panopticon to Disney World: the development of discipline': in Doob, Anthony and Greenspan, Edward (eds), *Perespectives in Criminal Law: Essays in Honour of John Ll. J. Edwards*: Canada Law Book, Inc.

Skocpol, Theda, 1985, 'Bringing the State Back In: Strategies of Analysis in Current Research' in Theda Skocpal, Peter Evans and Dietrich Rueschemeyer (eds), *Bringing the State Back In*: Cambridge University Press

Skocpol, Theda, 1979, *States and Social Revolutions*: Cambridge University Press

Smith, Martin, 1995, *Pressure Politics*: Baseline Books

Sowell, Thomas, 2002, *A Conflict of Visions: Ideological Origins of Political Struggles*: Basic Books

Sparrow, Andrew, 2004, 'Labour membership sinks to an all-time low', http://news.telegraph.co.uk

Spretnak, Charlene, 1990, 'Ecofeminism: Our roots and flowering' in Irene Diamond and Gloria Orenstein (eds), *Reweaving the World: The Emergence of Ecofeminism*: Sierra Club Books

Stephenson, Mary-Ann, 1998, *The Glass Trapdoor: Women, politics and the media during the 1997 General Election*: Fawcett Society

Strafford, John, 1999, *Michael Ashcroft*: Campaign for Conservative Democracy

Toffler, Alvin, 1991, *Powershift: Knowledge, Wealth, and Power at the Edge of the 21st Century*: Bantam

Wall, Derek, Doherty, Brian and Plows, Alex, 2002, 'Capacity building in the British direct action environmental movement': Paper for the 'Workshop on Direct Action at the Local Level', Manchester, June

Weber, Max, 1978, *Economy and Society* (Guenther Roth and Claus Wittich, eds): University of California Press (first published 1922)

Welsh, Ian, 2001, 'Anti-nuclear Movements: Failed Projects or Heralds of a Direct Action Milieu?': Sociological Research Online, http://www.socresonline.org.uk/6/3/welsh.html

White, Michael, 2005, 'Cameron Surges into Tory Lead and Answers Cocaine Question': *The Guardian*, 21 October

Williamson, Judith, 2002, 'Tough on horridness': *The Guardian*, 14 November

Wilson, Graham, 1990, *Interest Groups*: Oxford University Press

Wintrobe, Ronald, 2002, *Dictatorship*: University of Western Ontario

Zweig, Ferdynand, 1961, *The Worker in an Affluent Society*: Heinemann

## Chapter 3: World sociology

ActionAid, 2005, 'Power hungry: six reasons to regulate global food corporations', www.actionaid.org

Aisbett, Emma, 2003, 'Globalization, Poverty and Inequality: are the criticisms vague, vested, or valid?': NBER Pre-conference on Globalization, Poverty and Inequality, University of California at Berkeley

Anand, Sudhir and Sen, Amartya, 1995, 'Gender Inequality in Human Development': Occasional Paper 19, Human Development Reports, http://hdr.undp.org

Anderson, Sarah and Cavanagh, John, 2000, 'The Rise of Global Corporate Power': Corporate Watch, http://www.corpwatch.org/

Appadurai, Arjun, 1990, 'Disjuncture and Difference in the Global Cultural Economy' in Mike Featherstone (ed.), *Global Culture: Nationalism, Globalization and Modernity*: Sage

Archer, David (with Jeng, Yaikah), 2006, 'Writing the Wrongs: International Benchmarks on Adult Literacy': ActionAid International

Badri, Belghis, 1994, 'The Concept of Sustainable Development': United Nations Non-Governmental Liaison Service (NGLS), http://www.un-ngls.org/index.html

Barbanti, Olympio, 2004, 'Development and Conflict Theory' in Guy Burgess and Heidi Burgess (eds), *Beyond Intractability*: Conflict Research Consortium, University of Colorado, http://www.beyondintractability.org/m/development_conflict_theory.jsp

Barro, Robert and Lee, Jong-Wha, 1994, 'Sources of economic growth': Carnegie-Rochester Series on Public Policy, No. 40

Baudrillard, Jean, 1998, 'Simulacra and Simulations' in Mark Poster (ed.), *Selected Writings*: Stanford University Press

Baudrillard, Jean and Patton, Paul, 1995, *The Gulf War Did Not Take Place*: Indiana University Press

Bauer, Peter, 1971, *Dissent on Development: Studies and Debates in Development Economics*: Weidenfeld and Nicolson

Beck, Ulrich, 1992, *Risk Society – Towards a New Modernity*: Sage

Berger, Peter and Hsiao, Hsin-Huang Michael (eds), 1988, *In Search of an East Asian Development Model*: Transaction Books

Borrego, John, 1995, 'Models of Integration, Models of Development in the Pacific': *Journal of World-Systems Research*, Vol. 1, No. 11

Boseley, Sarah, 2006, 'Britain defies US with funding to boost safe abortion services': *The Guardian*, February 6

Braveman, Paula and Gruskin, Sofia, 2003, 'Poverty, equity, human rights and health': *Bulletin of the World Health Organization*

Breinlich, Holger, 2004, 'Geography and Industrialisation': London School of Economics and Centre for Economic Performance

British Medical Association, 2005, 'Improving health, fighting poverty': BMA

Browne, Anthony, 2006, 'The Retreat of Reason: Political correctness and the corruption of public debate in modern Britain': Civitas, http://www.civitas.org.uk

Browne, John, 2000, 'Business': BBC Reith Lectures, http://newsbbc.co.uk/hi/english/static/events/reith_2000/default.stm

Brundtland Commission (World Commission on Environment and Development), 1987, *Our Common Future*: Oxford University Press

Bryman, Alan, 1999, 'The Disneyisation of Society': *The Sociological Review*, Vol. 47, No. 1

Bush, George W., 2001, 'Letter to Senators Hagel, Helms, Craig, and Roberts': White House, Office of the Press Secretary

Cameron, John and Cameron, Stuart, 2006, 'The Economic Benefits of Increased Literacy': UNESCO, Education For All (EFA) Global Monitoring Group Report

Capitán, Antonio Luis Hidalgo and Lambie, George, 1994, 'A Background to Development Theory and some Practical Applications', http://www.uhu.es/antonio.hidalgo/documentos/Econ-Des-Ingl.pdf

Capra, Fritjof, 1983, *The Turning Point*: HarperCollins

Cassel, Andrew, 2002, 'Why U.S. Farm Subsidies Are Bad for the World', *Philadelphia Inquirer*, May 6

Castells, Manuel, 1997, 'The Power of Identity' in *The Information Age: Economy, Society and Culture*, Vol. 2: Blackwell

Chaliand, Gerard, 1977, *Revolution in the Third World*: Viking

Chase-Dunn, Christopher and Grimes, Peter, 1995, 'World-Systems Analysis': *Annual Review of Sociology*, Vol. 21

Clemens, Michael, Kenny, Charles and Moss, Todd, 2004, 'The Trouble with the MDGs: Confronting Expectations of Aid and Development Success': Working Paper 40, Economics Working Paper Archive, http://econwpa.wustl.edu:80/eps/dev/papers/0405/0405011.pdf

Collier, Paul and Dollar, David, 2002, 'Aid, Allocation and Poverty Reduction': *European Economic Review*, Vol. 45, No. 1

Comte, Auguste, 1853, *The Positive Philosophy*

Congressional Budget Office, 1997, 'The Role of Foreign Aid in Development': Congress of the United States

Connelly, Patricia, Murray Li, Tania, MacDonald, Martha and Parpart, Jane, 2000, 'Feminism and Development: Theoretical Perspectives': Commonwealth of Learning

Contreras, Arnoldo, 1987, 'Transnational corporations in the forest-based sector of developing countries', *Unasylva*, Vol. 39, No. 157/158

Coury, Ralph, 1997, 'Neo-Modernization Theory and Its Search for Enemies: The Role of the Arabs and Islam': Left Curve No. 21, http://www.leftcurve.org/index.html

d'Addio, Anna and d'Ercole, Marco, 2005, 'Trends and Determinants of Fertility Rates in OECD Countries: The Role of Policies': OECD (Social, Employment and Migration Working Papers No. 27)

Dalmiya, Nita and Schultink, Werner, 2003, 'Combating hidden hunger: the role of international agencies', *Food and Nutrition Bulletin*, Vol. 24, No. 4

Demographic and Health Surveys (1991–1999), 2000, http://www.measuredhs.com

Dovers, Stephen and Handmer, Johyn, 1992, 'Uncertainty, sustainability and change', *Global Environmental Change*, 2 (4)

Easterly, William, Levine, Ross and Roodman, David, 2003 'New Data, New Doubts: Revisiting Aid, Policies and Growth': Centre for Global Development, Working Paper 26

Ebeltoft, Nini, 1998, 'Reflexive Modernity and Modern Reflexivity' in 'Everywhere and Nowhere – Social Interaction on a Global Computer Network for Young People': unpublished thesis (http://folk.uio.no/ninie)

Economic Commission for Africa, 2005, 'Mainstreaming Trade in National Development Strategies': United Nations

*The Economist*, 2004, 'The Big Mac Index', http://www.economist.com/markets/Bigmac/Index. cfm

European Commission, 2005, 'The 2005 Review of the EU Sustainable Development Strategy: Initial Stocktaking and Future Orientations': European Commission

Ferraro, Vincent, 1996, 'Dependency Theory: An Introduction': Mount Holyoke College, http://www.mtholyoke.edu/acad/intrel/depend.htm

Fonseca, Gonçalo, 2001, 'The History of Economic Thought: Economic Development', http://cepa.newschool.edu/het/

*Fortune Magazine*, 2005, 'Fortune Global 5000', http://money.cnn.com/magazines/fortune/global500/ 2005

Frank, Andre Gunder, 1995, 'The Abuses and Some Uses of World Systems Theory in Archaeology': American Anthropological Association, http://www.rrojasdatabank.org/agfrank/abuses_and_uses.html

Freund, Peter and Martin, George, 2005, 'Fast Cars/Fast Foods: Hyperconsumption and Its Health and Environmental Consequences': Montclair State University, http://www.cnsjournal.org/documents/cnslfast2.doc

Friedman, Milton, 1962, *Capitalism and Freedom*: University of Chicago Press

Gardner, Gary, Assadourian, Erik and Sarin, Radhika, 2004, 'The State of Consumption Today' in Linda Starke (ed.), *State of the World*: W.W. Norton

Gatley, David, 2001, 'The Stoke-upon-Trent Parish Listing of 1701': Victorian Census Project, http://www.staffs.ac.uk/schools/humanities_and_soc_sciences/census/vichome.htm

Gershuny, Jonathan, 2002a, 'Life-course, social position and life-chances': Institute for Social and Economic Research, University of Essex

Gershuny, Jonathan, 2002b, 'Beating the Odds (1): intergenerational social mobility from a human capital perspective'; 'Beating the Odds (2): a new index of intergenerational social mobility': Institute for Social and Economic Research, Working Papers 2002–17 and 2002–18

Ghose, Ajit, 2000, 'Trade and International Labour Mobility': *International Labour Review*, Vol. 139, No. 3, International Labour Organization

Giddens, Anthony, 1990, *The Consequences of Modernity*: Polity Press

Gladwin, Christina, 1993, 'Women and structural adjustment in a global economy': Women and International Development Annual

Global Campaign for Education, 2004, 'Learning to Survive: How Education for All would save millions of young people from HIV/AIDS': www.campaignforeducation.org

Gray, John, 2002, 'What Globalization Is Not': Turkish Time, http://www.turkishtime.org/agustos/86_en_1.htm

Gray, John, 1999, *False Dawn:The delusions of global capitalism*: Granta

Greenhill, Romilly, 2004, 'Urban Poor are Neglected in World Bank Project': ActionAid

GTZ, 2004, 'Who We Work For', http://www.gtz.de/en/unternehmen/1732.htm

Hanlon, Joseph, 2005, 'Reconstructing Peace', http://www.open2.net/development/peace.html

Hanlon, Joseph, 2004, 'How Northern Donors Promote Corruption: Tales From the New Mozambique': The Corner House, Briefing No. 33, http://www.thecornerhouse.org.uk/pdf/briefing/33mozamb.pdf

Harvey, David, 1990, *The Condition of Postmodernity: An Enquiry into the Origins of Cultural Change*: Blackwell

Haub, Carl and Cornelius, Diana, 2000, '*World Population Data Sheet*': Population Reference Bureau

Hawley, Susan, 2000, 'Exporting Corruption: Privatisation, Multinationals and Bribery': The Corner House, Briefing No. 19, http://www.thecornerhouse.org.uk/pdf/briefing/19bribes.pdf

Held, David, McGrew, Anthony, Goldblatt, David and Perraton, Jonathan, 1999, *Global Transformations – Politics, Economics and Culture*: Polity Press

Hettne, Björn, 1995, *Development Theory and the Three Worlds: Towards an international political economy of development* (2nd edition): Longman

Hillyard, Mick and Miller, Vaughne, 1998, 'Cuba and the Helms-Burton Act': Library Research Paper 98/114, House of Commons

Hirst, Paul and Thompson, Graham, 1996, *Globalization in Question*: Polity Press

Hobsbawm, Eric with Polito, Antonio, 2000, *The New Century*: Little, Brown

Hong, Evelyne, 2000, *Globalisation and the Impact on Health*: Third World Network

Independent Commission on International Development Issues (the Brandt Report), 1980, *North-South: A Programme for Survival*: Pan Books

International Labour Office, 2003, 'Working out of poverty: Views from Africa': Tenth African Regional Meeting

International Labour Office, 1987, 'International Conference of Labour Statisticians': ILO

International Labour Organization, 2006, 'Global Employment Trends': ILO

International Labour Organization, 2005, 'Employment Analysis: Poverty, income and working poor': ILO

Jackson, Cecile, 1997, 'Gender Analysis of Environmental Change in Developing Countries': Economic and Social Research Council

Jahan, Selim, 2001, 'Measuring Human Development: Evolution of The Human Development Index': UN Human Development Resource Centre, http://hdrc.undp.org.in/APRI/Event/Colombo/resources/bgppr/Measuring%20HD-Evolution%20of%20HDI%20.pdf

Justino, Patricia, 2001, 'Social Security and Political Conflict in Developing Countries, with special reference to the South Indian state of Kerala': PhD dissertation, School of Oriental and African Studies

Khosla, Romi (with Hasan, Sikandar, Samuels, Jane and Mulyawan, Budhi), 2002, 'Removing Unfreedoms: Citizens as Agents of Change': Department for International Development

Kinsella, Kevin and Velkoff, Victoria, 2001, 'An Aging World': US Census Bureau

Kodoth, Praveena and Eapen, Mridul, 2005, 'Looking beyond Gender Parity: Gender Inequities of Some Dimensions of Well-Being in Kerala', *Economic and Political Weekly*, July

Labour Party National Policy Forum, 2003, 'A future fair for all': The Labour Party

Lebel, Louis and Steffen, Will (eds), 1998, 'Global Environmental Change and Sustainable Development in Southeast Asia: Science Plan for a SARCS Integrated Study': Southeast Asian Regional Committee for START (SARCS)

Lechner, Frank, 2001, 'Globalisation Issues': The Globalisation Website, http://www.sociology.emory.edu/globalization/issues.html

Leinbach, Thomas, 2005, 'The Concept of Development: Definitions, Theories and Contemporary Perspectives': University of Kentucky, http://www.uky.edu/AS/Courses/GEO260/Powerpoint/Concept_of_Development.ppt

Lewis, Arthur, 1954, 'Economic Development with Unlimited Supplies of Labour': *Manchester School*, Vol. 22, No. 2

Looney, Robert, 2005, 'Rethinking Iraq's Neo-liberal Reforms: Implications for State Formation': MIT Centre for International Studies

Lorenz, Edward, 1972, *The Butterfly Effect*: American Association for the Advancement of Science

Madeley, John, 2003, 'Transnational corporations and developing countries: big business, poor peoples': The Courier ACP-EU No. 196

Malena, Carmen, 1995, 'A Practical Guide to Operational Collaboration between The World Bank and Non-governmental Organizations': World Bank Operations Policy Department

Matheson, Jill and Babb, Penny (eds), 2002, 'Social Trends 32': Office for National Statistics, The Stationery Office

Mathews, Marsha, 2001, 'Health Spending Per Capita By Level of Development': Global Forum for Health Research, http://www.globalforumhealth.org/forum5/abstracts/plenarygrowthfeachem/sld003.htm

Matthews, Sally, 2005, 'Attaining a Better Society: Critical reflections on what it means to be "developed"', *Theoria*, Vol. 52, No. 1, Issue 106: Berghahn Books

McMichael, Philip, 2004, *Development and Social Change* (3rd edition): Pine Forge Press

Meadows, Donella, 2000, 'A World Food Production Quiz': The Global Citizen, http://www.pcdf.org/meadows/

Meadows, Donella, 1999, 'The World's Top Five Consumers in Many Categories': The Global Citizen, http://www.pcdf.org/meadows/

Mol, Arthur and Sonnenfeld, David, 2000, 'Ecological Modernization Around the World: An Introduction', *Environmental Politics*, Vol. 9, No. 1

Moore, Thomas, 1993, *Lifespan*: Simon and Schuster

Morrison, Wayne, 2000, 'China's Economic Conditions': Issue Brief for US Congress

Naudé, Willem, 2003, 'The Effects of Policy, Institutions and Geography on Economic Growth in Africa: An Econometric Study Based on Cross-Section and Panel Data', *Journal of International Development*, No. 16

Noah, Harold and Eckstein, Max, 1988, 'Dependency Theory in Comparative Education: Twelve Lessons from the Literature' in Jürgen Schriewer and Brian Holmes (eds), *Theories and Methods in Comparative Education:* Peter Lang Publishers

OECD Development Assistance Committee, 1995, 'Development Cooperation 1994: Efforts and Policies of the Members of the Development Assistance Committee': Organization for Economic Cooperation and Development

Ohmae, Kenichi, 1995, *The End of the Nation-State: The Rise of Regional Economies*: HarperCollins

Organisation for Economic Co-operation and Development, 2005, 'Health Data 2005: How Does the United States Compare', OECD

Oxaal, Zoë with Baden, Sally, 1997, 'Gender and empowerment: definitions, approaches and implications for policy': briefing prepared for the Swedish International Development Cooperation Agency (Sida)

Palacios, Robert, 2002, 'The Future of Global Ageing', *International Journal of Epidemiology*, Vol. 31, No. 4

Parsons, Talcott, 1951, *The Social System*: RKP.

Peace, Mark, 2005, 'Gender and Development', www.sociologystuff.com

Peace, Mark, 2005, 'Globalisation', www.sociologystuff.com

Peet, Richard with Hartwick, Elaine, 1999, *Theories of Development*: Guilford Press

Polaski, Sandra, 2004, 'Job Anxiety Is Real – and It's Global': Carnegie Endowment for International Peace

Porritt, Jonathon, 2000, 'Sustainable Development: The Argument': BBC Reith Lectures, http://news.bbc.co.uk/hi/english/static/events/reith_2000/argument.stm

Psacharapoulos, George and Patrinos, Harry, 2002, 'Returns to

Investment in Education: A further update': World Bank Policy Research Working Paper 2881, World Bank

Quebec Institute of Statistics, 2005, 'Comparative Table: Gross Domestic Product', http://www.stat.gouv.qc.ca/default_an.htm

Raghavan, Chakravarthi, 1996, 'TNCs Control Two-Thirds of World Economy': Third World Network Features

Redding, Gordon, 1990, *The Spirit of Chinese Capitalism*: De Gruyter

Reich, Robert, 1991, *The Work of Nations*: Vintage Books

Rice-Oxley, Mark, 2004, 'In 2,000 Years, Will the World Remember Disney or Plato?': *Christian Science Monitor*, 15 January

Ritzer, George, 1996, *The McDonaldization of Society*: Pine Forge Press.

Robbins, Richard, 2005, *Global Problems and the Culture of Capitalism* (3rd edition): Allyn and Bacon

Robertson, Roland, 1992, *Globalization*: Sage

Rosamond, Ben and Booth, Jane, 1995, *The Globalisation of the State*: Political Studies Association

Rostow, Walter, 1960, *The Stages of Economic Growth: A Non-Communist Manifesto*: Cambridge University Press

Rugman, Alan, 2001, 'The Myth of Global Strategy': *Insights* (Academy of International Business newsletter), Vol. 1, No. 1

Rugman, Alan and Hodgetts, Richard, 2000, *International Business* (2nd edition): Pearson Education

Scholte, Jan Aart, 2000, *Globalization. A critical introduction*: Palgrave

Schuh, Trish, 2005, 'Covert Ops to Overthrow Iran's Government': Aljazeera News Agency, http://aljazeera.com/cgi-bin/review/article_full_story.asp?service_ID=9847, September 26

Schultz, Theodore, 1960, *Capital Formation by Education*: JPE

Seers, Dudley, 1983, *The Political Economy of Nationalism*: Oxford University Press

Sen, Amartya, 1999, *Development as Freedom*: A.A. Knopf

Sethuraman, Salem, 1976, 'The urban informal sector: concept, measurement and policy': *International Labour Review*

Shah, Anup, 2005, 'Non-governmental Organizations on Development Issues': Global Issues, http://www.globalissues.org/TradeRelated/Poverty/NGOs.asp

Shaw, Martin, 1997, 'The state of globalization': *Review of International Political Economy*, Vol. 4, No. 3

Short, Clare, 2001, 'Globalisation, Trade and Development in the Least Developed Countries': Department for International Development, http://www.dfid.gov.uk/news/files/sp-globaltrade190301.asp

Sklair, Leslie, 1999, 'Competing Conceptions of Globalisation', *Journal of World-Systems Research*, Vol. 5, No. 2

Smith, Cynthia, Cowan, Cathy, Heffler, Stephen and Catlin, Aaron, 2006, 'National Health Spending In 2004', *Health Affairs*, Vol. 25, No. 1

Smith, Mark and Doyle, Michelle, 2002, *Globalization*: The Encyclopedia of Informal Education, www.infed.org/biblio/globalization.htm

Smith, Lisa and Haddad, Lawrence, 2001, 'Overcoming Child Malnutrition in Developing Countries: Past Achievements and Future Choices': Food, Agriculture and the Environment, Discussion Paper 30, International Food Policy Research Institute

Sporer, Zeljka, 2000, *Controversies of Globalisation*: University of South Australia

Standing, Gary, 1999, 'Global Feminization through Flexible Labour: A Theme Revisited', *World Development*, Vol. 27, No. 3

Stern, Paul, 2000, 'Toward a Coherent Theory of Environmentally Significant Behavior': *Journal of Social Issues*

Summerfield, Carol and Babb, Penny (eds), 2005, 'Social Trends 35': Office for National Statistics, The Stationery Office

Symons, Elizabeth (Baroness), 2002, 'Trade and its Role in Sustainable Development': Department for Trade and Industry

Thirlwall, Anthony, 2002, *The Nature of Economic Growth: An Alternative Framework for Understanding the Performance of Nations*: Edward Elgar

Thomas, Alan, 2000, 'Meanings and Views of Development' in Tim Allen and Alan Thomas (eds), *Poverty and Development into the 21st Century*: Oxford University Press

Thompson, Grahame, 2000, 'Economic globalization?' in David Held (ed.), *A Globalizing World?: Culture, Economics and Politics* (2nd edition): Routledge

Thompson, John, 2004, 'The Emergence of Contemporary North America': Duke University, http://www.dlt.ncssm.edu/lmtm/index.htm

Todero, Michael and Smith, Stephen, 2005, *Economic Development* (9th edition): Addison-Wesley

Tooley, James, 2005, 'Is Private Education Good for the Poor?', http://www.ncl.ac.uk/egwest

True, Jacqui, 2002, 'Engendering international relations: What difference does second-generation feminism make?': Department of International Relations, Working Paper 2002/1

UK Communication and Information Management Resource Centre, 2006, 'About Urbanisation': Department for International Development

UN Demographic Yearbook, 2003, United Nations Statistics Division

UN-Habitat, 2004, 'Urban Indicators Guidelines: Monitoring the Habitat Agenda and the Millennium Development Goals': United Nations Human Settlements Programme, http://www.unchs.org/programmes/guo/documents/urban_indicators_guidelines.pdf

UN-Habitat, 2001, 'The World's Largest Cities': United Nations Human Settlements Programme, http://hq.unhabitat.org/Istanbul+5/20-27.pdf

United Nations, 2002, 'International Migration Report': United Nations Population Division

United Nations, 2001, 'Human Development Report': United Nations

United Nations, 2000, 'National Sustainable Development Strategy': UN Department of Economic and Social Affairs

Urry, John, 2002, *Global Complexity*: Polity Press

US Census Bureau (Population Division), 2005, 'Population Pyramid Summary for India': http://www.census.gov/ipc/www/idbpyr.html

US Central Intelligence Unit, 2005, 'The World Factbook', http://www.cia.gov/cia/publications/ factbook/

US General Accounting Office, 2002, 'Foreign Assistance: AID Strategic Direction and Continued Management Improvements Needed': NSIAD

US Population Reference Bureau, 2006, 'Human Population: Fundamentals of Growth: Three Patterns of Population Change': http://www.prb.org

US Population Reference Bureau, 2005, 'Improving the Health of the World's Poorest People', http://www.prb.org

USAID, 2005, 'Frequently Asked Questions', http://www.usaid.gov/faqs.html

Veseth, Michael, 1998, *Selling Globalization: The Myth of the Global Economy*: Lynne Rienner Publishers

Virilio, Paul, 2000, 'The Kosovo War Took Place in Orbital Space', www.ctheory.net/articles.aspx?id=132

von Hayek, Friedrich, 1973, *Law, Legislation and Liberty: A New Statement of the Liberal Principles of Justice and Political Economy: Vol. 1, Rules and Order*: Routledge & Kegan Paul

von Stokar, Thomas and Steinemann, Myriam, 2004, 'Sustainable development: definition and constitutional status in Switzerland': Swiss Agency for Development and Cooperation, http://www.are.admin.ch/are/en/nachhaltig/definition/index.html

Wallerstein, Immanuel, 1974, 'The Rise and Future Demise of the World Capitalist System: Concepts for Comparative Analysis', *Comparative Studies in Society and History*, 16

Weber, Max, 1958, *The Protestant Ethic and Spirit of Capitalism*: Charles Scribner and Sons (first published 1904/05)

Weintraub, Irwin, 1994, 'Fighting Environmental Racism': Electronic Green Journal, Vol. 1, Issue 1, http://egj.lib.uidaho.edu/egj01

World Bank, 2005, 'Urbanisation': World Bank, http://youthink.worldbank.org/issues/urbanization

World Bank, 2002, 'A Sourcebook for Poverty-reduction Strategies: Cross-Cutting Issues: Gender': World Bank

World Bank, 2002, *A Sourcebook for Poverty-reduction Strategies: Cross-cutting Issues*: World Bank

World Bank, 1987, *World Development Report*: Oxford University Press

World Bank Gender and Development Group, 2003, *Gender Equality and the Millennium Development Goals*: World Bank

World Health Organization/UNAIDS, 2005, 'AIDS epidemic update: Special Report on HIV Prevention': WHO

World Health Organization, 2003, 'Obesity and overweight': WHO

World Health Organization, 2003, 'World Health Report 2003: Shaping the Future': WHO

Yip, George, 1995, *Total Global Strategy*: Prentice Hall

Zachariah, K.C., 1998, 'Models of Development and Demographic Change: A Case Study of Kerala', *Demography India*, Vol. 27, No. 1

# Chapter 4: Theory and method

Adomaitiene, Ruta, 1999, 'The conceptualization of sociology of disability as a part of mainstreamed sociology': *Education. Physical Training. Sport*, Vol. 2, No. 31

Barthes, Roland, 1977, 'The Death of the Author' in *Image, Music, Text*: Noonday Press (first published 1968)

Becker, Howard, 1967, 'Whose Side Are We On?': *Social Problems*, 14

Becker, Howard, 1963, *Outsiders: Studies in the Sociology of Deviance*: Free Press

Bell, Daniel, 1999, *The Coming of Post-Industrial Society: A Venture in Social Forecasting*: Basic Books (first published 1973)

Bellah, Robert, 1985, *Habits of the Heart: Individualism and Commitment in American Life*: Harper and Row

Bilton, Tony, Bonnett, Kevin, Jones, Pip, Skinner, David, Stanworth, Michelle and Webster, Andrew 1996, *Introductory Sociology* (3rd edition): Macmillan

Blackburn, Sheila, 1995, 'How Useful are Feminist Theories of the Welfare State?': *Women's History Review*, Vol. 4, No. 3

Blunt, Adrian, 1994, 'The Future of Adult Education Research' in Garrison, D. Randy (ed.), *Research Perspectives in Adult Education*: Krieger Publishing Company

Boles, Derek, 2003, 'The Language of Media Literacy: A Glossary of Terms': Centre for Media Literacy, http://www.medialit.org

Bowker, Natilene Irain, 2001, 'Understanding Online Communities Through Multiple Methodologies Combined Under a Postmodern Research Endeavour': *Qualitative Social Research*, Vol. 2, No. 1, http://www.qualitative-research.net/fqs-texte/1-01/1-01bowker-e.htm

Calvert, Susan and Calvert, Peter, 1992, *Sociology Today*: Harvester Wheatsheaf

Campbell, Lee, 1996, *Postmodernism and You: Science*: Xenos Christian Fellowship

Carpi, Anthony, 2003, 'The Scientific Method': *Visionlearning* Vol. SCI-1 (1), http://www.visionlearning.com

Carter, Greg, 2001, *Analyzing Contemporary Social Issues* (2nd edition): Allyn and Bacon

Chambliss, William, 1985, 'The Saints and the Roughnecks' in James Henslin, *Down To Earth Sociology*: The Free Press (first published 1978)

Chiu, Stephen, Ho, KC, Lui, Tai-Lok, 1997, *City-States in the Global Economy: Industrial Restructuring in Hong Kong and Singapore*: Westview Press

Clarke, John and Layder, Derek, 1994, 'Let's Get Real: The Realist Approach in Sociology': *Sociology Review* Vol. 4, No. 2

Clarke, Ronald and Mayhew, Patricia, 1980, *Designing Out Crime*: HMSO

Coffey, Michael, 2000, 'The Educators' New(ish) Clothes?': unpublished thesis, http://www.spin.net.au/~mifilito/ednewclothescont.html

Cook, James, 2001, *Social Networks: A Primer*: Duke University

Coser, Lewis, 1977, *Masters of Sociological Thought: Ideas in Historical and Social Context* (2nd edition): Harcourt Brace

Craig, Robin, 2005, 'Philosophical Reflections XXXI': January http://www.thoughtware.com.au/philosophy/philref/PHILOS.31B.html

Crebbin, Wendy, 2000, 'Revisioning learning – contributions of postmodernism, constructivism and neurological research': University of Ballarat

Curran, Jeanne and Takata, Susan, 2004, 'Positivism to Postmodernism: An Explanation and Example': California State University, http://www.csudh.edu/dearhabermas/postmod01.htm

Davis, Nanette, 1985, 'Becoming a Prostitute' in James Henslin, *Down To Earth Sociology*: The Free Press

Davis, Nanette, 1967, 'Prostitution and Social Control', unpublished thesis: University of Minnesota

Davis, Peter, 2000, 'Rethinking the Welfare Regime Approach: The Case of Bangladesh': Conference Paper, European Network of Bangladesh Studies, University of Oslo

Dawe, Alan, 1970, 'The Two Sociologies': *British Journal of Sociology*, Vol. 21

Deleuze, Gilles and Guattari, Felix, 1987, *Capitalism and Schizophrenia*: University of Minnesota Press

Dentler, Robert, 2002, *Practicing Sociology: Selected Fields*: Praeger

Durkheim, Emile, 1964, *The Division of Labour in Society*: Free Press (first published 1893)

Durkheim, Emile, 1951, *Suicide: A Study in Sociology*: Free Press (first published 1897)

Durkheim, Emile, 1938, *The Rules of Sociological Method* (8th edition): Collier-Macmillan (first published 1895)

Etzioni, Amitai, 1993, *The Spirit of Community*: Crown Books

Feyerabend, Paul, 1975, *Against Method*: Verso

Feyerabend, Paul, 1992, 'Atoms and Consciousness', *Common Knowledge*, Vol. 1, No. 1

Fiske, John, 1987, *Television Culture: popular pleasures and politics*: Methuen

Fleischmann, Martin and Pons, Stanley, 1989, 'Electrochemically Induced Nuclear Fusion of Deuterium': *Journal of Electroanalytical Chemistry*, No. 261

Fonseca, Gonçalo and Ussher, Leanne, 1999, 'The History of Economic Thought', http://cepa.newschool.edu/~het/home.htm

Foucault, Michael, 1972, *The Archaeology of Knowledge and the Discourse on Language*: Pantheon

Francis, David and Hester, Stephen, 2004, *An Invitation to Ethnomethodology*: Sage Publications

Fuller, Steve, 1998, 'Who's Afraid of Science Studies?': *Independent on Sunday*, magazine, 28 June

Garfinkel, Harold, 1967, *Studies in Ethnomethodology*: Prentice-Hall

Gewirtz, Sharon, 2004, 'Taking a Stand: Education Policy, Sociology and Social Values': King's College Lecture, 5 February

Giddens, Anthony, 1991, *Modernity and Self Identity: Self and Society in the Late Modern Age*: Stanford University Press

Giddens, Anthony, 1998, 'Sociology Review', Vol. 8, No. 2: Philip Allan

Giddens, Anthony, 2001, *Sociology* (4th edition): Polity

Gillborn, David and Youdell, Deborah, 2000, *Rationing Education: policy, practice, reform and equity*: Open University Press

Goldman, Steven, Nagel, Roger, and Preiss, Kenneth, 1995, 'Agile Competitors and Virtual Organisations: Strategies for Enriching the Customer': Van Nostrand Reinhold

Gouldner, Alvin, 1975, 'Anti-Minotaur: The Myth of a Value-Free Sociology' in Alvin Gouldner, *For Sociology*: Basic Books (first published 1962)

Gouldner, Alvin, 1973, *For Sociology: Renewal and Critique in Sociology Today*: Basic Books

Habermas, Jurgen, 1992, *Postmetaphysical Thinking*: Polity

Hanmer, Jalna and Statham, Daphne, 1999, *Women and Social Work – Towards A Woman-Centred Practice* (2nd edition): Macmillan

Harvey, David, 1990, *The Condition of Postmodernity: An Enquiry into the Origins of Cultural Change*: Blackwell

Heise, David, 1996, 'Social order through macroactions: An Interactionist approach': Presentation at Panel on Micro-Macro Processes and Social Order, Ninth Annual Group Processes Conference, August 21

Heise, David and Durig, Alex, 1997, 'A frame for organizational actions and macroactions': *Journal of Mathematical Sociology*, Vol. 22 (2)

Horowitz, Irving (ed.), 1967, *The Rise and Fall of Project Camelot: Studies in the Relationship Between Social Science and Practical Politics*: MIT Press

How, Alan, 2005, 'Sociology: new thinking for a changing world': *University of Warwick Course Handbook 2005–06*

Hudgins, Clyde and Richards, Michael, 2000, 'Individual, Family and Community: An Interdisciplinary Approach to the Study of Contemporary Life': San Antonio College, http://www.accd.edu/sac/interdis/2370/text.htm

Jamrozik, Adam and Nocella, Luisa, 1998, *The Sociology of Social Problems*: Cambridge University Press

Jones, Geoff, 2002, 'Scientific Fraud': *Socialism Today*, No. 70, November

Keat, Russell and Urry, John, 1975, *Social Theory as Science*: Routledge and Kegan Paul

Kharkhordin, Oleg, 1991, 'Postmodern Ghosts in Sociology': University of Kent, http://lucy.ukc.ac.uk/csacpub/russian/oleg.html

Krippendorff, Klaus, 1986, *A Dictionary of Cybernetics*: University of Pennsylvania

Kuhn, Thomas, 1962, *The Structure of Scientific Revolutions*: University of Chicago Press

Labossiere, Michael, 1995, 'Fallacies': The Nizkor Project http://www.nizkor.org/features/fallacies/

Lechner, Frank, 1998, 'Modernism' in William Swatos, Jr (ed.), *Encyclopedia of Religion and Society*: Hartford Institute for Religion Research

Lee, David, 1992, 'Unreason and Uncertainty in the Practice of Sociology': *The Raven*, No. 19, Freedom Press

Lorenz, Edward, 1972, 'Deterministic Nonperiodic Flow': *Journal of Atmospheric Science*, No. 20

Lorenz, Edward, 1963, 'The Butterfly Effect': American Association for the Advancement of Science

Luhmann, Niklas, 1995, *Social Systems (Writing Science)*: Stanford University Press

Luhmann, Niklas, 1997, 'Globalization or World Society?: How to conceive of modern society': *International Review of Sociology*, Vol. 7, No. 1

Lyon, David, 1994, *Postmodernity*: Open University Press

Lyotard, Jean-François, 1984, *The Postmodern Condition: A Report on Knowledge*: University of Minnesota

Malik, Kenan, 1998, 'An annotated bibliography of nonsense': *Independent on Sunday*, 1 February

Mann, Steve, Nolan, Jason and Wellman, Barry, 2001, 'Sousveillance': *Surveillance & Society*, Vol. 1, No. 3

Marling, William, 2001, 'Hard-Boiled Fiction': Case Western Reserve University, http://www.cwru.edu/artsci/engl/marling/hardboiled/Glossary.htm

Marshall, Thomas, 1950, *Citizenship and Social Class and Other Essays*: Cambridge University Press

Marsland, David, 1995, 'Which Sociology? A Consumer's Guide', Subjectivism and the Socialist Intellectual': *Sociological Notes*, No. 23, Libertarian Alliance

Marsland, David, 1994, 'Sociologists and Social Policy: The Need for Intelligent Involvement': Sociological Notes, No. 21, Libertarian Alliance

Martin, Brian, 1992, 'Scientific fraud and the power structure of science': *Prometheus*, Vol. 10, No. 1, June

Martinson, Brian, Anderson, Melissa and de Vries, Raymond, 2005, 'Scientists behaving badly': *Nature 435*, 09/06/05

Marx, Karl, 1998, 'Theses on Feuerbach' (1845) in Robert Baird and Stuart Rosenbaum (eds), *The German Ideology*: Prometheus Books

Marx, Karl, 1977, *Capital*: Lawrence and Wishart (first published 1867–1895)

Maturana, Humberto and Varela, Francisco, 1980, *Autopoiesis and Cognition*: D. Reidel

Medawar, Peter, 1991, 'Is the scientific paper a fraud?' in Peter Medawar, *The Threat and the Glory: Reflections on Science and Scientists*: Oxford University Press (first published in *The Listener*, 12 September 1963)

Merton, Robert, 1973, 'The Normative Structure of Science' in Norman Storer, *The Sociology of Science*: University of Chicago Press (first published 1942)

Michels, Robert, 1962, *Political Parties*: Crowell-Collier Publishing (first published 1911)

Mills, C. Wright, 1959, *The Sociological Imagination*: Oxford University Press

Misra, Joya, 2000, *Cross-Cultural Perspectives on Family, Economy, and the State*: University of Massachusetts

Misztal, Barbara, 2001, 'Trust and cooperation in the democratic public sphere': *Journal of Sociology*, Vol. 37, No. 4

Moore, Roderick, 1993, 'Sociology, Subjectivism and the Socialist Intellectual Establishment': *Sociological Notes*, No. 17, Libertarian Alliance

Morris, Estelle, 2004, 'Progressive Party Politics', www.policy-network.net

Morris, Susannah, 2004, *Social Policy: From the Victorians to the Present Day*

Mulder, Dwayne, 2004, 'Objectivity': The Internet Encyclopedia of Philosophy, http://www.iep.utm.edu/o/objectiv.htm

Murphy, John, 1988, 'Making Sense of Postmodern Sociology': *British Journal of Sociology*, Vol. 9, No. 4

O'Donnell, Mike, 1997, *Introduction to Sociology* (4th edition): Nelson

Paine, Thomas, 1988, *The Age of Reason*: Citadel Press (first published 1795)

Parsons, Talcott, 1959, *The School Class as a Social System*: Harvard Educational Review

Parsons, Talcott, 1951, *The Social System*: RKP

Parsons, Talcott, 1937, *The Structure of Social Action*: McGraw Hill

Pascall, Gillian, 1997, *Social Policy: A New Feminist Analysis*: Routledge

Pearce, Frank (with Steve Tombs), 1998, *Toxic Capitalism: Corporate Crime and the Chemical Industry*: Ashgate

Polyani, Michael, 1958, *Personal Knowledge. Towards a Post Critical Philosoph*: Routledge

Polyani, Michael, 1967, *The Tacit Dimension*: Anchor Books

Popper, Karl, 1972, *Objective Knowledge*: Oxford University Press (first published 1966)

Popper, Karl, 1968, *The Logic of Scientific Discovery*: Hutchinson (first published 1934)

Popper, Karl, 1963, *Conjectures and Refutations*: Routledge

Postero, Nancy, 2005, 'Neoliberal Restructuring in Bolivia': University of California, http://www.ncsu.edu/project/acontracorriente/spring_05/Postero.pdf

Prelli, Lawrence, 1989, 'The Rhetorical Construction of Scientific Ethos' in Herbert Simons (ed.), *Rhetoric in the Human Sciences*: Sage

Putnam, Robert, 2001, *Bowling Alone: The Collapse and Revival of American Community*: Simon and Schuster

Ritzer, George, 2000, *Classical Sociological Theory* (3rd edition): McGraw-Hill

Ritzer, George, 1996, *The McDonaldization of Society*: Pine Forge Press

Rorty, Richard, 1995, *The Cambridge History of Literary Criticism, Vol. 8: From Formalism to Poststructuralism*: Cambridge University Press

Sabel, Charles, 1991, 'Moebius – Strip Organizations and Open Labor Markets: Some Consequences of the Reintegration of Conception and Execution in a Volatile Economy' in James Coleman and Pierre Bourdieu (eds), *Social Theory for a Changing Society*: Westview

Sarup, Madan, 1993, *An Introductory Guide to Post-Structuralism and Postmodernism*: Harvester Wheatsheaf

Scambler, Graham and Higgs, Paul (eds), 1998, *Modernity, Medicine and Health*: Routledge

Schutz, Alfred, 1962, *Collected Papers, Vol. 1: The problem of social reality*: Martinus Nijhoff

Sewell, Tony and Majors, Richard, 2001, 'Black boys and schooling: an intervention framework for understanding the dilemmas of masculinity, identity and underachievement' in R. Majors (ed.), *Educating Our Black Children: New Directions and Radical Approaches*: Routledge

Simkin, Mikhail and Roychowdhury, Vwani, 2002, 'Read Before You Cite': *New Scientist*, December

Sokal, Alan, 1996, 'Transgressing the Boundaries: Towards a Transformative Hermeneutics of Quantum Gravity': Social Text No. 46/47

Sokal, Alan, 1998, 'What the Social Text Affair Does and Does Not Prove' in Koertge, Noretta (ed.), *A House Built on Sand: Exposing Postmodernist Myths about Science*: Oxford University Press

Solomon, Paul, 2000, *Information Mosaics: Patterns of Action that Structure*: University of North Carolina

Solovey, Mark, 2001, 'Project Camelot and the 1960s Epistemological Revolution: Rethinking the Politics–Patronage–Social Science Nexus': *Social Studies of Science*, Vol. 31, No. 2

Soothill, Keith and Grover, Chris, 1995, 'The Social Construction of Sex Offenders': *Sociology Review*

Stanley, Geoffrey, 2004, *Contemporary Social Problems*: Staffordshire University

Stephens, Paul, 2000, 'The "good social policy" – lessons from the Nordic countries': http://www5.his.no/kompetansekatalog/visCV.aspx?ID=06229&sprak=ENGELSK

Taylor, Paul, Walton, Ian and Young, Jock, 1973, *The New Criminology: for a social theory of deviance*: Routledge and Kegan Paul

Taylor, Peter, 2000, 'A Metageographical Argument on Modernities and Social Science': Globalization and World Cities Study Group and Network, Research Bulletin 29

Thio, Alex, 1991, *Sociology: A Brief Introduction*: HarperCollins

Thomas, W.I. and Thomas, D.S., 1928, *The Child in America: Behaviour Problems and Programs*: Alfred A. Knopf

Tilley, Nick and Laycock, Gloria, 2002, 'Working out what to do: Evidence-based crime reduction': Crime Reduction Research Series, Paper 11, Home Office

Tombs, Steve and Whyte, Dave, 2003, 'Unmasking the Crimes of the Powerful': Conference Paper, Centre for Studies in Crime and Social Justice

Townsend, Peter and Abel-Smith, Brian, 1965, *The Poor and the Poorest: A New Analysis of the Ministry of Labour's Family Expenditure Surveys of 1953–4 and 1960*: Bell

Troest, Mads Orbesen, 1999, *Linguistic Relativity – Revisiting Whorf in the Postmodern Era*: Aalborg University

Trochim, William, 2002, 'Positivism and Post-Positivism': Research Methods Knowledge Base, Cornell University, http://www.socialresearchmethods.net/kb/

Usher, Robin, 1996, 'A Critique of the Neglected Epistemological Assumptions of Educational Research' in David Scott and Robin Usher (eds), *Understanding Adult Educational Research*: Routledge

Vaillancourt-Rosenau, Pauline, 1991, *Post-modernism and the Social Sciences: Insights, Inroads, and Intrusions*: Princeton University Press

Vandenberghe, Frederic, 1998, 'Niklas Luhmann, 1927–1998': *Radical Philosophy*, http://www.radicalphilosophy.com

Weber, Max, 2001, *The Protestant Ethic and the Spirit of Capitalism*: Routledge (first published 1905)

Weber, Max, 1954, *Economy and Society* (Max Rheinstein, ed.): Simon and Schuster (first published 1922)

Wilkins, Leslie, 1964, *Social Deviance*: Tavistock

Williams, Malcolm, 2005, 'Situated Objectivity': *Journal for the Theory of Social Behaviour*, Vol. 35, Issue 1

Wilson, Bryan, 1982, *Religion in Sociological Perspective*: Oxford University Press

Wilson, Tom, 2002, 'Alfred Schutz, phenomenology and research methodology for information behaviour research': Paper delivered to Fourth International Conference on Information Seeking in Context, Lisbon

Yeatman, Anna, 1994, *Postmodern Revisionings of the Political*: Routledge

Young, Jock, 1971, 'The Role of the Police as Amplifiers of Deviancy, Negotiators of Reality and Translators of Fantasy' in Stan Cohen (ed.), *Images of Deviance*: Penguin

Youngson, Robert, 1998, *Scientific Blunders*: Robinson

## Chapter 5: Crime and deviance

Agnew, Robert, 2000, 'An Overview of General Strain Theory' in Raymond Paternoster and Ronet Bachman (eds), *Explaining Criminals and Crime: Essays in Contemporary Criminological Theory*: Roxbury Press

Agnew, Robert, 1985, 'A Revised Strain Theory of Delinquency': *Social Forces*, Vol. 64, No. 1

Akers, Ronald and Sellers, Christine, 2004, *Criminological Theories: Introduction, Evaluation, and Application* (4th edition): Roxbury Press

Atkinson, J. Maxwell, 1978, *Discovering Suicide: Studies in the Social Organization of Sudden Death*: Macmillan

Baechler, Jean, 1979, *Suicides*: Basic Books (first published 1975)

Barton, Ben and Barton, Marthalee, 1993, 'Modes of Power in Technical and Professional Visuals': *JBTC*, Vol. 7, No. 1

Bennett, Andy, 1999, 'Subcultures or Neo-Tribes?: Rethinking the Relationship Between Youth, Style and Musical Taste': *Sociology*, Vol. 33, No. 3

Berard, Tim, 'Evaluative Categories of Action and Identity in Non-Evaluative Human Studies Research: Examples from Ethnomethodology': *Qualitative Sociology Review*, Vol. 1, No. 1, www.qualitativesociologyreview.org

Becker, Howard, 1963, *Outsiders: Studies in the Sociology of Deviance*: Free Press

Blalock, Hubert, 1967, *Toward a Theory of Minority-Group Relations*: John Wiley and Sons

Blumstein, Alfred, Cohen, Jacqueline, Roth, Jeffrey and Visher, Christy, 1986, *Criminal Careers and Career Criminals*: National Academy Press

Bose, Anuradha, George, Kuryan, Prasad, Jasmine, Minz, Shantidani and Abraham, Vinod, 2004, 'Suicides in Young People in Rural Southern India': *The Lancet*, Vol. 363

Bottoms, Anthony and Wiles, Paul, 1992, 'Explanations of Crime and Place' in David Evans, Nicholas Fyfe and David Herbert, *Crime, Policing and Place: Essays in Environmental Criminology*: Routledge

Box, Stephen, 1983, *Power, Crime and Mystification*: Tavistock

Burke, Roger Hopkins, 1999, 'From Idealism to Realism: Politics, Criminology and the Triumph of the Respectable Working Class': Scarman Centre for the Study of Public Order, University of Leicester

Carlen, Pat, Hicks, Jenny, O'Dwyer, Josie, Christina, Diana and Tchaikovsky, Chris, 1985, *Criminal Women*: Polity

Chambliss, William, 1975, 'The Political Economy of Crime: A Comparative Study of Nigeria and the United States' in Paul Taylor, Ian Walton and Jock Young (eds), *Critical Criminology*: Routledge and Kegan Paul

Charlton, John, 1995, 'Trends and Patterns in Suicide in England and Wales': *International Journal of Epidemiology*, Vol. 24

Clancy, Anna, Hough, Mike, Aust, Rebecca and Kershaw, Chris, 2001, 'Crime Policing and Justice: the Experience of Ethnic Minorities': Home Office Research Study, No. 223

Clarke, Graham, Evans, Andrew and Kongmuang, Charatdao, 2004, 'Modelling social determinants of crime in Leeds': University of Leeds, Conference Paper, Second National Crime Mapping Conference, March

Clarke, Ronald, 1980, '"Situational" crime prevention: theory and practice': *British Journal of Criminology*, Vol. 20, No. 2

Clarke, Ronald and Mayhew, Patricia (eds), 1980, 'Designing Out Crime': Home Office and Research Planning Unit, HMSO

Cloward, Richard and Ohlin, Lloyd, 1960, *Delinquency and Opportunity*: Free Press

Cohen, Albert, 1955, *Delinquent Boys*: Free Press

Cohen, Phil, 1972, 'Subcultural Conflict and Working Class Community': University of Birmingham: Centre for Cultural Studies, Working Papers in Subcultural Studies

Cohen, Stanley, 2002, *Folk Devils and Moral Panics*: Routledge (first published 1972)

Cohen, Stanley, 1979a, 'The Punitive City: notes on the dispersal of social control': *Contemporary Crises*, Vol. 3, No. 4: Elsevier Publishing Co.

Cohen, Stanley, 1979b, 'Guilt, justice and tolerance: Some old concepts for a new criminology' in David Downes and Paul Rock (eds), *Deviant Interpretations*: Barnes & Noble

Coleman, Alice, 1985, *Utopia on trial: Vision and reality in planned housing*: Hilary Shipman

Commission for Racial Equality, 2004, 'Race equality impact assessment: Criminal Justice': CRE, http://www.cre.gov.uk/duty/reia/statistics_justice.html

Congdon, Peter, 1996, 'Suicide and Parasuicide in London: a small area study': *Urban Studies*, Vol. 33, No. 1

Conrad, Peter and Schneider, Joseph, 1992, *Deviance and Medicalization: From Badness to Sickness* (2nd edition): Temple University Press (first published 1980)

Corrigan, Paul, 1979, *Schooling the Smash Street Kids*: Macmillan

Costello, Barbara, 1997, 'On the Logical Adequacy of Cultural Deviance Theories', *Theoretical Criminology*, Vol. 1, No. 4

Crawford, Adam, Jones, Trevor, Woodhouse, T. and Young, Jock, 1990, 'Second Islington Crime Survey': Centre for Criminology, Middlesex Polytechnic

Critcher, Chas, 2000, 'Still raving: social reaction to Ecstasy': *Leisure Studies*, Vol. 19

Darwin, Charles, 1998, *The Origin of Species*: Gramercy Books (first published 1859)

Davies, Pamela, 1997, 'Women, Crime and an Informal Economy: Female Offending and Crime for Gain' in Mike Brogden (ed.), *The British Criminology Conferences: Selected Proceedings, Vol. 2*: British Society of Criminology

De Haan, Willem, 1990, *The Politics of Redress*: Unwin Hyman

Dearlove, John and Saunders, Peter, 2001, *Introduction to British Politics*: Blackwell

Diekstra, Rene, 1989, 'Suicide and Attempted Suicide: An International Perspective': *Acta Pyschiatrica Scandinavica*, Vol. 80

Douglas, Jack, 1967, *The Social Meanings of Suicide*: Princeton University Press

Downes, David, 1966, *The Delinquent Solution: A Study in Subcultural Theory*: Routledge and Kegan Paul

Durkheim, Emile, 1938, *The Rules of Sociological Method* (8th edition): Collier-Macmillan (first published 1895)

Durkheim, Emile, 1951, *Suicide: A Study in Sociology*: Free Press (first published 1897)

Easteal, Patricia Weiser, 1991, 'Women and Crime: Premenstrual Issues': Trends and Issues in Crime and Criminal Justice, Australian Institute of Criminology

Featherstone, Richard and Deflem, Mathieu, 2003, 'Anomie and Strain: Context and Consequences of Merton's Two Theories': *Sociological Inquiry*, Vol. 73, No. 4

Feely, Malcolm and Simon, Jonathon, 1992, 'The New Penology: Notes on the Emerging Strategy of Corrections and Its Implications': *Criminology*, Vol. 30, No. 4

Felson, Marcus and Clarke, Ronald, 1988, 'Opportunity Makes the Thief: Practical Theory for Crime Prevention': Police Research Series Paper 98: Home Office Research, Development and Statistics Directorate

Field, Andy, 2000, 'Suicide and Parasuicide': University of Sussex, http://www.sussex.ac.uk/Users/andyf/teaching/clinical/suicide.pdf

FitzGerald, Marian, Stockdale, Jan and Hale, Chris, 2003, 'Young People & Street Crime: Research into young people's involvement in street crime': Youth Justice Board for England and Wales

Forrester, David, Chatterton, Mike and Pease, Ken (with Brown, Robin), 1988, 'The Kirkholt Burglary Prevention Project, Rochdale': Crime Prevention Unit, Paper 13: Home Office

Foucault, Michel, 1983, *Beyond Structuralism and Hermeneutics* (2nd edition): University of Chicago Press

Foucault, Michel, 1980, *Power/Knowledge: Selected Interviews and Other Writings, 1972–1977*: Pantheon

Fowler, Robert, 1991, *Language in the News*: Routledge

Gilling, Daniel, 1999, 'Community Safety: A Critique' in Mike

Brogden (ed.), *The British Criminology Conferences: Selected Proceedings*, Vol. 2: British Society of Criminology

Gottfredson, Michael and Hirschi, Travis, 1990, *A General Theory of Crime*: Stanford University Press

Greek, Cecil, 2001, 'Robert Agnew's General Strain Theory': Florida State University, http://www.criminology.fsu.edu/crimtheory/agnew.htm

Grossberg, Lawrence, 1997, 'Re-placing Popular Culture' in Steve Redhead, Derek Wynne and Justin O'Connor (eds), *The Club Cultures Reader*: Blackwell

Hale, Chris, Hayward, Keith, Wahidin, Azrini and Wincup, Emma, 2005, *Criminology*: Oxford University Press

Hall, Stuart, 1973/1980, 'Encoding/decoding' in the Centre for Contemporary Cultural Studies (ed.), *Culture, Media, Language: Working Papers in Cultural Studies*: Hutchinson

Hall, Stuart and Jefferson, Tony (eds), 1976, *Resistance Through Rituals*: Hutchinson

Hall, Stuart, Critcher, Chas, Jefferson, Tony, Clarke, John and Roberts, Brian, 1978, *Policing the Crisis: mugging, the State and law and order*: Macmillan

Hargreaves, David, 1967, *Social Relations in a Secondary School*: Routledge and Kegan Paul

Hebdidge, Dick, 1979, *Subculture: The meaning of style*: Methuen

Henry, Stuart and Milovanovic, Dragan (eds), 1999, *Constitutive Criminology at Work: Applications to Crime and Justice*: State University of New York Press

Hirschi, Travis and Gottfredson, Michael, 1983, 'Age and the Explanation of Crime': *American Journal of Sociology*, 89

Hirst, Paul Q., 1975, 'Marx and Engels on law, crime and morality' in Paul Taylor, Ian Walton and Jock Young (eds), *Critical Criminology*: Routledge and Kegan Paul

Home Office, 2005, 'Long-term national recorded crime trend': Research Development and Statistics (Crime Reduction & Community Safety Group)

Home Office, 2004, Statistics on Race and the Criminal Justice System

Home Office, 1998, 'Reducing Offending': Research Study 187

Jessor, Richard, 1998, *New Perspectives on Adolescent Risk Behaviour*: Cambridge University Press

Jones, Trevor, MacLean, Brian and Young, Jock, 1986, *Islington Crime Survey: Crime, Victimization and Policing in Inner-City London*: Gower

Jupp, Victor, 1989, *Methods of Chronological Research*: Unwin Hyman

Jurgen-Tas, Josine, Terlouw, Gert-Jan and Klein, Malcolm (eds), 1994, *Delinquent Behaviour of Young People in the Western World*: Kugler Publications

Kanazawa, Satoshi and Still, Mary, 2000, 'Why Men Commit Crimes (and Why They Desist)': American Sociological Association *Sociological Theory* 18:3

Kidd-Hewitt, David and Osborne, Richard, 1995, *Crime and the Media: The Postmodern Spectacle*: Pluto Press

Kleiman, Mark, 2000, 'Crime Control Policy in California' in Daniel Mitchell (ed.) *California Policy Options*, UCLA School of Public Policy and Social Research, http://www.anderson.ucla.edu/x6450.xml

Klein, Dorie, 1973, 'The Etiology of Female Crime: a review of the literature': *Issues in Criminology*, Vol. 8, No. 2. Updated 1996 in John Muncie, Eugene McLaughlin and Mary Langan, 2001, *Criminological Perspectives: A Reader*: Sage

Kooistra, Paul and Mahoney, John, 1999, 'The Historical Roots of Tabloid TV Crime' in Jeff Ferrell and Neil Websdale (eds), *Making Trouble: Cultural Constructions of Crime, Deviance, and Control*: Aldine De Gruyter

Lagassé, Paul (ed.), 2005, *The Columbia Encyclopedia*. (6th edition): Columbia University Press

Lea, John and Young, Jock, 1984, *What Is To Be Done About Law and Order – Crisis in the Eighties*: Penguin

Lemert, Edwin, 1967, *Human Deviance, Social Problems and Social Control*: Prentice Hall (first published 1951)

Lombrosso, Cesare and Ferrero, William, *The Female Offender*: Fisher Unwin

Macpherson, William, 1999, 'The Stephen Lawrence Inquiry' (The Macpherson Report)

Maguire, Mike, 2002, 'The 'data explosion' and its implications' in Mike Maguire, Rod Morgan and Rob Reiner (eds), *The Oxford Handbook of Criminology* (3rd edition): Oxford University Press

Maruna, Shadd, 1997, 'Desistance and Development: The Psychological Process of "Going Straight"' in Mike Brogden (ed.), *The British Criminology Conferences: Selected Proceedings*, Vol. 2: British Society of Criminology

Mason, Timothy, 1997, 'Delinquency': Lecture Notes, University of Paris, http://www.timothyjpmason.com/WebPages/Deviance/Deviance3.htm

Matza, David, 1964, *Delinquency and Drift*: Wiley

McIvor, Gill, 1998, 'Exploring Diversity: Understanding and Responding to Offending Among Young Women and Girls': Scottish Executive, Conference Paper, http://www.scotland.gov.uk/cru/kd01/crime-01.htm

McMillan, Lesley, 2004, 'Gender, Crime & Criminology': University of Sussex, http://www.sussex.ac.uk/sociology/documents/gender_lecture_5.rtf

McRobbie, Angela, 1994, *Postmodernism and Popular Culture*: Routledge

McRobbie, Angela and Thornton, Sarah, 1995, 'Rethinking "moral panic" for multi-mediated social worlds': *British Journal of Sociology*, Vol. 46, No. 4

Merton, Robert, 1938, 'Social Structure and Anomie': *American Sociological Review*, 3

Miller, David and Reilly, Jacquie, 1994, 'Food "Scares" in the Media': Glasgow Media Group, Glasgow University

Miller, Walter, 1958, 'Lower Class Cultures as a Generating Milieu of Gang Delinquency': *Journal of Social Issues*, 14

Milliband, Ralph, 1973, *The State In Capitalist Society*: Quartet (first published 1969)

Milovanovic, Dragan, 1997, 'Dueling Paradigms: Modernist v. Postmodernist Thought' in Dragan Milovanovic, *Postmodern Criminology*: Garland Publishing

Morcillo, Aurora, 2005, *The Gendered History of the Body*: Florida International University

Mugford, Stephen and O'Malley, Pat, 1990, 'Policies Unfit for Heroin: A Critique of Dom and South': *International Journal on Drug Policy*, Vol. 2, No. 1

Muncie, John, 2000, 'Decriminalising Criminology' in George Mair and Roger Tarling (eds), *British Criminology Conference: Selected Proceedings, Vol. 3*: British Society of Criminology

Neeleman, Jan, Wesseley, Simon and Lewis, Glyn, 1998, 'Suicide Acceptability in African and White Americans: The Role of Religion': *Journal of Nervous & Mental Disease*, January

Newman, Oscar, 1996, 'Creating Defensible Space': US Department of Housing and Urban Development, Office of Policy Development and Research

Newman, Oscar, 1972, *Defensible Space*: The Macmillan Company

Nisbet, Robert, 1967, *The Sociological Tradition*: Heinemann

Osborn, Steve and Shaftoe, Henry, 1995, 'Safer Neighbourhoods? Successes and failures in crime prevention': Safer Neighbourhoods Unit

Park, Robert, 1915, 'The City: Suggestions for the Investigation of Human Behavior in the City Environment': *American Journal of Sociology*, 20

Park, Robert and Burgess, Ernest, 1921, *Introduction to the Science of Sociology*, University of Chicago Press.

Parker, Howard, 1974, *A View from the Boys*: David & Charles

Parsons, Talcott, 1967, *Sociological Theory and Modern Society*: Free Press

Parsons, Talcott, 1937, *The Structure of Social Action*: McGraw Hill

Payne, Sarah and Lart, Rachel, 1998, 'Researching Suicidal Behaviour': *Radical Statistics*, 70, Winter

Pfohl, Stephen, 1998, *Deviance and Social Control*: Boston College

Platt, Stephen, 1992, 'Epidemiology of suicide and parasuicide', *Journal of Psychopharmacology*: Vol. 6, No. 2

Plummer, Ken, 1979, 'Misunderstanding Labelling Perspectives', in David Downes and Paul Rock (eds), *Deviant Interpretations*: Oxford University Press

Pollack, Otto, 1950, *The Criminality of Women*: University of Pennsylvania Press

Poulantzas, Nicos, 1973, *Political Power and Social Classes*: New Left Books

Power, Anne and Tunstall, Rebecca, 1995, *Swimming Against the Tide: Progress or polarisation on 20 unpopular estates*: Joseph Rowntree Foundation

Roberts, Mark, 2003, 'Related to Bigotry: The Repression of Swingers in Early 21st Century Britain': *Sociological Notes*, No. 28, Libertarian Alliance

Røn, Katrina and Scourfield, Jonathan, 2005, 'The cultural context of youth suicide: Identity, gender, and sexuality': http://www.cf.ac.uk/socsi/whoswho/ scourfield-cultural-context-suicide.html

Sale, Anabel Unity, 2003, 'The Bigger Picture on Suicide': www.communitycare.co.uk

Sarup, Madan, 1989, *Post-Structuralism and Postmodernism*: University of Georgia Press

Scaton, Phil and Chadwick, Emma, 1991, 'The Theoretical and Political Priorities of Critical Criminology' in Kevin Stenson and David Cowell (eds), *The Politics of Crime Control*: Sage

Schwendinger, Herman and Schwendinger, Julia, 1975, 'Defenders of order or guardians of human rights?' in Paul Taylor, Ian Walton and Jock Young (eds), *Critical Criminology*: Routledge and Kegan Paul

Searle, John, 1995, *The Construction of Social Reality*: Free Press

Shaw, Clifford and McKay, Henry, 1969, *Juvenile Delinquency and Urban Areas*: University of Chicago Press (first published 1932)

Shaw, Susan, Caldwell, Linda and Kleiber, Douglas, 1996, 'Boredom, stress and social control in the daily activities of adolescents': *Journal of Leisure Research*, No. 4

Shearing, Clifford and Stenning, Philip, 1985, 'From Panopticon to Disney World: the development of discipline': in Anthony Doob and Edward Greenspan (eds), *Perspectives in Criminal Law: Essays in Honour of John Ll. J. Edwards*: Canada Law Book, Inc.

Simmons, Jon, 2000, 'Review of Crime Statistics: A Discussion Document': Home Office (Research Development and Statistics)

Skidelsky, Robert, 2000, 'Institutional Racism and the Police: Fact or Fiction?' in David Green (ed.), *The Age of Inequality*: Institute for the Study of Civil Society

Smith, David, McAra, Lesley, McVie, Susan, Holmes, Lucy, Palmer, Jackie, Brown, Alison and Penman, Mark, 2005, 'Edinburgh Study of Youth Transitions and Crime': University of Edinburgh, http://www.law.ed.ac.uk/cls/esytc/index.htm

Stahl, Geoff, 1999, 'Still Winning Space?: Updating Subcultural Theory': Invisible Culture, http://www.rochester.edu/in_visible_culture/issue2/stahl.htm

Stark, Rodney, 1987, 'Deviant Places: A Theory of the Ecology of Crime': *Criminology*, 25

Summerfield, Carol and Babb, Penny (eds), 2005, 'Social Trends 35': Office for National Statistics, The Stationery Office

Sutherland, Edwin and Cressey, Donald, 1939, *Principles of Criminology*: Lippincott

Tatz, Colin, 1999, 'Aboriginal suicide is different: Aboriginal youth suicide in New South Wales, the Australian Capital Territory and New Zealand: towards a model of explanation and alleviation': Criminology Research Council

Taylor, Paul, Walton, Ian and Young, Jock, (eds), 1975, *Critical Criminology*: Routledge and Kegan Paul

Taylor, Paul, Walton, Ian and Young, Jock, 1973, *The New Criminology: for a social theory of deviance*: Routledge and Kegan Paul

Thomas, W.I., 1923, *The Unadjusted Girl*: Little, Brown and Co.

Thornberry, Terence, 1997, *Developmental Theories of Crime and Delinquency*: Transaction

Thornberry, Terence and Krohn, Marvin, 2000, 'The Self-Report Method for Measuring Delinquency and Crime': *Criminal Justice*, Vol. 4

Thornton, Sarah, 1996, *Club Cultures: Music, Media and Subcultural Capital*: Wesleyan University Press

Tonnies, Ferdinand, 1957, *Community and Society: Gemeinschaft und Gesellschaft* (Charles Loomis, ed.): Michigan State University Press (first published 1887)

Town, Stephen, 2001, 'Crime Displacement: The perception, problems, evidence and supporting theory', unpublished dissertation

Van Egmond, M., Garnifski, N., Jonker, D. and Kerkhof, A., 1993, *The Relationship Between Sexual Abuse and Female Suicidal Behaviour*: Crisis

Weitekamp, Elmar, 1989, 'Some problems with the use of self-reports in longitudinal research' in Malcolm Klein (ed.), *Cross-National Research in Self-reported Crime and Delinquency*: Kluwer Academic Publishers

Wekstein, Louis, 1979, *Handbook of Suicidology*: Brunner/Mazel

White, Rob, 1993, 'Young people, community space and social control' in Lynn Atkinson and Sally-Anne Gerull (eds), 'National Conference on Juvenile Justice': Australian Institute of Criminology

Wilcox, Pamela and Augustine, Michelle, 2001, 'Physical Environment and Crime in Kentucky Schools': American Society of Criminology Conference, University of California

Wiles, Paul and Costello, Andrew, 2000, 'The "Road to Nowhere": The Evidence for Travelling Criminals': Home Office Research Study 207, Home Office Research, Development and Statistics Directorate

Wilkins, Leslie, 1964, *Social Deviance*: Tavistock

Willis, Paul, 1977, *Learning to Labour*: Saxon House

Wilson, James Q., 1983, 'Thinking About Crime: The debate over deterrence', *Atlantic Monthly*, Vol. 252, No. 3

Wilson, James Q. and Kelling, George, 1982, 'Broken Windows: The police and neighborhood safety', *Atlantic Monthly*, Vol. 249, No. 3

Young, Jock, 2003, 'The Left and Crime Control'; 1997, 'Left Realist Criminology: Radical in its Analysis, Realist in its Policy'; 2001, 'The Extent of Crime'; 1994, 'Self Report Studies', www.jockyoung.org.uk

Young, Jock, 2001, 'Sub-cultural Theory: Virtues and Vices': http://www.malcolmread.co.uk/JockYoung/subculture.htm

Young, Jock, 1994, 'Policing the Streets: Stop and Search in North London': Centre for Criminology, Middlesex University

Young, Jock, 1971, 'The Role of the Police as Amplifiers of Deviancy, Negotiators of Reality and Translators of Fantasy' in Stan Cohen (ed.), *Images of Deviance*: Penguin

Young, Jock and Mooney, Jayne, 1999, 'Social Exclusion and Criminal Justice: Ethnic Minorities and Stop and Search in North London': Middlesex University, Centre for Criminology

Zaki, Sania, 2003, 'Comparing the effects of socio-economic and spatial factors on crime patterns at the macro level of a London borough': 4th International Space Syntax Symposium, University College London

# Chapter 6: Stratification and differentiation

Abrams, Dominic, 2005, 'Ageism': Conference Paper: British Association for the Advancement of Science

Ahmed, Kamal, 2002, 'Britain "to scrap retirement age"': *The Observer*, May 12

Ainley, Patrick, 2004, 'The new "market-state" and education': *Journal of Education Policy*, Vol. 19, No. 4

Aldridge, Stephen, 2004, 'Social Mobility: A Discussion Paper': Performance and Innovation Unit, Cabinet Office

Aldridge, Stephen, 2001, 'Life Chances and Social Mobility: An Overview of the Evidence': Prime Minister's Strategy Unit

Alexander, Jeffrey, 1995, 'Modern, Anti, Post, Neo': *New Left Review* No. 210, March/April

Avramov, Dragana and Maskova, Miroslava, 2003, 'Active ageing in Europe': *Population Studies*, Vol. 1, No. 41, Council of Europe Publishing

Barker, Martin, 1981, *The New Racism*: Junction Books

Barratt, Will, 2005, 'Social Class: The Inequitable Campus': American College Personnel Association, Indiana State University

Baudrillard, Jean, 1998, 'Simulacra and Simulations' in 'Mark Poster (ed.), *Selected Writings*: Stanford University Press

Becker, Howard, 1963, *Outsiders: Studies in the Sociology of Deviance*: Free Press

Bly, Robert, 1990, *Iron John: A Book About Men*: Perseus Books

Bonney, Norman, 1988, 'Gender, Household and Social Class': *British Journal of Sociology*, No. 39

Bourdieu, Pierre, 1977, 'Cultural Reproduction and Social Reproduction' in Jerome Karabel and Albert Halsey (eds), *Power and Ideology in Education*: Oxford University Press

Braverman, Harry, 1974, *Labor and Monopoly Capital: The Degradation of Work in the Twentieth Century*: Monthly Review Press

Breen, Richard, 1997, 'The Significance of Social Mobility: Inequality, economic growth and social mobility': *British Journal of Sociology*, Vol. 48, No. 3

Breen, Richard and Goldthorpe, John, 1999, 'Class inequality and meritocracy: a critique of Saunders and an alternative analysis': *British Journal of Sociology*, Vol. 50, No. 1

Bruce, Steve, 1994, *The Edge of the Union: The Ulster Loyalist Political Vision*: Oxford University Press

Bulmer, Martin (ed.), 1975, *Working Class Images of Society*: Routledge and Kegan Paul

Burnham, James, 1962, *The Managerial Revolution*: Penguin (first published 1941)

Capra, Fritjof, 1982, *The Turning Point: Science, Society, and the Rising Culture*: Bantam Books

Chapman, Sydney and Abbott, W., 1913, 'The tendency of children to enter their fathers' trades', *Journal of the Royal Statistical Society*, 76

Chattoe, Edmund and Heath, Anthony, 2001, 'A New Approach to Social Mobility Models: Simulation as Reverse Engineering': Department of Sociology, University of Oxford

Cohen, Don and Prusak, Larry, 2001, *In Good Company. How social capital makes organizations work*: Harvard Business School Press

Coleman, James, 1988, 'Social Capital in the Creation of Human Capital': *American Journal of Sociology*, 94

Cowgill, Donald, 1974, 'Ageing and Modernisation: Revision of the Theory' in Jaber Gubrium (ed.), *Late Life: Communities and Environmental Policy*: Charles C. Thomas

Creighton, Colin, 1999, 'The rise and decline of the "male breadwinner family" in Britain': *Cambridge Journal of Economics*, 23

Crompton, Rosemary, 1993, *Class and Stratification*: Polity Press

Dahrendorf, Ralf, 1979, *Life Chances*: University of Chicago Press

Dahrendorf, Ralf, 1959, *Class and Class Conflict in Industrial Society*: Stanford University Press

Davis, Gerald and McAdam, Doug, 2000, 'Corporations, Classes and Social Movements After Managerialism': *Research in Organizational Behaviour*, Vol. 22

Davis, Kingsley and Moore, Wilbert, 1967, 'Some Principles of Stratification' in Reinhard Bendix and Seymour Martin Lipset (eds), *Class, Status and Power* (2nd edition): Routledge and Kegan Paul (first published 1945)

Demers, David and Merskin, Debra, 2000, 'Corporate News Structure and the Managerial Revolution': *Journal of Media Economics*, Vol. 13, No. 2

Dowd, James, 1986, 'The Old Person as Stranger' in Victor Marshall (ed.), *Later Life: The Social Psychology of Aging*: Sage

Draper, Hal, 1978, *Karl Marx's Theory of Revolution, Vol II: The Politics of Social Classes*: Monthly Review Press

Duffy, Mary and Evans, Geoffrey, 1997, 'Class, Community Polarisation and Politics' in Lizanne Dowds, Paula Devine and Richard Breen (eds), *Social Attitudes in Northern Ireland: The Sixth Report*: Appletree Press Ltd

Dunbar, Roxanne, 1970, 'Female Liberation as the Basis for Social Revolution' in Robin Morgan (ed.), *Sisterhood is Powerful: An Anthology of Writings from the Women's Liberation Movement*: Vintage Books

Duncombe, Jean and Marsden, Dennis, 1993, 'Love and Intimacy: The Gender Division of Emotion and "Emotion Work"': *Sociology*, Vol. 27

Economic and Social Research Council, 2005, 'Knowledge Economy in the UK', http://www.esrcsocietytoday.ac.uk

Eichler, Margrit, 1980, *The Double Standard. A Feminist Critique of Feminist Social Science*: St Martin's Press

Erikson, Robert and Goldthorpe, John, 1992, *The Constant Flux: A Study of Class Mobility in Industrial Societies*: Clarendon Press

Evans, Geoffrey, 1993, 'The decline of class divisions in Britain? Class and ideological preferences in the 1960s and the 1980s': *British Journal of Sociology*, No. 44

Farkas, George and Beron, Kurt, 2001, 'Family Linguistic Culture and Social Reproduction: Verbal Skill from Parent to Child in the Pre-school and School Years', Working Paper 01–05: Population Research Institute, March

Ferree, Myra and Hall, Elaine, 1996, 'Rethinking Stratification from a Feminist Perspective: Gender, Race and Class in Mainstream Textbooks': *American Sociological Review*, No. 61

Ferree, Myra, Khan, Shamus and Morimoto, Shauna, 2005, *Assessing the Feminist Revolution: The presence and absence of gender in theory and practice*: University of Wisconsin

Fukuyama, Francis, 1989, *The End of History?*: The National Interest

Galbraith, John Kenneth, 1983, *The New Industrial State*: Penguin (first published 1967)

Gallie, Duncan, 2001, 'Skill Change and the Labour Market: Gender, Class and Unemployment': National Institute for Economic and Social Research Conference Paper, 'Disadvantage in the Labour Market: Diversity and Commonality in Causes, Consequences and Redress'

Gauntlett, David, 2002, 'Anthony Giddens: Lifestyle – Choose your future', http://theory.org

General Household Survey, 2005, Office for National Statistics

Gershuny, Jonathan, 2002a, 'Life-course, social position and life-chances': Institute for Social and Economic Research, University of Essex

Gershuny, Jonathan, 2002b, 'Beating the Odds (1): intergenerational social mobility from a human capital perspective'; 'Beating the Odds (2): a new index of intergenerational social mobility': Institute for Social and Economic Research, Working Papers 2002–17 and 2002–18

Giddens, Anthony, 2001, *Sociology* (4th edition): Polity

Gingrich, Paul, 2002, 'Class, Status, and Party', http://uregina.ca/~gingrich/318n2202.htm

Glass, David and Hall, John, 1954, 'Social mobility in Great Britain: a study of inter-generation changes in status' in David Glass (ed.), *Social Mobility in Britain*: Routledge & Kegan Paul

Goldthorpe, John, 1983, *Women and Class Analysis*: BSA Publications Ltd

Goldthorpe, John, 1980, *Social Mobility and Class Structure in Modern Britain*: Clarendon Press

Goldthorpe, John (with Llewellyn, Catriona and Payne, Clive), 1980, *Social Mobility and Class Structure in Modern Britain*: Clarendon Press

Goldthorpe, John, Lockwood, David, Bechhofer, Frank and Platt, Jennifer, 1968, *The Affluent Worker in the Class Structure*: Cambridge University Press

Grusky, David, 1996, 'Theories of Stratification and Inequality' in David Grusky, James Baron and Donald Treiman (eds), *Social Differentiation and Inequality*: Westview Press

Hacker, Helen, 1951, 'Women as a Minority Group': *Social Forces*, Vol. 31

Hakim, Catherine, 2000, *Work-Lifestyle Choices in the 21st century: Preference Theory*: Open University Press

Hall, Stuart, 1996, 'New Ethnicities' in David Morley and Kuan-Hsing Chen (eds), *Stuart Hall: Critical Dialogues in Cultural Studies*: Routledge

Hall, Stuart, 1973/1980, 'Encoding/decoding' in the Centre for Contemporary Cultural Studies (ed.), *Culture, Media, Language: Working Papers in Cultural Studies*: Hutchinson

Hall, Stuart, Hobson, D., Lowe, A. and Willis, Paul (eds), 1980, *Culture, Media and Language*: Hutchinson

Halsey, Albert, Heath, Anthony and Ridge, John, 1980, *Origins and Destinations*: Oxford University Press

Harris, Dave, 2005, 'Reading Guide to Davis and Moore', http://www.arasite.org/dandm.htm

Harris, Dave, 2003, 'Social Mobility in Modern Britain: Class versus Merit', http://www.arasite.org/saunders.html

Harrison, Carolyn and Davies, Gail, 1998, 'Lifestyles & the Environment': Environment & Sustainability Desk Study, Economic and Social Research Council

Hauknes, Johan, 1996, 'Innovation in the Service Economy': STEP Group Report, http://www.step.no/reports/Y1996/0796.pdf

Heath, Anthony, 2002, 'Introduction To Sociology': Nuffield College, Oxford

Heath, Anthony and Payne, Clive, 1999, 'Twentieth Century Trends in Social Mobility in Britain': University of Oxford, Centre for Research into Elections and Social Trends, Working Paper No. 70

Heath, Anthony, McMahon, Dorren and Roberts, Jane, 1999, 'Ethnic Differences in the Labour Market: a comparison of the SARs and LFS': Centre for Research into Elections and Social Trends, Working Paper No. 71

Hendricks, Fred and Vale, Peter, 2004, 'Who Owns the Jewels? And What Lies Beyond Them?: The Continuing Relevance of Race and Class in Democratic South Africa': Rhodes University, http://www.ru.ac.za/research/pdfs/vale_hendricks_thought_paper.pdf

Hicks, Joe and Allen, Grahame, 1999, 'A Century of Change: Trends in UK statistics since 1900': House of Commons Library, Social and General Statistics Section: Research Paper 99/111

Hockey, Jenny and James, Allison, 1993, Growing Up and Growing Old: ageing and dependency in the life course: Sage

Hodges Persell, Caroline, 2000, 'Wright and Perrone's Expanded Marxian Criteria for Class': New York University, Dept of Sociology

Husmo, Marit, 1999, Cementing the Gender Stratification System: Total Quality Management in Norwegian Fish Processing: Women's World

Hutton, Will, 1995, The State We're In: Cape

ICM, 1998, 'Social Class Poll': BBC Today programme

Jeremy, David, 1998, A Business History of Britain 1900–1990s: Oxford University Press

Johnson, Hans and Saitoti ole Tumanka, Simon, 2004, 'Maasai: Age Sets', http://www.laleyio.com

Kan, Man Yee, 2005, 'Work Orientation and Wives' Employment Careers: An Evaluation of Hakim's Preference Theory': Institute for Social and Economic Research, GeNet Working Paper No. 12

Kane, Richard, 2004, The Sociology and Politics of Fernando Henrique Cardoso: Illinois State University

Karlsen, Saffron and Nazroo, James, 2002, 'Relation between racial discrimination, social class, and health among ethnic minority groups': American Journal of Public Health, 92

Kiemo, Karatu, 2004, 'Towards A Socio-Economic and Demographic Theory of Elderly Suicide: A Comparison of 49 Countries At Various Stages of Development', doctoral dissertation: University of Uppsala

Lawson, Tony and Garrod, Joan, 2003, Complete A–Z Sociology Handbook (3rd edition): Hodder and Stoughton

Lenski, Gerhard, 1994, 'New Light on Old Issues: The Relevance of "Really Existing Socialist Societies," for Stratification Theory' in David Grusky (ed.), Social Stratification: Class, Race, and Gender in Sociological Perspective: Westview Press

Leonardo, Zeus, 2004, 'The Unhappy Marriage between Marxism and Race Critique: political economy and the production of racialized knowledge': Policy Futures in Education, Vol. 2, Nos 3 and 4

Liu, William Ming, 2004, 'Using Social Class in Counselling Psychology Research': Journal of Counselling Psychology, University of Iowa

Luhmann, Niklas, 1997, 'Globalization or World Society?: How to conceive of modern society': International Review of Sociology, Vol. 7, No. 1

Luhmann, Niklas, 1995, Social Systems (Writing Science): Stanford University Press

Marshall, Gordon and Swift, Adam, 1996, 'Merits and Mobility: a Reply to Peter Saunders': Sociology, Vol. 30, No. 2

Marshall, Victor, 1996, 'The Stage of Theory in Aging and the Social Sciences' in Robert Binstock and Linda George (eds), Handbook of Aging and the Social Sciences (4th edition): Academic Press

Maturana, Humberto and Varela, Francisco, 1980, Autopoiesis and Cognition: D. Reidel

Mazur, Robert, 1996, Dictionary of Critical Sociology: Iowa State University

Meadows, Pamela, 2003, 'Retirement ages in the UK: a review of the literature': Employment Relations Research Series, No. 18

Miles, Andrew, 1996, 'Social Mobility in nineteenth-century England': Economic History Society, Refresh 23

Miliband, David, 2005, 'Life Chances: the positive agenda': Institute of Education lecture

Millet, Kate, 1970, Sexual Politics: Doubleday

Mills, C. Wright, 1963, 'The Sociology of Stratification' in Irving Horowitz (ed.), Power, Politics and People: The Collected Essays of C. Wright Mills: Oxford University Press (first published 1951)

Mills, C. Wright, 1959, The Sociological Imagination: Oxford University Press

Mitchell, Barbara, 2003, Life Course Theory: The Gale Group

Modood, Tariq, Berthoud, Richard, Lakey, Jane, Nazroo, James, Smith, Patten, Virdee, Satnam and Beishon, Sharon, 1997, 'Ethnic Minorities in Britain: Diversity and Disadvantage – Fourth National Survey of Ethnic Minorities': Policy Studies Institute

Moriarty, Jo and Butt, Jabeer, 2004, 'Inequalities in quality of life among older people from different ethnic groups': Ageing & Society, 24, Cambridge University Press

Mortimore, Roger and Robinson, Jane, 2003, 'Changing Social Values': MORI http://www.mori.com

Murphy, Jim, 1990, 'A Most Respectable Prejudice: Inequality in Educational Research and Policy': British Journal of Sociology, 41

Murray, Charles and Phillips, Melanie, 2001, The British Underclass 1990–2000: Institute for the Study of Civil Society

National Statistics Online, 2005, http://www.statistics.gov.uk

Neville, Peter, 1998, 'Norbert Elias: Civilisation and De-civilisation': Total Liberty, Vol. 1, Issue 4

Nicholas, Tom, 1999, 'The myth of meritocracy: an inquiry into the social origins of Britain's business leaders since 1850': London School of Economics, Working Paper No. 53/99

Nyíri, Lajos, 2002, 'Knowledge-Based Society and Its Impact on Labour-Market Values': *Society and Economy*, Vol. 24, No. 2

Office for National Statistics, 2002, 'The Jobs People Do', www.statistics.gov.uk

Pakulski, Jan and Waters, Malcolm, 1996, *The Death of Class*: Sage

Parenti, Michael, 1997, *Blackshirts and Reds: Rational Fascism and the Overthrow of Communism*: City Lights Books

Parkin, Frank, 1971, *Class Inequality and Political Order*: McGibbon and Kee

Parsons, Talcott, 1971, *The System of Modern Societies*: Prentice Hall

Paterson, Lindsay and Iannelli, Cristina, 2004, 'Patterns of Social Mobility: A Comparative Study of England, Wales and Scotland': ESRC Research Project 'Education and Social Mobility in Scotland in the Twentieth Century', Working Paper 3

Piskorski, Mikołaj Jan and Anand, Bharat, 2002, 'Resources, Power and Prestige: Formation of Structural Inequality in Social Exchange Networks': Harvard Business School, http://www.people.hbs.edu/ mpiskorski/papers/VC-Money.pdf

Platt, Lucinda, 2005, *Migration and Social Mobility: The life chances of Britain's minority ethnic communities*: Policy Press

Platt, Lucinda, 2003, 'The Intergenerational Social Mobility of Minority Ethnic Groups': ISER Working Papers, No. 2003–24, Institute for Social and Economic Research

Poulantzas, Nicos, 1978, *Classes in Contemporary Capitalism*: Verso (first published 1974)

Poulantzas, Nicos, 1973, *Political Power and Social Classes*: New Left Books

Powell, William, 2002, 'Finding closure': *Families in Society* – the Journal of Contemporary Human Services, Vol. 83, No. 3

Quarterly Economic Review, 2005, Department of Enterprise, Trade and Investment, January

Rajamanickam, Balakrishnan, 2004, 'Transcultural health care practice: Core practice module, chapter five: Mental health and minority ethnic groups': Royal College of Nursing, http://www.rcn.org.uk/resources/transcultural/mentalhealth/index.php

Riley, Matilda, 1994, 'Introduction: the Mismatch between People and Structures' in Matilda Riley (ed.), *Aging and Structural Lag: Society's Failure to Provide Meaningful Opportunities in Work, Family and Leisure*: John Wiley & Sons

Rose, David and Pevalin, David (with O'Reilly, Karen), 2005, 'The National Statistics Socio-economic Classification: Origins, Development and Use': Palgrave Macmillan (with the permission of the Controller of Her Majesty's Stationery Office)

Sabel, Charles, 1991, 'Moebius-Strip Organizations and Open Labor Markets: Some Consequences of the Reintegration of Conception and Execution in a Volatile Economy' in James Coleman and Pierre Bourdieu (eds), *Social Theory for a Changing Society*: Westview

Sandomierski, David, 2003, 'Canadian Environmental Policy in a post-Newtonian World': ISYP Conference 'Advancing Human Security', Nova Scotia

Saunders, Peter, 2005, quoted in John-Paul Flintoff, 'Going down': *Sunday Times*, December 4

Saunders, Peter, 2002, 'Reflections on the meritocracy debate in Britain: a response to Richard Breen and John Goldthorpe': *British Journal of Sociology*, Vol. 53, No 4

Saunders, Peter, 1997, 'Social Mobility in Britain: an empirical evaluation of two competing explanations': *Sociology*, Vol. 31, No. 2

Saunders, Peter, 1995, 'Might Britain be a Meritocracy?': *Sociology*, Vol. 29, No. 1

Saunders, Peter, 1990, *Social Class and Stratification*: Routledge

Savage, Mike, 2002, *Social Exclusion and Class Analysis*: Blackwell Publishing

Savage, Mike, Bagnall, Gaynor and Longhurst, Brian, 2001, 'Ordinary, ambivalent and defensive: class identities in the North West of England': *Sociology*, Vol. 35, Cambridge Journals Online

Scott, Jacqueline, 2004, 'Gender Inequality in Production and Reproduction: A New Priority Research Network': University of Cambridge, GeNet Working Paper No. 1

Scott, John, 1999, 'Class and Stratification' in Geoff Payne (ed.), *Social Divisions*: Macmillan

Shapiro, Thomas, 2004, *The Hidden Cost of Being African American: How Wealth Perpetuates Inequality*: Oxford University Press

Stanworth, Michelle, 1984, 'Women and Class Analysis: A Reply to John Goldthorpe': *Sociology*, Vol. 18, No. 2, BSA Publications Ltd

Stanworth, Philip and Giddens, Anthony, 1974, 'An economic elite: a demographic profile of company chairmen' in Philip Stanworth and Anthony Giddens (eds), *Elites and Power in British Society*: Cambridge University Press

Sullivan, Alice, 2001, 'Cultural Capital and Educational Attainment': British Sociological Association, *Sociology*, Vol. 35, No. 4

Summerfield, Carol and Babb, Penny (eds), 2004, 'Social Trends 34': Office for National Statistics, The Stationery Office

Townsend, Peter, 1986, 'Ageism and Social Policy' in Chris Phillipson and Alan Walker (eds), *Ageing and Social Policy*: Gower

Tumin, Melvin, 1953, 'Some Principles of Stratification: A Critical Analysis': *American Sociological Review*, 18

Turner, Bryan, 1989, 'Ageing, Status Politics and Sociological Theory': *British Journal of Sociology*, Vol. 40, No. 2

Vincent, Carol, Martin, Jane and Ranson, Stewart, 2000, 'Class, Culture and Agency: Researching Parental Voice': Institute of Education Conference Paper 'Education for Social Democracies'

Waters, Malcolm, 1997, 'Inequality after Class' in David Owen (ed.), *Sociology after Post-Modernism*: Sage

Weber, Max, 1978, 'Economy and Society': Guenther Roth and Claus Wittich (University of California Press (first published 1922)

Westergaard, John and Resler, Henrietta, 1976, *Class in Capitalist Society*: Basic Books

Whitehead, Steve, 1997, 'Class Inequality Revisited': *Reviewing Sociology*, Vol. 10, No. 2

Wolf-Light, Paul, 1994, 'The Shadow of Iron John': *Men & Families*, 17, http://www.achillesheel. freeuk.com/issue17.html

Wright, Eric Olin and Perrone, Luca, 1977, 'Marxist Class

Categories and Income Inequality': *American Sociological Review*, No. 42

Yaqub, Shahin, 2000, 'Intertemporal Welfare Dynamics': Sussex University (Background Paper for HDR)

Young, Jock, 2000, 'The Maintenance of Order Amongst Lightly Engaged Strangers', http://www.malcolmread.co.uk/JockYoung/lightlye.htm

Zhou, Peterson, 1997, ' Influences in the Timing of Retirement: Age Norms, Perception of Age and Life Course Events', http://wwwsuperdirector.com

Zweig, Ferdynand, 1961, *The Worker in an Affluent Society*: Heinemann

# Name Index

# Index